3/99

 **St. Louis Community
College**

Forest Park
Florissant Valley
Meramec

Instructional Resources
St. Louis, Missouri

A Jane Austen
Encyclopedia

Jane Austen, 1775–1817. Based on an unfinished watercolor portrait by her sister, Cassandra, c. 1810. Drawing by Barbara Wilamowska. Reproduced with permission.

A JANE AUSTEN ENCYCLOPEDIA

Paul Poplawski

Greenwood Press
Westport, Connecticut

Library of Congress Cataloging-in-Publication Data

Poplawski, Paul, 1957–
    A Jane Austen encyclopedia / Paul Poplawski.
       p.   cm.
    Includes bibliographical references and index.
    ISBN 0–313–30017–8 (alk. paper)
    1. Austen, Jane, 1775–1817—Encyclopedias. 2. Women novelists,
English—19th century—Biography—Encyclopedias. 3. Austen, Jane,
1775–1817—Bibliography. 4. Austen, Jane, 1775–1817—Chronology.
I. Title.
PR4036.A28   1998
823'.7—dc21   97–44880

British Library Cataloguing in Publication Data is available.

Library of Congress Catalog Card Number: 97–44880
ISBN: 0–313–30017–8

First published in 1998

Greenwood Press, 88 Post Road West, Westport, CT 06881
An imprint of Greenwood Publishing Group, Inc.

Printed in the United States of America

The paper used in this book complies with the
Permanent Paper Standard issued by the National
Information Standards Organization (Z39.48–1984).

10 9 8 7 6 5 4 3 2 1

I will not say that your Mulberry trees are dead, but I am afraid they are not alive. We shall have peace soon—I mean to have them with a couple of Ducks from Wood Barn & Maria Middleton towards the end of next week.

—*Letter to Cassandra Austen, 31 May 1811*

Where Edward in the name of wonder . . . did you pick up this unmeaning Gibberish? You have been studying Novels I suspect.

—*"Love and Friendship"*

(I hope somebody cares for these minutiae) . . .

—*Letter to Cassandra Austen, 20 May 1813*

Contents

An illustration essay follows page 24

Preface

This book aims to present the known facts about Jane Austen's life and works in as uncluttered and straightforward a manner as possible, without duplicating the structures, approaches, and assessments of previous books of a similar sort (see, e.g., *Apperson 1932, Copeland and McMaster 1997, Grey 1986, Halperin and Kunert 1976, Hardwick 1973, Leeming 1974, Pinion 1973*). It undoubtedly has many features in common with earlier reference guides on Austen, and it certainly owes a scholarly debt to several of them, but in almost every instance of similarity there are key differences that I believe make this work a worthwhile addition to what is, admittedly, already a fairly crowded market. This is not the place to point out every one of these differences, but one or two examples may help to justify the appearance of yet another book on Austen to the skeptical observer.

To begin at the end, as it were, very few (if any) other general reference works contain the sort of comprehensive and up-to-date bibliographies presented here; and for many scholars, this alone would justify the publication of this book. Similarly, although there are chronologies of Austen's life and works in abundance, very few of them provide more than a skeleton outline of the life, and none of them systematically trace the steps and stages in the composition and publication of *all* her writings. My chronology—for the first time, I believe—does this, while providing a full account of the life at the same time. The chronology presented by Deirdre Le Faye (*1989*) is an outstanding exception to the general rule, and I acknowledge an important debt to her meticulous biographical research in the construction of my own chronology; but even Le Faye (because she is primarily concerned with biographical matters) does not deal systematically with *all* the writings in her chronology, though she does do so discursively in the course of the rest of her book. There have also, previously, been several dictionary-style guides to the plots and characters of Austen's novels, and these have generally been of a very high standard. But, again, few of them can boast the comprehensive coverage of both texts and characters that my version of this genre presents (there have been more complete *listings* than mine, but that has been gained only at the expense of analytical elaboration).

This book has three separate but interdependent parts. The first part presents information about Jane Austen's life and times in the form of detailed chronologies, a map, a genealogical chart, and various illustrations. The second part, which forms the core of the book, is an alphabetical encyclopedia devoted mainly to the works and characters of Jane Austen, though it also includes short biographical sketches of the author and her immediate family. The third part contains three comprehensive bibliographies listing all of Austen's work, all significant books of criticism written about her, and selected critical essays and articles.

Part I, the chronology of Jane Austen, provides a year-by-year and, where possible, month-by-month account of her life and writing career. Where relevant, it also includes details of the lives of her immediate family and friends. For the reader unfamiliar with the outline of Austen's life and with the full range of her writing, this chronology provides an essential orientation point for exploring the rest of the book. All of Austen's writings referred to in this chronology, along with most of the family members who are mentioned here, have separate entries in Part II, so that the chronology can be used as a type of index to the encyclopedia. The chronology is supplemented by a map that locates all the important places associated with Jane Austen, as well as by a genealogical chart of her immediate family and sketch-portraits of her father and brothers.

The second chronology provides social and historical information about the period in which Jane Austen lived, and this is supplemented by fashion illustrations and by illustrations of a selection of carriages that were in use at the time (most of which are mentioned in Austen's novels). Within the inherent constraints and limitations of the chronology form, I have attempted to make this chronology a readable narrative rather than simply a list of disconnected "facts," in the hope that it will provide genuine insight into some of the main events and trends of the period. Clearly, any chronology can only skate over the surface of events, and it would require several books of detailed historical scholarship to do full justice to the many complex developments touched on here. But I hope the reader will recognize a pattern of deliberate selection here that attempts to focus attention on the main economic and political developments of the time, as well as on those events that impinged significantly on the lives of the Austen family (the Revolutionary and Napoleonic Wars being the most obvious of these, given that her two sailor brothers were actively involved).

The third chronology attempts to provide an at-a-glance overview of the literary context in which Jane Austen was embedded, and I have made this serve an additional purpose by marking those books that it is known Jane Austen read or was familiar with. Hopefully, this will provide a useful source of quick reference for scholars and students alike, though, again, one would need to refer to more detailed histories of literature to understand the full significance of the context sketched here.

Part II aims to provide a comprehensive guide to the works of Jane Austen, concentrating principally on the plots and characters of her novels, though including what are, in effect, short essays on their main themes and on the critical reception of Austen's work since the early nineteenth century. The entries cover the whole of Austen's output: every single one of her texts, including all her juvenilia and minor works, has a separate entry. Entries on the main novels and most of the minor novels all contain the following information: full details of the composition and initial publication of the work in question; brief critical comments on its place in Austen's oeuvre and its general nature; a fully detailed plot summary that incorporates critical comment where appropriate and that is designed to clarify the dramatic structure and thematic ramifications of the work; an appended list of all the characters, usually subdivided between major and minor characters; a summary, where relevant, of the volume structure of the work, with equivalent chapter numbers of modern editions (where continuous chapters are used); and an appended list of bibliographical references for further reading, abbreviated using the author-date citation system and cross-referenced to the bibliographies in Part III of the book. (Note: Italicized citations, such as *Tucker 1983*, indicate that the reference is to a book and that full details can be found in Chapter 5. Citations in roman type, as in Copeland 1996, indicate that the reference is to an essay or article and that full details can be found in Chapter 6.)

For all the major novels and nearly all the minor and unfinished novels, there are also separate entries for every character. At the start of the entry, the location of the character's first appearance in the novel is indicated, (sometimes along with subsequent significant appearances), using a simple chapter reference for modern editions of the novel and a volume, chapter, and page reference for the standard Oxford editions of Austen, which retain the original volume divisions of the novels. Character-entries should ideally be read in conjunction with the parent-novel entries, as they are written (with the obvious exception of some short ones that simply serve to identify very minor characters) with a view to extending or deepening the reader's understanding both of the nature of the parent-novel and of the character's role and position in it. As the major characters in a novel will have been treated at length in the main novel-entry, they are often dealt with more briefly in these entries, while certain often overlooked minor characters are given more detailed treatment. Collectively, these entries are intended to serve as a sort of gazeteer to Austen's fiction and to provide a useful source of quick reference; but, as just indicated, I hope that the majority of them will also serve a critical function in revealing something of the craft of Austen's often-admired depiction and deployment of her fictional characters.

Part III, the bibliographical section, is organized into three main parts: (1) a bibliography of Jane Austen's writings that gives full details of all initial publications of her work, along with related information (such as first translation and first publication in America) and including details of all scholarly editions; (2) a bibliography of critical books that, to the best of my knowledge, includes every work, published up to 1996, devoted solely or largely to Jane Austen (with the exception of minor study guides and including one or two 1997 publications)—this bibliography is followed by a chronological listing of the same works, with abbreviated citations, designed to indicate the development of Austen studies over two centuries; and (3) a selective bibliography of critical essays and articles, with key nineteenth-century essays and reviews listed separately and with twentieth-century studies selected mainly from the past two decades. The bibliographies in this part of the book should be consulted for full details of all abbreviated citations made in the body of the work.

Limitations of space have inevitably prevented me from exploring the full range of issues that generations of critics and readers have responded to in Jane Austen's works. However, under the headings of "Criticism" and "Themes and Concerns" (and the two entries should really be read together), I have attempted to provide a critical overview of the dominant themes of both her novels and her critical reputation. If nothing else, these two entries offer the reader a developed starting point from which to explore Austen's works further. In a sense, that is what this book is all about anyway, for, despite the ambition to "guide" the reader through both familiar and unfamiliar Austen terrain, its nonhierarchical organization actually leaves a lot of the pathfinding up to the reader, and I hope this will prove conducive to new ways of looking at Austen and to new ideas for research into her life and works.

I would like to thank the following for various sorts of help and encouragement during the completion of this book: Trinity College Carmarthen, for allowing me a period of study leave in which to begin the work; my colleagues in the English Department there, in particular Ian Fisher and Katie Gramich, who facilitated the process; Trevor Harris for the map; Barbara Wilamowska for the portrait drawings and Emily Smith for the fashion and carriage drawings; Conway Davies for help with the historical chronology; Martin Rhys for some last minute printing; Julie Rees and other support staff at Trinity College for ever-cheerful technical assistance; George Butler for suggesting and encouraging the project; Brian Hollingworth for introducing me to the joys of Jane Austen in the first place; Angela Smith for many stimulating discussions and suggestions—and simply for being there.

Part I

CHRONOLOGICAL CONTEXTS

1

Chronology of Jane Austen's Life and Works

1731	1 May: Birth of George Austen (Jane Austen's father) in Tonbridge, Kent, to the surgeon William Austen (1701–1737) and Rebecca (Walter) Austen, née Hampson (c.1695–1733).
1732	February: Death of Rebecca Austen.
1736	May: William Austen marries Susannah Kelk (1688–1768).
1737	December: Death of William Austen. Susannah (Kelk) Austen apparently refuses to look after George and his two sisters, Philadelphia (1730–1792) and Leonora (b.1732), who are left under the guardianship of William's elder brother, Francis (1698–1791), a prosperous solicitor in Sevenoaks, Kent; as he is unmarried, however, they go to live with his married brother, Stephen (1704–1751), a bookseller and publisher in St. Paul's Churchyard, London.
1739	Cassandra Leigh (Jane Austen's mother) born at Harpsden, near Henley-on-Thames in Oxfordshire, to Rev. Thomas Leigh (1696–1764) and Jane Leigh, née Walker (1704–1768).
1741	George Austen becomes a pupil at Tonbridge School.
1747	July: George Austen enters St. John's College, Oxford, and receives fellowship of the college reserved for a Tonbridge School scholar.
1751	George Austen awarded bachelor of arts degree.
1752	18 January: Philadelphia Austen, George Austen's sister, sails for India on the *Bombay Castle*, arriving at Madras on 4 August.
1753	22 February: Philadelphia Austen marries Tysoe Saul Hancock (1711–1775), a surgeon with the East India Company at Fort St. David on the Coromandel Coast south of Madras.
1754	George Austen becomes master of arts at Oxford and is ordained deacon. Becomes curate of Shipbourne, near Tonbridge, and a second master, or usher, at Tonbridge School (both until the end of 1757).
1755	May: George Austen ordained priest at Rochester, Kent.

1758	George Austen returns to Oxford to prepare for bachelor of divinity degree.

1759   The Hancocks move to Fort William in Calcutta, where they become friends with Warren Hastings (1732–1818), later governor-general of India (1773–1785).

1760   George Austen awarded bachelor of divinity degree.

1761   November: Thomas (Brodnax, May) Knight I of Godmersham, Kent (1702–1781), husband of a second cousin of George Austen's, presents the latter with the living (ecclesiastical tenure) of Steventon, near Basingstoke, in Hampshire, worth about £100 per annum (though George Austen does not take up duties there until after his marriage in 1764).

22 December: Birth of Elizabeth Hancock in Calcutta: Warren Hastings, now a business partner of Mr. Hancock, becomes her godfather. His own four-year-old child, George, whose mother had died in 1759, has been sent back to England for his education (where, eventually, he will be taught by George Austen).

1764   26 April: Marriage, in Bath, of George Austen and Cassandra Leigh. They go to live in Hampshire, where George Austen is finally to take up duties as rector of Steventon. As the Steventon rectory is dilapidated and unfit for occupation, however, they rent Deane parsonage, two miles north of Steventon, where they live until 1768. Mr. Austen is allowed to supplement his income from farming the 200-acre Cheesedown Farm in the north of the parish.

Spring–Summer: Mrs. Austen's widowed mother, Mrs. Leigh, comes to live with the Austens, bringing along Warren Hasting's seven-year-old son, George, to be a boarding pupil with Mr. Austen.

Autumn: George Hastings dies of "putrid sore throat" (diphtheria).

1765   13 February: James Austen born.

June: The Hancocks return from India to settle in London.

1766   26 August: George Austen born.

1767   7 October: Edward Austen born.

1768   26 January: Death of Susannah (Kelk) Austen, Mr. Austen's stepmother. His father's Tonbridge properties are sold, providing the Austens with some £1,200 later in the year.

July–August: The Austens move into the renovated and enlarged Steventon rectory. (This to remain the family home until 1801.) Mrs. Austen's mother, Mrs. Leigh, dies here on 29 August, leaving her daughter about £1,000. (This, along with other family moneys, was invested in £3,350 of Old South Sea Annuities to provide Mrs. Austen's widow's portion: by 1820 this was yielding about £116 per annum, which, along with rent from a little land she owned—worth £6 per year in 1820—was Mrs. Austen's only personal income after her husband's death.)

Summer–Autumn: Mr. Hancock sails for India to try to restore his dwindling fortune, the family having lived beyond its means in London; his wife and daughter remain in London.

1770   Mr. and Mrs. Austen's second son, George, has been subject to fits, and it starts to become clear that he is mentally disabled. (Like all the Austen children, George was sent out to be nursed by a local family after being weaned; but, unlike the others, he never returned to become a regular member of the Austen household. He remained in care outside the family circle for the rest of his life, and though that care seems always to have been supervised by the family, there is little mention of him after this date in the family tradition.)

1771   8 June: Henry Thomas Austen born.

1773   9 January: Cassandra Elizabeth Austen born.

February: The Austens apparently experience financial problems: a payment of £300 into Mr. Austen's bank account by his wife's brother, James Leigh Perrot (1735–1817), prevents insolvency.

March: The Austens' financial problems further eased when Mr. Austen becomes rector of Deane as well as of Steventon, the living (worth about £110 per annum), having been bought for him by his uncle Francis. Mr. Austen also begins to take in boarding pupils at Steventon (until 1796), preparing them for university entrance.

1774   23 April: Francis William Austen born.

1775   5 November: Death of Mr. Hancock in Calcutta.

16 December: Jane Austen born.

1777   Winter: Mrs. Hancock and Eliza leave for the continent, traveling in Germany and Belgium before settling in Paris in the autumn of 1779.

1779   23 June: Charles John Austen born.

July: James Austen, aged fourteen, enters St. John's College, Oxford, on a "Founder's Kin" scholarship (his maternal grandmother, seven times removed, was the sister of Sir Thomas White (1492–1567), the founder of St. John's).

1781   Autumn: In Paris, Eliza Hancock marries Jean Capot de Feuillide (1750–1794), a captain of Dragoons in the queen's regiment (and self-styled "Comte de Feuillide").

1782   December: Austen family and friends, under the general direction of Jane Austen's eldest brother, James, perform *Matilda* (1775), a tragedy by Dr. Thomas Francklin—the first of several amateur theatricals to be produced at Steventon rectory over the next six years (either in the dining room or in the barn across the road).

1783   Edward Austen adopted by Thomas Knight II (1735–1794) of Godmersham and his wife Catherine, née Knatchbull (1753–1812). (Godmersham is about eight miles southwest of Canterbury in Kent.)

Spring: Jane Austen, aged seven, and Cassandra, ten, along with their cousin, Jane Cooper, twelve, are sent to a boarding school in Oxford run by Jane Cooper's aunt, Mrs. Ann Cawley.

May: Rev. George Lefroy (1745–1806) becomes rector of Ashe, next to Steventon, and he and his wife, Anne, née Brydges (1749–1804), move into Ashe rectory. They soon become close acquaintances of the Austens. (The intelligent and sophisticated ''Madam Lefroy'' later—from about 1786—became an intimate friend of Jane Austen's and an important formative influence on her.)

Summer: Mrs. Cawley moves to Southampton with her pupils, where they fall seriously ill with typhus fever. The girls are taken home by their mothers and eventually recover, but Jane Cooper's mother (Jane Austen's maternal aunt) contracts the fever and dies in October. Jane Austen and Cassandra remain at home in Steventon until 1785.

1784

July: *The Rivals* (1775), by R. B. Sheridan (1751–1816), performed at the Steventon rectory.

Eliza de Feuillide goes with her husband to visit his family for the first time at his estate at Guienne in the southwest of France; she remains here until 1786.

1785

Spring: Jane Austen, Cassandra, and Jane Cooper go to the Abbey School in Reading, Berkshire. (The school overlooks the ruins of the twelfth-century Reading Abbey, and its premises include the abbey's surviving inner gatehouse.)

1786

Edward Austen sent on the Grand Tour by his adoptive parents; visits Switzerland and Italy and spends a year in Dresden, returning to England in 1788.

April: Frank Austen, nearly twelve, enters Royal Naval Academy, Portsmouth.

May: Mrs. Hancock and Eliza de Feuillide return to London, where Eliza's son, Hastings, is born on 25 June.

November: James Austen leaves for the continent, where he travels until the autumn of 1787, visiting France and, possibly, Spain and Holland.

December: Jane Austen and Cassandra leave the Abbey School around this time and from now on are educated at home. Mr. Austen's sister, Mrs. Hancock, along with Eliza and Hastings de Feuillide, is part of the Christmas and New Year family gathering at Steventon. Over the holiday, two plays are performed, with Eliza taking the leading female roles: *The Wonder—A Woman Keeps a Secret* (1714), by Mrs. Susannah Centlivre (c.1667–1723), and *The Chances*, a comedy of 1647 by John Fletcher (1579–1625), adapted by David Garrick (1717–1779) in 1773.

1787

Jane Austen, aged eleven, begins her literary writing sometime this year. (The composition of the juvenilia is generally agreed to have taken place between now and June 1793. The original manuscripts are now lost, but these writings were transcribed by Jane Austen over many years—with evidence of revision as late as 1809—into three notebooks: *Volume the First, Volume the Second, Volume the Third.*)

Autumn–Winter: James Austen returns from continental travels, and in December he is ordained deacon at Oxford.

1787–1790   The following of Jane Austen's juvenilia probably written (all from *Volume the First*): "Frederic and Elfrida," "Jack and Alice," "Edgar and Emma," "Henry and Eliza," "Mr. Harley," "Sir William Mountague," "Mr. Clifford," "The Beautifull [*sic*] Cassandra," "Amelia Webster," "The Visit," "The Mystery."

1788   March: A burlesque play by Henry Fielding (1707–1754), *The Tragedy of Tragedies, or The Life and Death of Tom Thumb the Great* (1731), performed at Steventon.

July: Henry Austen, aged seventeen, joins his brother James as a scholar at St. John's College, Oxford.

July–August: Jane Austen taken on a family visit to her great-uncle Francis Austen at the Red House in Sevenoaks, Kent. In August the Austens return to Hampshire via London, where they dine at the Orchard Street home of Eliza de Feuillide and Mrs. Hancock.

September: Eliza and her mother return to France, where they remain until 1790. (They live in Paris for at least some of this period, perhaps for all of it, and quite possibly witness some of the events of the French Revolution.)

Autumn: Edward Austen returns from his Grand Tour and goes to live permanently at Godmersham with the Knights.

December: Frank Austen completes technical studies at Portsmouth and, to continue his training as a seaman, sails for the East Indies on board HMS *Perseverance* (returning to England only at the end of 1793).

1788–1789   Winter: Two farces performed at Steventon, *The Sultan, or a Peep into the Seraglio* by Isaac Bickerstaffe (c.1735–1812) (first performed, 1775; published 1784) and *High Life below Stairs* (1759) by Rev. James Townley: these, it seems, were the last of the theatricals at the rectory.

1789   31 January: First issue of James Austen's weekly Oxford magazine, *The Loiterer*. Produced with the help of his brother Henry and largely written by the two of them, it ran for sixty issues until 20 March 1790, when James left Oxford to become curate at Overton (three miles or so from Steventon). (It has been suggested—and disputed—that Jane Austen submitted a burlesque letter to the editor for the issue of 28 March 1789, under the name of Sophia Sentiment—a name from a play by William Hayley [1745–1820], *The Mausoleum*, but whether or not this is true, Jane Austen would certainly have read and discussed her brothers' periodical.)

Spring: Mr. Austen lets Deane parsonage to the recently widowed Mrs. Lloyd (1728–1805) and her two daughters, Martha (1765–1843) and Mary (1771–1843), who soon become close friends with Jane Austen and Cassandra. (A third daughter, Elizabeth Lloyd [1768–1839] was recently married to her cousin, Rev. Fulwar Craven Fowle [1764–1840], a former pupil of Mr. Austen's and brother of Cassandra Austen's future fiancé, Tom Fowle.)

June: James Austen ordained as priest at Oxford.

December: Frank Austen becomes midshipman on HMS *Perseverance*.

1790   Mrs. Hancock and Eliza de Feuillide return to England from revolutionary France sometime this year.

June: Jane Austen writes "Love and Friendship" (*Volume the Second*).

1791   June: Eliza de Feuillide and Mrs. Hancock are now settled at Orchard Street in London again; Mrs. Hancock has begun to suffer from breast cancer.

July: Charles Austen, aged twelve, enters the Royal Naval Academy at Portsmouth; his parents and sisters possibly take this opportunity for a seaside holiday nearby.

November: Jane Austen writes "The History of England" (*Volume the Second*). James Austen is made vicar of Sherborne St. John, just north of Basingstoke, Hampshire. Still in the East Indies, Frank Austen moves to HMS *Minerva*.

27 December: Edward Austen marries Elizabeth Bridges (1773–1808), daughter of Sir Brook and Lady Fanny Bridges of Goodnestone Park (near Wingham, about seven miles east of Canterbury); they live at Rowling House, a mile from Goodnestone.

?1791–1792   "A Collection of Letters" probably written by Jane Austen in late 1791 or early 1792 (*Volume the Second*). Jane Austen's dramatic skit, *Sir Charles Grandison*, possibly begun in this period. (It has been suggested [*Fergus 1991*: 180] that "Lesley Castle," transcribed between "Love and Friendship" [June 1790] and "The History of England" [November 1791], may also have been written in 1791, but its first letter is dated January 1792, and this has generally been taken as its year of composition.)

1792   Jane Austen writes the following pieces: "Lesley Castle" (*Volume the Second*), possibly between January and April; "The Three Sisters" (*Volume the First*); "Evelyn," between May and August, and, in August, "Catharine" (both *Volume the Third*).

January: The Lloyds leave Deane parsonage and move to Ibthorpe, just north of Andover and about sixteen miles from Steventon. As part of a leaving present for Mary Lloyd (who would later marry James Austen), Jane Austen writes her "Verses Given with a Needlework Bag to Mrs. James Austen.'' (Most of Jane Austen's verse titles were given posthumously. As with this purely descriptive title, I follow the now-familiar titles given in the Oxford edition of Jane Austen's *Minor Works* (1954). For variant titles, see *Selwyn 1996*.)

26 February: Death of Mrs. Hancock.

27 March: James Austen marries Anne Mathew (1759–1795); they live first at Overton before moving, later in the year, into Deane parsonage, where James acts as his father's curate.

August: Eliza de Feuillide stays with the Austens at Steventon until at least the end of October.

October: Jane Austen and Cassandra visit the Lloyds at Ibthorpe House, from where Jane Austen attends her first balls at Enham House, near Andover, and at the earl of Portsmouth's Hurstbourne Park, five miles east of Andover.

December: Frank Austen promoted to lieutenant on HMS *Minerva*. It is possibly at this time, also, that Cassandra Austen becomes engaged to Rev. Tom Fowle (1765–1797), a former pupil of her father's at the Steventon rectory and son of Rev. Thomas Fowle (1727–1806) of Kintbury, just west of Newbury in Berkshire.

1793	23 January: Birth of Edward Austen's first child, Fanny (Jane Austen's first niece). Soon after, presumably, Jane Austen writes the pieces collected as ''Scraps,'' which are dedicated to her newborn niece (''The Female Philosopher,'' ''The First Act of a Comedy,'' ''A Letter from a Young Lady,'' ''A Tour through Wales,'' ''A Tale''; *Volume the Second*).

Spring: Henry Austen joins Oxfordshire Militia as lieutenant.

15 April: Birth of James Austen's first child, Anna.

2–3 June: Jane Austen writes last of the juvenilia: ''Detached Pieces,'' dedicated to her second niece, Anna (''A Fragment,'' ''A Beautiful Description of the Different Effects of Sensibility on Different Minds,'' ''The Generous Curate''), and ''Ode to Pity'' (both *Volume the First*).

December: Frank Austen returns from the East Indies. Jane Austen and Cassandra, possibly with Frank, visit relations at St. Mary's, Southampton.

1793–1795	Within this period, Jane Austen probably writes *Lady Susan* (posthumously titled by her nephew J. E. Austen-Leigh in the 1871 edition of his *A Memoir of Jane Austen*).
1794	22 February: Eliza de Feuillide's husband sent to the guillotine in Paris after being found guilty of trying to bribe a witness in the trial of an aristocratic friend charged with conspiracy against the republic.

Midsummer: Jane Austen and Cassandra stay with their uncle and aunt, Rev. Thomas Leigh and his wife, Mary (both of them first cousins to Mrs. Austen), at the rectory in Adlestrop, Gloucestershire.

They also then visit (possibly in August) their brother Edward at Rowling, Kent.

September: Charles Austen, aged fifteen, leaves the Naval Academy in Portsmouth and, as a midshipman, joins HMS *Daedalus* under the command of Captain Thomas Williams (1761–1841), husband of his cousin Jane (Cooper). (Charles continues to serve with Captain Williams, on the ships *Unicorn* and *Endymion*, until his promotion in December 1797.)

October: Death of Thomas Knight II, Edward Austen's adoptive father. His estates in Kent and Hampshire are left to his widow, to be inherited by Edward Austen after her death.

1795   ''Elinor and Marianne,'' an early epistolary version—now lost—of *Sense and Sensibility*, probably written this year.

3 May: Death of James Austen's wife, Anne.

December: Tom Lefroy (1776–1869), from Ireland and on his way to study law in London, visits his uncle, Rev. George Lefroy, at Ashe rectory. He becomes romantically involved with Jane Austen between now and mid-January when he leaves, apparently sent away by the Lefroys.

1796   January: Tom Fowle, Cassandra's fiancé, sails for the West Indies as private chaplain to Lord Craven.

April: Jane Austen and Cassandra visit their cousin Edward Cooper (1770–1835) and his family at Harpsden, Oxfordshire (birthplace and childhood home of Mrs. Austen), where he has been curate since 1793.

June: Charles Austen, on HMS *Unicorn*, is involved in a dramatic sea chase and battle after three French ships are intercepted in British home waters; one of the ships is eventually captured, and Captain Williams is knighted as a result of this action.

August–September/October: Jane Austen stays with Edward Austen at Rowling, Kent, with, on the outward journey, an overnight stay in London, at Cork Street, Mayfair, and a brief visit to Greenwich.

October: ''First Impressions,'' an early version of *Pride and Prejudice*, begun. Jane Austen possibly works intermittently on *Sir Charles Grandison* between this year and 1800.

1797   January: James Austen marries his second wife, Mary Lloyd (1771–1843).

February: Tom Fowle dies of yellow fever at San Domingo, West Indies. He had made a will before sailing and has left his fiancée his savings of £1,000, the interest on which would provide Cassandra Austen with a small personal income (about £35 per annum if invested in government stocks). (Cassandra was to maintain close contact with the Fowle family, and she and Jane Austen continued to make regular visits to the Kintbury rectory in future years.)

August: Jane Austen completes "First Impressions."

Autumn: Mrs. Knight, Edward Austen's adoptive mother, decides to retire to Canterbury on an annual income of £2,000 and arranges for Edward to come into immediate inheritance of the Knight estates in Kent and Hampshire. He and his family move from Rowling to Godmersham.

November: "First Impressions" offered to a publisher (Cadell and Davies) by Mr. Austen but rejected. Jane Austen begins to rewrite the epistolary "Elinor and Marianne" in the form of *Sense and Sensibility*.

November–December: Mrs. Austen, Jane Austen, and Cassandra stay in Bath with Mrs. Austen's brother, James Leigh Perrot, and his wife, Jane (née Cholmeley, 1744–1836), at 1 Paragon Buildings. (This is Jane Austen's first recorded visit to Bath, though she has possibly been there before.)

December: Charles Austen promoted to rank of lieutenant and transferred to HMS *Scorpion*.

31 December: Henry Austen marries Eliza de Feuillide in London.

1798	*Sense and Sensibility* presumably finished sometime this year. In midsummer, Jane Austen possibly begins the novel "Susan" (posthumously published and titled *Northanger Abbey* by Henry Austen).
	9 August: Death of Jane Austen's cousin, Jane Cooper (now Lady Jane Williams) in a carriage accident.
	Late August–24 October: Jane Austen, Cassandra, and their parents stay with Edward Austen at Godmersham Park in Kent.
	24–27 October: Jane Austen and her parents return to Steventon via Sittingbourne, Dartford, Staines, and Basingstoke.
	December: Frank Austen promoted to rank of commander on HMS *Peterel* (which he joins in Gibraltar in February 1799).
1799	17 May–late June: Jane Austen and Mrs. Austen visit Bath with Edward Austen and his wife, staying at 13 Queen Square. "Susan" (*Northanger Abbey*) probably finished by the end of June.
	Late summer: Jane Austen and family visit the Leighs at Adlestrop, the Coopers at Harpsden, and another of Mrs. Austen's cousins, Cassandra Leigh (1744–1826), wife of Rev. Samuel Cooke (1741–1820), at Great Bookham in Surrey. After these visits the Austens seem to have remained at Steventon for the rest of the year.
1799–1800	Jane Austen possibly completes her burlesque play, *Sir Charles Grandison*, in this period.
1800	(Jane Austen's movements for most of this year are unknown; there are no surviving letters from her between June 1799 and late October of this year.)

29 March: Trial and acquittal of Jane Austen's aunt, Mrs. Leigh Perrot, accused of stealing a one-pound card of lace from a shop in Bath in August 1799. (As the theft involves goods above twelve pence in value, this is grand larceny at this time, a crime punishable by death or transportation.)

May: Frank Austen promoted to rank of post-captain (though he does not hear of this until October).

November: Jane Austen visits the Lloyds at Ibthorpe, staying from the end of the month to mid-December.

December: Mr. Austen decides to retire and move to Bath with his wife and two daughters, leaving James as his deputy at Steventon.

1801   January: Henry Austen resigns his commission in the militia and establishes himself as a banker and army agent in London.

January–February: Jane Austen visits her old friends Catherine and Alethea Bigg (1775–1848, 1777–1847) at the Bigg-Wither family home, Manydown Park, near Basingstoke. (Jane Austen had often previously stayed overnight here after attending balls at the Basingstoke assembly.)

May: Mrs. Austen, Jane Austen, and Cassandra leave Steventon for Bath, visiting the Lloyds at Ibthorpe on the way. At Bath, they first stay with the Leigh Perrots at 1 Paragon Buildings, before leasing 4 Sydney Place at the end of May. James Austen and his family move into the Steventon rectory.

June–September: Jane Austen and family go on holiday to the West Country, probably visiting Sidmouth and Colyton on the Devon coast. They visit James Austen at Steventon toward the end of September and return to Bath on 5 October.

August: Frank Austen is appointed captain of HMS *Neptune*.

Autumn: Hastings de Feuillide dies in London, aged fifteen.

1802   Jane Austen seems to have spent most of the first half of the year at Bath.

Summer: Jane Austen and family, including the recently demobilized Charles Austen (the Peace of Amiens was declared in March), go on holiday to Devon (to Dawlish and, probably, Teignmouth) and then also possibly to Wales, where they may have visited Tenby and Barmouth.

Late August: Jane Austen and Cassandra possibly visit friends near Steventon, while their parents, together with James and Mary Austen, visit Frank Austen in Portsmouth.

1–3 September: Jane Austen and family stay at Steventon.

3 September–28 October: Jane Austen, Cassandra, and Charles stay at Godmersham with Edward Austen.

28 October–25 November: Jane Austen and Cassandra stay at Steventon.

25 November–3 December: Jane Austen and Cassandra stay with the Bigg sisters at Manydown Park. On 2 December Jane Austen apparently accepts a proposal of marriage from their brother (the only surviving son of the family and heir to Manydown Park), Harris Bigg-Wither (1781–1833). However, Jane Austen withdraws her consent on the following morning. She and Cassandra cut short their visit and return to Steventon.

4 December: Jane Austen and Cassandra return to Bath.

Sometime in 1802 or early in 1803, Jane Austen makes a second copy of "Susan" (*Northanger Abbey*), with revisions.

1803

Spring: Through a business associate of Henry Austen's, Jane Austen sells the copyright of "Susan" (*Northanger Abbey*) for ten pounds to a London publisher, Richard Crosby & Company. Crosby does not publish the novel, however.

May: Henry and Eliza Austen travel to France and narrowly escape detainment following Napoleon's termination of the Peace of Amiens this month. Frank and Charles Austen return to active service. Frank is put in charge of organizing the "Sea Fencibles" (volunteer coastal defense forces) for the southeast coast down from Ramsgate, where he is stationed.

Summer: Possibly, the Austens go on holiday to the West Country again, to the Devon and Dorset coast.

September–October: The Austens stay at Godmersham, and Jane Austen possibly visits Frank Austen at Ramsgate at this time. Jane Austen and Cassandra visit the Lefroys at Ashe rectory on the way back to Bath, where they arrive on 24 October.

November: The Austens take an autumn holiday at Lyme Regis in Dorset.

?1803–1804

Jane Austen writes *The Watsons* (unfinished; titled posthumously by J. E. Austen Leigh).

1804

May: Frank Austen returns to sea as captain of HMS *Leopard*, flagship of Rear Admiral Thomas Louis, and is stationed off Boulogne as part of the blockade of Napoleon's flotilla there.

Midsummer to October: The Austens, along with Henry and Eliza Austen, holiday on the Devon and Dorset coast, Jane Austen and her parents staying mainly in Lyme Regis.

October: Charles Austen promoted to the command of HMS *Indian* and sent to patrol the Atlantic seaboard of America to prevent trade with France by neutral countries such as the United States. Charles remains on duty here, with headquarters at Bermuda, until 1810–1811.

25 October: Back at Bath, the Austens move to 3 Green Park Buildings East.

16 December: Death of Madam Lefroy following a riding accident.

1805

21 January: Death of Mr. Austen.

25 March: Jane Austen moves, with her mother and sister, to 25 Gay Street, Bath.

March–August: Frank Austen, now in the Mediterranean in command of Admiral Louis' flagship HMS *Canopus*, takes part in the chase after Admiral Villeneuve's fleet to the West Indies and back.

16 April: Mrs. Lloyd dies at Ibthorpe, and it is agreed that Martha Lloyd should come to live with the Austens from now on. Probably just after this date, Jane Austen composes "Lines *Supposed* to Have Been Sent to an Uncivil Dressmaker."

June–September: The Austens go to Godmersham, via Steventon, in June. Jane Austen and Cassandra remain in Kent until 17 September, mainly at Godmersham, but with short stays at Goodnestone Farm (with Lady Fanny Bridges, Edward Austen's widowed mother-in-law) in late August and at Sandling (near Maidstone) with Edward's sister-in-law in September.

17 September: Jane Austen and Cassandra go to join Mrs. Austen and Martha Lloyd at lodgings in Worthing on the Sussex coast, where they remain until at least November and possibly until early January 1806.

Jane Austen possibly makes a fair copy of *Lady Susan* sometime this year, at which time the narrated conclusion may also have been added.

October: Frank Austen narrowly misses the Battle of Trafalgar after having been sent on escort duty to Malta.

1806

3 January–mid-March: The Austens go to Steventon for most of January, and then Jane Austen and Cassandra visit the Bigg sisters at Manydown until late February. They stay at Steventon again before returning, in mid-March, to Bath, where Mrs. Austen has taken new lodgings in Trim Street.

May–June: Frank Austen, to be married in July to Mary Gibson, arranges to set up home in Southampton along with his mother, sisters, and Martha Lloyd.

2 July: The Austens leave Bath for the last time. They travel first to Clifton, Bristol, and then, toward the end of the month, to visit the Leighs at Adlestrop, where they remain until 14 August. Jane Austen composes "Lines to Martha Lloyd" while at Clifton and, for her niece Fanny, some verses on the marriage of her brother, Frank (written on or near 24 July).

24 July: Marriage of Frank Austen and Mary Gibson at Ramsgate in Kent.

5–14 August: The whole Adlestrop house party go to stay at Stoneleigh Abbey in Warwickshire.

	14 August–late September: The Austens stay with the Coopers (formerly of Harpsden) at Hamstall Ridware in Staffordshire, where Jane Austen's cousin, Edward, has been rector since 1799.
	September–October: From Staffordshire, the Austens visit Steventon before traveling, on 10 October, to Southampton, where they live in lodgings with Frank Austen and his wife until March 1807.
1807	March: The Austen household moves into a house in Castle Square, Southampton. Frank Austen is appointed to the command of HMS *St. Albans* for convoy duties to and from South Africa, China, and the East Indies.
	27 April: Frank's wife gives birth to their first child, Mary Jane. Jane Austen presumably writes the verse "On Sir Home Popham's Sentence, April 1807" around this time.
	19 May: Charles Austen marries Fanny Palmer (1790–1814) in Bermuda.
	30 June: Frank Austen sets sail for the Cape of Good Hope.
	1–11 September: Jane Austen, Cassandra, and Mrs. Austen go to Chawton, Hampshire, for a family gathering organized by Edward Austen at Chawton Great House, part of his Hampshire estate. "Verses to Rhyme with 'Rose,' " by Jane Austen, Mrs. Austen, Cassandra, and Edward's wife, Elizabeth, possibly written during this visit.
1808	January–March: Jane Austen and Cassandra stay at Steventon and Manydown Park and, from 25 February, with the Fowle family at Kintbury in Berkshire.
	16 May–14 June: Jane Austen stays with Henry and Eliza Austen in London at 16 Michael's Place, Brompton (traveling there via Steventon on 15 May).
	14 June–8 July: Jane Austen stays at Godmersham, traveling back to Southampton, via Guildford, on 8–9 July. She remains in Southampton until April 1809.
	26 August: Jane Austen writes the short verse "To Miss Bigg with Some Pockethandkerchiefs." In this month, Frank Austen is sent on escort duty to the coast of Portugal, where he witnesses the Battle of Vimeiro at the start of the Peninsular War.
	10 October: Death of Edward Austen's wife, Elizabeth. Sometime later this month, Edward offers to provide his mother and sisters with a house, either near Godmersham or at Chawton; they opt for Chawton.
	16 December: On the fourth anniversary of Mrs. Lefroy's death (and Jane Austen's thirty-third birthday) Jane Austen writes her verses "To the Memory of Mrs. Lefroy."

1809   April: Jane Austen (using a pseudonym) writes to Crosby inquiring
            after "Susan" (*Northanger Abbey*) and offering to supply a second
            copy if the first has been lost; Crosby appears to have no immediate
            plans to publish but will not relinquish the copyright (unless it is
            bought back from him). (The reference to another copy of the man-
            uscript—presumably the original one written in 1798–1799, from
            which Crosby's copy was made in 1803—means that the novel may
            have been revised at anytime between 1803 and 1816, when the
            Crosby copy was bought back from him. Jane Austen's renewed in-
            terest in April 1809 may suggest some revision around this time.
            Judging by Jane Austen's own 1816 advertisement to the novel, how-
            ever, it seems unlikely that there were any *major* changes after 1803.)

            15 May–30 June: Jane Austen, Cassandra, and Mrs. Austen stay at
            Godmersham.

            7 July: Jane Austen, her sister, mother, and Martha Lloyd move into
            Chawton Cottage.

            26 July: Jane Austen writes a letter in verse on the birth of Frank
            Austen's first son.

            August: Some minor changes made to *Volume the Third* of the ju-
            venilia. Revision of *Sense and Sensibility* probably begins around this
            time.

1810   Revision of *Sense and Sensibility* continues.

            May: Charles Austen promoted to post-captain on the flagship HMS
            Swiftsure.

            May–July: Jane Austen possibly composes the verses "Mock Pane-
            gyric on a Young Friend."

            July: Frank Austen returns from China.

            July–August: Jane Austen and Cassandra visit Manydown and Stev-
            enton.

            Sense and Sensibility accepted for publication in late 1810 or early
            1811 by Thomas Egerton on a commission basis (i.e., at the author's
            expense, with the publisher receiving a commission on any profits
            and the author retaining the copyright).

1811   7 February: Jane Austen writes "Lines on Maria Beckford." She
            possibly begins *Mansfield Park* this month.

            Late March–early May: Jane Austen corrects proofs of *Sense and
            Sensibility* while staying in London with Henry and Eliza Austen
            (now at 64 Sloane Street, Knightsbridge). At the end of April, Jane
            Austen writes the verse "On the Weald of Kent Canal Bill" and
            possibly also the brief rhyme "I am in a Dilemma."

            May: Jane Austen returns to Chawton via Streatham (south London),
            where she visits her old friend Catherine Bigg (formerly of Many-
            down), now married to the rector of Streatham, Rev. Herbert Hill
            (1749–1828), uncle of Robert Southey.

July: Frank Austen given command of HMS *Elephant* and serves as part of the North Sea Fleet until May 1813.

August: Eliza Austen visits Chawton Cottage in the first half of the month. She appears in good health, but between now and the following year she develops some form of terminal illness and is seriously ill by the start of 1813. Charles Austen returns to England with his wife and two children, his first visit in seven years. Later in the year, he is given command of HMS *Namur*, a guardship stationed at the Nore, off Sheerness, where he and his family live on board (until Fanny's death in 1814).

27 October: Jane Austen writes the verse "On a Headache." Possibly also around this time, she writes the verse "Mr. Gell and Miss Gill."

30 October/November: Publication of *Sense and Sensibility* in three volumes, with "By a Lady" on the title page (none of Jane Austen's novels were published under her name during her lifetime). The price of the novel is fifteen shillings. (The size of the edition is not known for certain but was probably 750 copies.)

November: Jane Austen visits Steventon briefly at the end of the month.

1811–1812   "First Impressions" substantially revised and retitled *Pride and Prejudice*; revision must have been complete by early autumn 1812 and may have begun soon after Jane Austen's return to Chawton from London in May 1811.

1812   9–25 June: Jane Austen and Mrs. Austen visit Steventon.

14 October: Death of Mrs. Knight, Edward Austen's adoptive mother; Edward now takes the name of Knight.

November: Jane Austen probably writes the verse "A Middle-Aged Flirt."

Copyright of *Pride and Prejudice* sold to Egerton sometime before 29 November for £110. Proofs presumably corrected sometime in December and January 1813.

1813   28 January: Publication of *Pride and Prejudice* ("by the Author of 'Sense and Sensibility' ") in an edition of at least 1,000 copies, at a price of eighteen shillings per copy. *Mansfield Park* half-finished.

22 April–1 May: Jane Austen stays with Henry in London through Eliza Austen's final illness and death on 25 April.

19 May–early June: Jane Austen returns to London to help Henry in settling Eliza's affairs and in preparing to move house. (He goes in June to live above his banking premises at 10 Henrietta Street, Covent Garden.)

June–July: *Mansfield Park* finished. First edition of *Sense and Sensibility* sold out, netting Jane Austen a clear profit of £140.

14–17 September: Jane Austen goes to London with Edward Austen and his eldest daughters, where they stay with Henry at 10 Henrietta Street.

October: Second editions of *Sense and Sensibility* (with some authorial revisions) and *Pride and Prejudice* (apparently with no involvement of Jane Austen) issued at the end of the month.

17 September–13 November: Jane Austen stays at Godmersham.

13 November: Jane Austen returns to London and stays with Henry for two weeks, during which time they probably negotiate publication terms for *Mansfield Park* with Egerton, who agrees to publish the novel on a commission basis. Jane Austen is then at Chawton until March 1814.

1814

21 January: *Emma* begun.

February: Proofs for *Mansfield Park* probably corrected.

March: Jane Austen travels to London with Henry Austen on 1 March and stays with him there (possibly continuing with the proofs of *Mansfield Park*) until early April, when she returns to Chawton with Cassandra, via a visit to Catherine (Bigg) Hill at Streatham.

9 May: *Mansfield Park* published in a probable edition of 1,250 copies, at eighteen shillings each.

June–July: Jane Austen spends two weeks with her aunt and uncle Cooke at Great Bookham, Surrey.

August–3 September: Jane Austen stays in London with Henry, who has now moved to 23 Hans Place, off Sloane Street.

6 September: Charles Austen's wife, Fanny, dies on board the HMS *Namur* following the birth of her fourth child.

25 November–5 December: The first edition of *Mansfield Park* has sold out by November, giving Jane Austen a profit of between £310 and £350. She goes to London with Henry to try to arrange a second edition, but Egerton refuses to issue one.

26 December–2 January 1815: Jane Austen and Cassandra stay at 12 Cathedral Close, Winchester, with Alethea Bigg and her widowed sister, Elizabeth Heathcote (1773–1855).

1815

2–16 January: Jane Austen and Cassandra stay with James Austen and family at Steventon, spending three days of the visit at Ashe rectory with the family of Rev. George Lefroy (1782–1823), Madam Lefroy's eldest son, who had become rector of Ashe on the death of his father in 1806.

29 March: *Emma* finished.

8 August: Jane Austen begins *Persuasion* (posthumously published and titled by Henry Austen). Sometime after 30 July, Jane Austen copies out, with her own alterations, ''Lines of Lord Byron, in the Character of Buonoparté'' (Byron's ''Napoleon's Farewell,'' first printed on 30 July).

August–September: In late August and early September, Jane Austen is possibly in London with Henry, negotiating for the publication of *Emma*; they call at Steventon on 3 September, presumably on the return journey to Chawton. A favorable reader's report on the manuscript of *Emma* is with the publisher John Murray by the end of September.

4 October–16 December: Jane Austen stays in London. Henry Austen falls seriously ill on 16 October, and, though his life is out of danger by the end of the month, Jane Austen stays in London longer than planned in order to nurse him through his convalescence. In October, Murray offers £450 for the copyright of *Emma* if the copyrights of *Sense and Sensibility* and *Mansfield Park* are included. Henry and Jane Austen reject this offer in early November; Murray refuses to increase his offer but agrees to publish an edition of 2,000 copies on commission; at the same time, he also agrees to bring out, on commission, a second edition of 750 copies of *Mansfield Park*. The production of *Emma* now proceeds rapidly, Jane Austen correcting proofs probably from mid-November to the second week of December. Revisions for the second edition of *Mansfield Park*, possibly made in a marked copy of the first edition, are completed by 11 December. *Emma* is published, priced twenty-one shillings, at the end of the month (though the title page is dated 1816).

Jane Austen's presence in London during this period comes to the attention of the prince regent (later, George IV), a great admirer of her novels. He arranges for her to visit his Carlton House residence, and the visit takes place on 13 November, Jane Austen being escorted by Rev. James Stanier Clarke (c.1765–1834), the regent's domestic chaplain and librarian at Carlton House. He indicates that the regent would like Jane Austen to dedicate one of her novels to him, and, though with misgivings (she had never approved of the prince and sympathized with Princess Caroline), she obliges a few days later with the dedication of *Emma*. A special presentation set of the novel is dispatched to Carlton House in mid-December, just prior to its general publication. (Subsequent correspondence from Rev. Clarke, who clearly had a strong desire to be immortalized in fiction, provided Jane Austen with the basis for her comic *Plan of a Novel, according to Hints from Various Quarters*, probably written in 1816.)

1816 Early in the year, Jane Austen, through Henry, buys back the manuscript and copyright of "Susan" (*Northanger Abbey*) from Crosby, with the intention of finding another publisher for it. The title is changed to "Catherine," and some slight revisions are possibly made; the "Advertisement, by the Authoress" is also presumably written sometime this year.

19 February: Second edition of *Mansfield Park* published, with revisions made by Jane Austen. During this month, Charles Austen's ship, HMS *Phoenix*, is wrecked off the coast of Asia Minor by a hurricane, though he and his crew survive.

March: Collapse of Henry Austen's banking business and army agency; among others, several members of the family suffer serious losses, most notably his uncle Perrot (£10,000) and brother Edward (£20,000).

May: Jane Austen possibly writes *Plan of a Novel, according to Hints from Various Quarters* during a three-week visit to Chawton by her brother Edward and niece Fanny (who contributed some of the "hints").

22 May–15 June: Jane Austen, feeling unwell from early this year, goes for two weeks to take the waters at Cheltenham Spa, accompanied by Cassandra; they visit the Fowle family at Kintbury on the return journey and Steventon on both the outward and return journeys.

18 July: First draft of *Persuasion* completed.

6 August: Ending of *Persuasion* revised.

October: *Emma* has sold 1,248 copies by this date, giving Jane Austen a notional profit of £221 on this novel so far—but losses from the second edition of *Mansfield Park* are offset against this sum, and she actually receives only some £38 for *Emma* in her lifetime. (The edition did not sell out: 539 copies were remaindered in 1821, along with 498 copies of the second edition of *Mansfield Park*.)

December: Henry Austen is ordained deacon and becomes curate of Chawton. (He is ordained as a priest in early 1817.)

1817

17 January: Jane Austen begins *Sanditon* (posthumously titled by the Austen family, though Jane Austen's intended title seems to have been "The Brothers").

18 March: Work on *Sanditon* abandoned because of illness.

27 April: Jane Austen makes her will, leaving everything to Cassandra, subject to funeral expenses, apart from two legacies of fifty pounds each to her brother Henry and his housekeeper, Madame Bigeon.

24 May: Jane Austen is moved by Cassandra to Winchester for better medical care; they lodge at 8 College Street.

15 July: Jane Austen writes "Venta," her verses on Winchester Races and St. Swithun.

18 July: Jane Austen dies at about 4:30 A.M.

22 July: Jane Austen identified as the author of her novels for the first time in public in an obituary in the *Hampshire Courier*.

24 July: Jane Austen buried in Winchester Cathedral.

10 September: Jane Austen's will is proved: after £239 funeral costs and other payments are deducted, Cassandra is left with £561.2.0. (Jane Austen's earnings from her novels, at the time of her death, amount to about £630; posthumous profits, including the sale price

of the five remaining copyrights in 1832 to the publisher Richard Bentley, bring her total literary earnings to somewhere in excess of £1,625.)

Late December: *Northanger Abbey* and *Persuasion* published together in four volumes by Murray, along with a "Biographical Notice of the Author" by her brother, Henry (who negotiated the publication on Cassandra's behalf—on a commission basis once more—and who probably gave the novels these titles). 1,750 copies are printed, priced twenty-four shillings each, and most are sold in the following year, providing Cassandra with a profit of nearly £519 by the start of 1821 (in which year 283 copies of the novels were remaindered).

The second edition of *Pride and Prejudice* is sold out sometime this year, and a third edition issued by Egerton.

1866	First publication of Jane Austen's verses "To the Memory of Mrs. Lefroy."
1869	*A Memoir of Jane Austen* by her nephew James Edward Austen-Leigh (actually published on 16 December 1869, but with 1870 on the title page and usually cited under the latter date); prints some of Jane Austen's letters and verses for the first time and sparks increased interest in Jane Austen after a period of general neglect.
1871	Enlarged second edition of *A Memoir* published, including first printing of *Lady Susan*, *The Watsons*, the so-called "canceled" chapter from *Persuasion*, "The Mystery" (*Volume the First*), further letters, and extracts from *Plan of a Novel* and from "The Last Work" (*Sanditon*).
1884	*Letters of Jane Austen*, 2 vols., edited by Edward, Lord Brabourne, eldest son of Jane Austen's niece, Fanny Austen-Knight (later, Lady Knatchbull); prints letters unavailable to J. E. Austen-Leigh for his *Memoir* and some of her verses.
1895	*Charades, Written a Hundred Years Ago by Jane Austen and Her Family*: this publication includes three charades by Jane Austen (reprinted in *Minor Works* [see under 1954], p. 450).
1902	*Jane Austen: Her Homes and Her Friends* by Constance Hill provides further biographical and background information based on personal contacts and visits and drawing on Austen family manuscripts.
1906	*Jane Austen's Sailor Brothers* by J. H. and E. C. Hubback (Frank Austen's grandson and his daughter): provides much new family information and prints, for the first time, Jane Austen's letters to her brother Frank and the poem "Venta."
1913	*Jane Austen: Her Life and Letters, A Family Record* by William Austen-Leigh (son of J. E. Austen-Leigh) and his nephew Richard Arthur Austen-Leigh: based on the 1869–1871 *Memoir* but drawing on newly available material and many unpublished family papers. (This largely factual biography has come to be seen as the standard *Life* of the author and as a primary source of reference for Austen

scholarship. Drawing on R. A. Austen-Leigh's own much-annotated copy of the book and on further papers collected by him (and, indeed, on the complete Austen family archive) and incorporating new material published since 1913, along with findings from her own original researches, Deirdre Le Faye has recently revised and enlarged this work as *Jane Austen: A Family Record [1989].)*

1920   *Personal Aspects of Jane Austen* by Mary Augusta Austen-Leigh (daughter of J. E. Austen-Leigh): includes material not included in the 1913 *Life*.

1922   *Volume the Second* of the juvenilia first published under the title of *Love and Freindship* [*sic*].

1923   Oxford edition of *The Novels of Jane Austen*, 5 vols., edited by R. W. Chapman: the first scholarly edition and now generally cited as standard (reprinted with revisions and corrections, but from the 1923 plates, in 1926 and 1932–1934 as the second and third editions respectively; and subsequently reprinted many times, with further revisions, corrections, and additions).

1925   *Sanditon* first published in full, edited by R. W. Chapman.

            Lady Susan reprinted from the original, edited by R. W. Chapman.

1926   *Two Chapters of Persuasion*, edited by R. W. Chapman, reprints the original manuscript ending of the novel (Chapters 10 and 11 of vol. 2). It corrects errors in the transcript of Chapter 10 that was included in the 1871 *Memoir* and points out that not all of this chapter had been "canceled" (as suggested by the *Memoir*); it also reveals that the manuscript Chapter 11 differs in details from its printed version (where it becomes Chapter 12) and that there had therefore been some further revision of this chapter, too.

            Plan of a Novel, according to Hints from Various Quarters first published in full, edited by R. W. Chapman, and accompanied by the first printing of Jane Austen's collection of comments, "Opinions of *Mansfield Park*" and "Opinions of *Emma*" (dates of composition unknown but probably in the year or so following publication of each novel: 1814–1815 and 1816 respectively); and also her notes on the dates of composition of three novels and on profits from her novels to March 1817.

            "Mr. Gill and Miss Gell" and "On a Headache" first published in *Two Poems by Jane Austen*.

1927   *The Watsons* reprinted from the original, edited by R. W. Chapman.

1932   *Jane Austen's Letters to Her Sister Cassandra and Others*, 2 vols., edited by R. W. Chapman: prints all letters then known. (A second edition in 1952 added five letters; a third edition, edited by Deirdre Le Faye [1995], represents a thorough revision of Chapman's edition and brings the record right up to date.)

1933   *Volume the First* first published, edited by R. W. Chapman.

1940	*Three Evening Prayers* by Jane Austen, edited by W. M. Roth.
1942	*Austen Papers 1704–1856* collected and edited by R. A. Austen-Leigh: previously unpublished materials collected as part of the continuing researches into Jane Austen's life by the coauthor of the 1913 *Life*.
1951	*Volume the Third* first published, edited by R. W. Chapman.
1952	*My Aunt Jane Austen: A Memoir* (written in 1867) by Caroline Mary Craven Austen (1805–1880), daughter of Jane Austen's eldest brother James.
	Second enlarged edition of Chapman's 1932 *Letters*.
1954	*Minor Works*, vol. 6 in the Oxford edition of *The Works of Jane Austen*, edited by R. W. Chapman; this volume collects all of Jane Austen's writings (then available) apart from the six novels and the letters. (The edition was reprinted in 1958, with revisions in 1963 and 1965 and with further revisions by B. C. Southam in 1969 and at several subsequent dates.)
1963	*Volume the Second* reprinted (see entry for 1922) in a recollated text, edited by B. C. Southam.
1975	*The MS of Sanditon*, edited by B. C. Southam.
1975–1976	First publication of complete text of manuscript of "Lines to Martha Lloyd," edited by Donald Greene, in *Nineteenth-Century Fiction* 30 (1975–1976): 257–60. (Eleven stanzas: *Minor Works* prints only three.)
1980	First publication of *Jane Austen's "Sir Charles Grandison,"* transcribed and edited by Brian Southam; this provides a reading text and a transcription of the manuscript of Jane Austen's burlesque play, "Sir Charles Grandison or The Happy Man, a Comedy in Five Acts." Although in Jane Austen's hand, the play had traditionally been ascribed to Jane Austen's niece, Anna, by the Austen family; however, when the manuscript came to auction in the autumn of 1977 and became open to scholarly inspection for the first time, its length, nature, and apparent chronology of composition provided strong (though not conclusive) evidence of Jane Austen's authorship.
1987	First publication of Jane Austen's "Lines *Supposed* to Have Been Sent to an Uncivil Dressmaker" (April 1805) and her verses on Frank Austen's marriage to Mary Gibson (July 1806), both edited by Deirdre Le Faye, *Times Literary Supplement* (20 February 1987): 185.
1989	The *Life* of 1913 revised and enlarged by Deirdre Le Faye.
1995	*Letters of Jane Austen*, third edition, edited by Deirdre Le Faye.
1996	*Jane Austen: Collected Poems and Verse of the Austen Family*, edited by David Selwyn.

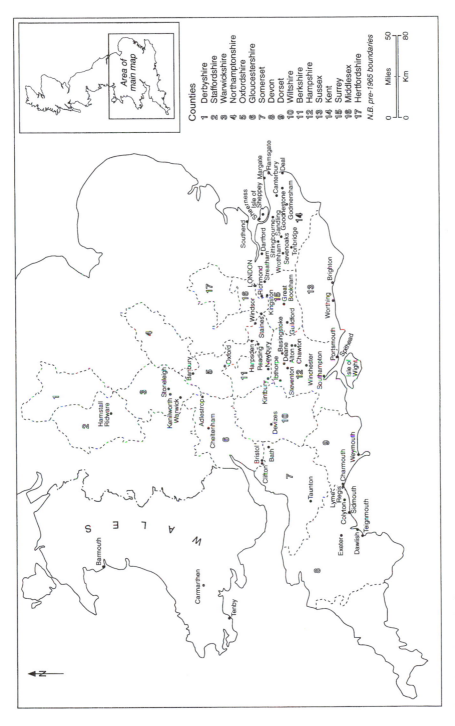

Jane Austen's England.

Miles
0   50

Km
0   80

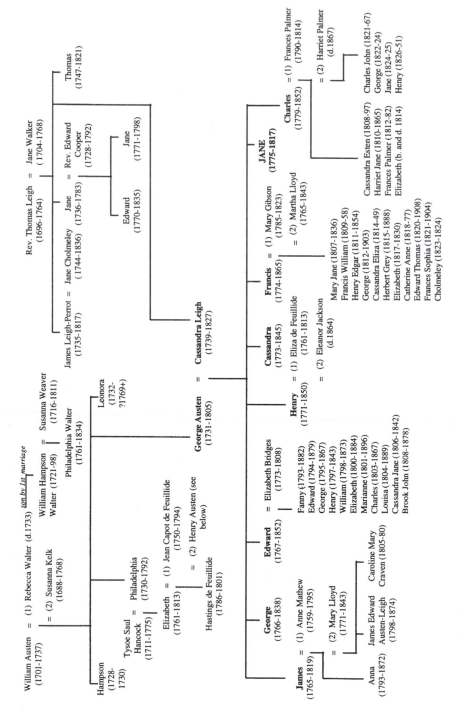

The Austen Family.

Jane Austen's brothers (left to right). Henry (1771–1850) at about fifty; James (1765–1819) at about twenty-five; Frank (1774–1865) at about twenty-two; Charles (1779–1852) at about thirty; and Edward (1767–1852) at about thirty. Drawing by Barbara Wilamowska. Reproduced with permission.

Reverend George Austen, 1731–1805 (Jane Austen's father). Drawing by Barbara Wilamowska. Reproduced with permission.

1790 — Chemise gown of patterned muslin

1800 — High waisted muslin with low décolletage

1810 — High waisted muslin in empire line style with hem frills

1820 — White gauze gown

Female Fashion, 1790–1820. Drawing by Emily Smith. Reproduced with permission.

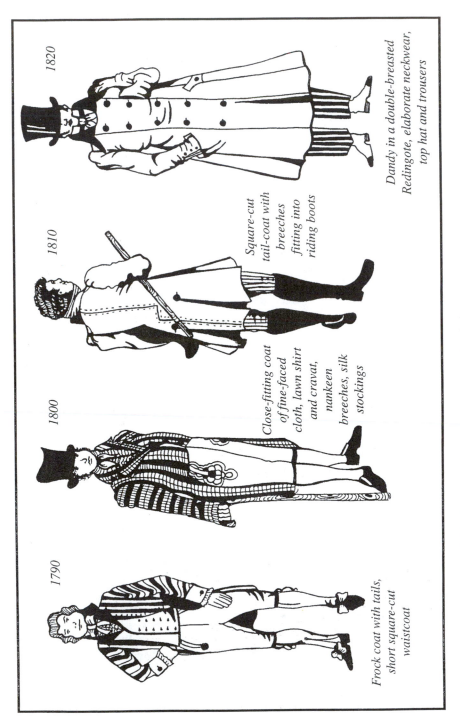

1790

Frock coat with tails, short square-cut waistcoat

1800

Close-fitting coat of fine-faced cloth, lawn shirt and cravat, nankeen breeches, silk stockings

1810

Square-cut tail-coat with breeches fitting into riding boots

1820

Dandy in a double-breasted Redingote, elaborate neckwear, top hat and trousers

Male Fashion, 1790–1820. Drawing by Emily Smith. Reproduced with permission.

Elaborate Walking Dress with bustle and puffed bodice and sleeves

Army Officer's Uniform

Fashion, c. 1780. Drawing by Emily Smith. Reproduced with permission.

One-piece thin muslin day dress with cashmere shawl - the "Naked Style"

Admiral's Uniform

Fashion, c. 1804. Drawing by Emily Smith. Reproduced with permission.

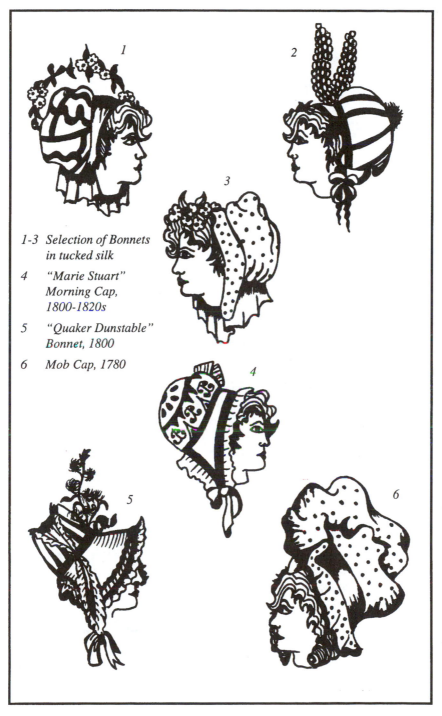

1-3 *Selection of Bonnets in tucked silk*

4 *"Marie Stuart" Morning Cap, 1800-1820s*

5 *"Quaker Dunstable" Bonnet, 1800*

6 *Mob Cap, 1780*

Female Headwear, 1780–1820. Drawing by Emily Smith. Reproduced with permission.

Travelling Coach

Gig

Barouche Landau

Landaulet

Carriages, c. 1800. Drawing by Emily Smith. Reproduced with permission.

Queen Square, Bath. On Jane Austen's second recorded visit to the city in 1799, she stayed at No. 13 which is the house on the corner with the arched doorway.

Chawton Cottage, where Jane Austen lived from July 1809 until shortly before her death in 1817. It was here that she completed her major novels. The house is now open to the public as a museum dedicated to the author.

"Granny's Teeth," the steps on the Cobb at Lyme Regis from which Louisa Musgrove fell in Chapter 12 of *Persuasion*.

No. 8 College Street, Winchester, where Jane Austen died on 18 July 1817. She had been moved into lodgings here in May 1817 in order to receive better medical treatment.

Winchester Cathedral. Jane Austen was buried in the north aisle of the church on 24 July 1817.

2

Historical Chronology, 1750–1820

1750–1850	Some 4,000 enclosure acts, mainly in the years 1755–1780 and 1790–1815, enclose approximately 6 million acres of open field and common land in Britain. Food output is increased (helped by growing imports), but land and wealth become concentrated in the hands of a relatively small number of powerful landlords, while thousands of small farmers, cottagers, and squatters are dispossessed and forced off the land. (In Wales, for example, 90 percent of the land is owned by less than 10 percent of the population.) Though there are regional variations, the dominant pattern of agricultural production becomes one whereby large estates are worked by tenant farmers employing landless laborers. In 1790, approximately 25,000 families own most of the land, with ownership concentrated in the hands of around 400 large land owners (whose average yearly income is about £10,000 each).
	This is also the main period of the Industrial Revolution, marked by extensive technical innovation and increasing mechanization, especially in the textile and iron industries; increased output and productivity and the creation of new industries such as engineering; expansion and improvement of transport systems; the growth of industrial capitalism, wage-labor, and the factory system; major population growth and shifts in centers of population, with greater urbanization and rapid expansion of workforces in the industrial heartlands (mainly in the Midlands and the north of England and in parts of South Wales and Scotland); many new social and political tensions; and increasing agitation for reform arising from wretched living and working conditions and lack of rights of the new industrial proletariat.
1756	Start of Seven Years' War (French and Indian War): Britain allied with Prussia against France, Austria, Russia, and, later, Spain, with fighting in Europe and the colonies.

1757	Battle of Plassey, West Bengal (23 June): British troops, led by Robert Clive (1725–1774), defeat the nawab of Bengal, giving East India Company mastery of Bengal and making Britain the dominant power in India.
1760	Death of George II (b.1683); accession of George III (b.1738), who rules until 1820.
1761	The Bridgewater Canal opens in Lancashire. Built by James Brindley (1716–1772) to connect the duke of Bridgewater's collieries at Worsley to Manchester (a distance of eight miles), this is the most spectacular canal of the period, and its engineering and commercial success greatly encourages further canal construction. (The Sankey Brook Canal, built in 1751, also in Lancashire, was the first modern canal in Britain; the development of the canal system continues until railways begin to dominate from around 1840, there being some 4,000 miles of canals by 1830.)
1763	February: Treaty of Paris ends Seven Years' War: Britain emerges as leading world power, but with national debt almost doubled from £76 million to £133 million.
	April: George Grenville (1712–1770) becomes prime minister (to 1765).
1764	James Hargreaves (d.1778) invents the spinning jenny around this time.
1765	March: Stamp Act passed to raise tax revenues from American colonies; meets strong resistance ("no taxation without representation") and begins decade of crisis in Anglo-American relations, culminating in rebellion and war.
	July: Marquess of Rockingham, Charles Wentworth (1730–1782), becomes prime minister (to 1766).
	In India, Mughal emperor Shah Alam grants East India Company right to collect Bengal land revenues (*diwani*); this effectively gives company direct political control of Bengal.
	James Watt (1736–1819) improves design of Newcomen steam pump with invention of condenser (patented 1769), leading to construction and manufacture of his improved steam engine from 1775.
1766	March: Repeal of Stamp Act, but a new act declares right to tax American colonies (Declaratory Act).
	July: Rockingham dismissed by the king: 1st earl of Chatham, William Pitt the Elder (1708–1778), becomes prime minister (to 1767).
1767	February: Reduction of land tax from four to three shillings in the pound reflects strength of landed interest in Parliament.
	September: Chatham suffers a breakdown, and, though he does not formally resign until October 1768, the duke of Grafton, Augustus Fitzroy (1735–1811), becomes effective prime minister (to 1770).

1768	James Cook (1728–1779) charts coasts of New Zealand and western Australia.
1769	Richard Arkwright (1732–1792) invents water-powered spinning frame, allowing pure cotton cloth to be woven for first time; leads to rapid expansion of mechanized cotton manufacture. James Watt (1736–1819) patents his improved steam engine.
1770	Some 15,000 miles of roads are administered by turnpike trusts by this date (22,000 miles by 1830); often employing skilled engineers and road makers such as Thomas Telford (1757–1834) and John Macadam (1756–1836), turnpikes are the main means of road improvement, though often unpopular locally because of tolls. (London to Cambridge takes about two days by coach in 1750 and about seven hours in 1820.)
	January: Lord North (1732–1792) becomes prime minister (until 1782).
	Cook names Botany Bay in Australia.
1771	Luigi Galvani (1737–1798) discovers electric nature of nervous impulse.
	First edition of *Encyclopaedia Britannica*.
1772	Warren Hastings (1732–1818) appointed governor of Bengal in April.
	Slavery effectively outlawed in England by the Somerset case, in which the lord chief justice, Lord Mansfield (1705–1793), rules that slaves cannot be sold abroad by their masters.
	Britain imports 5.3 million pounds of raw cotton and exports 11.6 million yards of linen and 91,000 pounds of silk.
1773	May: Regulating Act, designed to increase government control over East India Company, establishes post of governor-general of India; Warren Hastings the first appointee in September.
	16 December: Boston Tea Party: American colonists destroy East India Company shipment of tea in protest against "arbitrary" taxation and legislation by Britain, a landmark event whose repercussions contribute to outbreak of American War of Independence.
1774	March: Coercive Acts passed by Parliament against Massachusetts.
	April: Quebec Act defines governance of the colony (taken from France in 1759 during the Seven Years' War) and aims to reconcile French to British rule.
	May: Louis XVI accedes to throne in France.
	September: First Continental Congress of the American colonies meets at Philadelphia. Decides in December to refuse imports of British goods into the colonies.
1775	American War of Independence begins: first hostilities in April, with the Battle of Bunker Hill in June.

James Watt, in partnership with Matthew Boulton (1728–1809), begins manufacture of improved steam engine.

Thomas Spence (1750–1814) advocates land nationalization in Britain, attacking the power of the landlords as the root cause of contemporary distress in the country.

Cook returns from second South Seas voyage, having discovered the Sandwich Islands and conquered scurvy.

Sarah Siddons (1755–1831) makes her debut at the Drury Lane Theatre as Portia.

Population of England and Wales about 6.7 million.

[16 December: Birth of Jane Austen.]

1776	4 July: Declaration of American Independence.
1778	France declares war on Britain in support of America.
1779	Spain enters war on American side: siege of Gibraltar begins (continues until February 1783).

Samuel Crompton (1753–1827) invents his "mule," a cross between the water frame and the spinning jenny, capable of spinning cotton that is at once strong and fine.

1780   Holland enters war on American side.

June: Gordon Riots in London: anti-Catholic demonstration escalates into full-scale rioting over ten days; some 700 die, with 450 arrests and twenty-five subsequent executions.

Society for Constitutional Information founded in London to promote parliamentary reform.

1782   March: Marquess of Rockingham becomes prime minister until his death later in the year, when he is replaced by the earl of Shelburne, William Petty (1737–1805).

November: Preliminary peace treaty signed with America (in January 1783 with France and Spain).

1783   April: Duke of Portland, William Bentinck (1738–1809), becomes prime minister.

3 September: Peace of Versailles. Britain recognizes American independence and ends war.

December: William Pitt the Younger (1759–1806) becomes prime minister (until 1801).

The Montgolfier brothers, Joseph (1740–1810) and Jacques Etienne (1745–1799), launch hot-air balloons in June, September (in Versailles), and, manned, in Paris on 21 November. The first piloted hydrogen balloon flight takes place on 1 December, the balloon traveling twenty-seven miles in two hours.

Charles Simeon (1759–1836) starts Evangelical movement at Cambridge.

1784	February: John Wesley (1703–1791) begins to ordain ministers, and his deed of declaration becomes the charter of Wesleyan Methodism.

March: Pitt is reelected prime minister.

August: India Act establishes Board of Control in London to supervise activities of East India Company. Also in August, the first mail coach, brainchild of John Palmer (1742–1818), runs from Bristol to London in sixteen hours, inaugurating the systematic carriage of mail by road throughout the country; by 1800, 400 towns receive a daily post, with coaches traveling at an average of six miles an hour.

Andrew Meikle (1719–1811) invents threshing machine.

Henry Cort (1740–1800) develops his puddling process, a key invention in advancing the manufacture of iron.

1785   Hastings resigns as governor-general of India and returns to England amid accusations of corruption and extortion; there begins a concerted Whig campaign for his impeachment, led by Edmund Burke (1729–1797).

Jean-Pierre Blanchard (1753–1809) and John Jeffries make first air crossing of English Channel in a hot-air balloon.

Edmund Cartwright (1743–1822) invents and patents a mechanically driven ''power loom''; completes mechanization of weaving and brings about demise of the hand-loom weavers. Cartwright opens a cotton factory in Doncaster, Yorkshire, in 1787.

15 December: George, Prince of Wales, secretly and illegally marries Mrs. Maria Fitzherbert, née Smythe (1756–1837).

1786   Registered tonnage for British merchant shipping is 1,150,000 tons.

1787   May: Warren Hastings impeached by Edmund Burke.

September: U.S. Constitution signed.

Start of major public campaign in Britain for the abolition of the slave trade.

1788   January: The *Times* founded by John Walter (1739–1812) (though a forerunner, the *Daily Universal Register*, has been published since 1785).

February: Trial of Warren Hastings begins.

May: Motion in Parliament for abolition of slave trade.

June: Joseph Banks (1743–1820) founds Africa Association to encourage exploration and trade.

November–December: ''Regency crisis'': George III suffers severe mental breakdown and precipitates political dispute about what the powers of the prince regent should be.

Watt perfects steam engine.

1789   February: Regency crisis ends without resolution when the king makes a sudden recovery.

April: Mutiny on HMS *Bounty*. George Washington (1732–1799) takes office as first president of the United States (in office until 1797).

In France, Estates General meet at Versailles (May–June); storming and fall of Paris Bastille (14 July) set in motion French Revolution. In its reformist and antiabsolutist aspects, it is widely welcomed in Britain, especially by radicals, but conservative opposition gradually mounts over the next two years as fears of British "Jacobinism" grow.

1790   Popular radical corresponding societies are founded around the country to debate and campaign for parliamentary reform.

At the start of November, the Whig politician and writer Edmund Burke, highly critical of the French Revolution, publishes *Reflections on the Revolution in France*. This sparks a major war of ideas that continues throughout the decade, with its opposite pole most notably represented by *The Rights of Man* (Part I published in March 1791) by Tom Paine (1737–1809). Conservative upper- and middle-class opinion sides with Burke, while radicals and reformers, intellectuals, and the educated working classes generally support Painite ideals. One of the earliest of the many "replies" to Burke, published at the end of November, is *Vindication of the Rights of Men, in a Letter to the Right Honourable Edmund Burke* by Mary Wollstonecraft (1759–1797).

1791   July: "Church and King" riots in Birmingham, in protest at a dinner held by prominent Dissenters and reformers to mark the anniversary of the fall of the Bastille.

Ordnance Survey, official British mapmaking organization, founded for defense purposes (first one inch: one mile maps published in 1801).

Jeremy Bentham (1748–1832) designs his "Panopticon," a model prison allowing for the central observation of convicts.

1791–1794   "Canal mania": more than forty canals built; reduces cost of transporting goods inland, particularly in areas without navigable rivers.

1792   January: London Corresponding Society founded, partly in order to link existing corresponding societies and to coordinate radical activity throughout Britain. *A Vindication of the Rights of Woman* by Mary Wollstonecraft published.

In revolutionary France: war declared on Austria (April); royal palace stormed, and king imprisoned; first Paris commune comes to power under Danton (August); monarchy abolished, and France declared a republic (September); peoples of other nations offered support to overthrow their monarchies (November).

The radicalization and increased violence of the French Revolution alarm even erstwhile supporters in Britain, and, from now on, there are increasing hostility toward, and increasingly repressive legislation against, British "Jacobin" activity and opinion. In May, George III

issues a proclamation against seditious writings, and legal intimida-
tion of radical newspaper printers and booksellers begins (made easier
by special legal powers held by the attorney-general in prosecutions
for libel). Part II of *The Rights of Man* (published in February) is
suppressed, and a warrant for Paine's arrest issued; he flees to France.

November: The loyalist Association for the Preservation of Liberty
and Property against Republicans and Levellers is founded as part of
the growing government propaganda campaign against radicals.

December: Paine is tried in absentia and convicted of seditious libel.
The Association for Preserving the Liberty of the Press is formed,
though it disbands again in June 1793, having had little impact.

Slave trade abolished in Denmark.

Dollar coinage introduced in United States.

1793	In France: Louis XVI guillotined (21 January); start of Revolutionary Wars with declaration of war on Britain, Holland, and Spain (February); moderate Girondins overthrown by radical Jacobins (June), and Committee of Public Safety under Robespierre comes to power— period of "Terror" follows, with aggressive prosecution of war abroad and severe repressive measures at home, including mass executions; Marie Antoinette executed in October.

In Britain, sedition trials of leading radicals and reformers in Scotland
result in harsh sentences of up to fourteen years' transportation to
Botany Bay. A British convention of reformers meets in Edinburgh
in November and December but is broken up by the authorities, and
its leaders arrested; further trials and convictions follow, including
those of delegates from England.

Voluntary Board of Agriculture set up to promote agricultural improvements.

1793–1794	Some 40,000 men enlist in voluntary civil defense forces.
1794	Habeas corpus suspended, allowing government to imprison suspects for long periods without trial. Leaders of the London Corresponding Society (which has been infiltrated by government spies) are arrested and charged with treason; they are tried between October and December but are acquitted, much to the government's embarrassment.

Fall of Robespierre and end of Terror in France (July).

1795	8 April: George, Prince of Wales, marries his cousin Princess Caroline of Brunswick (1768–1821) (despite his "marriage" to Mrs. Fitzherbert in 1785; the marriage to Caroline was one of convenience, and the couple effectively separated after the birth of their daughter in January 1896).

23 April: Trial of Warren Hastings ends; he is acquitted on all charges
but is left bankrupt.

General food shortages and rising prices lead to nationwide food riots.

May: A new form of poor relief is adopted at Speen near Reading
in Berkshire whereby wages are made up from local parish rates to

equal the cost of subsistence (linked to the price of a gallon loaf of bread); adopted by other counties in the southeast of England and known as the Speenhamland system.

Methodist secession from Church of England.

October–November: George III's coach apparently attacked on the way to open Parliament; this provides a pretext for the government to pass a Treasonable Practices and Seditious Meetings Acts ("Two Acts"), which limit political freedoms and curtail the activities of radical societies.

Napoleon Bonaparte comes to prominence as commander of French armed forces.

1796   First successful vaccination against smallpox carried out by Edward Jenner (1749–1823).

Society for Bettering the Condition and Increasing the Comforts of the Poor founded.

October: Spain, originally Britain's ally, reenters war on French side.

December: Abortive attempt by French fleet to invade Ireland, partly in support of United Irishmen attempting to foment rebellion against British rule. Heightened fears of French invasion of Britain throughout following year.

1797   February: Abortive French landing in Pembrokeshire, Wales, by some 1,400 French troops led by an American colonel (the last invasion of mainland Britain).

Government forced to abandon gold standard because of cost of war—paper money introduced nationally for the first time; devaluation of currency and higher prices follow.

March: John Adams (1735–1826) becomes second president of United States.

April–June: Naval mutinies at Spithead, Plymouth, and Nore (in protest against appalling conditions and brutal discipline) effectively put home fleet out of action and increase danger of French invasion. Men's demands largely granted at Spithead and Plymouth, but Nore mutiny suppressed amid suspicions of Jacobin involvement; over thirty ringleaders executed.

October: British victory over Dutch fleet at Camperdown ends immediate danger of invasion.

November: *The Anti-Jacobin* magazine starts publication and runs until July 1798 with an influential campaign against radicals and revolutionary sympathizers; succeeded by the *Anti-Jacobin Review and Magazine* (1798–1821).

1798   April: Entire committee of London Corresponding Society imprisoned (some to remain in prison for nearly three years without trial).

May: Income tax introduced for the first time, as an emergency war measure: 10 percent on incomes over £200. (Abolished again in 1816 but becoming a permanent fixture of fiscal policy after 1842.) This year, also, the government increases tax on newspapers and prohibits import of foreign newspapers.

May–June: Irish Rebellion suppressed by British; up to 20,000 killed. French expeditionary force arrives belatedly in August and is repelled.

August: Nelson destroys French fleet at Battle of the Nile.

Volunteer movement gathers force in face of renewed fears of invasion; there are mass enlistments this year, and by 1803 approximately a fifth of men of military age belong to some form of voluntary civil defense force or "home guard."

Mechanization of paper manufacture quickly leads to reduction in costs of printing, and rates of production increase further by introduction of iron presses.

1799   Government Act (strengthening a similar one passed in 1798) imposes system of registration on printers of books, pamphlets, and newspapers "for better preventing treasonable and seditious practices" and to facilitate suppression of "Jacobinical" societies.

July: London Corresponding Society and similar radical organizations are made illegal. Combination Act forbids workers to act together for improved wages and conditions (effectively outlawing trade unions).

Victory over the French-backed Tipu, sultan of Mysore, at Seringapatam ends Mysore Wars and gives Britain control of most of south and west India.

November: Napoleon seizes power in France and becomes first consul.

Church Missionary Society and Religious Tract Society founded under Evangelical influence.

1800   Act of Union between Britain and Ireland passed in August, effective from January 1801.

Widespread food riots.

Approximately 2,500 steam engines in production: now a major source of power in textile, coal, and other industries.

Robert Owen (1771–1858), an early advocate of socialism, takes over mills at New Lanark in Scotland and develops model community with improved working conditions, housing, sanitation, and educational provision.

Royal College of Surgeons founded in London.

1801   March: Henry Addington (1757–1844) becomes prime minister (until 1804). Thomas Jefferson (1743–1826) becomes president of United States (until 1807) in new capital of Washington.

April: Habeas corpus suspended.

First census in Britain: population of England and Wales, 8.9 million; 30 percent live in towns.

General Enclosure Act simplifies process of enclosing common land.

1802   March: Treaty of Amiens brings peace between Britain and France,
                ending the Revolutionary Wars.

                First purpose-built stock exchange opens in London.

                Richard Trevithick (1771–1833) invents high-pressure steam engine,
                which leads to development of steam locomotives.

                First successful use of steam engine to propel a vessel, the *Charlotte
                Dundas*, on the Forth and Clyde Canal in Scotland.

                Health and Morals of Apprentices Act pioneers health and safety
                legislation in British factories.

                Britain imports 56 million pounds of raw cotton and exports 15.7
                million yards of linen and 78,000 pounds of silk.

1803   May: Start of the Napoleonic Wars as hostilities are resumed between
                Britain and France.

1804   May: William Pitt becomes prime minister again (until his death in
                January 1806). Napoleon proclaimed emperor of France.

                Spain declares war on Britain at instigation of France.

                Richard Trevithick builds the first steam locomotive to run on rails
                and runs it on the track at Pen-y-darren ironworks, Merthyr Tydfil,
                South Wales.

                First British savings bank opened.

                British and Foreign Bible Society founded.

1805   Napoleon amasses an "Army of England" at Boulogne and plans to
                invade Britain across the channel as soon as the Royal Navy can be
                diverted elsewhere. The plan largely fails by July, and Napoleon's
                fleet is destroyed at the Battle of Trafalgar in October, effectively
                ending the threat of French invasion.

                British power in India is consolidated with the defeat of the Maratha
                princes (1803–1805); almost the whole of India is under British rule
                by 1818.

1806   23 January: Death of William Pitt.

                February: Coalition government formed, led by William Grenville
                (1759–1834) ("All-the-Talents" ministry).

                A royal commission is established to make a "Delicate Investiga-
                tion" into the conduct of Caroline, Princess of Wales, who is sus-
                pected of sexual profligacy and of having borne an illegitimate child

                (who might later have claims to the throne); the latter charge is dis-
                proved, but there is sufficient evidence for the former to prompt a
                royal reprimand from the king—though not sufficient to give the
                Prince of Wales grounds for the divorce he was hoping for. In the
                public eye, the prince's own reputation for loose living makes this
                attempt to discredit his wife seem unfair and hypocritical; she gains
                some popular sympathy, while his standing sinks even lower.

November: Napoleon issues Berlin Decrees, which begin a trade blockade of Britain (the "Continental System") and a five-year period of mutually damaging economic warfare between the two sides as Britain retaliates with its own Orders in Council (from 1807) and a blockade of France and its satellites.

December: Grenville ministry reelected.

Registered tonnage of British merchant shipping is 2 million tons.

British iron production stands at 243,851 tons. The cotton industry employs 90,000 factory workers and 184,000 hand-loom weavers.

1807

March: Duke of Portland (1738–1809) becomes prime minister (until 1809).

August: The *Clermont*, designed by Robert Fulton (1765–1815) and built by Matthew Boulton and James Watt, sails up the Hudson River and becomes first commercially successful steamboat.

November: France invades Portugal, and the Braganzas, the Portuguese royal family, flee to Brazil.

Slave trade abolished in British Empire (slavery abolished, 1833).

1808

January: United States prohibits import of slaves from Africa.

February: France invades Spain.

August: Start of Peninsular War. Early victory against the French in Portugal, at Vimeiro, by Arthur Wellesley (1769–1852), future Duke of Wellington, followed by abortive invasion of Spain by Sir John Moore; chased by the French to Corunna, his army suffers heavy losses before a successful rearguard action (in which Moore dies) allows a sea evacuation in January 1809.

Royal Lancastrian Institution set up to promote education of the poor on the educational model of Joseph Lancaster (1778–1838).

1809

March: James Madison (1751–1836) becomes president of United States (until 1817).

May: Wellesley defeats French at Oporto and forces retreat from Portugal.

June: Curwen's Act prohibits sale of parliamentary seats.

July: Wellesley created first Duke of Wellington following victory at Talavera.

Following the failure of the Walcheren expedition to capture Antwerp, two cabinet ministers, Viscount Castlereagh (Robert Stewart, 1769–1822) and George Canning (1770–1827), fight a duel after the latter attempts to have the former removed from office for incompetence.

October: Spencer Perceval (1762–1812) becomes prime minister (until 1812).

Pall Mall in London is lit by gas.

1810   Riots in London in support of Sir Francis Burdett (1770–1844),
                    prominent and popular radical member of Parliament, imprisoned for
                    breach of parliamentary privilege.

                    George III suffers a complete breakdown.

1811   February: Regency Act appoints the Prince of Wales to the regency:
                    the prince rules from now until his father's death in 1820, when he
                    becomes George IV.

                    Population of England and Wales, 10.2 million (12 million in 1821).
                    Population of London exceeds 1 million.

                    National Society for Educating the Poor in the Principles of the Es-
                    tablished Church founded.

1811–1812   General economic depression with widespread food riots.

                    Luddite riots in Nottinghamshire and Yorkshire lead to breaking of
                    machines being made punishable by death.

1812   11 May: Assassination of the prime minister, Spencer Perceval.

                    May–June: Lord Liverpool, Robert Jenkinson (1770–1828), becomes
                    prime minister (until 1827).

                    June: Anglo-American "War of 1812" begins.

                    October: Napoleon's retreat from Moscow begins.

                    Orders in Council and Continental System abandoned by Britain and
                    France, respectively; a freeing of trade follows.

                    A renewed interest in parliamentary reform is signaled by the for-
                    mation, in April and June, respectively, of the Hampden Club and
                    the Union for Parliamentary Reform by well-to-do radicals, such as
                    Francis Burdett and Major John Cartwright (1740–1824): these or-
                    ganizations have little immediate impact, though similar, less exclu-
                    sive clubs become more numerous after 1815.

                    Main streets of London lit by gas.

                    Britain imports 73 million pounds of raw cotton and exports
                    15,275,000 yards of linen.

                    Repeal of Conventicle Act eases position of Protestant Dissenters in
                    Britain.

1813   17 Luddites executed in York.

                    East India Company's trade monopoly in India ended, though its
                    monopoly in China continues.

1814   Britain and allies invade France, entering Paris on 31 March. Napo-
                    leon abdicates and is banished to Elba.

                    Treaty of Ghent ends Anglo-American War in December (though the
                    Battle of New Orleans takes place in January 1815).

                    George Stephenson (1781–1848), developing Trevithick's pioneering
                    work (see 1802 and 1804), constructs the most effective steam lo-
                    comotive so far—it operates at Killingworth colliery.

First steam press, used to print the *Times*: nearly four times as fast as the best hand presses.

1815   March: Corn Law Act sets artificially high price on wheat by increasing the price level at which foreign corn is allowed to enter the country. This serves the interests of the landowning classes and reflects their continuing hegemony in Britain. The consequent increase in the price of bread creates hardship for the masses. (This Corn Law not repealed until 1846.)

Napoleon escapes from Elba and, in March, raises French army once more but is finally defeated at the Battle of Waterloo on 18 June and sent into exile on St. Helena. Congress of Vienna draws up peace treaty and establishes Quadruple Alliance between Britain, Austria, Prussia, and Russia, with an agreement to retain a system of diplomatic congresses.

Apothecaries Act forbids unqualified doctors from practicing medicine.

USN *Fulton* the first steam warship.

1816   Britain's national debt stands at around £900 million (before the wars, in 1792, it was around £250 million).

Repeal of income tax (introduced in 1798 on incomes over £200): leads to increased indirect taxation on many common goods, disproportionately burdening those with lower incomes.

William Cobbett (1763–1835) starts to publish his radical *Political Register*: at twopence, the first cheap periodical.

Registered tonnage of British merchant shipping is 2,504,000 tons.

1816–1817   Start of economic slump and of renewed working-class and radical agitation for reform in response to low wages, poor factory conditions, growing unemployment, heavy indirect taxation, and the Corn Law. The Spa Fields Reform Meetings of December 1816, the Blanketeers' march of March 1817, and other disturbances lead to increasingly repressive governmental measures such as the "Gagging Bills" of March 1817, whereby, among other things, habeas corpus is suspended, and severe restrictions are placed on public meetings.

1817   January: Prince regent fired at on his return from opening Parliament.

March: James Monroe (1758–1831) becomes president of United States.

June: Riots in Derbyshire in protest of low wages and unemployment.

[18 July: Jane Austen dies.]

September: Spain agrees to end slave trade.

November: Third Mahratta War against British in India.

1818   September: First European Congress to meet in peacetime, held in France at Aix-la-Chapelle: agrees to withdrawal of occupying troops from France and the admittance of France to the Congress System.

October: Border between United States and Canada established at 49th parallel.

British iron production stands at 325,000 tons.

1819   March: Assassination of August von Kotzebue (b.1761), influential playwright (author of German original of *Lovers' Vows*, the play performed in Austen's *Mansfield Park*) and reactionary journalist, by a student in Mannheim: this precipitates the signing of the Karlsbad Decrees by German states, suppressing liberal movements and bringing in strict censorship of publications.

July: Act passed for a return to the gold standard (abandoned in 1797), allowing for gradual resumption of cash payments between now and May 1823.

August: Peterloo massacre: a mass reform meeting on St. Peter's Field, Manchester, is broken up by troops, who kill eleven people, including two women and a child, and seriously wound 400 others.

As a response to Peterloo and similar reformist agitation, the government increases the army by 10,000 men and, in December, drastically curtails remaining political liberties in perhaps the most repressive legislation of the period, the ''Six Acts'' (which include tight controls on the press, on other freedoms of speech, and on the size of public meetings). Sir Francis Burdett is imprisoned once more, for criticizing the government's actions at Peterloo.

Thomas Telford (1757–1834) begins construction of Menai suspension bridge.

The *Savannah*, fitted with a steam engine, crosses the Atlantic in twenty-six days.

1820   29 January: Death of King George III and accession of George IV.

February: Cato Street Conspiracy: a plot to assassinate government ministers is foiled, and the leaders of the conspiracy are tried and executed (in April and May).

June: George IV's estranged wife, Caroline, returns to England to claim her place as queen. She receives a rousing reception from the populace, but the government introduces a Bill of Pains and Penalties to divorce her from the king and take away her title. A major public controversy ensues over succeeding months, including mass meetings and public demonstrations in support of the queen that conveniently allow for a revival of radical and reformist agitation. The bill is effectively defeated in November (to the great glee of the London crowds), leaving the affair unresolved and the already unpopular monarchy in further disrepute. (The queen is later prevented from attending the king's coronation, in July 1821, and she dies in August of that year.)

3

Literary Chronology, 1749–1820

In general terms, the following chronology is designed to outline the literary and intellectual context of Jane Austen's life and work. More specifically, it aims to do three things: to provide a list of the *major works and authors* of the period, so that anyone with a reasonable grasp of the traditional literary canon will be able to pick out the main pathways of development that contributed not only to Jane Austen's art but to the art of the later nineteenth century generally; to provide a sense of the *range of writing, thought, and drama* that was actually available at the time (to some extent regardless of its retrospective status as "major" or "minor"); and to provide an overview of *Jane Austen's own reading*. To the latter end, I have included some works *solely* because they were known to Jane Austen, and, where there is evidence (in the letters, novels, or biographical record) that she read, or was familiar with, a particular work or with several works of a particular author, I have asterisked* that work or author. (Of course, the lack of an asterisk does not necessarily mean that Austen was not familiar with the work or author in question but simply that there is no clear evidence for such familiarity.) But this should be seen as only a *selective* overview of Austen's reading, partly because it has other aims, too, but also partly because it does not cover works from earlier periods or common cultural texts that were very important to Austen, such as the Bible, the Book of Common Prayer, Shakespeare, and Milton.

1749	Henry Fielding, *Tom Jones*.* Sarah Fielding, *The Governess, or the Little Female Academy*.
1750	Thomas Gray, *Elegy in a Country Churchyard*.* Charlotte Lennox, *The Life of Harriot Stuart*. Samuel Johnson,* *The Rambler* (1750–1752).

1751   Henry Fielding, *Amelia*. Eliza Haywood, *The History of Miss Betsy Thoughtless*. David Hume, *An Enquiry concerning the Principles of Morals*. Tobias Smollett, *The Adventures of Peregrine Pickle*.

1752   David Hume, *Political Discourses*. Charlotte Lennox, *The Female Quixote*.*

1753   Sarah Fielding, *The History of Betty Barnes*. Eliza Haywood, *The History of Jemmy and Jenny Jessamy*. Samuel Richardson, *The History of Sir Charles Grandison** (1753–1754). Tobias Smollett, *Ferdinand Count Fathom*.

1754   David Hume, *History of England* (1754–1761).

1755   Samuel Johnson, *Dictionary of the English Language*.

1756   *Critical Review* (1756–1817).

1757   Edmund Burke, *Philosophical Enquiry into the Origin of Our Ideas of the Sublime and Beautiful*.

1758   Robert Dodsley, *A Collection of Poems in Six Volumes by Several Hands*.* David Hume, *An Enquiry concerning Human Understanding*. Samuel Johnson, *The Idler** (1758–1760). Charlotte Lennox, *Henrietta*.

1759   Alexander Gerard, *Essay on Taste* (1759). Samuel Johnson, *Rasselas*. Adam Smith, *The Theory of Moral Sentiments*. James Townley, *High Life below Stairs** (first produced). Voltaire, *Candide*. Edward Young, *Conjectures on Original Composition*.

1760   Laurence Sterne, *Tristram Shandy*,* vols. 1–2 (further vols. 1761, 1762, 1765, 1767).

1761   George Colman (the Elder), *The Jealous Wife* (first produced). Jean-Jacques Rousseau, *Julie, ou la nouvelle Héloïse*.

1762   Isaac Bickerstaff, *Love in a Village* (first produced). Oliver Goldsmith, *The Citizen of the World*. Charlotte Lennox, *Sophia*. Jean-Jacques Rousseau, *Emile, ou de l'éducation*, and *Du contrat social*.

1763   Samuel Foote, *The Mayor of Garratt* (first produced).

1764   Oliver Goldsmith, *The Traveller, An History of England in a Series of Letters from a Nobleman to His Son*. Kane O'Hara, *Midas: An English Burletta** (first produced). Thomas Reid, *An Inquiry into the Human Mind on the Principles of Common Sense*. Horace Walpole, *The Castle of Otranto*.

1765   Isaac Bickerstaff, *The Maid of the Mill* (first produced). Samuel Johnson's edition of *The Plays of William Shakespeare*; also Johnson's *Preface*. Thomas Percy, *Reliques of Ancient English Poetry*. Sarah Scott, *The Man of Real Sensibility; or, The History of Sir George Ellison*.

1766   Henry Brooke, *The Fool of Quality*, 5 vols. (publication begins; completed 1772). George Colman (the Elder) and David Garrick, *The Clandestine Marriage** (first produced). James Fordyce, *Sermons to*

*Young Women.** Oliver Goldsmith, *The Vicar of Wakefield.** Tobias Smollett, *Travels through France and Italy.*

1768   Joseph Baretti, *Account of the Manners and Customs of Italy.** Isaac Bickerstaff, *The Hypocrite** (first produced). Oliver Goldsmith, *The Good Natur'd Man* (first produced). Thomas Gray, *Poems.* Joseph Priestley, *Essay on the First Principles of Government.* Laurence Sterne, *A Sentimental Journey.** Horace Walpole, *The Mysterious Mother, Historic Doubts on Richard III.*

1769   Thomas Moss, *Poems on Several Occasions.** Clara Reeve, *Original Poems on Several Occasions.* Thomas Secker, *Lectures on the Catechism of the Church of England.**

1770   Joseph Baretti, *Journey from London to Genoa.** James Beattie, *An Essay on the Nature and Immutability of Truth.* Oliver Goldsmith, *The Deserted Village.* The *Lady's Magazine* begins publication (to 1832).*

1771   James Beattie, *The Minstrel, or the Progress of Genius** (Book 2, 1774). Sophia Briscoe, *Miss Melmoth or The New Clarissa.* Richard Cumberland, *The West Indian* (first produced). Robert Henry, *Henry's History of England** (6 vols. to 1793). Oliver Goldsmith, *The History of England, from the Earliest Times to the Death of George II** (4 vols.). Henry Mackenzie, *The Man of Feeling.* Tobias Smollett, *The Expedition of Humphry Clinker.*

1772   Choderlos de Laclos, *Les Liaisons Dangereuses.*

1773   Anna Laetitia Barbauld, *Poems.* Georgiana, duchess of Devonshire, *Emma; or The Unfortunate Attachment.* Johann Wolfgang von Goethe, *Götz von Berlichingen* (Goethe's "Sturm und Drang" play first produced). Oliver Goldsmith, *She Stoops to Conquer* (first produced). Henry Mackenzie, *The Man of the World.* Phyllis Wheatley, *Poems on Various Subjects.*

1774   J. W. Goethe, *Die Leiden des jungen Werther (The Sorrows of Young Werther).** Oliver Goldsmith, *History of England** (abridged version of 1771 work). Thomas Warton, *History of English Poetry* (publication completed 1781).

1775   David Garrick, *Bon Ton; or High Life above Stairs** (first produced). Samuel Johnson, *A Journey to the Western Islands of Scotland.** Richard Brinsley Sheridan, *The Rivals** (first produced).

1776   Jeremy Bentham, *A Fragment on Government.* Edward Gibbon, *The Decline and Fall of the Roman Empire* (publication completed 1788). Richard Price, *Observations on the Nature of Civil Liberty, the Principles of Government, and the Justice of Policy of the War with America.* Adam Smith, *An Inquiry into the Nature and Causes of the Wealth of Nations.*

1777   Hugh Blair, *Sermons** (5 vols. to 1801). Elizabeth Bonhote, *Hortensia.* Henry Mackenzie, *Julia de Roubigné.* Hannah More, *Percy* (first produced). Clara Reeve, *The Champion of Virtue, a Gothic Story* (republished as *The Old English Baron* in 1778). Richard Brinsley Sheridan, *The School for Scandal** (first produced).

1778   Anna Laetitia Barbauld, *Lessons for Children*. Fanny Burney, *Evelina.**

1779   David Hume, *Dialogues concerning Natural Religion*. Samuel Johnson, *Lives of the Poets* (publication completed 1781). Henry Mackenzie's periodical, *The Mirror,** begins publication (January to May 1780). Richard Brinsley Sheridan, *The Critic** (first produced).

1780   Elizabeth Blower, *The Parsonage House*. Hannah Cowley, *The Belle's Strategem** (first produced). Thomas Holcroft, *Alwyn*.

1781   Robert Bage, *Mount Henneth*. Anna Laetitia Barbauld, *Hymns in Prose for Children*. George Crabbe,* *The Library*. Thomas Holcroft, *Duplicity* (first produced). Charles Macklin, *The Man of the World* (first produced). Jean-Jacques Rousseau, *Confessions* (posthumous). Friedrich Schiller, *Die Räuber* (first produced).

1782   Fanny Burney, *Cecilia.** Hannah Cowley, *Which Is the Man?** (first produced). William Cowper, *Poems.** William Gilpin,* *Observations on the River Wye and Several Parts of South Wales*.

1783   William Blake, *Poetical Sketches*. George Crabbe, *The Village.** Richard Cumberland, *The Mysterious Husband* (first produced). Madame de Genlis, *Adelaide and Theodore.** Sophia Lee, *The Recess, or A Tale of Other Times* (–1785). Harriet Meziere, *Elmar and Ethlinda; A Legendary Tale*. Clara Reeve, *The Two Mentors*.

1784   Robert Bage, *Barham Downs*. Eliza Bromley, *Laura and Augustus*. Madame de Genlis, *Les Veillées du Château** (later translated as *Tales of the Castle*). Charlotte Smith,* *Elegiac Sonnets, and Other Essays*.

1785   Agnes Maria Bennett, *Anna; or Memoirs of a Welch Heiress*. Elizabeth Blower, *Maria*. James Boswell, *The Journal of a Tour to the Hebrides with Samuel Johnson.** William Cowper, *The Task.** Elizabeth Inchbald, *I'll Tell You What* (first produced). Samuel Johnson, *Prayers and Meditations* (posthumous). William Paley, *The Principles of Moral and Political Philosophy*. Rudolf Eric Raspe, *Baron Munchausen's Narrative*. Clara Reeve, *The Progress of Romance*. Thomas Reid, *Essays on the Intellectual Powers of Man*.

1786   William Beckford, *Vathek, an Arabian Tale*. Agnes Maria Bennett, *Juvenile Indiscretions*. John Burgoyne, *The Heiress* (first produced). Robert Burns, *Poems, Chiefly in the Scottish Dialect*. Anne Rice Hughes, *Zoraida, or, Village Annals*. William Gilpin,* *Observations on . . . the Lakes*. Harriet Meziere, *Moreton Abbey; or, The Fatal Mystery*.

1787   Robert Bage, *The Fair Syrian*. Elizabeth Bonhote, *Olivia*. Mrs. Burke, *Ela; or The Delusions of the Heart*. George Colman (the Younger), *Inkle and Yarico* (first produced). Elizabeth Helme, *Louisa; or, The Cottage on the Moor*. Anne Rice Hughes, *Caroline;*

or, The Diversities of Fortune. Harriet Lee, *The Errors of Innocence.* Harriet Thomson, *Excessive Sensibility.* Elizabeth Tomlins, *The Victim of Fancy.* John Whitaker, *Mary Queen of Scots Vindicated.** Mary Wollstonecraft, *Thoughts on the Education of Daughters.*

1788   Robert Bage, *James Wallace.* Elizabeth Blower, *Features from Life.* Mrs. Burke, *Emilia de St. Aubigne.* Elizabeth Helme, *Clara and Emmeline.* Elizabeth Hervey, *Melissa and Marcia; or, The Sisters.* Thomas Holcroft, *Seduction* (first produced). Anne Rice Hughes, *Henry and Isabella.* Hannah More,* *Thoughts on the Importance of the Manners of the Great.* Hester Lynch Piozzi (Mrs. Thrale), *Letters to and from the Late Samuel Johnson.** Clara Reeve, *The Exiles.* Charlotte Smith, *Emmeline, the Orphan of the Castle.** Mary Wollstonecraft, *Mary, a Fiction.*

1789   Agnes Maria Bennett, *Agnes De Courci: A Domestic Tale.* Jeremy Bentham, *An Introduction to the Principles of Morals and Legislation.* William Blake, *Songs of Innocence.* Edmund Burke *Reflections on the Revolution in France.* Mrs. Cowley, *Belinda.* William Gilpin, *Observations Relative to Picturesque Beauty . . . on . . . the Highlands of Scotland.** Vicesimus Knox, *Elegant Extracts, or Useful and Entertaining Pieces of Poetry.** Richard Price, *A Discourse on the Love of Our Country.* Ann Radcliffe,* *The Castles of Athlin and Dunbayne.* Charlotte Smith, *Ethelinde, or The Recluse of the Lake.** Gilbert White, *The Natural History and Antiquities of Selborne.* Mary Wollstonecraft, *Vindication of the Rights of Men.*

1790   Joanna Baillie, *Fugitive Verses.* William Blake, *The Marriage of Heaven and Hell.* Elizabeth Hervey, *Louisa.* Dorothy Kilner, *Anecdotes of a Boarding School.** Charlotte Lennox, *Euphemia.* William Paley, *Horae Paulinae.* Ann Radcliffe, *The Sicilian Romance.*

1791   Arnaud Berquin,* *The History of Little Grandison* (for children). James Boswell, *The Life of Samuel Johnson.** Robert Burns, "Tam o'Shanter." Mary Hays, *Cursory Remarks.* Elizabeth Inchbald, *A Simple Story.* Eliza Parsons, *The Errors of Education.* Tom Paine, *The Rights of Man* (Part I). Ann Radcliffe, *The Romance of the Forest.** Clara Reeve, *The School for Widows.* Marquis de Sade, *Justine.* Charlotte Smith, *Celestina.*

1792   Robert Bage, *Man as He Is.* William Gilpin, *Three Essays: On Picturesque Beauty; On Picturesque Travel; and On Sketching Landscapes.* Thomas Holcroft, *Anna St. Ives, The Road to Ruin* (first produced). Anna Maria Mackenzie, *Slavery, or, The Times.* Hannah More, *Village Politics.* Tom Paine, *The Rights of Man* (Part II). Mary Robinson ("Perdita"), *Vancenza; or, The Dangers of Credulity.* Charlotte Smith, *Desmond.* Jane West,* *The Advantages of Education, or The History of Maria Williams.* Mary Wollstonecraft, *A Vindication of the Rights of Woman.* William Wordsworth,* "An Evening Walk," "Descriptive Sketches." Arthur Young, *Travels in France.*

1793   William Godwin, *An Enquiry concerning Political Justice*. Elizabeth
                        Inchbald, *Every One Has His Fault* (first produced). Charlotte Ma-
                        thews, *Simple Facts; or, The History of an Orphan*. Tom Paine, *The
                        Age of Reason* (completed 1795). Eliza Parsons, *Woman as She
                        Should Be, The Castle of Wolfenbach,** *Ellen and Julia*. Clara Reeve,
                        Memoirs of Sir Roger de Clarendon. Charlotte Smith, *The Old Manor
                        House, D'Arcy* (novels), *The Emigrants* (poetry).

1794   Agnes Maria Bennett, *Ellen, Countess of Castle Howel*. William
                        Blake, *Songs of Innocence and of Experience*. Stephen Cullen, *The
                        Haunted Priory*. Richard Cumberland, *The Wheel of Fortune, a Com-
                        edy** (first produced). Lawrence Flammenberg, *The Necromancer**
                        (translated by Peter Teuthold). William Godwin,* *Things as They
                        Are; or, The Adventures of Caleb Williams*. Elizabeth Helme, *Duncan
                        and Peggy: A Scottish Tale*. Thomas Holcroft, *The Adventures of
                        Hugh Trevor*. Elizabeth Inchbald, *The Wedding Day* (first produced).
                        Charlotte Mathews, *Perplexities, or The Fortunate Elopement*. Han-
                        nah More, *Cheap Repository Tracts* (series published to 1798). Rich-
                        ard Payne Knight, *The Landscape*. William Paley, *A View of the
                        Evidences of Christianity*. Uvedale Price, *An Essay on the Pictur-
                        esque*. Ann Radcliffe, *The Mysteries of Udolpho*.* Maria Elizabeth
                        Robinson, *The Shrine of Bertha*. Charlotte Smith, *The Wanderings of
                        Warwick, The Banished Man*.

1795   Mrs. Bullock, *Susanna*. Maria Edgeworth,* *Letters for Literary La-
                        dies*. Mary Anne Hanway, *Ellinor; or The World as It Is*. Isabella
                        Hedgeland, *The Abbey of St. Asaph*. Anne Rice Hughes, *Jemima*.
                        Mary Meek, *The Abbey of Clugny*. Friedrich Schiller, *Letters con-
                        cerning the Aesthetic Education of Mankind*. Charlotte Smith, *Mon-
                        talbert*.

1796   Robert Bage, *Hermsprong; or, Man as He Is Not*. Mrs. Burke, *Adela
                        Northington, The Sorrows of Edith; or, The Hermitage of the Cliffs*.
                        Fanny Burney, *Camilla*.* Sarah Burney, *Clarentine*.* Samuel Taylor
                        Coleridge, *Poems on Various Subjects*. George Colman (the
                        Younger), *The Iron Chest* (first produced). Maria Edgeworth, *The
                        Parent's Assistant*, six vols. (1796–1801). Edward Gibbon, *Memoirs*.
                        J. W. Goethe, *Wilhelm Meister*. Carl Grosse, *Horrid Mysteries**
                        (translated by Peter Will). Mary Hays, *Memoirs of Emma Courteney*.
                        Elizabeth Inchbald, *Nature and Art*. Matthew Gregory Lewis, *The
                        Monk*.* Eliza Parsons, *The Mysterious Warning,** *Women as They
                        Are*. Mary Robinson (''Perdita''), *Angelina, Hubert de Sevrac, The
                        Wanderings of the Imagination*. Charlotte Smith, *Marchmont*. Robert
                        Southey, *Joan of Arc*. Jane West, *A Gossip's Story, and A Legendary
                        Tale*.

1797   *The Anti-Jacobin* begins publication (November to July 1798). Eliz-
                        abeth Bonhote, *Bungay Castle*. George Colman (the Younger), *The
                        Heir at Law** (first produced). Isaac D'Israeli, *Vaurien; or, Sketches
                        of the Times*, and *Flim-Flams; or, The Life of My Uncle*. Joseph Fox,

Santa-Maria; or, The Mysterious Pregnancy. Thomas Gisborne, *An Enquiry into the Duties of the Female Sex.** Elizabeth Inchbald, *Wives as They Were and Maids as They Are* (first produced). Samuel Egerton Leigh, *Munster Abbey.* Ann Radcliffe, *The Italian.** Robert Southey,* *Poems and Letters Written during a Short Residence in Spain and Portugal.*

1798   *Anti-Jacobin Review and Magazine,* a successor to *The Anti-Jacobin,* begins publication (to 1821). Joanna Baillie, *Plays on the Passions,* vol. 1 (vols. 2 and 3, 1802, 1812). Samuel Egerton Brydges, *Arthur Fitz-Albini.** Samuel Taylor Coleridge and William Wordsworth, *Lyrical Ballads.* Maria and Richard Edgeworth, *Practical Education.* William Godwin, *Memoirs of the Author of "A Vindication of the Rights of Woman."* Mary Hays, *Appeal to the Men of Great Britain in Behalf of Women.* Francis Lathom, *The Midnight Bell.** Thomas Malthus, *An Essay on the Principle of Population.* Regina Maria Roche, *Clermont.** Friedrich Schiller, *Wallenstein* trilogy (–1799). Eleanor Sleath, *The Orphan of the Rhine.** Mary Wollstonecraft, *The Wrongs of Woman.* William Wordsworth, *The Prelude* (begun; completed 1805, published 1850).

1799   Robert Burns,* "Holy Willie's Prayer." Thomas Campbell, *Pleasures of Hope.** Mrs. Cassandra Cooke (née Leigh, Mrs. Austen's first cousin), *Battleridge, an Historical Tale Founded on Facts.** William Godwin, *St. Leon.* Mary Hays, *The Victim of Prejudice.* Hannah More, *Modern Female Education.* Clara Reeve, *Destination.* Robert Southey, *Poems.* Jane West, *A Tale of the Times.*

1800   Maria Edgeworth, *Castle Rackrent.* Coleridge and Wordsworth, second edition of *Lyrical Ballads* (with preface). Thomas Morton, *Speed the Plough* (first produced; introduces character of Mrs. Grundy). Friedrich Schiller, *Maria Stuart.*

1801   Maria Edgeworth, *Belinda,** *Early Lessons, Moral Tales for Young People.* Uvedale Price, *A Dialogue on the Distinct Characters of the Picturesque and the Beautiful.* Friedrich Schiller, *Die Jungfrau von Orleans.* Robert Southey, *Thalaba the Destroyer.*

1802   *The Edinburgh Review* begins publication (to 1929). William Paley, *Natural Theology.* Walter Scott,* *Minstrelsy of the Scottish Border* (vols. 1 and 2; vol. 3 published in 1803). Madame de Staël,* *Delphine.*

1803   William Blake, *Milton* (begun; completed 1808). Mary Hays, *Female Biography.* Mrs. Rachel Hunter, *Letters from Mrs. Palmerstone to Her Daughters, Inculcating Morality by Entertaining Narratives.** Thomas Malthus, *The Principles of Population.* Humphrey Repton,* *Observations on the Theory and Practice of Landscape Gardening.*

1804   William Blake, *Jerusalem* (begun; completed 1820). Maria Edgeworth, *Popular Tales.* Anna Maria Porter, *Lake of Killarney.** Friedrich Schiller, *Wilhelm Tell.*

1805   Maria Edgeworth, *The Modern Griselda*. William Godwin, *Fleet-wood*. William Hazlitt, *An Essay on the Principles of Human Action*. Richard Payne Knight, *An Analytical Inquiry into the Principles of Taste*. Walter Scott, *The Lay of the Last Minstrel*.* Robert Southey, *Madoc*.

1806   Maria Edgeworth, *Leonora*. Madame de Genlis,* *Alphonsine, ou la Tendress maternelle* (translated 1807 as *Alphonsine, or Maternal Affection*).* William Hazlitt, *Free Thoughts on Public Affairs*. Mrs. Rachel Hunter, *Lady Maclairn, the Victim of Villainy* (8 vols.).* Sydney Owenson (Lady Morgan), *The Wild Irish Girl*.* Walter Scott, *Ballads and Lyrical Pieces*. Jane West, *Letters to a Young Lady*.

1807   Lord Byron,* *Poems on Various Occasions, Hours of Idleness*. George Crabbe, *The Parish Register*. Madame de Staël, *Corinne* (translated 1807 as *Corinna*).* Mrs. Anne Grant (of Laggan), *Letters from the Mountains . . . between the Years 1773–1807*.* William Hazlitt, *A Reply to the Essay on Population by the Rev. T. R. Malthus*. Charles and Mary Lamb, *Tales from Shakespeare*. Lord Macartney, *Journal of the Embassy to China*.* Robert Southey, *Letters from England: By Dom Manuel Alvarez Espriella*.* William Wordsworth, *Poems in Two Volumes*.

1808   Thomas Clarkson, *History of the Abolition of the African Slave Trade*.* J. Debrett, *The Baronetage of England*. J. W. Goethe, *Faust* 1 (completed; 2, 1832). Mrs. Anne Grant (of Laggan), *Memoirs of an American Lady*.* Elizabeth Hamilton, *The Cottagers of Glenburnie*.* Rev. T. Jefferson, *Two Sermons*.* Charles Maturin, *The Wild Irish Boy*. Thomas Moore, *A Selection of Irish Melodies* (ten parts published between now and 1834). Hannah More, *Coelebs in Search of a Wife*.* Walter Scott, *Marmion*.* Mrs. S. Sykes, *Margiana, or Widdrington Tower** (5 vols.).

1809   Rudolph Ackermann's *Repository of Arts, Literature, Fashions, Manufactures* begins publication (to 1828; makes first extensive use of lithography in Britain). Lord Byron, *English Bards and Scotch Reviewers*. Rev. Edward Cooper (Jane Austen's first cousin), *Practical and Familiar Sermons. . . .* * Richard and Maria Edgeworth, *Essays on Professional Education*. Maria Edgeworth, *The Absentee*, and *Tales from Fashionable Life* (two series, 1809, 1812*). Sydney Owenson (Lady Morgan), *Woman, or Ida of Athens*.* The *Quarterly Review* begins publication (to 1967).*

1810   Mary Brunton, *Self-Control, a Novel*.* George Crabbe, *The Borough*.* Sir Charles William Pasley, *Essay on the Military Policy and Institutions of the British Empire*.* Walter Scott, *The Lady of the Lake*.* Anna Seward, *Poetical Works*.

1811   Samuel Beazley, *The Boarding House; or, Five Hours at Brighton** (first performed; musical farce). Claudius Buchanan, *Christian Researches in Asia*.* Sir John Carr, *Descriptive Travels in the Southern*

and Eastern Parts of Spain and the Balearic Isles, in the Year 1809.*
Sir George Steuart Mackenzie, *Travels in Iceland.** Hannah More,
Practical Piety. Anna Seward, *The Letters of Anna Seward, 1784–
1807* (six vols.).

1812   Lord Byron, *Childe Harold's Pilgrimage* (1 and 2; 3 and 4 published
1816 and 1818). Maria Callcott, *Journal of a Residence in India.*
William Combe and Thomas Rowlandson, *The Tour of Dr. Syntax
in Search of the Picturesque** (first published in *The Poetical Magazine* in 1809). George Crabbe, *Tales in Verse.** Jakob and Wilhelm
Grimm, *Fairy Tales.* Elizabeth Hamilton, *Popular Essays on the Elementary Principles of the Human Mind.** Charles Maturin, *The Mi-
lesian Chief.* Thomas Sherlock, *Several Discourses Presented at the
Temple Church* (1754–1797; new edition).* Horatio and James
Smith, *Rejected Addresses: or the New Theatrum Poetarum.** Robert
Southey, *The Curse of Kehama.* Jane West, *The Loyalists.*

1813   Eaton Stannard Barrett, *The Heroine, or Adventures of Cherubina.**
Claudius Buchanan, *Apology for Promoting Christianity in India.**
Lord Byron, *The Giaour,* The Bride of Abydos.** Percy Bysshe Shel-
ley, *Queen Mab.* Robert Southey, *Life of Nelson.** Madame de Staël,
De l'Allemagne (translated and published in Britain—first published
1810: introduces German Romanticism to wider public).

1814   Fanny Burney, *The Wanderer, or Female Difficulties* (5 vols.).* Lord
Byron, *The Corsair,* Lara.* Maria Callcott, *Letters on India.* Charles
Dibdin, *The Farmer's Wife** (first produced). Maria Edgeworth, *Pa-
tronage,* Continuation of Early Lessons.* Laetitia Matilda Hawkins,
Rosanne, or a Father's Labour Lost.* Walter Scott, *Waverley.** P. B.
Shelley, *Alastor.* Jane West, *Alicia de Lacey, an Historical Ro-
mance.** William Wordsworth, *The Excursion.*

1815   Walter Scott, *Guy Mannering, The Field of Waterloo,* Paul's Letters
to His Kinsfolk.** Thomas Skinner Surr, *The Magic of Wealth.* Helen
Maria Williams, *A Narrative of the Events Which Have Lately Taken
Place in France.** William Wordsworth, *Poems.*

1816   Lord Byron, *The Siege of Corinth, Parisina.* Samuel Taylor Coleridge, *Kubla Khan* (written c.1797). Rev. Edward Cooper, *Two Sermons Preached at Wolverhampton.** William Hazlitt (ed.), *Memoirs
of the Late Thomas Holcroft.* Thomas Love Peacock, *Headlong Hall.*
Walter Scott, *The Antiquary,* Old Mortality.* Robert Southey, *Poet's
Pilgrimage to Waterloo.**

1817   Maria Edgeworth, *Ormond, Harrington.* *Blackwood's Edinburgh
Magazine* begins publication (to 1980). Lord Byron, *Manfred.* Sam-
uel Taylor Coleridge, *Biographia Literaria, Sybilline Leaves.* William
Godwin, *Mandeville.* William Hazlitt, *Characters of Shakespeare's
Plays, The Round Table.* John Keats, *Poems.* Thomas Moore, *Lalla
Rookh.* Thomas Love Peacock, *Melincourt.* P. B. Shelley, *The Revolt
of Islam.*

1818   Lord Byron, *Beppo*. Susan Ferrier, *Marriage*. William Hazlitt, *Lectures on the English Poets, A View of the English Stage*. John Keats, *Endymion*. Charles Maturin, *Women; or, Pour et Contre*. Thomas Love Peacock, *Nightmare Abbey*. Walter Scott, *Heart of Midlothian, Rob Roy*. Mary Shelley, *Frankenstein*.

1819   Lord Byron, *Mazeppa*. George Crabbe, *Tales of the Hall*. William Hazlitt, *Lectures on the English Comic Writers and Political Essays*. Walter Scott, *The Bride of Lammermoor, The Legend of Montrose*. William Wordsworth, *Peter Bell, The Waggoner*.

1820   Lord Byron, *Don Juan* (begun). William Hazlitt, *The Dramatic Literature of the Age of Elizabeth*. John Keats, *Lamia, Isabella, The Eve of St. Agnes, and Other Poems*. Charles Maturin, *Melmoth the Wanderer*. Walter Scott, *Ivanhoe, The Monastery, The Abbot*. P. B. Shelley, *Prometheus Unbound*. William Wordsworth, *The River Duddon*.

Part II

ENCYCLOPEDIA OF JANE AUSTEN'S LIFE AND WORKS

A

Abbotts, the two (*Emma* Ch.9; I:9:75). Harriet Smith's fellow pupils at Mrs. Goddard's school.

Abdy, John (*Emma* Ch.44; III:8:383). Son of old John and head man and ostler at the Crown Inn.

Abdy, Old John (*Emma* Ch.44; III:8:383). Ex-clerk to the former vicar of Highbury, Rev. Bates (Miss Bates' deceased father). Now bedridden with rheumatism and gout.

"The Adventures of Mr. Harley" (*Volume the First* of Jane Austen's juvenilia). This "short, but interesting Tale" was probably written early in the period 1787–1790 and transcribed from the lost original probably in early 1790, judging from the dedication, which was addressed to Frank Austen after he had become a midshipman on HMS *Perseverance* in December 1789. The essential joke of the "tale" is that it compresses an eventful plot—a miniparody of conventional novelistic plots—into only three very short paragraphs. It tells how Mr. Harley becomes a ship's chaplain and then returns to England to find himself sitting in a stagecoach with a young wife whom he suddenly remembers having married before going to sea. The three named characters are Emma Harley, Mr. Harley, and Sir John.

"Advertisement, by the Authoress." This was written in early 1816 as a brief preface to *Northanger Abbey* when Jane Austen was thinking of having the novel published shortly after having recovered the copyright and manuscript that she had sold in 1803 to the publisher, Crosby and Company. The preface apologizes for any anachronisms that may appear and explains that the novel had been completed thirteen years earlier. See under *Northanger Abbey*.

Alice (*Northanger Abbey* Ch.28; II:13:228). Probably Eleanor Tilney's maid-servant. Just before Catherine leaves Northanger Abbey, Eleanor asks her to write to her at Lord Longtown's, but "under cover to Alice" for fear of being found out by General Tilney. At first, Catherine's pride is hurt by this suggestion that she can no longer write to her friend as an equal, and she refuses, then almost immediately relents when she sees the "look of sorrow" on Eleanor's face.

Alicia, Lady (*Persuasion* Ch.19; II:7:179). One of two acquaintances of Lady Russell—the other being Mrs. Frankland—who have told her to look out for some particularly handsome and well-hung window curtains in Pulteney Street; at least, this is what Lady Russell says to Anne Elliot to explain her intent gaze from the carriage window as they drive along that street past Captain Wentworth. Anne, who has seen Captain Wentworth for herself, clearly believes that Lady Russell is just making up an excuse for not mentioning him to her, but we cannot be sure that this is, in fact, the case.

Allen, Mr. (*Northanger Abbey* Ch.1; I:1:17). Mr. Allen is a friend of the Morland family and chief property owner around the village of Fullerton in Wiltshire, where the Morlands live. His apothecary orders him to Bath for a period "for the benefit of a gouty constitution," and this is the immediate cause of Catherine Morland's visit there, as Mrs. Allen invites her to accompany them on their visit. Mr. Allen is "a sensible, intelligent man," with an educated interest in politics and history. He is concerned to take good care of Catherine while she is in his charge and to provide her with appropriate advice and guidance when necessary, though he is indulgent of his shallow-minded wife and does not actively interfere in her arrangements for Catherine. While at Bath, Mr. Allen tends to escape from the "mob" of the assemblies into the quiet of the cardroom.

Allen, Mrs. (*Northanger Abbey* Chs.1, 2; I:1:17; I:2:20–21). Frivolous and empty-headed, Mrs. Allen seems a somewhat surprising choice of wife for the sensible Mr. Allen, though she is a placid, good-natured, and kindly woman. It is her idea to invite Catherine to Bath when she and her husband go to stay there, and, being as giddily interested in fashionable dress and manners as any young person, she is "admirably fitted to introduce a young lady into public." As a chaperon, however, she proves to be rather careless of the company Catherine keeps and negligent in the advice she gives to her young charge, particularly on the matter of being driven in an open phaeton by John Thorpe. Mrs. Allen's "trifling turn of mind" generally means that she pays more attention to her own clothes than to "the comfort of her protegée."

"Amelia Webster" (*Volume the First* of Jane Austen's juvenilia). Probably written and copied from the lost original between 1787 and 1790, this piece is subtitled "an interesting & well written Tale" and is dedicated to Mrs. Austen. A spoof on epistolary fiction of the period, the "tale" consists of seven very short letters by means of which three courtships are conducted, and as many marriages made. The correspondents among whom the matches are arranged are Benjamin Bar, Henry Beverley, George Hervey, Matilda (Maud) Hervey, Miss Sarah (Sally) Hervey, and Amelia Webster. We hear of the newspaper marriage announcements in a final letter from Tom to Jack (whoever they are).

Amyatt, Lord and Lady ("Catharine," *Minor Works* 204). The brother and sister-in-law of Rev. Dudley.

Andersons, the (*Mansfield Park* Ch.5; I:5:49–50). Acquaintances of Tom Bertram, living in Baker Street, London. When Tom was first introduced to the family by his friend Charles Anderson, the latter's sister, Miss Anderson, was not yet "out" in society, and she behaved very awkwardly, hardly saying a word to him. However, when he next met her a year later, she *was* out, and this time she embarrassed him by her brash and forward behavior.

Andrew (*Sanditon, Minor Works* 381–82). The old gardener at Sanditon House who supplies the Parkers with any fruit or vegetables that their garden in their old country house fails to supply. Mr. Parker considers buying more foodstuffs from the Stringers as he encouraged them to set up in Sanditon, but he would not like to withdraw all his custom from Andrew, as this might mean his losing his daily job (even though the Parkers' cook complains that Andrew never brings her what she wants). This apparently minor discussion, in fact, neatly captures the novel's central concern with social and economic change and Mr. Parker's ambivalent position as both a traditional, paternalistic landowner (he wants to maintain the "estate" way of doing things by using Andrew) and an entrepreneurial businessman keen to promote local trade (by using the Stringers).

Andrews, Miss (*Northanger Abbey* Ch.6; I:6:40–42). Miss Andrews is the "particular" friend of Isabella Thorpe, who reads all the "horrid" novels she can get hold of but finds difficulty reading even the first volume of *Sir Charles Grandison*. Miss Andrews, we are told by Isabella in typically sentimental style, is "a sweet girl, one of the sweetest creatures in the world" and "as beautiful as an angel," though, as Isabella is at that moment keen to flatter Catherine Morland for her "animation," she also admits what we have already deduced, that Miss Andrews is "amazingly insipid."

Anne, or Nanny ("Catharine," *Minor Works* 213). Catharine Percival's impressionable young maid, whose heart is set aflutter by the arrival of the "vastly handsome" Edward Stanley. Edward Stanley, for his part, rakishly refers to her as "the prettiest little waiting maid in the world."

Annesley, Mrs. (*Pride and Prejudice* Ch.45; III:3:267). Mrs. Annesley is the refined and discreet companion of Miss Darcy, with whom she lives in London. Mrs. Annesley endeavors "to introduce some kind of discourse" during Elizabeth Bennet's visit to Miss Darcy at Pemberley and thus shows herself to be "more truly well bred" than either Mrs. Hurst or Miss Bingley.

Atkinson, Miss (*Persuasion* Ch.19; II:7:177). After unexpectedly meeting Captain Wentworth at Molland's shop in Milsom Street, Bath, Anne Elliot leaves on the arm of Mr. William Elliot, and the ladies of Wentworth's party speculate about the possibility of an engagement between the two. Someone refers to Miss Atkinson as having once dined with Mr. Elliot at the house of Colonel and Mrs. Wallis and having found him "the most agreeable man she ever was in company with." Captain Wentworth begins to be jealous of Mr. Elliot from this moment.

Austen, Anna (1793–1872). Daughter of James Austen by his first marriage to Anne Mathew, and Jane Austen's second-born niece; known as "Anna," though her full name was Jane Anna Elizabeth Austen. After the death of her mother in May 1795, Anna Austen lived at Steventon rectory with her aunts and grandparents until January 1797, when her father remarried. Even then, she continued to be a regular visitor at Steventon, and she was often in Jane Austen's company in later life, too. Anna had a somewhat strained relationship with her stepmother, Mary Lloyd (and because of that, with her father, too, it appears), and she is represented in the family tradition as a rather troublesome and temperamental child and adolescent. But she was also obviously a spirited, intelligent, and independent-minded girl who—especially when she showed signs of artistic creativity herself—was recognized as something of a kindred spirit by her literary aunt. (Indeed, it was long thought that Anna was the youthful author of the short play *Sir Charles Grandison or The Happy Man*, having dictated it to Jane Austen at the age of seven; but this view has now been challenged and the play reascribed to Jane Austen herself.)

When Anna became engaged without her parents' approval in 1809, at the age of sixteen, she was sent away for several months to her Uncle Edward's house at Godmersham, and then, when she caused further embarrassment by breaking off the engagement just as her parents had acknowledged it, she was sent to stay with the Austens at Chawton for three months. From around this time, in the summer of 1810, Anna started to become close to her aunt Jane, who may have composed her verses for Anna, "Mock Panegyric on a Young Friend," during this visit. The relationship between the two developed most significantly, however, during another extended visit by Anna to Chawton in the summer of 1812, when they began to recognize their shared literary interests. Thereafter, until Jane Austen's death in 1817, Anna kept in close contact with her aunt. Fifteen letters from Jane Austen to Anna have been preserved, and of particular importance are those of 1814 that deal with Anna's attempt at writing a novel ("Enthusiasm" and "Which Is the Heroine?" were two working titles).

Anna evidently sent her aunt manuscript drafts of each chapter of the novel as she wrote it, and these elicited some rare critical comments on the art of fiction by Jane Austen, including her famous comment about "3 or 4 Families in a Country Village" being "the very thing to work on." Not long after her marriage in November 1814 to Benjamin Lefroy (1791–1829), Anna abandoned her novel and later destroyed the manuscript. With an eventual family of seven children, she clearly had little time to devote to writing over the next fifteen years or so, but she did eventually publish a novella, *Mary Hamilton*, in 1833 and then two books for children, *The Winter's Tale* (1841) and *Springtide* (1842). She also attempted to complete Jane Austen's own unfinished novel, *Sanditon*, when the manuscript was left to her on the death of Cassandra Austen, though she abandoned the attempt after writing about 20,000 words. In the mid-1860s, Anna wrote down her memories of Jane Austen so that her half brother, James Edward Austen-Leigh, could use them in his 1869–1870 *Memoir* of their aunt. Anna Austen's contemporary drawings of Steventon rectory and its environs have also been useful for the biographical record of Jane Austen.

See: Lane 1984, Le Faye 1989, Tucker 1983.

Austen, Caroline Mary Craven (1805–1880). Born at Steventon on 18 June 1805, Caroline Austen was the second child of James and Mary Austen, sister to James Edward and half sister to Anna Austen. She knew her aunt Jane very well and, most important, wrote down her memories of her in *My Aunt Jane Austen: A Memoir* (1867; published 1952), and *Reminiscences* (1872; published 1986). The first of these works was drawn on by her brother for his 1869 *Memoir*. Like her siblings, Caroline also took to creative writing and submitted her efforts to her aunt for comments and advice, which, she remembers, were always patiently and sympathetically given. In commenting on Caroline's writing, Jane Austen confessed to wishing she had read more and written less before she was sixteen. Several of Jane Austen's letters to Caroline survive, as Caroline took great care to preserve them and pass them on in the family.

See: Lane 1984, Le Faye 1989, Tucker 1983.

Austen, Cassandra, née Leigh (1739–1827). Jane Austen's mother. Cassandra Leigh was the third surviving child of Rev. Thomas Leigh (1696–1764) and Jane Walker (1704–1768). The large Leigh family of Adlestrop in Gloucestershire and its younger branch, the Leighs of Stoneleigh Abbey in Warwickshire, had a common ancestor in Sir Thomas Leigh (1498–1571), lord mayor of London from 1558 (elected just before the death of Queen Mary Tudor; he presided over the coronation festivities of Elizabeth I and was knighted by her shortly afterward). On Jane Walker's side of the family, two important kinship connections were with Sir Thomas White (1492–1567), the founder of St. John's College, Oxford (Jane Austen's brothers were able to enter St. John's on "Founder's Kin" scholarships because of this connection), and with the Perrot family of

Northleigh in Oxfordshire (Jane Austen's uncle James eventually inherited the Perrot estate and changed his name from Leigh to Perrot).

Cassandra Leigh's father was a fellow of All Souls, Oxford (from such an early age that he was nicknamed "Chick Leigh"), and, from 1731 until his death, he was rector of Harpsden near Henley-on-Thames, Oxfordshire. He married Jane Walker in 1732, and they had six children. Two of these died young, leaving James (1735–1817), Jane (1736–1783), Cassandra, and Thomas (1747–1821) (who was mentally disabled and looked after outside the family—in later years, apparently along with Jane Austen's disabled brother, George). Cassandra grew up in the rectory at Harpsden and soon gained a reputation for her cleverness and quick way with words; when she was only six, another academic member of the family, her uncle, Rev. Dr. Theophilus Leigh (1693–1784), master of Balliol College, Oxford, referred to her in a letter as having a precocious talent for acting and as "the poet of the family." Both she and her sister were renowned for their good looks, and Cassandra was later said to be especially proud of her aristocratic nose—something, along with her quick wit, that she seems to have passed on to many of her children. Toward the end of his life, Cassandra's father retired to Bath, and she seems to have lived there for about two years before her marriage to George Austen on 26 April 1764. (Her father died in January 1764, and her mother lived with the Austens until her death in August 1768.)

Mr. and Mrs. Austen had eight children (between 1765 and 1779), the first three while they were living at Deane parsonage between 1764 and 1768 and the rest at Steventon rectory, which was the family home for thirty-three years, until Mr. Austen retired to Bath in 1801. The Austens were never rich, and, especially in the early days of their marriage, Mrs. Austen needed to marshal all her housekeeping skills to make ends meet, but she was a robust and practical-minded woman who managed the home efficiently and even contributed to its finances by careful oversight of the domestic garden, dairy, and poultry yard. A kind, loving, but firm parent, she certainly played her part in ensuring that the Austen children were brought up in a materially and emotionally secure environment. Though her scholarly husband provided for the more formal education of the children, she also clearly contributed a great deal to their intellectual and social formation, too, for she was a naturally intelligent and sociable woman who enjoyed good company and who loved reading and writing almost as much as her famous daughter did. Mrs. Austen's love of society—she enjoyed trips to London and Bath, going to balls, visiting friends and relatives, and having them visit her—ensured that her children had a stimulating social life and were exposed to a wide and varied acquaintance. She encouraged and greatly enjoyed the amateur theatricals that took place at Steventon in the 1780s; and, along with the rest of the family, she was an avid novel reader and letter writer, and she continued to live up to her early reputation as the poet of the family by regularly composing light verses and charades for family entertainment. Mrs. Austen's zest for life and her general liveliness of wit and humor seem clearly to have rubbed off onto most of her children, not least onto her youngest daughter, whose prodigious talent for comic irony may well have come from her shrewd mother.

After the death of Mr. Austen in 1805, Mrs. Austen left Bath with her daughters and lived first in Southampton with Frank Austen and his wife, between 1806 and 1809, and then at Chawton, where she died, aged eighty-seven, on 17 January 1827.

See: Lane 1984, Le Faye 1989, Tucker 1983.

Austen, Cassandra Elizabeth (1773–1845). Born on 9 January 1773, Cassandra Austen was the elder sister of Jane Austen by almost three years. She became engaged to Rev. Tom Fowle, possibly in 1792, but he died of yellow fever in the West Indies in 1797 before they could afford to marry, and Cassandra remained single thereafter. Cassandra and Jane shared most of their lives together until parted by Jane's death, and Cassandra was clearly Jane's closest sibling, friend, and confidante. Even as children they were inseparable, and this is why, when Cassandra was sent away to school in Oxford in 1783, Jane had to be sent, too, even though she was only seven. In later life, when they were not together physically, they wrote to each other more or less on a daily basis, and what remains of this correspondence (Cassandra later destroyed much of it) provides one of the main sources of biographical information about Jane Austen. Cassandra was an accomplished amateur artist, and we are also indebted to her for our only visual record of what Jane Austen looked like, in the form of two watercolor pictures, one a back view from 1804, and the other an unfinished portrait from around 1810 (both are frequently reproduced in biographical works; the frontispiece to this book is an artist's adaptation of the portrait, the original of which is in the National Portrait Gallery, London; the other picture is still within the Austen family). Ironically, apart from a silhouette, no pictures of Cassandra herself survive. Cassandra painted a series of watercolor caricatures of British royalty to illustrate her sister's juvenile burlesque "The History of England," and several other pieces of Jane Austen's juvenilia are dedicated to Cassandra. Indeed, the sisters' shared experiences, shared reading, and shared jokes almost certainly provided much of the initial inspiration and material for these early writings. In later life, Cassandra was in on the secret of her sister's authorship from the start, and she no doubt acted as Jane Austen's first reader, critic, and adviser.

Jane Austen seems always to have looked up to her elder sister as a wiser, stronger, and better character than herself, and she seems to have become increasingly dependent on her as she grew older. Cassandra certainly seems to have been quietly reliable and efficient in all practical matters and to have had a reassuringly calm, controlled, and rational disposition. She was noted for her stoicism, particularly in the face of her fiancé's death, and this seems to have reflected an increasingly devout faith in Christianity (perhaps influenced by the Evangelical movement). Cassandra clearly felt things very deeply, as witnessed

by the moving letters she wrote to her niece just after Jane Austen's death
(included in *Jane Austen's Letters*, 1995), but because she was not customarily
demonstrative of her feelings, it seems that she was sometimes considered cold
and reserved by those who did not know her well.

Cassandra inherited the estate of Jane Austen and was responsible, through
Henry Austen, for the posthumous publication of *Persuasion* and *Northanger
Abbey* as well as for the sale, in 1832, of the remaining copyrights of her sister's
novels to the publisher Richard Bentley. After her own death, she was also
responsible for passing on her sister's surviving manuscripts and letters to various other members of the family. After Jane's death, Cassandra lived at Chawton for the rest of her life. She looked after her mother until the latter's death
in 1827 and died herself, while staying with her brother Frank in Portsmouth,
on 22 March 1845. One of her great-nieces remembered Cassandra as "a pale,
dark-eyed old lady, with a high arched nose and a kind smile."

See: *Hubback & Hubback 1906, Lane 1984, Le Faye 1989, Tucker 1983.*

Austen, Charles John (1779–1852). Jane Austen's younger brother and the
youngest of the Austen family. Referred to by Jane Austen in a letter of 1799
as "our own particular little brother" (a phrase adapted from Fanny Burney's
novel *Camilla*), Charles was clearly a great favorite in the family and is said to
have had something of her own happy and affectionate disposition. He also later
won the respect and admiration of all who served with, and under, him during
his long and distinguished naval career, for he seems to have been a very brave
and skillful sailor and, later, a fair, caring, and compassionate captain. Educated
at home by his father until the age of twelve, he then followed in the footsteps
of his brother, Frank, by attending the Royal Naval Academy in Portsmouth
between 1791 and 1794. On completing his studies there, he went to sea immediately as a midshipman and thereafter was on active service throughout the
Revolutionary and Napoleonic Wars with France. He was promoted to the rank
of lieutenant in December 1797 and then to that of commander in October 1804,
when he was appointed to HMS *Indian* and stationed in Bermuda to patrol the
North American Station to prevent neutral countries from trading with France.
Here, he married Frances Palmer (1790–1814), the daughter of a former attorney
general of Bermuda, on 19 May 1807; and he was promoted to the rank of post-
captain, on HMS *Swiftsure*, in May 1810. On his return to England in 1811, he
was appointed to a guardship stationed at the Nore, off Sheerness, where he and
his wife and children lived until late 1814. After his wife died, in September
1814, Charles went to sea again in command of HMS *Phoenix*. On duty in the
Mediterranean, he became involved in the renewed hostilities with France following Napoleon's escape from Elba in March 1815. After the war, in early
1816, his boat was shipwrecked in a storm off the coast of Asia Minor, and
though there were no fatalities, and he was cleared of blame by a court-martial
in April 1816, he did not go to sea again for some ten years. In February 1820,
he was appointed to land-based duties in the coast guard service and stationed

at Padstow in Cornwall. He married his first wife's sister, Harriet Palmer (d.1867), on 7 August 1820. He was given the command of HMS *Aurora* on the Jamaica Station in 1826, and his main duties here had to do with the suppression of the slave trade; he was made flag-captain on the *Winchester* in December 1828 and continued to serve on the North American and West Indies Station until December 1830, when a severe injury forced him to return to Britain. He made a full recovery, however, and returned to sea again in 1838 (till 1841) as captain of the *Bellerophon* on duty in the Mediterranean, where he was involved in the Levant campaign against Mehemet Ali, viceroy of Egypt; for his services during this campaign, Charles was made a Companion of the Bath. In November 1846, he was made a rear admiral and, in February 1850, commander in chief of the East India and China Station. While in this post and on active service in Burma, Charles Austen died of cholera on 8 October 1852, at the age of seventy-three. He had four daughters by his first marriage and three sons and one daughter by his second (though only four of his children survived him).

See: *Hubback & Hubback, 1906, Lane 1984, Le Faye 1989, Tucker 1983.*

Austen, Edward (1767–1852). Jane Austen's third brother, born on 7 October 1767 at Deane, Hampshire, a few months before the Austens moved to Steventon Rectory. In 1779, when Edward was nearly twelve, Mr. Austen's distant cousin, Thomas Knight II (1735–1794) of Godmersham Park, Kent, visited Steventon as part of a wedding tour with his new wife, Catherine, née Knatchbull (1753–1812). The couple took a liking to the young Edward and asked him to accompany them on the rest of their tour. Sometime later, the Knights also invited him to spend a holiday with them at Godmersham. Their fondness for him clearly grew, for, as they remained without children of their own, they eventually agreed with the Austens, in or around 1783, that they should adopt Edward as their heir. From this time on, he was increasingly at Godmersham, and in 1786 he was sent by the Knights to finish his education (gained so far entirely from his father at Steventon) on the Grand Tour. On this trip, he visited Switzerland and Italy and spent a year at Dresden. On his return, in the autumn of 1788, he went to live permanently at Godmersham with the Knights, where he was gradually prepared for the life of a country squire as the prospective owner of three large estates in Kent and Hampshire (Godmersham, Chawton, and Steventon).

On 27 December 1791, Edward married Elizabeth Bridges (1773–1808), daughter of Sir Brook and Lady Fanny Bridges of Goodnestone Park in Kent, and they began their married life together at Rowling House on the Goodnestone estate. In October 1794, Edward Austen's adoptive father died, leaving his estates to his widow but to be inherited by Edward after her death. In the autumn of 1797, Edward's adoptive mother decided to retire to a smaller property in Canterbury, and she arranged for Edward to come into his inheritance straightaway. He and his family moved to Godmersham shortly afterward. On 10 October 1808, Edward's wife, Elizabeth, died some twelve days after giving birth to her eleventh child by Edward. Sometime shortly after this sad event Edward gave his mother and sisters the cottage at Chawton to live in. It can be said, then, that Edward thus indirectly promoted the writing and publication of Jane Austen's novels, for only after the move to the congenial surroundings of Chawton did she return in earnest to her writing after several barren years, and it was during her time here that her novels first began to be published.

Edward adopted the name of Knight following the death of Mrs. Knight in October 1812, and he lived on at Godmersham until the age of eighty-five. He died in his sleep on 19 November 1852. Edward seems to have been a gentle and mild-mannered man with an amiable and cheerful disposition that made him generally well liked. With a good head for business and without the scholarly leanings of some of his other siblings, he seems to have been well suited to the life of a country squire that so fortunately fell to him.

See: Lane 1984, Le Faye 1989, Tucker 1983.

Austen, Elizabeth, née Bridges (1773–1808). One of thirteen children and the third daughter, after Fanny (1771–1805) and Sophia (1772–1844), of Sir Brook and Lady Bridges of Goodnestone Park, Kent. She married Edward Austen on 27 December 1791 at Goodnestone in a double wedding ceremony that also saw the marriage of her sister, Sophia, to William Deedes of Sandling. Her other elder sister had also married earlier in the same month, and all three sisters had become engaged at various points throughout 1791 (Elizabeth's engagement to Edward had been announced on 1 March). Jane Austen's early burlesque piece, "The Three Sisters" (?1792), is dedicated to her brother Edward and would seem to have been inspired by the symmetrical romantic progress of the three Bridges girls at this time. Elizabeth had eleven children and died suddenly on 10 October 1808, less than a fortnight after the birth of her last one.

Austen, Frances (Fanny) Catherine (1793–1882). Eldest daughter of Edward and Elizabeth Austen and Jane Austen's firstborn niece. On Fanny's birth on 23 January 1793, Jane Austen dedicated to her the juvenile pieces known as "Scraps." Fanny was born just four months before her cousin Anna Austen, and though both nieces were very close to their aunt, Fanny is usually referred to as Jane Austen's favorite, possibly because, in a letter to Cassandra of 7 October 1808, she referred to Fanny as "almost another Sister" and continued that she "could not have supposed that a neice [sic] would ever have been so much to me. She is quite after one's own heart." Only two days after this letter, Fanny's mother died, and the sixteen-year-old Fanny was left "to be companion to her father, mistress of a large household, and surrogate mother to her [ten] younger brothers and sisters" (*A Family Record*, 1989, p. 151). Jane Austen and Fanny corresponded regularly, and eight of Jane Austen's letters to Fanny survive. One of these, written around 24 July 1806, is a letter in verse on the marriage of Francis Austen and Mary Gibson; and later letters, of 1814 and

1817, responding to Fanny's requests for advice on romantic matters, are important for recording some of Jane Austen's few direct, personal thoughts on love and marriage. In fact, Fanny did not marry in Jane Austen's lifetime, but, on 24 October 1820, she became the second wife of Sir Edward Knatchbull, with whom she eventually had nine children. In 1845, Fanny inherited most of the surviving letters of Jane Austen from her other aunt, Cassandra. She did not make these available to J. E. Austen-Leigh for his 1869 *Memoir*, but after her death, on 24 December 1882, they were found by her eldest son, Edward (1829–1893; first Lord Brabourne, 1880), and published by him in 1884. Fanny's own surviving letters to her former governess, Miss Chapman, and her diaries, which survive in an unbroken sequence, 1804–1872 (both deposited in the Kent Archives Office), are themselves a useful source of information about Jane Austen and the Austen family generally. Fanny contributed four of the "hints" for Jane Austen's *Plan of a Novel, according to Hints from Various Quarters*, possibly in the spring of 1816, while she was on a visit to Chawton with her father; and her views on her aunt's work appear in the two collections of comments, "Opinions of *Mansfield Park*" and "Opinions of *Emma*."

See: Lane 1984, Le Faye 1989, Tucker 1983.

Austen, Francis (1698–1791). Uncle and guardian of Rev. George Austen and Jane Austen's great-uncle. A prosperous solicitor at Sevenoaks, Kent, he paid for his nephew's schooling and later bought him the living of Deane, which fell vacant in 1773, making George Austen rector of both Steventon and Deane. Francis Austen's second wife, Jane, née Chadwick (d.1782), was one of Jane Austen's godmothers. A brief early description of Jane Austen comes in a letter written by her half cousin, Philadelphia Walter, following a family gathering at Francis Austen's home in Sevenoaks, the Red House, in July 1788. Francis Austen died on 21 June 1791 at the age of ninety-three, leaving £500 to each of his nephews, including Jane Austen's father.

Austen, Francis William (1774–1865). Jane Austen's fifth brother, born on 23 April 1774. Along with his younger brother, Charles, Frank had the most varied and adventurous life of all the Austen children in his long career in the navy. He was on active service throughout the whole of the Revolutionary and Napoleonic Wars with France and during that time traveled almost the whole world over, from the Baltic to the Cape of Good Hope, from America and the West Indies to China and the East Indies, and all over the Mediterranean. He eventually rose to the highest ranks of his profession and received high public recognition for his services to the country when he was knighted in 1837. Yet, despite living much more dangerously than the other Austen children, he outlived all his brothers and sisters by many years (indeed, he also outlived six of his eleven children).

Frank Austen entered the Royal Naval Academy in Portsmouth just before his twelfth birthday in April 1786. He left the academy in December 1788 with glowing reports about his academic and technical progress and about his exemplary behavior. To continue his training, he set sail immediately as a volunteer on HMS *Perseverance* bound for the East Indies, not returning home until five years later. He graduated to the rank of midshipman in December 1789, moved to HMS *Minerva* in November 1791, and was made lieutenant in December 1792, while still in the East Indies. He returned to Britain at the end of 1793 and was assigned to ships on the home station between 1794 and 1796. He joined HMS *Lark* in March 1794 and later that year took part in the evacuation of British troops from the Netherlands following its fall to the French. In March 1795, he was part of a squadron sent to escort Princess Caroline of Brunswick from Germany to England for her marriage to the Prince of Wales. Frank transferred to HMS *Andromeda* in May 1795 and then again to HMS *Glory* in the autumn of that year; on this ship he sailed to the West Indies as part of an escort convoy for a large expeditionary force led by Sir Ralph Abercromby (during this military campaign Cassandra Austen's fiancé, Tom Fowle, died of yellow fever). Frank served on HMS *Triton* in 1796, and on HMS *Seahorse* from 1797 to February 1798, when he was appointed to HMS *London*, one of the ships blockading Cadiz at that time. In 1798, through the good offices of General Edward Mathew, the father of James Austen's first wife, the late Anne Mathew, Mr. Austen had succeeded in gaining for Frank the patronage of Admiral James Gambier, a member of the Admiralty Board, and in December the admiral wrote to Mr. Austen informing the family of Frank's promotion to the rank of commander on HMS *Peterel*. Frank joined this ship in the Mediterranean in February 1799. Now that he had command of his own vessel, Frank would be able to claim prize money from captured enemy ships, and over the next two years he captured some forty vessels. Following a particularly spectacular engagement off Marseilles in March 1800, when he drove two French ships onto the rocks and captured a third, without any losses among his own crew, he was promoted to the rank of post-captain, though he did not hear of this promotion until his replacement on the *Peterel* arrived to relieve him in October. His next appointment was as flag-captain on HMS *Neptune* under his patron, Admiral Gambier, and he remained on this ship until the Peace of Amiens in March 1802. When the war resumed again in May 1803, there seemed to be a bigger danger than ever of a French invasion from across the channel, and Frank was put in charge of the North Foreland unit of "Sea Fencibles," a home guard set up to defend the coast in the event of a French landing. He was headquartered at Ramsgate in Kent and remained there until May 1804, when he returned to sea as captain of HMS *Leonard*, the flagship of Rear Admiral Thomas Louis. In the following year, 1805, he went with Admiral Louis to join HMS *Canopus* in the Mediterranean and, between March and July, took part in Nelson's famous sea chase after Villeneuve to the West Indies and back—a decisive action that foiled Napoleon's plan to invade Britain. However, to Frank's everlasting regret, he was not part of the even more decisive Battle of Trafalgar in October of the same year, for, some three weeks before the battle, the *Canopus* was sent away from Nelson's main fleet on supply and convoy duties, and the battle was over by the time it returned. Frank gained some consolation in February 1806, when he took part in the British victory at the Battle of San Domingo in the West Indies—for this, he and the other officers received gold medals and votes of thanks from both houses of Parliament. Soon after his return to Britain, on 24 July 1806, Frank married Mary Gibson (1785–1823) whom he had met during his period at Ramsgate three years earlier. As he would soon be away at sea again, and his wife left alone, and as his mother and sisters had no permanent home, it was arranged that he and Mary would set up home together with the Austen women in Southampton, and they all moved there together in October, staying first in lodgings before removing, in March 1807, to a house in Castle Square. In that very month, Frank received a new appointment, to the command of HMS *St. Albans*, and, after the birth of his first child in April, he set sail in June for a period of convoy duty to and from South Africa, China, and the East Indies. Within this period he was also briefly involved with events in the Peninsular War when, in July 1808, he escorted some troopships to Portugal and, on 21 August, observed the Battle of Vimeiro from the deck of his ship, afterward taking the wounded and some French prisoners back to Britain with him. At the start of 1809, he was also involved in the disembarkation of troops at Portsmouth following Sir John Moore's retreat to Corunna in northern Spain. Between April 1809 and July 1810, Frank convoyed East Indiamen to China and back again, and on their safe return to Britain he was commended by the Admiralty and given a gratuity of 1,000 guineas by a grateful East India Company. In December 1810, after some months' leave, Frank was appointed to HMS *Caledonia* as flag captain to Admiral Gambier and engaged in blockading the French coast. Between July 1811 and May 1813 he was in command of HMS *Elephant* and stationed with the North Sea Fleet. Here, he was mainly involved in helping to blockade Napoleon's dockyard at Flushing, but during the War of 1812 with America he also captured an American privateer off the Western Islands of Scotland. In May 1813, still with the *Elephant*, he was sent on convoy duty to Sweden and the Baltic, where he remained until his demobilization in May 1814, following Napoleon's abdication and exile to Elba in April. Frank did not return to sea again for about another thirty years, during which time he rose steadily through the ranks, becoming rear admiral in 1830 and vice admiral in 1838. Between 1844 and 1848 he was commander in chief of the North American and West Indies station, and he became a full admiral in 1848. In 1862 he was vice admiral of the United Kingdom and in 1863 admiral of the fleet. In addition to his promotions in the navy, he was also honored as a Companion of the Bath in 1815 and a Knight Commander of the Bath in 1837.

After his return to shore in 1814, Frank lived on half-pay and, with a steadily growing family, clearly found it impossible to buy a house of his own. He was fortunate in that his brother, Edward, frequently allowed him to live at Chawton Great House (where, of course, he was close to his mother and sisters at Chawton cottage), and at other times he lived either at Alton or Gosport. His wife died in 1823 while giving birth to their eleventh child (who also died soon afterward). On 24 July 1828, Frank married his second wife, Martha Lloyd (1765–1843), the long-standing friend and companion of Jane, Cassandra, and Mrs. Austen. At this time, too, Frank received a gift of £10,000 from his rich aunt, Mrs. Leigh Perrot, and this enabled him to buy Portsdown Lodge, near Portsmouth, where he lived for the rest of his life. Martha died in 1843, and Frank lived on at Portsdown with his daughters and grandchildren until he died, at the age of ninety-one, on 10 August 1865.

Frank Austen seems to have been cut out for the life he actually led: physically robust and fearless from infancy, placid and controlled in temperament though resolute in action, precise and methodical in thought, and with a strong sense of duty and morality. If other of her brothers initially appeared more glamorous to Jane Austen, Frank's steady good sense, orderly way of life, and quiet determination to succeed seem to have been more appealing to her at the last—at least, this would seem to be the case if we judge by the strength of positive feeling associated with the naval characters in her last completed novel, *Persuasion*: with "their friendliness, their brotherliness, their openness, their uprightness," they have "more worth and warmth than any other set of men in England" (99).

See: Hubback & Hubback 1906, Lane 1984, Le Faye 1989, Tucker 1983.

Austen, George (1766–1838). Jane Austen's second brother, born at Deane on 26 August 1766. Very little is known about George, except that he was disabled in some way, probably mentally, though he was also possibly deaf and dumb and epileptic. In a letter of 1788, Eliza de Feuillide compared her disabled two-year-old son, Hastings, to George, saying that he was outwardly healthy but subject to fits and unable to walk or talk. George did not grow up with the rest of the family at Steventon but was boarded out locally under the supervision of his parents. Later, his care was supervised by his brothers, and it seems he may have lived with a family called Culham, together with Mrs. Austen's disabled brother, Thomas Leigh (1747–1821), at Monk Sherborne, Hampshire, near to Sherborne St. John, where James Austen was vicar from 1791. George died here on 17 January 1838.

The suggestion that George may have been deaf is often supported by reference to one of Jane Austen's letters from 1808 (*Letters* 1995: 160), where she describes talking to a deaf man by means of her fingers. The implication here is that, in order to thus communicate, she must have learned to do so previously and that the only reason she would have had to do this would have been in order to talk to her brother. But this does not necessarily follow.

See: Lane 1984, Le Faye 1989, Tucker 1983.

Austen, Rev. George (1731–1805). Jane Austen's father. As Henry Austen suggested in 1817 in his introduction to *Northanger Abbey* and *Persuasion*

(p. 3), it is not in the least surprising that Jane Austen became a writer and such a careful stylist and lover of language, given the example of her learned father, who, as a preacher, worked constantly with language and who, Henry states, was "a profound scholar" with "a most exquisite taste in every species of literature." But Rev. George Austen was not only a learned, skillful, and high-principled clergyman but also an infectiously enthusiastic and kindly teacher, a loving husband and father, and an energetic, practical-minded man with a lively sense of humor who cared deeply for the success and happiness of his children and who, indeed, provided them with all the necessary preconditions for happy and successful lives: a secure and loving home, a good education, sound advice and guidance, and a lifelong willingness to promote their best interests.

Born on 1 May 1731, in Tonbridge, Kent, to a surgeon, William Austen (1701–1737), and Rebecca (Walter) Austen, née Hampson (c.1695–1733), George Austen was the third of four children: Hampson, who died in infancy (1728–1730), Philadelphia (1730–1790), and Leonora (b.1732). His mother died not long after George's birth, in February 1732, and his father took a second wife, Susannah Kelk (1688–1768), in May 1736. His father died in December 1737 without further issue but also without having changed his will to take account of his second marriage. His second wife was thus under no legal obligation to keep the children with her in the Tonbridge home, and she seems to have passed them on to her Austen brothers-in-law with undignified haste. William Austen's will had left the children under the guardianship of William's elder brother, Francis (1698–1791), a prosperous solicitor in Sevenoaks, Kent; but as he was a bachelor at this time, they were sent to live with his married brother, Stephen (1704–1751), a bookseller and publisher in St. Paul's Churchyard, London. Although little is known of this period in George Austen's life, it appears that his uncle Stephen resented having his brother's children and treated them harshly; but George was eventually sent back to Tonbridge when he was about ten years old, and he seems not to have been badly affected by this unhappy episode. He appears to have lost touch with his younger sister from this point on (we know only that she was still alive in 1769), but he retained contact with Philadelphia, who was later to become part of Jane Austen's regular family circle.

In 1741, then, he went to live at Tonbridge with an aunt, Betty Hooper, and became a pupil at Tonbridge School, his fees apparently being paid by his uncle Francis. In July 1747, at the age of sixteen, George entered St. John's College, Oxford, and received a fellowship of the college specifically reserved for a Tonbridge School scholar. He graduated in 1751, and in 1753 he received another scholarship related to Tonbridge School that allowed him to remain at Oxford for another seven years to study divinity. In 1754 he obtained his M.A. and was also ordained as a deacon. At this time, while still a fellow at Oxford, he became perpetual curate of Shipbourne, near Tonbridge (possibly through the influence of his uncle Francis Austen), and a second master, or usher, at Tonbridge School, holding both posts until the end of 1757. In May 1755 he was ordained as a priest at Rochester in Kent, and in 1758 he returned to Oxford to prepare for his bachelor of divinity degree. He became assistant chaplain of the college and was junior proctor for the academic year 1758–1759, when his good looks gained him the nickname of "the Handsome Proctor." He was awarded his bachelor of divinity degree in 1760. In November 1761, George was presented with the living of Steventon, in Hampshire, by Thomas Knight I of Godmersham, Kent (1702–1781), husband of George's second cousin, Jane Monk. The living was worth about £100 per annum. However, George did not take up his duties in the parish until after his marriage in 1764, instead employing a deputy to officiate on his behalf (another cousin, Rev. Thomas Bathurst). George probably became engaged to his future wife, Cassandra Leigh, in 1763. It is not clear when, where, or how they first met, but it was probably in the early 1760s and may have been at Oxford, where Cassandra's uncle Theophilus was master at Balliol College (Cassandra's sister, Jane, later married Edward Cooper, who was also at Oxford at this time, as a fellow of All Souls, and this, too, may have been a reason for Cassandra's being at Oxford). In any case, George and Cassandra were married in Bath on 26 April 1764 and went to live in Hampshire, where George finally took up his duties as rector of Steventon.

The Steventon rectory was in poor repair, however, and unfit for occupation, so the Austens began their married life by renting the parsonage at Deane, two miles north of Steventon, where they lived until 1768. The glebe land of the parish (land set aside for the maintenance of the incumbent) amounted to only three acres, so George Austen was allowed by Mr. Knight to supplement his income (derived from the living, the glebe land, and the parish tithes) by farming the 200-acre Cheesedown Farm in the north of Steventon parish. Still, the newlyweds' lifestyle was modest (Mrs. Austen is said to have had no new dress for the first two years of her married life), and, as children began to arrive, their finances had to stretch even further. Three sons, James, George, and Edward, were born in quick succession, in 1765, 1766, and 1767. In the summer of 1768 the Austens moved into the renovated and enlarged Steventon rectory, and this was to remain the much-loved family home until 1801.

From 1770, financial problems loomed ever larger for George and his growing family (Henry was born in 1771), and it seems that he was on the verge of insolvency in early 1773 (when his first daughter, Cassandra, was born). He was saved from this by a gift, in February of that year, of £300 from his wife's rich brother, James Leigh Perrot; and his position was further improved in March, when he became rector of Deane as well as of Steventon, the living of Deane (worth about £110 per annum) having been bought for him by his uncle Francis. George also began to take in boarding pupils at Steventon from this time (until 1796), mainly teaching them classics to prepare them for university entrance. This neatly served a double purpose in that he was able to educate his own children at the same time. From now on, his financial position steadily improved, and he was always able to keep his family in comfortable circumstances thereafter. He was by no means ever rich, however, and there were more children to come (Francis in 1774, Jane in 1775, and Charles in 1779). For most of his career at Steventon his annual income fluctuated somewhat unpredictably from year to year; he seems to have been able to rely on £310 (his two livings plus £100 from dividends and a small annuity), and this was then supplemented by parish dues, the sale of produce from his farming, and whatever he made from teaching (in 1778, he charged about £35 per annum per pupil for tuition, board, and lodging, and this had gone up to about £65 in the 1790s), but his income never exceeded £600. It is perhaps indicative of his uncertain position on the margins of the gentry that, though he was briefly wealthy enough to keep a carriage in late 1797, it had to be given up again before the end of the following year. But, in terms of his children's upbringing, what George Austen lacked in reliable, fixed income he more than made up for by his prodigious intellectual wealth, which ensured that the Austen children all had an exceptional early education for the time (and there was always money enough for books: George Austen's library contained more than 500 volumes by 1800). Moreover, as a highly respected scholar (many of the pupils George took in at the rectory were from wealthy, titled families), as the perceived representative of the owners of the Steventon estate (his relations, the Knights, never lived there themselves—they also eventually adopted his third son, Edward), and as the husband of a wife with her own highborn connections, George Austen had a significantly higher standing in local society than his actual income or position warranted. Thus his children had access to social circles that would normally have been closed to them as sons and daughters of a humble country parson.

In late 1800, George Austen decided to retire and remove to Bath with his wife and daughters, leaving his son, James, as his curate at Steventon. The reasons for this were probably the obvious ones to do with the elder Austens' age and health and their desire to spend their last years together in a favorite old haunt from which they could also conveniently make holiday excursions to the west country and Wales. Jane and Cassandra, who were away from home when the decision was made and seem not to have been consulted about it, were not so happy about the idea, and Jane is said to have fainted on hearing the news that she would have to leave her comfortable home and beloved country-side for the enervating urban environment of Bath; there is a suggestion, also, that she suspected that her father had been persuaded to make the move by the James Austens, by Mary in particular, who lost little time in establishing herself as mistress at the rectory.

George Austen's years of retirement at Bath seemed to pass pleasantly enough. The family did, indeed, make several holiday excursions to the west country and Wales, and they also visited at Godmersham and Steventon. But it was a fairly short retirement, for George Austen died in Bath, following a brief illness, on 21 January 1805.

George Austen provided his famous daughter, Jane, not only with a loving home and a rich intellectual and literary environment in which to develop her talent but also with the positive encouragement to seek a novelistic career at a time when fiction was viewed with suspicion, and professional independence for women seen almost as a perversion of nature. Although he never saw his daughter's books in print, he was clearly proud of her writing and ever keen to encourage it; apart from sharing in the family's communal delight in her early literary efforts, he gave her perhaps the biggest vote of confidence possible when, in November 1797, he offered the early version of *Pride and Prejudice* ("First Impressions") to the publishing house of Cadell and Davies. It was rejected sight unseen by Cadell, but the very fact that someone of George Austen's scholarship and reading believed the novel to be worthy of publication must have counted for a great deal with his daughter and possibly gave her the self-assurance, later in life, to return to the quest for publication.

If, in her writing, Jane Austen inherited her ironic wit and acute observation of human foibles from her mother, then from her father she inherited her intellectual and moral judiciousness, her elegance and precision of style, and the compassion of a gentle humor that always allowed for the redemption of even the most unsympathetic character.

See: Lane 1984, Le Faye 1989, Tucker 1983.

Austen, Henry Thomas (1771–1850). Jane Austen's fourth brother, born on 8 June 1771. Henry is usually referred to as Jane Austen's favorite brother, and he is certainly the member of the family who had the most direct practical involvement with her literary career, for he effectively acted as her literary agent and arranged for the publication of her novels. Intellectually, Henry seems to have been the most naturally gifted of the Austen family, and he was renowned for his brilliant conversation and quick wit. Described by one of his nieces as the handsomest and most talented of the family, he was also liked for his sociability and his sunny and sanguine temperament. At the same time, he seems also to have been the least steady of the Austens, and he experienced a far less settled and, in some ways, less successful career than his brothers.

He entered St. John's College, Oxford, at the age of seventeen in July 1788 (on a Founder's Kin scholarship like James Austen before him) and graduated in 1792, gaining his M.A. in 1796 and retaining his fellowship until 1798. It was expected that he would eventually follow his brother into the church, but he was not old enough to be ordained when he left Oxford, and then, when the war with France broke out in 1793, he joined the Oxfordshire Militia—a home defense force—as a lieutenant. He remained in the militia until 1801, becoming a captain and adjutant in 1797. Sometime in 1796, Henry became engaged to Mary Pearson of Greenwich, London, but she broke off the engagement in the autumn of that year, and Henry turned his thoughts once more to Eliza de Feuillide, the glamorous cousin he had first been attracted to some ten years earlier. She seems to have flirted with him during the Christmas festivities at Steventon in 1786, shortly after her return from France and the birth of her son, Hastings, and Henry, still not quite sixteen, stayed with her in London in the following spring. There was clearly a mutual attraction between the two cousins, but nothing came of it immediately: Eliza was already married, of course, and, in any case, she was back in France between 1788 and 1790. However, on her return to England, there appears to have been a renewal of their intimacy (such as it was), particularly in the autumn of 1792. Then, following the death of Eliza's husband in 1794, a more definite courtship seems to have developed from around 1795. This was interrupted by Henry's short-lived engagement to Mary Pearson in 1796, but Henry and Eliza were finally married in London on 31 December 1797.

Eliza enjoyed the life of an officer's wife until 1801, at which point Henry resigned his commission and established himself as a banker and army agent in London. In 1804 and 1807, respectively, two fellow ex-officers, Henry Maunde, and James Tilson, joined Henry as partners, and their bank became Austen, Maunde, and Tilson, with premises, from 1807, at 10 Henrietta Street, Covent Garden. Henry also formed other banking partnerships in Alton, Hampshire (1806–1815 and 1814–1815), Petersfield, Hampshire (1810–1814) and Hythe, Kent (1810–1814).

In 1813, in addition to his banking concerns, Henry was made receiver general for taxes for Oxfordshire. This post required a surety of £30,000, and this was pledged for him by his brother Edward and by his uncle, Mr. Leigh Perrot (£20,000 and £10,000, respectively). Unfortunately, the postwar economic depression led to the failure of Henry's Alton bank at the end of 1815, and this, in turn, led to the failure of his London bank, so that in March 1816 he became bankrupt. This meant that his uncle and brother had to pay the large amounts they had pledged as surety. Other members of the family who had money tied up in Henry's banks also suffered financial losses, although Jane Austen herself lost only about £13 (she had already invested the bulk of her profits from her first three novels—between about £530 and £600—in Navy 5 percent stock). For his part, Henry seems to have taken the disaster in his ever-optimistic stride, and he quickly turned his mind to other things. He decided to return to his earlier vocation for the church, and, by December 1816, he had been ordained as a deacon and had become curate of Chawton. According to Jane Austen's letters of this time, he was soon preaching as if he had done it all his life and writing "very superior sermons." He was ordained as a priest in early 1817 and seems to have quickly established a reputation as an earnest evangelical preacher—something that may account for the tone of the "Biographical Notice" of Jane Austen, which he wrote in 1817 as an introduction to the posthumous edition of *Northanger Abbey* and *Persuasion*.

In 1818 Henry served as chaplain to the British in Berlin, where he delivered a series of *Lectures upon Some Important Passages in the Book of Genesis*, which were published in 1820. When his brother James died in December 1819, Henry became rector of Steventon, where he remained until 1822. Eliza had died, following a long illness, in 1813, and now, on 11 April 1820, Henry married Eleanor Jackson (d.1864). In 1822, Henry moved to Farnham in Surrey, where he was curate (and, from 1823, master at the grammar school) until 1827. In 1824 he was made perpetual curate of Bentley in Hampshire, where he eventually settled until 1839. After this, Henry and his wife lived alternately at Colchester in Essex and at Tunbridge Wells, Kent. Henry died at Tunbridge Wells on 12 March 1850, aged seventy-eight. He left no issue from either of his marriages.

Henry Austen had a significant influence on Jane Austen's writing in terms of both its composition and its publication.

In terms of initial composition, Jane Austen certainly cut her writer's teeth partly in dialogue with Henry and her eldest brother James, her two Oxford-educated brothers, who, through their academic studies, their wide reading, and their own efforts at writing, clearly helped her to define and refine her literary talents at a formative stage of her development. Henry's undergraduate days (1788–1792) coincide almost exactly with the period in which Jane Austen is thought to have composed her juvenilia (1787–1793), and it is likely that some of these burlesque pieces were written as a result of literary exchanges between brother and sister. Indeed, at Oxford, Henry collaborated with his elder brother James in the production and writing of the latter's periodical, *The Loiterer*, and critics have noted clear echoes of some of the essays Henry published there in Jane Austen's juvenilia. In later life, too, Henry continued to be close to his sister's writing as it was being composed and revised, for, once she began to have her work published, in the period after 1810, she frequently stayed with him in London, and at this time he was probably, after Cassandra, the first person to whom she would show her work as it was completed and the main person with whom she could discuss proof corrections. Finally, here, given Henry's reputation as a spirited and eloquent conversationalist, one might also speculate on how many of his speeches or arguments eventually found their way (adapted, of course) into the mouths of his sister's characters (Henry Tilney from *Northanger Abbey* most immediately springs to mind, though aspects of Henry Crawford in *Mansfield Park* also suggest themselves).

Henry's involvement with his sister's publishing career could be said to have begun in the spring of 1803, when, through a business associate named Mr. Seymour, he sold the manuscript of "Susan," the novel that later became *Northanger Abbey*, to a London publisher, Richard Crosby and Company, for ten pounds. Crosby did not publish the novel, but the pattern was set for Jane Austen's future dealings with publishers through her brother. Henry wrote letters and negotiated terms with publishers on Jane's behalf and was directly responsible for the publication of all six of her major novels. Interestingly, almost his last business negotiation for his sister before her death was the repurchase of "Susan" from Crosby early in 1816. After Jane Austen's death, he arranged for the publication of *Northanger Abbey* and *Persuasion* and included in it his "Biographical Notice of the Author"—the earliest published source of biographical information about her. Immediately after her death, he also provided the obituaries for the local newspapers and for the first time in public revealed her identity as the author of her novels.

As a banker, Henry may have had something of a checkered career, but any material losses he was responsible for have been fully repaid to posterity by the cultural riches he invested for us as his sister's literary agent. As Jane Austen herself exclaimed, with a touch of exasperation, on hearing that he had got himself invited to an exclusive ball to mark the end of the war in 1814: "Oh! what a Henry."

See: Lane 1984, Le Faye 1989, Tucker 1983.

Austen, James (1765–1819). Jane Austen's eldest brother, born 13 February 1765. If Mrs. Austen was playfully referred to as the poet of the Austen family for her ready ability to turn a witty verse, the studious and scholarly James Austen made a more plausible claim to the title through his lifelong commitment to exploring his feelings and experiences through writing serious poetry. From youthful, imitative verses on the beauties of nature, through the blank verse prologues and epilogues written for the Steventon theatricals in the 1780s and the romantic eulogies written on his second wife and family, to the more didactic and brooding religious poetry of his later years and the touching (if strained) elegy he wrote on Jane Austen's death, James seems to have turned to poetry as naturally as his sister turned to prose fiction to make sense of his life and world.

Educated at home by his father until the summer of 1779, James, at the early age of fourteen, then became a scholar and fellow of St. John's College, Oxford, on a Founder's Kin scholarship. He graduated in 1783 and obtained his M.A. in 1788. A career in the church had been planned for him from the start, but it also clearly accorded with his own temperament and intellectual bent, and, following a year or so traveling on the continent, from November 1786, he was ordained deacon on 10 December 1787. He obtained his first curacy in July 1788—that of the village of Stoke Charity near Winchester, Hampshire—but he continued to reside at Oxford, where he was ordained as a priest in June 1789. In the spring of 1790 he moved back to the Steventon area to become curate of Overton. He became vicar of Sherborne St. John, near Basingstoke, in September 1791 and his father's curate at Deane in 1792, on his marriage to Anne Mathew (b.1759) in March of that year. He moved with his new wife from Overton to Deane parsonage later in 1792, and here their daughter, Anna, was born, on 15 April 1793. For his marriage in 1792, James was also presented with the vicarage of Cubbington in Warwickshire by his uncle Leigh Perrot; this was worth about £100 and seems to have smoothed the path to the marriage, but James employed a curate to act for him in this parish and seems never to have gone there himself. In 1793, James' father-in-law, General Mathew, bought him the chaplaincy of a new regiment raised as a result of the outbreak of war with France, but this, too, was effectively a sinecure for which James could afford to appoint a deputy.

On 3 May 1795, tragedy struck in James' life when his wife, aged only thirty-six and apparently in good health, suddenly died. James evidently could not cope alone with his distraught infant daughter, Anna, and she was looked after by the Austens at Steventon rectory for most of the following two years, until James remarried on 17 January 1797. His second wife was Mary Lloyd (1771–1843), of the Lloyd family, who had already once lived at Deane parsonage, 1789–1792, and who had become close friends with the Austen family. With Mary, James had two further children, James Edward and Caroline, born in 1798 and 1805, respectively. When James' father decided to retire to Bath with his wife and daughters, James became his curate at Steventon and moved into the rectory there with his young family. In January 1805, when Mr. Austen died, James succeeded him as rector of Steventon. In that year, he was also made perpetual curate of Hunningham in Warwickshire, though again there is no evidence that he ever officiated there.

James seemed to become increasingly introspective and melancholy as he grew older and less involved with other branches of the family. Indeed, relations with other members of the family had become somewhat strained after his marriage to Mary Lloyd. In earlier days, she had been well liked by Jane Austen and the rest of the family, but as James' wife she seems to have developed an officious and overbearing streak that clearly grated with the others. Moreover, her jealousy over James' previous marriage seems to have spilled over into her treatment of her stepdaughter, Anna, and there was a great deal of friction between Mary and Anna, not helped (from the latter's point of view certainly) by James' overeager attempts to appease his wife by doting on his other two children. Perhaps the quickest way of suggesting how Mary Lloyd came to be seen—at times at least—by some of her Austen relations is to say that she has been suggested as a possible source for Mrs. Norris in *Mansfield Park* (though the comparison is a little harsh and does not reflect the more charitable aspects of Mary's character, which are also acknowledged in the family tradition). James, however, seems to have been largely happy with his second wife, at least if a sequence of eulogizing poems he wrote about her are anything to go by (though there is a sense of his protesting a little too much in these).

Despite James' literary pretensions, none of his poetry was published, but between January 1789 and March 1790 he published a weekly periodical at Oxford on the model of well-known earlier periodicals such as *The Spectator* and *The Rambler*. This was *The Loiterer*, and, produced with the help of his younger brother, Henry, James was here able to find an outlet for his writing in prose at least, and a great many of the essays that appeared over the periodical's sixty issues were written by him (a smaller number by Henry). The essays are revealing for what they tell us about some of the common reading matter of the time and of the Austen family in particular, and it seems clear that Jane Austen, just starting to learn her craft, took her cue in the juvenilia from the largely satirical and burlesque style of her brother's periodical. Jan Fergus, in *Jane Austen* (1991: 60–63), suggests, moreover, that there are distinct similarities between *The Loiterer* and the juvenilia in their treatment of questions of money, class, and education, though Jane Austen approaches these from the perspective of an unendowed woman in an economically more marginal position than her brothers. Fergus also suggests that one of the most important aspects of *The Loiterer* in terms of its influence on Jane Austen was the very fact of its publication by a member of the family and the implicit message ''that publication was a real, available goal for a writer.''

James' final few years were marred by illness, and, the firstborn of the Austen children, he was also, with the exception of Jane, the first to die. His health was in serious decline from around September 1817, though he became bedridden only in November 1819, a few weeks before his death on 13 December 1819.

Jane Austen was extremely fortunate in her family for many reasons, but not least for the tremendous amount of intellectual stimulus she received from her university-educated father and brothers, James and Henry. James, in particular, is usually credited with having had a large part in her intellectual development and, in particular, in the formation of her literary tastes, as, apart from the influences of his general scholarship, his bringing live theater into the home, and his publication of *The Loiterer*, he seems also to have encouraged and guided much of her early reading, which was, as the juvenilia testifies, the initial spur to her own literary production. It is as Jane Austen's early literary mentor that James is so important to us, and thus he should perhaps be remembered primarily for possessing, ''in the highest degree,'' as his mother put it, ''Classical Knowledge, Literary Taste, and the power of Elegant Composition'' (*Le Faye 1989*: 50).

See: Lane 1984, Le Faye 1989, Tucker 1983.

Austen, Jane (1775–1817). Jane Austen was born at Steventon, Hampshire, on 16 December 1775 to Rev. George Austen and Cassandra Austen (née Leigh). She was the second of their two daughters and the seventh child in a family of eight. It was generally a very close-knit family, but Jane became especially close to her elder sister, Cassandra. Jane and Cassandra were sent away to school for two brief periods. First of all, in the spring of 1783 (when Jane was seven), they went, along with their cousin Jane Cooper, to a school in Oxford run by Jane Cooper's aunt, Mrs. Cawley. She moved the school to Southampton in the summer of that year, but unfortunately there was an outbreak of typhus fever there, and the girls fell seriously ill and had to be taken home (Jane Cooper's mother, Jane Austen's maternal aunt, subsequently contracted the fever and died of it in October). Second, Jane and Cassandra were sent to the Abbey School in Reading in the spring of 1785, and they then attended this school until around the end of 1786. Apart from this, Jane Austen's education was received at home from her scholarly father and from her brothers, James and Henry.

Jane Austen seems to have started writing from a very early age, and the first of her writings that have come down to us date from around 1787, when she was eleven (it is useful to remember that she was born in December when considering her age in different years; biographers and critics often simply round out her age according to the years, so that one often sees her earliest writings ascribed to her twelfth year). Between 1787 and 1793 she wrote the pieces of her juvenilia that she transcribed into three manuscript notebooks called simply *Volume the First, Volume the Second*, and *Volume the Third*. Most of these are short, burlesque pieces that parody the established literature of the time, especially sentimental fiction. The earliest pieces, mainly (but not exclusively) in *Volume the First*, are often *very* short and quite clearly the work of a small child, though a very talented one. In the later juvenilia of 1790–1793, the voice and style of the mature artist become more evident; the Jane Austen of the major novels is unmistakable in "Catharine" (1792), for example, though critics usually identify the minor work *Lady Susan* (1793–1794) as the key transitional one between Jane Austen's literary apprenticeship and her "serious" writing.

The six novels by which she is mainly known fall into two groups in terms of their composition. The first three were all first written in the 1790s: *Sense and Sensibility* (begun about 1795, apparently in epistolary form under the title "Elinor and Marianne"), *Pride and Prejudice* (written as "First Impressions" between October 1796 and August 1797), and *Northanger Abbey* (written about 1798 or 1799, under the title "Susan"). The second three were all written in the 1810s: *Mansfield Park* (written 1811–1813), *Emma* (written 1814–1815), and *Persuasion* (written 1815–1816). In between these two periods, Jane Austen wrote only the unfinished *The Watsons*. In terms of publication there is only one period, however, the 1810s: *Sense and Sensibility* (1811), *Pride and Prejudice* (1813), *Mansfield Park* (1814), *Emma* (1815), *Northanger Abbey*, and *Persuasion* (1817). All of these works were published anonymously.

For the first twenty-five years of her life, Jane Austen lived at Steventon in rural Hampshire, where all her early writing was done. In 1801, however, her father retired to Bath, and this was the start of what seems to have been a rather unsettled period in Jane Austen's life and a barren period in her writing. She lived with her parents and sister in Bath until 1806. Then, with her mother and Cassandra (her father died in 1805) she moved to Southampton, where they moved in with Frank Austen and his wife. In 1809, they moved back to the Hampshire countryside when Edward Austen provided them with a cottage (really a large house) on his Chawton estate. Jane Austen was to spend most of the rest of her life here, and, almost as soon as she had moved in, she returned to her writing by revising *Sense and Sensibility* (1809–1810). The next seven years were extremely productive, as we have seen. In the spring of 1816, Jane Austen began to show symptoms of the disease (generally assumed to be Addisc 's) that was eventually to kill her. She wrote *Persuasion* in the summer of that year, however, and in the first three months of 1817 she worked on her unfinished novel, *Sanditon*. In May of that year, Cassandra took her to stay in Winchester so that she could receive better medical care, but this was to no avail, and she died on 18 July 1817. (See also the detailed Chronology of Jane Austen's Life and Works in Part I.)

See: Adams 1891, C. M. C. Austen 1952, H. Austen 1817, E. Austen-Leigh 1937, 1939, J. E. Austen-Leigh 1869, 1871, J. Austen-Leigh 1983, 1986, 1989a, b, 1990, *M. A. Austen-Leigh 1920, R. A. Austen-Leigh 1940, 1941, 1942, 1949, W. and R. A. Austen-Leigh 1913, Brabourne 1884, Brown 1966, Cecil 1978, Chapman 1932, 1950, Fergus 1991, Freeman 1969, Greene-Armytage 1968, Halperin 1984, Hawkridge 1995, Hill 1902, Hodge 1972, Honan 1987, Hubback and Hubback 1906, Irons 1975, Jenkins 1938, Johnson 1930,* Kaplan 1984, *Lane 1984, 1986, 1988, 1994, 1996, Laski 1969,* Le Faye 1979, 1985, 1988, 1992, *Le Faye 1989, 1995, Mitton 1905, Myer 1980, 1997, Nicolson 1991, Nokes 1997, Pilgrim 1971, 1989, Radovici 1995, Sisson 1962, Smith and Anderson 1890, Smithers 1981, Tomalin 1997, Tucker 1983, 1994, Warner 1951, Watson 1960, Wilks 1978.*

Austen, Philadelphia (1730–1792). *See* Hancock, Philadelphia.

Austen-Leigh, James Edward (1798–1874). Born on 17 November 1798, James Edward Austen was the only son of Jane Austen's eldest brother, James, by his second marriage to Mary Lloyd. He became a great favorite of his aunt's, especially when, at around eighteen, he began to write a novel of his own and consulted her closely about it. Three of her letters to him survive, and one of them (from December 1816), in commenting on his writing and contrasting it with hers, includes the now famous statement about her "little bit (two inches wide) of Ivory" on which she works "with so fine a Brush, as produces little effect after much labour." James Edward was ordained in 1823 and became curate of Newtown in Berkshire. He married Emma Smith in 1828 and had ten children with her. In 1837 he assumed the additional name of Leigh, having inherited the estate of his great-aunt, Jane Leigh-Perrot. He became vicar of Bray in Berkshire in 1852 and lived there as vicar until his death on 8 September 1874. As George Holbert Tucker says, James Edward Austen was Jane Austen's most important nephew as far as posterity is concerned, for "with the publication of his *Memoir of Jane Austen* it was he who laid the foundation upon which all future biographies of his aunt have been built" (*1983*: 201). The *Memoir* was first published at the end of 1869, and there was a revised and enlarged edition in 1871. James Edward's youngest son, William (1843–1921), and his grandson, Richard Arthur (1872–1961), continued the work he had begun when they collaborated to produce *Jane Austen, Her Life and Letters, a Family Record* in 1913. His daughter, Mary Augusta (1838–1922), also contributed significantly to the handing down of information about Jane Austen through a privately published memoir of her father (1911) and through *Personal Aspects of Jane Austen* (1920).

See: Lane 1984, Le Faye 1989, Tucker 1983.

Aylmers, the (*Mansfield Park* Ch.45; III:14:434). A family from Twickenham with whom Maria (Bertram) Rushworth becomes friendly after moving to London and with whom she spends the fateful Easter holidays that give rise to her elopement with Henry Crawford. He has a house in the same neighborhood and has easy access to Maria while she is there without Mr. Rushworth. The clear implication is that the Aylmers have acted irresponsibly in allowing and possibly even encouraging the affair to develop; they are, we are told, ''a family of lively, agreeable manners, and probably of morals and discretion to suit'' (Ch.16; III: 16:450).

B

Baddeley (*Mansfield Park* Chs.19, 32; II:1:180; III:1:344). Sir Thomas Bertram's butler at Mansfield Park.

Baldwin, Admiral (*Persuasion* Ch.3; I:3:20). In the course of discussing the possibility of renting out Kellynch Hall to a naval commander, Sir Walter Elliot explains his objections to the naval profession, one being that a seafaring life "cuts up a man's youth and vigour most horribly." He goes on to hold up Admiral Baldwin, someone he had been in company with recently, as a perfectly "wretched" example of this: "the most deplorable looking personage you can imagine, his face the colour of mahogany, rough and rugged to the last degree, all lines and wrinkles, nine grey hairs of a side, and nothing but a dab of powder at top." Sir Walter assumed Admiral Baldwin to be sixty or sixty-two years old when, in fact, he was only forty.

Barlow, Augusta ("Catharine," *Minor Works* 200, 204). An acquaintance and correspondent of Camilla Stanley. Her sister or sisters are also mentioned, and together they are casually compared by Camilla—as "just such other sweet Girls"—to Catharine's dearest friends, the Wynne sisters.

Barlow, Sir Peter ("Catharine," *Minor Works* 200, 204). Father of Camilla Stanley's friends, the Barlow sisters. Camilla "cannot bear" Sir Peter, however, partly because he is always ill with gout.

Bates, Jane (*Emma*). *See* Fairfax, Mrs.

Bates, Miss Hetty (*Emma* Chs.2, 3; I:2:17; I:3:20–21). Middle-aged daughter of Mrs. Bates and aunt to Jane Fairfax. Her life is spent in caring for her mother and in trying to make ends meet, but she remains bright and cheerful and contented with her lot, and she is generally popular in the neighborhood for her simple and cheerful nature and for her "contented and grateful spirit." She takes a sympathetic and kindly interest in the lives of other people and always tries to see the best in others—"quick-sighted to every body's merits." She is, however, somewhat simple-minded and "a great talker upon little matters" (which is why Mr. Woodhouse enjoys her company so much!), and her garrulity is often the occasion for comedy in the novel; but, though her gossiping can seem tedious and interfering at times, her friends are usually happy to humor her for her underlying good nature and because of her straitened circumstances. (Of course, her apparently vacuous speeches are almost always highly functional to the development of the plot.) For all the comedy associated with Miss Bates, she is nevertheless a key figure in the novel (as the critical Box Hill episode shows), in that she serves to test the charitability of the other characters (and, to some extent, of the reader, too). In this light, it is important to note Jane Austen's ironic comment on superficial social attitudes of the time when she notes that Miss Bates' "uncommon degree of popularity" exists despite the fact that she is "neither young, handsome, rich, nor married."

Bates, Mrs. (*Emma* Chs.2, 3; I:2:17; I:3:20–21). Elderly widow of the former vicar of Highbury, Rev. Bates. She lives with her single daughter, Hetty, in genteel poverty and is "almost past every thing but tea and quadrille." She is grandmother of Jane Fairfax, the child of her deceased younger daughter, Mrs. Jane Fairfax.

Beard, Mr. (*Sanditon, Minor Works* 389). On his return to Sanditon, Mr. Parker's first port of call is Mrs. Whitby's circulating library, where he inspects the subscription list to see how many—and what sort of—visitors have been attracted to Sanditon for the season. The list proves to be "but commonplace" to Mr. Parker (who wants Sanditon to be both popular *and* exclusive), but in a sense that is Jane Austen's point, as it demonstrates the rise of the middle classes at the time. It also provides us with a convenient "snapshot" of the broad social scene at Sanditon. Mr. Beard's is one of the names on the list: he is a solicitor at Grays Inn, London.

Beaufort, Miss, and Letitia (*Sanditon, Minor Works* 421–23). Two of the three young ladies brought to Sanditon by Mrs. Griffiths. They are showy, shallow, and conceited and clearly enjoy being the center of attention in sleepy Sanditon, even if that only means the leering attention of the usually recumbent Arthur Parker. The Miss Beauforts' education so far has meant acquiring the usual female "accomplishments" of music and drawing, but otherwise they are "very Ignorant."

"The Beautifull Cassandra" (*Volume the First* of Jane Austen's juvenilia). Written sometime between 1787 and 1790, probably in 1787–1788, this piece is subtitled "A Novel in Twelve Chapters" and is dedicated to Cassandra Austen. The London setting of the story was possibly inspired by a brief stay in London by the Austen family in August 1788 (which would suggest a composition date around that period). The "chapters" of the piece are *very* short, most of them consisting of just one sentence, and the whole "novel" is less than three pages long. Such comical reduction is a feature common to many of Jane Austen's juvenile pieces, and here the narrative can be seen as a parody of picaresque adventure stories.

The main character is the somewhat anarchic but formidable Cassandra, the sixteen-year-old daughter of a celebrated milliner of Bond Street in London. She takes an elegant bonnet her mother has just made for a Duchess and goes out in it to seek her fortune. During a seven-hour ramble around the city, she brazenly curtsies to a young Viscount but otherwise ignores him; refuses to pay for six ices she consumes and then knocks down the pastry cook who had provided them; goes to Hampstead and back in a Hackney Coach and then, having no money on her, runs away from the coachman after putting her bonnet on his head; passes someone called Maria in a mutually embarrassed silence; greets her friend the Widow; and returns home to her mother's bosom saying to herself, "This is a day well spent."

See: McMaster 1988, 1993 (in addition to references cited under "Juvenilia").

Bennet, Elizabeth (*Pride and Prejudice* Ch.1; I:1:4–5). The Bennets' second daughter at twenty years of age and the heroine of the novel. She eventually marries Fitzwilliam Darcy, despite their initial prejudices against one another that arise from their different forms of pride. Elizabeth is a spirited, intelligent, and independent-minded woman with a strong sense of her own inherent worth. Extremely sharp-witted and not afraid to speak her mind, she is easily capable of holding her own in any conversation, whether with man or woman, and she rarely lets anyone get the better of her, as we see when she stands up fearlessly to the attempted bullying of Lady Catherine de Bourgh. She is a sensible, steady, and reliable character—and therefore her father's favorite—though she also has a lively sense of fun and a playful disposition that delights in "anything ridiculous." For all her usual perspicacity, however, Elizabeth's judgment is clouded when it comes to Wickham, partly because he appears so plausible, partly because she is flattered by his attentions, and partly because her prejudice against Darcy predisposes her to sympathize with Wickham in his dispute with the other man. But she is quick to recognize and learn from her mistakes and honest enough to admit to them.

Bennet, Jane (*Pride and Prejudice* Ch.1; I:1:4). The eldest Bennet daughter at twenty-two years of age and, by common consent, the most beautiful. There is not the slightest trace of vanity in her, however, and her composed and cheerful temperament is as attractive as her appearance. An affectionate and loving sister and daughter, her outward calm often conceals strong feelings—as becomes evident in the period of her separation from Bingley when she thinks he has forgotten her. Jane always tries to look on the bright side of things and to see the good in everyone, and this can sometimes lead to naive errors of judgment. In the end, Jane's patience and stoicism in the face of her apparently broken romance pay off when Bingley returns to propose and reveals that he has, in fact, never stopped thinking about her.

Bennet, Kitty (*Pride and Prejudice* Ch.2; I:2:6). The fourth daughter of Mr. and Mrs. Bennet, Kitty is a weak, impressionable character, to begin with, who is easily led astray by her younger sister, Lydia. But she can also be influenced for the better, and, once separated from Lydia and guided by her elder sisters, she becomes more steady and sensible.

Bennet, Lydia (*Pride and Prejudice* Ch.1; I:1:4). Self-willed, headstrong, and heedless and, at fifteen, the youngest daughter of the Bennet family, Lydia is, in many ways, a typical teenager, full of "high animal spirits" and determined to enjoy herself whatever the consequences. She is her mother's favorite and has therefore been allowed to "come out" in public earlier than usual. Elizabeth Bennet fears that nothing good will come of this, and she warns her father that if Lydia is not better controlled, her silly and simple-minded behavior will soon make her and her family look ridiculous. Elizabeth's fears prove to be well founded, for Lydia does bring scandal to the family when, at sixteen, she elopes with Mr. Wickham and narrowly escapes being abandoned by him. Even then, Lydia seems not to recognize her own foolishness, and she remains unrepentant, especially as Wickham does marry her in the end, and she is able to boast of having secured a husband before her elder sisters.

Bennet, Mary (*Pride and Prejudice* Ch.2; I:2:7). Mary is the third daughter of Mr. and Mrs. Bennet. Overearnest, studious, and moralistic, she is the exact opposite of Lydia in most ways, though she, too, likes to make an exhibition of herself in public, but with her "accomplishments" rather than with her looks, wit, or high spirits. Unfortunately, however, Mary has little real talent and tends to embarrass her family when she insists on performing in public for any of them. The younger girls regard her as a bore.

Bennet, Mr. (*Pride and Prejudice* Ch.1; I:1:3). The father of Elizabeth Bennet and her four sisters and owner of Longbourne. He is a dry, ironical man who maintains a detached and sardonic attitude toward his witless wife and silly younger daughters, and he is especially satirical about his wife's overzealous concern to see their girls married off. However, the reckless behavior of the youngest girl, Lydia, finally shocks him into realizing the dangers of too great a detachment from the education and upbringing of his daughters and, ironically, forces him into becoming directly involved in the marrying off of at least one daughter, though in a manner even less desirable than what his wife might have contrived. Urbane, witty, and intelligent, Mr. Bennet does not suffer fools gladly, and something of his own character is reflected in that of his sensible and independent-minded favorite daughter, Elizabeth.

Bennet, Mrs., née Gardiner (*Pride and Prejudice* Ch.1; I:1:3, 5). Mrs. Bennet is clearly a comic figure with various exaggerated characteristics—garrulity, obtuseness, vulgarity, peevishness—and she develops little throughout the novel. Jane Austen's masterly initial description of the character sums her up: ''She was a woman of mean understanding, little information, and uncertain temper. When she was discontented she fancied herself nervous. The business of her life was to get her daughters married; its solace was visiting and news.''

Benwick, Captain James (*Persuasion* Ch.11; I:11:96). Captain Benwick had once served as first lieutenant under Captain Wentworth, who praises him as ''an excellent young man and an officer.'' When we first hear of him from Wentworth, he is living with the family of another naval friend, Captain Harville, at Lyme. He had been engaged to Harville's sister, Fanny, but she had died the previous summer while he was away at sea, and he is still mourning her loss. Indeed, Captain Wentworth describes him as ''deeply afflicted'' and as having a disposition ''which must suffer heavily, uniting very strong feelings with quiet, serious, and retiring manners, and a decided taste for reading, and sedentary pursuits.'' When we actually meet him and see him through the eyes of Anne Elliot, however, his youthful suffering appears rather forced and exaggerated, especially when set beside her own long years of suppressed sorrow over Wentworth. In company, Benwick affects a typically romantic pose of melancholic gloom, and, in conversation with Anne, he demonstrates an intimate knowledge of the poetry of Scott and Byron, reciting especially those lines ''which imaged a broken heart, or a mind destroyed by wretchedness.'' Benwick brightens a little on being able to share his interest in literature with Anne Elliot, and it seems for a brief while that he has begun to transfer his affections to her from his dead fiancée, but he surprises everybody when he eventually falls in love with, and marries, the high-spirited Louisa Musgrove. The attachment was formed while Louisa was recuperating from her fall from the Cobb at Lyme and living at the Harvilles' house. Anne, reflecting on this apparently odd match, concludes that Benwick would have fallen in love with ''any tolerably pleasing young woman who had listened and seemed to feel for him,'' for, above all, ''he must love somebody.'' She also suspects that the couple had fallen in love over Romantic poetry, and we see here the presence of a favorite theme of Jane Austen's: the distorting influence that sentimental and romantic literature can have on the day-to-day actions and emotions of susceptible characters. For in Benwick, especially, we have a character of impressionable temperament who allows the intensified feelings of Romantic poetry to dictate his actions in real life (though the fact that Anne Elliot has some affinities with Benwick—despite her prescription of "a larger allowance of prose in his daily study"—suggests a less clear-cut anti-Romanticism than first meets the eye).

Beresford, Colonel (*The Watsons, Minor Works* 330). Little Charles Blake is downcast at the ball when Miss Osborne breaks her promise to dance with him and dances instead with Colonel Beresford.

Bertram, Edmund (*Mansfield Park* Ch.1; I:1:6–7). Edmund is the younger son of Sir Thomas Bertram of Mansfield Park. A sober, sensible, and morally upright character with a vocation for the church, Edmund serves (for most of the time, at least) as a model of sound judgment and correct principles in the novel. His "excellent nature" is immediately established for us when we see him comforting his homesick cousin, Fanny, shortly after her arrival at Mansfield Park as a young girl of ten. His kindly and considerate attention at this time helps her to overcome her loneliness and to become reconciled to her new family and surroundings. Edmund thereafter remains her principal friend, protector, adviser, and confidant and proves to be a major formative influence on the growth of her character. Much to Fanny's chagrin, Edmund becomes romantically involved with the attractive but worldly Mary Crawford, and his judgment becomes temporarily clouded by his infatuation for her. Temperamentally unsuited to the life of a clergyman's wife and never fully appreciating the sincerity of Edmund's vocation, Mary Crawford does her best to talk him out of becoming a priest, but he remains steadfast in his commitment to the church, despite his passionate feelings for her. Edmund finally realizes Mary's true shallowness and lack of principle when he is able to observe her in her natural milieu among her fashionable and superficial London friends and, above all, when she makes light of her brother's adulterous elopement with Edmund's sister, Maria. He breaks off the relationship and soon forgets Mary Crawford as he begins to appreciate the deeper feelings and regard he holds for his devoted and ever-loving Fanny, who, he finally sees, has been his true soul mate all along. Edmund marries Fanny, and they settle at Thornton Lacey, the parish where Edmund has his first living, before eventually moving back to the parsonage at Mansfield when that living falls vacant on the death of Dr. Grant.

Bertram, Julia (*Mansfield Park* Ch.1; I:1:6–7). Julia Bertram is the younger daughter of Lady and Sir Thomas Bertram, a year younger than her sister and two years older than Fanny Price. She possesses many of the selfish and superficial characteristics of her sister, Maria, but to a lesser degree, partly because of a more easygoing and controllable temperament and partly because she has been less spoiled by Mrs. Norris. Julia becomes jealous of her sister when Henry Crawford seems to prefer her, even though Maria is already engaged, and Julia peevishly withdraws from the Mansfield theatricals as a result of this. However, she makes friends with Maria again after the latter's wedding, and she is happy to accompany Maria on her honeymoon trip to Brighton and then, later, to

London. Here she meets up again with Mr. Yates, who had been attracted to her earlier at Mansfield during the theatricals. She had not encouraged his attentions then and does not do so now, but she allows him to pay court to her and eventually agrees to elope with him—through motives of "selfish alarm"—in order to escape the increased severity she expects of her father following the scandal that breaks around Maria and Henry Crawford. At the time, of course, this second elopement aggravates the general situation for Sir Thomas and his family, but after her marriage to Mr. Yates, Julia seems genuinely "humble and wishing to be forgiven," and, with signs of reform from her husband, too, she eventually becomes reconciled with her father.

Bertram, Lady Maria, née Ward (*Mansfield Park* Ch.1; I:1:3). The wife of Sir Thomas and sister of Mrs. Norris and Mrs. Price, Lady Bertram is an unthinking woman with an easy and indolent nature that remains largely passive in the face of events. With her husband, she is clearly culpable of abandoning the education and formation of her children to the vitiating influence of their aunt Norris. But Lady Bertram is not actively or positively a bad influence on anyone, and in herself she is a kindly and largely good-humored woman who, though needing to be guided by her husband, generally thinks and feels justly "on all important points." She is shocked into a more active awareness of things toward the end of the novel when faced by the serious illness of her eldest son and then by the scandal caused by her daughters, and here she most fully appreciates the true value of her dependable "dear Fanny."

Bertram, Maria (*Mansfield Park* Ch.1; I:1:6–7). The elder daughter of Lady and Sir Thomas Bertram and three years older than Fanny Price. Spoiled, conceited, and headstrong, she gains little from her expensive education and finds her character formed more by her small-minded and materialistic aunt Norris than by her governess, teachers, or parents. Blinded by the lure of wealth and status (and freedom from parental constraint), she allows herself to be matched to the rich Mr. Rushworth, even though she feels no love for him. She soon regrets her engagement, however, when she meets the attractive and eligible Henry Crawford, whose urbane manners and sharp wit contrast markedly with those of the lumbering Mr. Rushworth. She flirts brazenly with Henry Crawford during the Mansfield theatricals, and, though this comes to nothing at the time, her attraction to Crawford brings downfall in the end when she elopes with him after her marriage to Mr. Rushworth. Mr. Rushworth promptly divorces her, and, contrary to her expectations, Crawford steadfastly refuses to marry her, so she is forced to return to her father, who exacts an appropriate punishment for the scandal and shame she has brought to the family, by sending her to live, at a distance from Mansfield Park, with her aunt Norris—"where, shut up together with little society, on one side no affection, on the other, no judgment, it may be reasonably supposed that their tempers became their mutual punishment."

Bertram, Sir Thomas (*Mansfield Park* Ch.1; I:1:3). A baronet and member of Parliament, Sir Thomas is the wealthy owner of Mansfield Park, father of Tom, Edmund, Maria, and Julia, and, later, guardian and benefactor to his niece, Fanny Price. He is also the owner of properties in the West Indies, in Antigua, and he travels there during the course of the novel to deal with problems that have arisen with his estates. During this absence domestic problems occur in his family at home, and the private theatricals are organized. Distant, reserved, and somewhat severe with his children, his daughters in particular, Sir Thomas later lives to regret the fact that he paid scant attention to the details of their education and development, for his eldest son and both daughters turn out to be selfish and lacking in good sense and sound principles. Rather too concerned with the outer forms of respectability, responsibility, and morality, he neglects to nurture the inner substance that gives these things their meaning.

Bertram, Tom (*Mansfield Park* Ch.1; I:1:6–7). Tom Bertram, the eldest son and heir of Sir Thomas Bertram, "had easy manners, excellent spirits, a large acquaintance, and a great deal to say." As this suggests, though not without charm, he is a somewhat superficial character, and he is certainly irresponsible and extravagant in his youth, squandering his father's money in high living and incurring debts that eventually require the sale of the Mansfield living that had been earmarked for his younger brother, Edmund. Tom has some force of character, as he shows in the determined way in which he promotes and organizes the Mansfield theatricals, but this whole episode also shows that he really has nothing better to do with his time and that he has no clear sense of his duties and responsibilities as the head of the household in his father's absence. Later, however, at the age of twenty-six, Tom becomes a reformed character following a serious illness from which he almost dies: "He had suffered, and he had learnt to think, two advantages that he had never known before. . . . He became what he ought to be, useful to his father, steady and quiet, and not living merely for himself."

Betty (*Sense and Sensibility* Ch.25; II:3:153). Mrs. Jennings' maid. When Mrs. Jennings invites Elinor and Marianne to go to London with her, her only inconvenience is to have to pay for Betty's journey by coach, as there is insufficient room in her chaise for four. Betty has a sister whom Mrs. Jennings asks Elinor to recommend as a housemaid to Edward Ferrars and Lucy Steele when they seem on the point of marrying.

Betty (*The Watsons, Minor Works* 346). The Watsons' maid.

Bickerton, Miss (*Emma* Ch.39; III:3:333–34). Harriet Smith's fellow parlor-boarder at Mrs. Goddard's school. She is walking with Harriet on the night after the Crown Inn ball, which they had both attended, when they are frightened by the appearance of some Gypsies, though mainly children, who approach them to beg for money. Miss Bickerton panics, screams, and runs away up a steep bank and over a hedge, leaving Harriet, suffering from cramp brought on by the previous night's dancing and therefore unable to follow, alone and "exceedingly terrified." This initial display of fear and panic merely exacerbates the situation and emboldens the Gypsy children in their demands for money. This is when Frank Churchill appears on the scene to save the day for Harriet: he chases off the Gypsies and takes Harriet back to Hartfield, where he expresses indignation at "the abominable folly of Miss Bickerton."

Bingley, Caroline (*Pride and Prejudice* Ch.3; I:3:10–11). The proud and conceited younger sister of Mr. Bingley. She becomes jealous of Elizabeth Bennet when she perceives Mr. Darcy's interest in her, as she hopes to win Mr. Darcy for herself.

Bingley, Mr. Charles (*Pride and Prejudice* Ch.1; I:1:3). The tenant of Netherfield Park, Mr. Bingley is introduced as the prototypical "single man in possession of a good fortune" who must be in want of a wife. His large fortune, of £4,000 or £5,000 a year (and property worth nearly £100,000), derives originally from his family's success in trade in the north of England, and he has none of the haughty reserve of his richer and higher-born friend, Mr. Darcy, having a lively and unreserved temperament and "easy, unaffected manners." Well mannered, sensible, and good-humored, Mr. Bingley "was sure of being liked wherever he appeared," whereas the reserved and distant Mr. Darcy "was continually giving offence." Bingley falls in love with Jane Bennet almost at first sight but is eventually persuaded by his sisters and Mr. Darcy that she is not good enough for him. His feelings for Jane remain constant, however, and when Darcy later admits his mistaken views of both Jane and her sister, Elizabeth, Bingley and Jane are reunited and marry at the same time as Darcy and Elizabeth.

Bird, Mrs. (*Emma* Ch.33; II:14:277). Originally Miss Milman, sister of Mrs. James Cooper, a friend of Mrs. Elton's, used by the latter as an example (along with Mrs. Cooper and Mrs. Jeffereys) of married women's being "too apt to give up music."

Blake, Charles (*The Watsons, Minor Works* 329). Ten-year-old son of Mrs. Blake with whom Emma dances at the ball after he is let down by Miss Osborne.

Blake, Mrs. (*The Watsons, Minor Works* 329–31). The widowed sister of Mr. Howard and mother of Charles and three other children. Mrs. Blake is about thirty-five or thirty-six and a lively, friendly woman.

Bragge, Mr. (*Emma* Ch.36; II:18:306). A cousin of Mr. Suckling. Illustrating her observation to Mr. Weston, "what is distance . . . to people of large fortune,'' Mrs. Elton says that Mr. Bragge and her brother-in-law once went to London and back twice in one week with four horses.

Bragge, Mrs. (*Emma* Ch.35; II:17:299). A cousin of Mr. Suckling living near Maple Grove and mentioned by Mrs. Elton as having ''an infinity of applications'' from hopeful governesses anxious to be part of her family—''for she moves in the first circle.''

Brand, Admiral (*Persuasion* Ch.18; II:6:170). While walking with Anne Elliot along Milsom Street in Bath, Admiral Croft points out Admiral Brand and his brother on the other side of the street. He describes them as ''shabby fellows'' for once tricking him out of some of his best sailing men.

Brandon, Colonel (*Sense and Sensibility* Ch.7; I:7:34). A friend of Sir John Middleton who is staying at Barton Park on the Dashwoods' first visit there shortly after their moving into Barton Cottage. His ''silent and grave'' manner sits oddly beside the ebullience of Sir John, and Marianne and Margaret Dashwood are quick to dismiss him as a tedious and lackluster ''old bachelor.'' Marianne later talks of him as an infirm old man—despite his being only just past thirty-five years—because he complains of some rheumatism in one shoulder and talks of wearing flannel waistcoats. However, he is, from the first, identified as ''sensible'' and gentlemanlike, and Elinor Dashwood soon learns to appreciate his ''good-breeding and good nature'' as well as the strength and depth of his character amid the general superficiality of Barton society. While Marianne (influenced by Willoughby and her own romantic imagination) dislikes him for his lack of ''genius, taste . . . spirit . . . brilliancy . . . ardour,'' Elinor values his experience and sincerity, his well-informed and ''thinking mind,'' and the fact that he is ''on every occasion mindful of the feelings of others.'' Moreover, she astutely recognizes that his reserved and serious manner is the result of ''some oppression of spirits'' rather than a ''natural gloominess of temper.'' This, of course, turns out to be the case, as we later learn of his blighted past—of his doomed love for his cousin, Eliza Williams, who was married off to his elder brother against her inclination and who was then mistreated, forced into infidelity, and divorced by her husband before sinking into a life of general dissipation that led to poverty, sickness, and an early death; of his subsequent care for Eliza's illegitimate daughter; and of her recent elopement with, and seduction by, Willoughby. His suffering is increased now as he falls in love with the seventeen-year-old Marianne (who reminds him of the first Eliza) and has to stand by as she becomes more and more besotted by the dashing young Willoughby. However, though never encouraged by Marianne, he remains steadfast and selfless in his love for her, and, when she is jilted by Willoughby and becomes seriously ill, he is able to provide support and comfort to her and her family and thereby gradually to gain in her affections and finally to win her hand in marriage.

Brandon, Miss (*Sense and Sensibility* Chs.12, 13; I:12 & 13:62–63). Colonel Brandon's sister, who is married to the owner of the Whitwell estate. She appears to be ill and is abroad with her husband (at Avignon, France) when Lord Middleton proposes one of his annual parties to visit the grounds at Whitwell.

Brandon, Mr. (deceased) (*Sense and Sensibility* Ch.31; II:9:205). Elder brother of Colonel Brandon who marries his cousin Eliza Williams for her fortune. He mistreats her and divorces her when she is unfaithful to him. He dies five years before the main action of the story, leaving Colonel Brandon to inherit the family estate of Delaford in Dorset.

Brandon, Mrs. Eliza, née Williams (deceased) (*Sense and Sensibility* Ch.31; II:9:205). Eliza Williams, an heiress, was orphaned at infancy and brought up at Delaford in Dorset, under the guardianship of her uncle, Mr. Brandon. Nearly the same age as her younger cousin, later Colonel Brandon, she was his playfellow, friend, and then sweetheart. However, because of the failing fortunes of the Brandon estate, her uncle forced her, at the age of seventeen, into a marriage of convenience with Colonel Brandon's elder brother. Strongly attached to her younger cousin, she at first resisted the match and even attempted to elope to Scotland with the young Colonel Brandon. However, when this attempt was foiled, he was banished to the house of a distant relation, and she was pressed into the marriage. Her husband felt no real love for her, and the relationship was immediately unhappy: "his pleasures were not what they ought to have been, and from the first he treated her unkindly." With this provocation and "without a friend to advise or restrain her" (Colonel Brandon had left for the East Indies, and her uncle died a few months after the wedding), she was soon unfaithful to her husband, and he then divorced her. From her first illicit affair, she bore a child, Eliza, and thereafter apparently sank "deeper in a life of sin" until, about three years later, she was discovered by Colonel Brandon dying of consumption in a debtor's prison. He removed her to more comfortable lodgings and agreed to take the little Eliza into his care.

Brandon, Old Mr. (deceased) (*Sense and Sensibility* Ch.31; II:9:205). Father of Colonel Brandon and uncle and guardian to Eliza Williams, whom he forces into marriage with his eldest son in order to save the family's failing fortune. He dies shortly after the wedding.

Brereton, Clara (*Sanditon, Minor Works* 375, 377–79, 391). Clara Brereton is Lady Denham's poor but beautiful cousin. She had originally been invited to Sanditon House for a visit of six months, but she had been so well received that it is now tacitly understood that she will remain indefinitely as the old lady's companion, and this has led to fears in other parts of the family that Clara may now be a contender for Lady Denham's fortune. Clara Brereton is something of a Jane Fairfax figure. She is elegant, refined, and sensible and is universally well liked for her even temperament and steady conduct; but she is poor, possibly destined to become a governess, and dependent on the patronage of others, and there is also, as with Jane Fairfax, a certain mysterious reserve about her that possibly suggests some hidden romance. Although Sir Edward Denham is paying court to her, she seems distinctly unimpressed by him (in public anyway—the final scene of the novel leaves the situation a little more uncertain). Later, we learn that he has plans to seduce her (partly because he wants to ruin her chances of inheriting Lady Denham's money), but she sees through him and has "not the least intention of being seduced."

Brigden, Captain (*Persuasion* Ch.18; II:6:169). A friend of Admiral Croft, seen by the latter at Bath while walking in the street with Anne Elliot.

"The Brothers." *See Sanditon*: "The Brothers" was Jane Austen's working title for her unfinished last novel.

Brown, Dr. and Mrs. (*Sanditon, Minor Works* 389). Visitors to Sanditon noted by Mr. Parker in the subscription list at the circulating library. *See* Beard, Mr.

Brown, Mrs. (*Emma* Ch.22; II:4:182). Following a dinner given by "Mr. Green," the rapidly developing relationship between Mr. Elton and Miss Hawkins at Bath is further advanced at a party given by "Mrs. Brown."

Brown, Mrs. (*Mansfield Park* Ch.24; II:6:235). Referring to his sister Fanny's fashionable hairstyle, William Price remembers having thought it outlandish when he saw it worn by "Mrs. Brown, and the other women, at the Commissioner's, at Gibraltar"—but, he goes on, "Fanny can reconcile me to any thing."

Burgess, Mrs. (*Sense and Sensibility* Ch.49; III:13:371). Anne Steele goes to stay with this friend in Exeter after she is left stranded in London by her sister's elopement with Robert Ferrars.

C

Campbell, Colonel, and Mrs. Campbell (*Emma* Chs.12, 20; I:12:104; II:2: 163–65). Colonel Campbell was an army friend of Lieutenant Fairfax. He had a very high regard for his younger officer and, moreover, felt indebted to him for once saving his life during an outbreak of camp fever. When he returned to England, therefore, some years after the death in action of Lieutenant Fairfax, he sought out the latter's orphaned daughter, Jane, and "took notice" of her before taking her entirely into his care when she was nine years old, partly as a companion for his own young daughter and partly to provide her with an education. Colonel Campbell's fortune was not sufficient to secure Jane an independent future, but he hoped, in educating her, to provide at least the means to a respectable living, eventually, as a governess. Jane was given an excellent education and received nothing but kindness from the Campbells, who grew to love her almost as a second daughter: "Living constantly with right-minded and well-informed people, her heart and understanding had received every advantage of discipline and culture." When their own daughter marries, and Jane comes of age, the Campbells are loath to part with her; they would be happy for her to remain with them "for ever," but their good sense tells them that "what must be at last, had better be soon," and they reluctantly accept the inevitability of her becoming a governess at last (though they still prolong the separation on the pretext of Jane's apparent ill health in the period following their daughter's marriage—which is why Jane has not yet found a position when we first meet her).

Campbell, Miss. *See* Dixon, Mrs.

Campbell, Mr. (*Mansfield Park* Ch.38; III:7:377, 384). William Price's friend and fellow officer, the surgeon of the *Thrush*. He is "a very well behaved young man'' who comes to call for William (shortly after he and Fanny arrive in Portsmouth), so that they can go together to join their ship.

Capper, Miss (*Sanditon, Minor Works* 408). The particular friend of Diana Parker's particular friend, Fanny Noyce, and an intimate of Mrs. Darling.

Careys, the (*Sense and Sensibility* Ch.13; I:13:65). Neighboring acquaintances of the Middletons from Newton. Two Miss Careys come over to Barton for the party to Whitwell, and, when that is abandoned, they stay for dinner and are joined by other members of their family.

Carr, Fanny (*The Watsons, Minor Works* 329, 340). Miss Osborne's friend.

Carter, Captain (*Pride and Prejudice* Ch.7; I:7:29). An officer of the militia stationed at Meryton who, along with others, is admired by Lydia Bennet.

Carteret, the Honourable Miss (*Persuasion* Ch.16; II:4:148–50). Daughter of the Dowager Viscountess Dalrymple and a cousin of the Elliots but otherwise undistinguished. She is, according to Anne Elliot, a plain and awkward woman with even less to say for herself than her mother.

Cartwright (*Sense and Sensibility* Ch.26; II:4:163). When Mrs. Jennings returns to her London home after her visit to the Middletons and a long period away, she has various ''little odd things'' to attend to, including having ''Cartwright to settle with''; this has connotations of some sort of business or financial dealing, though Cartwright could simply be Mrs. Jennings' housekeeper.

''Catharine, or the Bower'' (*Volume the Third* of Jane Austen's juvenilia). The dedication to Cassandra Austen of this unfinished fragment is dated August 1792, and it was presumably written around this time. ''Catharine'' is generally considered one of the most important of Jane Austen's juvenile writings, as it contains the clearest indications yet of the novelist's mature style and represents a distinct (if not absolute) shift away from the out-and-out burlesque mode of the earlier juvenilia and toward the later novelistic modes of domestic realism and social comedy. This is undoubtedly still an apprentice piece (there is some unevenness in the characterization of the heroine in particular), but, as Brian Southam has written, we see here for the first time ''the mark of an ambitious novelist. . . . The range and depth of the characterization, and the fullness of dialogue and action, are far in advance of anything she had attempted before'' (*Jane Austen's Literary Manuscripts*, Oxford, 1964, p. 38).

   Catharine (or Kitty) Percival, orphaned at an early age, has been strictly brought up by her overprotective aunt, Mrs. Percival (originally Peterson in the manuscript), at her large house, the Grove, in the village of Chetwynde in Devon. Although Catharine is often constrained in her behavior (and especially at social events when men are present) by the ever-watchful eye and excessive caution of her aunt, she is a lively, good-humored girl whose spirits are not easily depressed. Moreover, whenever she is seriously upset, there is a secluded and shady bower in the garden where she can always find comfort and consolation. This bower was constructed by her in childhood with the help of her two close friends, Cecilia and Mary Wynne, the daughters of the local clergyman of that period, Mr. Wynne. Now that the girls have been separated, perhaps forever, Catharine finds that the bower always brings her comfort and relief from distress by evoking happy childhood memories of times spent with her two friends. Two years ago, Mr. Wynne had died (not long after the death of Mrs. Wynne), and, although he had provided well for his children during his life (there are also two sons whom we hear of briefly later on) and in particular had given them all an excellent education, he did not have the means to provide for them after his death. Thus the Wynne girls were left wholly dependent on relations, who were only grudgingly willing to provide for them. The eldest girl, Cecilia, had been shipped off to India to find a husband (somewhat like Jane Austen's aunt, Philadelphia) and has been married now for nearly a year—respectably but unhappily married to a man twice her age whom she does not care for. Mary, meanwhile, has been taken to Scotland by the dowager Lady Halifax as a companion for her daughters, and it is clear to Catharine from Mary's letters that she is not kindly treated by the family and is generally in depressed spirits.

The family of the man who had come to replace Mr. Wynne as the incumbent of Chetwynde had proved to be haughty, vain, and quarrelsome, and Catharine had not become friendly with their only daughter, who had inherited "the ignorance, the insolence, & pride of her parents." Since the departure of the Wynne girls, therefore, Catharine's life with her straitlaced aunt has been lonely and tedious. A spinster herself, Mrs. Percival has always been so frightened of Catharine's marrying imprudently that, as far as possible, she avoids making visits to neighbors or receiving visitors herself. In recent years, she has been particularly anxious to put off some distant relations, the Stanleys, who have been regularly offering to visit. This is because the son of the family has a reputation as a lady's man. Now, however, it appears that this son is traveling on the continent and so unlikely to accompany his parents and sister, and Kitty is finally able to prevail on her aunt to invite the Stanleys for the summer.

The Stanleys are people "of Large Fortune and high Fashion," and they spend six months of each year in London, as Mr. Stanley is a member of Parliament. Their daughter, Camilla, is a handsome, fashionable young girl of about eighteen, and Catharine, happy to have a companion of her own age in the house again, is immediately predisposed to like her. However, over the past twelve years, Camilla has been given a typically genteel girl's education for the time. This, we are told, means that, at a time when she ought to have been developing her intellect and understanding, extending her range of useful reading and knowledge, she has merely acquired a set of surface "accomplishments" primarily designed to enable her to "display" herself as an attractive and fashionable (and marriageable) young lady. Thus, although she has a veneer of sophistication and can make relevant references to some of the same books that Catharine has read, it is not long before Catharine realizes that she is essentially empty-headed and shallow, interested only in her own appearance and trivial gossip about her well-to-do acquaintances in London and elsewhere. Interestingly—given Austen's reputation as an apolitical writer—Catharine's first clear sign of this is during a discussion of politics by the whole family group after supper one evening. Catharine herself is not frightened to state her own views with force and conviction, but Camilla observes the period conventions of female decorum by immediately disclaiming any knowledge of, or interest in, political matters. Catharine sees this as a reflection of Camilla's ignorance and suspects that she is not, after all, going to make a satisfactory replacement for the Wynne girls. Catharine's suspicions about Camilla's shallowness are confirmed over the next few days as the latter's small reserve of witty conversation peters out in a sequence of formulaic descriptions of acquaintances as "either the sweetest Creature in the world, and one of whom she was doatingly [sic] fond, or horrid, shocking and not fit to be seen."

Camilla, however, is still good for one thing from Catharine's point of view, and that is to provide her with some information about Mary Wynne and the Halifax family, as the latter turn out to move in the same social circle as the Stanleys when they are in London. Camilla does, indeed, know the Halifax family, and she is familiar, at secondhand, with the whole history of the Wynnes' recent fortunes, but her perspective on this is entirely different from that of Catharine, as Camilla can see only the *good* fortune of the Wynne children in having been taken in by their rich relatives. She presents a very positive picture of the Lady Halifaxes and the Sir Fitzgibbons (who had sent Cecilia to India) and generally praises them for their great benevolence. Catharine sharply challenges her representation of the matter and draws attention to the underlying meanness and cruelty of these rich people, who clearly begrudge every penny spent on their poor relations and who then have the self-righteous gall to pretend to benevolence. Camilla has obviously been keen to ingratiate herself with her rich friends, and, being well-off herself, she finds it difficult to understand Catharine's indignation or to sympathize with the Wynnes. Catharine and Camilla agree to differ on the subject, and Catharine retires to her bower, where she gives vent to her feelings of anger and frustration at how shabbily her childhood friends have been treated by their relations.

Not long after, Camilla rushes out excitedly to break the news of a ball to be held in a few days at the house of the Dudleys, to which they have all been invited. This news also raises Catharine's spirits, as a ball is a far greater novelty to her than it is to Camilla, though it immediately gives the latter an excuse to indulge her favorite occupation of talking about her clothes. The girls both wait impatiently for the day of the ball, but when it arrives, Catharine awakes in the morning with a violent toothache. She tries every remedy available to her, but to no effect, and as the day wears on, it looks increasingly as though she will be forced to miss the ball. Camilla is sympathetic to Catharine's plight, but she is equally concerned about the danger of the whole party's having to stay at home on Catharine's account. When her fears about this are allayed by Catharine's insistence that they should all go without her, Camilla gives free rein to her vacuous expressions of pity for Catharine ("I wish there were no such things as Teeth in the World; they are nothing but plagues to one, and I dare say that People might easily invent something to eat with instead of them"). These persecute Catharine as much as her toothache, and she spends most of the rest of the day trying to escape from Camilla. She stoically resigns herself to missing the ball and is finally relieved to be left alone in the house once her aunt and the Stanleys have gone. She settles down to write a letter to Mary Wynne and finds that by the time she has finished it, her toothache has passed. She decides that she can now follow the rest of the party to the ball, and she quickly dresses and orders her aunt's carriage (the others having gone in the Stanleys' carriage). At that moment, Catharine hears another carriage draw up before the house, and her maid, Anne, soon rushes into her dressing room in great agitation to announce the arrival of "one of the handsomest young men you would wish to see." Catharine is amused at the impression this man has made on Anne but also intrigued on her own behalf, though she is also slightly suspicious of the stranger, especially given that he has not announced his name and has arrived with no servants. She goes down to meet him and finds that Anne was not exaggerating about his good looks. But she is also taken aback at the casualness of his address to her and at his general ease of manner in the house: when she comes in, he is already sitting reading a newspaper, and he then jumps up, confirms what her name is, and offers her a chair—all without introducing himself. However, he makes it clear that he is familiar with the Percival family and with the Stanleys, too; indeed, it soon emerges that he is, in fact, the notorious son of the Stanleys, unexpectedly returned from France on business. Catharine has been confused and disconcerted by him, and she is not pleased by his free manner toward her; but, at the same time, his liveliness, good humor, and lack of reserve chime with something of the same nature in her, and she soon adopts his style of witty banter. When Stanley discovers that Catharine is on her way to the Dudleys' ball, he quickly invites himself to it, offers to take her in his carriage, and engages her for her first dance. Catharine is flattered by his attentions now and prepared to overlook questions of propriety and decorum, so she happily acquiesces to each of these proposals. First, though, Stanley asks to be able to spruce himself up a little, and Catharine directs him to Mr. Stanley's dressing room, expecting to see him again in a few minutes. But it is more than half an hour later before he emerges, and Catharine is amazed to hear him boast of how quick he has been. He then takes her by the hand and leads her to his carriage. On the way to the Dudleys' house, Stanley talks of what an impression they will make on entering the ballroom, but Catharine tries to remind him that he is a total stranger to the Dudleys and that it would be indecorous for him to enter without a proper introduction to them. Moreover, she is also concerned about her own impropriety, in the eyes of her aunt at least, in coming to the ball unchaperoned and with a total stranger. Stanley, however, breezily dismisses all these conventional decorums, and, when they arrive at the house, he prevents Catharine from forewarning her aunt or his parents of their arrival, and he more or less forcibly rushes Catharine up the stairs. "Half angry & half laughing," Catharine finally manages to extricate herself from his grasp just before they enter the room. This saves her from major embarrassment, but their entrance still causes great consternation on the part of Mrs. Percival, all the more so given that the couple arrive during a break in the dancing when everybody is sitting down and able to observe the spectacle. Catharine hurries over to her aunt to explain matters, while Stanley is greeted effusively by Camilla and Mr. Stanley. He is much more coldly received by the Dudleys, who are indignant at his uninvited presence, though he is too insensitive to notice their disapproving manner. He then goes into the cardroom to greet his mother.

Camilla now comes to sit with Catharine (who has survived "a severe lecture" from Mrs. Percival) and reveals that the "melancholy" business that had brought her brother back from Lyons in such haste was the illness of his favorite hunting mare. The horse had died on his return, and he had then decided to call on his family at Chetwynde before going back to France. Edward Stanley then returns to the room and immediately invites Catharine to lead off the next dance with him. This once more provokes general indignation as it places Catharine, who has only just arrived at the ball and who, though an heiress, is "only" a merchant's daughter, above all the other ladies in the room. In particular, it enrages Camilla, who feels that her own superior breeding has been insulted. Catharine, however, remains totally oblivious to any offense she may have caused, and she thoroughly enjoys the rest of the evening, mainly spent with Edward Stanley as her dancing partner. Not until she is in the carriage home with the other ladies of her party does she become aware of the reason for Camilla's ill humor, and she is only too willing to apologize and smooth over the affair, as she has "too much good Sense to be proud of her family, and too much good Nature to live at variance with any one." Camilla and Mrs. Stanley are quickly placated, but Mrs. Percival has fallen into a silent gloom because of the events of the evening, particularly because of the arrival of Edward Stanley, whom she sees as a major threat to Catharine.

The next morning, Mrs. Percival makes it clear to Mr. Stanley that she expects him to send his son away as soon as possible. Mr. Stanley explains the situation to Edward and urges him to leave the next day, but Edward will not give his word on this. In fact, though he has no intention of seriously courting Catharine, he is highly amused at hearing of the disturbing effect he has had on Mrs. Percival, and he now gleefully considers how he might provoke her jealous fears further. For the rest of the day, with one eye constantly on Mrs. Percival, he purposely pays extra attention to Catharine, talking only to her, praising her drawing and her playing, and seeming to be distracted by her absence when she leaves the room. The problem is that, while this has the desired effect on Mrs.

Percival, who is "in tortures the whole Day," Catharine herself believes Stanley to be genuine in his attentions to her, and her romantic disposition inclines her to think that an intimate relationship is developing on both sides. In the course of the evening, Stanley contrives to walk alone with Catharine in the garden, and they discuss books and history together. Catharine, influenced by her growing attraction to him, is impressed by his range of knowledge and conversation, but we can see that though he has something to say on every subject, he dwells on nothing for long, and his opinions are, in fact, as unfixed and fleeting as his feelings for Catharine evidently are. She, on the other hand, argues her points with genuine passion and takes their historical debate seriously. In the middle of a discussion on the character of Richard III, Stanley suddenly seizes Catharine's hand, kisses it, and rushes out of the bower in which they had seated themselves. Catharine is bemused by this odd behavior but soon realizes its cause when she sees her aunt bearing down on her along another path leading to the arbor. Mrs. Percival grossly overreacts to the situation and berates Catharine for her "profligate" behavior, repeating one of her favorite catchphrases, "every thing is going to sixes & sevens and all order will soon be at an end throughout the Kingdom" (this may be Jane Austen's joking reference to contemporary events, of course: Edward has recently come over from revolutionary France). Catharine manages to defuse her aunt's anger by reminding her of her hypochondriacal fear of catching cold by being out in the "damp" garden late in the evening. This has the desired effect of sending Mrs. Percival straight to bed, and Catharine can return to the rest of the company to try to fathom out Edward Stanley's strange behavior for herself.

Back in the house, Stanley has no qualms whatsoever about telling Catharine straight out that he had behaved as he had and pretended an affection for Catharine merely to antagonize Mrs. Percival. Catharine is at first understandably offended at this admission, but it is not long before his charming manners and witty ways again work their effect on her. By the end of the evening, she is almost convinced once more that he really is in love with her, and she goes to bed in high spirits, dismissing any reservations she has about his apparent "thoughtlessness & negligence." When she rises in the morning, however, she finds that Edward Stanley has already departed for France without even taking his leave of her. She immediately reflects on her own foolishness and vanity in believing that he could have seriously fallen in love with her after only twenty-four hours' acquaintance; but she still regrets his going. Camilla then comes into her room and puts a new gloss on the matter when she tells Catharine that Edward had been forced to leave by his father and that he had made a special point of expressing his regrets at having to leave Catharine, who he hoped would not be married before he returned. Camilla assures Catharine that her brother is genuinely in love with her, and Catharine is happy once more to entertain the possibility of this being the case.

(The final page or so of the manuscript was probably not written by Jane Austen herself, but by another member of her family, possibly by one of her literary nephews or nieces. However, it continues as follows.) Catharine remains in good spirits for the rest of the Stanleys' stay at Chetwynde, and after their departure her bower is even more important to her than it had been before because of its new associations with Edward Stanley. Although Camilla subsequently writes to Catharine, her letters give the latter little pleasure once they stop referring to Edward, as they quickly do once he is back in France. The manuscript ends inconclusively with Catharine and Mrs. Percival on the verge of a theater visit to Exeter.

Major Characters: Mrs. Percival (sometimes Mrs. Peterson in the manuscript), Catharine (Kitty) Percival, Mr. and Mrs. Stanley, Camilla Stanley, Edward Stanley.

Minor Characters: Lord Amyatt, Lady Amyatt, Anne, or Nanny, Augusta Barlow, Sir Peter Barlow, Sir Harry Devereux, Rev. and Mrs. Dudley, Miss Dudley, Sir George Fitzgibbon, Dowager Lady Halifax, Miss Halifax, Caroline and Maria Halifax, Sarah Hutchinson, John (Mrs. Percival's servant), Mr. and Mrs. Lascelles, the Bishop of M——, Lady Susan, Tom (Mrs. Percival's servant), Rev. and Mrs. Wynne, Cecilia Wynne, Mary Wynne, Charles Wynne.

See: in addition to *Southam 1964, Grey 1989* and Derry 1990.

"Catherine." *See* "Susan" and *Northanger Abbey*. "Susan" was Jane Austen's original title for this novel, which was titled and published as *Northanger Abbey* only posthumously. Jane Austen had sold the manuscript to a publisher in 1803, but it had never been printed. When she bought it back in 1816 and was thinking of trying another publisher, she changed the title to "Catherine."

Chamberlayne, Mr. (*Pride and Prejudice* Ch.39; II:16:221). One of the militia officers stationed in Meryton with whom Lydia and Kitty Bennet become familiar. At one of Colonel and Mrs. Forster's house parties, they dress Chamberlayne "to pass for a lady," using one of their aunt Phillips' gowns.

Chapman, Mrs. (*Mansfield Park* Ch.27; II:9:271). Lady Bertram's maid, who, as a special favor, is sent up by Lady Bertram to help Fanny dress on the evening of the ball—but "too late of course to be of any use."

Charades &c. Written a Hundred Years Ago by Jane Austen and Her Family. This publication of Austen family miscellanea, possibly collected and published by Jane Austen's great-niece, Mary Augusta Austen-Leigh, includes three short riddles attributed to Jane Austen—on "hemlock," "agent," and "banknote." They are in the style of the charade on "courtship" by Mr. Elton in Chapter 9 of *Emma*. They are reprinted in Jane Austen's *Minor Works* (p. 450) and also in the recent edition of her *Collected Poems and Verse* edited by David Selwyn (p. 18).

Charles (*Mansfield Park* Ch.20; II:2:189). A postilion at Mansfield Park (i.e., someone who rides the near horse of the leaders drawing a coach).

Charles, Sir (*Mansfield Park* Ch.31; II:13:299). An acquaintance of Admiral Crawford. Solicited by the latter on behalf of his nephew, Henry Crawford, who wants to impress Fanny, he helps to get William Price made a lieutenant through his connections in the Admiralty.

Churchill, Frank C. Weston (*Emma* Ch.2; I:2:16). Son of Mr. Weston and his first wife but adopted, on the death of his mother when he was three years old, by Mr. and Mrs. Churchill of Enscombe, Yorkshire. It is tacitly understood that Frank will be heir to the wealthy Churchill estate, and he takes the name of Churchill when he is twenty-one. On his first appearance in the novel he is twenty-three, a lively, spirited, and handsome young man with an easy and charming manner. He is generally admired in Highbury but particularly by Emma, who enjoys his witty company and is flattered by his attentions to her. They flirt with one another, and she begins to fancy herself in love with him, though she soon recognizes that this is, indeed, just a passing fancy. Doubts about Frank's true character and motives slowly accumulate, though they are expressed early on by Mr. Knightley, who wonders at the fact that Frank visits his father so rarely: when we first meet him, he has come to Highbury for the very first time, and apart from that he sees his father in London only once a year. One of his main excuses for this is that his aunt demands so much of his time and attention and does not permit him to visit as freely as he might want to. But Knightley finds it difficult to believe that a grown man can be so much under the thumb of an elderly aunt. Apart from this, even Emma registers an air of duplicity and affectation in some aspects of his behavior: he sometimes seems to be trying too hard to please everybody (a little like Mr. Weston, in fact), and yet when it boils down to it, he mainly pleases himself—for example, in his erratic comings and goings at Highbury. Although much of the uncertainty surrounding his character is later explained by the fact of his secret engagement to Jane Fairfax, serious doubts remain about his manners and morals, given his unnecessarily involved flirtation with Emma and his sometimes downright cruel exploitation (apparently for his own gratification) of Jane's awkward position at Highbury. He is largely forgiven by both Jane and his Highbury acquaintances when the truth about the engagement is made known, but all three of the novel's most reliable and trustworthy "voices"—those of Knightley, Mrs. Weston, and Emma herself at the end—continue to express reservations about him.

Churchill, Miss. *See* Weston, Mrs.

Churchill, Mr. (*Emma* Ch.2; I:2:15). Mr. Churchill of Enscombe in Yorkshire is the rich uncle and adoptive guardian of Frank Churchill. Although he disapproved of his sister's marriage to Captain Weston, it would seem that their consequent estrangement was provoked more by the nouveau riche snobbery of his wife than by his own true feelings. Being childless, he and his wife were drawn back toward his sister by the birth of her son, Frank, and then also by her last lingering illness, so that there was "a sort of reconciliation" between them; and, after her death, he and Mrs. Churchill undertook the care and upbringing of Frank, tacitly making him their heir. After the death of Mrs. Churchill toward the end of the novel, Mr. Churchill is easily persuaded to agree to Frank's marriage to Jane Fairfax and is happy to have them live with him at Enscombe, thus further suggesting a more easygoing nature than his wife's and also his previous subservience to her.

Churchill, Mrs. (*Emma* Ch.2; I:2:15). Frank Churchill's capricious and ill-tempered aunt and adoptive guardian; and sister-in-law to the first Mrs. Weston. According to Mr. Weston, a proud and arrogant "upstart" who married into the wealth of the Churchill family and then "out-Churchill'd them all in high and mighty claims." Her domineering interference, he suggests, was the true cause of the quarrel between Mr. Churchill and his sister that led to the estrangement of the Westons from the Churchills. Though she never actually appears in person, her possessive influence over Frank motivates much of the plot intrigue surrounding him and Jane Fairfax, and her death sets in motion the final unraveling of the plot.

Clarke family (*Lady Susan, Minor Works* 268). Friends of Frederica Vernon in Staffordshire. They are apparently the only acquaintances she has apart from the friends of her mother, and Lady Susan assumes she was trying to go to them when she tries to run away from school.

Clarke, Mrs. (*Sense and Sensibility* Ch.38; III:2:271). A close acquaintance of Mrs. Jennings, whom she and Elinor meet at Kensington Gardens.

Clay, Mrs. Penelope, née Shepherd (*Persuasion* Ch.2; I:2:15–16). The daughter of Sir Walter Elliot's agent, Mr. Shepherd, Mrs. Clay is a young and artful widow who, "after an unprosperous marriage," returns to her father's house with her two children and quickly insinuates herself into a close friendship with Elizabeth Elliot at Kellynch Hall, with the ulterior motive of becoming a second wife to Sir Walter. However, in Bath, Mr. William Elliot, aware of the danger of his being disinherited by such a match, contrives to make her his mistress instead.

Cole, Mr. and Mrs. (*Emma* Chs.9, 19, 25; I:9:75; II:1:156–57; II:7:207). The Coles are "very good sort of people—friendly, liberal, and unpretending." They have been settled in Highbury for some years and are active and respected members of the local community. Mr. Coles is closely involved in parish business, along with Mr. Knightley, Mr. Weston, and others; and Mrs. Coles is a close and charitable friend to Miss Bates and her mother, taking special interest in the welfare of Jane Fairfax. They have made their fortune in trade and have recently increased their profits quite substantially, so that at the time of the main events in the novel, they have become, "in fortune and style of living," second only to the Woodhouse family in Highbury society. Emma acknowledges the Coles as "respectable in their way" but snobbishly considers them below herself because of their origins in trade; when she expects a dinner party invitation from them, she plans to refuse it in order to teach them "that it was not for them to arrange the terms on which the superior families would visit them." In the event, of course, she accepts the invitation when it comes, largely for her own personal reasons (Frank Churchill will be there), but also because it is so well expressed and so considerate with regard to the comfort and convenience of Mr. Woodhouse.

"A Collection of Letters" (*Volume the Second* of Jane Austen's juvenilia). Written probably in late 1791 or early 1792 and dedicated to Jane Austen's cousin, Jane Cooper, this "collection" contains five unconnected letters, each experimenting with different styles and voices. Together, these letters provide a neat overview of the development of Jane Austen's writing over the whole of her juvenilia, for we have here examples of her earliest style of literary burlesque and parody (especially in the exaggerated sentimentalism of the second, fourth, and fifth letters) as well as examples of her later move toward a more realistic mode of social comedy and criticism (especially in the third letter). The first letter, "From a Mother to Her Freind [*sic*]," lies somewhere between these two poles and "mocks the tradition of the moral and didactic epistle, perfected by Richardson and subsequently used as an editorial device in the periodicals" (*Southam 1964*: 31). The third letter is notable for its anticipation of the clash between Elizabeth Bennet and Lady Catherine De Bourgh in *Pride and Prejudice*, as it presents a rich and haughty dowager, Lady Greville, constantly patronizing and trying to "mortify" the young, proud, but poor Maria Williams, who, like Eliza Bennet, is perfectly prepared to stand up to her pompous antagonist. The titles of the letters give an indication of the range of voices and scenarios: "From a Mother to Her Freind," "From a Young Lady Crossed in Love to Her Freind—," "From a Young Lady in Distress'd Circumstances to Her Freind," "From a Young Lady Rather Impertinent to Her Freind," "From a Young Lady Very Much in Love to Her Freind."

Characters (Letters 1–5): 1. A. F., Augusta, Mrs. Cope and daughter, Margaret, the Misses Phillips, Mr. Stanly, Sir John Wynne. 2. Belle, the two Mr. Crawfords, Lady Bridget Dashwood, Captain Henry Dashwood, Admiral Annesley (deceased), Miss Jane Annesley, Fitzowen, Colonel Seaton, Edward Willoughby, Sophia. 3. Mr. Ashburnham, Mr. Bernard, Lord and Lady Clermont, Lady Greville, Ellen and Miss Greville, Miss Mason, Mrs. Williams, Maria Williams, Sir Thomas Stanley. 4. Miss Dawson, Dr. Drayton, Mr. and Mrs.

Evelyn, Miss Greville. 5. Henrietta Halton, Matilda, Thomas Musgrove, Lady Scudamore.

Collins, Mr. William (*Pride and Prejudice* Chs.13, 15; I:13:61; I:15:70). Mr. Bennet's oafish cousin and heir to Longbourn. "Mr. Collins was not a sensible man, and the deficiency of nature had been but little assisted by education or society." He is twenty-five years old when we first meet him and has been recently ordained as a priest. Moreover, "by fortunate chance" he has also recently obtained the valuable rectorship of Hunsford in Kent from his patron, Lady Catherine de Bourgh. Having been brought up to a humility of manner by "an illiterate and miserly father," this was now counteracted by "the self-conceit of a weak head" brought on by his early preferment, so that Mr. Collins is "a mixture of pride and obsequiousness, self-importance and humility." Pompous, arrogant, and overbearing toward those he sees as his inferiors (such as the Bennets), abjectly servile toward his perceived superiors (such as Lady Catherine de Bourgh), he lacks any sort of self-awareness and critical understanding and appears consistently foolish in all situations. One of the most famous scenes in English literature occurs when he proposes to Elizabeth Bennet. Smugly confident, as the heir to Longbourn, of being gratefully accepted by her, he is swiftly cut down to size by Elizabeth's forthright and indignant rejection of him. He later saves face somewhat (and, he thinks, revenges himself on the Bennets) by being accepted by Charlotte Lucas. But, as an Austen character, he is damned for all time when, on being asked to read aloud from a circulating library book, he starts back and protests in horror that "he never read novels."

Cooper, Mrs. James (*Emma* Ch.32; II:14:277). Originally Miss Milman, sister of Mrs. Bird; a friend of Mrs. Elton, used by the latter as an example (along with Mrs. Bird and Mrs. Jeffereys) of married women's being "too apt to give up music."

Courteney, General (*Northanger Abbey* Ch.17; II:2:139). An old friend of General Tilney who fails to show up in Bath.

Courtland, Lord (*Sense and Sensibility* Ch.36; II:14:251–52). A friend of Robert Ferrars, mentioned by the latter in the course of his absurd little disquisition to Elinor on the virtues of cottages. Lord Courtland had been seeking advice on some building plans by the architect Joseph Bonomi (1739–1808), and Robert Ferrars claims to have thrown these on the fire while enjoining his friend to build a cottage instead.

Cox, Mr. (*Emma* Ch.26: II:8:214). The lawyer of Highbury.

Cox, Mr. William (*Emma* Ch.27; II:9:233). The eldest son of Mr. Cox the lawyer and presumably the same character referred to earlier in the novel as

William Coxe, the "pert young lawyer." Also mentioned is "a second young Cox" (Ch.29; II:11:248).

Coxe, William (*Emma* Ch.16; I:16:137). Emma, in the immediate aftermath of Elton's proposal to her, guiltily contemplates the damage done by her foolish attempt to make a match between Harriet Smith and Elton; but even here she suffers a brief "relapse" and for a moment imagines yet another potential match for Harriet in William Coxe—before snobbishly dismissing him as "a pert young lawyer."

Coxes, the Miss (*Emma* Ch.27: II:9:232). Anne Cox and her younger sister are daughters of Mr. Cox, the lawyer. Reviewing the Coles' dinner party (II:8) with Emma, Harriet Smith says that the Coxes, particularly Anne, had talked a great deal about Robert Martin and that Miss Nash had commented that either of the Coxes would be happy to marry Martin. Emma immediately recognizes the warmth of feeling Harriet obviously still feels for her erstwhile sweetheart, and she tries once again to demean him in Harriet's eyes by suggesting that the Coxes would, indeed, be a good match for him, as "they are, without exception, the most vulgar girls in Highbury."

Crawford, Admiral (*Mansfield Park* Ch.4; I:4:46). The paternal uncle of Mary and Henry Crawford and their guardian after they are orphaned. Although unhappily married, the Crawfords provide Henry and Mary with a good, kindly home, and the Admiral takes special delight in Henry. He mistreats his wife and, after her death, brings his mistress into the house so that Mary feels obliged to leave for the sake of her aunt's memory, and this is the immediate cause for her going to stay at Mansfield with her half sister, Mrs. Grant.

Crawford, Henry (*Mansfield Park* Ch.4; I:4:40). Henry Crawford owns the estate of Everingham in Norfolk, and he comes with his sister, Mary, to visit their half-sister, Mrs. Grant, at Mansfield Parsonage. Like his sister, Henry is immediately admired by others for his elegant manners, sparkling wit, and stylish looks, but his surface glamour veils a lack of scruple and a vein of cynical egotism. His superb acting skills, which even Fanny Price admires, are suggestive here, for in some ways he is always playing a part, always masking his true motives; yet, at the same time, there is never any real substance of personality beneath the various parts he plays—the masks are all there is to him. He clearly enjoys luring women into relationships with him for the thrill of conquest and for satisfaction of his own "cold-blooded" vanity, but he has no thought for the consequences of his actions for those women. He trifles with the feelings of Julia Bertram; he flirts with Maria Bertram in full knowledge of her engagement to Mr. Rushworth but then drops her once he has won her affections; he doggedly pursues Fanny and then compromises her position by proposing to her and enlisting the support of the Bertram family; and, partly on the rebound from his rejection by Fanny, he takes up again with the now-married Maria, cuckolds Rushworth, and then leaves Maria in the lurch. We should perhaps remember that Henry Crawford was brought up by his dissolute uncle, Admiral Crawford, for it is suggested that this "bad domestic example," along with a premature access to his own fortune, may have "ruined" him.

Crawford, Mary (*Mansfield Park* Ch.4; I:4:40). The sister of Henry Crawford and in many ways from the same moral pedigree, Mary Crawford is again, though perhaps to a lesser extent than Henry, a character of surface glamour and inner corruption. She is a fashionable, sophisticated, and vivacious woman, exceptionally pretty and witty. But, though she is perhaps less egotistical than her brother, she shares some of his cynicism and his desire for control over others, and she is, if anything, more materialistic than he is, with her values fixed firmly to a monetary scale: she believes everything worth having can be bought. The essential incompatibility of her materialism with the religious idealism of Edmund dooms their relationship from the start. But her attraction to Edmund does seem largely genuine and not inspired by motives of financial gain, for, after all, as the younger brother, he does not stand to inherit the family estate, and his future as a priest does not hold the promise of great riches. On the other hand, she does not relish the likely constraints on her enjoyment of being a clergyman's wife, and she insensitively tries to talk Edmund out of his vocation (and, of course, there is always a chance of his eventually inheriting the estate, especially if something happens to Tom, as Mary later realizes when Tom is ill). Part of her role in the novel, like that of her brother, is to tempt others to relax their judgment and moral sense and pursue some form of "forbidden" pleasure. She tempts Edmund in a variety of ways—to take part in the theatricals, to abandon his vocation, to temper his moral censure (of Maria), to marry her. Mary is finally judged by Edmund to have a "corrupted, vitiated mind" when she first comments casually on Maria's elopement, as if it were a mere indiscretion, and then also tries to blame Fanny for Henry's behavior, for not having accepted his proposal of marriage. Edmund qualifies his judgment of Mary, to some extent, by saying that Mary's are not faults of a temper that would "voluntarily give unnecessary pain to any one," but faults of principle.

Crawford, Mrs. (deceased) (*Mansfield Park* Ch.4; I:4:40). Wife of Admiral Crawford who, with him, had brought up Henry and Mary Crawford. Out of the two children, she had paid special attention to Mary, who had become her protégée. Mrs. Crawford seems to have had an unhappy marriage, for, apart from their common affection for the two orphaned children, she and her husband did not agree, and he is said to have mistreated her.

Criticism (Note: All works referred to in this entry can be found in Chapters 5 and 6. As elsewhere in the book, italicized name and date citations indicate a reference to a book, and therefore to Chapter 5, while normal-type citations indicate an essay to be found in Chapter 6. Lists of references are chronologically ordered to indicate the development of critical comment through time, but where there are long lists of essay citations, these are in alphabetical order to aid the reader in locating items in the bibliography.)

It has become customary to consider the history of Jane Austen criticism in terms of three main periods: 1812–1870, the period between the first contemporary reviews and J. E. Austen-Leigh's *A Memoir of Jane Austen*; 1870–1939, a period of gradually developing popular and critical interest in Austen, initially sparked by the *Memoir*, fueled by growing academic discussion and scholarly research, and culminating in the first fully developed analytical study of her works, *Jane Austen and Her Art* by Mary Lascelles; and 1940 to the present, a period of exponential growth both in professional academic criticism of Austen and in the general popularity of her works (a popularity that shows no signs of abating if we are to judge by the recent spate of television and movie adaptations of the novels).

1812–1870. As far as we know, Jane Austen received only sixteen reviews or notices during her lifetime: two for *Sense and Sensibility*, three for *Pride and Prejudice*, and eleven for *Emma* (though two of these appeared in Germany and one in Russia, and there is no evidence that Austen knew of them). Most of the reviews were short, but they were largely favorable, with most reviewers commenting in some way on the novels' verisimilitude, on their entertaining nature, and on their unexceptionable morality. The most important and most fully developed review was the essay written on *Emma* in 1816 by Sir Walter Scott (though published anonymously). This is usually seen as the first landmark in Austen criticism for its recognition of Austen's technical virtuosity and for its systematic emphasis on her realism, dramatic characterization, and narrative control. Scott's discussion was to remain one of the most perceptive of his century, and it certainly established the pattern for much future criticism. However—not surprisingly, perhaps—Scott expressed some reservations about Austen's anti-Romanticism at the end of his essay, and, as Margaret Kirkham has argued, these mark the limits of his understanding of Austen's art and indicate his "hostility" to its essentially feminist morality (*Kirkham 1983*: 162).

The next major discussion of Austen's work came in 1821, in what was ostensibly a review of *Northanger Abbey* and *Persuasion* but actually a wide-ranging general assessment of her work by Archbishop Richard Whately. This clearly built on Scott's essay but went further than Scott in its praise of Austen and, in particular (as Kirkham usefully points out in the work just cited), in its serious and sympathetic consideration of the values implicit in all six of her novels (Scott had discussed only three of the four novels published by 1816 and neglected even to mention *Mansfield Park*).

Apart from some brief notices of Richard Bentley's collected edition of the novels in 1833, there was little developed critical comment on Jane Austen in the decades immediately following Whately's work. Another full-length essay devoted solely to her did not appear until 1852, and between then and 1870 there were only five further such essays, the most important by George Henry Lewes in 1859. From this handful of essays and other scattered comments, however, it is clear that, though Austen was not a popular author in this period, she had an influential following within literary circles and a small but devoted band of private readers. This was to stand her in good stead in the period following the publication of the *Memoir*, which gave her admirers a convenient pretext to proselytize about their "forgotten" author.

1870–1939. J. E. Austen-Leigh's elegantly written *Memoir* of his aunt first appeared in 1869 (with 1870 on the title page), but it met with such interest that a second revised and enlarged edition was published in 1871, which, in addition to the letters and verses of the first edition, brought into print for the first time several of Jane Austen's minor writings. The *Memoir* was relatively short but important for several reasons: as indicated, it brought previously unpublished works by Austen into the public domain for the first time, and it demonstrated the existence of other such materials still in the family's possession; it provided a detailed account of Austen's life in its domestic, social, and cultural contexts, which has been the starting point for nearly all subsequent biographies; it provided an overview of her development as a writer and of her publishing career, and it gave a useful general assessment of her artistic achievement and of her reputation up to that time; but perhaps most important of all, it told a fascinating "human interest" story about a writer who until that time had been little more than a name to most people—in short, the *Memoir* constructed an engaging identity for "Jane Austen" and thereby generated a revival of public and critical interest in both her life and works.

But Austen-Leigh's Jane Austen was no more (and no less) than a construction, and, as many critics have pointed out, it was very much an idealized Victorian construction of what a good Christian maiden aunt ought to be like. This was perhaps inevitable, given Austen-Leigh's place in time and position in society as an elderly clergyman; and, by creating a figure congenial to Victorian sensibilities, the *Memoir* certainly facilitated the growth of critical debate and publication around Austen's work. However, it may also have had a stalling effect on the development of a truly sophisticated and searching style of Austen criticism, in that the demure "dear Aunt Jane" figure of the *Memoir* tended to encourage a congruently decorous type of criticism that largely eschewed detailed analysis and serious moral or ideological debate in favor of a generalized appreciation of Austen's "genius" and "perfection." This genteel and self-consciously amateurish form of criticism somewhat dominated the field in this period, and it eventually became known as the Janeite tendency in Austen studies (the word seems to have come into the language around 1896 and was later popularized by Kipling's short story "The Janeites," first published in 1924). Nevertheless, many valuable critical contributions emerged from the widespread interest generated by the *Memoir*, including one of the classics of Jane Austen criticism, the review-essay by Richard Simpson of April 1870, later described by Lionel Trilling as "perhaps the very first consideration of the subject undertaken in the spirit of serious criticism'' (quoted in *Southam 1987*: 17). Other notable contributions at this time came from R. H. Hutton (December 1869 and July 1871) and Margaret Oliphant (March 1870), and something like a critical consensus emerged that, taking its cue from Scott and Whately, praised Austen's novels "for their elegance of form and their surface 'finish'; for the realism of their fictional world, the variety and vitality of their characters; for their pervasive humour; and for their gentle and undogmatic morality and its unsermonising delivery'' (*Southam 1987*: 13).

The first book-length studies of Austen now began to appear (from 1880 onward). Most of these were firmly in the Janeite mold of criticism and designed mainly to introduce Austen to a wider popular audience; but there were notable exceptions, such as the works by W. George Pellew (*1883*) and Goldwin Smith (*1890*), who took a more sober and scholarly approach to their subject. Smith's book was also significant for being published in a series called *Great Writers*, a clear indication of the new status now given to Jane Austen as an accepted classic.

The next major examples of serious criticism come with A. C. Bradley's scholarly lecture of 1911 and, in 1917, Reginald Farrer's centenary essay in the *Quarterly Review*, which brilliantly confounded the dominant Janeite image of Austen at the time by celebrating not her quaint artlessness and gentility but her consummate artistry and protomodernistic impersonality and complexity. The publication of the scholarly Oxford edition of the novels in 1923 gave a further boost to Austen's reputation, as did the accumulating and usually admiring commentaries of contemporary writers such as Woolf, Priestley, Wharton, West, and Muir. Aided by these developments, critical discussion of Austen's works shifted firmly onto a professional academic footing by the end of the 1920s with a spate of learned books and articles all increasingly concerned with Austen's "craft of fiction'' (following Percy Lubbock's call for a new approach to novel-criticism in his *The Craft of Fiction* [first published in 1921], where, significantly, he refers to Austen in the same breath, so to speak, as Dickens and George Eliot [London: Cape, 1954, pp. 272–273]). Geoffrey Keynes produced the first major bibliography of Jane Austen in 1929, and this, in a sense, set the seal on the growing professionalization of Austen studies and provided a spur to further scholarship and research on the author.

Two major works of the 1930s brought this phase of Austen criticism to a culmination: Elizabeth Jenkins' *Jane Austen: A Biography* (1938) and Mary Lascelles' *Jane Austen and Her Art* (1939). Jenkins' eloquent biography provided not only a fresh, compelling, and evocative account of Austen's life and times but also the first sustained consideration of Austen's growth and development specifically as a creative artist. Mary Lascelles' work was groundbreaking in providing the first full-length, *formal* study of Jane Austen's novels, considering them in detail both separately and together in order to trace Austen's technical and thematic development from the very start of her career. The study took into account Austen's early sources and influences and discussed her ju-

venilia and minor writings within the overall trajectory of her work; it also
engaged critically with previous writers on Austen and thus provided a useful,
if partial, survey of Austen's critical reputation to that point. This was really
the first monograph on Austen that we would now recognize as fully critical
and rigorous in an academic sense, and it clearly marked the start of a new
phase in Austen criticism and scholarship. By this time, Jane Austen was firmly
established as a popular author and a "great" writer; Mary Lascelles' book had
now also firmly established her as a subject eminently worthy of detailed academic study and scholarly research: the ensuing period of criticism would see
a steady consolidation, growth, and development in the professional academic
study of Austen's works.

1940–present. Austen criticism in this third period largely reflects general
trends in literary studies and is as complex and varied as the criticism of any
other major author over the same period—a period, clearly, of rapid developments in literary-critical theory and methodology. The essentially New Critical,
close reading mode of approach heralded by Mary Lascelles was to be the
dominant one in Austen studies in the 1940s, 1950s, and 1960s as the fashionable formalist aesthetics of the era concentrated attention on just those technical
qualities that Austen's works exhibited in abundance: tight structural design and
self-contained focus; stylistic density; close, impersonal narrative control; complex verbal, dramatic, and structural ironies. The complacent, nostalgic popular
image of Jane Austen as a quaint chronicler of a more leisured and refined
bygone age now came under attack, as her subversive ironies and cool-eyed
exposure of pettiness and hypocrisy took center stage in critical discussion of
her work. Earlier critics had often commented on the tough-minded iconoclasm
inherent in much of Austen's humor; and, as recently as 1937, in his poem
"Letter to Lord Byron," W. H. Auden—amazed at Austen's audacious critique
of her society's materialistic values—had bluntly declared, "You could not
shock her more than she shocks me" (quoted in *Southam 1987*: 299). But these
views seem to have been overwhelmed by the general Janeite celebration of
Austen's "gentle" charm, and it took a combative essay by D. W. Harding in
1940 to reclaim for criticism what he called, in his title, the "Regulated Hatred"
of Austen's works. This highly controversial essay divided the critics in obvious
ways, but it was a seminal influence on a new generation of Austen readers,
and it helped to place the issue of irony right at the heart of Jane Austen studies
for many years to come. Marvin Mudrick's *Jane Austen: Irony as Defense and
Discovery* (1952) explored in detail this darker, more "angry" version of Jane
Austen and took Harding's argument to probably its most developed, if perhaps
overstated, point. After this book, serious critics might still wish to disagree
with Harding's version of Jane Austen, but they would now have to do so in
the same spirit of rigorous analysis and argumentation as Mudrick. Though the
traditional, "gentle-Jane" view of Austen has continued to find expression right
up to the present in a steady stream of subcritical, if often fascinating,
publications on a wide range of topics to do with her life and works, most

serious criticism after Mudrick has been marked by its sophistication in teasing out a balanced view of Austen as a complex and elusive ironist.

The other notable publications in the 1940s, apart from Harding's essay, were R. W. Chapman's biobibliographical *Jane Austen: Facts and Problems* (1948), which conveniently summarized the current state of scholarly information about Austen and remained a major source of reference for the next three decades; and R. A. Austen-Leigh's *Austen Papers* (1942), an invaluable source of biographical information to this day. (Austen-Leigh also published three other works on Austen's life and family in this period.)

The 1950s and 1960s saw a marked increase in academic criticism of Austen, and most of the book-length studies still have a great deal to offer to the contemporary reader. Of the many valuable critical discussions of Austen in the 1950s and 1960s, the following should be noted in particular: *Wright 1953*, a close and insightful reading of all six novels; Trilling, 1954, 1957, seminal revaluations of *Mansfield Park* and *Emma*, respectively; *Bradbrook 1961*, on *Emma*, the first single-novel monograph; *Babb 1962*, an early focus on Austen's strategic use of dialogue and character idiolect; *Southam 1964*, a magisterial account of Austen's surviving manuscripts, still authoritative and still the most elegant and incisive critical study of the juvenilia and minor works; *Litz 1965*, in the mold of Mary Lascelles' work, another landmark general study that neatly synthesizes the period's understanding of Austen with a penetrating exploration of her artistic development; *Bradbrook 1966* and *Moler 1968*, pioneering studies of Austen's sources and influences (see also the more general work of *Steeves 1965* and Birkhead 1925, Crundell 1941, Dodds 1948, Duncan-Jones 1954, Litz 1961); *Fleishman 1967* on *Mansfield Park; Burrows 1968* on *Emma*; and *Wiesenfarth 1967*, another stimulating general reading of the novels. Several important essay collections in this period provided useful critical surveys: *Watt 1963, Lodge 1968* (the first single-novel "casebook"—on *Emma), Southam 1968* (two separate collections: one general collection of contemporary essays and the first of Southam's indispensable *Critical Heritage* volumes, this one covering the years 1811–1870), *Rubinstein 1969, O'Neill 1970.*

From around 1970, recognizably contemporary critical trends began to show themselves in Austen studies (as in literary studies generally), and, throughout this period, two trends in particular have established themselves (often in relation to one another) as probably the dominant modes of approach to Austen's works: historicism (sociocultural and ideological contextualization of various sorts) and feminism.

The seminal historicist works (though see also *Rubinstein 1969*) were *Duckworth 1971* and *Butler 1975*, which both attempted to position Austen's works very precisely within the moral and political discourses of her time, Duckworth using the symbol of the "estate" to explore what he sees as Austen's conservatively reformist ethical outlook, and Butler rigorously interrogating Austen's works in relation to the polarized "war of ideas" of the revolutionary period— and placing her firmly in the anti-Jacobin camp. These works were followed by what is now a long line of detailed historical-cum-cultural studies that have investigated different aspects and phases of Austen's period in order to enrich our understanding of her works' contemporary meanings and significance. Some of the most important of these studies are as follows: Sulloway 1976, Lovell 1978, Monaghan 1978, Robinson 1978, *Brown 1979, Roberts 1979, Monaghan 1980, Morgan 1980*, Aers 1981, *Monaghan 1981*, Spring 1983, Stepankowsky and Harper 1988, *Thompson 1988, Handler and Segal 1990, Fergus 1991, MacDonagh 1991, Singh 1991, Stewart 1993, Sales 1994, Ruderman 1995*.

Historical contextualization on specific topics has also been provided by more specialized studies (not all of them adopting a thoroughgoing historicist perspective): *Nardin 1973*, Richards 1990 (on manners); Buck 1971, *Byrde 1979, Watkins 1990* (on fashion); *Piggott 1979, Wallace 1983*, La Rue 1994 (on music), *Devlin 1975, Fergus 1983, Mooneyham 1988, Horwitz 1991* (on education); Jackson 1975, Cheng 1978, Willis 1987, *Koppel 1988, Collins 1994*, Waldron 1994, and *Jarvis 1996* (on religion); Dodds 1949. Gornall 1966–67, Macey 1983 Garside 1987, Copeland 1989, 1993, and 1996, Erickson 1990, Heldman 1990, Hopkins 1994 (on money, economics and consumerism); *Wiltshire 1992, Gorman 1993* (on medicine and health); Sutherland 1990, *Lane 1994* (on food). Another form of historical inquiry in this period has been the continued study (following *Bradbrook 1966* and *Moler 1968*) of Jane Austen's literary context, of her intellectual and artistic "dialogue" with other writers. Important studies of this sort are: *De Rose 1980, Polhemus 1980, 1990, Wilt 1980, Cottom 1985, Spencer 1986, Spender 1986, Harris 1989, Johnson 1995*. See also Banerjee 1990, Barfoot 1995, Barker 1985, Barry 1986, Beasley 1973–1974, Bilger 1995, Bloom 1994, Brower 1975, Butler 1980, 1981b, Cohen 1994, Conger 1987, 1988, Copeland 1983, Crawford 1983, Derry 1990a, b, c, 1991, 1992, 1993, 1994, Doody 1986, Dorsey 1990, Drew 1980, Ehrenpreis 1970–1971, Epstein 1985, Fischer 1993, Frost 1991, Galperin 1990, Gross 1989, Halperin 1975, Harris 1993, Hoeveler 1995, Honan 1984, 1986, Keith 1984, Kelly 1986, 1995, Kirkland 1987, Knox-Shaw 1993, Lock 1976, Lucas 1992, Magee 1975, Maxwell 1974, Mellor 1990, Meyers 1986, Millgate 1996, Moon 1987, Morrow 1980, Myer 1982, Nath 1980, Nollen 1984, Parke 1982–1983, Paulson 1981, Perry 1994, Pinion 1977, Ram 1977, 1985, B. Roberts 1989, Saisselin 1994, Scholes 1975, Shaffer 1992, Siskin 1984–1985, Smith 1992, Swingle 1979, Thomas 1987, Ty 1986, Viveash 1991, Webb 1981, Weedon 1988.

Austen cropped up frequently as a focus for discussion in seminal feminist literary works of the 1970s, perhaps most notably in *The Madwoman in the Attic* by Sandra Gilbert and Susan Gubar (1979); but, apart from some scattered essays (such as those by Sulloway [1976] and Robinson [1978] already mentioned in different context), the devoted feminist study of Austen began in earnest with Margaret Kirkham's crusading *Jane Austen, Feminism and Fiction* (1983), a work that argued forcefully for a historically grounded reevaluation of Austen as a self-conscious feminist in the main tradition of Enlightenment feminism running from Mary Astell to Mary Wollstonecraft. Since Kirkham's book, there has been a steady flow of feminist or feminist-related studies of Austen, and these have almost all provided exhilarating new leads in the field and have rapidly transformed received notions of how to read and understand Austen. Significant book-length works in this category are as follows: *James 1983, Smith 1983, Poovey 1984, Weldon 1984, Evans 1987, Johnson 1988, Sulloway 1989, Mukherjee 1991, Hudson 1992, Kaplan 1992, Castellanos 1994, Johnson 1995, Looser 1995*. See also *Beer 1974* and the following essays: Auerbach 1983, Bilger 1995, Booth 1983, Brown 1973, Brown 1982, Brown 1990, Brownstein 1982, 1988, Butler 1980, Cohen 1994, Epstein 1985, Ferguson 1991, Fowler 1974, 1980, Fraiman 1989, 1995, Frost 1991, Fullbrook 1987, Gillooly 1994, Giobbi 1992, Giordano 1993, Giuffre 1983–1984, Goodwin 1990, Greenfield 1994, Hunt 1986, Hutcheson 1983, Kelly 1995, Laurence 1994, Lenta 1981a, b, 1983, Marshall 1992, McDonnell 1984, Meyersohn 1983, 1990, Moffat 1991, Morgan and Kneedler 1990, Okin 1983–1984, Perry 1994, Potter 1994, Shaffer 1992, 1994, J. Smith 1987, 1993, P. Smith 1993, Snyder 1992, Spacks 1988, 1989b, Sulloway 1986, Swords 1988, Todd 1983, 1991, Uphaus 1987, Warhol 1992.

What might be considered a third dominant trend in this period of Austen criticism is the sustained focus on her language and style. The precision and "finish" of her works had been commented on from the very earliest reviews, of course, but, with the exception of David Lodge's pioneering study of the language of *Mansfield Park* in his *Language of Fiction* (1966), systematic and detailed stylistic analysis did not appear until the 1970s with the works of *Phillips 1970, Kroeber 1971, Page 1972, Brown 1973, Tave 1973, Schapera 1977,* and *Petersen 1979*. More recent full-length studies of Austen's language and narrative technique include *Konigsberg 1985*, the unique, computer-based statistical study of *Burrows 1987, Stokes 1991, Kuwahara 1993*, and *Wallace 1995*. See also Bevan 1987b, Boyd 1983, 1984, Finch and Bowen 1990, Flavin 1987, 1991, Frazer 1983, Heyns 1986, McMaster 1996, Moler 1984, 1991, Neumann 1986, Pascal 1977, Schmidt 1981, Shaw 1990, Spacks 1983, Tandrup 1983, Thompson 1986c, Tsomondo 1985, 1987, 1990, Weissman 1988.

Of course, parallel to all the preceding, traditional critical studies of Austen have continued to appear in the past three decades. Some useful general studies that provide stimulating interpretations of Austen's novels or that explore them in relation to particular themes are *Gooneratne 1970, Mansell 1973, Hardy 1975, McMaster 1978, Paris 1978, Odmark 1981, Hardy 1984, Tanner 1986, Williams 1986, Odom 1991, Gard 1992*. Comprehensive scholarly guides to Austen's life, times, and works are offered by *Pinion 1973, Grey 1986*, and *Copeland and McMaster 1997*; while more selective introductory surveys are provided by *Hardwick 1973, Gillie 1974, Bush 1975, Southam 1975, Handley 1992*, and *Lauber 1993*.

There has been steady progress in the development of the biographical and bibliographical record on Austen in this period, and biographies and biographical materials have steadily accumulated since the early 1970s. Most of the popular biographies and coffee-table introductions to Jane Austen's life, times, and environment are basically reliable and readable, and many of them are particularly valuable for their photographs and illustrations; good examples are *Laski 1969, Cecil 1978, Wilks 1978, Lane 1986, Watkins 1990, Nicolson 1991, Howard 1995, Batey 1996, Lane 1996* (see also *Hughes-Hallett 1990* for a finely illustrated selection of Austen's letters). However, mostly, these works are simply fresh versions of existing biographical accounts, and they add little that is genuinely new to the biographical scholarship on Austen. The most important new advances have been made in the four outstanding biographical works of this period, all of which incorporate substantial original research: *Tucker 1983* (on Jane Austen's family; see also *Lane 1984* and *Tucker 1994), Honan 1987* (a comprehensive, scholarly biography), *Le Faye 1989* (a thoroughgoing revision of the standard *Life and Letters* of 1913 by W. and R. A. Austen-Leigh, this is now by far the most objective, balanced, and elegantly written general account of Austen's life), and *Fergus 1991* (probably one of the best short introductions to Austen's life and works, this is a superbly focused and incisive account of Austen's professional career; it considers the day-to-day details and difficulties of being a female author at the time, while also providing a stimulating critical commentary on Austen's novelistic development). The two most recent biographies, *Nokes 1997* and *Tomalin 1997*, also contain some original research and provide a reliable account of Austen's life, though without breaking any radically new ground in our understanding of her works. Other interesting, though sometimes more tendentious, biographies of this period are *Hodge 1972, Rees 1976, Halperin 1984* and *Myer 1997*. The major biobibliographical event of this period has been the appearance of a third edition of Austen's collected letters. The two previous editions of 1932 and 1952 (edited by R. W. Chapman) have now been wholly revised and brought up-to-date by Deirdre Le Faye in *Jane Austen's Letters* (1995). In addition to incorporating new letters and new manuscript information that have come to light since Chapman's editions, Le Faye provides an invaluable new source of information by including a comprehensive and detailed list of places and people known to Jane Austen. (An important source and stimulus for this new edition of the letters was the manuscript research of *Modert 1990*).

The bibliographical landmark of Austen studies in this period was the appearance of David Gilson's magisterial *A Bibliography of Jane Austen* (1982), which is now the standard primary bibliography, also containing a complete list of secondary materials published up to 1978. Other important bibliographical works are *Roth and Weinsheimer 1973* (criticism 1952–1972), *Roth 1985* (criticism 1973–1983), *Southam 1987* (criticism 1870–1940), and Gilson and Grey 1989 (criticism on the juvenilia and *Lady Susan*). The many collections of essays that have appeared in this period often provide bibliographical surveys or essays in addition to presenting a representative sample of critical views in their main contents. Inevitably, there was a spate of bicentenary collections in 1975 (*Halperin, Lee, Nineteenth-Century Fiction, Weinsheimer;* and *McMaster 1976,*

Ruoff 1976), and these offered a convenient focus for reviewing Austen's reputation and the "state of the art" in Austen criticism—see, for example, Duckworth 1975. Other key essay collections were *Monaghan 1981* (Austen in a social context), *Todd 1983* (new perspectives on Austen; again, see Duckworth's essay in this collection for a review of critical approaches), *Grey 1989* (an invaluable addition to criticism of the juvenilia and *Lady Susan), Looser 1995* (feminist perspectives), *McMaster and Stovel 1996* (a general collection but with an emphasis on *Persuasion*); and see also Jane Austen Society, *Collected Reports of the Jane Austen Society* (1977, 1989) both for their main essays and for their annual bibliographies. Casebook-style collections on specific Austen works have proliferated since the 1970s and, because of their narrower focus, these are often particularly valuable in demonstrating how critical responses to Austen have developed. Southam's two 1976 *Casebooks* cover all the novels except *Emma* (which was dealt with in Lodge's separate volume in 1968), and a series of *New Casebooks* has recently started to appear: so far, we have had *Monaghan 1992* (on *Emma*) and *Clark 1994* (on *Sense and Sensibility* and *Pride and Prejudice*)—both volumes contain excellent introductions that neatly survey the critical scene since the 1970s, and Monaghan's volume in particular has a very useful annotated list of further reading. Similar volumes are *Petersen 1979* (on *Pride and Prejudice*), *Bloom 1987* (three volumes in the Modern Critical Interpretations, on *Emma, Mansfield Park,* and *Pride and Prejudice*), *Cookson and Loughrey 1988* (on *Emma*), *Folsom 1993* (on *Pride and Prejudice*), and *Wood 1993* (on *Mansfield Park*). To these collections can be added several monograph studies and study guides on individual novels: *Havely 1973* (on *Mansfield Park), Whitten 1974* (on *Persuasion), Jefferson 1977* (on *Emma), Smith 1978* (on *Mansfield Park), Gard 1985* (on *Emma* and *Persuasion), Armstrong 1988* (on *Mansfield Park), Moler 1989* (on *Pride and Prejudice), Berendsen 1991* (on *Emma), Ruoff 1992* (on *Sense and Sensibility), Armstrong 1994* (on *Sense and Sensibility), Sacco 1995* (on *Sanditon*).

For essay surveys of Austen criticism and Austen's critical reputation not mentioned elsewhere in this entry, see Allen 1995, Armstrong 1990, Bald 1923, Brown 1973, Brown 1990, Child 1915, Dillon 1992, Duckworth 1991, Harris 1981, Lee 1990, Leighton 1983, MacCarthy 1947, Marshall 1992, Neill 1987, Odom 1989, Parker 1990, Pickrel 1985, 1987, Rosmarin 1984, Roth 1985, 1994, Sabor 1991, Said 1989, Sandock 1993, Southam 1969, 1971, 1974, Thompson 1994, Weinsheimer 1983.

Croft, Admiral (*Persuasion* Ch.3; I:3:21). An unsophisticated but direct, open-hearted, and honest man with an illustrious sea career behind him, including action at the Battle of Trafalgar. He rents Kellynch Hall from Sir Walter Elliot, and, as an unaffected, sensible, and successful man of action, he serves as a foil for the vain, foolish, and ineffectual baronet.

Croft, Mrs. Sophia, née Wentworth (*Persuasion* Ch.3; I:3:22–23). Wife of Admiral Croft and sister of Captain Wentworth. She is similar to her husband in her frank good nature and sociability, as well as in her physical vigor and robustness, having lived on board ships with him for much of their married life and being capable of surviving his regular carriage accidents.

Curtis, Mr. (*The Watsons, Minor Works* 321). The surgeon at Guildford with whom Sam Watson is employed.

D

Dalrymple, the Dowager Viscountess (*Persuasion* Ch.16; II:4:148–50). The Elliots' rich cousin, whose friendship they seek to reestablish after a period of estrangement. She is an unremarkable woman, "without any superiority of manner, accomplishment or understanding," though because she has a smile "and a civil answer for every body," she has gained a reputation for being "charming." She is the mother of the Honorable Miss Carteret.

Dalrymple, Viscount (deceased) (*Persuasion* Ch.16; II:4:148–49). A relative of the Elliots whose death was the cause of a breach between the two families, as no letter of condolence was written to his widow by the Elliots, owing to Sir Walter's own dangerous illness at the time. This omission was repaid in kind by the Dalrymples on the death of Lady Elliot, and the two families had not communicated since.

Darcy, Lady Anne, née Fitzwilliam (*Pride and Prejudice* Ch.16; I:16:83). Mr. Fitzwilliam Darcy's late mother and sister to Lady Catherine de Bourgh. Lady Anne and Lady Catherine had planned a match between their respective children, Fitzwilliam and Anne, almost as soon as they were born, and it is this "tacit engagement" that Lady Catherine insists upon later when trying to dissuade Eliza Bennet from marrying Darcy.

Darcy, Miss Georgiana (*Pride and Prejudice* Chs.8, 44; I:8:36, 38–39; III:2: 261). Mr. Darcy's younger sister, who is sixteen years old when we first meet her. Our first substantial information about Miss Darcy comes from Mr. Wickham, who, talking to Elizabeth Bennet, describes her as a handsome and highly accomplished young girl who, since her father's death, has lived in London with a companion (Mrs. Annesley) who superintends her education. He also describes her as "much like her brother,—very, very proud," and this view of her is later corroborated by other, less prejudiced sources. However, her reputation for being "exceedingly proud" turns out to be unfounded and based on a misperception of what is actually extreme shyness, and when Elizabeth finally meets Miss Darcy for herself, she is pleasantly surprised to find her entirely unassuming and good-natured. We later learn, from Mr. Darcy, that when his sister had first gone to live in London, she had been in the care of a Mrs. Younge, who, on a trip with her fifteen-year-old charge to Ramsgate, had helped Mr. George Wickham insinuate himself into Miss Darcy's affections to the point at which she believed herself in love and ready to elope with him. Fortunately, Miss Darcy's concern for the feelings of her brother had obliged her to inform him of her situation, and he had arrived in time to rescue her from almost certain ruin at the hands of Wickham, whose main object had been her fortune of £30,000.

Darcy, Mr. (deceased) (*Pride and Prejudice* Chs. 16, 35; I:16:78–81; II:12: 199–200). Fitzwilliam Darcy's father and previous owner of Pemberley. He has been dead for five years at the start of the main action of the story. The steward of his estates at Pemberley, Mr. Wickham (senior), had discharged his duties so honorably and efficiently that Mr. Darcy had been "naturally inclined . . . to be of service to him," and he had taken particular interest in the progress of his son, George, whose godfather he had become. Mr. Darcy had "liberally bestowed" his kindness on George, paying for his education through school and Cambridge University and informally providing for him in his will. As we learn later, of course, George Wickham's engaging manners in the company of the late Mr. Darcy had been a front for his real personality and his real motives, which were entirely mercenary.

Darcy, Mr. Fitzwilliam (*Pride and Prejudice* Ch.3; I:3:10). The son of the late Mr. Darcy and Lady Anne (Fitzwilliam) Darcy and present owner of Pemberley in Derbyshire, with an income of £10,000 a year. Mr. Darcy is initially presented as a cold, reserved, even arrogant character, disdainful of those beneath him in the social hierarchy, and full of his own self-importance. His apparent class pride, his general aloofness, and his rudeness to her at the Meryton assembly immediately turn Elizabeth Bennet against him, and in several subsequent exchanges between these two characters, this initial impression of Darcy is consolidated. However, later in the book, another picture emerges as the integrity and nobility of his character are gradually illustrated—through revelations about his true role in the Wickham affair; through his high reputation as the benevolent custodian of Pemberley; through his charitable and tactful management of the Lydia–Wickham affair; through his readiness to admit, and make amends for, his mistakes of officiousness, pride, and prejudice in his dealings with Elizabeth and Jane Bennet; and last, but certainly not least, through the depth and sincerity of his passion for Elizabeth.

Darling, Mrs. (*Sanditon, Minor Works* 408). Apparently a close friend of Mrs. Griffiths and the last link, after Fanny Noyce and Miss Capper, in Diana Parker's chain of connections to Mrs. Griffiths in her aspect as "the West Indians."

Dashwood, Elinor (*Sense and Sensibility* Ch.1; I:1:6). The central character of *Sense and Sensibility*, through whose consciousness most of the action is filtered and appraised (even though the novel is narrated in the third person). If the novel is viewed as a type of dramatized debate between the competing claims of "sense" and "sensibility," then Elinor is clearly intended to represent a balanced fusion of both sets of qualities, though her self-restraint and down-to-earth good sense are most immediately apparent. At nineteen, she is the eldest daughter of Mr. and Mrs. Henry Dashwood and the most well balanced personality of all the Dashwood women, with "strength of understanding, and coolness of judgment," but also with an affectionate disposition and strong but controlled feelings. She falls in love early on with Edward Ferrars while they are both at Norland, but, though the attraction seems mutual, he does not openly declare his feelings for her and allows her to leave for Devonshire with her mother and sisters without indicating any desire to continue the relationship. Elinor realistically acknowledges that she is probably too poor to be considered an eligible match for Edward, but she continues to love him and maintains a secret hope that they may one day be married. When she learns of his secret engagement to Lucy Steele, she is deeply mortified and disappointed, though she retains her outward composure and does not speak to anyone about her feelings. She soon reasons out for herself the likely circumstances of Edward's youthful engagement to Lucy, and she consoles herself with the thought that he does not genuinely love Lucy as he loves her—indeed, imagining *his* predicament (in feeling duty-bound to marry Lucy but without loving her), Elinor selflessly feels more pity for Edward than she does for herself. Elinor stoically resigns herself to her loss and in this goes on to present a stark contrast to her sister, Marianne, whom she calmly and steadily comforts through her own uninhibited distress at losing Willoughby. Elinor's patience and fortitude and her constancy in love are eventually rewarded when Lucy Steele unexpectedly marries Robert Ferrars (for his money) and thus finally clears the way for Edward and Elinor to marry.

Dashwood, Fanny, née Ferrars (*Sense and Sensibility* Ch.1; I:1:5). Wife of John Dashwood and sister of Edward and Robert Ferrars. More selfish, snobbish, materialistic, and mean-spirited than her husband, Fanny Dashwood is also much more calculating than he is and much more clever, so that she is almost always able to manipulate him into the actions and opinions that suit her. The best example of this (and a classic example of Jane Austen's ability to have her characters expose and condemn themselves through their own mouths) is the famous scene at the start of the book (Ch.2) where, with coldhearted persistence, Fanny slowly and skillfully brings her husband to reason falsely that his father in fact wished him *not* to give financial help to his stepmother and sisters when he asked him to promise to help them.

Dashwood, Harry (*Sense and Sensibility* Ch.1; I:1:4). The only son of John and Fanny Dashwood, who, as an infant, had become such a favorite with old Mr. Dashwood that the latter had bequeathed Norland Park to him, despite the apparently stronger claim of Henry Dashwood's family.

Dashwood, Henry (*Sense and Sensibility* Ch.1; I:1:3). Nephew of old Mr. Dashwood and the immediate legal heir to the estate of Norland Park. He is the father of John Dashwood by his first marriage and of Elinor, Marianne, and Margaret Dashwood by his second. As his son is well provided for, Henry Dashwood is anxious to inherit Norland in such a way as to be able to make adequate provision for his second family, but his uncle entails the estate to John and Harry Dashwood so that when Henry himself dies, one year after his uncle, the estate passes to his son rather than to his wife and daughters. Henry Dashwood's last act before his death, therefore, is to secure his son's promise to look after Mrs. Dashwood and the three girls—though this is a promise that is not kept.

Dashwood, John (*Sense and Sensibility* Ch.1; I:1:3). Son of Henry Dashwood by the latter's first marriage. He inherits a large fortune from his mother on her death and increases his wealth when he marries Fanny Ferrars shortly after reaching the age of twenty-one. On the death of his father, he inherits the Norland estate, which is entailed on his four-year-old son, Harry. At his father's deathbed, he had been prevailed upon to promise to make adequate provision for his stepmother and half sisters, but he is "rather cold hearted, and rather selfish," and he is easily persuaded to break this promise by his mean and grasping wife, who, we hear, is "a strong caricature of himself—more narrow-minded and selfish." He initially intended to give Mrs. Dashwood and her daughters £1,000 each, but, under the influence of his wife, he soon talks himself out of this idea by means of some absurd reasoning, and he finally gives them nothing at all. This early impression of John Dashwood as a heartless, mercenary, and somewhat stupid character remains more or less constant throughout the rest of the novel, though as the narrative progresses, his crass materialism becomes more a source of satiric humor than of serious moral censure.

Dashwood, Margaret (*Sense and Sensibility* Ch.1; I:17). Youngest daughter of Mr. and Mrs. Henry Dashwood. Margaret is "a good-humoured well-disposed girl" whose nature, at thirteen, already shows a marked resemblance to that of her romantically inclined sister, Marianne, though Margaret lacks Marianne's understanding.

Dashwood, Marianne (*Sense and Sensibility* Ch.1; I:1:6). One of the two heroines of the novel, Marianne, who is only just seventeen when the main part of her story begins, is the second daughter of Mr. and Mrs. Henry Dashwood and sister of Elinor and Margaret. Marianne is the novel's chief representative of "sensibility," and, as such, she is gently satirized throughout the novel for her excessive emotionalism and unrealistically romantic notions about love. But it is clear from the start that we are also intended to admire her for her many positive qualities, too, and to recognize that most of her faults are the faults of youth and inexperience rather than of any fundamental weakness of character. Her "sensibility," moreover (her spontaneity, outspoken disregard of convention, and romantic idealism), is not seen in entirely negative terms either, for if it is excessive at times and leads her into much suffering, it is at least more honest and less calculating than the so-called sense of coldhearted characters such as John and Fanny Dashwood, Mrs. Ferrars, and Lucy Steele. Indeed, in some ways, Marianne's "excessive" demands on life stand as a sort of critique of her society's narrow concern with money, manners, and social position (and, in a more complex way, they can also be seen to represent a type of feminist protest against the rationalized constraints that the society of the time imposed upon women's emotional lives). Marianne's character at the start of the novel, with its uneven blend of sense and sensibility, is neatly summed up by the narrator as follows: "Marianne's abilities were, in many respects, quite equal to Elinor's. She was sensible and clever; but eager in every thing; her sorrows, her joys, could have no moderation. She was generous, amiable, interesting: she was every thing but prudent." Marianne's "eager" disposition, indeed, leads her into an immoderate and imprudent romance with the duplicitous John Willoughby, who encourages her to fall in love with him and then abandons her to marry an heiress for her money. Her romantic dreams shattered by this, Marianne becomes listless and withdrawn; she falls seriously ill with pneumonia after catching a cold, and she very nearly dies. She survives, however, and, out of her disillusionment and suffering, comes to understand the folly of her previous actions and attitudes and, in particular, the dangers of a sensibility insufficiently informed by sense. She resolves in the future to temper her passions and to control her romantic imagination by a "calm and sober judgment." At the end of the novel, Marianne is a much wiser, more mature, and more balanced person than she was at the beginning, and, at nineteen, she happily marries her long-standing admirer, the steady and reliable Colonel Brandon, whom she had initially rejected as being too old and dull and unromantic for a husband.

Dashwood, Miss (*Sense and Sensibility* Ch.1; I:1:3). The sister of old Mr. Dashwood and his constant companion and housekeeper for many years until her death ten years before his own.

Dashwood, Mr. (deceased) (*Sense and Sensibility* Ch.1; I:1:3–4). The late owner of the long-established Dashwood estate in Sussex centered on Norland Park. After the death of Miss Dashwood, he invited the family of his nephew and legal inheritor, Henry Dashwood, to come live with him. Old Mr. Dashwood's death provides the initial complicating action of the plot, for, although he does leave the estate to his nephew in the first instance, the terms of his will are such as, in effect, to disinherit his nephew's second wife and three daughters in favor of the son of a first marriage, John Dashwood, and *his* son, Harry Dashwood. Thus when Henry Dashwood dies just a year after his uncle, Mrs. Dashwood and her daughters have no rights at Norland, and they are soon forced out of their home by John Dashwood and his wife, Fanny.

Dashwood, Mrs. (deceased) (*Sense and Sensibility* Ch.1; I:1:3). First wife of Henry Dashwood and mother of John Dashwood. The whole of her large fortune was secured to her son (although Henry Dashwood had a life interest in half of it), and therefore he and his family are already amply provided for even before inheriting the Norland estate, while Henry Dashwood's second family are left, on the latter's death, with no home of their own and only £10,000 between them.

Dashwood, Mrs. Henry (*Sense and Sensibility* Ch.1; I:1:3–4). Second wife of Mr. Henry Dashwood and mother of Elinor, Marianne, and Margaret. She has no fortune of her own and is therefore left in relatively straitened circumstances by the death of her husband. Mrs. Dashwood resembles her impetuous second daughter, Marianne, more than her sensible first daughter, Elinor. She has "an eagerness of mind" and immoderately "strong feelings" that would together invariably lead to imprudent behavior if it were not for the restraining influence of Elinor. In fact, Mrs. Dashwood positively values Marianne's romantic "sensibility" and frequently encourages her in her excessive emotionalism. But if, in some ways, she fails to give her daughters sensible advice and guidance (and therefore contributes to Marianne's near-downfall at Willoughby's hands), Mrs. Dashwood is a kindly and warmhearted soul whose childlike eagerness is also often endearing. She is certainly a tender, loving, and selfless mother to all three of her daughters and, with others, considerate almost to a fault, with rarely a harsh word for anyone.

Davies, Doctor (*Sense and Sensibility* Ch.32; II:10:218). A supposed admirer of Miss Anne Steele, about whom she likes to be teased.

Davis, Charlotte (*Northanger Abbey* Ch.27; II:12:217). Captain Tilney's partner at the end of his stay at Bath, preferred by him to Isabella Thorpe.

Davis, Mrs. (*Sanditon, Minor Works* 389). A visitor to Sanditon noted by Mr. Parker in the subscription list at the circulating library. *See* Beard, Mr.

Dawson (*Pride and Prejudice* Ch.37; II:14:211). Lady Catherine de Bourgh's maid, who "does not object to the Barouche box"—that is, she is happy to travel in the outside box of Lady Catherine's carriage if it is necessary to make room inside for guests.

De Bourgh, Lady Catherine (*Pride and Prejudice* Chs.13, 29, 56; I:13:62–63; II:6:161–62; III:14:351–59). Mr. Fitzwilliam Darcy's maternal aunt and owner of the estate of Rosings in Kent. She is a member of the lesser aristocracy and full of her own self-importance. An extreme snob, she deals with others in an insufferably overbearing and arrogant manner, best illustrated by her bullying attempt to frighten Elizabeth Bennet away from any romantic involvement with Mr. Darcy (Ch.56; III:14). Lady Catherine has, of course, long cherished the mercenary hope of uniting the estates of Rosings and Pemberley by making a match between Darcy and her own daughter, Anne. Elizabeth's spirited and intelligent response to the vulgar presumption of Lady Catherine is one of the most satisfying scenes in the novel as we see reason and personal integrity triumph over the insolence of wealth and social position. As things turn out, moreover, Lady Catherine makes matters worse for herself when she tells Darcy of Elizabeth's response, for this encourages him to propose to Elizabeth once more.

De Bourgh, Miss Anne (*Pride and Prejudice* Chs.14 29; I:14:67; II:6:162). Lady Catherine de Bourgh's only daughter and heiress to Rosings and other extensive property. Dominated by her mother, spoiled and overprotected by her former governess and present companion, Mrs. Jenkinson, Miss de Bourgh has little to say for herself and is, in appearance, thin, pale, sickly, and cross-looking. From the moment Miss de Bourgh was born, her mother had planned for her to marry Mr. Darcy, and when Elizabeth Bennet first sees her, at a time when she is still prejudiced against Darcy, she thinks mischievously to herself that Miss de Bourgh will make the proud Mr. Darcy "a very proper wife." But, of course, Mr. Darcy has no intention of marrying his cousin and in the end, much to Lady Catherine's annoyance, marries Elizabeth herself.

De Bourgh, Sir Lewis (deceased) (*Pride and Prejudice* Ch.13; I:13:62). Lady Catherine de Bourgh's late husband, mentioned only in passing.

De Courcy, Catherine (*Lady Susan, Minor Works*). *See* Vernon, Mrs. Catherine.

De Courcy, Lady C. (*Lady Susan, Minor Works* 246, 263). Wife of Sir Reginald De Courcy of Parklands, Sussex, and mother of Reginald and Mrs. Catherine Vernon.

De Courcy, Reginald (*Lady Susan, Minor Works* 247, 248). The eldest son of the De Courcy family of Parklands, Sussex. He is a handsome, lively, clever young man about twenty-three years old when we meet him, and he becomes, for a time, the besotted lover of Lady Susan, although he is skeptical of her allure before he meets her. In fact, it is precisely because he feels so confident of resisting her charms and so confident of being her superior that she becomes so determined to subdue his "insolent" spirit and make him acknowledge *her* superiority. His doubts about Lady Susan are rekindled later by her harsh treatment of her daughter, Frederica (who has fallen in love with him herself), though it is not until he finds out about her continuing affair with Mr. Manwaring in London that the "spell" of Lady Susan is removed, and he sees clearly that she has made a fool of him. He remains disillusioned about love for some time after this experience, but we are given to believe that he will eventually marry Frederica Vernon.

De Courcy, Sir Reginald (*Lady Susan, Minor Works* 256, 260). Owner of the Parklands estate in Sussex and father of Reginald and Mrs. Catherine Vernon.

De Feuillide, Eliza. *See* Hancock, Eliza.

Denham, Lady, née Brereton (*Sanditon, Minor Works* 375–77, 399–402). Lady Denham of Sanditon House owns a large part of the parish of Sanditon and is Thomas Parker's "Colleague in Speculation" in promoting its development as a fashionable seaside resort. She had been born to money (though not to education, we are told) and then had increased her wealth substantially by means of her first marriage to the elderly Mr. Hollis, who, on his death shortly afterward, left her all his extensive properties in the area. She then married Sir Harry Denham of Denham Park, from whom she acquired her title but to whom she relinquished none of her money or property, so that after his death she returned to Sanditon House with her fortune intact. At the start of the novel, she is seventy years old with three families more or less discreetly vying for her favor and fortune: the Breretons, the Denhams, and the Hollises. We hear of her first when Mr. Parker describes her to Charlotte Heywood as an active, spirited, and essentially good-natured woman but one whose self-importance and love of money sometimes overshadow her better qualities. He puts any faults she may have down to her lack of education and culture, though he makes clear that she is a naturally shrewd and quick-witted woman. When Charlotte herself meets her, however, and hears her talk coldly and calculatingly about money and relatives, she soon decides that Mr. Parker's "mild" judgment of Lady Denham has more to do with his own good nature than with her real character, which she finds arrogant and overbearing and downright mean.

Denham, Miss Esther (*Sanditon, Minor Works* 394, 396). The hypocritical and grasping sister of Sir Edward Denham. She is haughty, cold, and reserved when she visits the Parkers and meets Charlotte, but shortly afterward, when seen in the company of Lady Denham, she has suddenly become animated and attentive, clearly intent on sucking up to her rich relative. Such guile, we are told, can be seen as either amusing or sad, depending on whether we read it satirically or morally.

Denham, Sir Edward, Bart (*Sanditon, Minor Works* 377, 394). Sir Edward fancies himself as a dashing, dangerous seducer "quite in the line of the Lovelaces." He feels duty-bound to flatter any young lady he finds himself with and to try to dazzle her with the range of his literary allusions. He is handsome and, at first, agreeable, and Charlotte is, indeed, flattered by his eloquent and apparently sincere attentions to her. But when she sees him behaving in a similar fashion with Clara Brereton, she realizes he is not to be trusted. In talking about poetry and fiction with Charlotte, he becomes something of a caricature through which Jane Austen parodies the excesses of sentimental and romantic literature. When he rants about novels of "strong Passion" where our hearts are paralyzed, and our reason "half-dethroned," Charlotte coolly thinks to herself that he has read more sentimental novels than are good for him; and when she hears his nonsensical perorations on Romantic poetry and the sublimity of the sea, she thinks him just "downright silly."

Denham, Sir Harry, Bart (deceased) (*Sanditon, Minor Works* 375). Second husband of Lady Denham and the uncle of Sir Edward and Esther Denham. His full-length portrait has pride of place in the sitting room at Sanditon House.

Dennison, Mrs. (*Sense and Sensibility* Ch.36; II:14:248, 252). A London acquaintance of Mrs. Fanny Dashwood's. When she calls at the Dashwoods' house in Harley Street one day, her visit happens to coincide with that of Elinor and Marianne. She naturally assumes that the sisters are staying there as guest of their half brother and sister-in-law, so she later includes them in an invitation for a musical evening she has organized, thus obliging Fanny Dashwood to send her carriage for them and, "what was still worse," to appear as though she were treating them with attention.

Denny, Mr. (*Pride and Prejudice* Ch.14; I:14:68). Mr. Denny is one of the officers in the militia regiment stationed at Meryton under the command of Colonel Forster. He introduces his friend Mr. Wickham into the regiment and is frequently mentioned by Lydia Bennet in her vacuous chatter about the Meryton officers. After Wickham elopes with Lydia, it becomes clear that Denny has been party to Wickham's intentions, though he pretends not to have known anything about the matter when questioned by Colonel Forster.

"Detached Pieces" (*Volume the First* of Jane Austen's juvenilia). Called "Miscellanious [*sic*] Morsels" by Jane Austen herself, these short pieces were dedicated on 2 June 1793 to her second niece, Anna (born on 15 April 1793)—and presumably copied from the lost originals on or around that date and possibly written around that time, too. There are three pieces or morsels, although the first is canceled in the manuscript. "A Fragment, Written to Inculcate the Practise of Virtue" is a very short mock-sermon that appears to criticize the leisured elite who "perspire away their Evenings in crouded [*sic*] assemblies" with no thought for those who "sweat under the fatigue of their daily Labour" (*Minor Works* 71). "A Beautiful Description of the Different Effects of Sensibility on Different Minds" is a burlesque of a sentimental sickbed scene as might have appeared in popular novels of the time. Although only just over a page long, it is quite remarkable for the rapidity with which it sets the scene and evokes a sense of each of its nine characters: the first-person narrator; the sickly Melissa and (presumably) her family, Sir William, Mrs. Burnaby, Julia, Maria, Anna; the "melancholy" Charles, who is possibly Melissa's lover; and the punning Dr. Dowkins, who, on hearing that Melissa is "very weak," responds with, "aye indeed it is more than a very *week* since you have taken to your bed" (*Minor Works* 72). "The Generous Curate, a Moral Tale, Setting Forth the Advantages of Being Generous and a Curate" is an inconclusive (possibly unfinished) "history" of Mr. Williams and his family of six. His eldest son (like Jane Austen's two sailor brothers, Frank and Charles) becomes a sailor after attending the naval academy at Portsmouth and, while stationed in Newfoundland, sends home a large Newfoundland dog every month (unlike Jane Austen's brothers!).

Devereux, Sir Henry ("Catharine," *Minor Works* 199). An acquaintance of the Stanleys who has promised to go with them on their autumn trip to the Lake District.

Dixon, Mr. (*Emma* Ch.19; II:1:159–61). The "rich and agreeable" young man, owner of Balycraig in Ireland, who marries Colonel Campbell's daughter, Jane Fairfax's adoptive sister. Jane Fairfax's visit to Highbury arises partly as a result of the Campbells' going to stay with their daughter in Ireland. Although Jane had also been invited to Ireland, she chose to come to Highbury instead. Miss Bates describes Mr. Dixon as "a most amiable, charming young man," and when Emma also hears about his rescue of Jane, when she nearly fell from a boat during a water party in Weymouth, Emma starts to imagine a secret affair between Jane and Mr. Dixon. Frank Churchill later encourages her in this fantasy, as it helps him to keep hidden his own relationship with Jane.

Dixon, Mrs. (*Emma* Chs.12, 20; I:12:104; II:2:163–65). Daughter of Colonel and Mrs. Campbell and devoted girlhood companion to Jane Fairfax. Her "warm attachment" to Jane encouraged her parents in their idea of adopting Jane, and they lived together almost as sisters and with "unabated regard" until the marriage of Miss Campbell to Mr. Dixon.

Donavan, Mr. (*Sense and Sensibility* Ch.37; III:1:257). The apothecary or physician who is called in to confirm that Mrs. Palmer's newborn child is suffering from nothing worse than "red-gum" or teething rash. Before calling at Mrs. Palmer's house, it happens that Mr. Donavan had just been to the Dashwoods' home in Harley Street, where he had been called to attend to Fanny Dashwood, who had fallen into violent hysterics after learning about her brother's secret engagement to Lucy Steele. Mr. Donavan is therefore able to pass this gossip on to Mrs. Palmer's mother, Mrs. Jennings.

"Dorothy" (*Northanger Abbey* Ch.20; II:5:158–60). An imaginary "ancient housekeeper" conjured up by Henry Tilney as part of the teasing parody of gothic romance that he relates to the credulous Catherine Morland on their journey to Northanger Abbey from Bath in his curricle.

Drew, Sir Archibald (*Persuasion* Ch.18; II:6:170). An old friend of Admiral Croft, seen walking along Milsom Street in Bath with his grandson. He kisses his hand to Anne Elliot, mistaking her for Admiral Croft's wife.

Drummond, Miss (*Northanger Abbey*). *See* Tilney, Mrs.

Dudley, Rev. and family ("Catharine," *Minor Works* 195). Rev. Dudley is the replacement for Rev. Wynne at Chetwynde, but he and his wife and daughter are no replacement for the Wynnes as far as Catharine Percival is concerned. The Dudleys are quarrelsome, conceited, and ill educated. Both Mr. and Mrs. Dudley come from distinguished families (he is the younger brother of Lord Amyatt), and they bear a grudge about their present lowly position and lack of standing in the local community; this is the cause of much of their antagonism toward that community. The daughter had merely inherited her parents' disagreeable qualities.

Duke of—, the (*Mansfield Park* Ch.13; I:13:122). Referred to by the Hon. John Yates as a leading actor in the private theatricals held at Lord Ravenshaw's seat, Ecclesford, in Cornwall; for his acting, "the duke was thought very great by many."

Dupuis, Mrs. Charles (*Sanditon, Minor Works* 411). The friend of Diana Parker who, through friends of friends, has helped to have Sanditon recommended to a Camberwell girls' school (i.e., Mrs. Griffiths).

Durands, the little (*Persuasion* Ch.21; II:9:193). Mrs. Smith talks of them as familiar faces in Bath who never miss a concert. She describes them as baby sparrows with their mouths constantly open as though trying to catch the music.

E

"Edgar and Emma, a Tale" (*Volume the First* of Jane Austen's juvenilia). A satire on sentimental fiction containing three very short chapters, this piece was probably written early in the period 1787–1790 and copied from the lost original shortly afterward. The tale ends in abrupt bathos when Emma Marlow, hoping for a visit from her beloved Edgar Willmot, learns of his absence from home and retires to her room to spend the rest of her life in tears. Other characters are Emma's parents, Sir Godfrey and Lady Marlow of Marlhurst in Sussex and her unnamed sister; neighbors of the Marlows, Mr. and Mrs. Willmot of Willmot Lodge and their innumerable family of more than twenty children, fifteen of whom are named, including the Edgar of the title; and Thomas, who appears to be a servant in the Marlows' home.

Edward(e)s, Mary (*The Watsons, Minor Works* 320–21, 322–23). Mary Edwards is twenty-two years old and an only daughter, with about £10,000 settled on her. Elizabeth Watson suggests that she is rather prim, but, once her initial reserve has dropped, Emma finds her quite friendly, unpretentious, and sensible. Emma's brother, Sam, is a great admirer of Mary, but it seems he stands little chance of winning her hand because of his lowly status. Another contender for Mary's hand is Captain Hunter, with whom she dances at the ball.

Edward(e)s, Mr. (*The Watsons, Minor Works* 314, 323). A well-to-do gentleman in the town of D. in Surrey. He always invites the Watsons to stay over at his house when there is a ball in the town. He is an easygoing and friendly man who puts Emma at her ease after her rather stiff reception by his wife and daughter—though he also appears to be something of a gossip and busybody. He also seems keen to impress upon Emma that her brother Sam is not a suitable match for his daughter.

Edward(e)s, Mrs. (*The Watsons, Minor Works* 319, 322–23, 338–39). Emma Watson at first finds Mrs. Edwards a little intimidating; she is friendly but restrained and reserved in her manner. However, she becomes more relaxed with Emma as the evening of the ball wears on, and on the following day she supports Emma in her refusal to be driven home by Tom Musgrave by diplomatically offering her the family carriage to go home in.

"Elinor and Marianne." An early epistolary version of *Sense and Sensibility*. Nothing of this version survives. It was probably written in 1795, and it was revised as the later novel in 1797–1798.

Elliot, Anne (*Persuasion* Ch.1; I:1:3, 5–6). The second daughter of Sir Walter Elliot and the novel's principal character, whose stalled and gradually renewed romance with Captain Frederick Wentworth provides the narrative with its main focus and direction. The most mature of Jane Austen's major heroines, Anne Elliot is twenty-seven at the start of the novel, and, though she had once been very pretty, she has suffered "an early loss of bloom and spirits" as a result of the broken engagement with Wentworth that took place when she was nineteen. She is, moreover, marginalized by the other members of her family, who are snobbish, conceited, and almost wholly dominated by materialistic values that make her seem a "nobody" in their eyes. But she slowly moves to the center of the stage—growing in self-confidence and regaining her bloom and spirits as she does so—as circumstances serve to foreground her strength of character and her elegance of mind and manners and as she becomes an object of desire for Mr. Elliot and then of renewed love for Captain Wentworth, whom she finally marries.

As well as being the main character, Anne is the center of consciousness in the novel, through whose eyes most of the events are perceived and judged (even though the novel is narrated in the third person). Her essential reliability as a sort of second narrator is established early on as we learn of her "elegant and cultivated mind" and "sweetness of character" and see evidence of her sound judgment and practical good sense when she advises her father over the retrenchments necessary at Kellynch Hall. There are times when Anne is gently mocked by the actual narrator's irony for some naïveté or priggishness, but on the whole we trust to her qualities of mind and outlook to guide us throughout the novel: to her sensible, rational intelligence and penetrating moral discernment, to her love of honesty and openness, and to her dislike of affectation and snobbery.

Elliot, Elizabeth (*Persuasion* Ch.1; I:1:3, 5–10). Eldest daughter of Sir Walter Elliot and almost his equal in terms of vanity, pride, and snobbish self-importance. She is twenty-nine at the start of the novel, and, for the thirteen years since the death of her mother, she has been able to indulge her sense of superiority by acting as the first lady of Kellynch Hall and its surrounding neighborhood. In fact, her life seems to have been a mindless round of "prosperity and . . . nothingness," and that effectively sums up her character, too, for although she has pretensions to elegance and gentility, she is actually an empty-headed, vulgar woman, lacking in any real refinement, judgment, or talent. The only fly in the ointment of her privileged existence so far has been her failure to find a husband, a fact made more painful by the bitter memory of having been snubbed some ten years ago by the cousin she had hoped to marry, Mr. William Walter Elliot. She is still angry about his disdainful treatment of her and of her family name, so that even when she hears that his wife has died, "she could not admit him to be worth thinking of again." But this apparently firm resolution is quickly forgotten when Mr. Elliot turns up at Bath, apparently eager to renew his contact with the family. Elizabeth mistakenly assumes his intention is to court her, and thus she is led, partly by her own vanity and lack of insight, to a second humiliation at his hands, when he eventually elopes with Mrs. Clay. This, of course, is doubly ironic in showing up Elizabeth's lack of judgment, as she had adopted the scheming Mrs. Clay as a companion and confidante in preference to her own sister, Anne.

Elliot, Lady Elizabeth, née Stevenson (deceased) (*Persuasion* Ch.1; I:1:3). Sir Walter Elliot's late wife, who had died in 1800 after seventeen years of marriage when her second daughter, Anne, was fourteen years old. A sensible woman of sound judgment and understanding and with a character far superior to that of her husband, Lady Elliot had been a loving and conscientious mother and a dutiful, if not very happy, wife. She had done her best to establish and maintain the respectability of the family, despite the many failings of Sir Walter, and she had been especially careful and efficient in her management of the estate of Kellynch Hall. The family had had no financial problems while she lived; but as soon as her steadying hand had gone, Sir Walter had begun to live beyond his means, and matters had deteriorated rapidly until the point of the retrenchments at the start of the novel. Lady Elliot is very fondly remembered and missed by Anne Elliot, who appears to have inherited much of her mother's sensible character.

Elliot, Mary (*Persuasion*). *See* Musgrove, Mary.

Elliot, Mrs. (deceased) (*Persuasion* Chs.1, 15, 21; I:1:8; II:3:139; II:9:202). The wife of William Walter Elliot. Though of humble birth, being the daughter of a grazier and the granddaughter of a butcher, Mrs. Elliot was nevertheless very rich, and Mr. Elliot had married her solely for her money (preferring this immediate access to wealth to the more distant prospects offered by a marriage to Elizabeth Elliot). Mrs. Elliot seems genuinely to have loved her husband, but he treated her badly—Mrs. Smith later describes her as having been "too ignorant and giddy" for his respect—and their marriage was a very unhappy one. She has only recently died when the novel begins.

Elliot, Sir Walter (*Persuasion* Ch.1; I:1:3–5). Fifty-four-year-old widower and baronet of Kellynch Hall in Somersetshire, father of Elizabeth, Anne, and Mary. To some extent a comic caricature, with vanity his overriding vice, Sir Walter nevertheless represents one of Jane Austen's most sustained and forthright attacks on inherited wealth and position—on the "elegant stupidity," arrogance, and idleness of the old order of landed gentry. For although there are perhaps sharper satirical portraits of a similar type in other of the major novels, and although in some ways Sir Walter is only a minor character in the book, he and his foolishness open the novel and remain as important foreground presences throughout. His conceited, silly, and shallow character is summed up bluntly in both the first and the last chapters of the novel as if to emphasize his lack of development in between: we hear at the start that "vanity was the beginning and the end of Sir Walter Elliot's character . . . vanity of person and of situation" and at the end that he is "a foolish, spendthrift baronet, who had not had principle or sense enough to maintain himself in the situation in which Providence had placed him." Obsessed by the surface trappings of social rank, Sir Walter has none of the inner qualities—of intelligence, discrimination, prudence, or industry—that might justify his own high position, particularly as a large land owner; and his replacement at Kellynch by the self-made Admiral Croft (recently returned from helping to save the country from Napoleon) is clearly suggestive of Jane Austen's disdain of Sir Walter's class.

Elliot, William Walter (*Persuasion* Chs.1, 12, 17, 21; I:1:4, 7–9; I:12:104–7; II:5:160–61; II:9:199–211). Mr. Elliot is the great-grandson of a previous Sir Walter Elliot ("the second Sir Walter"), nephew of the present Sir Walter, and heir presumptive to the baronetcy of Kellynch Hall. He is about thirty-four years old at the start of the main action of the novel (his letter of 1803 in Ch.21; II:9 states that he was twenty-three then, and the novel begins in 1814, though he is described as being about thirty in Ch.12). He had become estranged from the Elliots some eleven years earlier after snubbing Elizabeth Elliot and marrying instead "a rich woman of inferior birth." He had been a poor law student, but this marriage had made him very wealthy and financially independent regardless of his future Kellynch inheritance; as we learn later, he had a strong dislike of the Kellynch Elliots and was only too glad to break off any contact with them at this time. At the start of the novel, his wife has recently died, and he is in mourning when, at Lyme, he first meets and becomes attracted to Anne Elliot (though he does not know she is his cousin at this point). Shortly afterward, Anne learns that he has unexpectedly reestablished contact with Sir Walter and Elizabeth in Bath. We later learn that this is because he has now set his heart on Sir Walter's title and has heard from his Bath friend, Colonel Wallis, that Mrs. Clay seems to have marital designs on the old man; if they were to marry and have offspring, this would prevent Mr. Elliot's inheriting the baronetcy, so he has decided to insinuate himself into the family in order to prevent Mrs. Clay from making any further advances with Sir Walter. His apparent reform of attitude toward the family leads Elizabeth to renew her hopes of a possible match with him, but he is delighted to find that the woman he had admired in Lyme turns out to be his cousin Anne, and it soon becomes quite clear that she, not Elizabeth, is the true focus of his romantic intentions. Anne is flattered by his interest, and she finds him superficially attractive: he is good-looking, sensible, well mannered, and generally charming. But she is suspicious of his sudden reappearance in the family and cannot entirely forget the apparent dissoluteness of his past life. In particular, though he is "rational, discreet, polished," he is "too generally agreeable" and not "open." When she later becomes reacquainted with Mrs. Smith and hears the history of the latter's acquaintance with Mr. Elliot, the whole truth about his character is finally revealed, and Anne's suspicions about him turn out to be well founded. Mrs. Smith describes him as "a man without heart or conscience; a designing, wary, cold-blooded being, who thinks only of himself." He is, she says, "black at heart, hollow and black." Anne now realizes the full extent of his dissembling behavior with her and realizes that he had hoped to marry her largely in order to maintain a watchful eye over Mrs. Clay. The duplicity of his character becomes clear to everyone at the end of the novel when it emerges that, having failed in his designs on Anne, he has seduced Mrs. Clay away from Sir Walter and has set up with her in London. We are left to understand that, being an able schemer herself, Mrs. Clay would probably soon find a way of making him marry her.

Elliotts, the (*Sense and Sensibility* Ch.36; II:14:252). Robert Ferrars' friends who live near Dartford in what is evidently a large house but which he describes as a "cottage." While he was staying there, he says, he succeeded in demonstrating to Lady Elliott how she might arrange the rooms so as to be able to hold a dance, thereby disproving (by his strange logic) the common assumption "that there can be no accommodations, no space in a cottage."

Ellis (*Mansfield Park* Ch.1; I:1:10). Maid to Maria and Julia Bertram at Mansfield Park.

Ellison, Mr. and Mrs. (*Sense and Sensibility* Ch.30; II:8:194–95). Guardians to Sophia Grey who are happy to see her married to Willoughby because of a persistent antagonism between her and Mrs. Ellison.

Elton, Mr. (Rev. Philip) (*Emma* Ch.1; I:1:13–14). Vicar of Highbury. Misled into believing Emma is attracted to him by her meddlesome matchmaking for Harriet Smith, he is indignant at finding himself forcefully rejected by Emma when he proposes to her. He then rushes into what appears to be a face-saving marriage to the rich but vulgar Miss Augusta Hawkins. Presented at first (by Mr. Knightley) as "a very good young man" (14) of six or seven and twenty years and "a great favourite wherever he goes" (66), in speech, manner, and action he actually shows himself to be a foolish, foppish, and quite ruthless social climber. He appears at his worst at the Crown Inn ball when he tries to avenge himself on Emma by humiliating Harriet Smith—though the attempt is foiled by Mr. Knightley.

Elton, Mrs. Augusta, née Hawkins (*Emma* Chs.21, 22, 32; II:3:174; II:4 & 14). The youngest of two daughters of a Bristol merchant (though having, fashionably, spent part of each winter at Bath), with an independent fortune "of so many thousands as would always be called ten." After her marriage to Mr. Elton, following his rejection by Emma Woodhouse, she high-handedly promotes herself as the first lady of Highbury (in conscious competition with Emma), largely by means of her constant bragging about the wealth of her sister, Selina, and brother-in-law, Mr. Suckling of Maple Grove near Bristol (who keeps two carriages). She imposes herself onto the local community and, among other things, presumes to patronize Jane Fairfax by finding her a post as a governess. Vain, showy, insensitive, and rude, she represents a classic early example of the vulgar nouveau riche character who would become such a mainstay of later nineteenth-century fiction.

Emily (*Northanger Abbey* Ch.14; I:14:115). With Sophia, one of two new "dear" friends that Anne Thorpe quickly acquires as a means of displacing her obvious resentment at being left out of the Clifton excursion party. It is typical of the overfamiliar Thorpes that she is already calling these friends by their first names, even though she has known them only for the morning.

Emma. A novel in three volumes, composed by Jane Austen between 21 January 1814 and 29 March 1815 and published by John Murray in December 1815 (though 1816 was printed on the title page). *Emma* was dedicated to the prince regent, later George IV, at his request. Jane Austen had ambivalent feelings about this, as she had never approved of the prince's behavior, and, in his notorious dispute with his estranged wife, Princess Caroline of Brunswick, she was rather more sympathetic to the latter. Nevertheless, Austen was advised by her family that the request was, in fact, something of a command (and she must also have realized that such a dedication would do no harm to sales of the book or to her general reputation), and so she went ahead with it. At this time (November 1815), Jane Austen was also shown around the prince regent's luxurious palace in London, Carlton House, and her contact there with the prince's chaplain and librarian, Rev. James Stanier Clarke, led to a humorous subsequent correspondence that provoked her composition of *Plan of a Novel*.

The fifth of her major novels (though the fourth to be published), *Emma* is considered by many to be her masterpiece, especially in terms of novelistic technique (and narrative technique in particular). Shortly after its publication, it elicited a highly laudatory and, subsequently, highly influential review from the writer Sir Walter Scott, who, praising it for its verisimilitude, its narrative control, and its precision of language and characterization, saw it as an important new departure for fiction toward greater realism. Scott's seminal insights into the craft of Austen's fiction have been echoed, in variously elaborated forms, down to the present day by other critics (and practitioners of fiction) who typically cite *Emma* as one of the first (if not *the* first) fully achieved modern novels, as well as one of the best. In an incisive essay from 1917, Reginald Farrer neatly sums up a common feeling about the novel: "Take it all in all, 'Emma' is the very climax of Jane Austen's work; and a real appreciation of 'Emma' is the final test of citizenship in her kingdom. . . . Only when the story has been thoroughly assimilated can the infinite delights and subtleties of its workmanship begin to be appreciated, as you realise the manifold complexity of the book's web, and find that every sentence, almost every epithet, has its definite reference to equally unemphasised points before and after in the development of the plot" (quoted in *Southam 1987*: 266).

The novel's opening sentence is almost as well known and as notoriously ironic as that of *Pride and Prejudice*, and, as with the latter, it yields its full significance only gradually as we progress through the novel: "Emma Woodhouse, handsome, clever, and rich, with a comfortable home and happy disposition, seemed to unite some of the best blessings of existence; and had lived nearly twenty-one years in the world with very little to distress or vex her." Much hinges on the initially innocent-looking word "seemed," of course, for, as in all of Austen's novels, nothing is quite as it appears at first, and the rest of the novel slowly but surely tests that simple "seeming" against a progressively more complex sense of the reality of Emma's situation. The sentence is, in part, a rendering of Emma's own complacent view of herself, and the novel is centrally concerned with her education into a more critical self-awareness and self-understanding (just as it is concerned with *our* education into a more critical and discriminating mode of reading and interpretation).

Emma Woodhouse is the mistress of her father's house, Hartfield, in Highbury, Surrey. Mrs. Woodhouse died when Emma and her elder sister, Isabella, were children, and they were brought up by their governess, Miss Taylor. After Isabella's marriage to John Knightley, brother to the Woodhouses' neighbor at Donwell Abbey, Mr. George Knightley, Miss Taylor became more of a friend and companion to Emma than a governess, and from around the age of sixteen Emma has been used to governing her own life and having more or less her own way. This and "a disposition to think a little too well of herself" are, we hear, the chief dangers that "threaten alloy to her many enjoyments." She, of course, is oblivious of these dangers, and, as we get to know more about her, we realize that her perceptions of herself and others are not as reliable as she believes.

Now, when Emma is almost twenty-one, there is a change at Hartfield, as Miss Taylor marries a well-to-do local man, Mr. Weston, and Emma is left in sole charge of the house with only her valetudinarian father for company. Emma fondly believes that she made the match between Miss Taylor and Mr. Weston, but when Mr. Knightley arrives and hears her make this boast, he questions its validity and reproves Emma for thinking that she can organize other people's lives for them. This only inflames Emma's passion for matchmaking further, and she declares her intention of finding a bride for the new vicar of Highbury, Mr. Elton.

At one of Mr. Woodhouse's regular card evenings at Hartfield, Mrs. Goddard, headmistress of a local school, brings along one of her young boarders, Harriet Smith, a seventeen-year-old girl of unknown parentage. Emma decides to take Harriet under her wing, to introduce her into "good" society, and generally to "improve" her. She also soon fixes upon her young protégée as a likely wife for the said Mr. Elton—even though Emma finds that Harriet already has a suitor in Robert Martin, a tenant farmer of Abbey Mill Farm on Mr. Knightley's estate. Harriet seems to be genuinely taken with Robert Martin and has already become friendly with his family, so Emma tries to weaken this attachment by giving Harriet a false sense of her own importance. On the basis of no evidence whatsoever, Emma suggests to her impressionable friend that, though her parentage is unknown, she must surely be the daughter of a gentleman and that it is therefore improper to associate so closely with such a "low" family as the Martins. Mr. Knightley, in conversation with Mrs. Weston, expresses strong reservations about Emma's intimacy with Harriet, saying that Emma is only satisfying her own vanity in "noticing" Harriet and is doing Harriet no good by raising her expectations unrealistically.

Emma quickly elevates the charms of Mr. Elton in Harriet's mind and makes her believe herself in love with him. She similarly tries to elevate Harriet in Mr. Elton's esteem, though it soon becomes clear that Elton is much more interested in Emma herself. Emma draws a picture of Harriet that Mr. Elton fulsomely admires and promptly takes off to London to be framed. This action is intended to impress Emma, but she takes it to mean that he has fallen for Harriet and that her matchmaking scheme is progressing smoothly.

Robert Martin then proposes to Harriet by means of an admirably expressed letter whose fluency surprises Emma. Emma perseveres with her scheme, however, and by a subtle mixture of innuendo and emotional blackmail, succeeds in persuading Harriet to refuse her suitor. When Knightley hears of this, he is extremely angry with Emma for interfering and, in his view, ruining Harriet's chances of marrying respectably. In fact, it emerges that Robert Martin had sought his advice before making his proposal, and Knightley, impressed by the young farmer's good sense, had assured him that Harriet would accept. Knightley and Emma quarrel over the affair, and Emma is ruffled by Knightley's confident sense of her wrongdoing.

Emma and Harriet start a collection of riddles and charades, and Emma invites Elton to compose one for them. He does so willingly, taking the opportunity to make a veiled request to Emma to accept his courtship of her. But she interprets Elton's charade as being aimed at Harriet and continues to believe that he is preparing to propose to her young friend. After a charity visit to some of the local poor, Emma and Harriet bump into Elton, and Emma contrives to separate herself from the other two to give Elton time to declare himself to Harriet, but, of course, he has no intention of doing so, and she is a little puzzled at his apparent overcautiousness.

Emma's sister, Isabella, arrives for Christmas with her husband and five children, and the whole Hartfield set is invited by the Westons to a dinner party on Christmas Eve at the Westons' house, Randalls. Harriet comes down with a cold and is unable to attend, so Emma assumes that Elton will not want to go either and offers to give his apologies to the Westons. She is somewhat taken aback, however, to find that he has no intention whatsoever of missing the party, and he accepts with alacrity when John Knightley offers him a seat in his carriage. At Randalls, what is more, Emma soon becomes uneasy at the signal attention Elton pays her. During the evening there is a light fall of snow, and, when this is made known, the timorous Mr. Woodhouse becomes nervous of the journey home, and the Hartfield party decide to leave as quickly as possible to preserve his peace of mind. In the hurried arrangements for the return, Emma, much to her consternation, finds herself in a carriage alone with Mr. Elton. Rather too full of Mr. Weston's good wine, he has no hesitation, once the carriage sets off, in seizing Emma's hand, making a passionate declaration of love, and proposing to her. Their mutual and most embarrassing misperception of each other is soon revealed, however, as Emma refuses him in no uncertain terms, and he, when challenged about Harriet, disdainfully denies even the slightest interest in her, especially given her lowly status. The remainder of the journey passes in angry silence on the part of both characters.

Emma is mortified to realize how badly she has misjudged matters, especially as the effects of her foolishness will be felt most keenly by the innocent Harriet. She spends a restless night of self-criticism and self-recrimination, mixed with resentment at what she considers to be Mr. Elton's arrogant presumption in proposing to her. She finally admits to herself that her attempt at matchmaking was misconceived from the start, and, ashamed of herself, she resolves "to do such things no more." For the next few days, the weather keeps people indoors and saves Emma from any further embarrassment for the time being. When the weather improves, the John Knightleys return to London, Mr. Elton leaves to spend some weeks in Bath, and Emma finally goes to confess her mistakes to Harriet. As might be expected, Harriet is extremely upset about Mr. Elton, though, to her credit, she does not seek to apportion blame to Emma or anyone else for what has happened. Rather, she self-disparagingly accepts that "she never could have deserved him." Emma feels more ashamed of herself than ever in the face of Harriet's artless tears and touching humility, and she resolves henceforth to be "humble and discreet" and to repress her overactive imagination.

A new development in the plot is signaled by discussion of Frank Churchill, Mr. Weston's twenty-three-year-old son by his first marriage. After the death of his mother when he was a young child, he was brought up by his rich aunt and uncle, Mr. and Mrs. Churchill of Enscombe in Yorkshire, and he has now taken their name and become their adopted heir. He has been expected to pay a visit to his newly married father for some time but has not yet managed to do so. At his Christmas Eve dinner party, Mr. Weston had made it known that Frank had definitely arranged to visit in the second week of January, but now we learn that he has put off his visit yet again, apparently because of his guardian aunt's illness. Despite Emma's determination never to marry and despite never having met him, Emma has always harbored a fancy for Frank Churchill as a possible match for herself, and so she is disappointed to hear of this further postponement of his visit. When she communicates her disappointment to Mr. Knightley, he begins to criticize Frank Churchill for his apparently casual attitude to his father, and, though Emma actually agrees with Knightley on this, she thinks he is unduly prejudiced against Frank and therefore springs to the latter's defense. An argument ensues, and they eventually agree to differ about Frank Churchill, but Emma remains puzzled by Knightley's strength of feeling on the subject.

The second volume of the novel opens with a visit by Emma and Harriet to the home of Mrs. and Miss Bates, where they are bombarded with news of Miss Bates' niece, Jane Fairfax. She is an orphan who had been brought up by her aunt and grandmother until she was nine, when she went to live with Colonel and Mrs. Campbell to finish her education and to be a companion for their daughter. Miss Campbell has recently married Mr. Dixon and removed to Ireland. Her parents have now gone to visit her there, and Jane is coming to Highbury to stay with the Bateses for three months. She is Emma's exact contemporary, but she has no independent fortune, and, at the end of this period, she has resolved to seek a post as a governess. On hearing of the Campbells' trip to Ireland, Emma wonders why Jane has not accompanied them, and she immediately starts to fantasize about some form of illicit relationship between Jane and Mr. Dixon, a fantasy encouraged by hearing that Mr. Dixon had once, on a family trip to Weymouth, saved Jane from falling into the sea from a boat. Otherwise, Emma finds Miss Bates' constant chatter about Jane tiresome, partly because of Miss Bates' long-windedness but also partly because she does not really like Jane Fairfax. From past acquaintance she has found her to be somewhat cold and reserved. However, Jane is often praised in Highbury for her looks, elegance, and accomplishments, and there is a distinct touch of jealousy in Emma's attitude toward her, especially as people frequently talk of the two women as though they were close friends and equals, which both pricks her conscience for not being more friendly with Jane and offends her sense of being the leading young lady in Highbury.

When Jane arrives, Emma finds her even more elegant and beautiful than she remembered, and in admiring her looks and manner while simultaneously musing on her unpromising prospects as a governess, Emma initially determines to be more friendly toward her. This frame of mind does not outlast their second meeting, however, for Emma soon finds her pique rising at what she sees as Jane's willful reluctance to share any intimate information with her, particularly on the subjects of Mr. Dixon and Mr. Frank Churchill, whom, it emerges, she met at Weymouth at the time of the boat party mentioned earlier.

It is only some four weeks since Mr. Elton's departure for Bath, but now news arrives that he is shortly to be married to Miss Augusta Hawkins, the younger daughter of a Bristol merchant, with an independent fortune of some £10,000. This news confirms Emma's belief that his proposal to her had been motivated more by a desire for self-advancement than by any genuine feelings of love, and it also allows her to believe once more that her hopes for Harriet had not been entirely misplaced, given that Miss Hawkins does not appear to be particularly wellborn (though Emma conveniently sets aside the matter of her fortune).

Frank Churchill finally arrives in Highbury and is brought to Hartfield by his father to meet the Woodhouses. Emma finds him very good-looking and extremely charming and gallant—indeed, so much so on their first meeting that she is slightly suspicious of his sincerity, though she is clearly ready to be won over by him and is rather pleased to discern Mr. Weston's all-too-evident hopes for a match between them. At the end of this visit, Frank explains that he feels duty-bound to pay a courtesy call to a slight acquaintance of his in Highbury, Jane Fairfax. In her second meeting with Frank, the next day, Emma continues to find him very agreeable, and she is particularly gratified to see that he appears to share her critical view of Jane and to corroborate, to some extent, her suspicions about Jane and Mr. Dixon. On the following day, her good opinion of him is shaken somewhat by the news that he has suddenly left for London for the sake of a haircut, as, to her, this smacks of "foppery and nonsense." But this is only a minor blemish on his good conduct so far, and, especially after comparing notes with Mrs. Weston, Emma is happy to think of him as a worthy suitor for her, even though meeting him has not shaken her resolution, disclosed earlier, of never marrying. Only Mr. Knightley, of all Emma's acquaintances, remains critical of Frank.

At a dinner party given by Mr. and Mrs. Cole, Frank sits beside Emma and, throughout the evening, pays particular attention to her. As the company converse, we learn that Jane Fairfax has received the present of a piano from an unknown source. Colonel Campbell is generally thought to be the sender, but Emma, continuing with her fanciful idea, speculates that it may be none other than Jane's supposed lover, Mr. Dixon—and Frank Churchill seems happy to support her in this view. Jane Fairfax is among a new set of guests to arrive after dinner, and she is immediately quizzed about the piano. Her evident embarrassment at this is taken by Emma to corroborate her suspicions, and Emma now feels that she has established a private understanding with Frank over Jane. Mrs. Weston tells Emma that Mr. Knightley had sent his carriage to bring Jane and Miss Bates to the party and that this may suggest a desire on Knightley's part to court Jane Fairfax. Emma is horrified at this suggestion and brings forward a range of reasons to doubt it, though none of them seem quite to justify her strength of feeling on the matter.

The next day, Emma and Harriet are at Ford's shop in Highbury, when Miss Bates and Mrs. Weston come over to ask them to come to hear Jane's new piano. Frank is already with Jane, having stayed to mend Mrs. Bates' spectacles while the other two women went to fetch Emma and Harriet. Jane then plays, while Frank, taking his cue from Emma's comments the evening before, makes pointed comments about Ireland. Emma is flattered at sharing this private joke with him but becomes worried that he may be overdoing things when she sees Jane blush and smile slightly to herself. Knightley passes in the street, and Miss Bates calls out to thank him for a large basket of apples he had given them. When he hears that Emma is there, he agrees to come in but then changes his mind when he gathers that Frank is also there.

Emma and Frank make plans for a ball to be held at the Crown Inn, but the event has to be put off when Frank is peremptorily recalled to Enscombe, where his aunt has become ill. Emma is disappointed by his departure and by the cancellation of the ball, and her feelings make her wonder whether she has not, after all, started to fall in love with Frank, for all her conscious resistance to such an idea. However, after some careful self-examination, she decides that this is not actually the case, that though she has enjoyed flirting with him, her real feelings have not been truly engaged. With Frank gone, Emma turns to Harriet again as Mr. Elton's marriage and wife become the main topic of Highbury gossip. Mrs. Elton turns out to be a vain, vulgar, and arrogant woman who immediately starts vying for position with Emma as the principal lady of Highbury. Her first gesture in this direction is to take it upon herself to promote the welfare of Jane Fairfax and to find her a post as a governess. Emma, Mrs. Weston, and Mr. Knightley are amazed at her presumption in this, but they are equally amazed to find Jane Fairfax apparently accepting Mrs. Elton's attentions. Knightley suggests that this may be partly because nobody else of equal standing in the community pays her any attention—and his reproachful look at Emma here makes it clear whom he means. Emma then archly provokes him to declare his interest in Jane, and he states quite plainly that he has no intention whatsoever of courting or proposing to Jane.

For propriety's sake, Emma organizes a dinner party at Hartfield for the Eltons, and she is happy to take this early opportunity of making some amends for her previous neglect of Jane Fairfax by inviting her, too, along with Knightley and the Westons. While waiting for dinner, it emerges in conversation that Jane had walked to the post office that morning in the rain. Mrs. Elton makes a large show of being concerned for Jane's health and more or less tells her not to do such a thing again and that she would arrange for a servant to collect the mail for her. But Jane will not agree to this. Emma suspects that this is because she is receiving letters from Mr. Dixon and wants no one else to see them, but Emma resolves to try not to embarrass Jane again on this matter, and the two young women go into dinner arm-in-arm. After the meal, Mrs. Elton corners Jane and pesters her about applying for governess posts, but Jane again resists Mrs. Elton's officious interference and remains firm in her determination not to make any applications until later in the summer (it is now April). Mr. Weston (who had been called away on business earlier in the day) then arrives carrying a letter from his son, Frank, announcing that the Churchills are moving to London for an extended stay on account of Mrs. Churchill's illness and that Frank will be able to be at Highbury for half of the time.

Frank reappears in Highbury, two months after his last visit. Emma is now confident of having no strong feelings for him, and she is relieved to find that his feelings for her seem also to have cooled, for, although he appears nervous, he spends only fifteen minutes with her before rushing off to see other acquaintances. After ten days in London, Mrs. Churchill decides that London is too noisy for her, and the Churchills take a house in Richmond for two months (May and June). This means that Frank will now be only some nine miles from Highbury, and this enables him to resurrect the idea of a ball at the Crown Inn. This is duly organized.

The ball, one of Jane Austen's most memorable set-piece scenes, opens with a bravado performance from Miss Bates, who, as she enters and moves into the large assembled company (she and Jane had been "forgotten" by Mrs. Elton, and the carriage had to be sent back for them), sets the scene for us by introducing almost every single guest present in a veritable flood of words that drowns out all other voices. Before the dancing begins, Mrs. Elton—who arrogantly assumes the ball is being held in her honor—speaks to Jane Fairfax with great familiarity, and Frank, who overhears her, reacts with visible annoyance. Emma has already noticed him behaving somewhat nervously, and though his frown turns into a smile as soon as he realizes she has seen it, she cannot help wondering about his odd behavior. Emma is Frank's partner for the first dance, but as she moves around the room with him, her attention is constantly drawn to the onlooking Mr. Knightley. She muses on his handsome, youthful figure and on the grace with which he carries himself, and she thinks to herself that he ought to be dancing, too, rather than placing himself with the husbands, fathers, and whist players. For the two last dances before supper, Emma notices that Harriet Smith has no partner and is the only young lady sitting down; as everybody has been equally matched thus far, this can only mean that one of the gentlemen has purposely dropped out. She then sees that it is none other than Mr. Elton, who is sauntering about the room and making a very obvious show of *not* asking Harriet to dance. When Mrs. Weston comes over and politely urges him to partner Harriet, he adds insult to injury by making clear that he would be happy to dance with Mrs. Weston herself or even with Mrs. Gilbert, but not with Harriet. He exchanges knowing grins with his wife as he talks to Mrs. Weston and then also as he walks over to talk to Mr. Knightley, and Emma realizes that this very public put-down of Harriet (and of Emma herself as Harriet's mentor) has been premeditated. Emma can hardly contain her anger, but she is then surprised and delighted to see Mr. Knightley gallantly coming to the rescue by asking Harriet to dance himself. Harriet is overjoyed by his gesture and dances with more gusto than ever, while Emma does her best to communicate her gratitude to Knightley by beaming at him across the room. Elton slinks shamefacedly into the cardroom. At supper, Knightley and Emma join in censure of the Eltons and come thereby to settle their previous differences over Emma's involvement with Harriet and Elton. After supper, Knightley dances with Emma.

The next day, Emma reviews the evening with great satisfaction, taking particular pleasure in her reconciliation with Knightley. But no sooner has she acknowledged one set of matchmaking mistakes, than she invites another, for an incident now occurs that leads her to believe that Frank Churchill and Harriet might be destined for one another. While she is walking in the garden thinking about the ball, Frank suddenly appears with Harriet on his arm, and it emerges that he has just rescued her from some Gypsy children she had encountered while out walking with a friend, Miss Bickerton. Miss Bickerton had managed to run away, but Harriet had developed a cramp. She had just been surrounded by the clamorous Gypsy children, who were demanding money from her, when Frank appeared and frightened the Gypsies away. Emma, ever the "imaginist," immediately sees the possibility of a match here in the romantic encounter between gallant rescuer and grateful young girl. However, she has learned something from her previous experience, and Emma here resolves not to interfere in any positive way; it will be "a mere passive scheme" this time. Shortly after this, Harriet burns all her surviving mementos of Elton and acknowledges to Emma her silliness and self-deception in that affair. Now, she declares, she admires someone far superior to Elton but someone whom she can never hope to marry. Emma thinks she knows who this paragon is, and, though much more circumspect this time, she cannot help raising Harriet's hopes just a little by suggesting that matches of even greater disparity have been known.

It is now June, and we hear that Jane Fairfax's stay at Highbury has been prolonged at least until August. During an informal gathering of the principal characters, Knightley starts to suspect that there is some sort of attachment between Frank Churchill and Jane Fairfax: Frank says something about Mr. Perry's plans to set up a carriage, which only Miss Bates and Jane could have known about, and he later makes Jane blush with the words "blunder" and "Dixon" when the party play word games with a child's alphabet. Knightley notices these things but cannot work out their significance. He broaches the subject with Emma later on, but she is confident that there can be no attachment between Frank and Jane, and this leaves Knightley perplexed and worried that Frank may be playing on the affections of Jane and Emma simultaneously.

A planned outing to Box Hill, a local beauty spot, has to be postponed, and, as an alternative, Knightley invites the party to come and pick strawberries at Donwell Abbey. Here, Mrs. Elton tells Jane that she has found her a position as a governess, and Jane becomes increasingly agitated and upset as Mrs. Elton presses her to accept it. Emma sees Knightley and Harriet walking together and is pleased that he seems now to have accepted her protégée as an acceptable companion, though she worries a little about her being reminded of Knightley's tenant, Robert Martin, whose farm is easily seen from the Abbey grounds. Frank Churchill has been expected to join the party at any time, but there is still no sign of him as the day wears on to late afternoon. Emma wanders into the hall of the house and discovers Jane there, evidently in some distress and determined to walk home by herself. Emma offers to call a carriage for her, but she begs to be allowed to walk and asks Emma to give her apologies to the others. For the first time, she confides in Emma a little, telling her how weary and unhappy she feels at present and how comforting it can be to have some time alone. Emma is moved by this and sees Jane off with the tender feelings of a friend. When she is gone, she thinks to herself that Jane's unhappiness must derive partly from having to live at close quarters with Miss Bates all the time. A quarter of an hour later, Frank Churchill finally arrives, extremely hot after a long ride in the sun and in a very bad temper. Emma finds his irritability objectionable and feels glad that any feelings she may have had for him have faded, though she thinks to herself that Harriet's "sweet easy temper" will probably be able to put up with it. Frank briefly mentions having met Jane on his way, and he comments on her "madness" at walking in such heat. After he has something to eat, he settles down somewhat, and Emma manages to persuade him to stay for the Box Hill party, which has been reorganized for the next day.

On the excursion to Box Hill, there is a general air of tension and irritability among the group. Frank and Emma both strain to be jolly and witty with one another, and this leads to Emma's being cuttingly rude to Miss Bates. Frank makes pointed remarks about the Eltons, referring to unsuitable matches being made at public places, and he then jokingly asks Emma to find and educate an appropriate wife for him, something that she takes semiseriously, thinking, of course, of Harriet. At that moment, Jane takes her aunt and walks away from the main party. Before they all set off for home, Knightley talks to Emma alone and tells her quite plainly that her words to Miss Bates were insolent, arrogant, and cruel and that Miss Bates was deeply hurt by them. Emma immediately recognizes the truth of his reproach and feels so ashamed of herself that she is at a loss for anything to say in reply. He hands her into her carriage and turns away before she can say anything, and her only means of expression now are her tears.

Full of remorse, Emma goes to see Miss Bates the very next morning to apologize. Here, she finds that Jane Fairfax has unexpectedly accepted the post of governess that Mrs. Elton had found for her and that she will be leaving within a fortnight. Miss Bates is extremely grateful for Emma's kindness in coming to see them and for inquiring after Jane, but Jane seems strangely determined not to see Emma and keeps herself out of the way. Miss Bates explains that they had spent the previous evening with the Eltons, and it was there that Jane had finally made up her mind. As it turns out, during the evening, the ostler of the Crown Inn had come to see Mr. Elton, and it had emerged that Frank had left for Richmond almost immediately after returning from Box Hill, even though he was not expected there until the next morning.

When Emma returns home, Knightley and Harriet are there. Knightley is very happy to learn that Emma has been to visit Miss Bates, and she is relieved to be restored to his good opinion. He is going away to stay with his brother in London for a few days, and when he leaves, he almost kisses her hand; she is disappointed that he does not actually do so, but she is gratified at the effort.

We learn of the sudden death of Frank's aunt, Mrs. Churchill. Emma thinks that there is now nothing in the way of a match between Frank and Harriet, but she detects no signs of new hope on Harriet's part. Emma thinks again of Jane Fairfax's plight in having to become a governess, and she wants now more than ever to be of use to her. She invites Jane to come to stay for a day, she offers to take her out in her carriage, and she sends her a present of arrowroot, but everything is rejected by Jane, and Emma concludes that it is too late; after all this time, Jane does not want kindness from *her*. But Emma consoles herself with the thought that her intentions have been good and her motives, on this occasion at least, selfless.

About ten days after the death of Mrs. Churchill, Emma is called to Randalls by the Westons, and, with trepidation as to its effect on her, they break the news that Frank has only that morning broken to them—that he has been secretly engaged to Jane Fairfax for eight months, since their being together the previous October in Weymouth. He had not dared to make the engagement public while his aunt was alive, as she would have refused to consent to it, and he may not have done so now had not matters come to a head in his relationship with Jane, as he later explains in a long and detailed letter to Mrs. Weston. In that letter, also, many of the puzzles about his previous behavior become clear, as do the many errors of judgment made about him by Emma. The strains of keeping their liaison secret, he explains, coupled with such things as his flirtatious behavior with Emma (justified by him as a cover for his real motives in being there), had led him to quarrel with Jane on the day of the strawberry-picking party at Donwell, when he had met Jane on her walk back to Highbury (hence, his agitated state when he arrived at Donwell). Relations between them had deteriorated even further on the trip to Box Hill when, as we understand in retrospect, many of their comments were coded jibes at one another. At her lowest ebb on the evening of that day, Jane, under pressure from Mrs. Elton, had resigned herself to the fate of becoming a governess and had written to Frank to break off their engagement. When, after Mrs. Churchill's death, Frank learned of Jane's decision to take up a position as governess near Bristol, he decided finally to bring things out into the open with his uncle, hoping that the latter would be more sympathetic to his plight than his aunt would have been. This turned out to be the case, and Mr. Churchill readily gave his consent and blessing to a match between Frank and Jane. Frank had then gone to see Jane, to repropose, as it were, and they had been reconciled. He had then come to tell the Westons about the affair, as we have seen.

On hearing of this long-standing engagement, Emma immediately thinks of her ''private'' understanding with Frank about Jane and of all the foolish things she had said to him about her; and she thinks also of Harriet, whom she presently believes to be in love with Frank. Emma puts Mrs. Weston's mind at ease as far as her own feelings for Frank are concerned, but she is highly critical of Frank for his duplicity and for his having toyed with her emotions. Mrs. Weston agrees with Emma, but she says that Frank is going to write with fuller details of the affair and that perhaps they should wait to hear the full story before judging him too harshly.

Emma is now once again angry with herself for her inept behavior, particularly with regard to Harriet, who, for the second time, has been ''the dupe of her [Emma's] misconceptions and flattery.'' But when Harriet appears, having heard the news from Mr. Weston, she shows no signs of upset at all, and it quickly emerges that Harriet and Emma had been talking at cross-purposes when discussing Harriet's ''superior'' person: it was not Frank, but Mr. Knightley that she meant. This truly shocks Emma, and when she stops to analyze why it shocks her so, the answer comes to her ''with the speed of an arrow, that Mr. Knightley must marry no one but herself.'' Emma now becomes seriously concerned that Knightley may, indeed, have fallen in love with Harriet and that, largely through her own interference, she may have caused to come about the only match she had never fantasized about and never wanted to happen. She now wishes she had never met Harriet or that she had not stopped her marrying Robert Martin. In this chastened state of mind, Emma goes through a period of intense self-criticism, and, for the first time, she pulls no punches in admitting and taking full responsibility for all her previous faults of vanity, arrogance, self-deception, and misjudgment—''the blunders, and blindness of her own head and heart.''

Mrs. Weston calls and tells Emma that she has been to see Jane Fairfax, who feels ashamed of the deception she has practiced with Frank and guilty for her rejection of Emma's attempted kindnesses. However, Emma understands better now the predicament that Jane has been in and cannot blame her for any resentment she may have felt toward her, especially given Frank's teasing attentions to Emma, which must have been hurtful to Jane. (Emma is later reconciled with both Jane and Frank, after a mutual exchange of appropriate apologies, although, prompted by Knightley, she—along with the reader—retains lingering doubts about Frank's character. We also hear later that Frank and Jane will live with Mr. Churchill at Enscombe in Yorkshire after their marriage.)

Though it is July, gloomy weather prevails, neatly reflecting Emma's mood of dejection in the face of what she now fears may be a gloomy future for her, especially if it means being without Mr. Knightley. Her only consolation is that she will at least be a more rational and more self-critical person in the future and will therefore have fewer regrets to live with than she has at the moment. The next day brings brighter weather, however, and, with it, Mr. Knightley's return from London. He comes to Emma as she is walking in the garden, and he seems preoccupied. He has only just heard the news about Frank that morning, and he fears that Emma has been upset by it because of her own feelings for Frank. He is relieved to hear that Frank had meant nothing to her, and this encourages him to talk more animatedly to her. Emma fears that he is now going to raise the matter of his love for Harriet, and she tries to prevent him from speaking too freely. But eventually, he comes to the issue and speaks not of Harriet but, to Emma's relief and delight, of his love for her, Emma. Needless to say, she accepts his proposal of marriage.

Two serious problems remain for Emma: what to do with her father and how to win him over to the idea of her marriage (he hates change of any kind); and how to deal with Harriet, given her attachment to Knightley. With Harriet, Emma decides that it may help matters if they were separated for a short while, and so she procures an invitation for Harriet to go to stay with her sister, Isabella, in London for two weeks. In the course of her stay, Robert Martin happens to go to London on business, and, at the request of Mr. Knightley, he calls at John Knightley's house to deliver some papers. This leads to invitations for him to join the Knightley party, first for an evening out and then for dinner; and this, in turn, leads to a renewal of his relationship with Harriet and then to a renewed proposal of marriage—which, this time, she accepts. When she returns to Highbury and meets Emma again, their initial awkwardness with one another is soon overcome by their mutual sense of how well things have turned out for both of them, and, at the end of September, Emma is only too happy to attend Harriet to the church to see her married at last to the steadfast Robert Martin.

The first part of the problem with Emma's father is solved by Mr. Knightley, who agrees to come and live at Hartfield after he and Emma are married. The second part takes a little longer to solve, but Mr. Woodhouse is slowly won over by the combined persuasive powers of Isabella Knightley, Mrs. Weston, Emma, and Mr. Knightley—though it is not until just before the wedding that he finally accepts the situation, and this is only because a series of poultry thefts in the neighborhood makes him appreciate the potential benefits of having Mr. Knightley in the house! A date for the wedding can now be set, and, it takes place, in "perfect happiness," in October.

Main Characters: Miss Hetty Bates, Frank C. Weston Churchill, Mr. (Rev. Philip) Elton, Mrs. Augusta Elton (née Hawkins), Jane Fairfax, Mr. George Knightley, Mr. John Knightley, Mrs. Isabella Knightley (née Woodhouse), Harriet Smith, Robert Martin, Mr. Weston, Mrs. Anne/a Weston (née Taylor), Emma Woodhouse, Mr. Henry Woodhouse.

Minor Characters: the two Abbotts, Old John Abdy, John Abdy, Mrs. Bates, Jane Bates (Mrs. Fairfax), Miss Bickerton, Mrs. Bird, Mr. and Mrs. Bragge, Mrs. Brown, Colonel and Mrs. Campbell, Miss Campbell (Mrs. Dixon), Mr. and Mrs. Churchill, Miss Churchill (first Mrs. Weston), Mr. and Mrs. Cole, Mrs. James Cooper, Mr. Cox, Mr. William Cox, William Coxe, the Miss Coxes (Anne and her younger sister), Mr. and Mrs. Dixon, Lieutenant Fairfax, Mrs. Jane Fairfax, Mrs. Ford, Mrs. Gilbert, the two Gilberts, Mrs. Goddard, Mr. Graham,

Mr. Green, Hannah, Harry, Mrs. Hodges, the Hughes family (Dr. and Mrs. Hughes and their son, Richard), James, Mrs. Jeffereys, the Knightley children (Henry, John, Bella, George), William Larkins, the Martin family (Elizabeth Martin and her sister, Mrs. Martin), the two Milmans (Mrs. Bird and Mrs. James Cooper), Farmer Mitchell, Miss Nash, Mr. and Mrs. Otway and family, Mrs. Partridge, Patty, Mr. Perry, Miss Prince, Miss Richardson, John Saunders, Serle, Mrs. Smallridge, Mrs. Stokes, Mr. and Mrs. Suckling, Miss Taylor (Mrs. Anne Weston), Tom, the Tupmans, Mrs. Wallis, Mrs. Weston (the first), Anna Weston, Mr. Wingfield, Wright.

Volume and chapter divisions (numbers in brackets are for editions with continuous chapter numbers): Volume 1: Chapters 1–18, volume 2: Chapters 1–18 [19–36], volume 3: Chapters 1–19 [37–55].

See: Alexander 1988, *Berendsen 1991, Birtwistle and Conklin 1996, Bloom 1987a,* Boles 1981, Booth 1983, *Bradbrook 1961, Burrows 1968, Canby 1931,* Conrad 1980, *Cookson and Loughrey 1988,* Crosby 1989, Dash 1983, Davies 1986, Davis 1988, DeForest 1987, Derry 1992, Finch and Bowen 1990, Flavin 1991, Fleishman 1983, Fletcher 1992, *Gard 1985,* Graham 1987, Groves 1983, Halperin 1975, Havely 1993, Hayes 1949–1950, Hilliard 1979, Hogan 1977, Holly 1989, *Jefferson 1977,* Kenney 1991, Knoepflmacher 1967, *Lauritzen 1981,* Lenta 1981b, Litvak 1985, *Lodge 1968,* Loveridge 1983, Mallett 1992, Mandel 1991, Marie 1985, McAleer 1991, McMaster 1991, 1992, Merrett 1980, Moffat 1991, *Monaghan 1992,* Monk 1990, Myer 1982, Neill 1987, O'Keefe 1994, Page 1984, Parker 1992, *Parrish 1972,* Perry 1986, Pickrel 1985a, b, Potter 1994, Preus 1991, Reid-Walsh 1991, Restuccia 1994, Rogers 1994, Rosmarin 1984, Sabor 1991, Smith 1984, Spacks 1989, Stewart 1982, Stovel 1991, Sulloway 1976, Thaden 1990, Tobin 1988, 1990, Tsomondo 1987, Tumbleson 1992, Weinsheimer 1983, Wilkes 1987–1988, Wilt 1983, Wiltshire 1985, Zaal 1988.

"Evelyn" (*Volume the Third* of Jane Austen's juvenilia). Jane Austen transcribed this short and unfinished fantasy novel into the notebook known as *Volume the Third* sometime between 6 May and August of 1792, and it was probably written around this time, too (the notebook was given to her by her father on 6 May 1792, and the work that follows "Evelyn" is "Catharine," dated August 1792). She later changed a date in the manuscript to 19 August 1809, shortly after she moved to Chawton, and this may suggest some later revisions, though there is no evidence of major changes.

The events of "Evelyn" are wholly absurd and principally designed to burlesque various conventions of sentimental and early gothic fiction. They include a mock-epic journey, the sudden acquisition of a house and fortune, a romance thwarted by disapproving parents, enforced separation of lovers, chance encounters, sudden marriages, and equally sudden and sensational deaths. Along with the surreal events, there is a sort of fairy tale atmosphere in the piece, with settings (an idyllic village, a "Gloomy Castle," storms at sea) that serve to parody elements of romantic fiction again but also the contemporary fashion for the picturesque and the sublime in landscape description. Frederic Gower finds himself in the perfect village of Evelyn in Sussex, where there is no sickness, misery, or vice. He decides he must rent a house there but learns that all accommodations are taken. However, Mrs. Willis, the landlady of the inn he is staying at, sends him to see Mr. and Mrs. Webb. They welcome him warmly, feed him lavishly, give him gifts of money, and then agree also to hand over possession of the whole house and grounds. Before they leave, they also agree to his marrying their eldest daughter, Maria, and provide her with a handsome portion into the deal. After a few months of perfect happiness, Mr. Gower sees a rose on the ground that reminds him of his sister Rose and of the reason he had set out from the family home in Carlisle in the first place: to visit the family of his sister's dead lover, Henry, and to obtain a picture of him for Rose. Henry's family had prohibited him from marrying Rose and had sent him to the Isle of Wight, hoping to cure him of his love for her by a period of separation and ''Absence in a foreign Country.'' Unfortunately, he had died when his ship was wrecked in a storm. Frederic now writes to Rose to apologize for his delay in writing. He receives a reply from another member of the family telling him of Rose's death six weeks previously. Following an attack of gout brought on by this news, Mr. Gower goes to see Henry's parents at their ancient castle. He berates them over the death of the young lovers and storms out, leaving them ''unanimous in their opinion of his being Mad.'' As it is now night, and he is terrified of seeing Gypsies or ghosts, he closes his eyes and gallops all the way back to Evelyn. There, he finds that his wife had been so grieved at his departure that she had died of a broken heart three hours after he had left. After arranging for her funeral, Mr. Gower leaves for Carlisle, where he is astonished to find not only that Rose is alive after all but that she is now married to Mr. Davenport, who had arrived two days ago and had proposed to her after delivering the news of Henry's death. Mr. Gower then goes into town for some beer and is served by his old Evelyn friend Mrs. Willis, who is in Carlisle visiting her cousin. Mr. Gower immediately proposes to her, and they are married the next day. They return to Evelyn and settle to enjoy ''the just reward of their virtues.'' Mr. and Mrs. Davenport also come to settle at Evelyn and become the proprietors of Mrs. Willis' old inn. (The manuscript ends here.)

Main characters: Mr. Davenport, Frederic Gower, Maria Gower (née Webb), Rose Gower (later, Davenport), Henry, Lord and Lady—(parents of Henry), Mr. and Mrs. Webb, William (servant in the Webbs' house), Mrs. Sarah Willis (later, Gower).

F

Fairfax, Jane (*Emma* Chs.10, 12, 20; I:10:86; I:12:104; II:2:163–68). Born at Highbury, Jane Fairfax was orphaned at the age of three and brought up by her grandmother and aunt, Mrs. and Miss Bates, until the age of nine, when she was informally adopted by Colonel and Mrs. Campbell. When we first meet her, she is nearly twenty-one, the same age as Emma. Elegant, graceful, and beautiful, Jane Fairfax is also highly accomplished, having had an excellent education provided for her by Colonel Campbell. Living with the Campbells, moreover, has given "her heart and understanding" every advantage of "discipline and culture." She has no independent fortune, however, and her education has accordingly been designed to enable her to earn a respectable living as a governess. She is, apparently, on the verge of seeking a post when she arrives at Highbury. Emma has never really liked Jane, but for no very clear reason: partly (according to Knightley) because of envy, partly because Jane is always "made such a fuss with by every body" (and particularly Miss Bates), partly because "every body had supposed they must be so fond of each other," and partly because of what Emma sees as Jane's "coldness and reserve." On her first meetings with Jane on this occasion, however, Emma is genuinely impressed by her elegance and sympathetic to her plight at having to become a governess; but, though she briefly determines that "she would dislike her no longer," she finds Jane colder and more reserved than ever, and she soon reverts to her customary feelings of mixed dislike and jealousy. We later learn that Jane's manner at this time is largely the result of her secret engagement to Frank Churchill, who cannot make the engagement public for fear of being cast off by his rich aunt. They had become engaged some months earlier when they had met at Weymouth, where Jane had gone for a visit with the Campbells. When all the secrecy surrounding the engagement is finally dispelled, Jane's true warmth of personality emerges when she apologizes to Emma for her previous behavior, and they become friends.

Fairfax, Lieutenant (*Emma* Ch.20; II:2:163). Father of Jane Fairfax who died while on active duty abroad. Considered by Colonel Campbell to be "an excellent officer and most deserving young man."

Fairfax, Mrs. Jane (*Emma* Ch.20; II:2:163). Younger daughter of Mrs. Bates and mother of Jane Fairfax. Her husband, Lieutenant Fairfax, died in action abroad, and she died soon afterward, when Jane was three years old.

Fanny (*Sense and Sensibility* Ch.13; I:13:64). Colonel Brandon's cousin, mentioned only in passing.

Ferrars, Edward (*Sense and Sensibility* Ch.3; I:3:15). Brother to Mrs. Fanny Dashwood and Robert, Edward Ferrars is the eldest son of a man "who had died very rich," though his fortune depends on the will of his ill-natured mother, to whom he is something of a disappointment. She would like to see him make a name for himself in the world, to enter Parliament or become connected with "some of the great men of the day," but he is a retiring, naturally shy character whose aspirations "centered in domestic comfort and the quiet of private life." Despite the lack of any immediately outstanding qualities, however, and an initial reserve in public, he is a character of "solid worth," of whose "sense" and "goodness" no one can be in any doubt, according to Elinor Dashwood. A sound education has improved a good natural intelligence; he is well read and well informed, with a lively imagination and refined taste, and he has "an open affectionate heart." He and Elinor clearly feel a strong attraction for one another while he is staying at Norland with his sister, before the Dashwoods' removal to Devon; but Edward seems strangely reluctant to declare his feelings openly or to allow the relationship to develop into an unequivocally romantic one, and Elinor is confused by his changeable manner toward her. Later, the reason for this is revealed to be that he is already secretly engaged to Lucy Steele and has been, at this point, for about four years. He had come to know his fiancée during the four years he was at school under the care of her uncle, Mr. Pratt, and the engagement was formed in the idle year he spent between leaving school and entering Oxford University at the age of nineteen. We also learn later that he had soon come to regret the attachment—"the consequence of ignorance of the world—and want of employment"—but had felt duty-bound to continue the engagement, and this accounts for his contradictory behavior with Elinor at Norland and again when he visits her at Barton Cottage some weeks later. When the secret engagement becomes public through the indiscretion of Lucy's sister Anne, Mrs. Ferrars, who had been planning a match for Edward with the rich Miss Morton, predictably disowns and disinherits him. He then takes holy orders and apparently agrees with Lucy that they should be married as soon as he obtains a satisfactory living. On hearing of Edward's situation, Colonel Brandon, through Elinor, offers him the living of Delaford, which he gratefully accepts. However, while he is at Oxford preparing for ordination, Lucy Steele marries his brother instead and unexpectedly releases Edward from "an entanglement which had long formed his misery." Finally free to profess his love openly to Elinor, he rushes to Barton to explain all and to ask for her hand in marriage—which she gladly gives. There follows a partial reconciliation between Edward and his mother, who, after "an ungracious delay," gives her grudging consent to the match and even grants him a small allowance, though without reinstating the full inheritance he might have had if he had married Miss Morton. We are given to believe, however, that in future life he never has cause to regret his reduced circumstances nor to envy the wealthy but fractious life of his brother with Lucy, Mrs. Ferrars, and the John Dashwoods, for he finds professional fulfillment in his duties as a clergyman and real domestic happiness in his loving marriage with Elinor.

Ferrars, Mrs. (*Sense and Sensibility* Chs.3, 34; I:3:131; II:12:232–36). The proud, pompous, and dictatorial mother of Edward and Robert Ferrars and of Fanny Dashwood. Driven by materialistic values only and full of her own wealth and self-importance, she is rude and condescending to anybody she considers beneath her. She haughtily tries to force her son, Edward, to marry the rich Miss Morton for her wealth and rank, and, when he refuses, she disinherits and disowns him. She is eventually partly reconciled with him after his marriage to Elinor Dashwood, but she meanly refuses to restore him to his full rights as the eldest son, illogically favoring her foolish younger son, Robert, and his scheming wife, Lucy Steele.

Ferrars, Robert (*Sense and Sensibility* Chs.3, 33; I:3:16; II:11:220–21). When Lucy Steele, without ever having met him, says of Robert Ferrars, "I fancy he is very unlike his brother—silly and a great coxcomb," she clearly speaks more truly than she knows. For he turns out to be the conceited fop observed by Elinor at Gray's (the London jewelers) who spends a quarter of an hour ostentatiously choosing a toothpick case. "Adorned in the first style of fashion," his surface display is immediately penetrated by Elinor, who notes "the puppyism of his manner" and a face of "strong, natural, sterling insignificance." She later receives clear confirmation of her initial impressions when he is formally introduced to her as Robert Ferrars at Mrs. Dennison's musical party. Here, she finds him to be "exactly the coxcomb" described by Lucy Steele: empty-headed, opinionated, and unworthy even of "the compliment of rational opposition." Elinor marvels at the difference between him and his sensible and serious-minded brother, Edward, but Robert blithely boasts about his superiority over Edward and explains it as being down to his having had the "advantage" of a public school education (Westminster, apparently), while Edward was privately educated. Perhaps appropriately, Robert is his pompous mother's favorite, and at the end of the novel, after she has forgiven him for marrying Lucy Steele, she irrationally elevates him to the status and income of eldest son, even though, earlier, the true eldest son, Edward, had been cast off merely for *proposing* to marry the same woman—but, then, marriage to the manipulative Lucy evidently carried its own costs, for we hear that there were "frequent domestic disagreements" between them.

Ferrars, Sir Robert (*Sense and Sensibility* Ch.36; II:14:251). The uncle of Edward and Robert Ferrars who, according to Robert, was responsible for persuading Mrs. Ferrars not to send Edward to public school. With Robert standing as an example of the ill effects of a public school education, Sir Robert would seem to be a sensible man.

"First Impressions." An early version of *Pride and Prejudice*, begun in October 1796 and completed in August 1797. In this form, it was read by Cassandra Austen, Martha Lloyd, and Rev. George Austen and read aloud to other members of Jane Austen's family. It seems to have been the most popular of her early writings with the family, and her father evidently thought it worthy of publication, as in November 1797 he wrote to offer it to the publishers Cadell and Davies, though they declined even to read the manuscript. No manuscript of "First Impressions" survives, and it is therefore impossible to know just how much it was revised before it became *Pride and Prejudice* (published in January 1813). Jane Austen certainly revised it (if it was still "First Impressions" at that point) between 1811 (possibly from May) and the autumn of 1812, when, she suggests in a later letter, she "lop't and crop't" it extensively; but we cannot absolutely rule out the possibility that she had already revised "First Impressions" sometime between 1797 and 1811 (though it is generally thought unlikely).

Fisher, Miss and Mrs. Jane (*Sanditon, Minor Works* 389). Visitors to Sanditon noted by Mr. Parker in the subscription list at the circulating library. *See* Beard, Mr.

Fitzgibbon, Sir George ("Catharine," *Minor Works* 203). The wealthy cousin of the Wynne girls who arranges for Cecilia to go to India to find a husband.

Fitzwilliam, Colonel (*Pride and Prejudice* Ch.30; II:7:170–71). Colonel Fitzwilliam is Mr. Darcy's cousin and joint guardian, with Darcy, of Miss Georgiana Darcy. He is a well-bred, well-mannered man of about thirty years of age who becomes friendly with Elizabeth Bennet while she is staying with Charlotte and Mr. Collins at Hunsford, Kent. However, he is the younger son of an earl and, he says, must marry with "some attention to money."

Fletcher, Sam (*Northanger Abbey* Ch.11; I:11:76). John Thorpe's hunting acquaintance who has a horse to sell for forty guineas. They plan to rent a house together for the next hunting season.

Ford, Mrs. (*Emma* Chs.21, 27; II:3:178; II:9:235). The "obliging" proprietor of Ford's drapery and haberdashery shop, Highbury's "first in size and fashion."

Forster, Colonel (*Pride and Prejudice* Ch.6; I:6:24). Colonel Forster is the commander of the militia regiment that arrives in Meryton for the winter period in the early stages of the book. When the regiment removes to Brighton, his wife, Harriet (whom he marries while at Meryton), invites Lydia Bennet to come to stay with them there, and Colonel Forster is therefore later drawn into the scandal when Lydia elopes with Mr. Wickham. However, he is a sensible and honorable man, and there is no suggestion that he was at fault in this affair. Indeed, he demonstrates his integrity when, on hearing of how matters stand, he immediately leaves Brighton to give chase to the errant couple, and when, after losing their trail, he continues on to Longbourn to break the bad news to the Bennets, "in a manner most creditable to his heart."

Forster, Mrs. Harriet (*Pride and Prejudice* Ch.39; II:16:221). A young woman, only recently married to Colonel Forster, who resembles Lydia Bennet in "good humour and good spirits" and, it seems, in giddiness. She and Lydia become "intimate" friends after a month's acquaintance, and Lydia is overjoyed when Mrs. Forster invites her to accompany her to Brighton with her husband's regiment. Elizabeth Bennet warns her father that Lydia will gain little advantage "from the friendship of such a woman as Mrs. Forster," especially with the relative freedoms open to them at Brighton, but he allows Lydia to go anyway, with the unfortunate results we see later on. Although Mrs. Forster's part in Lydia's elopement with Wickham is never made explicit, it seems clear that, as Elizabeth feared, she turned out to be an irresponsible chaperon for Lydia.

Frankland, Mrs. (*Persuasion* Ch.19; II:7:179). One of Lady Russsell's acquaintances. *See* Alicia, Lady.

Fraser, Margaret (*Mansfield Park* Ch.36; III:5:360–61). Mr. Fraser's daughter by a first marriage. The second Mrs. Fraser is "wild" to see her married, according to Mary Crawford, preferably to Henry Crawford.

Fraser, Mr. (*Mansfield Park* Ch.36; III:5:360). A moderately rich widower who marries the much younger Janet Ross, Mary Crawford's friend, and then turns out (according to Mary Crawford) "ill-tempered, and *exigeant*," wanting his young wife "to be as steady as himself." Given the character of his wife as Edmund Bertram describes her, however, this would seem to be a reasonable response on Mr. Fraser's part.

Fraser, Mrs. Janet, née Ross (*Mansfield Park* Ch.36; III:5:359–61). Mary Crawford's old friend from London. As Mary presents it to Fanny at Mansfield

Park, the friendship seems to have cooled on Mary's side since her friend's marriage, which, she comments cynically, is as unhappy as most others. It is clear that Mrs. Fraser married solely for financial convenience, but Mary exposes her own confused or hypocritical set of values when she both implicitly applauds this fact and then also bewails the marriage's lack of love and affection. It at first seemed a good match, she tells Fanny, because "he was rich, and she had nothing," and "we were all delighted"; but now the evident mismatch in age and temperament has led to "a spirit of irritation" in the relationship. Apparently without any irony, Mary argues that "poor Janet has been sadly taken in," especially as she did not rush into the marriage: "she took three days to consider of his proposals." When, later in the novel, Mary is once more amicably socializing with her friend in London, Edmund describes Mrs. Fraser as coldhearted and vain and "the determined supporter of every thing mercenary and ambitious," and it becomes clear that where she was "taken in" was in believing Mr. Fraser to be richer than he actually was.

Frasers, the Lady (*Northanger Abbey* Ch.26; II:11:209). General Tilney's neighbors at Northanger Abbey. They are away at the time of Catherine's visit; otherwise, he says, they would have provided some entertainment for her.

"Frederic and Elfrida, a Novel" (*Volume the First* of Jane Austen's juvenilia). Jane Austen probably wrote this short burlesque early in the period 1787–1790, adding a dedication to Martha Lloyd after the spring of 1789, when they first became friends. This is the first piece in the volume and contains five short chapters, which variously burlesque the unlikely courtship and marriage scenarios of popular sentimental fiction of the time. We have, for example, an exaggerated version of the age-old structure of comic romance where young lovers are obstructed in their progress toward marriage by a disapproving parent; only here, the lovers are not young—Rebecca Fitzroy is thirty-six, and her suitor, Captain Roger, is sixty-three. The absurdity of the situation is increased by the fact that Mrs. Fitzroy objects to the marriage "on account of the tender years of the young couple." The situation is summarily resolved when Mrs. Fitzroy is forced to give her approval more or less on the point of a dagger (though it is not entirely clear who is holding it). A different version of a similar scenario—one that makes fun of artificial stalling devices in romantic fiction—involves the eponymous hero and heroine (who are cousins), whose marriage is delayed for nearly twenty years because Elfrida's delicate frame of mind cannot face the shock of naming a wedding day. In fact, it is not until Rebecca and Captain Roger return to Crankhumdunberry with Eleanor, their beautiful daughter of eighteen, and Frederic starts to fall for her, that Elfrida suddenly changes her tune and presses Frederic to marry her the very next day. He now refuses to do so, but when Elfrida falls into such a succession of fainting fits "that she had scarcely patience enough to recover from one before she fell into another," he relents, and they are married after all.

Another plotline in the novel involves Charlotte Drummond, a friend of Frederic, Elfrida, and Rebecca (we are told that the Fitzroy, Drummond, and Falknor families are such good friends that they are able "to kick one another out of the window on the slightest provocation"). Charlotte is so concerned to oblige everyone that, on a visit to her aunt's house in London, she agrees to marry two different suitors on the same evening (neither of whom she had ever seen before). The next morning, realizing what she has done, she commits suicide by throwing herself into a stream, which takes her body back to Crankhumdunberry, where her friends bury her and compose a doggerel epitaph for her.

Characters: Rev. Drummond, Charlotte Drummond, Elfrida Falknor, Frederic Falknor, Mrs. Fitzroy, Jezalinda Fitzroy, Rebecca Fitzroy, Captain Roger, Eleanor Roger, Mrs. Williamson (Charlotte's aunt).

Freeman (*Northanger Abbey* Ch.7; I:7:46). John Thorpe's acquaintance from Christchurch College, Oxford, who sells his gig to John Thorpe for fifty guineas cash. This is the carriage whose ironwork John Thorpe describes as "new, or better."

G

Gardiner, Mr. Edward (*Pride and Prejudice* Chs.1, 25; I:7:28; II:2:139). The brother of Mrs. Bennet and Mrs. Philips. He is a prosperous businessman "in a respectable line of trade," and he and his family live in Gracechurch Street, London, in view of his own warehouses. Intelligent, well bred, and good-humored, he is "greatly superior to his sister as well by nature as education." He and his wife take Elizabeth Bennet with them on their tour of Derbyshire, and they are thus instrumental in promoting the romance between Elizabeth and Darcy. Up to this point, Darcy's view of Elizabeth's family has been strongly colored by his impressions of the vulgar Mrs. Bennet, so Elizabeth is pleased to be able to introduce him to the more refined Gardiners. Equally, the occasion provides Darcy with an opportunity to demonstrate his lack of prejudice through his courteous treatment of the Gardiners. After their marriage, Darcy and Elizabeth continue on intimate terms with the Gardiners, whom they love both for themselves and for the fact of their having helped bring about the match. Mr. Gardiner is also important as a relatively new fictional type in that he represents a positive picture of the self-made tradesman, able to hold his own with the gentry.

Gardiner, Mrs. M. (*Pride and Prejudice* Ch.25; II:2:139). The wife of Mr. Gardiner and "an amiable, intelligent, elegant woman" who is a great favorite with Elizabeth and Jane Bennet. She is much younger than Mrs. Bennet and has four young children.

Gibson, Old (*Sense and Sensibility* Ch.33; II:11:225). A former resident of East Kingham Farm, a property adjoining the Norland estate that John Dashwood buys.

Gilbert, Mrs. (*Emma* Chs.29, 38; II:11:248; III:2:327). Part of the Highbury social set. She attends the Coles' dinner party and the Crown Inn ball. At the latter event, Elton refers to her as the only suitable dancing partner for him as a pointed means of foiling Mrs. Weston's attempt to have him dance with Harriet Smith.

Gilberts, the (*Sense and Sensibility* Ch.20; I:20:111). Neighbors of the Middletons at Barton. Sir John complains about his wife's not inviting the Gilberts to dinner so as to make a larger party, but she reminds him that it would have been improper to do so, as it is the turn of the Gilberts to invite *them* to dinner.

Gilberts, the two (*Emma* Ch.29; II:11:248). Mrs. Gilbert's sons and eligible young dancing partners who can be relied upon to make up numbers for Mr. Weston's ball. Their sister, a Miss Gilbert, is also mentioned.

Godby, Miss (*Sense and Sensibility* Ch.38; III:2:272). An acquaintance of the Miss Steeles in their London circle. Anne Steele refers to her as one source of gossip that is suggesting that Edward Ferrars will forsake Lucy Steele now that his mother has found out about their secret engagement.

Goddard, Mrs. (*Emma* Ch.3; I:3:20–23). Part of the "second set" of Highbury society that frequents Mr. Woodhouse's drawing room of an evening, Mrs. Goddard is the respected mistress of the girls' school where Harriet Smith is a parlor-boarder. She is a "motherly kind of woman" who gives her pupils plenty of good food and exercise and "a reasonable quantity of accomplishments . . . at a reasonable price." Mrs. Goddard first introduces Harriet Smith to Emma.

Goulding family (*Pride and Prejudice* Chs.50, 51; III:8:310; III:9:316). The Gouldings of Haye-Park are neighbors of the Bennet family. On hearing of Lydia's coming marriage to Wickham, Mrs. Bennet sets to considering where they might live in the vicinity of Longbourn, and, she muses, Haye-Park would be just the place, "if the Gouldings would quit it." A little later, Lydia, on her triumphant way home after the wedding, drives past William Goulding and makes an extravagant show of her wedding finger out of the window of her carriage to ensure that her neighbors are aware of her new status.

Graham, Mr. (*Emma* Ch.12; I:12:104). An acquaintance of John Knightley who intends to appoint a bailiff from Scotland to look after his new estate. Emma queries the wisdom of this, suggesting that "the old prejudice" may be too strong.

Grant, Dr. (*Mansfield Park* Ch.3; I:3:24). Dr. Grant is Mr. Norris' successor as rector of Mansfield, and there is a certain Dickensian symmetry in noting that Dr. Grant the gourmand replaces the pinched and parsimonious Norrises at the parsonage. Dr. Grant is "a short-neck'd, apoplectic sort of fellow" of forty-five, "an indolent, stay-at-home man" who, though learned and gentlemanly, seems more concerned with his food and drink than with the morals of his parishioners. Mary considers him a gentleman, a good scholar, clever and respectable but also an indolent, selfish bon vivant. He is later made a dean of Westminster and dies of apoplexy after eating three great dinners in one week.

Grant, Mrs. (*Mansfield Park* Ch.3; I:3:24). Wife to Dr. Grant and half sister, by a common mother, to the Crawfords, Mrs. Grant is a good-humored and kindly woman of about thirty. She always does her best for her demanding husband—indeed, she is perhaps too much at his gluttonous beck and call—and after his death she goes to live with Mary Crawford.

Grantley, Miss (*Pride and Prejudice* Ch.11; I:11:48). An acquaintance of Miss Bingley's. When Darcy is writing to his sister, Georgiana, Miss Bingley asks him to tell her that she liked a table design she had done better than one done by Miss Grantley.

Gray's (*Sense and Sensibility* Ch.33; II:11:220). A jeweler's shop in Sackville Street, London, where Elinor goes to negotiate for the exchange of some of her mother's jewelry and where she first sees Robert Ferrars as he deliberates over the purchase of a toothpick case.

Green, Mr. (*Emma* Ch.22; II:4:182). Their mutual attendance in Bath at a dinner given by "Mr. Green" is one of the "steps so quick" toward the marriage of Mr. Elton and Miss Hawkins; a party given by "Mrs. Brown" is the next step.

Green, Mr. (*Mansfield Park* Ch.7; I:7:73). Briefly mentioned by Mrs. Norris when making excuses to Edmund for having sent Fanny out into the hot sun on an unnecessary errand. She says she had to talk to Mr. Green about Lady Bertram's dairymaid, so Mr. Green presumably has something to do with the running of the estate.

Gregorys, the (*Mansfield Park* Ch.25; II:7:249). Old acquaintances of Fanny and William Price from Portsmouth. William, at that point still only a midshipman, tells Fanny that "Portsmouth girls turn up their noses at any body who has not a commission" and then, by way of example, refers to the Gregorys, who, he says, have grown into "amazing fine girls" but will hardly speak to him now, as one of them, Lucy, is being courted by a lieutenant.

Grey, Miss Sophia (*Sense and Sensibility* Chs.30, 44; II:8:192, 194–95; III:8:326). An heiress with £50,000 whom John Willoughby marries for her fortune. She is reportedly "a smart, stilish girl . . . but not handsome." Her relationship with her guardians, Mr. and Mrs. Ellison, appears to have been strained, and the suggestion that this may have been on account of her willful character is reinforced by Willoughby's later descriptions of her possessive jealousy and by the fact that she dictates his letter breaking off contact with Marianne.

Grierson, Lady Mary (*Persuasion* Ch.8; I:8:68). On a voyage back to England from Lisbon, Captain Wentworth once almost had to give passage to this lady and her daughter, but he was glad to have avoided the obligation, as he does not hold with carrying women on his ships.

Griffiths, Mrs. (*Sanditon, Minor Works* 408, 420). The genteel proprietor of a girls' school in Camberwell who brings three of her charges to Sanditon for the summer, apparently at the suggestion of some friends of Diana Parker. Diana has been misled by her friends into believing that this "Ladies Seminary" is a different group from the wealthy West Indian one she has also been told to expect at Sanditon. It is the latter group she associates with Mrs. Griffiths, and this leads to confusion when *only* the girls' school arrives but headed by Mrs. Griffiths. The misunderstanding has arisen because of there being a West Indian girl, Miss Lambe, among Mrs. Griffiths' party.

Groom, John (*Mansfield Park* Ch.7; I:7:73). "Groom" is almost certainly a reference to the work that the said John does at Mansfield Park rather than his actual surname. Mrs. Norris refers to a letter she is to write for him to a Mrs. Jefferies about his son.

H

Haggerston (*Pride and Prejudice* Ch.49; III:7:303). The attorney who prepares Lydia Bennet's marriage settlement on Mr. Gardiner's instructions.

Halifax, Dowager Lady, and daughters ("Catharine," *Minor Works* 195). The family of relations who, after Mr. Wynne's death, take in Mary Wynne as a companion for the girls. They take her to Scotland with them, but her letters to Catharine suggest that she is not treated very kindly by them. The Halifaxes are also well known to Camilla Stanley.

Hamiltons, the (*Lady Susan, Minor Works* 298). Acquaintances of Mrs. Johnson, mentioned only in passing.

Hancock, Elizabeth (Eliza) (1761–1813). Jane Austen's first cousin, Eliza Hancock, was born on 22 December 1761 in Calcutta to Philadelphia and Tysoe Saul Hancock. She was the goddaughter of Warren Hastings, who later made handsome financial provision for her when her father's fortunes fell. She came to England with her parents in 1765 and never returned to India. After her father's death in 1775, she traveled on the continent with her mother from 1777 and settled in Paris in 1779, where she was able to gain entry into high society in both Paris and Versailles. In 1781, Eliza married Jean Capot de Feuillide (1750–1794), a captain of dragoons in the queen's regiment and self-styled comte de Feuillide. In 1786, Eliza returned to London, where she gave birth to her only child, Hastings, on 25 June. Later that year, she was part of the Christmas festivities at the home of her Steventon cousins. Her acting talents were given full scope during her visit, as she took the leading female roles in the theatricals that were organized, and these also seem to have given her plenty of scope to flirt with her male cousins, James and Henry Austen, who seem both to have become enamored of her at this time. Jane Austen was only eleven, but she also seems to have been enchanted by her glamorous and cosmopolitan "French" cousin. Eliza and her mother then settled in a fashionable house on Orchard Street, London (where Henry stayed with them in April 1787). She was again part of the Steventon Christmas theatricals in 1787–1788, and Jane Austen and her family dined with her on Orchard Street in the summer of 1888, just before she and her mother returned again to France in September of that year. They stayed in Paris for at least some of that time and therefore presumably witnessed some of the main events in the French Revolution of 1789, and they returned to England in 1790. For much of the time leading to her mother's death in February 1792, Eliza was occupied full-time in not only nursing her mother but also caring for her son, who, it was now clear, had been born disabled. From 1792 on, until the end of her life, Eliza became increasingly part of Jane Austen's regular family circle. For one thing, in the autumn of 1792, she seems to have renewed her flirtation with Henry Austen, whom she would later marry. In 1794, events in the French Revolution were, for the first time, brought close to the Austen family through Eliza, in a tragic way, when her husband, who had become embroiled in political developments in France as part of the aristocratic faction, was guillotined in Paris on 22 February. From around 1795, a more definite courtship between Eliza and Henry Austen seems to have developed, and they were finally married in London on 31 December 1797. From this point on, obviously, the events of Eliza's life overlap with those of Henry Austen, which are detailed in the entry on him. Eliza's son, Hastings, died in the autumn of 1801 at the age of fifteen, and she had no further children with Henry. Eliza herself died after a long illness on 25 April 1813, the extent of her closeness to Jane Austen by this time being demonstrated by the fact that Jane Austen helped to nurse her through her last days. With her intelligence, vivacity, and glamour (as well as her flirtatiousness and talent for acting), Eliza is often suggested by biographers and critics as a possible source for Maria Crawford in Jane Austen's *Mansfield Park* (though also—less frequently and more harshly—as a possible source for the title character in *Lady Susan*).

See: R. A. Austen-Leigh 1942, Lane 1984, Le Faye 1989, Tucker 1983.

Hancock, Philadelphia (1730–1792). Younger sister of Jane Austen's father. Little is known of Philadelphia's early life, but at the age of twenty-one she seems to have been sent to India to find a husband (somewhat like Cecilia Wynne in Jane Austen's "Catharine"). She arrived at Madras in August 1752 and, in February 1753, was duly married to Tysoe Saul Hancock (1711–1775), a surgeon with the East India Company. The Hancocks moved to Calcutta in 1759, where they became acquainted with Warren Hastings (1732–1818) who was later to become governor-general of India (1773–1785) and the subject of a famous impeachment trial back in England (1788–1795). When the Hancocks' daughter, Eliza, was born on 22 December 1761, Warren Hastings stood as godfather to her, and he later (in 1775) settled £10,000 on her. At the time, there were apparently rumors of an affair between Warren Hastings and Philadelphia, and this act of generosity, along with other hearsay evidence, has led to some speculation over the possible illegitimacy of Eliza Hancock, though there is no clear evidence of this.

In June 1765, the Hancocks returned to England and settled in London, and Philadelphia was able to renew her contact with George Austen and his family. Mr. Hancock returned to India in 1768, when he started to experience financial difficulties, but Philadelphia and Eliza remained in London. Mr. Hancock died in November 1775. Between 1777 and 1779, Philadelphia and Eliza traveled on the continent, visiting Germany and Belgium. They then settled in Paris in the autumn of 1779 and remained in France until May 1786, when they returned to London and once more became part of Austen family life at Steventon and elsewhere. They returned to France in 1788 and presumably witnessed some of the events of the French Revolution in 1789, as they did not return to England until 1790. In the summer of 1791, Philadelphia began to suffer from breast cancer, and she died on 26 February 1792.

See: Lane 1984, Le Faye 1989, Tucker 1983.

Hanking, Rev. (*Sanditon, Minor Works* 389). A visitor to Sanditon noted by Mr. Parker in the subscription list at the circulating library. *See* Beard, Mr.

Hannah (*Emma* Ch.1; I:1:9). Housemaid at Randalls, the home of Mr. and Mrs. Weston. She is the daughter of Mr. Woodhouse's coachman, James, and sometimes comes to Hartfield to help with needlework. Mr. Woodhouse thinks she will make an excellent servant, as she has always been polite and attentive to him; he observes that "she always turns the lock of the door the right way and never bangs it." He suggested her employment at Randalls and takes pleasure at the thought that Miss Taylor will have a familiar face from Hartfield in her new home.

Harding, Dr. (*The Watsons, Minor Works* 317). A rich old man from Chichester whom Penelope Watson is hoping to marry.

Harding, Mr. (*Mansfield Park* Ch.47; III:16:450). Sir Thomas Bertram's "old and most particular friend" in London who writes to Sir Thomas to apprise him of the developing scandal involving his daughter, Maria, and Henry Crawford.

Harrington, Miss Harriet, and Miss Pen (*Pride and Prejudice* Ch.39; II:16: 221). Acquaintances of Lydia and Kitty Bennet who are invited to Mrs. Forster's home at Meryton for an informal dance. In the event, Harriet is too ill to attend, and Pen comes alone.

Harris, Mr. (*Sense and Sensibility* Ch.43; III:7:307). Mr. and Mrs. Palmer's apothecary at Cleveland who is brought in to treat Marianne when she falls ill.

He is an optimistic soul who talks encouragingly of a speedy recovery and who blithely tries out various medicines on Marianne without much obvious effect.

Harrison, Colonel (*Mansfield Park* Ch.29; II:11:283). A guest at the Mansfield Park ball. Lady Bertram could not be sure whether he had been talking about Henry Crawford or William Price when he talked to her of "the finest young man in the room."

Harry (*Emma* Ch.32; III:16:458). One of Mr. Knightley's menservants at Donwell Abbey, of whom Mrs. Elton loftily remarks to Emma, "I would not have such a creature . . . stand at our sideboard for any consideration."

Harville, Captain (*Persuasion* Chs.8, 11; I:8:67; I:11:96–99). Captain Wentworth's friend and former fellow officer on the *Laconia*. He had been wounded in action two years previously to our introduction to him, and he has been suffering from ill health ever since. He and his family have settled in Lyme for the winter, and it is there that we first meet him, when he is introduced to the Musgrove party and hospitably invites them back to his lodgings. He is described as a perfect gentleman—well mannered, "unaffected, warm, and obliging." His considerate and generous nature is made evident by the fact that he continues to care and provide accommodations for his late sister's fiancé, Captain Benwick, as well as by the way in which he arranges for Louisa Musgrove to be nursed at his home following her fall from the Cobb. Although slightly lame on account of his wound and struggling somewhat to maintain his wife and three children, Harville does not dwell on his difficulties (unlike Captain Benwick) and remains cheerful, lively, and active. He is clearly quite a handyman around the house, making toys for the children and furniture for the rooms, and Anne Elliot is full of warm admiration for his skill and ingenuity in making the lodgings so comfortable and homely for his family.

Harville, Fanny (deceased) (*Persuasion* Ch.11; I:11:96–97). The late fiancée of Captain Benwick. The couple had been engaged for some time and were waiting for Captain Benwick to gain promotion and fortune at sea before marrying, when Fanny suddenly died while he was away on duty.

Harville, Mrs., and her three children (*Persuasion* Chs.8, 11; I:8:67 & 69; I: 11:97–98). Though she is "a degree less polished," Mrs. Harville has the same friendly openness and warmth as her husband, and she is as spontaneously hospitable and welcoming to others. She is an experienced nurse and provides excellent care for Louisa Musgrove while she is recuperating at Lyme, despite also having three children to look after.

Hawkins, Miss Augusta. *See* Elton, Mrs.

Hayter, Mr. (*Persuasion* Ch.9; I:9:74). The owner of the small estate of Winthrop in Somerset, just two miles away from the Musgroves' Uppercross. He and his wife, the sister of Mrs. Musgrove (senior) live an "inferior, retired, and unpolished" life, and their children are looked upon as poor relations by the Musgroves, though the two families remain on excellent terms.

Hayter, Mrs. (*Persuasion* Ch.9; I:9:74). Wife of Mr. Hayter and sister of Mrs. Musgrove. Like her sister, Mrs. Hayter had had a reasonable fortune settled on her, but, unlike her sister, she had married a man with relatively little property, and this had rather reduced her social consequence.

Hayter, Rev. Charles (*Persuasion* Ch.9; I:9:73–76). Eldest son of Mr. and Mrs. Hayter of Winthrop. He is "a very amiable, pleasing young man" who has a decided superiority of mind and manner over the rest of his family, owing to his profession and scholarly education. He is a suitor for Henrietta Musgrove's hand and is therefore dismayed to return from a brief absence to find her fascinated by Captain Wentworth. His suit eventually prevails, however, and he and Henrietta are later engaged.

Hayters, the Miss (*Persuasion* Ch.8; I:8:71). Cousins of the Musgrove girls but of a lower social standing. They have had a "defective education" and would have belonged "hardly in any class" were it not for their connection with the Musgrove family. There is no pride or envy between the two sets of cousins, however, and they all socialize together quite happily.

Heeley, William (*Sanditon, Minor Works* 383). The shoemaker at old Sanditon whose window display of blue shoes and nankeen boots delights Mr. Parker, as it suggests the increasingly fashionable nature of Sanditon.

Hemmings, Mr. (*The Watsons, Minor Works* 353). An acquaintance of Robert and Jane Watson in Croydon; he apparently dresses for dinner every day, as does Mr. Marshall.

"Henry and Eliza, a Novel" (*Volume the First* of Jane Austen's juvenilia). This piece was dedicated to Jane Austen's cousin Jane Cooper, possibly around the start of 1789 while the Coopers were visiting with the Austens. The story itself, however, may have been written earlier, though probably not before 1787. Almost every trick in the book of sentimental fiction is packed in to this "novel" of seven pages. A beautiful baby is discovered in a haycock by Sir George and Lady Harcourt, who have no children of their own. They adopt the child, Eliza, and bring her up as their own, giving her a good education and teaching her to be virtuous. Admired by everyone and adored by the Harcourts, she has a life of "uninterrupted Happiness" until she reaches the age of eighteen. At this time, she is caught one day stealing a fifty-pound banknote and thrown out of the house by her adoptive parents (it is later indicated that such stealing has been a regular source of her "happiness"). Eliza goes to see her best friend, Mrs. Wilson, the proprietor of the local inn, and she gives her a letter of introduction to the Dutchess [*sic*] of F. The latter lady takes Eliza in as a companion, and both she and her daughter Harriet immediately resolve to treat Eliza as a member of the family. Harriet is on the point of marrying Henry Cecil, but he now falls in love with Eliza, and they are secretly married by the chaplain of the house (who has also fallen in love with Eliza and will do anything she asks, even if it means marrying her to someone else!). The couple then escape to France, while the enraged Dutchess organizes a group of 300 armed men to go to find them and bring them back, dead or alive. In France, Henry and Eliza live for three years and have two sons before Henry dies, leaving Eliza destitute. She returns to England and is imprisoned by the Dutchess in a private prison she has built specially for her—"a snug little Newgate." Eliza escapes, however, by sawing through the bars of the window in her cell. She then makes her way back, with her little boys, to the town where she had been brought up by the Harcourts. Outside an inn, she approaches a carriage for charity and finds that it is the carriage of her adoptive parents. When Lady Harcourt hears her voice, she suddenly realizes that Eliza is, in fact, her natural daughter. She explains to her astonished husband that she had given birth to a daughter while he had been away in America but that she had abandoned her in a haycock for fear of his being annoyed that the child was not a boy. When they had later come across Eliza, Lady Harcourt had forgotten about the "other" baby, and it is only now, on being reminded of that baby's voice by hearing Eliza's, that she has remembered it. Sir George is impressed at the rationality of this explanation (!) and forgives Eliza for stealing his money. She returns with them to Harcourt Hall to pick up where she left off. The story ends with her raising an army and demolishing the Dutchess of F.'s private Newgate, an act that gains her "the Blessings of thousands."

Characters: Henry Cecil, Dutchess of F., Lady Harriet F., Eliza Harcourt, Sir George Harcourt, Lady Polly Harcourt, Mrs. Sarah Wilson.

Henry, Sir (*Mansfield Park* Ch.13; I:13:122). An acquaintance of Mr. Yates from Lord Ravenshaw's house party. According to Mr. Yates, Sir Henry complained about the Duke's acting of the part of Frederick in *Lovers' Vows*, but only because he wanted the part for himself.

Henshawe, Biddy (*Sense and Sensibility* Ch.29; II:7:194). Rich aunt of Sophia Grey.

Heywood, Charlotte (*Sanditon, Minor Works* 374). At twenty-two, Charlotte Heywood is the eldest of the Heywood daughters still at home. She is particularly helpful to the Parkers during their enforced stay at Willingden, and they are pleased to be able to take her back with them to spend a holiday at Sanditon.

Although prone to brief flights of fancy and as susceptible to flattery as the next young person, she is, on the whole, a sensible character who weighs evidence carefully and rationally and relies on her own judgment. She quickly sees through the artifice and guile of characters like Sir Edward and his sister, Esther, and recognizes the partiality of Mr. Parker's assessment of Lady Denham, whose meanness she reacts against very strongly. In what we have of the novel, Charlotte Heywood seems to be developing clearly as its central character, and all the other characters are, as it were, refracted through her consciousness, though she herself remains somewhat undeveloped.

Heywood, Mr. and Mrs. (*Sanditon, Minor Works* 365, 370). Mr. Heywood is a solidly respectable gentleman farmer of Willingden in Sussex. He has lived there for the whole of his fifty-seven years and, though not rich, has a comfortable home in which he and his wife have raised fourteen children. When Mr. Parker's carriage overturns outside the Heywoods' house, they are quick to offer their help and hospitality. They are a homely and steady couple who have become accustomed to, and happy with, a quiet and prudent lifestyle. They have neither of them traveled far from home, and they have no intention of starting now, so they politely demur when Mr. Parker invites them to Sanditon—though they are only too happy to send their daughter, Charlotte.

Hill, Mrs. (*Pride and Prejudice* Ch.13; I:13:301). The Bennets' housekeeper at Longbourn.

Hillier, Mr. and Mrs. (*Sanditon, Minor Works* 380). Thomas Parker's tenant farming family who have taken over the Parkers' comfortable old family home two miles inland from the sea.

"The History of England from the Reign of Henry the 4th to the Death of Charles the 1st" (*Volume the Second* of Jane Austen's juvenilia). This spoof history, an exuberant parody of popular histories of the time (and Oliver Goldsmith's in particular), is announced as being "by a partial, prejudiced, & ignorant Historian." It was completed on 26 November 1791 and dedicated to Jane Austen's sister, Cassandra, who painted illustrations for it in the form of miniature portraits of the various monarchs dealt with. The comedy of the piece derives from its extreme informality of style and tone, its chatty trivialization of important historical matter, and its absurd reduction of whole reigns and sweeps of time into short paragraphs made up largely of throwaway lines such as—on Henry VIII—"his abolishing Religious Houses . . . has been of infinite use to the landscape of England in general, which probably was a principal motive for his doing it"; or, on Edward V, "This unfortunate Prince lived so little a while that no body had time to draw his picture." On a slightly more serious note, Jan Fergus suggests that the intentions of the "History," particularly in its treatment of Mary Queen of Scots and Elizabeth I, are revisionist:

Jane Austen "is revising conventional views of Elizabeth's and Mary's characters. But more important, in offering these unconventional images of two powerful women, and in making them central to her narrative, she is revising history itself, which (as Catharine Morland laments) has 'hardly any women at all' " (*1991*: 42).

Hodges, Mrs. (*Emma* Ch.27; II:9:239). Mr. Knightley's housekeeper at Donwell Abbey. She is annoyed to hear of his giving away the last of his apples, as "she could not bear that her master should not be able to have another apple-tart this spring." Mrs. Hodges is included in Mrs. Elton's general censure of the Donwell servants as "extremely awkward and remiss": *her* housekeeper, Wright, she assures Emma, holds Mrs. Hodges "very cheap indeed" (partly because she forgot to send a promised recipe); and, later, after hearing the news of Emma's marriage to Knightley, Mrs. Elton declares herself glad to have "abused" his housekeeper in Emma's hearing.

Hodges, the (*Northanger Abbey* Chs.16, 27; II:1:130; II:12:217). Some friends of Isabella Thorpe, including Charles Hodges, who appears to be her admirer. She expects him to pester her at the assembly at which she first meets Captain Tilney. Later, after losing Captain Tilney to Charlotte Davis, she goes to see a play with the Hodges in order to prove that she is not shutting herself away from company.

Holford, Mrs. (*Mansfield Park* Ch.5; I:5:50). At a Mrs. Holford's house in London, Tom Bertram finds himself embarrassed by the recently "out" and suddenly overfamiliar Miss Anderson.

Hollis, Mr. (*Sanditon, Minor Works* 385). The first husband of Lady Denham. Mr. Hollis was a wealthy landowner in the area of Sanditon and already an elderly man when Lady Denham married him. He left her all his property, much to the annoyance of other members of his family, who seem to have considered her a fortune hunter.

Howard, Rev. (*The Watsons, Minor Works* 330). A clergyman of the parish of Wickstead, former tutor to Lord Osborne, and brother of Mrs. Blake. Mr. Howard is just over thirty. When Emma dances with him, she finds him to be as agreeable in manner and conversation as he is in looks. When Mr. Watson later attends a religious service, he reports to his daughters that the preacher was Mr. Howard and that he had preached an excellent sermon. Mr. Howard had also helped Mr. Watson up a steep flight of steps and had asked after one of his daughters. (Although the novel was never finished, it appears that Jane Austen had intended Mr. Howard to marry Emma Watson in the end.)

Hughes family (Dr. and Mrs. Hughes and their son, Richard) (*Emma* Ch.38; III:2:323). Guests at the Crown Inn ball and acquaintances of Miss Bates.

Hughes, Mrs. (*Northanger Abbey* Chs.8, 9; I:8:54–55; I:9:68–69). An acquaintance of Mrs. Thorpe and an old school friend of the late Mrs. Tilney. Mrs. Hughes is part of the Tilney party at Bath, and, via Mrs. Thorpe and Mrs. Allen, she provides Catherine with background information about the Tilney family. At the second ball at which Catherine meets Henry, Mrs. Hughes escorts Eleanor Tilney onto the dance floor and finds a place for her beside Catherine, who is therefore able to speak to Eleanor for the first time.

Hunt, Captain (*Northanger Abbey* Ch.6; I:6:40). One of Isabella Thorpe's dancing partners at the assemblies at her home in Putney. She tells Catherine that she once threatened not to dance with him unless he agreed with her about the beauty of her friend, Miss Andrews.

Hunter, Captain (*The Watsons, Minor Works* 320). Sam Watson's rival for Mary Edwards' hand.

Hurst, Mr. (*Pride and Prejudice* Ch.3; I:3:10). The husband of Mr. Bingley's sister and an indolent man of little account who has no sensible conversation and "who lived only to eat, drink, and play at cards." He appears to have married his wife only for her money and, with her, lives parasitically on Darcy and Bingley, even though he has a house of his own on Grosvenor Street, London.

Hurst, Mrs. Louisa, née Bingley (*Pride and Prejudice* Ch.3; I:3:10). The older sister of Mr. Bingley who, though in possession of a large fortune of her own, appears content to live off him. Like her sister, Caroline Bingley, she is a "fine" lady, fashionable, proud, and conceited. But she is less actively manipulative than her sister and, in fact, plays little part in the main action.

Hutchinson, Sarah ("Catharine," *Minor Works* 233). Mrs. Percival's particular friend who literally caught her death of cold.

I, J

Ibbotsons, the (*Persuasion* Ch.21; II:9:193). A family mentioned by Mrs. Smith as familiar faces at social gatherings in Bath.

"Jack and Alice, a Novel" (*Volume the First* of Jane Austen's juvenilia). Probably written early in the period 1787–1790 and transcribed from the lost original shortly after, this piece was later dedicated to Frank Austen (probably early in 1790 just after Frank had become a midshipman on HMS *Perseverance*— he is given this title in the dedication). It contains nine short chapters and parodies, often hilariously, the typical excesses of the sentimental novel of the period, both through the outrageous events of its plot and through its stylized characterization, with most characters being summed up by one or two dominating features that are clearly identified as a vice or a virtue. The Johnson family are "addicted to the Bottle & the Dice," Caroline Simpson is ambitious, Sukey Simpson is envious and spiteful, Cecilia Simpson is affected and vain, Charles Adams is a paragon of beauty, Lady Williams a paragon of virtue, and Lucy a paragon of loveliness and amiability. There is, though, a slightly more complex development of one or two of the characters, and this anticipates the more subtle technique of Jane Austen's later fiction (particularly in its controlled release of ironies). For example, the scheming nature of the apparently honest Lady Williams is made fully clear only at the end of the story, when we realize that she has been plotting all along to capture the dazzling Charles Adams for herself and that her earlier words and behavior have been entirely disingenuous (indeed, she exhibits some of the ruthless aplomb of Lady Susan Vernon in the way she deceives and manipulates others for her own ends). Similarly, the apparent perfections of Charles Adams' character are gradually undermined by references to his arrogance, snobbery, and coldheartedness, not to say cruelty (Lucy's falling into the mantrap is suggestive here).

Following a masquerade party held by the Johnson family to celebrate Mr.

Johnson's fifty-fifth birthday (which ends with everyone's being carried home "Dead Drunk"), Alice Johnson becomes infatuated with Charles Adams, though he shows no interest in her. She seeks the advice of Lady Williams, who appears to be sympathetic to her but who craftily plays on her sensitivities, making fun of her high color and drunkenness and provoking her to a rage. Nevertheless, Alice continues to visit Lady Williams (drawn by her claret as much as by anything else), and while they are walking one day on the grounds of Charles Adams' estate, they come across a lovely young woman caught in a mantrap. This turns out to be Lucy, a tailor's daughter from North Wales. She tells them her life story, which includes having fallen in love with Charles Adams when he was staying on his estate in North Wales (which happened to be near to her home), before anybody pays attention to the leg she has had broken by Charles Adams' steel mantrap. Lady Williams now sets the leg, and Lucy is immediately able to walk back with them to Lady Williams' house! Lady Williams is careful to prevent a friendship's forming between Lucy and Alice but tells Lucy of Alice's bad-tempered drunkenness; and when, the next day, the three Simpson girls call and invite Lucy to come with them to Bath the next morning, Lady Williams effectively encourages her to accept the invitation (thus removing another potential rival for the affections of Charles Adams).

In the seventh chapter, the supposed hero of the novel, Jack Johnson, is briefly introduced when we hear that he has drunk himself to death. This means that his sister, Alice, is now the heir to the family fortune, and this encourages her to ask her father to propose to Charles Adams on her behalf. He does so but receives a disdainful refusal in which Charles Adams, after running through Alice's various deficiencies, states that he will contemplate only a wife who is as perfect as he is. On hearing of this refusal, Alice "flew to her Bottle & it was soon forgot."

Once in Bath, Lucy soon forgets how Charles Adams had broken her heart and leg and becomes engaged to a rich old Duke. This, however, causes the envious Sukey Simpson to threaten Lucy's life. In a letter to Lady Williams, Lucy reports that Sukey has often "endeavoured to cut my throat," and before she can receive a reply from Lady Williams, she is, in fact, poisoned to death by the said Sukey. The bereaved Duke mourns Lucy's death for two weeks before marrying Caroline Simpson. She is thus raised to the rank of Duchess while her miscreant sister, Sukey, is "speedily raised to the Gallows." Back in the neighborhood of Pammydiddle, there is general astonishment at the news of Charles Adams' impending marriage—to Lady Williams.

Characters: Charles Adams, Miss Dickins (Lady Williams' former governess), Mr. Johnson, father of Jack and Alice Johnson, Mr. and Mrs. Jones, Lucy, the sisters Caroline, Sukey, and Cecilia Simpson, Mrs. Susan (Charles Adams' cook), Mrs. Watkins, Lady Kitty Williams.

Jackson (*Northanger Abbey* Ch.7; I:7:47). One of John Thorpe's cronies from Oxford—he offered sixty guineas for John Thorpe's new gig and horse.

Jackson, Christopher (*Mansfield Park* Ch.13; I:13:127). The carpenter at Mansfield Park commissioned by Tom Bertram to prepare the "theatre" for the private theatricals. His ten-year-old son, Dick, also features briefly when Mrs. Norris catches him on an errand for his father, which, it being dinnertime, she immediately interprets as a ruse to get him a free meal in the servants' hall; she considers the Jacksons to be "encroaching people . . . just the sort of people to get all they can," and she sends the "greedy," "marauding" lad away with a flea in his ear (Ch.15; I:15:141–42). Mrs. Norris' "triumph" over Dick Jackson is heavily ironic, of course, when one considers *her* position and behavior at Mansfield Park.

James (*Emma* Ch.1; I:1:8). Mr. Woodhouse's overprotected coachman— "James will not like to put the horses to for such a little way"—and father of the Westons' housemaid, Hannah.

James (*Lady Susan, Minor Works* 283). Reginald De Courcy's manservant.

James (*The Watsons, Minor Works* 319). Mr. Watson's coachman.

Jebb (*Sanditon, Minor Works* 381). One of the shopkeepers at Sanditon, possibly a milliner, as Mrs. Parker talks of buying her daughter a bonnet there.

Jeffereys, Mrs. (*Emma* Ch.32; II:14:277). A friend of Mrs. Elton—"Clara Partridge, that was" (presumably the daughter of Mrs. Elton's "particular friend" at Bath, Mrs. Partridge)—used by the latter as an example (along with Mrs. Bird and Mrs. Cooper) of married women's being "too apt to give up music."

Jefferies, Mrs. (*Mansfield Park* Ch.7; I:7:73). An acquaintance of Mrs. Norris, mentioned only briefly.

Jemima (*Persuasion* Ch.6; I:6:45). Mary Musgrove's nursemaid at Uppercross cottage. Mary considers her to be steady and trustworthy, even though (Mary claims) she is often tempted to go "gadding about the village" by Mrs. Musgrove's upper housemaid and laundry maid. On the other hand, Mrs. Musgrove complains that Jemima is extravagant and showy, "a fine-dressing lady," and that she has a bad influence on *her* servants.

Jenkinson, Mrs. (*Pride and Prejudice* Chs.19, 29; I:19:105; II:6:161–62). Former governess and present companion to Miss Anne de Bourgh, Mrs. Jenkinson is an "unremarkable" old lady who appears to be entirely devoted to her charge and grossly overprotective of her.

Jennings, Charlotte (*Sense and Sensibility*). *See* Palmer, Mrs.

Jennings, Mary (*Sense and Sensibility*). *See* Middleton, Lady.

Jennings, Mr. (deceased) (*Sense and Sensibility* Chs.11, 25; 1:11:54; II:3:153). A successful tradesman "in a less elegant part" of London—presumably an important piece of background information by which to understand the character of Mrs. Jennings.

Jennings, Mrs. (*Sense and Sensibility* Ch.7; I:7:34). A widow with "an ample jointure," mother of Lady Middleton and Charlotte Palmer, and cousin to the Steele girls, Mrs. Jennings is "a good-humoured, merry, fat, elderly woman, who talked a great deal, seemed very happy, and rather vulgar." Having married off her only two daughters, she is now a zealous matchmaker for any other young people she comes across, and she rarely spares them any blushes in making crude jokes about the love affairs she imagines for them. As with Sir John Middleton, one of her favorite intensifiers—"monstrous"—serves to characterize her robust manner.

John ("Catharine," *Minor Works* 210). Mrs. Percival's servant.

John (*Pride and Prejudice* Ch.37; II:14:212). Manservant to Mr. Collins at Hunsford Parsonage.

John (*Pride and Prejudice* Chs.37, 46; II:14:212; III:4:280). The Gardiners' servant who accompanies them on their tour of Derbyshire.

Johnson, Alicia (*Lady Susan, Minor Works* 244). Lady Susan's intimate friend and confidante and sometime companion in coquetry. She is married and lives at Edward Street in London. Seventeen of the forty-one letters of the novel are exchanged between Lady Susan and Mrs. Johnson, and, because Lady Susan writes openly and honestly to her friend, these serve a type of soliloquy function whereby her "true" thoughts and feelings can be set against her dissimulating words and actions with others.

Johnson, Mr. (*Lady Susan, Minor Works* 245, 249). Gouty husband of Lady Susan's intimate friend, Alicia Johnson, and guardian to Mrs. Manwaring. He is apparently a respectable man, and, under no illusions about Lady Susan's bad influence on his wife, he is constantly vigilant about the possibility of the two friends' meeting up, even, it seems, to the point of feigning attacks of gout to interfere with their suspected plans. He has forbidden his wife from ever inviting Lady Susan to Edward Street, and, after the events of the novel, he also forbids her from even writing to her. He is instrumental in the final denouement, as he breaks the news of Lady Susan's affair with Manwaring to Reginald De Courcy and provides Reginald with reliable proof of her previous misconduct. But in terms of wit, if not morality, Lady Susan perhaps has the last word with her memorable quip about her archenemy: "too old to be agreable [*sic*], & too young to die."

Jones, Mr. (*Pride and Prejudice* Ch.6; I:6:31). The apothecary at Meryton who attends Jane Bennet when she is ill at Netherfield Park. Mrs. Phillips later learns of Jane's return home from Mr. Jones' shop boy, whom she meets in the street.

Juvenilia. What has come to be known as Jane Austen's juvenilia are the pieces written roughly between 1787 and 1793 (when she was between eleven and seventeen years old) and transcribed by her over that period and later (continuing until possibly as late as 1809) into three notebooks entitled *Volume the First, Volume the Second*, and *Volume the Third*. To these should now be added *Sir Charles Grandison or The Happy Man*, a *Comedy* in *Five Acts*, possibly begun around 1791–1792 (attributed to Jane Austen only in 1977 and published for the first time in 1980). The juvenilia consist mainly of short burlesque pieces that parody the fictional conventions of the period, and, as such, they demonstrate that Jane Austen's literary apprenticeship was essentially that of a creative literary critic with a keen eye for the leading formal and thematic features of the eighteenth-century novel (particularly the sentimental novel). Indeed, one could do far worse than to use her juvenilia as an entertaining introduction to the study of that period's fiction, for her comical exaggerations and absurdist condensations make the popular period conventions stand out very clearly. The two best-known pieces in the juvenilia—among the funniest—are "Love and Friendship" and "The History of England," while the most important piece for our understanding of Jane Austen's later development is "Catharine, or the Bower." The contents of the three volumes are as follows (see separate entries for each individual title).

Volume the First: "Frederic and Elfrida," "Jack and Alice," "Edgar and Emma," "Henry and Eliza," "Mr. Harley," "Sir William Mountague," "Mr. Clifford," "The Beautifull Cassandra," "Amelia Webster," "The Visit," "The Mystery," "The Three Sisters," "Detached Pieces" ("A Fragment," "A Beautiful Description of the Different Effects of Sensibility on Different Minds," "The Generous Curate"), and "Ode to Pity."

Volume the Second: "Love and Friendship," "Lesley Castle," "The History of England," "A Collection of Letters," "Scraps" ("The Female Philosopher," "The First Act of a Comedy," "A Letter from a Young Lady," "A Tour through Wales," "A Tale").

Volume the Third: "Evelyn," "Catharine, or the Bower."

See: Epstein 1985, Gilbert and Gubar 1979, *Grey 1989*, Johnson 1989a, Kaplan 1988a, Knuth 1987, 1989b, Southam 1962, *Southam 1964*.

K

King, Miss Mary (*Pride and Prejudice* Chs.3, 26; I:3:13; II:3:149–50). A young lady of Meryton who suddenly inherits £10,000 and equally suddenly attracts the attentions of Mr. Wickham, who up to that point seemed to be paying court to Elizabeth Bennet. We hear later, however, that Mary King is removed from Meryton by her family to an uncle in Liverpool in order to be out of Wickham's grasping reach.

King, Mr. (*Northanger Abbey* Ch.3; I:3:25, 27). The master of ceremonies at the Lower Assembly Rooms in Bath who first introduces Henry Tilney to Catherine Morland.

Knightley, Henry, John, Bella, George (*Emma* Ch.6; I:6:45), and **Emma** (Ch.12; I:12:98). Children of John and Isabella Knightley. Of her sketches of the first four, Emma Woodhouse is particularly proud of the youngest, "little George." When the eight-month-old Emma visits Hartfield for the first time, her aunt Emma and uncle George admire her together and, despite their disagreement over Harriet and Elton, unite again in "perfect amity."

Knightley, Mr. George (*Emma* Ch.1; I:1:9). Owner of the Donwell Abbey estate just outside Highbury, an old and intimate friend of the Woodhouse family, and elder brother of John Knightley, husband to Emma's sister, Isabella. Generally respected by everybody, Knightley takes a serious and responsible attitude toward his role as the leading landowner in the area, managing his estate conscientiously and efficiently, taking good care of his tenant farmers and employees, playing a full part in the general life of the parish, and dealing kindly and courteously with all members of the community, regardless of class or wealth. A cheerful and sensible man of about thirty-seven or -eight, he has known Emma from when she was a child and has always taken a great interest in her development; in fact, as the novel develops, it becomes clear—to us, if not immediately to Emma—that this interest is motivated by love. While he never flatters her and often bluntly states her faults and weaknesses, he is always honest with her and is one of the few people she can truly trust and rely upon—something she fully appreciates only toward the end of the novel, after her various misadventures in matchmaking lead her to a better understanding of herself and of her true feelings for Knightley. Ironically, their marriage is the one match Emma had never imagined beforehand.

Knightley, Mr. John (*Emma* Chs.5, 11; I:5:40; I:11:92). Younger brother of George Knightley, husband of Emma's older sister, Isabella, and rising in his profession as a lawyer in London. He is a clever, quick-witted man, but is sometimes impatient and irritable, especially in the face of some of Mr. Woodhouse's irrational complaints: this does not endear him to Emma, with whom he has a somewhat strained relationship.

Knightley, Mrs. Isabella, née Woodhouse (*Emma* Chs.1, 11; I:1:5–6; I:11:92). Emma's elder sister and married to John Knightley, with whom she has had five children. A tender and loving sister and daughter, a devoted wife and doting mother, Isabella is a placid, easygoing, and "amiable" woman but, unlike Emma, without any real independence of mind or spirit and without "strong understanding or any quickness." In this, she rather resembles her father, whose constitution she also seems to have inherited, for she "was delicate in her own health, over-careful of that of her children, had many fears and many nerves."

L

Lady Susan. A novel in forty-one letters, with a brief narrated conclusion, probably written about 1793–1794 and transcribed as a fair copy by Jane Austen about 1805. But there is no conclusive evidence for a date of composition, as only the fair copy survives. There is a watermark of 1805 on two leaves of the surviving manuscript of the transcribed copy, and this, therefore, indicates the period of the work's transcription, but it does not tell us when it was first composed beyond suggesting that it was completed sometime before 1805. The novel was first published in the 1871 edition of J. E. Austen-Leigh's *Memoir of Jane Austen,* when it was given its present title, and in a scholarly edition edited by R. W. Chapman in 1925. As the novel is an epistolary one, and Jane Austen seems to have rejected this form of novel after the first version of *Sense and Sensibility* (''Elinor and Marianne'') in 1795, this would seem to suggest that a date around this time is the most likely. The mode of writing is often referred to as a transitional one, in that there are very clear traces of the juvenilia in the novel's parodic exaggeration of the stock formulas of sentimental fiction, while there are also distinct signs of Austen's more mature art in the (on the whole) psychologically realistic characterization of Lady Susan and of one or two of the other characters, as well as in aspects of the novel's ironic social observation (though the exposé of decadent high society is much more direct than anything we have in the major novels). This apparently transitional nature of the novel probably also accounts for its mixed critical reception, particularly as regards interpretations of the character of Lady Susan herself. For although one can debate the relative pros and cons of this formidable lady (heartless psychopath or early feminist beating the men at their own game), one's final view will probably be determined by the degree to which one reads the novel as a comedy—a comedy of literary conventions, in particular—or as a serious work of psychological, social, or moral realism.

Lady Susan Vernon is staying with the Manwarings of Langford following the death of her husband some four months ago. She writes to her late husband's brother, Charles Vernon, accepting a long-standing invitation to stay with him and his family at their house, Churchill, in Sussex. She explains in her letter that she finds life at the Manwarings' too lively for a woman in mourning. She also refers to her worries at being separated from her daughter, Frederica, whom she is to leave at a private school in London on her way to Churchill. She tells her brother-in-law that she is looking forward to meeting his wife and children for the first time. Her next letter, to a close friend, Mrs. Alicia Johnson of Edward Street in London, reveals a different side to Lady Susan's character and her true feelings about the Manwarings and also her own daughter, for whom she seems to have little genuine affection. During her stay at Langford, it emerges, she has seriously offended both Mrs. Manwaring and Mr. Manwaring's sister, Maria, by flirting with Mr. Manwaring and with Maria's admirer, Sir James Martin. Although Lady Susan appears to be genuinely enamored of Mr. Manwaring, the latter flirtation, she claims, was for the benefit of her own daughter, as she was hoping to detach Sir James from Maria so that he might take an interest in Frederica. However, although she succeeded in persuading Sir James to make a proposal to Frederica, the latter—the "greatest simpleton on Earth"—was violently opposed to the match and refused to have anything to do with him. Sir James has now left the house, and Maria Manwaring is furious at Lady Susan, while Mr. Manwaring hardly dares speak to Lady Susan because of Mrs. Manwaring's jealousy. In fact, Lady Susan has fomented a veritable "war" in the family, and it is clearly time for her to be gone, and this is the real reason she has decided to leave. She certainly has no positive inclination to go to Churchill, for she dislikes "that insupportable spot, a Country Village," feels an aversion for Charles Vernon himself, and is apprehensive about how his wife might receive her, as she, Lady Susan, had originally tried to prevent their match.

A letter from Mrs. Vernon to her mother, Lady De Courcy, explains that the Charles Vernons will be unable to pay their usual Christmas visit to the De Courcys' home because of this unexpected visit from Lady Susan. Mrs. Vernon is clearly suspicious of Lady Susan's motives in coming, and she is aware of the need to be on her guard against Lady Susan's famous ability to ingratiate herself with others while actually taking advantage of them. Mrs. Vernon's brother, Reginald De Courcy, replies to this letter. He evidently knows all about Lady Susan and calls her "the most accomplished Coquette in England." He has heard about Lady Susan's escapades at Langford from Mr. Smith, a neighbor of the Manwarings, and he expresses his fascination in this woman who seems to have such "bewitching powers," despite being no longer young. He accepts his sister's invitation to come to stay at Churchill and says it will be interesting to witness Lady Susan's "captivating Deceit" in action. He also expresses relief at the fact that Frederica Vernon will not be accompanying her mother, as he has heard that she has little to recommend her and is proud and stupid in equal measure.

At Churchill, Lady Susan is determined to insinuate herself into the affections of the family, as she reports to Mrs. Johnson, but she quickly senses that Mrs. Vernon will not easily fall for her wiles, so she plans to win her over by attaching herself to the children. Lady Susan reports that she has had a letter from Mr. Manwaring but that she passed it off to her hosts as a letter from his wife. She intends to reply to him via Mrs. Johnson. We then hear Mrs. Vernon's account of her initial impressions of Lady Susan, in a letter to Reginald De Courcy. She gives Lady Susan her due in terms of surface charms—she is remarkably good-looking, with a winning manner and eloquent conversation—but her reputation for deceit precedes her, and Mrs. Vernon is careful to note any contradictions or inconsistencies that appear in Lady Susan's account of things.

Lady Susan confides in Mrs. Johnson that she has sent Frederica to school mainly to teach her the lesson that marriage to Sir James Martin would be a more comfortable option and less humiliating for a girl of sixteen than being at school. She is not at all seriously interested in Frederica's education (and, anyway, assumes that Frederica, whom she often accuses of stupidity, is incapable of learning much) but simply wants to marry her off as quickly and conveniently as possible. She reports that so far life has been very dull at Churchill but that her interest has now been piqued by the arrival of Reginald De Courcy. She recognizes that, under the influence of his sister, he has been predisposed to dislike her, but she views this as a challenge and determines to subdue the "insolent" spirit of the De Courcys by making him fall in love with her and acknowledge her superiority. This does not take long, for within a fortnight of his arrival at Churchill, Mrs. Vernon is writing to her mother in bewilderment at the change in Reginald's attitude toward Lady Susan: he was originally wholly set against her but is now praising her in the most exaggerated terms and ready to excuse any of her previous indiscretions by reference to her neglected education or her early marriage. At the same time as bemoaning the apparent perversion of Reginald's judgment, however, Mrs. Vernon has to admit that Lady Susan has so far acted in an exemplary way and that, given this, it is no surprise that he has been beguiled by her other manifest charms. Mrs. Johnson writes to Lady Susan advising her to marry Reginald for his fortune. She also reports that she has seen Sir James Martin and has worked to keep his interest in Frederica alive, as requested by Lady Susan—though it appears that he would just as happily marry Lady Susan herself. "He is as silly as ever," as Mrs. Johnson says. Lady Susan replies that she really has no intention of marrying Reginald De Courcy and that she is motivated in this flirtation mainly by a desire for revenge on Mrs. Vernon for her superior attitude toward her. In any case, she claims, she does not need Reginald's money, and she still finds Mr. Manwaring the more attractive of the two men. However, she is extremely proud of her success so far and believes that she could make Reginald marry her if she wanted to. She is particularly pleased that she has managed to win him over "entirely by sentiment & serious conversation" rather than by any more obvious means of coquetry, thus outmaneuvering both Reginald and his sister.

Mrs. Vernon is becoming more alarmed at Lady Susan's growing power over Reginald, and she writes to her mother asking for her help in trying to get him away from Churchill and Lady Susan's influence. Sir Reginald De Courcy now writes his son a long, fatherly letter warning him off from becoming too embroiled with Lady Susan, who, he emphasizes, would never be acceptable to him as a daughter-in-law. Lady De Courcy, it emerges, was too sick to read Mrs. Vernon's last letter when it arrived, and her husband had read it aloud to her and had thus found out about the liaison between his son and Lady Susan. It had alarmed him so much, Lady De Courcy now explains to Mrs. Vernon, that he had immediately written the letter just mentioned. A reply from Reginald has just been received, which has set Sir Reginald's mind at rest, and Lady De Courcy encloses this reply with her present letter to Mrs. Vernon. Reginald's letter assures his father that he has no intention of marrying Lady Susan, but he spends a good deal of time defending Lady Susan's good name against even the accusations that he was previously wont to make about her. She has been misrepresented by malicious gossips, he suggests, and she is, in fact, a respectable and intelligent woman with remarkable abilities and tender affections for her family and daughter. Mrs. Vernon returns the letter to her mother enclosed with her own reply. She is glad that her father has been reassured by Reginald's letter, but she herself is still worried about the longer-term prospects of a marriage between Reginald and Lady Susan. However, she is unsure how to react to what Reginald has said about Lady Susan's character, for, though she still finds it hard to believe that Lady Susan is not being duplicitous, she does not want to disbelieve her brother or to be uncharitable to Lady Susan, who has, after all, behaved well while at Churchill. Moreover, Catherine is at present feeling sorry for Lady Susan, as is everyone else, because she has just had a letter from Frederica's schoolmistress, Miss Summers, reporting that her daughter has tried to run away and asking that she be removed from the school forthwith. Mr. Vernon has gone to London to see what can be done: if he cannot persuade Miss Summers to keep Frederica at the school, he will bring her back to Churchill with him. Lady Susan emphasizes that this should be only a last resort, and she makes out to the Vernons that her daughter is an ill-tempered and wayward girl who needs to be treated with severity: her attempt to run away is just one more example of her willfulness. Lady Susan adds to the plausibility of her case by suggesting that she herself has been to blame for being too indulgent of her daughter in the past. Mrs. Vernon, however, is suspicious of a mother who talks so harshly about her own daughter. Indeed, when Lady Susan next writes to Mrs. Johnson, the truth is revealed that Frederica had tried to run away in response to a letter from her mother once more insisting on Frederica's marrying Sir James Martin. Lady Susan is annoyed with her ''horrid'' daughter and, if anything, now even more determined to force her to marry Sir James as a punishment for her action. She boasts to Mrs. Johnson about her powers of

eloquence and persuasion and feels confident that, even if Frederica should dare
to tell the Vernons the truth about her plan, she will easily be able to undermine
her story. She also reports on her continuing success with Reginald De Courcy,
though she finds his constant soul-searching over her somewhat irritating, declaring that she "infinitely" prefers the more robust lovemaking of Mr. Manwaring, whom she considers far superior to Reginald. Manwaring himself is
apparently riven by jealousy over Lady Susan's affair with Reginald, and she
has had to put him off from coming to see her at Churchill.

Mrs. Vernon reports to her mother that Frederica has, indeed, returned to
Churchill with Mr. Vernon and that, far from being a wild and ill-tempered girl,
she is extremely timid and withdrawn and totally in awe of her mother. For her
part, Lady Susan shows not the slightest sign of affection for her daughter,
continuing to blame her for her actions and affecting a distressed state herself
for the benefit of the Vernons, particularly Reginald. Mrs. Vernon is distinctly
unimpressed by this, and she views Frederica's tearful and despondent state as
further proof of Lady Susan's heartless character. As Mrs. Vernon gets to know
Frederica better, so Lady Susan's earlier descriptions of her become less plausible: Frederica has natural abilities, a pleasant disposition, an affectionate heart,
and a studious interest in books. She also soon notes that Frederica is developing
a romantic interest in Reginald De Courcy, and she wants to encourage this as
a means of weaning Reginald away from Lady Susan; she even suggests that
Frederica might make Reginald a good wife.

Much to Frederica's horror, however, her weak-headed suitor, Sir James Martin, now unexpectedly arrives at Churchill. He impertinently invites himself to
stay for a few days and generally shows up his foolish character in front of the
Vernons. Lady Susan is annoyed to see him there, as his presence may jeop-
ardize her plans for Frederica, but she is careful not to show this and treats him
with a respect she clearly does not feel. She decides to preempt any adverse
consequences arising from his appearance by pretending to take Mrs. Vernon
into her confidence and telling her of Sir James' devotion to Frederica; she hopes
Mrs. Vernon will congratulate her on gaining such an eligible match for her
daughter. Mrs. Vernon is impressed by Lady Susan's apparent earnestness in
this, but she is not fooled by her and determines to find out the real truth from
Frederica herself. Frederica is given her own voice for the first and only time
in the novel when she writes to Reginald De Courcy and asks him to intervene
on her behalf with Lady Susan. She tells him that she has been forbidden to
talk to her aunt and uncle on the matter but that she is desperately miserable at
the prospect of marrying Sir James. Reginald had already had his suspicions
about Frederica's dislike of Sir James, and he now confronts Lady Susan about
the whole affair. They quarrel and part in anger, and, when we next hear from
Mrs. Vernon, she is happily writing to her mother to announce Reginald's imminent departure. He has told Mrs. Vernon about Frederica's plight and hopes
that she will be able to protect her niece from the fate Lady Susan is planning
for her. However, no sooner has Mrs. Vernon sent this letter, than she has to

follow it with another withdrawing the news of the first; Reginald has not left, after all, and is suddenly on good terms with Lady Susan again. Her remarkable powers of persuasion have evidently prevailed, and now it looks more likely than ever that he will eventually marry her. Lady Susan now also tries to persuade Mrs. Vernon to see things her way, but her convoluted account of recent events, although almost plausible, simply confirms Mrs. Vernon's view of her as a deceitful and manipulative woman.

The only positive consequence of Frederica's letter to Reginald is that Lady Susan decides to send Sir James Martin away, though, as she tells Mrs. Johnson, she has still not given up on her plan to have Frederica marry him; after ten weeks at Churchill, she has decided to leave for London, for "a little Dissipation," and she will continue with her plan there. However, in her reply, Mrs. Johnson advises Lady Susan to forget about her daughter and to come to London alone—partly because Mr. Manwaring is there and increasingly desperate to see her and partly because Mr. Johnson will be away at Bath, and they will be able to have fun together—though she apologizes for not inviting Lady Susan to stay with her, as her husband has previously extracted a promise from her never to invite Lady Susan to their house.

Mrs. Vernon tells Lady De Courcy that Reginald is finally leaving Churchill but that, as Lady Susan is leaving for London at the same time, he will probably soon follow her there. She confirms that Frederica is to stay behind at Churchill. Mrs. Johnson reports to Lady Susan that Mr. Johnson has "contrived" to have a sudden attack of gout (possibly as a result of hearing about Lady Susan's visit) and will therefore not be going to Bath after all; this means that Mrs. Johnson will not be able to spend much time with Lady Susan (presumably, Mr. Johnson's main aim). She has, however, arranged for some lodgings for Lady Susan nearby. Lady Susan's next letter to Mrs. Johnson is from those lodgings. She has always detested Mr. Johnson anyway, she says, but now her aversion to him is even greater, and she cruelly sums up her feelings for him when she refers to him as "too old to be agreable, & too young to die." She has already seen Manwaring and has put his mind at rest in relation to her affair with Reginald De Courcy, whom she again compares unfavorably to Manwaring. She and Reginald seem to have become engaged, but she now expresses reluctance to go through with the marriage, especially as there is not yet any sign of Reginald's father's dying and leaving Reginald his estate.

She next writes to Reginald trying to put him off from coming to see her in London, but this has the effect of making him come immediately. When he arrives, Lady Susan sends him over to see Mrs. Johnson in order to keep him out of the way during a visit from Manwaring, but this turns out to be a fatal mistake, for Mrs. Johnson is out when he arrives, and he turns up at the same time as Mrs. Manwaring, who has come to see her guardian, Mr. Johnson, to ask for his help in extricating her husband from Lady Susan's clutches. Mrs. Manwaring had found out from a servant about her husband's daily visits to Lady Susan and has just watched him to the door with her own eyes. Reginald now learns of all this from Mr. Johnson, who, having heard of Reginald's possible marriage to Lady Susan, is only too happy to enlighten him as to her true character. Reginald's illusions about Lady Susan are now shattered once and for all, and he breaks off their relationship. She protests her innocence and tries to entice him back in a cajoling letter, but when this fails, she writes more curtly in her true character and, in effect, jeers at him for having fallen for her stratagem. Mrs. Johnson writes to Lady Susan to say that she has now been forced by her husband to stop corresponding with her. She tells her that the Manwarings are to separate but that Mrs. Manwaring is so distraught by it all that she may not live much longer. She also mentions that Miss Manwaring has just arrived in London in the hope of reclaiming the affections of Sir James Martin. Lady Susan's last letter to Mrs. Johnson is both defiant and callous. She is totally unrepentant about her recent escapades; she "despises" Reginald and, with no thought for Mrs. Manwaring, expresses herself happy with her present devoted lover, Mr. Manwaring. She even considers the prospect of marrying him and asks Mrs. Johnson to expedite matters by helping to "wear out" Mrs. Manwaring. She looks forward to the time she might once again be intimate with Mrs. Johnson—that is, when Mr. Johnson has died—and she hopes that "the next Gouty Attack" may be favorable to such a circumstance. Finally, she reveals a renewed and even more vindictive determination to marry Frederica to Sir James Martin, despite Miss Manwaring's aspirations in that direction and despite Frederica's hopes of marrying Reginald.

Lady De Courcy writes to Mrs. Vernon informing her that Reginald has returned home and has parted from Lady Susan for good. She invites the Vernons, along with Frederica, to come to stay, and she suggests that they may, after all, be able to make a match between Reginald and Frederica. Unfortunately, Mrs. Vernon replies, Frederica has already been taken away by her mother, much to the girl's distress and the rest of the family's dismay.

The novel ends with a conclusion narrated in the third person. This informs us that Mr. and Mrs. Vernon eventually succeed in rescuing Frederica from her mother and taking her back to live at Churchill with them. Three weeks later, Lady Susan marries Sir James Martin herself. She soon seems to lose all interest in Frederica, who then becomes a fixed member of the Vernon family—at least until such time as Reginald can be encouraged to take her off their hands, which, we are told, should be within about a year. As for Lady Susan's later happiness, "she had nothing against her, but her Husband, & her Conscience."

Main Characters: Reginald De Courcy, Alicia Johnson, Mr. and Mrs. Manwaring, Maria Manwaring, Sir James Martin, Catherine Vernon (née De Courcy), Charles Vernon, Frederica Susanna Vernon, Lady Susan Vernon,

Minor Characters: the Clarke family, Lady C. De Courcy, Sir Reginald De Courcy, the Hamiltons, James, Mr. Johnson, Charles Smith, Miss Summers, the Vernon children (including Catherine and Frederic), Mr. Frederic Vernon, Wilson.

See: Anderson 1989, Gard 1989b, Horwitz 1989, Jackel 1977, Kaplan 1987, Knuth 1989b, Leavis 1941–1942b, Levine 1961, M. G. Marshall 1989, McKellar 1989.

Lambe, Miss (*Sanditon, Minor Works* 408, 421). A Creole heiress of about seventeen who is under the charge of the schoolmistress Mrs. Griffiths. She is the one who gives rise to the false rumor that Mrs. Griffiths is bringing a West Indian family to Sanditon. When Lady Denham hears about the presence in Sanditon of an eligible heiress, she immediately thinks of trying to arrange a match with her nephew, Sir Edward Denham.

Larkins, William (*Emma* Ch.27; II:9:238). Mr. Knightley's bailiff on the Donwell estate who "thinks more of his master's profit than any thing."

Lascelles, Lady (*Mansfield Park* Ch.40; III:9:394). The previous tenant of the house on Wimpole Street, London, where Maria Bertram establishes herself after her marriage to Mr. Rushworth. Mary Crawford had stayed there with Lady Lascelles and calls it "one of the best houses in London."

Lascelles, Mr. ("Catharine," *Minor Works* 194, 239). The respectable but unpleasant elderly man Cecilia Wynne marries in Bengal.

Lascelles, Mrs. ("Catharine," *Minor Works*). *See* Wynne, Cecilia.

"The Last Work" *See Sanditon.*

Lee, Miss (*Mansfield Park* Ch.1; I:1:9). The governess at Mansfield Park, first to Maria and Julia Bertram and then to Fanny Price.

"Lesley Castle, an Unfinished Novel in Letters" (*Volume the Second* of Jane Austen's juvenilia). The range of dates of the ten letters that make up this unfinished novel—January–April 1792—would suggest that it was written within that period (though not necessarily so: for the possibility of a slightly earlier date, see *Fergus 1991*: 180, n.73). The work is dedicated to Jane Austen's brother, Henry.

The main interest of the piece lies more in the style and content of the individual letters than in the somewhat rambling and unfocused plot. That plot, such as it is, deals mainly with the consequences of Sir George Lesley's second marriage to Susan Fitzgerald, particularly for his two adult daughters, Margaret and Matilda. Sir George spends most of his time carousing in London while his daughters live in contented seclusion at Lesley Castle near Perth in Scotland. However, because of his marriage, he now returns to Perthshire in order to introduce his new wife to his daughters. She finds the castle bleak and forbidding and too cut off from society. Jealous tensions also soon manifest themselves between her and her stepdaughters, and so the whole family remove again to

London, where the novel finishes. Humor arises mainly from the fact that Charlotte Lutterell is a friend and correspondent of both Margaret Lesley and Lady Lesley, so that in the letters she receives from them we can clearly see a clash of perspectives as each woman presents her biased and jealous opinions of the other. But Charlotte herself has a somewhat inconsistent voice in the novel and one that is sometimes satirized itself for its vapidity and silliness. There is a sense in which this novel is really a continuation of the stylistic experimentation evident in ''A Collection of Letters'' (if, indeed, that was composed first), and this stands out particularly in the eighth and ninth letters, where two new correspondents are introduced (Eloisa Lutterell and Mrs. Marlowe) with distinctly different tones of voice from those of the other three correspondents. In these two letters, which pick up a type of subplot about the sudden death of Eloisa's fiancé, the dominant effect is no longer that of satirical comedy but of serious and sincere feeling.

Main Characters: William Fitzgerald, Sir George Lesley, Margaret Lesley, Matilda Lesley, Charlotte Lutterell, Eloisa Lutterell, Mrs. Marlowe.

Minor Characters: Louisa Burton (Lesley), Mr. Cleveland, Danvers, Rakehelly Dishonour Esq., Colonel and Mrs. Drummond, Lady Flambeau, Sir James Gower, Diana Hervey, Henry Hervey, the Honorable Mrs. Kickabout, Louisa Lesley, Mr. Lesley, Lady Susan, M'Leods, M'Kenzies, M'Phersons, M'Cartneys, M'donalds, M'Kinnons, M'lellans, M'Kays, Macbeths and Macduffs (all neighbors of the Lesleys in Perthshire), the Marlowe family, William (servant in the Lutterell house).

Letters. Only 161 of Jane Austen's letters have survived to the present day, and even of this number several survive only as copies of original manuscripts that have now been lost. Like many women of her class at that time, Jane Austen wrote letters almost on a daily basis, and it is clear that the surviving record of her correspondence must represent only a fairly small proportion of the letters she actually wrote. The earliest known letter dates from January 1796—so that there are no letters from the first twenty years of her life—and the last one from the end of May 1817, some six weeks before her death. The period in between is represented only patchily, with major gaps in the correspondence as follows: 1797 (no letters); 1799 and 1800 (six letters each); June 1801–September 1804 (no letters); 1804 (one letter); 1806 (one letter in verse); 1807 (three letters); July 1809–April 1811 (no letters); June 1811—January 1813 (two letters). The last three and a half years of Austen's life account for over half of the surviving letters, or eighty-three of them—which is still a small record for a relatively long period.

One of the reasons that the overall record of Austen's correspondence is not larger is that her sister, Cassandra, is reputed to have destroyed many of the letters in her possession two or three years before she died in 1845 (as well as to have censored others that she bequeathed to nieces and other family members). The reasons for Cassandra's reported actions are not known and have been the subject of intense speculation ever since. But, of course, it must also have been the case that, in the natural course of things, many other letters by Jane Austen were discarded, lost, or destroyed by her other correspondents, including other close family members, and it is perhaps unnecessary to exaggerate Cassandra's importance in this matter—though there is little doubt that she was her sister's closest confidante. A constant stream of letters would pass between the two sisters whenever they were apart, even if that were only for a day or two, and the distance of their separation only a matter of a few miles, so that, even despite Cassandra's apparent burning of many of them, the vast majority of the letters that have come down to us are, indeed, a record of this particular correspondence. Partly as a result of this—because most of the letters naturally enough deal with private family matters and workaday domestic details—little in Jane Austen's surviving correspondence directly illuminates her art, though the letters clearly remain a primary, if fragmentary, source of biographical information. Ironically, if the surviving letters are anything to go by, it is not the lost letters to Cassandra that should concern us, so much as the lost letters to other correspondents. For, although the letters to Cassandra obviously help to inform our understanding of Jane Austen's life and personality, only in the few surviving letters written to people other than Cassandra do we find material of any direct critical relevance to her novels (though, even here, Austen's ''critical'' comments tend to be more in the nature of lighthearted asides than seriously considered statements). The letters in question are, primarily, letters to her eldest nephew, James Edward, and to her nieces, Fanny, Anna, and Caroline (see, e.g., letters 103–4, 107–18, and 146 in *Jane Austen's Letters* 1995), though the correspondence with James Stanier Clarke that inspired her *Plan of a Novel* also contains important ironic comments about her novelistic preferences (see letters 125, 132, and 138 in the *Letters*). The letters as a whole are, of course, often indirectly important for our understanding of Austen's art, not least in that they provide information about her reading (Chapman's 1932 edition of the letters contains a detailed appendix listing all her references to authors and books) and about the stages in the composition of some of her works; but also because, particularly in their often playful nature, we can detect in many of them the sources of the more carefully crafted comic style of the novels (see, e.g., the first quotation at the head of this book).

The first appearance in print of any of Jane Austen's correspondence came when her brother, Henry, quoted from some of her last letters in his ''Biographical Notice'' to the posthumously published *Northanger Abbey* and *Persuasion* (1817). But not until the two editions of J. E. Austen-Leigh's *Memoir* (1869, 1871) were a substantial number of the letters published for the first time, though few of these appeared in their entirety. The first devoted collection of *The Letters of Jane Austen* was published, in two volumes, by her great-nephew, Edward, Lord Brabourne, in 1884. Five new letters, all to Jane Austen's brother, Frank, appeared in 1906, in *Jane Austen's Sailor Brothers* by J. H. and E. C. Hubback; and several more new letters were published for the first time in 1913 in the

Life and Letters by W. and R. A. Austen-Leigh. The first scholarly edition of Austen's letters, collecting all the letters then known, was R. W. Chapman's 1932 Oxford edition in two volumes. A second edition in 1952 added five letters, and further additions were made in subsequent reissues. A third, wholly revised edition of Chapman's work, edited and collected by Deirdre Le Faye as *Jane Austen's Letters*, appeared in 1995 with further additions, bringing the total of extant letters up to 161. This authoritative edition contains, among other things, an extensive bibliography of relevant sources, comprehensive indexes of the people and places mentioned in the letters, and a list of the locations of the surviving letters.

Full details of the works mentioned in this entry, along with other relevant works, can be found in Chapter 4 in Part III of this book.

See also: Austen 1952, Austen-Leigh 1942, Cahoon 1975, Copeland and McMaster 1997, Grey 1986, Juhasz 1987, Kaplan 1988b, Le Faye 1992, Leavis 1944–1945, *Modert 1990*, Stepankowsky and Harper 1988, Vick 1994, Ward 1885.

Little, Captain (*Sanditon, Minor Works* 389). A visitor to Sanditon from Limehouse, noted by Mr. Parker in the subscription list at the circulating library. *See* Beard, Mr.

Lloyd, Martha (1765–1843). Martha Lloyd became the intimate friend of Jane and Cassandra Austen from 1789, when she, her sister Mary, and their mother moved into Deane parsonage, which they rented from Mr. Austen. After the death of her mother in 1805, she also became their house companion, and she lived with them and Mrs. Austen, sharing the housekeeping, at Southampton and Chawton. Her manuscript book of food and health recipes still survives to provide us with a fascinating insight into the domestic life of the Austens and of similar families of the period (see *Hickman 1977*). After Jane Austen's death, Martha Lloyd lived on at Chawton with Cassandra and Mrs. Austen until the latter's death in 1827. Then, on 24 July 1828, at the age of sixty-three, she married for the first time when she became the second wife of Jane Austen's brother, Frank. As Frank was knighted in 1837, Martha was Lady Austen when she died in 1843.

Jane Austen dedicated her juvenile piece "Frederic and Elfrida" (*Volume the First*) to Martha and wrote the verse "Lines *supposed* to have been sent to an uncivil dressmaker" for her. Four of Jane Austen's letters to Martha have survived and are printed in *Jane Austen's Letters*.

See: Hickman 1977, Le Faye 1989.

Lloyd, Mary (1771–1843). Sister of Martha Lloyd and second wife of Jane Austen's eldest brother, James, with whom she had two children, James Edward and Caroline Mary Craven. She first became acquainted with Jane Austen and her family when she and her sister and mother rented Deane parsonage from Mr. Austen in the spring of 1789, just after the death of her father, Rev. Noyes

Lloyd of Enborne near Newbury, Berkshire. Jane Austen dedicated the unfinished piece of juvenilia, "Evelyn," to Mary and wrote "Verses Given with a Needlework Bag . . ." as part of a leaving present for her when the Lloyds moved from Deane to Ibthorpe in 1792. Mary Lloyd was at first good friends with Jane and Cassandra Austen, but after her marriage to James Austen on 17 January 1797, it seems that Mary became somewhat aloof and self-important and somewhat grasping, and her relationship with the rest of the Austen family deteriorated, though there was never any serious breach among them. References to her in Jane Austen's surviving letters are not wholly explicit about the author's views on Mary, and it is clear that she retained a dutiful, sisterly love for her, but they frequently convey a sense of exasperation with her: "she is in the main *not* a liberal-minded Woman," she commented in one of her last letters (22 May 1817). (For further comments on Mary's character, see the entry on James Austen.)

Long, Mrs. (*Pride and Prejudice* Chs.1, 2; I:1:3; I:2:6). Mrs. Long is a neighbor of Mrs. Bennet's who first brings news of the imminent arrival of Mr. Bingley at Netherfield Park. Mrs. Bennet worries that Mrs. Long will put her own two nieces forward as potential marriage partners for Mr. Bingley before she has a chance of introducing her daughters to him, and she calls Mrs. Long "a selfish, hypocritical woman." However, later, when it seems clear that Mr. Bingley will propose to her daughter, Jane, after all, Mrs. Bennet can afford to be magnanimous, and she says, "I do think Mrs. Long is as good a creature as ever lived." Mrs. Long's two nieces are also referred to again at this point as Mrs. Bennet compliments them with typically faint praise: "and her nieces are very pretty behaved girls, and not at all handsome: I like them prodigiously" (Ch.54; III: 12:342).

Longtown, Marquis of (*Northanger Abbey* Chs.17, 28; II:2:139; II:13:224). General Tilney is disappointed not to see his old friend, Lord Longtown, at Bath. He later gives the excuse of a visit to Lord Longtown's home near Hereford as a pretext for sending Catherine Morland away from Northanger Abbey.

"Love and Friendship" (*Volume the Second*). "A novel in a series of Letters" with an inscription, "Deceived in Friendship & Betrayed in Love." Completed on 13 June 1790 and dedicated to Jane Austen's cousin, Eliza de Feuillide. First published in the volume *Love and Freindship* (with an introduction by G. K. Chesterton, London: Chatto and Windus, 1922) and then in the scholarly edition of *Volume the Second* (edited by B. C. Southam, Oxford: Clarendon Press, 1963), which, corrected, forms the basis for the version printed in *Minor Works*, volume 6 of the Oxford edition of Jane Austen's works. The third word of the title is customarily spelled "freindship" following Jane Austen's own juvenile spelling, though she did later correct this on the transcript manuscript.

The novel, an often hilarious burlesque on the conventions of sentimental fiction and the cult of "sensibility," is one of the best-known and most highly regarded of Jane Austen's juvenilia and certainly repays attention as a lively introduction to her major works. It consists of fifteen letters: an initial one from Isabel to her friend, Laura, a brief reply from Laura to Isabel, and then thirteen from Laura to Isabel's daughter Marianne. Isabel's first letter prepares us for what is to come, for she writes to remind Laura of a promise to tell the story of "the Misfortunes and Adventures" of her life to Isabel's daughter, Marianne, once she (Laura) is past the dangers of experiencing any further such misfortunes; as it is Laura's fifty-fifth birthday, Isabel judges that this time has come, for Laura is now surely safe from "the determined Perseverance of disagreable Lovers and the cruel Persecutions of obstinate Fathers." Laura cannot agree that her "misfortunes" have entirely ceased, but she agrees anyway to satisfy the curiosity of Marianne, and her strange narrative begins.

Born in Spain of an Irish father and an illegitimate Scottish-Italian mother, she was educated at a convent in France before returning, at the age of eighteen, to her parents' home in the Vale of Usk in Wales, where she first became friends with Isabel, then twenty-one. Isabel had "seen the World," having lived in London for two years, in Bath for a fortnight, and in Southampton for one night, and she advises Laura against the "idle Dissipations" of the first, the "unmeaning Luxuries" of the second, and "the Stinking fish" of the third. One December evening, there is a violent knocking at the cottage door, and, after much pointless debate about the source and nature of this noise, Laura and her parents decide to admit the visitors, a young man and his servant, who, having lost their way to Middlesex, seek shelter for the night. Laura finds the young man "the most beauteous and amiable Youth" she had ever seen, and her "natural Sensibility" immediately recognizes that "on him the happiness or Misery of my future Life must depend." The youth in question introduces himself as Edward Lindsay (though Laura, for no clear reason, gives him the alias of Edward Talbot), the son of a baronet from Bedfordshire. He explains that he had left home for his aunt's in Middlesex following a quarrel with his father, who was insisting that he should marry the "lovely and Engaging" Lady Dorothea. Edward had no objection whatsoever to Lady Dorothea, but he could not bear the thought of obeying and obliging his father, and he told him so in no uncertain terms before storming off with his faithful servant, William.

Now, Edward proposes to Laura. She accepts him, and they are instantly married by Laura's father, Polydore, who, though not a priest, "had been bred to the Church." A few days later, the newlyweds go to the home of Edward's Aunt Philippa in Middlesex. She greets them warmly, but Edward's sister, Augusta, is also there, and she is angered and amazed by her brother's rash actions. She argues with him and asks the obvious question of how he hopes to support his wife without the help of Sir Edward, whereupon Edward replies, in his "nobly contemtuous Manner," "Can you not conceive the Luxury of living in every Distress that Poverty can inflict, with the object of your tenderest Affection?" They are interrupted by the entrance of Lady Dorothea, whose visit, however, lasts for only half an hour and is entirely inconsequential, notable only to Laura for the fact that Lady Dorothea fails to confide any secrets to her. Sir Edward Lindsay then arrives, but before he can say anything, Edward, with "undaunted Bravery," bluntly confirms that he has married without his father's consent and that he glories in the fact. Leaving his father speechless, he leads Laura to his father's carriage, and they drive to the home of Edward's close friend, Augustus.

He, too, has recently married a young girl, Sophia, against the wishes of his father. In Sophia, Laura immediately recognizes a kindred spirit: "She was all Sensibility and Feeling. We flew into each others arms & after having exchanged vows of mutual Friendship for the rest of our Lives, instantly unfolded to each other the most inward Secrets of our Hearts—." Edward's reunion with Augustus is equally affecting: they fly into each other's arms, and, Laura writes, "It was too pathetic for the feelings of Sophia and myself—We fainted Alternately on a Sofa." Aunt Philippa writes to say that Edward's father and sister have returned to Bedfordshire, and she invites Edward and Laura to return to Middlesex at their convenience. They reply that they will certainly return "whenever we might have no other place to go to" and are surprised to hear shortly afterward that Philippa, "either to revenge our Conduct, or releive her own solitude," has married "a young and illiterate Fortune-hunter" (which will probably deprive Edward of any inheritance from his aunt). Augustus and Sophia had set up home on the basis of some money that Augustus had stolen from his father, and now that this has been exhausted and with the increased expense of maintaining Edward and Laura, Augustus falls into serious debt and is eventually arrested and imprisoned in London. This brings on another bout of sighing and fainting on the sofa for Laura and Sophia, while Edward goes off to London to comfort his friend.

Laura and Sophia abandon the house and, following an abortive trip to London in search of Edward, repair to Scotland, where Sophia has a relation who she believes will take them in. (In passing, we are told of the death of Laura's parents, Polydore and Claudia, and of the marriage and removal to Ireland of Isabel; these facts explain why Laura could not return to Usk.) They prepare to stay the night at an inn in the vicinity of Sophia's Scottish relation, when a coroneted coach drives into the yard, and an elderly gentleman descends from it. This is Lord St. Clair, and, by "an instinctive Sympathy" whispered to her heart, Sophia recognizes the man as her grandfather. When she presents herself to him, he immediately recognizes her resemblance to his wife, Laurina, and his daughter Claudia and acknowledges her as his granddaughter. Moreover, when he sees Sophia, he also recognizes her as another of his granddaughters, by his second daughter, Matilda. At that moment "a most beautifull Young Man" enters, and Lord St. Clair recognizes yet another grandchild, Philander, the son of his third daughter, Bertha. No sooner has he expressed a wish now to find his fourth grandchild, Gustavus, son of Agatha, his fourth daughter, than the very same "Gracefull Youth" enters the room. Lord St. Clair then gives each of his grandchildren a banknote of fifty pounds and leaves abruptly. His sudden departure induces another fit of fainting in the two girls, and when they recover, they find that Philander and Gustavus have also gone, taking all four banknotes with them.

Macdonald, Sophia's relation (her cousin), then arrives and escorts them to his mansion, Macdonald Hall, where they are introduced to his fifteen-year-old daughter, Janetta, and her fiancé, Graham. Graham is said to be sensible, well informed, and agreeable, but Laura and Sophia immediately take a dislike to him for not having auburn hair, for never having read "the Sorrows of Werter," for having no soul, and, above all, for being approved by Janetta's father. They go to work on the impressionable Janetta and soon persuade her that she cannot love Graham and that she is violently in love with another acquaintance, Captain M'Kenzie (of whom she had hardly thought anything before). They write an anonymous letter to the "amiable M'Kenzie," who arrives forthwith to whisk Janetta off to Gretna Green, where they are married. Macdonald learns of the elopement at the same time as he catches Sophia "depriving" him of some of the banknotes that she "accidentally" came across while opening his private drawers in his library. Despite their indignation at Macdonald's "criminal" accusations, Sophia and Laura are unceremoniously thrown out of the house.

They leave on foot and, after about a mile and a half, stop to rest beside a stream, a place "suited to meditation." Laura begins to wax lyrical about the beauties of nature, but everything she says reminds Sophia of her poor imprisoned Augustus. Then occurs, on the road behind them, "the lucky overturning of a Gentleman's Phaeton." Two men are thrown out of the vehicle and lie "weltering in their blood," both apparently dead. As the women approach, they recognize Edward and Augustus: Sophia faints, and Laura screams and "instantly ran mad." They continue in this manner for an hour and a quarter, when they hear a groan from Edward and rush to comfort him, but he dies almost immediately afterward. Sophia again falls into a swoon, and Laura returns to her manic ravings. After two hours, they realize that night is falling, and it is becoming damp, so they ask for shelter at a nearby cottage, where they are welcomed by an old widow and her seventeen-year-old daughter, Bridget. As the latter is good-tempered, civil, and obliging but lacking in "exalted Ideas, Delicate Feelings or refined Sensibilities," Laura and Sophia can but view her as an "Object of Contempt." The next morning finds Sophia suffering from an illness that develops into galloping consumption, and within days she, too, is dead, her dying breath given over to advising Laura to "Beware of swoons. . . . Run mad as often as you chuse; but do not faint—."

Laura then boards a stagecoach bound for Edinburgh. At first, she cannot make out her traveling companions, as it is dark, but when day breaks, she is disconcerted to find that the coach is full of her "nearest Relations and Connections": Sir Edward Lindsay, Augusta, Lady Dorothea, and Isabel inside and Philippa and her husband on the coach box, with Philander and Gustavus in the basket. Laura informs the company of "the whole melancholy Affair" since she ran away with Edward and then, to deflect "unjustifiable Reproaches" to herself, inquires after the others. She learns that the stagecoach they are on runs between Stirling and Edinburgh and belongs to Philippa's husband, who, having spent her fortune, has reverted to the only trade he knows, which is driving. Sir Edward, Augusta, and Lady Dorothea, inspired by the writings of Gilpin, have come to make a tour of Scotland, though, because they feel obliged to patronize Philippa's husband, they are mainly visiting the countryside between Edinburgh and Stirling. During a breakfast stop, Laura also hears the life history of Gustavus and Philander. Illegitimate children of Laura's aunts Bertha and Agatha (the one to a bricklayer, the other to a stay maker), they ran away from home at the age of fifteen after stealing £900 from their mothers. This money was spent within two months, whereupon they joined a traveling company of actors with whom they performed *Macbeth* (their only play) all over England and Wales. They had come to Scotland to extend their tour, when they had come across their grandfather, along with Laura and Sophia. With the £200 they acquired on that occasion, they had left their manager and his wife to perform *Macbeth* on their own and had gone to Stirling, where they spent the money "with great *eclat*." They are now returning to Edinburgh to find work as actors again.

At Edinburgh, Sir Edward gives Laura, as his son's widow, £400 to live on. With this she was able to retire to "a romantic Village in the Highlands of Scotland," where she has continued ever since to indulge her "unceasing Lamentations" for the death of her parents, husband, and friend. Laura finishes her narrative by tying up some loose ends. She tells Marianne that Augusta married Graham, and Sir Edward married Lady Dorothea (in the hope of a new heir); Philander and Gustavus became successful actors and still perform at Covent Garden under the names of Lewis and Quick (real actors of the period, in fact); and Philippa has long since died, but her husband continues to drive the stagecoach from Edinburgh to Stirling.

Main Characters: Augustus, Edward Lindsay, Laura Lindsay, Sophia.

Minor Characters: Agatha, Bertha, Bridget, Claudia, Lady Dorothea, Mr. Graham, Gustavus, Isabel, Philip Jones, Augusta Lindsay, Sir Edward Lindsay, Mr. Macdonald, Janetta Macdonald, Captain M'kenzie, Marianne, Matilda, Philander, Philippa, Polydore, Lord St. Clair, Lady Laurina St. Clair, Gregory Staves, William (Edward Lindsay's manservant).

See: Derry 1990c, Hopkins 1925, McMaster 1989, Pinion 1977.

Lucas, Charlotte (*Pride and Prejudice* Chs.3, 5; I:3:13; I:5:18). At twenty-seven, the eldest daughter of Sir William and Lady Lucas and the intimate friend of Elizabeth Bennet. Charlotte is sensible and intelligent, but she has a wholly unromantic view of marriage, which leads her to marry the foolish Mr. Collins purely for the material security he can provide her.

Lucas, Lady (*Pride and Prejudice* Chs.1, 5; I:1:4; I:5:18). Lady Lucas is summed up by the suggestion that she is "not too clever to be a valuable neighbour to Mrs. Bennet.'' She appears to be as frivolous and status-conscious as Mrs. Bennet and takes great pleasure in flaunting the fact that her daughter has married before any of the Bennet girls.

Lucas, Maria (*Pride and Prejudice* Chs.3, 27; I:3:13; II:4:152). The second daughter of Lady and Sir William Lucas, ''a good-humoured girl, but as empty-headed'' as Sir William himself. When she visits Rosings while staying with her sister at Hunsford, she is ''frightened almost out of her senses'' by the grandeur of the place and made speechless by the company of Lady Catherine and her daughter.

Lucas, Sir William (*Pride and Prejudice* Chs.1, 5; I:1:4; I:5:18). A former Meryton tradesman and now the knighted owner of Lucas Lodge. Feebleminded at times and overimpressed by material wealth and rank, Sir William is nevertheless ''inoffensive, friendly and obliging.''

Lucases, younger (*Pride and Prejudice* Chs.5, 22; I:5:18 & 20; I:22:122). In addition to Charlotte and Maria, there are several other Lucas children, but these are mentioned only in passing and include both boys and girls.

M

M—, Bishop of ("Catharine," *Minor Works* 203). The man who sent Charles Wynne to the army rather than finding him a place in the church, as might have been expected, and as both Mr. Wynne and Charles would have liked.

Mackenzie (*Persuasion* Ch.5; I:5:38). Sir Walter's gardener at Kellynch.

Maclean, Lady Mary (*Persuasion* Ch.21; II:9:193). Mrs. Smith refers to this lady as never missing a Bath concert.

Maddison (*Mansfield Park* Chs.41, 42; III:10:404; III:11:411–12). Henry Crawford's agent for his estate at Everingham, Norfolk, whom he suspects of some underhanded dealing. He is "a clever fellow," and Henry does not want to lose him, but neither does he want to be duped by him. He provides Henry with a convenient reason to take a renewed interest in his estate just when he wants to impress Fanny (whom he hopes to marry at this point) as being a dutiful and responsible landlord. Talking of Maddison, he observes: "The mischief such a man does on an estate, both as to the credit of his employer, and the welfare of the poor, is inconceivable."

Maddox, Charles (*Mansfield Park* Ch.15; I:15:148). A "gentlemanly" young man from Stoke, in the neighborhood of Mansfield Park, who, when the proposed production of *Lovers' Vows* is being planned, is suggested by Tom Bertram for the part of Anhalt, the clergyman.

Maddoxes, the Miss (*Mansfield Park* Ch.29; II:11:283). Guests at the ball at Mansfield Park and sisters of Charles Maddox. They are mentioned briefly by Lady Bertram on the day following the ball.

Mansfield Park. This is the first of the second wave of Jane Austen's major novels—that is, the novels of the 1810s that were not revised versions of her 1790s work. It was begun probably in February 1811 and completed in a first draft by July 1813. It was possibly revised later that year, and Jane Austen was apparently correcting proofs for it in February and March 1814. It was published in three volumes on 9 May 1814 by Thomas Egerton. The first edition was sold out by November 1814 and brought Jane Austen somewhere in the region of between £310 and £350 profit, the biggest profit she received on any of her novels in her lifetime. A second edition, incorporating revisions made by Austen in the late autumn of 1815, was published in February 1816 by John Murray.

The novel opens with the arrival of ten-year-old Fanny Price at Mansfield Park, the stately home of her aunt and uncle, Sir Thomas and Lady Bertram. Fanny is the eldest daughter in a family of eight children. Her mother, Lady Bertram's sister, had made an unfortunate marriage to a spendthrift naval lieutenant, Mr. Price (now retired), and this had been the cause of a breach between Mrs. Price and her sisters, Lady Bertram and Mrs. Norris (the wife of the rector of Mansfield, Rev. Norris). Unable to cope with her growing family—she is expecting another child (and will later have another)—Mrs. Price had finally swallowed her pride and had written to make up with her sisters, asking them for their help. Lady Bertram and Mrs. Norris responded by persuading Sir Thomas to take in Mrs. Price's eldest girl, Fanny.

Extremely diffident and withdrawn when she arrives at Mansfield, Fanny is overawed by her surroundings, by Sir Thomas and Lady Bertram, and by her bold, confident cousins, Tom, Edmund, Maria, and Julia (who are seventeen, sixteen, thirteen, and twelve, respectively). Bitterly unhappy at first, she becomes more comfortable when Edmund—who has a vocation for the church—befriends her, encourages her with her reading, and helps her to write to her beloved older brother William. Sir Thomas, learning of Fanny's homesickness and her special attachment to her brother, invites William to spend a week at Mansfield Park just before he sets off for a career at sea, and this helps to consolidate Fanny's growing sense of well-being at Mansfield. Indeed, by the time she is fifteen, she has come to think of it as her only true home, and when there is a danger of her being moved out to live with her aunt Norris after the death of Rev. Norris, she becomes extremely distressed for a time. As it turns out, though, the officious, miserly, and hypocritical Mrs. Norris has no intention of taking Fanny in. Even though she had been the prime mover in the adoption of Fanny, she has never intended to carry any of the financial burdens of looking after her, and she now wheedles her way out of what Sir Thomas and Lady Bertram had taken as an understood thing. Fanny, though, is hugely relieved at this reprieve.

Beneath the apparent stability and security of life at Mansfield Park, there are signs of disturbance. Sir Thomas' eldest son, Tom, the heir to the estate, has taken to living extravagantly away from home and has incurred so many debts that Sir Thomas has to sell the living of Mansfield to help pay them off. This living had been intended for Edmund once he had taken holy orders, but it is now lost to him, at least for the duration of the next incumbent's residence (Dr. Grant is Rev. Norris' replacement). At the same time, much of Sir Thomas' wealth seems to be bound up with properties he owns in the West Indies, in Antigua (presumably, sugar plantations worked by slaves), and these are currently proving problematic and failing to yield adequate profits. Therefore, when Fanny is sixteen, Sir Thomas decides to go to Antigua himself to try to deal with these difficulties. He takes Tom with him in order to remove him from the bad influences that have been leading him astray.

Maria and Julia Bertram are now "out" in society and attending balls and other social events chaperoned by their aunt Norris, who has taken it upon herself to promote their interests. By contrast, Mrs. Norris tries actively to suppress the interests of Fanny, and she is forever reminding Fanny of her second-class status in the household. Fanny's main role in the home is to provide company and comfort for the idle and largely couch-bound Lady Bertram, though she is also often bullied into doing chores for Mrs. Norris. As ever, the only person who seriously thinks of Fanny's well-being is Edmund, and Fanny's affection for him grows when he exchanges one of his own horses for a horse suitable for her to ride after the death of her old pony.

After about a year, Tom Bertram returns, but Sir Thomas remains in the West Indies. Partly egged on by the grasping Mrs. Norris, Maria becomes engaged to Mr. Rushworth of Sotherton, a wealthy young man with one of the largest houses and estates in the neighborhood. As he has little to recommend him other than his wealth, Edmund fears that Maria has accepted him only for his money.

Henry and Mary Crawford come to stay at Mansfield parsonage with the Grants, as they are related to Mrs. Grant. Wealthy, smart, and witty, they soon make friends with the Bertrams. Maria and Julia are both attracted to Henry, and Mary initially appears very taken with Tom, though she soon transfers her attentions to Edmund, who, for his part, is soon well on the way to becoming infatuated by her. He even offers Mary the horse that he had bought for Fanny to ride, and Fanny is again left without a means of regular exercise and frequently left behind with Lady Bertram while the others go out riding.

A visit to Mr. Rushworth's estate, Sotherton, is arranged. Edmund, feeling guilty that Fanny has been excluded from recent activities because of his having offered her horse to Mary, insists that she should be a member of the party, and he offers to stay behind to look after his mother himself. Mrs. Norris objects to this, and eventually Mrs. Grant offers to remain behind with Lady Bertram. At Sotherton, the party is shown around the house by Mrs. Rushworth, who takes great pride in trying to communicate a sense of its history to them. While in the former private chapel, Mary Crawford speaks slightingly of clergymen, not realizing at this point that Edmund is preparing to become one himself. Outside, on a tour of the grounds, the party divides into three groups: Edmund, Mary, and Fanny; Maria, Mr. Rushworth, and Henry; and Mrs. Rushworth, Mrs. Norris, and Julia. As they walk in the wood, known as "the wilderness," Mary talks to Edmund of her surprise at his choice of profession, and it becomes clear that she considers it a negligible one. He tries to convince her of his commitment to his vocation and of the general importance of the profession to the moral state of the nation. He wins the support of Fanny in this, but Mary remains unpersuaded: she clearly has little understanding of, or respect for, his vocation.

Fanny becomes tired, and Edmund and Mary leave her to rest on a bench while they walk on. A little while later she is joined by Maria, Mr. Rushworth, and Henry Crawford. Maria and Henry express a desire to go through a locked gate into the park beyond, and Mr. Rushworth goes back to the house to fetch the key. While he is gone, Fanny becomes alarmed to see Maria and Henry squeeze through the gate into the park and go off alone. A few minutes later, Julia arrives, looking hot and agitated and evidently annoyed at having been separated from Henry Crawford, first by the slow pace of Mrs. Rushworth and Mrs. Norris and now by the maneuverings of her sister. She is now determined to catch up with the errant couple, and she, too, squeezes past the locked gate. Mr. Rushworth returns, also looking hot and bothered, all the more so on finding that his fiancée has disappeared alone with Henry Crawford. He sits with Fanny and complains to her of Maria's behavior. She tries to console him and then persuades him to go in search of the others. She then goes off in search of Edmund and Mary, who have now been gone an hour together, even though Edmund had originally promised Fanny to be back within minutes. She finds that they, too, have been in the park, though they had found an open gate to go through. Eventually, everyone returns to the house for dinner, and the day ends with some restoration of face on the part of Julia and Mr. Rushworth as Henry chooses Julia to ride on the barouche box beside him, and Maria allows Mr. Rushworth to hand her into the compartment.

The Honourable John Yates, a fashionable friend of Tom Bertram's, visits Mansfield Park. He brings with him the idea of organizing some private theatricals. Edmund, knowing that his father would not allow such an event to take place in his house, initially opposes the idea, as does Fanny. However, on hearing that Mary is happy to take part, he allows himself to be persuaded into the scheme, too, and preparations for the play begin. The somewhat risqué choice of play, *Lovers' Vows*, again shocks both Edmund and Fanny, but, as before, Edmund allows himself to be persuaded to continue with the idea. Fanny becomes isolated from the others as she refuses to take part, while Henry and Maria become constant companions, much to the annoyance of Julia, who, prevented from playing the role of the heroine, withdraws from the whole enterprise. Fanny is gradually drawn back into the other's company as she is prevailed upon to listen to their lines, but she is pained to watch Edmund and Mary rehearsing together and evidently enjoying the intimacy this allows between them.

Volume 2 of the novel opens with the surprise early return of Sir Thomas from Antigua. He quickly puts a stop to the rehearsals and clears all evidence of the theatricals from the house. He is shocked at Mrs. Norris' approval for the scheme and pleased that Fanny had the sense not to become involved. Henry Crawford coolly takes his leave for Bath, and Maria, who had been expecting him to propose to her, is stunned to realize that he has, in fact, been trifling with her all this time. Sir Thomas then hurries away the foolish Mr. Yates, with whom Julia has been flirting as a reaction to being snubbed by Henry. Sir Thomas also discourages any further intimacy with the Grants and therefore with Mary Crawford, too. He is at first reasonably pleased to hear of Maria's engagement to Mr. Rushworth, whom he initially finds unexceptionable; but as he comes to know more of Mr. Rushworth, he revises this opinion and realizes that he is an ignorant and "inferior" young man. He also perceives Maria's indifference to her fiancé and suggests to her that she might think of breaking off the engagement. But Maria's pride has been hurt by Henry Crawford, and, though he may have destroyed her happiness, she does not intend to let him know it or to let him "destroy her credit, her appearance, her prosperity." Moreover, having tasted the liberty that her father's absence had allowed at Mansfield, she is loath to lose it again. She therefore intends to go through with the marriage to Rushworth in order to escape from Mansfield and her father and to seek consolation for her hurt pride "in fortune and consequence, bustle and the world." The marriage duly takes place, and Julia accompanies the newlyweds on their honeymoon trip to Brighton and London.

In the absence of Julia and Maria, Fanny enjoys a newfound status in the Mansfield household and becomes, for once, a center of attention there. She also finds herself particularly welcome at Mansfield parsonage, where Mary Crawford has started to feel isolated. She and Mary strike up a friendship of sorts and become frequent companions: Edmund is pleased to observe this apparently growing intimacy between them, but we are given to understand that inwardly Fanny continues to maintain a critical distance from Mary. Mrs. Grant invites Fanny and Edmund to dine at the parsonage, much to the surprise of Lady Bertram and the spiteful indignation of Mrs. Norris. At the parsonage, they find that Henry Crawford has unexpectedly returned to Mansfield. Fanny is amazed at his effrontery in returning so soon and at his apparent unconcern over any upset he may have caused on his previous visit. When he talks of past events, she is angered to hear him speak slightingly of Mr. Rushworth and disrespectfully of Sir Thomas. He is taken aback when (unusually for her) she speaks sharply to him in response.

Mary is vexed to realize that Edmund has been unaffected by her evident distaste for his priestly vocation—and for the type of life it would inevitably entail were she to marry him—and has continued to prepare for the church; he is to take orders within a few weeks and will then become priest of a nearby parish (Thornton Lacey), where his living will be a modest one only. She feels aggrieved that she seems to be of so little account to him, and she resolves to reply in kind by adopting a cooler attitude toward him.

Fanny's improved looks—on which both Sir Thomas and Edmund have already remarked—pique the interest of Henry Crawford, and we hear him, in conversation with Mary, planning to make Fanny fall in love with him. As with his flirtatious behavior with Maria and Julia, it seems clear that it is a type of game to him. He fails to realize, however, that Fanny is made of sterner stuff than Maria and Julia and that, in any case, she is already effectively in love with Edmund.

Fanny's brother William, home on leave from the navy, is invited again to visit Mansfield. Hearing him express a wish to see Fanny dance, Sir Thomas arranges for a ball to be held at Mansfield Park; effectively, this will be a "coming-out" ball for Fanny. Fanny is excited at the prospect but concerned about what to wear and particularly about her lack of ornament: she has recently been given an amber cross by William—her only piece of jewelry—but she has no chain to wear it on. She consults Mary Crawford on what she should wear, and Mary is only too happy to advise her. She also offers Fanny the gift of a fancy gold necklace, and, after Fanny has been persuaded to accept it, she tells her that it had originally been a gift to herself from Henry. On hearing this, Fanny tries to return the necklace but is pressed by Mary to keep it. Fanny has started to become aware that Henry has designs on her—as he had on her cousins—and, as she leaves the parsonage now, she suspects that Mary may be acting for him in this matter of the necklace. (This, indeed, turns out to be the case, and, as Fanny says later, if she had known the necklace was from Henry, she could never have accepted it; apart from her disinclination to encourage his attentions, it would have been a breach of decorum.) When Fanny returns to her room at Mansfield Park, she finds Edmund there in the process of writing her a note to accompany a gift he was intending to leave her. He now gives it to her in person, and it turns out to be a gold chain for her amber cross. But in contrast to Mary's necklace, this is just the sort of simple chain that she had originally wanted. She is delighted at Edmund's kindness but even more uncertain now as to what to do about Mary's necklace. She tells Edmund about it and asks if she should return it. Edmund, who has been wondering within himself whether Mary loves him enough to marry him despite her cosmopolitan tastes, takes this as a promising sign and urges Fanny to keep the necklace. He does not want there to be any coolness, he says, between "the two dearest objects I have on earth." Just as Fanny's heart soars to be considered so dear to Edmund, it sinks to realize he is seriously considering marrying Mary despite her manifest faults. Fanny is almost ashamed to admit that she has had hopes of Edmund herself, for that would be to admit presumption, and she has "not words strong enough to satisfy her own humility." But no sooner has she resolved to subdue her emotions than she snatches up the fragment of Edmund's note "as a treasure beyond all her hopes."

The next day begins with another of Henry's ploys to ingratiate himself with Fanny. William is due to leave the following evening, and he will have a long journey by mail coach; Henry now offers to take William to London in his carriage and also invites him to dine at Admiral Crawford's with him. Fanny is pleased to think that William will have a more comfortable journey, and Sir

Thomas points out that a meeting with Admiral Crawford may well be advantageous to William's career, for Admiral Crawford has important connections in the Admiralty. Later in the day, Fanny meets Edmund on the stairs as they go to dress for the ball. He seems dispirited and tells her that he has just called on Mary to engage her for the first two dances of the evening; she gladly accepted the offer but also added that it would be the last time she would dance with him, as she has never danced with a clergyman and does not intend ever to do so in the future. Edmund is leaving the following day to stay with a friend before his ordination, and Mary's words have vexed him. He now confides in Fanny that he fears that he and Mary are incompatible after all, that although Mary "does not *think* evil," she speaks it to the extent that "it appears as if the mind itself was tainted." Fanny is moved by Edmund's confiding in her and cheered to hear that he seems to be turning away from Mary. She now dresses for the ball in high spirits. She is relieved to find that Mary's necklace does not fit William's amber cross, and so she has a free conscience in following her inclination and attaching it to Edmund's chain instead, though, as an afterthought, she decides to wear Mary's necklace as well as the chain and cross.

Fanny is praised by Sir Thomas for her elegant appearance and good looks, and at the ball she is admired by all the guests. She is immediately claimed for the first two dances by Henry Crawford—about which she has mixed feelings: she is happy not to have to be part of the general "bustle" of engaging a partner, but she is not flattered by Henry's pointed attentions, especially as she notices his self-satisfied smile as he looks at her necklace. She is then embarrassed to find that she is expected to lead the first dance and thus open the ball. She had not expected to be placed in such an unwonted position of distinction, and she has to struggle hard to overcome her habitual shyness in taking to the floor under the gaze of the entire assembly. She acquits herself admirably, however, and attracts praise from all quarters, much to the satisfaction of her uncle. Henry continues to pay her particular attention throughout the evening, and she is obliged to dance with him several times, although the dances she anticipates with most pleasure are those she is to have with Edmund. He has danced twice with Mary, but they have quarreled again over his forthcoming ordination and have parted in "mutual vexation." Thus when Fanny does finally dance with him, she is, in a sense, happy because of his unhappiness: because he seems to take comfort from being with her, but also because she is pleased to see confirmation of a breakdown in his relationship with Mary.

The next day, after an early breakfast, Fanny bids a tearful farewell to William when he departs for Portsmouth, via London with Henry; and later Edmund also departs for Peterborough, where he will stay for a week with his friend, Mr. Owen, as they both await their ordination. Mary Crawford now begins to regret her peevishness with Edmund at the ball, and she is impatient for his return, especially as her planned departure for London draws near. Having heard that Mr. Owen has three grown-up sisters, moreover, Mary has started to feel jealous—an emotion quite new to her. When she hears that Edmund has, in fact, extended his stay at Peterborough, she cannot contain herself any longer, and she goes to Mansfield Park to see if Fanny can shed any light on Edmund's attitude and intentions toward her. Fanny remains largely noncommital, but Mary takes comfort from the fact that Fanny seems sure that Edmund has no immediate plans to marry.

Henry returns to Mansfield and breaks the news to Mary that he was mistaken in trying merely to flirt with Fanny, that he has, in fact, fallen in love with Fanny and is now resolved to marry her. Mary is at first disbelieving that her gadabout brother should have been finally smitten by such a steady and sober character as Fanny, but after hearing him eulogize Fanny, she is convinced that he is sincere. She also sees some benefit to herself in being thus attached to Edmund's family, and so she is quick to come round to the idea and to encourage it.

Henry goes to see Fanny early the next morning and first tries to soften her emotions toward him by telling her that, through his uncle the Admiral, he has secured William's promotion to the rank of lieutenant. She is overjoyed to hear this and is sincerely thankful for Henry's good offices on William's behalf. However, when Henry then declares his love for her and presses her to marry him, she becomes confused and distressed and begs him to stop. She neither believes him to be serious nor wants him to be so, and when he persists with his entreaties, she finally bursts out of the room and runs away upstairs to her isolated sitting room. After she has heard him go, she comes down again to share the good news of William's promotion with the rest of the family, but she is agitated again by the news that Sir Thomas has invited Henry to dine with them later in the day. When he arrives for dinner, he brings a note for Fanny from Mary. This congratulates Fanny and urges her to accept Henry's offer. Fanny is again confused by the apparent earnestness of both the Crawfords, as she had always been convinced that Henry was simply trifling with her in the same way he had trifled with Maria. But, in any case, she has no intention whatsoever of accepting Henry, and she tries to make this clear in a hurriedly written reply to Mary that she gives to Henry when he finally leaves after what has been for Fanny an extremely strained and awkward evening. Fanny hopes that her note will finally put an end to Henry's bothersome attentions.

However, volume 3 of the novel opens with yet another early morning visit to Mansfield Park by Henry. This time he has come to apply to Sir Thomas for his consent to the marriage. Sir Thomas goes to ascertain Fanny's feelings on the matter, clearly expecting her acceptance of Henry to be a mere formality. Not surprisingly, then, he is astonished to find that she is resolutely opposed to any engagement to Henry. He tries to reason with her about Henry's eminent suitability as a husband, not knowing, of course, of Henry's previous flirtations with his own daughters—something Fanny cannot bring herself to tell him about. He cannot believe that Fanny is prepared to pass up such an advantageous offer, especially given her unlikely prospects in marriage otherwise, and he gradually loses patience with her and accuses her of being willful and obstinate and, most hurtfully, ungrateful. She is now beside herself with emotion and begins to sob uncontrollably. Sir Thomas relents somewhat, thinking that a little quiet reflection may change her mind. He sends Henry away and arranges for him to see Fanny briefly the next day. As a result of his visit to Fanny's small sitting room, the east room, Sir Thomas gives instructions that a fire be lit there every day—a sign of her greatly improved status in the household, despite her refusal of Henry. On the following evening, when Fanny sees Henry alone, it becomes clear that despite her strongest disavowals of any shadow of feeling for him, Henry is determined to persist in his courtship of her; indeed, in some ways, her refusal of him has increased his determination to win her over, as he is unused to being rejected by women. Fanny is, to some extent, impressed by the change that seems to have come over Henry since the days of the theatri-cals—he does seem more sincere with her than he ever did with Maria, but his vanity and arrogance are still clearly in evidence in the way he assumes that she must inevitably fall in love with him as long as he perseveres in his efforts to win her. When Lady Bertram and Mrs. Norris come to hear of his proposal, the former is pleased for Fanny, but the latter is furious that Fanny has been preferred to Julia.

Edmund returns from Peterborough as a clergyman and is surprised to find Mary still at Mansfield parsonage. He is even more surprised to find that she gives him a warm reception and seems to have forgotten her angry objections to his becoming a priest. This revives his spirits and renews his earlier hopes of marrying her. Sir Thomas now enlists Edmund's support in trying to persuade Fanny to accept Henry's proposal, but Edmund is no more successful than Sir Thomas, even though he tries to play on Fanny's charitable nature by suggesting that if she were to marry Henry, she may well help to reform the weaker aspects of his character. On the eve of her departure for London, Mary Crawford, too, comes to see Fanny to press Henry's case, but she does him no real favor when she finally reveals the truth about the necklace she had given Fanny on his behalf. Fanny is relieved to see Henry and Mary leave for London at last, though she is once more fearful of Edmund's eventually marrying Mary, as there have recently been strong signs of a renewed warmth in their relationship.

William returns to Mansfield on ten days' leave. Sir Thomas, seeing no signs of Fanny's missing Henry, decides that it may help to concentrate her mind on what she might be giving up and on the possible implications of remaining unmarried or of marrying badly if she were to return with William for a visit to her family in Portsmouth. To put it bluntly, Sir Thomas wants to teach Fanny ''the value of a good income.'' She, however, sees the visit in a wholly positive light, as a valuable opportunity to renew and refresh the familial bonds of love that had been so suddenly broken all those years ago, and she looks forward with eager anticipation to seeing her parents, brothers, and sisters again. She also thinks that it may do her good to be separated from Edmund for two or three months, so that the pain of seeing him lured into marriage by Mary will not be so great.

When Fanny arrives at Portsmouth, Sir Thomas' hopes are vindicated almost immediately, for she is, indeed, taken aback by the dirt and noise of her family's house and disappointed to find that her parents have little time for her. The younger children are raucous and argumentative, her father is coarse and ill mannered, and her mother is careless of the home and described as a "dawdle" and a "slattern." Fanny's appreciation of Mansfield Park duly grows as she starts to pine for its elegance, comfort, and relative tranquillity. Her only consolation comes to be her growing friendship with her sister of fourteen, Susan, to whom she tries to pass on the education and culture she has herself acquired at Mansfield.

After about a month, Fanny is surprised to receive a visit at Portsmouth from Henry Crawford. His manners are now seen in their best light when set against the manners that Fanny is becoming accustomed to in the slovenly Price household. Henry also appears to have improved in terms of how he views his responsibilities as a landowner, for he makes clear to Fanny that he has recently become more actively and purposefully involved in the stewardship of his estate in Norfolk (Everingham). She is impressed by his charitable efforts on behalf of some of his tenants, but there are signs, as always with Henry, that this is just another persona he is adopting for his ulterior ends. Henry brings with him the news that Edmund is now in London and in contact with Mary; Fanny assumes that, therefore, Edmund must soon propose to Mary.

Fanny receives a meandering letter from Mary Crawford containing some London tittle-tattle and inconclusive comments about Edmund. It reinforces Fanny's sense of Mary's essential shallowness and of her unworthiness for Edmund; Mary talks only of external things and shows no understanding of Edmund's character or principles—and she again talks sarcastically of his being a clergyman. Fanny deduces from the letter that Edmund has not yet proposed to Mary, but she fears that when he does, Mary will probably accept him, for all her dismissive comments about his profession and even though her present fashionable lifestyle may temporarily disincline her to marry into the church. Also in Mary's letter is news of a party at the Frasers' house (where Mary is staying) that will bring Henry into contact with Maria for the first time since her marriage.

Fanny then receives a letter from Edmund. He writes from Mansfield Park again after having returned from three weeks in London. He tells Fanny that his hopes of marrying Mary are again at a low ebb. She seems to him to have become a different woman in London, and he has been greatly disappointed by what he has seen of her lax and frivolous manners there. He blames her altered conduct on the fashionable company she keeps and calls her principal friends, Mrs. Fraser and Lady Stornaway, coldhearted, vain, and mercenary. However, Edmund cannot quite give Mary up yet, and he tells Fanny that he is still considering proposing to her, possibly by letter. He also reports that he saw

Henry and Maria Rushworth at the Frasers' party but that they exchanged only unfriendly looks.

Letters now arrive for Fanny from Lady Bertram, breaking the news that Tom Bertram is seriously ill following a neglected fall and a heavy bout of drinking. For a while it seems as though Tom will not survive, but shortly after his return to Mansfield Park he begins to make a recovery. Lady Bertram's almost daily letters to Fanny over this trying period bespeak her strong reliance on Fanny, and she frequently expresses her wish to have Fanny back with her, especially as neither of her daughters has seen fit to come home to comfort her. But Sir Thomas will not be free to fetch her from Portsmouth for some time yet. Fanny now receives another letter from Mary Crawford, who is still in London. Shedding crocodile tears in anticipation of Tom Bertram's death, Mary effectively looks forward to the possibility of Edmund's inheriting his father's estate instead of Tom, an event that would, she implies, finally decide her to marry him and help her to overlook his being a clergyman. Mary also talks breezily about the fact that Henry is now often in the same company as Maria Rushworth and that Mr. Rushworth is out of town. Fanny is disgusted by this letter: for its callousness toward Tom, its mercenary attitude toward Edmund, and its irresponsible tone toward what Fanny suspects may be another flirtation between Henry and Maria. Indeed, another letter from Mary follows hard on the heels of this one, suggesting that some sort of scandal involving Henry and Maria may be about to break; Mary urges Fanny not to believe the "ill-natured rumour." But this so-called rumor is actually reported in Mr. Price's newspaper the following day—that Henry and Maria have run away together. Fanny is not sure whether or not to believe the report, and she waits anxiously for another letter that might confirm or refute the story. She has to wait three days before she receives one; it comes from Edmund, with a London postmark, and does, in fact, confirm the story. He tells her that Maria and Henry cannot be traced at the moment and also that a further calamity has befallen the family: Julia has eloped to Scotland with Mr. Yates. He tells Fanny that Sir Thomas has asked him to collect her from Portsmouth the following day; Sir Thomas wants her to return immediately to Mansfield to care for Lady Bertram, and he has invited Susan to accompany her and then to stay at Mansfield for a few months. Fanny and Susan travel back to Mansfield with Edmund, and they are greeted warmly by Lady Bertram on their arrival.

The whole household is in distress over the double scandal, but Lady Bertram at least now finds some consolation in being able to relate all she knows about the events to her beloved Fanny. After a few days, Edmund, too, confides in Fanny about his last interview with Mary before he left London. He tells her that he had become disillusioned with Mary once and for all when he realized how lightly she viewed what Henry and Maria had done. She had hardly objected to the adultery at all but had simply bewailed the fact that the couple had been foolish enough to allow their affair to be exposed in public. To add insult to injury, she had also more or less explicitly mocked Edmund's serious moral attitude toward the affair. He had left her, and their relationship was now over. Edmund admits to Fanny how badly he has been deceived in the characters of both Mary and Henry. He feels brokenhearted, however, and cannot envisage ever meeting another woman whom he could love as he loved Mary, but he ''clings'' to Fanny's friendship.

Despite the general gloom at Mansfield Park, Fanny is very happy. Now that the truth about Henry Crawford is known, she has been restored to her uncle's favor—especially as her exemplary conduct throughout contrasts so starkly with that of his two daughters; and she is, of course, overjoyed to know that Edmund is no longer attached to Mary. Maria lives with Henry Crawford for a time, but she soon realizes that he has no intention of marrying her, and they separate yet again amid mutual recriminations. In the meantime, Mr. Rushworth divorces her. Sir Thomas partly blames himself for what has happened because he feels he should have taken more careful interest in the education and upbringing of his daughters. But his has been a sin of omission rather than of commission, unlike that of Mrs. Norris, whom he holds directly responsible for the active inculcation of bad principles in his daughters. Eventually, Maria and Mrs. Norris are sent into a sort of exile by Sir Thomas, and they are forced to live at a long distance from Mansfield with only their bad tempers to keep each other occupied.

Julia's marriage to Mr. Yates turns out somewhat better than expected. They at least acknowledge their folly and seek forgiveness from Sir Thomas—and Mr. Yates turns out to have a larger estate and a larger degree of sense than had at first appeared. Tom Bertram recovers his health and, as a result of his suffering, turns over a new leaf, becoming less thoughtless and selfish and more sober, serious, and self-responsible. The main beneficiaries of Maria's disgrace, however, are the three eldest Price children, Fanny, William, and Susan. Edmund, finally realizing how much he relies on, and cares for, Fanny, asks her to marry him, and the match is approved by Sir Thomas. William Price's evident honesty, hard work, and good conduct win Sir Thomas' continuing support for him in his navy career. Susan is asked to remain at Mansfield in Fanny's place when Fanny goes to live with Edmund at Thornton Lacey. Sometime in the future, we hear, Dr. Grant dies, and Edmund receives his original birthright, as it were, when he returns to become the rector of Mansfield. In their married life, Fanny and Edmund achieve a happiness ''as secure as earthly happiness can be.''

Main Characters: Edmund Bertram, Julia Bertram, Maria Bertram, Tom Bertram, Sir Thomas Bertram, Lady Bertram, Henry Crawford, Mary Crawford, Mrs. Norris, Mr. Price, Mrs. Frances Price, Fanny Price, Susan Price, William Price, Mr. Rushworth, Mrs. Rushworth, Mr. Yates.

Minor Characters: Charles Anderson, Miss Anderson, the Aylmers, Baddeley, Mrs. Brown, Mr. Campbell, Mrs. Chapman, Sir Charles, Charles, Admiral Crawford, Mrs. Crawford, the Duke, Ellis, Mr. Fraser, Mrs. Fraser, Dr. Grant, Mrs. Grant, Mr. Green, the Gregorys, John Groom, Mr. Harding, Colonel Harrison,

Sir Henry, Mrs. Holford, Mrs. Jefferies, Lady Lascelles, Miss Lee, Maddison, Maddox, the Miss Maddoxes, Captain Marshall, Mrs. Maxwell, Nanny, Rev. Norris, Tom Oliver, Mr. Owen, the Miss Owens, Lady Prescott, Betsey Price, Charles Price, John Price, Mary Price, Richard Price, Sam Price, Lord Raven-shaw, Rebecca, Mr. Humphrey Repton, Robert, Flora Ross (Lady Stornaway), Janet Ross (Mrs. Fraser), Mr. Rushworth (deceased), the Saddler, Sally, Old Scholey, Smith, Sneyd, Mrs. Sneyd, Miss Sneyd, Augusta Sneyd, Stephen, Lord Stornaway, Lady Stornaway, Turner's, Captain Walsh, Mrs. Whitaker, Wilcox.

Volume and chapter divisions (numbers in brackets are for editions with continuous chapter numbers): Volume 1: Chapters 1–18, volume 2: Chapters 1–13 [19–31], volume 3: Chapters 1–17 [32–48].

See: Ahmad 1989, Anderson 1995, *Armstrong 1988*, Auerbach 1983, Bevan 1987, *Bloom 1987b*, Bowden 1992, Brissenden 1975, Cleere 1995, Collins 1949–1950, Conger 1988, *Cox 1970*, Dunn 1995, Ferguson 1991, Flahiff 1985, Flavin 1987, *Fleishman 1967*, Footerman 1978, Fowler 1991, Fowler 1974, Galperin 1992, Gard 1989a, Gardiner 1995, Garside and McDonald 1975, Gay 1987–1988, Gibbon 1982, Gillis 1985, Gillooly 1994, Giuffre 1983–1984, Goold 1987, Greenfield 1994, Grey 1980, Grove 1983, Halperin 1983a, *Havely 1973*, Heyns 1986, Hogan 1977, Hudson 1991, Jarvis 1988, Jordan 1987, Kaufmann 1986, Kearney 1988, Kelly 1982, Kilroy 1985, Kirkham 1975, Koppel 1983, Leavis 1941–1942, Lenta 1983, Lew 1994, Litvak 1986, Lougy 1988, MacDonagh 1986–1987, D. Marshall 1989, McDonnell 1984, McKenzie 1985, Meyers 1986, Meyersohn 1983, Miller 1992, Moler 1983, 1985, Monaghan 1978, Moore 1982, Pedley 1995, Perkins 1993, Pickrel 1987, Ram 1977a, Ray 1991, *Simons 1997*, Simpson 1987, Skinner 1992, *Smith 1978*, J. H. Smith 1987, Smith 1994, *Southam 1976b*, Southam 1995, Trickett 1986, Ty 1986, Vanita 1992, Waldron 1994, Willis 1987, *Wood 1993*, Worthington 1992, Yarrow 1991, Yeazell 1984, York 1987, Zelicovici 1983.

Manwaring, Maria (*Lady Susan, Minor Works* 245, 248). Mr. Manwaring's sister whose hopes of marrying Sir James Martin are foiled by Lady Susan's intervention, first on her daughter Frederica's behalf and later on her own behalf when she (Lady Susan) actually marries him.

Manwaring, Mr. (*Lady Susan, Minor Works* 243–45). He becomes Lady Susan's lover while she is staying at his family home in Langford; his wife's jealousy is the immediate cause of Lady Susan's removal to the Vernons' house at Churchill. Manwaring remains devoted to Lady Susan, however, and later follows her to London to continue the affair. He and his wife eventually separate as a result of this. Lady Susan seems genuinely to like Manwaring above all her other lovers and would even contemplate marrying him if he were free.

Manwaring, Mrs. (*Lady Susan, Minor Works* 245). The jealous wife of Mr. Manwaring, Lady Susan's lover. She follows her husband to London to try to prevent his continuing the affair with Lady Susan, but to no avail. She is genuinely distraught by her husband's infidelity and seems inconsolable when they finally separate, and she returns to the house of her former guardian, Mr. Johnson; there is even a suggestion that she may fret herself to death. Her extreme distress, although reported only secondhand, provides a serious measure against which to judge the behavior of Lady Susan and a sort of counterweight to the jaunty tone of Lady Susan's own account of events.

Marshall, Captain (*Mansfield Park* Ch.6; I:6:60). The captain of William Price's ship while he is still a midshipman.

Marshall, Mr. (*The Watsons, Minor Works* 353). A Croydon acquaintance of Robert and Jane Watson who, like Mr. Hemmings, changes for dinner every day.

Martin family (*Emma* Chs.3, 4; I:3:23; I:4:27–28). Elizabeth Martin and her sister are friends of Harriet Smith at Mrs. Goddard's school, and when Emma first meets Harriet, she has just returned from a two-month visit at the Martins' Abbey Mill Farm, where she has been treated with great kindness and hospitality by Mrs. Martin. During this visit she has obviously become romantically attached to the son of the family, Robert Martin, and it appears that the mother and sisters are hopeful of a marriage between the two.

Martin, Robert (*Emma* Chs.3, 4; I:3:23; I:4:28–34). Robert Martin is a young and successful tenant farmer at Abbey Mill Farm on the Donwell estate. Educated and widely read, good-humored, sensible, and hardworking, he is well liked and respected and held in high regard by Mr. Knightley. He falls in love with Harriet Smith when she comes to stay at the farm to visit his sisters. She returns his love but is later persuaded by Emma Woodhouse to view him as her social inferior and therefore to reject his proposal of marriage. Their love for one another survives Emma's misguided interference, however, and the young couple are finally married at the end of the novel.

Martin, Sir James (*Lady Susan, Minor Works* 245, 275–76). Sir James Martin is a wealthy but weak and foolish young man who "rattles" too much and who is mercilessly manipulated by Lady Susan. At Langford, she flirts with him herself to disengage him from Miss Manwaring and then persuades him to transfer his affections to her daughter, Frederica. She, however, finds him utterly repulsive and absolutely refuses to marry him. Eventually, Lady Susan once more steals him from Miss Manwaring and marries him herself for his money.

Mary (*Persuasion* Ch.21; II:9:202). Mrs. Smith's maid at her lodgings in Bath.

Mathews family (*Sanditon, Minor Works* 389). Visitors to Sanditon noted by Mr. Parker in the subscription list at the circulating library. *See* Beard, Mr.

"Matilda" (*Northanger Abbey* Ch.20; II:5:160). "The wretched Matilda" is an imaginary figure in the parody of gothic romance with which Henry Tilney teases Catherine on their journey to Northanger from Bath.

Maxwell, Mrs. (*Mansfield Park* Ch.38; III:7:387). An admiral's wife and god-mother to Mary Price, to whom she gives the silver knife that Mary bequeaths to her sister Susan.

"Memoirs of Mr. Clifford, an Unfinished Tale" (*Volume the First* of Jane Austen's juvenilia). Dedicated to the young Charles Austen, this very short piece was probably composed just after "Sir William Mountague" (also dedicated to Charles Austen), which, on internal evidence, can be dated to 1788. Mr. Clifford, who lives in Bath, has never been to London, and so he decides to pay a visit there in his coach-and-four. The tale, such as it is, merely recounts the details in each stage of the journey. Mr. Clifford makes a brisk start and covers nineteen miles in the first day, but, after this, his pace slows drastically. He becomes ill at Overton, Hampshire, and remains there for five months; from there he takes several days to reach Basingstoke, which is just a few miles away, and the piece ends there. Mr. Clifford is the sole character in the story, apart from the physician who treats him during his illness at Overton.

Merryweather, Miss (*Sanditon, Minor Works* 389). A visitor to Sanditon from Limehouse noted by Mr. Parker in the subscription list at the circulating library. *See* Beard, Mr.

Metcalfe, Lady (*Pride and Prejudice* Ch.29; II:6:165). An acquaintance of Lady Catherine de Bourgh. The latter had recommended a governess, Miss Pope, to her friend, and Lady Metcalfe had called to thank her for such a "treasure."

Middleton children (*Sense and Sensibility* Chs.7, 21; I:7:34; I:21:120–22). The Middletons have four somewhat spoiled, noisy, and unruly children; the eldest, John, is six years old, and the others are William, Annamaria (aged three), and an unnamed fourth. They are the means by which Lucy Steele and her sister ingratiate themselves with Lady Middleton, who dotes on her children, especially her "troublesome boys."

Middleton, Lady Mary, née Jennings (*Sense and Sensibility* Ch.6; I:6:30–31). Lady Middleton is the eldest daughter of Mrs. Jennings, though entirely unlike her rambunctious mother in being reserved and cold, with "nothing to say for herself beyond the most common-place inquiry or remark." She is elegant in appearance and graceful in manner, but the Dashwoods find her "cold insipidity" repulsive. She seems to have few interests apart from that of "humouring" or spoiling her four young children.

Middleton, Sir John (*Sense and Sensibility* Chs.4, 6; I:4:23–24; I:6:30). Mrs. Dashwood's cousin, of Barton Park in Devon. He provides Mrs. Dashwood and her daughters with a cottage on his estate, just outside Barton village, and entertains them at every available opportunity. A jovial, kindly, and "thoroughly good-humoured" man of about forty, though with few talents or refinements and fewer resources beyond hunting and organizing house parties, "he delighted in collecting about him more young people than his house would hold, and the noisier they were the better was he pleased." He and his wife make an odd couple in the eyes of the Dashwoods, for, apart from a shared lack of "talent and taste," they are very different in temperament and outward behavior: while she is graceful and elegant but cold, reserved, and taciturn, he is loud and boisterous but warm, outgoing, and spontaneous.

Millar, Colonel (*Pride and Prejudice* Ch.41; II:18:229). The commander of a regiment who had been stationed at Meryton in Mrs. Bennet's youth. When they left, Mrs. Bennet remembers feeling just as woeful as her younger daughters feel on the departure of Colonel Forster's regiment.

Milmans, the two. *See* Bird, Mrs., and Cooper, Mrs. James (*Emma*).

Minor Works. Jane Austen's minor writings, as collected in volume 6 of the Oxford edition of Jane Austen's works, *Minor Works*, include the juvenilia, *Lady Susan, The Watsons, Sanditon, Plan of a Novel, according to Hints from Various Quarters*, "Opinions of *Mansfield Park*," "Opinions of *Emma*," Verses and Prayers. *See* separate entries under these titles.

Mitchell, Farmer (*Emma* Ch.1; I:1:12). A Highbury farmer from whom Mr. Weston once borrowed two umbrellas for Emma and Miss Taylor; from this moment, Emma says, she began to plan a match between Miss Taylor and Mr. Weston.

Mitchells, the (*Northanger Abbey* Chs.11, 27; I:11:90; II:12:217). Acquaintances of Isabella Thorpe whom she describes as spiteful but who are friendly to her when she finds herself sitting next to them at a play. Isabella makes fun of Anne Mitchell's attempts to imitate her wearing of a turban.

Molland's (*Persuasion* Ch.19; II:7:174). A shop in Milsom Street, Bath (apparently an actually existing shop of the time, according to R. W. Chapman's note in the Oxford edition of the text).

Morgan (*Sanditon, Minor Works* 389). Butler to the Parker family at Trafalgar House.

Morland, Catherine (*Northanger Abbey* Ch.1; I:1:13). Catherine is the heroine of the novel, and that word is perhaps more applicable than usual here, as, though she has a normal, active childhood up to the age of fifteen, from fifteen to seventeen she goes into "training for a heroine" by reading all the books that heroines rely on for their stock of useful quotations—Pope, Gray, Shakespeare, and so on. But by the age of seventeen, she is still not a true heroine, as she had not yet had any romantic encounters that might inspire her passions and "call forth her sensibility." Fortunately, just at that time, Mr. and Mrs. Allen decide to pay a six-week visit to Bath, and they invite Catherine to accompany them. Thus starts the adventure that is sure to throw a hero in the path of our affectionate, cheerful, and unaffected young heroine with her as yet "ignorant and uninformed" mind.

Morland children (*Northanger Abbey* Chs.1, 13, 28; I:1:14; II:13:233, 240). Catherine's brothers and sisters mentioned by name in the book are George (six), Harriet (four), Sarah (Sally) (sixteen), and an older brother, Richard. *See also* Morland, James.

Morland, James (*Northanger Abbey* Ch.4, 7; I:4:33; I:7:44–45). Catherine's eldest brother, who comes to Bath with his Oxford friend John Thorpe. He becomes involved with Thorpe's sister, Isabella, whom he has met before on a Christmas visit to the Thorpes' house in London. He later becomes engaged to her, but when she discovers how little money he can bring to marriage, she starts to flirt with Captain Tilney and more or less jilts James.

Morland, Mrs. (*Northanger Abbey* Ch.1; I:1:13). Mother of Catherine Morland and nine other children. She is a healthy, good-tempered, and easygoing woman "of useful plain sense."

Morland, Rev. Richard (*Northanger Abbey* Ch.1; I:1:13). Catherine Morland's father—a very respectable man with an independent fortune in addition to two good livings.

Morley, Sir Basil (*Persuasion* Ch.3; I:3:20). A friend of Sir Walter Elliot, mentioned only in passing.

Morris, Mr. (*Pride and Prejudice* Ch.1; I:1:3). Mr. Bingley arranges the lease of Netherfield Park with Mr. Morris, who is therefore presumably the owner's agent.

Morton, the Honourable Miss (*Sense and Sensibility* Ch.33; II:11:224). Only daughter of the late Lord Morton, with £30,000 settled on her. Mrs. Ferrars is hopeful of a match between Miss Morton and her son, Edward, and is prepared to settle £1,000 on him if it takes place.

Mullins family (*Sanditon, Minor Works* 423). A Sanditon family in straitened circumstances for whom Mr. Parker would like to start a subscription fund.

Musgrave, Tom (*The Watsons, Minor Works* 318). A raffish, fashionable, womanizing young man with an independent fortune who likes to be seen in the company of Lord Osborne. Elizabeth tells Emma that most of the girls in the area are, or have been, in love with him, and he seems also to have had a flirtation with several of the Watson girls. When he meets Emma Watson, it is clear that he would like to add her to his list, too, but she finds him vain, conceited and overfamiliar, and she firmly blocks his attempts at establishing a connection with her.

Musgrove, Charles (*Persuasion* Chs.1, 6; I:1:3; I:6:43–44). Son and heir to Mr. Charles Musgrove and father of Charles and Walter. He had originally proposed to Anne Elliot (five years before the start of the novel), but when she refused him, he married her younger sister, Mary. He and his family live at Uppercross Cottage, a quarter of a mile from Uppercross Hall, and the two families are frequently at each other's house. Charles is a "civil and agreeable" man, bluff and easygoing, but with little substance to his character and few interests beyond shooting.

Musgrove, Charles (the younger) (*Persuasion* Chs.5, 7; I:5:38; I:7;53). The eldest of the two young sons of Charles and Mary Musgrove. When Charles dislocates his collarbone in an accidental fall, Anne Elliot quickly and coolly takes matters in hand (as she will do later after Louisa Musgrove's fall at Lyme): she attends to the child, calms his hysterical mother, organizes the servants, sends for the apothecary, Mr. Robinson, and sends messages to the child's father and to Uppercross Hall. A fortunate consequence of this accident, from Anne's point of view, is that it puts off her feared first meeting with Captain Wentworth at Uppercross, as the nursing of little Charles provides her with an excuse to stay at the cottage the next evening while Wentworth is entertained by the Musgroves (she realizes later that she would also have bumped into him at the hall on the day of the accident if it had not prevented her and Mary from visiting that day).

Musgrove, Harry (*Persuasion* Ch.13; II:1:122). The youngest and "long-petted" son of the elder Mr. and Mrs. Musgrove of Uppercross Hall.

Musgrove, Henrietta and Louisa (*Persuasion* Ch.5; I:5:40–41). The two grown-up daughters of Mr. and Mrs. Musgrove of Uppercross Hall. Louisa is the eldest at twenty, and Henrietta is nineteen, but, in terms of their characters, they are virtually indistinguishable, a point emphasized by Captain Wentworth's initial inability to choose which of them he prefers and by Admiral Croft's not being able to tell them apart. They are described together, too, as being open, affectionate, and good-humored, as having acquired "the usual stock of accomplishments" from their school in Exeter, and as "living to be fashionable, happy, and merry" like thousands of other young women. There is also a suggestion of youthful giddiness about them, and this becomes clearer as the plot unfolds, and their feelings are variously engaged by Captain Wentworth, Charles Hayter, and Captain Benwick. Henrietta is being courted by Charles Hayter when Captain Wentworth's appearance briefly turns her head, but Charles soon wins her back, and they are eventually engaged. Once it is clear that Henrietta has no serious interest in Wentworth, Louisa becomes the clear favorite for his hand—indeed, he has already started to prefer her for her apparent "decision and firmness" of character. However, their incompatibility emerges ironically from Louisa's accident at Lyme, when she is *foolishly* resolute in jumping down the steps of the Cobb, and when he, under her persuasion, is *ir*resolute in his efforts to stop her. During Louisa's recuperation at the Harvilles' house, she unexpectedly becomes attached to Captain Benwick and soon agrees to marry him. The rapid development of this romance underscores the capricious nature of both characters but also stands as an effective contrast to the slow process of the novel's central romance between Anne Elliot and Captain Wentworth. Thus it gradually becomes clear that, though Louisa and Henrietta are largely sympathetic characters, preferred by Anne to her own sisters, their function in the novel is partly to set off the maturity, constancy, and true firmness of mind of the heroine.

Musgrove, Mr. Charles (*Persuasion* Chs.1, 5; I:1:3; I:5:40). Wealthy owner of Uppercross Hall in Somerset and father of Charles, Louisa, and Henrietta Musgrove. He and his wife are both described as unaffected, being "in the old English style . . . friendly and hospitable, not much educated, and not at all elegant." Anne Elliot is constantly struck by the stark contrast between the hearty warmth and sincerity of the Musgrove family and her own family's coldness and artificiality.

Musgrove, Mrs. (*Persuasion* Ch.5; I:5:40). Wife of Mr. Musgrove and sister to Mrs. Hayter. A robust, matronly woman, Mrs. Musgrove is physically "of a comfortable substantial size" and, like her husband, temperamentally cheerful and sociable, though with a recently acquired tendency to become maudlin over her late son, Richard.

Musgrove, Mrs. Mary, née Elliot (*Persuasion* Chs.1, 5; I:1:3, 5; I: 5: 33, 37). Wife of Charles Musgrove of Uppercross Cottage and younger sister of Elizabeth and Anne Elliot. "Better endowed" than Elizabeth but without Anne's "understanding or temper," Mary is a self-centered and self-important woman who constantly complains of being "neglected and ill-used." Her better nature does shine through from time to time, but Austen's comic irony makes her memorable for her attention-seeking hypochondria.

Musgrove, Richard (deceased) (*Persuasion* Ch.6; I:6:50–51). The "troublesome, hopeless" son of the elder Musgroves, brother to Charles, Louisa, and Henrietta. He had been sent to sea because he was such a problem to his family and because he was too stupid for anything else. He had served for six months as a midshipman under Captain Wentworth but had been transferred as soon as Wentworth could get rid of him, and he had later been killed in action, some two years before the main action of the story. Although Richard Musgrove had been largely unloved and unwanted by his family during his life and not immediately lamented by them on his death, time has faded his faults, and he has become, when we first hear of him, "poor Richard," the subject of many "fat sighings" on the part of Mrs. Musgrove.

Musgrove, Walter (*Persuasion* Chs.5, 9; I:5:38; I:9:79–80). Mischievous younger son of Charles and Mary Musgrove. He is two years old and seems already to be taking after his brother, Charles, in largely flouting his mother's authority and behaving in a forward manner with other adults. When he climbs on Anne Elliot's back, while she is attending to his brother, and refuses to get off, she is rescued by Captain Wentworth, who gently but firmly removes the child; this is Captain Wentworth's first intimate gesture toward Anne since his return, and she is overcome by the confused emotions it revives in her for him.

Musgroves, the younger (*Persuasion* Ch.14; II:2:129). We are told that the elder Musgroves of Uppercross Hall have a "numerous" family, and, in addition to their named children, there seem to be at least some more young boys who, we are told, return from school at Christmas.

"The Mystery, an Unfinished Comedy" (*Volume the First*). Jane Austen dedicated this piece to her father, Rev. George Austen, and it was probably written about 1788. There are only three short scenes to the play, and it is a *complete* mystery because we hear only inconsequential snatches from the characters' conversations and never really know what they are talking about.

Characters: Corydon, Daphne, Colonel Elliott, Fanny Elliott, the Humbug family (Old, Young, and Mrs.), Sir Edward Spangle.

N

Nanny (*Mansfield Park* Ch.1; I:1:8). Mrs. Norris' housekeeper and "chief counsellor." She is sent to London to escort the young Fanny Price back to Mansfield Park on her first journey there.

Nanny (*The Watsons, Minor Works* 344). A servant, possibly the housekeeper, at the Watsons' house.

Nash, Miss (*Emma* Chs.4, 9; I:4:29; I:9:69–70). Head teacher at Mrs. Goddard's school who first gives Harriet the idea of making a collection of riddles and charades; she herself "had written out at least three hundred."

Nicholls, Mrs. (*Pride and Prejudice* Chs.11, 53; I:11:55; III:11:331). Mr. Bingley's housekeeper at Netherfield Park.

Norris, Mrs., née Ward (*Mansfield Park* Ch.1; I:1:3). Mrs. Norris is the sister of Lady Bertram and Mrs. Price and the widow of the former rector of Mansfield, Rev. Norris. One of Jane Austen's most memorable creations, Mrs. Norris represents a classic satire on self-important officiousness, hypocrisy, and miserliness. After the death of her husband, she gradually insinuates herself into the daily life of the Bertram family and takes on the self-appointed role of guardian and mentor to Julia and Maria. She indulges, flatters, and spoils the two sisters and does nothing for their real education and moral development; on the other hand, she is almost vindictively harsh on her poor relation Fanny Price. As Sir Thomas later recognizes, his daughters turn out in the way they do largely because of the vitiating influence of Mrs. Norris on their education. Mrs. Norris can also be held responsible for more specific misfortunes, too. In particular, she is the one who presses the case for Maria to marry Mr. Rushworth, even though it is fairly clear that they are incompatible. Mrs. Norris, of course, thinks only of the money and the reflected glory of such a match, not of the likely consequences or of the couple's happiness. When the marriage ends in disaster, she tries to make excuses on Maria's behalf and then reaps an appropriate harvest for all her interference over the years when she and Maria are banished from Mansfield Park and sent to live together in a remote place, with "their tempers . . . their mutual punishment." With the departure of Mrs. Norris, Sir Thomas feels relieved of "an hourly evil," and she is missed by no one at Mansfield.

Norris, Rev. (deceased) (*Mansfield Park* Ch.1; I:1:3). A friend of Sir Thomas Bertram, Rev. Norris marries Lady Bertram's sister, Miss Ward, some six years after the Bertrams' own marriage. Mr. Norris has no independent fortune, and so Sir Thomas presents him with the living of Mansfield, which has an income of a little less than £1,000. Mr. Norris develops a gouty condition and dies when Fanny is fifteen, at the start of the main action of the novel. Mrs. Norris, who seems to have married him for convenience rather than love, consoles herself that "she could do very well without him."

Northanger Abbey. This novel, in two volumes, was first written by Jane Austen in 1798–1799 under the title "Susan." It was possibly revised some time in 1802 or early 1803, when Jane Austen made a copy of it and then sold it for ten pounds to the publisher Richard Crosby and Company with the expectation of its being published soon after. However, although Crosby advertised the book, he never printed it. Jane Austen may have worked on her copy of the novel at any time after this (though in her later "Advertisement, by the Authoress" she suggests that no substantial changes were made after 1803), but there is no mention of it again in her correspondence until April 1809. At this date, she made inquiries about the novel to Crosby, using the pseudonym of Mrs. Ashton Dennis (which allowed her to sign herself M.A.D.), but Richard Crosby refused to return the manuscript or copyright (unless Jane Austen paid for it) or to commit himself to publication. Austen's renewed interest in the book at this time may indicate some revision of it, though, as no manuscript survives, we can only guess at this. Only in early 1816, after she had become a published author with four other novels, did Jane Austen again attempt to have this novel published. She arranged for the repurchase of the manuscript and copyright from Crosby and seemed to be preparing it for publication, perhaps revising it; she changed the title to "Catherine" (possibly because of the publication in 1809 of another novel called *Susan* by an anonymous author) and wrote a prefatory note to the text ("Advertisement, by the Authoress"), briefly explaining its history and apologizing for any anachronisms that might now stand out owing to its having been completed thirteen years previously. However, by March 1817, she appears to have abandoned this attempt at publication: "Miss Catherine is put upon the Shelve for the present, and I do not know that she will ever come out" (*Letters*, 1995: 333). It did eventually come out, of course, but only after Jane Austen's death, when her brother Henry entitled it *Northanger Abbey* and had it published, along with *Persuasion*, by John Murray in December 1817. Ironically, then, though it was the first of Austen's novels to be sold to a publisher, it was the last to be published.

If *Northanger Abbey* was not substantially revised after 1798–1799 (or 1802–1803), then it can be considered the first of Jane Austen's novels to be completed in the form that we know them. Indeed, in terms of both manner and content, it is perhaps the closest of all the major novels to the juvenilia, particularly in its aspects as a literary parody of the conventions of eighteenth-century novels of sentiment, sensation, and sensibility.

Catherine Morland is the daughter of a country clergyman living in the village of Fullerton in Wiltshire. The fourth child in a family of ten and the first daughter, she is introduced as our romantic heroine in ironically antiheroic and antiromantic terms. No one who had seen her as a young child, we are told, would have mistaken her for a heroine, as, quite simply, there is nothing remarkable about her: she is an average child living in an average family in average circumstances. She enjoys the usual pastimes of a child and has little time for books, except for those that are "all story and no reflection." Nevertheless, she is to be the heroine of this novel, and between the ages of fifteen and seventeen, we hear, she was "in training" as such, stocking up with the heroine's usual range of useful quotations from standard works of literature. Though at seventeen she has still had no "heroic" love affair that might have called forth her passions and "sensibility," things look up when she is invited to go to Bath for six weeks with some well-to-do neighbors, Mr. and Mrs. Allen. Catherine is delighted to accept the invitation and is excited at the prospect of her first visit to the town and her first introduction into fashionable society. In one respect, if not in many others, Mrs. Allen is well qualified to act as a chaperon for Catherine, as she is rather like a teenager herself, with "a trifling turn of mind" and a passion for matters of dress and social display.

Catherine's first ball is somewhat disappointing, as Mrs. Allen does not know anybody there and cannot find Catherine a dancing partner, but at her second ball she is introduced to Henry Tilney, a charming, witty, and intelligent young clergyman of about twenty-five years of age. Catherine finds him attractive and entertaining and looks forward eagerly to their next meeting, but she is disappointed on subsequent days when he fails to appear at any of the social gatherings she attends. At the Pump Room on the morning following the ball, however, Mrs. Allen meets an old school friend, Mrs. Thorpe, along with her three daughters, Isabella, Anne, and Maria. It soon emerges that the Thorpes know Catherine's eldest brother, James, as he is at college in Oxford with their brother, John, and the two young men have become friends. The eldest Thorpe girl, Isabella, who is twenty-one, quickly takes Catherine under her wing, and they are soon on intimate terms and spending every day together. In particular, they share a great interest in sensational gothic novels and spend much time reading and discussing these. Catherine's brother, James, then arrives in Bath with John Thorpe, who likes to affect the manner of a man-about-town and who rattles on incoherently about gigs, horses, and gothic novels. It becomes clear that James has fallen in love with Isabella Thorpe, and both he and Isabella are keen to pair Catherine off with John Thorpe. However, though she does not say so to either of them, Catherine finds John Thorpe ill mannered, vain, and foolish and is clearly not attracted to him at all. At the ball later that day, Henry Tilney reappears, this time with his sister, Eleanor. He asks Catherine to dance with him, but she is forced to refuse him as she has already been engaged to dance by John Thorpe. As she dances with John Thorpe, Eleanor Tilney joins in beside her, and they talk a little. Catherine would like to get to know Eleanor better, and she also hopes that Henry will ask her to dance again, but for the rest of the evening she finds herself monopolized by the Thorpes and prevented from mixing with the Tilneys as much as she would like to. The next day, she is taken for a ride by John Thorpe in his gig, with James and Isabella following in a separate carriage. As before, she finds his conversation tiresome and at times nonsensical—though we note that he is careful to discover how wealthy the Allens are—and she is relieved when the outing is over. When she returns to the Allens' house, she is sorry to find that she has missed an opportunity of meeting the Tilneys, whom Mrs. Allen had met while out walking with Mrs. Thorpe.

The next day, Catherine meets and talks with Eleanor Tilney at the Pump Room and makes clear her desire to be better acquainted with her and her brother: she asks if they will be at the ball the following evening and is pleased to hear that they will. On arriving at that event, Catherine is anxious to try to avoid the bothersome John Thorpe and anxious also lest Henry Tilney does not feel able to ask her to dance for a third time, but she is relieved and delighted when the latter gentleman does, in fact, appear and engage her to dance just as she senses John Thorpe about to pounce. For a while, John Thorpe peevishly stands behind her as she dances and tries to interest her in one of his inane conversations about horses and hunting, but he is soon moved along by the press of the crowd, and Catherine is left in peace to enjoy the more agreeable and more articulate conversation of her desired partner. In the course of the evening, Henry points out his father to her—General Tilney—and she is impressed by his handsome demeanor, which, she thinks to herself, clearly runs in the family. Before she leaves, she also talks again with Eleanor Tilney, and, together with Henry, they arrange to go for a country walk together the next day at midday. Catherine is so happy after this ball that, we are told, she dances in her chair all the way home.

The weather is inclement the next morning, however, and, unsurprisingly, the Tilneys do not call for Catherine at the arranged time. Half an hour later, the day begins to clear, but she does not know whether to expect them still, and just at that moment John and Isabella Thorpe arrive with her brother, James, to invite her to come with them on a drive to Bristol and Clifton. At first she refuses, but they press her and finally tempt her into agreeing by holding out the prospect of visiting Blaize Castle, which she imagines to be like the castles she has read of in novels such as Mrs. Radcliffe's *The Mysteries of Udolpho*. When she still hesitates on account of the Tilneys, John Thorpe tells her that he has just seen them driving off in a phaeton, and so Catherine finally agrees to the trip. However, as they set out, they drive past Henry and Eleanor, walking along the street. Eleanor sees Catherine, and Catherine is mortified to think of how rude she must appear to them for not having waited for them after all. She is angry at John Thorpe for tricking her and insists that he let her down to go and apologize to her friends, but he simply urges the horse on faster, and they continue on their way. Catherine is miserable on the rest of the drive, and she does not even have the pleasure of seeing Blaize Castle, as they make such slow time that they have to turn back before they are even halfway there.

The next morning, Catherine goes to the Tilneys' house hoping to apologize, but she suspects she has been rebuffed when she is told that Eleanor is not in but then sees her leaving the house with her father. However, at the theater that evening, Henry Tilney comes to talk to her, and she is at last able to explain herself. He is visibly cheered by her apology and explains in return that Eleanor had not, in fact, rebuffed her earlier that day and was herself eager to apologize for what must have seemed an incivility; she and her father were on the verge of going out just as she called, and General Tilney was impatient of any delay and insisted that they should not receive their visitor. Catherine is happy once more, and she and Henry agree that their proposed walk should be rearranged as soon as possible. While they are talking, she is surprised to see John Thorpe talking with General Tilney, apparently about her. When she later asks him about this, John Thorpe says that he is acquainted with the General from having played billiards with him, and he tells Catherine that the General thinks her the finest girl in Bath. He also adds that he agrees with this view, but Catherine is gratified only by the General's compliment.

While walking in the Crescent at Bath on Sunday afternoon, Catherine rearranges her walking appointment with Eleanor and her brother for the next morning, but no sooner has this been done than she is approached by her brother and the Thorpes to be told that they have decided to make another attempt at driving to Clifton the following morning and that they could not hear of leaving her behind. This time, Catherine is adamant that she will not put off the Tilneys again. John Thorpe then walks off and returns a short while later to tell her that he has talked to Eleanor Tilney and gained her agreement to a postponement of their walk. Catherine is furious that he should once again interfere in her arrangements and make her appear rude in the eyes of the Tilneys. She rushes after the Tilneys to explain and is just in time to see them entering their house; she hurries in after them before the servant can close the door and finds the family congregated in the drawing room, where she unceremoniously and breathlessly makes her apologies. They find it hard to follow the detail of what she says, but they respond warmly to the spirit in which it is expressed, and she once more feels confident of their friendship. She is formally introduced to

General Tilney, who is particularly gallant toward her. He invites her to stay for dinner, and, when she refuses on account of being expected by the Allens, he gains her agreement to come another day. When Catherine returns to the Allens' house, she is pleased to find that they approve of her actions regarding the Thorpes and Tilneys. Mr. Allen points out the impropriety of a young and unchaperoned girl driving out in an open carriage with a young man, and, when Mrs. Allen blithely agrees with him, Catherine is surprised that Mrs. Allen had not pointed this out to her before—she would not have gone with John Thorpe on the two previous occasions if she had known it was improper.

The postponed walk with the Tilneys finally takes place, and the three friends share a lively discussion on history, art, and especially novels. The next day brings a short note from Isabella Thorpe asking Catherine to come to see her. On her visit, Catherine learns that her brother James has proposed to Isabella and is just setting off to ask the consent of his father and to discuss what sort of income he might be able to marry on. He writes the next day briefly announcing that his father has given his consent and blessing, and the party at Bath are delighted at this. John Thorpe then hints to Catherine that he, too, would like to marry soon and that he has his eye on her as a potential wife— but she seems oblivious to his intended meaning.

The second volume of the novel opens with an account of Catherine's visit to the Tilneys' house in fulfillment of her promise to dine with them as soon as she has a free day. Although she goes with great expectations of enjoyment and in hopes of becoming more thoroughly acquainted with Eleanor and Henry, she is puzzled to find them apparently in low spirits and somewhat reserved with her, even though General Tilney seems to do his best to make her feel welcome. She cannot account for the strained atmosphere but later wonders, just for a brief moment, if it has something to do with General Tilney's almost exaggerated civility toward her. The episode is quickly forgotten, however, when she goes to the ball in the evening and finds that Henry and Eleanor are back to their usual charming and cheerful selves and clearly concerned once more to be open and friendly with her. On this occasion they have with them their elder brother, Captain Frederick Tilney. Catherine immediately recognizes in him the typical features of the handsome Tilney family, but, in comparing him to Henry, she also notes a certain inferiority of taste and manners. Isabella, who had earlier given the impression that she was coming to the ball only to humor Catherine (as James has gone to Fullerton) and who had then affected a firm disinclination for any dancing, soon becomes the object of Captain Tilney's attentions and agrees to dance with him as soon as he asks her.

A second letter arrives for Isabella from James, this time with details of the financial arrangements he has made with his father. Mr. Morland has been able to promise his son a living of about £400 per annum once he is old enough to take it, which will be in about two and a half years (and he will also eventually inherit an estate of at least equal value from Mr. Morland). Isabella and her mother are clearly less than overjoyed at this news, but they divert attention from their money-centered misgivings by suggesting that they are unhappy at the need for such a long engagement.

The six weeks that the Allens had intended to stay in Bath are now nearly over, and Catherine feels sad at the prospect of leaving, especially now that her relationship with the Tilneys is developing so well. Much to her relief, however, the Allens decide to extend their stay for a further fortnight, and Catherine has just begun to speculate happily on what this additional period may bring for her, particularly where Henry Tilney is concerned, when she is once more cast down by the news that General Tilney has decided to return home with his family at the end of another week. But this disappointment does not last long either, for she now receives an invitation from the Tilneys to return to Northanger Abbey with them and to stay for a period. Catherine is overjoyed at this development, not only because it will promote her intimacy with Henry Tilney but also because it will enable her to indulge "her passion for ancient edifices," which, we are told, is "next in degree to her passion for Henry Tilney."

A few days later, at the Pump Room, Isabella tells Catherine that she has just received a letter from her brother, John Thorpe, in which he talks of his love for Catherine. Catherine is astonished to hear this and quickly disabuses Isabella of any possibility of her returning his affections. Captain Tilney then appears and comes to sit beside Isabella (a meeting, we realize, that had clearly been planned beforehand). Catherine begins to suspect that an attachment is forming between Captain Tilney and Isabella, and she feels jealous for her brother's sake. Over the next few days, Catherine observes Isabella, especially when in company with Captain Tilney, and her suspicions grow apace. Isabella is unmistakably encouraging Captain Tilney's attentions, and Catherine is shocked at her inconstancy and apparent disregard for the feelings of her fiancé, James Morland. Catherine talks to Henry Tilney about this affair, and, though he confirms that his brother knows of Isabella's engagement and hints that Isabella cannot really love James if she is prepared to flirt as she does, he reassures Catherine that his brother is unlikely to stay in Bath for much longer and that he would not seriously countenance marrying Isabella Thorpe, because of her lack of fortune.

Catherine sets off with the Tilneys for Northanger Abbey. At first she rides in the chaise with Eleanor Tilney and her maid, but at the halfway stage she changes vehicle and travels the remainder of the journey with Henry in his curricle. As they go, he plays on her fiction-inspired fascination for all things gothic and romantic and teases her about what she might expect to find at Northanger. He also tells Catherine that he lives at Northanger for only part of each year, as he has his own house, the Parsonage at Woodston, about twenty miles from Northanger Abbey. Catherine is disappointed by her first views of the abbey, as it does not live up to her expectations of what an old abbey should be like as gleaned from the novels she has read. It is a low building with no high, gothic windows or antique chimneys, and it has a modern gate-lodge and a level, well-tended drive of fine gravel. Inside, the drawing room is elegantly furnished in an everyday, contemporary style, as is Catherine's bedroom, which is light and cheerful and unlike the gloomy chamber Henry had been playfully threatening her with in his curricle.

On her first night at the abbey there is a violent storm, and this somewhat revives her sense of the "gothic" potential of her situation. She has some misgivings as she prepares for bed and sees the curtains moving in the wind, but she is comforted by a cheerful fire and the fact that Eleanor Tilney is only two doors away. She comes across a previously unnoticed old cabinet in her bedroom, and she immediately starts to fantasize about its possible contents, imagining it to hold some secret ancient manuscript. She opens the cabinet and finds all its drawers empty; but there is also a locked inner compartment, and here, after some difficulty with the key, she discovers a roll of paper that seems to have been purposely concealed at the back of the compartment. In great excitement at the thought of what horrid mysteries the "manuscript" might reveal, Catherine prepares for a long night's reading, but in her nervous haste to snuff the candle, she accidentally extinguishes it and is left in total darkness, the fire having died away a little earlier. She has no choice but to wait for morning before she can peruse her document. But her excited imaginings are now added to by the darkness, the raging storm outside, and various other noises in the house, and she spends several restless hours shivering beneath her bedclothes before she falls asleep. When she wakes in the morning, the sun is streaming into her room, and everything seems secure and cheerful once more—and she is severely embarrassed to find that her great discovery of the night before turns out to be nothing more interesting than somebody's old laundry bills!

At breakfast, General Tilney drops strong hints about a possible match between Catherine and Henry when they discuss the breakfast set and Henry's living and home at Woodston, but Catherine fails to register these. Catherine is then shown around the grounds of the abbey, and she is impressed by their great size, though the General makes comments suggesting that he thinks she must be used to even bigger properties. When Eleanor takes Catherine down a narrow path leading through a grove of Scotch firs, the General takes a different path. Eleanor tells Catherine that it used to be a favorite walk of her late mother, who had died nine years ago, when Eleanor was thirteen. Catherine asks further questions about Mrs. Tilney and learns that her portrait is in Eleanor's bedroom rather than displayed in the drawing room, as might be expected. Adding this to the fact that the General had seemed disinclined to take his late wife's favorite path with them, Catherine's overactive imagination jumps to the conclusion that he had not loved his wife and that he had treated her cruelly in some way. Her suspicions are increased later while she is being shown around the house when General Tilney prevents Eleanor from showing Catherine a passage of rooms containing Mrs. Tilney's former bedroom (where she had died). Catherine learns from Eleanor that her mother had died suddenly and that she had been away from home when it happened. Catherine now begins to construct a truly gothic scenario around the General and his wife: after first thinking that the General may have actually murdered Mrs. Tilney, Catherine then imagines that Mrs. Tilney is not, in fact, dead but is being kept a prisoner by the General in a network of cells beneath the prohibited rooms.

Drawing on what she has read in sensational novels to embroider her fantasy, Catherine quickly convinces herself of the General's unquestionable guilt, despite seeing a monument he has erected to her memory in front of the family pew in the church. Another attempted visit to Mrs. Tilney's room is cut short by the last-minute appearance of the General, before Catherine decides to visit the room in secret by herself. As she enters the room, however, she is once more abashed and ashamed to find how mistaken she has been in her imaginings, for she sees not some gloomy shrine to torture or murder but a bright, handsomely furnished and cheerful-looking modern apartment. As she hurries out of the room and along the corridor, she is horrified to hear someone running up the stairs. She fears it will be the General, but it turns out to be Henry, who has arrived home from Woodston earlier than expected. She expresses surprise at seeing him and is momentarily recalled to her gothic fantasy as she realizes that he has come up from what she had thought were Mrs. Tilney's "cells." But, it emerges, the staircase leads up from the newly built part of the abbey that is in daily use for domestic purposes, and Henry was merely taking a shortcut to his room in this part of the house. Henry quickly guesses what Catherine has been thinking and briskly disembarrasses her of all her illusions and suspicions about his parents: his mother had died suddenly, but of natural causes; he and his brother had attended her in her last days, even though Eleanor had been absent; and his father had always loved Mrs. Tilney, in his own way, and had sincerely grieved her death. Deeply embarrassed by the foolish "extravagance of her late fancies," Catherine is crestfallen and ashamed and fearful of having lost Henry's good opinion of her. This is not the case, however; Henry continues to treat her affectionately and does not allude to the episode again. Catherine examines her conscience and acknowledges that, under the influence of the gothic romances of Mrs. Radcliffe and others, she has positively encouraged and welcomed her own self-delusion in willful pursuit of an experience of "terror." She resolves henceforth to act "with the greatest good sense."

"The anxieties of common life" now take over from "the alarms of romance," as Catherine receives a letter from her brother, James, announcing the breaking off of his engagement to Isabella Thorpe and his expectation that she will soon be engaged to Captain Tilney. Catherine is upset both for her brother's sake in being jilted for another man and for her own sake in having been so deceived in the character of Isabella, whom she now sees in her true light as an ambitious and calculating hypocrite. Henry and Eleanor discreetly agree with Catherine in this view, but they also assure her that it is highly unlikely that their brother will actually marry Isabella, as, apart from other considerations, she has no fortune, and General Tilney would therefore never agree to such a match. This sets Catherine's mind at rest about having to leave Northanger Abbey if Captain Tilney should arrive, but it raises some worrying thoughts about how the General might respond if Henry should propose to her, given her lack of fortune.

The General takes Catherine and Eleanor to visit Henry at his Woodston home. Catherine is enchanted by the parsonage house and grounds and flattered by increasingly emphatic hints from the General that she may one day be mistress there—something that she, indeed, dreams of as they depart for Northanger at the end of the day.

A letter arrives unexpectedly from Isabella Thorpe, full of ''shallow artifice,'' inconsistency, and contradiction. She pretends that nothing has changed in her relationship with Catherine and makes light of her so-called misunderstanding with James Morland, while it becomes abundantly clear that she has been jilted by Captain Tilney and now wants to wheedle herself back into the engagement with James through the good offices of Catherine. Catherine is no longer fooled by her former friend, however. She sees through her empty excuses and exaggerated expressions of affection and is flabbergasted at Isabella's impudence in asking her to write to James on her behalf.

General Tilney goes to London on business for a week, and Catherine enjoys herself more than ever in the sole company of Eleanor and Henry. She has been at Northanger for nearly a month now and is concerned not to outstay her welcome, but she is urged by Eleanor to stay for at least another month, and she is only too happy to agree to this. Before the end of the General's week in London, however, a carriage arrives late one night just as Eleanor and Catherine are going to bed. Eleanor assumes the visitor to be her brother, Frederick, who frequently arrives unexpectedly, and she goes down to greet him. But we soon learn that it is not Captain Tilney but the General himself, and he sends Eleanor to tell Catherine that he has suddenly remembered an engagement that will take the whole family away for a fortnight to Herefordshire and that she, Catherine, must leave for Fullerton the very next morning. To add insult to injury, the General has already arranged the time and means of her transport: she is to leave at seven o'clock by public post-chaise and without any of his servants to attend her on the seventy-mile journey. Eleanor is agitated and upset at her father's blatant rudeness to their guest and sorry to have to part with her dear friend, but she can give Catherine no further explanation beyond saying that the General has been greatly vexed by something and is in a foul temper. Catherine spends a sleepless night wondering what she might have done to offend him and then passes a miserable and lonely eleven hours on the journey home, anxiously reflecting on how Henry will react to their sudden separation.

Catherine is cheered somewhat by the affectionate and joyful reception she receives from her family at Fullerton, who have not seen her now for eleven weeks, though it is painful for her to recount the circumstances of her departure from Northanger, especially as she fears that it will predispose her family to think unkindly of Henry and Eleanor. Her parents are certainly discomposed by General Tilney's ill-natured treatment of their daughter and annoyed that he should have had such little thought for her comfort and safety on the journey home; but they do not dwell on the matter unduly and consider that, as Catherine is now safe, it can all be forgotten. But Catherine cannot dismiss the experience so lightly, and, in particular, she cannot help thinking about Henry. For the next two days, she remains in low spirits and unable to settle down to anything. Her mother fears that she has been spoiled by the diversions of Bath and her high life at Northanger, and, while they are working together at their needlework on the third day, Mrs. Morland remembers an essay in an issue of the journal *The Mirror* that may be pertinent to Catherine's condition. She goes upstairs to fetch it, and when she returns, she finds Henry Tilney sitting with Catherine, whose spirits have been so visibly raised by the unexpected visitor that Mrs. Morland can put *The Mirror* to one side. After apologizing to Mrs. Morland for his father's behavior to Catherine and chatting with her for a while, Henry suggests that Catherine might show him the way to the Allens' house, as he would like to pay his respects to them.

This gives Henry the chance to talk to Catherine in private. On the way to the Allens' house, he proposes to, and is accepted by, her. On the way back, he explains why his father had behaved as he had and what has happened subsequently. General Tilney had been misled by John Thorpe into believing that Catherine was rich, that she was to inherit between £10,000 and £15,000 from her father and stood also to inherit Mr. Allen's estate. This had motivated the General to invite Catherine to Northanger and to encourage a match between her and his son, but while he was in London during Catherine's fourth week at Northanger, he had again been in John Thorpe's company, and this time he exaggerated Catherine's situation in the opposite direction and made it clear that she was anything but rich. Believing the unreliable John Thorpe for a second time, the General had rushed off in a rage and, as we have seen, unceremoniously dispatched Catherine to Fullerton in order to prevent any further development of her relationship with Henry. When Henry returned from Woodston to find what had happened, he argued with his father, refused to go to Herefordshire with him, and insisted that he would marry Catherine. His father likewise insisted on withholding his consent, and the two had parted in disagreement. Because Henry has not had his father's consent, he had made a point of proposing to Catherine before telling her all this, as otherwise she may have felt obliged to refuse him.

Mr. and Mrs. Morland are surprised to hear of Henry's proposal, but they are happy for their daughter and immediately inclined to give the marriage their blessing; but when they learn of the opposition of General Tilney, they feel obliged to withhold their consent, too, at least until the General can be persuaded to change his mind. Though unhappy to have to delay their marriage, Henry and Catherine recognize the rightness of this decision, and they agree to wait for the General's consent. Happily, they do not need to wait long. Eleanor Tilney has herself had a secret lover for some time, but because of his lack of wealth and consequence, it had never been possible for them to marry. This lover now unexpectedly inherits both a title and a fortune, and all obstacles to their marriage are removed. General Tilney is so happy at this fortunate match that Viscountess Eleanor now has little difficulty in talking him round to giving his consent to Henry and Catherine. She is helped in this by the General's learning that Catherine's poverty is not as great as John Thorpe had led him to believe and that she will, in fact, bring £3,000 to the marriage; and also that, again contrary to what he had been told by John Thorpe, Mr. Allen's estate was still entirely at Mr. Allen's disposal and therefore still open "to every greedy speculation." With the General's consent, then, the wedding of Henry and Catherine is able to go ahead, and it takes place within a year of their first meeting.

Main Characters: Mr. Allen, Mrs. Allen, Catherine Morland, James Morland, Mrs. Thorpe, Isabella Thorpe, John Thorpe, General Tilney, Eleanor Tilney, Frederick Tilney, Henry Tilney.

Minor Characters: Alice, Miss Andrews, General Courteney, Charlotte Davis, Dorothy, Emily, Sam Fletcher, the Lady Frasers, Freeman, the Hodges, Charles Hodges, Mrs. Hughes, Captain Hunt, Jackson, Mr. King, Marquis of Longtown, Matilda, the Mitchells, Anne Mitchell, George Morland, Harriet Morland, Rev. Richard Morland, Mrs. Morland, Richard Morland, Sarah (Sally) Morland, Morland family, the Parrys, the Skinners, Miss Smith, Sophia, Anne Thorpe, Edward Thorpe, Maria Thorpe, William Thorpe, Mrs. Tilney (deceased), the Viscount, William.

Volume and chapter divisions (numbers in brackets are for editions with continuous chapter numbers): Volume 1: Chapters 1–15, volume 2: Chapters 1–16 [16–31].

See: Anderson 1984, Banerjee 1990, Bizzaro 1985, Boles 1981, Booth 1988, De Rose 1983, Edgecombe 1993, Ehrenpreis 1970–1971, *Farrar 1962*, Fowler 1980, Haney 1901, Hoeveler 1995, Hopkins 1978, Jerenic 1995, Lau 1985, Levine 1975, Looser 1993, Loveridge 1991, *Menon 1956*, Moler 1984, Morrison 1991, Morrow 1980, Pittock 1987, B. Roberts 1989, *Sadleir 1927*, Shaw 1990, Smith 1992, *Southam 1976a*, Tandrup 1983, *Varma 1968*, Williams 1987.

Norton, Mr. (*The Watsons, Minor Works* 337). A member of Captain Hunter's regiment.

Noyce, Fanny (*Sanditon, Minor Works* 408). Diana Parker's "very particular friend" and one link in the "short" chain of correspondence linking Diana Parker and the so-called West Indian family of Mrs. Griffiths.

O

O'Brien, Captain (*The Watsons, Minor Works* 326). An Irish army officer who becomes the second husband of Emma Watson's aunt Turner. There is a suggestion that Captain O'Brien may have married Mrs. Turner for her fortune, and it seems certain that Emma will not now inherit any of her aunt's money. As a result of this marriage Emma has to return to Stanton, as Captain O'Brien did not want her to accompany them to Ireland.

"Ode to Pity" (*Volume the First* of Jane Austen's juvenilia). Dated 3 June 1793 and dedicated to Cassandra Austen, this parody of an ode represents both the last piece in *Volume the First* and one of the last pieces of Jane Austen's juvenilia. The two rhymed verses quite skillfully burlesque the elevated lyricism and elaborate style and diction of the conventional eighteenth-century ode, playfully engaging a variety of typical rhetorical figures and prosodic patterns in the service of nonsense ("Gently brawling down the turnpike road,/Sweetly noisy falls the Silent Stream—"). (See *Selwyn 1996* for possible sources in the poetry of William Collins and Joseph Warton.)

Oliver, Tom (*Mansfield Park* Ch.15; I:15:148). Tom Oliver, "a very clever fellow," is a friend of Tom Bertram. He lives at Stoke in the neighborhood of Mansfield and is briefly considered for the part of Anhalt in the Mansfield Park production of *Lovers Vows*. His brother is also mentioned.

"Opinions of *Mansfield Park*" and **"Opinions of *Emma*."** These are collections of brief opinions on the named novels, gathered by Jane Austen herself (possibly out of frustration at the lack of critical reviews or notices) from family, friends, and acquaintances. The views on *Mansfield Park* date from 1814 and 1815; the ones on *Emma*, probably from 1816.

Osborne, Lady (*The Watsons, Minor Works* 329). Lady Osborne is the mother of Lord and Miss Osborne. She is a handsome, stately lady of around fifty.

Osborne, Lord (*The Watsons, Minor Works* 314, 329). Lord Osborne is quite a fine-looking young man, but he has an awkward social manner and little to say for himself. He is immediately attracted to Emma Watson, but she finds his brusque conversation and gauche behavior off-putting.

Osborne, Miss (*The Watsons, Minor Works* 329). Lord Osborne's sister. When Colonel Beresford asks her to dance, she has no qualms about breaking her promise to have the first two dances with little Charles Blake. This leads to Emma's offering herself instead and attracting everyone's admiration for her generous action.

Otway, Mr. and Mrs. (*Emma* Ch.38; III:2:323). Guests, with other members of their family, at the Crown Inn ball.

Owen, Mr. (*Mansfield Park* Chs.26, 29; II:8:255; II:11:287). Edmund Bertram's friend from Lessingby near Peterborough. He, like Edmund, is preparing to become a priest, and the two men go to be ordained at the same time.

Owens, the Miss (*Mansfield Park* Chs.29, 35; II:11:287; III:4:355). Mr. Owen's sisters, of whom Mary Crawford becomes jealous when Edmund extends his stay at their house during the period of his ordination. Edmund later describes them as "pleasant, good-humoured, unaffected girls" but not "sensible women" like Fanny and Mary Crawford.

P

Palmer, Mr. Thomas (*Sense and Sensibility* Chs.19, 20; I:19:105–9; I:20:110–13). Husband of Mrs. Jennings' daughter, Charlotte, and owner of Cleveland, near Bristol in Somerset—where he is standing for election to Parliament—and Hanover Square, London. He is a young man of twenty-five or -six with an exaggeratedly grave and offhand manner. He appears to be quite a sensible man and frequently makes sarcastic comments in response to his wife's fatuous conversation, but he refuses to make conversation himself and affects "indifference, insolence, and discontent." Elinor Dashwood judges that this is his way of trying to appear superior to others: "It was rather a wish of distinction she believed, which produced his contemptuous treatment of every body, and his general abuse of every thing before him." Initially, he and his wife make an almost absurdly contrasting pair, as he is surly, uncommunicative, unsociable, and uncompromising in his bad manners, while she is frothily cheerful and smiling and excessively friendly, talkative, and eager to please. However, when we see them at Cleveland after the birth of their son later in the book, the element of caricature in their presentation is modified somewhat, and Mr. Palmer now appears politer and more sociable, while the kindness and hospitality of his wife stand out more than her foolishness.

Palmer, Mrs. Charlotte, née Jennings (*Sense and Sensibility* Chs.19, 20; I:19:105–9; I:20:110–17). Daughter of Mrs. Jennings and sister to Lady Middleton. Mrs. Palmer has only recently married Mr. Palmer, and she is expecting their first child when she is first introduced to the Dashwood family at Barton. She later gives birth to a son while at her London home during the period, when Elinor and Marianne are staying with Mrs. Jennings. Short, plump, garrulous, and good-humored, Mrs. Palmer is very like her fat and "rather vulgar" mother and totally unlike her sister, who is tall and graceful but reserved, cold, and taciturn. Though warm and kindhearted, Mrs. Palmer is, to some extent, a caricature of silliness. She blithely takes her husband's seriously intended criticisms of her as a form of drollery, and her effusive speeches are full of inconsequential and illogical information: "Oh! dear, yes; I know him extremely well. . . . Not that I ever spoke to him indeed." When Elinor and Marianne stay at Cleveland on their way home from London to Barton, a more positive impression of her character is given, however, as we see her genuine warmth and kindness in making them feel welcome through her "constant and friendly good-humor."

Parker, Arthur (*Sanditon, Minor Works* 371, 385). Youngest of the three Parker brothers and, with his sisters, one of the trio of "invalid" Parkers. At the age of only twenty-one and with only a small fortune to live on, he has decided that he is too sickly to engage in any profession and has adopted the life of a valetudinarian. His complaints, such as they are, range widely: he is liverish, bilious, rheumatic, "subject to Perspiration," and of such a nervous disposition that drinking green tea can paralyze the whole of his right side. When Charlotte goes to have tea with the invalid Parkers, she expects to see a puny, sickly-looking man, but Arthur turns out to be the exact opposite—a very large, broad fellow whose only real problems seem to be those of gluttony and sloth and the "sodden complexion" arising therefrom. Like his siblings, talk is one activity he engages in with enthusiasm, and he is only too happy to discourse upon his health to Charlotte—that is, until the tea things arrive, at which point, in one of Jane Austen's funniest scenes, he abruptly stops talking and applies himself single-mindedly to the toast and cocoa.

Parker children, including Mary (*Sanditon, Minor Works* 371, 381). Thomas and Mary Parker have four young children, three born in their old family house and one, within the last two years, in their new Sanditon dwelling. When Mrs. Parker talks nostalgically of their "comfortable" and well-shaded old home, Mr. Parker rationalizes all the benefits of their new one, not the least of these being access to shops and the goods that can be bought there. For instance, the lack of shade can easily be dealt with for little Mary by buying her a parasol from Whitby's; this idea soon diverts Mrs. Parker's attention as she thinks of how proud Mary will be to have a new parasol.

Parker, Diana (*Sanditon, Minor Works* 371, 385, 406–7). The dominant character among the three hypochondriacal Parkers, Diana is about thirty-four years old and, though of slender build and delicate-looking and constantly complaining of "spasmodic bile" and other ailments, possessed of enormous energy when it comes to interfering in other people's business. Like her brother, Thomas, she is no mean talker, and her four-page soliloquy, on arrival at Sanditon, outdoes anything that even Miss Bates in *Emma* gives us. Her officiousness receives its just dessert when her plans to draw two prosperous families to Sanditon collapse after the Chinese-whisper effect of her overlong chain of correspondents and informants provides her with misleading information.

Parker, Mr. Thomas (*Sanditon, Minor Works* 363, 371). Mr. Parker is one of the principal landowners in Sanditon and the leading force behind attempts to turn Sanditon into a fashionable bathing resort. He is thus both a member of the traditional landed gentry and an entrepreneurial "speculator": as such, he reflects a general trend of the period for landowners to become more active capitalists by engaging in various forms of speculation in land, business, finance, and industry. Mr. Parker is about thirty-five years old; he has been married for seven years and has four children. As an eldest son, he had inherited the family estate and a comfortable, though not large, fortune. This has meant that he has had no need to adopt any profession, which, in turn, has enabled him, in recent years, to devote all his time to his speculative plans for Sanditon (there is a suggestion from Jane Austen that the Parkers generally have nothing better to do than pursue their various obsessions). Thomas Parker is "an Enthusiast" on the subject of Sanditon and spends all his time extolling its virtues and trying to persuade people to spend their holidays there. Indeed, he can hardly talk of anything else, and as he is also a great talker, the subject tends to dominate any conversation he is involved in. But though he enthusiastically lauds Sanditon, he has, it seems, "more Imagination than Judgement," and his great hopes for the village are clearly not materializing as fully or as quickly as he would have people believe. In this respect, his fall from the carriage at the start of the novel may be symbolic of the financial "fall" he may be heading for if business does not pick up—and the events of the story are not auspicious, given the nonappearance of the two supposedly large and prosperous families promised by Diana Parker. But although something of an obsessive and possibly ineffectual character, Mr. Parker is also presented as a loving, kindly, openhearted, and generous man who rarely has a bad word to say about anyone. In fact, he is in some ways too thoughtful and caring about others, too liberal-minded and gentlemanly ever to make a success as a hardheaded businessman. It is possibly a fault of the novel (though it is often conducive to humor and may be part of some scheme the author would have elaborated if the novel had been finished) that there is this odd mixture within Mr. Parker of the thrusting capitalist and the genial, jolly, gentleman-squire.

Parker, Mrs. Mary (*Sanditon, Minor Works* 363, 372). The following sentence sums up Mrs. Parker and represents a classic example of Jane Austen's elegantly controlled release of irony: "And Mrs P. was as evidently a gentle, amiable, sweet tempered Woman, the properest wife in the World for a Man of strong Understanding, but not of capacity to supply the cooler reflection which her own Husband sometimes needed, & so entirely waiting to be guided on every occasion, that whether he were risking his Fortune or spraining his Ancle, she remained equally useless."

Parker, Sidney (*Sanditon, Minor Works* 371, 382, 425). The dashing, fashionable younger brother of Thomas Parker. Sidney Parker makes only a brief appearance just before the end of the manuscript when Charlotte Heywood is impressed by his good looks and elegant manners. He is about twenty-seven or -eight and has an easy, lively air about him. We have learned earlier, from his brother, that he has an independent fortune and, it seems, a waggish sense of humor. When he drives on from Mrs. Parker and Charlotte, they are, we hear, "to meet again within a few hours": a promising meeting destined never to take place, unfortunately.

Parker, Susan (*Sanditon, Minor Works* 371, 385, 413). Susan is perhaps the most unfortunate of the Parker invalids in that she seems to be the only one who seriously "treats" her imagined illnesses, with fairly dire consequences. She is the one who, after failing to gain relief for a headache by applying six leeches a day for ten days, has three teeth pulled out. This cures the headache but deranges her nerves, not surprisingly. When Charlotte meets her, she sees no clear signs of ill health apart from all the quack medicines she surrounds herself with.

Parrys, the (*Northanger Abbey* Ch.2; I:2:23). Friends of Mr. and Mrs. Allen at Fullerton.

Parrys, the (*Sense and Sensibility* Ch.30; II:8:192). Acquaintances of Mrs. Jennings in London.

Partridge, Mrs. (*Emma* Ch.32; II:14:275). The "particular friend" at Bath with whom Mrs. Elton always used to reside when visiting the town. Mrs. Elton offers to provide Emma Woodhouse with a letter of introduction to this lady, much to Emma's horror.

Patty (*Emma* Chs.21, 27; II:3:173: II:9:236). The Bates' only servant.

Percival, Catharine ("Catharine," *Minor Works* 192). The eponymous heroine of the novel who, like many heroines before her, is orphaned in infancy and brought up in a large house by her maiden aunt. She is a bright, cheerful, and resourceful girl, but her life has been saddened in recent years by the departure of her two closest friends, Cecilia and Mary Wynne, following the death of their father. She is, however, reminded of her friends whenever she goes to the garden bower that they had all built together, and this bower is a great source of pleasure and comfort to her. She gains a new companion for a while with the arrival of the Stanleys and their daughter Camilla, but she proves to be a fairly empty-headed and shallow character, and not until Camilla's brother, Edward Stanley, turns up does Catharine find something seriously to occupy her heart and mind. But he, too, though in a different way, proves to be a trifling and unreliable character, and he disappears as unexpectedly as he arrived. Catharine's character seems to undergo some of its own rather sudden changes, too, particularly at the end of the fragment: in the company of Camilla Stanley, she appears to be an eminently sensible and steady girl, but in the company of Edward Stanley, she appears, at times, much more giddy and fanciful.

Percival, Mrs. ("Catharine," *Minor Works* 192, 230). Catharine's straitlaced maiden aunt who brings Catharine up with "jealous Caution" at her home, the Grove, in the village of Chetwynde, Devon. Mrs. Percival loves Catharine but is terrified of her meeting any men, as she immediately assumes she will make an inappropriate match. Mrs. Percival is old-fashioned and constantly harks back to some more orderly and civilized past when young ladies and gentlemen knew how to behave properly; now, she often says, "every thing is going to sixes & sevens." Mrs. Percival is also something of a hypochondriac and is particularly fearful of catching a cold.

Perry, Mr. (*Emma* Ch.2; I:2:19). The Highbury apothecary whose visits are "one of the comforts of Mr. Woodhouse's life." Mrs. Perry and "the little Perrys" also feature briefly (Ch.2; I:2:17 & 19). It would seem that Mr. Perry often simply humors Mr. Woodhouse with medical advice that suits Mr. Woodhouse's own eccentric opinions. Hence, he agrees with Mr. Woodhouse that wedding cake is unwholesome, but, shortly after Miss Taylor's marriage to Mr. Weston, "there was a strange rumour in Highbury of all the little Perrys being seen with a slice of Mrs. Weston's wedding-cake in their hands."

Persuasion. The first draft of the novel that was posthumously titled *Persuasion* was begun on 8 August 1815 and completed on 18 July 1816 (Jane Austen thought she had finished on 16 July and had written "Finis" with that date but had then added the final paragraph roughly as we have it in the printed version). Jane Austen then returned to the manuscript and substantially revised the final two chapters of the novel (at that point, Chapters 10 and 11 of the second volume), finishing this second draft on 6 August 1816. The manuscript of these original final chapters is the only surviving fragment of manuscript we have of Jane Austen's six major novels. In this revision of the novel's ending, Jane Austen largely retained the original Chapter 11 (the last chapter), with minor changes, but renumbered it as Chapter 12; and then rewrote about three-quarters of the original Chapter 10 and divided it into two new chapters—10 and 11—retaining about a quarter of it as part of the new Chapter 11. A fresh copy of the new Chapters 10, 11, and 12 was then made, and this must have been part of the manuscript (now lost) from which the printed edition derived (as there are minor differences between the surviving manuscript of the original Chapter 11 and the printed Chapter 12). There is no mention, in Jane Austen's letters or the family tradition, of any further rewriting or revision of the novel after 6 August 1816, but as the manuscript from which the novel was printed has not survived, we cannot be absolutely sure of this (there were eight months before the final onset of the illness that killed her in which changes could have been made). Moreover, in a letter of 13 March 1817, Jane Austen apparently refers to *Persuasion* when she says, "I have a something ready for Publication, which may perhaps appear about a twelvemonth hence." The facts that she had not tried to have the novel published before this date and that, even now, she was still talking of "twelvemonth hence" may suggest that she was still not entirely satisfied with the manuscript and was still revising it. On the other hand, she does say quite clearly that it is ready for publication, and, given that there are no other references to any revision (and she had started *Sanditon* in January 1817), it is most likely, as Jan Fergus suggests (*1991*: 167–68), that her postponement of the novel's publication was more a matter of financial expedience than anything else. In any case, she did not live to see the novel in print. It was finally seen through the press by her brother Henry, who probably also gave it its title, and was published with *Northanger Abbey* in late December 1817 (though 1818 was on the title page). This joint edition was published in four volumes, and the two volumes of *Persuasion* were volumes 3 and 4 (though throughout this book they are referred to as volumes 1 and 2 to avoid the impression that the novel itself has four volumes).

The so-called canceled chapter from the first draft of the novel (i.e., the original Chapter 10), which survives in manuscript, was first published in the second edition of J. E. Austen-Leigh's *Memoir of Jane Austen* (1871), though in an imperfect transcription and without the other part of the manuscript ending of the novel (the original Chapter 11). A scholarly edition of the whole of the manuscript ending was published in 1926, edited by R. W. Chapman (*Two Chapters of Persuasion*), and this transcription has now been incorporated into the Oxford edition of the novel as an appendix.

Uniquely among Jane Austen's novels, the action of *Persuasion* is precisely dated as taking place between the summer of 1814 and mid-February 1815. This specification of "real" time clearly adds to the verisimilitude of the novel (as does the "realistic" duration of the action—roughly seven months over twenty-four chapters); and this is further enhanced by the fact that we are given specific birth and marriage dates for the main characters at the very start. Sir Walter Elliot of Kellynch Hall was born on 1 March 1760. He had married Elizabeth Stevenson on 15 July 1784, and they had had three daughters: Elizabeth, born 1 June 1785, Anne, born 9 August 1787, and Mary, born on 20 November 1791. Lady Elliot had died in 1800. At the start of the novel, only the youngest daughter, Mary, is married; she had married Charles Musgrove, the son and heir of a wealthy neighbor, on 16 December 1810. Charles and Mary have two children, Charles and Walter, and they live at Uppercross Cottage near to the elder Musgrove family at Uppercross Hall, three miles from Kellynch. The heir to Kellynch Hall (given that Sir Walter has no male children) is his nephew, William Walter Elliot. Around 1802–1803, there had been hopes in the family that he might marry the eldest daughter, Elizabeth, but he had snubbed her and married into money elsewhere. Elizabeth, Sir Walter's favorite daughter, has since had to be content with being the first lady at Kellynch Hall, but, at twenty-nine, she is now becoming increasingly anxious about approaching "the years of danger," when she will be seen as no longer marriageable. She and her father are both full of snobbish self-importance and vanity, and they are both lacking in good sense. Thus, since the loss of the steadying hand of the eminently sensible Lady Elliot, Kellynch estate has been badly mismanaged, and now, in the summer of 1814, Sir Walter is in serious financial difficulties and is forced to consider radical measures of retrenchment.

The central character of *Persuasion*, however, is Sir Walter's second daughter, Anne. She had been very close to her mother and is the only one of the daughters to resemble Lady Elliot in character, being very sensible and steady, "with an elegance of mind and sweetness of character, which must have placed her high with any people of real understanding." To her foolish father and elder sister, though, she is of no consequence, "nobody," and she is always having to give way to their opinions and preferences. Anne's younger sister, Mary, values Anne a little more, but really only as someone she can impose upon, either to nurse her through her imaginary illnesses (she is a hypochondriac and constantly complaining) or to help her with the management of her children. The only person who truly values Anne for herself is Lady Elliot's former best friend and now a close neighbor and confidante of the Kellynch family, Lady Russell. When Lady Elliot died, she in many ways became a surrogate mother to the Elliot girls, and she has continued to play an important part in the life of the family ever since. Her favorite of all the girls, however, has always been her goddaughter, Anne (precisely because she takes after her mother), and as Anne grew to womanhood, she and Lady Russell became intimate friends. When Anne was nineteen, in the summer of 1806, she had become engaged to Frederick Wentworth, the visiting sailor brother of a neighboring curate, Rev. Edward Wentworth. Though "a remarkably fine young man, with a great deal of intelligence, spirit and brilliancy," Wentworth at that time was only twenty-three and had not yet progressed far in his career as a naval officer (he was then only a commander). He had no family connections to speak of, moreover. Therefore, on the grounds of both family and prospects, Anne's father had been against the match, and Lady Russell had finally persuaded Anne, against her better judgment—for she loved him passionately—to break off the engagement. Without blaming Lady Russell, who, she knows, was thinking of her own best interests at the time, Anne has always regretted this decision and has effectively pined for Wentworth ever since. Indeed, this is suggested as the reason for her early loss of looks and vivacity.

In considering the retrenchments proposed to him by his agent, Mr. Shepherd, Sir Walter is at first unwilling to make fundamental changes to his lifestyle; but he is finally persuaded by Mr. Shepherd, Lady Russell, and Anne that drastic action is necessary and that it would be best for him and his daughters to remove from Kellynch Hall altogether until all his debts are cleared. He is persuaded to move to more modest accommodations in Bath and to seek a suitable tenant for Kellynch. Lady Russell is enthusiastic to promote this move for other reasons beyond securing the Elliots' financial position. She also hopes that, in Bath, Anne will lead a more lively social life and perhaps meet some eligible suitors; and she also hopes that the move will be the means of separating Elizabeth from Mrs. Clay, the widowed daughter of Sir Walter's agent (Mr. Shepherd), whom Lady Russell considers a bad influence on both Sir Walter and Elizabeth.

With the end of the Napoleonic Wars, there are many returning naval officers who have made their fortunes during the conflict, and Mr. Shepherd points this out to Sir Walter, suggesting that such an officer might make an ideal tenant for Kellynch. Sir Walter is horrified at the thought of one of these self-made men usurping his position at Kellynch (never mind that they may have saved the country from invasion), but he is won over by the rank and respectability of the first applicant for the tenancy, who, indeed, turns out to be a naval man— Admiral Croft. Sir Walter is also won over by the news that Admiral Croft has local connections, in being married to the sister of Edward Wentworth, who, as we have seen, was formerly the curate of a neighboring parish (though he has now moved to Shropshire). Obviously, Mrs. Croft is also the sister of Anne's former fiancé, and Anne is now perturbed to realize that he may well soon be a visitor again at Kellynch. After the breaking off of their engagement, Wentworth had gone back to sea and had rapidly progressed to the rank of captain. Anne has followed his career in the navy lists and newspapers and knows that he has made a substantial fortune for himself and that he is still not married.

Sir Walter arranges to leave for Bath in September, and the Crofts are to move into Kellynch at the end of the month. Just before the Elliots leave, however, Mary Musgrove writes to insist that Anne should come to Uppercross for the autumn, as she feels sure she is going to be unwell for most of that time and that no one really wants her in Bath. Anne is actually quite relieved at this peremptory invitation, as she has no relish for Bath and would prefer to remain in her beloved countryside during the autumn months. She also recognizes the truth of what Mary says about not being wanted in Bath and takes solace in the thought that at least Mary thinks of her as being useful. Lady Russell is disappointed in her hopes of detaching Mrs. Clay from Elizabeth and Sir Walter, as they decide to take Mrs. Clay with them to Bath. Anne tries to warn Elizabeth that Mrs. Clay may be angling to catch Sir Walter as a husband—she is young and clever and knows how to flatter Sir Walter; but Elizabeth dismisses the suspicion as absurd, pointing out that Mrs. Clay has freckles, which Sir Walter cannot abide, a projecting tooth, and a "clumsy wrist."

Sir Walter, Elizabeth, and Mrs. Clay leave for Bath, and Anne, after a few days with Lady Russell at Kellynch Lodge, goes to stay with Mary at Uppercross Cottage. Here she finds Mary, who is always complaining, a tiresome companion and her children somewhat boisterous, but there is also much intercourse with the rest of the Musgrove family who live nearby. The older Mr. and Mrs. Musgrove are hearty, hospitable folk with a "numerous" family, including two lively and affable grown-up daughters, Louisa and Henrietta, who are nineteen and twenty, respectively. Although their conversation is not particularly cultivated, Anne nevertheless enjoys their company as a welcome break from Mary's constant whinings of discontent; she also admires their warmth toward one another, as that is something she misses in her own sisterly relationships.

The Crofts move into Kellynch Hall, and they eventually pay their compliments at Uppercross Cottage, where Anne immediately warms to them for their good humor and open, easy manners—again Anne is aware of a sharp contrast with the affected manners of her family. However, she is somewhat alarmed to learn from them that Captain Wentworth, only recently returned to England, is shortly expected to visit at Kellynch. She would like to avoid him, if possible, to avoid any mutual embarrassment but also because she is afraid a meeting may reactivate hopes of marriage and feelings of love she has learned to subdue over the years. However, it emerges that the elder Musgroves had had another son, Richard, who had died at sea two years previously and who had once spent six months under the benevolent command of a Captain Wentworth. When the Musgroves realize that this is the Captain Wentworth who is coming to Kellynch, they determine to pay their respects to him. Thus any hope Anne may have had of avoiding him is dashed, as he will now almost certainly also visit Uppercross. Indeed, he does, shortly after his arrival at Kellynch, and he soon becomes closely acquainted with the Musgrove family. Anne succeeds in absenting herself from the first occasion on which he is entertained at Uppercross Hall, but he stays overnight and then calls at the cottage briefly the next morning, where he and Anne exchange polite but strained greetings. Anne is disconcerted to find all her old emotions come flooding forth again and to realize that "to retentive feelings eight years may be little more than nothing." She is extremely distracted by the meeting and wonders what he might be thinking about her. In fact, she soon hears, via the tactless Mary, that he thought she had changed so much he almost failed to recognize her. Anne is obviously hurt by this reflection on her faded looks, but she also takes comfort from the fact that this at least confirms the breach between them so that she need no longer agitate herself over any possible renewal of their relationship. From Wentworth's point of view, we learn that this remark had not been hurtfully intended (indeed, it had not been intended for Anne at all) but that he does still resent Anne for having—to his mind—weakly succumbed to the shallow persuasions of Lady Russell all those years ago. He had dearly loved her at the time and had been deeply hurt by her rejection of him. He had not intended to meet with her again and certainly has no intention of courting her again. However, now that he has made his fortune and has been demobilized, he fully intends to marry and settle down. He jokingly tells his sister, Mrs. Croft, that he is there for the asking for any half-decent young lady, though he adds, more seriously, that his ideal match would be someone with "a strong mind" and "sweetness of temper."

Wentworth becomes a regular visitor to Uppercross, and Henrietta and Louisa Musgrove both become infatuated with him. Their cousin, Charles Hayter—part of a family of "poor relations" at nearby Winthrop—is unhappy with this situation, as he has been courting Henrietta for some time and clearly hopes to marry her eventually. Mary Musgrove is pleased that he seems to be displaced by Wentworth, as she snobbishly looks down on the Winthrop Hayters; but Charles Musgrove likes his cousin and would prefer Wentworth to marry Louisa. Needless to say, Anne is pained at the thought of a match either way and distressed to hear Wentworth constantly discussed in these terms in front of her. The frequency of Wentworth's visits means that he and Anne are often together in the same company now, but his behavior toward her continues to be reserved, and all trace of their former intimacy seems to have disappeared. There is, however, one tense moment of renewed contact between them when Wentworth calls at Uppercross Cottage one morning and is embarrassed to find himself alone with Anne and her sick nephew. Charles Hayter then arrives—like Wentworth, in search of the Musgrove girls, who are upstairs with Mary—but as he is displeased with Wentworth because of Henrietta, he simply picks up a newspaper and ignores the other two. Anne's youngest nephew then appears and climbs on her back as she is tending to his brother. She cannot shake him off but then feels him being firmly removed by someone else. When she realizes it was Wentworth who has helped her, she is strangely unnerved by the thought of his gentle and unassuming kindness and also, presumably, by his momentary physical closeness. Her mind and emotions in a whirl, she is unable even to thank him and is relieved when Mary and the Musgrove girls appear and allow her to slip out of the room.

It looks increasingly as though Captain Wentworth will soon decide seriously to court either Henrietta or Louisa Musgrove. The choice between them is made for him when Charles Hayter withdraws from the Musgroves' company for several days and thus provokes Henrietta into a confirmation of her love for him. Their imminent engagement becomes a settled thing, and the field is now left clear for Louisa to claim Wentworth. Indeed, Anne has already overheard Wentworth praising Louisa for her firm and decisive character—qualities she knows he desires in a wife.

The story moves next to Lyme Regis, where a naval friend of Captain Wentworth has settled for the winter. Captain Harville was wounded in action two years previously and has suffered poor health ever since. He has taken his family to Lyme for the winter partly for his health and partly for the cheapness of the accommodations. Living with him and his family is another of Captain Wentworth's former fellow officers, Captain Benwick. He had been engaged to Captain Harville's sister, Fanny, but she had died the preceding summer (in June), and he is still in mourning for her. Captain Wentworth's account of a brief visit to his friends at Lyme creates a general desire among the young people at Uppercross to visit, too, and so in mid-November Wentworth takes Charles, Mary, Anne, Henrietta, and Louisa with him on a second visit to Lyme. Here they meet up with the Harvilles and Captain Benwick, and Anne is deeply impressed by the warmth, openness, and hospitality of this little naval fraternity. She is, however, somewhat less impressed by the way in which the grieving Captain Benwick seems to wallow in self-pity, especially when she compares his future prospects for happiness with hers. The stoical forbearance she has shown over many years in the face of her broken romance with Wentworth contrasts sharply with Benwick's self-indulgence here, and the contrast is ironically pointed by his citation of Romantic poetry and her countervailing recommendation of the essays, memoirs, and letters of "our best moralists."

The Uppercross party spend the night at an inn, and the next morning they take a stroll before breakfast. They pass an elegant-looking gentleman who pays admiring attention to Anne. Wentworth notices this and looks at Anne as if he, too, sees her in an attractive light again. Back at the inn, Anne sees the same gentleman again and notices that he is in mourning; he again looks admiringly at her, and she is impressed by his agreeable looks and good manners. They later see the man leaving the inn in his curricle and learn from a waiter that it is none other than Anne's cousin, William Walter Elliot. Mary Musgrove is foolishly excited at the reflected glory of this brush with the future baronet of Kellynch, but Anne is quietly gratified simply to know that her cousin seems, after all, to be a respectable, sensible, and well-mannered gentleman.

The party is now joined by Captains Harville and Benwick, and they go for another walk, which takes them up onto Lyme's famous Cobb (an ancient harbor wall). Louisa insists on being "jumped down" some steps by Captain Wentworth. He reluctantly agrees the first time but remonstrates with her when she goes back up the steps in order to repeat the exercise. He has previously praised her for her firmness of mind, and thus she knowingly smiles and says, "I am determined I will." This time, however, she mistimes her jump and falls to the hard stone pavement unconscious. Everybody except Anne panics in one way or another—Mary becomes hysterical, Henrietta faints, Benwick and Charles Musgrove are haplessly rooted to the spot, while even Wentworth pales with shock and can do nothing but melodramatically exclaim, "Oh God! her father and mother!" Only Anne keeps her wits about her, and she quickly organizes the others to do something practical to help the concussed Louisa. A surgeon is sent for, and Louisa is taken to the Harvilles' home. The surgeon's opinion is that, apart from the severe concussion, Louisa has escaped other injury, and a period of rest should lead to a full recovery. Wentworth's relief is perhaps greater than anyone else's, as he holds himself responsible for the fall for not having been firmer in refusing to allow her to jump down the steps. The Harvilles insist that Louisa stay with them to recuperate, and Charles and Mary Musgrove stay to care for her, while Captain Wentworth accompanies Henrietta and Anne back to Uppercross. Just before they arrive there, Wentworth quietly consults Anne about how to present the news to the elder Musgroves; she is flattered at his deference to her judgment and takes great pleasure in what she sees as a gesture of friendship and trust. Having seen the Musgroves, Wentworth immediately returns to Lyme, leaving Anne to stay at Uppercross Great House with the Musgrove family for her final two days before going back to stay with Lady Russell at Kellynch Lodge.

Volume 2 opens with news that, though Louisa is out of any danger, a full recovery will take some time, and she will have to remain in Lyme for the time being. When Anne leaves for Kellynch Lodge, therefore, the Musgroves go to stay in Lyme in order to be near to Louisa. Anne is embarrassed at having to give full details of the Lyme accident to Lady Russell, as this involves talking of Wentworth, but tension is eased on both sides when she explains that she believes him to be in love with Louisa. They pay a visit to the Crofts at Kellynch Hall, where they are warmly received. Anne is amused to hear that Admiral Croft had had to remove most of the large number of mirrors he had found in Sir Walter's dressing room; and she reflects to herself that Kellynch has passed into more deserving hands than those of its owners.

Mary and Charles Musgrove return from Lyme with reports of Louisa's steady improvement. Charles teases Anne about Benwick, who he thinks is in love with her. The elder Musgroves return to Uppercross for the Christmas holidays with hopes that Louisa and Henrietta may be able to join them before the end of the holidays. They also bring the news that Wentworth has now gone to visit his brother in Shropshire. Lady Russell and Anne move to Bath. Anne goes to stay with her father and sister in Camden Place, while Lady Russell goes to lodgings of her own nearby. Anne is surprised to receive a warmer welcome than she expected from Sir Walter and Elizabeth, but this turns out to be mainly because they are proud to be able to show off their handsome new lodgings and furniture and to boast to her of how highly sought after they have been among Bath's high society. They have also been highly delighted by the fact that William Walter Elliot has paid court to them and has become fully reconciled with the family. They have been persuaded by him that the breach between them had been the result of a misunderstanding, and they are now firmly convinced of his excellent character and of his sincere respect for them. Anne is a little puzzled at Mr. Elliot's sudden desire to reestablish this family connection, as he seems to have little to gain by it. She assumes that he must be intending to woo Elizabeth. He calls later that evening and is surprised to recognize his cousin as the lady he had so admired at Lyme. Anne is again impressed by his looks and polished manners and charmed by his intelligent conversation. She finds herself starting to compare him quite favorably to Captain Wentworth, though she still retains a degree of suspicion about his motives in becoming involved with the family again. Lady Russell is even more impressed by him when she makes his acquaintance, and she tries to dismiss Anne's reservations about him. A clear point of difference between Anne and Mr. Elliot emerges with the appearance in Bath of some titled cousins of the Elliots, the Dowager Viscountess Dalrymple and her daughter, the Honourable Miss Carteret. There has been no contact between the families for many years owing to some past misunderstanding, and Anne sees no reason Sir Walter should go out of his way to reestablish the connection now. But Mr. Elliot shows himself to be every bit as snobbish and status-bound as Anne's father and sister when he enthusiastically supports their attempts to ingratiate themselves with Lady Dalrymple. Anne is even more ashamed of her father's toadying behavior when she finds

Lady Dalrymple and her daughter to be totally lacking in any real elegance of mind or manners; they have no attraction for her at all, whereas her father and sister, Mr. Elliot, and even Lady Russell seem mesmerized by their rank and riches.

The contrast between Anne and the others in this respect is nicely accentuated by Anne's renewal of a much more humble-sounding connection—that with an old school friend called Mrs. Smith, who, Anne discovers, is now resident in Bath, though fallen on hard times. She visits Mrs. Smith in her humble lodgings and finds her remarkably cheerful and stoical in the face of her various misfortunes. Her husband had died some two years previously and had left his finances in such a bad state as to make her almost destitute. To add to her difficulties, she has now developed a severe rheumatic fever in her legs that has, at least temporarily, crippled her. Anne's father strongly disapproves of her friendship with someone of no social standing like Mrs. Smith, but Anne continues to visit her friend. Mrs. Smith, we learn, is attended by the sister of her landlady, Nurse Rooke, who is also currently attending Mrs. Wallis, the wife of a close friend of Mr. Elliot, Colonel Wallis.

Lady Russell has become convinced that Mr. Elliot will wish to marry Anne once he is out of mourning for his first wife. Anne, however, realizes that there is still only one man for her and that Mr. Elliot's character is ''too generally agreeable'' to be trusted. He is not open enough for her, and she continues to be suspicious of his past behavior and of his present motives.

It is now the beginning of February, and Admiral and Mrs. Croft arrive in Bath, bringing Anne a letter from Mary Musgrove containing the surprising news that Louisa is to marry Captain Benwick. Their close proximity in the Harvilles' home had obviously drawn the two together despite their apparently opposite temperaments, and Anne amusedly decides that, with Louisa in a tender state owing to her illness, they must have ''fallen in love over poetry.'' But Anne herself is overjoyed to realize that Captain Wentworth is now ''unshackled and free.'' He soon arrives in Bath, moreover, and bumps into Anne while she is sheltering from the rain in a shop and waiting for Mr. Elliot to escort her home. Captain Wentworth is at first clearly embarrassed to see her, and she notes to herself that she has the advantage over him for once in this respect, even though her emotions are also inwardly tumultuous. He composes himself a little and eventually offers to accompany her home, but at that moment Mr. Elliot reappears, and she leaves with him. The ladies in Wentworth's group retail the received gossip that Anne and Mr. Elliot will eventually marry. Anne, however, looks forward to her next meeting with Captain Wentworth, which, after a few days of disappointed hopes, finally takes place at a concert evening.

Captain Wentworth is noticeably more relaxed with Anne when they first meet at the concert, and he talks animatedly to her. She takes her seat for the concert buoyant with inner happiness at her growing conviction that Wentworth's love for her has been rekindled, but, oblivious to what has been going on around her, she finds herself seated beside Mr. Elliot (who has maneuvered himself into this position), with Wentworth nowhere to be seen. Mr. Elliot proceeds to flatter her and to hint at a desire to marry her. Anne is uncomfortable with Mr. Elliot's attentions and constantly looks about her to try to catch Wentworth's eye. Eventually, after an interval in the concert, she manages to disengage herself from Mr. Elliot and to be in a position with a free seat beside her. Wentworth approaches, but he has now lost the relaxed and eager manner exhibited earlier; he is much more constrained and grave now. He edges toward Anne and begins to talk to her again, at one point almost breaking into a smile and almost taking the seat beside her; but then Mr. Elliot again addresses Anne and asks her to translate one of the songs for him. When she returns to talk to Wentworth, he coolly bids her good night and leaves. She now realizes, with mixed feelings, that he has become jealous of Mr. Elliot. She is overjoyed that he should be capable of such strong feelings for her again but concerned about how to communicate to him her real antipathy for Mr. Elliot and her true love for him.

The next morning, Anne visits Mrs. Smith, who, on hearing that Anne is not intending to marry Mr. Elliot, explains to Anne how her present poverty is partly the fault of Mr. Elliot. Apparently, he had led her husband into extravagance and, on her husband's death, had refused the responsibility of acting as a trustee to help her to benefit from her husband's property in the West Indies. Much of what Mrs. Smith tells Anne confirms her suspicions about Mr. Elliot, though his character actually appears to be much more disreputable than she had imagined. Mrs. Smith has also learned from Nurse Rooke, who has gleaned the information from Mrs. Wallis, that although Mr. Elliot has now become genuinely enamored of Anne, the initial reason for his sudden renewal of interest in the Elliot family was that he feared that Sir Walter might marry Mrs. Clay and possibly disinherit him by producing an heir to Kellynch after all.

Later that day, Anne sees Mr. Elliot but keeps him at arm's length. She is relieved to learn from him that he is leaving Bath the next morning to visit friends for a couple of days. However, the next day she sees him deep in conversation with his supposed enemy, Mrs. Clay, outside the White Hart Inn, where she has gone to visit the Musgroves, who have unexpectedly arrived in Bath. When this gives rise to some conversation about Mr. Elliot, Anne is embarrassed at the apparent assumption of members of the company (which by now includes Captain Wentworth) that she and Mr. Elliot are attached to one another. She does her best to make Captain Wentworth realize that she prefers his company to that of Mr. Elliot when she insists that she would rather go to the theater with the Musgroves the next evening than attend the party at Camden Place that has been proposed by her sister, Elizabeth.

The next day at the Musgroves' lodgings, Anne is again in the company of Wentworth. Wentworth seems absorbed in writing a letter, while Anne talks to Captain Harville. Their conversation turns to the relationship between Benwick and Louisa and to the apparent rapidity with which Benwick was able to switch his affections from Fanny Harville to Louisa. In the course of their discussion,

Harville and Anne make contrary claims about male and female constancy in love. Anne argues that women do not forget men as soon as men forget women and that women cannot help dwelling on their feelings, while men always have continual worldly occupations to weaken their emotional attachments. This, in effect, allows Anne, in Wentworth's hearing, to refer obliquely but feelingly to her own years of quiet suffering when her constancy had little hope of being repaid: "All the privilege I claim for my own sex . . . is that of loving longest, when existence or when hope is gone." It is made clear that Wentworth has been listening intently to this discourse, and, shortly after he leaves the room with Harville, he returns under the pretext of having forgotten his gloves and silently slips Anne a letter. In the letter, he, too, engages with the theme of constancy and declares *his* constancy in loving her. He has never stopped loving her, he declares, and he asks her for some sign to tell him whether or not it is too late for him to hope to win her back to him. Anne is overcome by the letter and experiences an "overpowering happiness" such that everybody in the room thinks her ill. Charles Musgrove then offers to escort her home. On the way, they are overtaken by Wentworth, who takes over as her escort as Charles goes off to honor a prior engagement with a gunsmith. Anne and Wentworth are finally openly able to share their true feelings of love for one another, feelings that they have only gradually been able to readmit to themselves over the preceding few months. Wentworth tells Anne that he had been foolish to embroil himself with Louisa, whom he had never really loved, but that as soon as he had heard of her engagement to Benwick, he had felt released of all obligations to her and had come straight to Bath to see Anne. Here, however, he had become jealous of Mr. Elliot, as Anne had guessed and, until this day, had almost given up hope of regaining her love.

At the Elliots' party that evening, the couple resume their conversation. Anne tries to explain and justify her fateful decision of eight years ago, but she makes clear that she had been wrong and that had he asked her again afterward, she would certainly have accepted him. This brings him to admit that he had thought of doing so in 1808, when he had started to make his fortune, but that he had been too proud and resentful to do so. This time Anne's family welcomes the match, as Captain Wentworth, with £25,000 and a glowing public reputation, "was no longer nobody." Lady Russell gracefully admits that she had been mistaken in her original advice to Anne and is soon affectionately attached to Wentworth as a type of son-in-law. Along with the other Elliots, she also has to admit that she has been mistaken about Mr. Elliot, for it becomes known that he has eloped to London with Mrs. Clay. This was his way of separating her from Sir Walter once and for all, but, we hear, he is now in danger of being wheedled into marriage himself by Mrs. Clay, who is every bit as cunning as he is. Captain Wentworth now acts for Mrs. Smith and manages to recover her husband's property in the West Indies, thus providing her with an improved income. She becomes one of the couple's best friends and, along with Lady Russell, one of the few people Anne can put forward from her side as being a worthy addition to Wentworth's own excellent family. Anne and Captain Wentworth live happily ever after, with Anne's only real anxiety being the fear of a future war.

Main Characters: Captain James Benwick, Mrs. Penelope Clay, Admiral Croft, Mrs. Croft, Anne Elliot, Elizabeth Elliot, Sir Walter Elliot, William Walter Elliot, Captain Harville, Charles Musgrove, Henrietta Musgrove, Louisa Musgrove, Mrs. Mary Musgrove (née Elliot), Lady Russell, Mrs. Smith, Captain Frederick Wentworth.

Minor Characters: Lady Alicia, Miss Atkinson, Admiral Baldwin, Admiral Brand, Captain Brigden, the Hon. Miss Carteret, Viscount Dalrymple, Sir Archibald Drew, the little Durands, Lady Elliot, the second Sir Walter Elliot, Mrs. Elliot, Mrs. Frankland, Lady Mary Grierson, Mrs. Harville, the little Harvilles, Mr. Hayter, Mrs. Hayter, Charles Hayter, the Miss Hayters, the Ibbotsons, Jemima, Mackenzie, Lady Mary Maclean, Molland's, Sir Basil Morley, Mr. Musgrove, Mrs. Musgrove, Charles Musgrove (the younger), Harry Musgrove, Richard Musgrove, the young Musgrove, the Pooles, Mr. Robinson, Nurse Rooke, Sir Henry Russell, Sarah, Mr. John Shepherd, Dr. Shirley, Mrs. Shirley, Charles Smith, Mrs. Speed, the Spicers, Lord St. Ives, Colonel Wallis, Mrs. Wallis, Edward Wentworth.

Volume and chapter divisions (numbers in brackets are for editions with continuous chapter numbers): Volume 1: Chapters 1–12, volume 2: Chapters 1–12 [13–24].

See: Astell 1987, Bander 1993, Benedict 1992, Booth 1988, Brown 1996, Burrows 1976–1977, *Coates 1969*, Collins 1984, Davison 1984, Derry 1990a, Fitzgerald 1988, *Gard 1985*, Giordano 1993, Grant 1983, Groves 1984, Gunn 1987, Harris 1983, Hart 1982, Heldman 1993, Heydt-Stevenson 1995, J. Johnson 1983, Kaplan 1993, Kastely 1991, Knox-Shaw 1993, Knuth 1993, Koppel 1984, Marshall 1984, Martin 1994, *May 1970*, McLean 1993, *McMaster and Stovel 1996*, Molan 1982, Moon 1987, O'Toole 1993, Orange 1989–1990, Parke 1983, Pinch 1993, Poovey 1983, Postlethwaite 1992, Ray 1993, Reid-Walsh 1993, Ruoff 1984, *Sherif 1968, Simons 1997, Southam 1976a, Spacks 1995*, Spence 1981, Sutherland 1993, Taylor 1989, Thomas 1987, Thomsen 1993, Warhol 1992, Weissman 1988.

Phillips, Mr. (*Pride and Prejudice* Ch.7; I:7:28). Mrs. Bennet's brother-in-law and successor to her father's attorney business in Meryton after having worked there as a clerk. He makes a point of visiting all the militia officers stationed at Meryton, much to the delight of his younger Bennet nieces, who thereby gain access to the officers themselves. However, in comparison to the officers, Mr. Phillips, broad-faced, stuffy, and smelling of port, appears to Elizabeth Bennet as distinctly inferior.

Phillips, Mrs., née Gardiner (*Pride and Prejudice* Ch.7; I:7:28). Mrs. Bennet's sister who lives in Meryton. She is as vulgar, foolish, and gossiping as her sister but of a somewhat lower social standing, having married her father's former clerk. She welcomes the frequent visits of her giddy nieces, Lydia and Kitty, and facilitates their flirtations with the Meryton officers by organizing supper parties for them. Indeed, she is almost as anxious as Mrs. Bennet to have her nieces married off.

Plan of a Novel, according to Hints from Various Quarters. This comic outline for a novel was inspired by Jane Austen's correspondence with Rev. James Stanier Clarke, domestic chaplain and librarian to the prince regent (later, George IV) at Carlton House. In October 1815, Jane Austen had come to stay in London with her brother, Henry, to negotiate for the publication of *Emma*. Henry fell seriously ill and happened to be treated at one point by one of the prince regent's physicians, who later informed the regent of Jane Austen's presence in London. The regent was a great admirer of her novels and arranged for Mr. Clarke to wait on her and to invite her to see the library at Carlton House. Mr. Clarke showed her around the small palace on 13 November and also let it be known that the regent would like to have one of her works dedicated to him; Jane Austen later dutifully obliged with the dedication of *Emma*. After this visit, Mr. Clarke, clearly not one to hide his light under a bushel, wrote to Jane Austen suggesting that she ought to write a novel about an English clergyman and that, if she did, she might like to take his career as a model. Jane Austen politely declined this offer, as well as a later suggestion that she should write a historical romance about the house of Saxe-Cobourg (Princess Charlotte had recently become engaged to a member of that line), but she later used some of the details of Mr. Clarke's letters as the framework for the brief but sharply pointed *Plan of a Novel*. As her eldest niece, Fanny, provided several of the "hints" that were added to Mr. Clarke's hints to create the piece, it would seem that it was probably written as a family entertainment around May 1816, when Fanny was staying with Jane Austen at Chawton. In addition to representing a shared family joke about Rev. Clarke, the *Plan* also harks back to the burlesque mode of writing that predominates in Jane Austen's juvenilia, for here once again she writes in exuberant parody of the excesses and artificiality of romantic fiction. Indeed, with the Clarke-figure expiring "in a fine burst of Literary Enthusiasm" and the heroine "having at least 20 narrow escapes" before running into the arms of the hero "in the very nick of time," the *Plan* presents us with a wonderfully condensed mock-prototype of the popular novel of Jane Austen's day. As well as provoking the *Plan of a Novel*, James Stanier Clarke should also be recognized by posterity for eliciting some of the few semicritical comments Jane Austen made about her own art (*Letters* 1995: 306, 312). Most important, perhaps, she stresses in these letters the quiet, domestic focus of her novels ("pictures of domestic Life in Country Villages) and the essentially *comic* nature of her writing: "I could no more write a Romance than an Epic Poem.—I could not sit seriously down to write a serious Romance under any other motive than to save my Life, & if it were indispensable for me to keep it up & never relax into laughing at myself or other people, I am sure I should be hung before I had finished the first Chapter."

Pooles, the (*Persuasion* Ch.5; I:5:39). Acquaintances of the Musgrove family, living in the vicinity of Uppercross.

Pope, Miss (*Pride and Prejudice* Ch.29; II:6:165). A young lady who had been recommended as a governess to Lady Metcalfe by Lady Catherine de Bourgh and who turns out to be "a treasure."

Pratt, Mr. (*Sense and Sensibility* Ch.22; I:22:130). Uncle of the Miss Steeles and former tutor of Edward Ferrars. His home is at Longstaples, near Plymouth.

Pratt, Mr. (*Pride and Prejudice* Ch.39; II:16:221). One of the militia officers staying at Meryton and part of the group, along with Wickham and Denny, with whom Lydia Bennet becomes friendly.

Pratt, Richard (*Sanditon, Minor Works* 389). A visitor to Sanditon from Limehouse, noted by Mr. Parker in the subscription list at the circulating library. *See* Beard, Mr.

"Prayers." Three short prayers of Jane Austen's survive in two sheets of undated manuscript, one of which, watermarked 1818, is inscribed "Prayers Composed by my ever dear Sister Jane." The handwriting on the manuscripts has not been definitively identified, but it appears that the prayers were copied out at two different times by Jane Austen's sister (who passed the manuscripts on at her death) and her brothers Henry and Charles; though some of the writing on the second sheet (which has no watermark or other clue as to date) has been ascribed to Jane Austen herself. Only the first prayer has a title, "Evening Prayer."

Given the preceding, we cannot know for certain the date of composition for these prayers, but it has been suggested that they were probably the work of Jane Austen's later life (*Le Faye 1989*: 274 n.57), most likely postdating the death of her clergyman father in 1805 (Stovel 1996: 200). The prayers were first published in a limited edition of 300 copies in 1940 (San Francisco: Colt Press) in a somewhat eccentric typed transcription by their then-owner, William Matson Roth. This version was then used as the basis for the texts that appear in the Oxford edition of the *Minor Works* (first published in 1954) as well as for those in *Catharine and Other Writings* (edited by Margaret Anne Doody and Douglas Murray. Oxford: World's Classics, 1993). As yet, therefore, there is no scholarly text based on the manuscripts (which are now at the F. W. Olin Library, Mills College, Oakland, California).

The prayers are clearly designed for communal family worship and are modeled on prayers—particularly the Collects—found in the *Book of Common*

Prayer, which Jane Austen obviously knew very well (and whose linguistic style may have been an important influence on her writing; see Doody 1986: 247–48). The prayers emphasize the importance of religion in Jane Austen's life and the sincerity with which she held her orthodox Christian beliefs. In the detail of the prayers there are also clues to the way in which some of her main novelistic concerns (e.g., the struggle for self-knowledge) are underpinned by Christian faith and morality.

Prescott, Lady (*Mansfield Park* Ch.29; II:11:283). A guest at the Mansfield Park ball held for Fanny. Lady Prescott seems to have noticed something about Fanny, but Lady Bertram cannot remember what it was.

Price, Betsey (*Mansfield Park* Ch.38; III:7:377). Five years old and the youngest of the Price children, Betsey is her mother's favorite and spoiled by her. She seems to have been "trained up to think the alphabet her greatest enemy," and Fanny despairs of being able to love her or to improve her character. Although there is little chance of her being spoiled any further by her godmother, Mrs. Norris (who only *almost* sends her a present of a prayer book), it is appropriate that Betsey is thus associated with her, as Mrs. Norris does spoil the Bertram girls and helps form their selfish and unprincipled natures.

Price, Charles and Tom (*Mansfield Park* Ch.38; III:7:381). At eight, Charles is the youngest boy in the Price family; he had been born just after Fanny had left for Mansfield Park. Tom is a year older than Charles, and Fanny remembers helping to nurse him when he was a baby, so that she takes special pleasure in greeting him again when she comes to stay with her family in Portsmouth. Both the boys are rosy-faced, ragged, and unruly, and Fanny soon realizes that she will be unable to make any impression on them: "they were quite untameable."

Price, Fanny (*Mansfield Park* Ch.1; I:1:5, 12–13). The heroine of the novel, Fanny Price is, in summary, physically slight and socially retiring but morally and intellectually robust and clear-sighted, with an affectionate and sweet-tempered disposition. She is the eldest daughter of Mr. and Mrs. Price and is brought up by them in Portsmouth until the age of ten, when she is taken to live with the Bertrams at Mansfield Park. Here, overawed by her imposing uncle, Sir Thomas Bertram, abashed in the face of her confident female cousins, Julia and Maria, and cowed by her shrewish aunt Norris, she is at first terribly homesick. But, with the help and sympathy of her kindly cousin Edmund, she eventually settles into her new home and becomes happy there, though she continues to lack confidence in her social self and remains rather passive and withdrawn in company.

As she grows up, she gradually falls in love with Edmund, though she cannot tell him this, and he suspects nothing. She then suffers to see him attracted by the glamorous and flamboyant Mary Crawford. Fanny herself becomes the object of Henry Crawford's romantic advances, but she does not trust his character and has no affection for him. Though externally diffident and submissive, Fanny, partly through the guidance of Edmund, has by this time developed a firm sense of her own mind and principles (as is shown by her resistance to the idea of the theatricals), and she is therefore resolute in refusing Henry's marriage proposal and in rejecting the attempts of the Bertrams to persuade her to marry purely for the convenience and consequence of a "good" match. Her uncle, Sir Thomas, is annoyed at her apparent willfulness and pride in this, and he sends her away to her parents' home in Portsmouth in order to teach her a lesson. Here, Fanny does, indeed, learn to appreciate anew the comforts and elegance of Mansfield Park, but she also learns to value her own capacity for positive action as she starts to educate her sister, Susan, and sees her making significant progress.

Fanny began the novel as a type of decentered personality, because of her depressed self-esteem in the Bertram household. Her return to Portsmouth is thus more than a literal homecoming, it represents also a psychological coming home to herself, a centering of herself in the final phase of her growth to maturity, when she can at last confidently see herself as useful and valuable (Henry Crawford's continuing pursuit of her in this period, however unwelcome, also contributes to her growing sense of womanly self-consequence). In addition, her period in Portsmouth represents an ironic shift of positions more generally within the book, for while she is there, physically marginalized by the Bertrams just as she has always been psychologically marginalized by them, the Bertrams come to recognize her as their true moral "center," and they are, as it were, forced to decenter themselves by sending Edmund to fetch her back. While she is away, their world symbolically collapses around them, and it is as though her removal has led to a loss of stability in their lives. Thus, while Fanny does learn Sir Thomas' intended lesson while away from Mansfield, during her absence Sir Thomas learns the more painful lesson about his daughters and about his own failures as a father. He and his wife (and, for other reasons, Edmund) are finally made to see just how important Fanny is to them, and her return to Mansfield (at the same time that Maria Bertram is banished from it) represents a suggestive realignment of center and periphery in the social and moral world of the novel: the poor little charity girl, whose highest price had been clearly fixed at the start (she would never have the "rank, fortune, rights, and expectations" of her cousins), has, by the end, become priceless. Moreover, when Edmund is disembarrassed of his illusions about Mary Crawford and finally realizes his more grounded love for Fanny, the girl who would never be "a *Miss Bertram*" nevertheless becomes a *Mrs.* Bertram (and therefore Price-less in another sense, too!).

Price, John and Richard (*Mansfield Park* Ch.39; III:8:389). Brothers of Fanny Price who live away from home and do not appear in the novel. One is a clerk in a public office in London, and the other a sailor on an East Indiaman.

Price, Mary (deceased) (*Mansfield Park* Ch.38; III:7:385–86). Fanny's younger sister, who was about four when Fanny left Portsmouth for Mansfield Park. She died a few years later without Fanny's seeing her again. Before she died, she gave the silver knife given to her by her godmother, Mrs. Maxwell, to Susan, and this is the source of the argument witnessed by Fanny between Susan and little Betsey, who keeps taking the knife out to play with.

Price, Mr. (*Mansfield Park* Ch.1; I:1:3). Fanny's father, Mr. Price, had been a lieutenant in the marines when he married Mrs. Price, but he was later disabled for active service and turned to drink. Although described as without "education, fortune or connections," he clearly possessed some positive qualities that first attracted his wife to him and that earned him a promotion in the marines, and we have a glimpse of this side to his character when Fanny introduces him to Henry Crawford at Portsmouth: "His manners now, though not polished, were more than passable; they were grateful, animated, manly; his expressions were those of an attached father, and a sensible man." However, this appears to be a different man from the one Fanny has come to recognize within the family home. There, loud, vulgar, and negligent of the others, "he swore and he drank, he was dirty and gross," with no interests or conversation beyond the narrow scope of dockyard and harbor. He seems never to have treated Fanny with any kindness or tenderness and during her visit "scarcely ever noticed her, but to make her the object of a coarse joke."

Price, Mrs. Frances, née Ward (*Mansfield Park* Ch.1; I:1:3). Fanny Price's mother and sister of Lady Bertram and Mrs. Norris. To the general dismay of her family, she marries the poor and lowly Lieutenant Price of the marines, and this becomes the source of a quarrel and breach with her sisters that continues for eleven years. However, after this time, the sisters are reconciled when Mrs. Price, finding herself with "a large and still increasing family, an husband disabled for active service, but not the less equal to company and good liquor, and a very small income to supply their wants," writes an apologetic letter to Lady Bertram and asks for some assistance with the upbringing of her children. The main result of this is the adoption of Fanny, Mrs. Price's second oldest child, by the Bertrams. When Fanny leaves the Portsmouth household, Mrs. Price has seven other children, with one more on the way; two or three years later, she gives birth again, to her tenth child, Betsey. When Fanny returns to Portsmouth some eight years later, she is shocked by the disorder of the house and disappointed in her mother, who, though initially warm and motherly toward her, soon more or less forgets her again as she slips back into the "slow bustle" of her messy life. Fanny likens her to Lady Bertram in having a kindly but basically lazy disposition that prevents her from doing anything properly and from engaging sensibly and rationally with others. Hurt by her mother's lack of real intimacy with her and missing the elegance and order of Mansfield Park, Fanny judges Mrs. Price unsentimentally, if not harshly: "her mother was a partial, ill-judging parent, a dawdle, a slattern, who neither taught nor restrained her children, whose house was the scene of mismanagement and discomfort from beginning to end, and who had no talent, no conversation, no affection towards herself.''

Price, Sam (*Mansfield Park* Ch.38; III:7:377). Fanny's eleven-year-old brother who leaves to begin his career at sea, on William's ship the *Thrush*, while Fanny is in Portsmouth. Although somewhat loud and overbearing, Fanny grows fond of him as the most intelligent and responsive of her three youngest brothers and regrets his departure just as she was beginning to establish rapport with him.

Price, Susan (*Mansfield Park* Ch.38; III:7:377). Susan is a physically and temperamentally robust fourteen-year-old when Fanny returns to the Price household in Portsmouth. Fanny becomes particularly close to Susan during her stay as she comes to recognize her determination to improve the home and herself. She begins to teach Susan and to guide her reading. When Fanny is sent for by Sir Thomas, he also invites Susan to come with her, and she eventually takes Fanny's place as Lady Bertram's companion.

Price, Tom (*Mansfield Park*). *See* Price, Charles and Tom.

Price, William (*Mansfield Park* Ch.2; I:2:15). William is the eldest son of Mr. and Mrs. Price and Fanny's closest and most loved brother. Only one year her senior, he is, in childhood, "her constant companion and friend; her advocate with her mother . . . in every distress," and when she first goes to Mansfield Park as a young girl, he is the one she misses most. He is also the only family member from Portsmouth to visit her there, first just before leaving to become a sailor at the age of about twelve and then once again seven years later, when he is nineteen and "had known every variety of danger, which sea and war together could offer." He is a warmhearted, well-mannered, and unaffected young man who immediately impresses Sir Thomas with his "good principles, professional knowledge, energy, courage, and cheerfulness." Even Henry Crawford silently acknowledges the great contrast between his own aimless and indulgent life and that of this young sailor, who, before the age of twenty, "had gone through such bodily hardships, and given such proofs of mind." Partly out of genuine respect and admiration for William but mainly in order to impress Fanny, Henry Crawford later uses his influence with his uncle, Admiral Crawford, to secure a promotion for William to the rank of lieutenant—though it is clear by then that this is nothing less than William deserves.

Pride and Prejudice. *Pride and Prejudice*, consistently Jane Austen's most popular novel and perhaps one of the most popular novels in the English language, was first written between October 1796 and August 1797 under the title of "First Impressions." It became the first of Jane Austen's works to be offered for publication when her father approached a London publisher, Cadell and Davies, in November 1797, though Cadell declined even to read the manuscript. There is no evidence of Jane Austen's working on the book again until 1811, though as no manuscript material survives, we cannot be entirely sure of this. Sometime between 1811 (possibly from May) and the autumn of 1812, she made a substantial revision of "First Impressions" and turned it into *Pride and Prejudice*. The copyright was sold to the publisher Thomas Egerton in November 1812 for £110, and the novel was published by him, in three volumes, on 28 January 1813. As with the other novels published in her lifetime, Jane Austen's name did not appear on the title page: it was presented as being "By the Author of Sense and Sensibility." A second edition was issued in October 1813, and a third, in two volumes, in 1817. The novel was published in America for the first time in 1832 under the title *Elizabeth Bennet*, and it was first translated, into French, in 1822.

Jane Austen was being ironically self-critical when she said that the novel was "rather too light & bright & sparkling" and in need of a long chapter of "sense if it could be had, if not of solemn specious nonsense . . . that would form a contrast . . . to the playfulness & Epigrammatism of the general stile" (letter of 4 February 1813)—but she identifies here precisely the stylistic and tonal qualities that have made the book such an appealing one to generations of readers. Moreover, the vivid characterization, the dramatic qualities of the dialogue, the superbly controlled buildup and release of tension in the plotting of the central romance, the sheer comedy of Mrs. Bennet, Mr. Collins, and others, the rousing satire on hypocrisy and snobbery represented by figures such as Lady Catherine de Bourgh, and the carefully modulated use of irony throughout (not least to expose "the economic basis of society" and "the amorous effects of 'brass,' " as W. H. Auden put it)—all these things, too, have contributed to the novel's enduring popularity and success.

The central characters in the novel are the Bennet family, leisured lesser gentry living in the village of Longbourn, near the town of Meryton in Hertfordshire. Their estate, however, which presently provides them with a comfortable living and an elegant home, is entailed to Mr. Bennet's nephew, Rev. William Collins, as the Bennets have five daughters and no male heir to inherit the property. Partly as a result of this situation, Mrs. Bennet is more than usually anxious to see all her five daughters well married, as they will otherwise be left unprovided for when Mr. Bennet dies, and the estate passes to Mr. Collins (there were, of course, no respectable careers for middle-class women at that time, and, when he inherits the estate, Mr. Collins will be under no obligation to provide anything for the Bennets).

The novel opens when Mrs. Bennet hears the news that a nearby country estate, Netherfield, has been rented by a Mr. Bingley, who, we learn, is young, rich, and single. Desperate that her daughters should meet with Mr. Bingley at the earliest opportunity, Mrs. Bennet pesters her husband to pay a formal call at Netherfield to pave the way for further acquaintance. After some prevarication and some teasing of his wife and daughters, Mr. Bennet visits Netherfield, and Mr. Bingley calls at Longbourn to return the compliment soon after. He is somewhat disappointed not to be introduced to the Bennet girls on this occasion, as he has heard of their reputed beauty. He meets them, however, at the next ball to be held at Meryton, where it becomes clear that he is especially attracted to Jane, the eldest and most immediately beautiful of the daughters.

Accompanying Mr. Bingley to the Meryton ball are his sisters, Caroline Bingley and Mrs. Hurst, with her husband Mr. Hurst, and a Mr. Darcy, a handsome, noble-looking, and, it is soon discovered, very wealthy man with a large estate in Derbyshire. Mr. Darcy, however, lacks Mr. Bingley's charm and good humor and signally fails to endear himself to the Meryton people, who soon judge him to be "the proudest, most disagreeable man in the world." For one thing, he refuses to be introduced to any of the ladies in the company and dances only with Mr. Bingley's sisters, but he also makes a particular enemy of Mrs. Bennet by passing a slighting remark about her second daughter, Elizabeth. Elizabeth herself overhears the remark, and it clearly does not endear Darcy to her either, but she is a spirited and confident young woman who laughs it off lightly.

Mr. Bingley continues to seek out the company of Jane Bennet, and they become increasingly attached to one another. This developing courtship inevitably throws Darcy and Elizabeth more into each other's company, too, and Darcy now begins to revise his former lukewarm opinion of Elizabeth and starts to admire her for her wit and intelligence, as well as for her "fine eyes." This interest is further developed at a party at the home of Sir William Lucas, a local baronet whose daughter, Charlotte, is Elizabeth's close friend. Elizabeth is unaware of Mr. Darcy's growing regard for her, and, assuming he still considers her to be beneath his notice, she enjoys herself in trying to outwit him in ironic verbal repartee. Her sharpness, eloquence, and confidence in this surprise and fascinate him and pique his interest in her further. Caroline Bingley, who clearly has designs on Darcy herself, recognizes a potential rival in Elizabeth and craftily appeals to the snobbery Darcy apparently shares with her by reminding him of the vulgarity of Mrs. Bennet.

Mr. Bingley's sisters invite Jane to spend an evening with them at Netherfield. Mrs. Bennet denies Jane the use of the family carriage, insisting that she go on horseback, hoping that the likelihood of rain will secure her an invitation to stay the night. Unfortunately, it rains sooner than expected, and Jane is soaked through. Mrs. Bennet's ploy is effective, therefore, but not exactly in the way she had expected, for Jane is forced to prolong her stay at Netherfield because of a bad cold. Elizabeth, concerned for her sister's welfare, goes to inquire after Jane's health and in doing so demonstrates a physical robustness to match her strength of personality by walking the three miles to Netherfield, partly across muddy fields. This meets with considerable censure from the Bingley sisters, who consider such behavior unbecoming of a lady and who clearly see it as yet another sign of the Bennets' lack of true gentility. Darcy, however, is silently impressed by the color the exercise has brought to Elizabeth's complexion.

Elizabeth, too, is now invited to stay at Netherfield so that she can nurse Jane through her illness. This provides the opportunity for a development in the relationship between her and Mr. Darcy, much to the annoyance of Miss Bingley, who is alarmed to observe Darcy's growing interest in Elizabeth. Despite this interest, however, Mr. Darcy has been made ever more acutely aware of Elizabeth's low social standing by an embarrassing visit to Netherfield by her witless mother and flighty sisters, Lydia and Kitty. This reminds him of the social barriers that would prevent him from marrying Elizabeth, and he resolves not to allow their relationship to develop any further. He remains aloof during the last days of Elizabeth's stay, and they part coolly.

Rev. Collins now comes to visit Longbourn, ostensibly to heal the breach that has existed between him and the Bennets over the issue of the entail but actually to marry one of the Bennet girls, of whom he has heard complimentary reports. He is, to an extremely sycophantic degree, in thrall to his wealthy patroness, Lady Catherine de Bourgh of Rosings in Kent, and she has recently advised him to marry, so that his visit is partly motivated by his desire to please Lady Catherine. Mr. Collins is a foolish, self-important, and tactless man whose pompous manners immediately invite ridicule from Mr. Bennet and his daughters, though Mrs. Bennet can think only of the prospects he offers as a potential match for one of her daughters. As Jane, Mrs. Bennet believes, is now spoken for by Mr. Bingley, she directs Mr. Collins' attentions to Elizabeth.

The younger Bennet girls, Kitty and Lydia, are particularly fond of socializing with the officers of the militia regiment stationed in Meryton and often go to visit their Meryton aunt, Mrs. Phillips, for this reason. On the day after Mr. Collins' arrival, they decide to go to Meryton to hear the latest gossip from Mrs. Phillips, and they are accompanied on the walk by Jane, Elizabeth, and Mr. Collins. In Meryton, they come across Mr. Denny, an officer known to Lydia and Kitty, and he introduces them to his friend, Mr. Wickham, who has just arrived from London to take a commission in Denny's regiment. Wickham is good-looking, urbane, and charming, and he clearly makes a strong impression on Elizabeth and the others. As the party stands talking, Bingley and Darcy appear riding down the street, and they come over to greet Jane and Elizabeth. When Darcy and Wickham see one another, they react awkwardly, and Elizabeth realizes that they must know one another and that there is clearly some tension between them, and she wonders what it could be. Mrs. Phillips later invites the Bennet party to dinner the following evening and agrees, under pressure from Lydia and Kitty, to invite Wickham along with the other officers she has already invited. At this dinner party, Elizabeth starts to be attracted by Wickham's easy manners and sociability, and she talks to him about his relationship with Darcy. She is shocked when Wickham tells her that Mr. Darcy has ruined his career prospects by denying him a living in the church reserved for him by Mr. Darcy's father. Darcy, Wickham says, was motivated in this by his jealousy of Wickham and also by his overweening pride. He also tells Elizabeth that Lady Catherine de Bourgh is Darcy's aunt and that she has long planned to join her estate to

Darcy's by promoting a match between him and her daughter. Wickham's description of Darcy's character seems to accord with Elizabeth's own impressions, and therefore she believes Wickham's story and feels sympathy for his plight. At the same time, her dislike for Darcy is reinforced.

Mr. Bingley is to host a ball at Netherfield, and Elizabeth happily anticipates an opportunity of gaining further in the affections of Mr. Wickham. She plans to have the first dances with him and in high spirits playfully asks Mr. Collins if he will be attending the ball and intending to dance. Much to her surprise, he responds enthusiastically, assuring her of his attendance and of a ready willingness to dance; indeed, he now takes this opportunity to engage her for the first two dances. She is dismayed at this not only because she had been hoping to dance those dances with Wickham but also because she senses an ulterior motive in Mr. Collins' manner and starts to realize that he has designs on her. At the Netherfield ball, Elizabeth is disappointed when Wickham fails to appear. She immediately suspects that Darcy is the cause of this, and her prejudice against him is increased. At the same time, the behavior of her family at the ball, particularly of her mother and her sister, Mary (who makes a spectacle of herself by singing too much), confirms Mr. Darcy in his view that the Bennet girls are not suitable marriage partners. Despite the love that has obviously developed between Bingley and Jane, Darcy, as we later discover, resolves to take Mr. Bingley away from the neighborhood to prevent the marriage that Jane and her family have now become confident of. Shortly after the ball, Jane is shocked to receive a letter from Caroline Bingley saying that the whole Netherfield party has departed for London and has no plans to return again that winter. Miss Bingley also mock-innocently refers to the high hopes she and her sister have of their brother's marrying Mr. Darcy's sister, Georgiana, with whom they will now be in close contact. Jane is obviously downcast at this, but Elizabeth reasons with her that this is probably only wishful thinking on the part of Miss Bingley, who, in any case, has ulterior motives in trying to encourage marriage between the Bingleys and the Darcys.

Meanwhile, on the day after the ball, in one of Jane Austen's most amusing scenes, Mr. Collins finally makes his marriage proposal to Elizabeth. She refuses him in no uncertain terms, but he is too conceited and insensitive to believe that she is serious, and he continues to press her until she leaves the room. Mrs. Bennet is horrified to hear of Elizabeth's refusal and insists that Mr. Bennet should force his daughter to accept the offer, but he firmly supports Elizabeth and is clearly mightily relieved to have avoided gaining Mr. Collins as a son-in-law. Mrs. Bennet can do nothing but retreat in ill humor to complain loudly and at length of her frayed nerves. Mr. Collins' hurt pride is salved somewhat by the appearance of Charlotte Lucas, who seems happy to pay him some attention, while the Bennet girls largely avoid him. When the Bennets dine with the Lucases shortly afterward, Charlotte again pays careful attention to Mr. Collins, and, though Elizabeth thinks she is doing this as a favor to her, it soon becomes clear that Charlotte has decided to woo him for herself. Indeed, the very next day, Mr. Collins proposes to her, and she willingly accepts him. When Charlotte tells Elizabeth about this, Elizabeth can barely conceal her astonishment and disapproval, but Charlotte, who dislikes Mr. Collins as much as anyone, is not, she says, "romantic," and she freely admits that her motives have been purely practical: "Without thinking highly either of men or of matrimony, marriage had always been her object; it was the only honourable provision for well-educated young women of small fortune, and however uncertain of giving happiness, must be their pleasantest preservative from want" (Ch.22; I:22:122–23). Even so, Elizabeth silently thinks to herself that her friend is seriously mistaken to sacrifice "every better feeling to worldly advantage." On top of the shock of Elizabeth's refusal of Mr. Collins, Mrs. Bennet is now further mortified to find that not only have her neighbors married off a daughter before her but that daughter will now in due course become the mistress of Longbourn; it takes her many months to forgive Elizabeth for this, we are told.

Volume 2 of the novel opens with a second letter to Jane from Caroline Bingley, confirming that Mr. Bingley will be staying in London for the winter and once again referring to his supposed intimacy with Georgiana Darcy. Jane resigns herself to thinking that she had been mistaken in supposing him to be genuinely in love with her. Elizabeth again suggests that the letter has been artfully designed to elicit exactly such a response, but Jane refuses to think badly of any of the Bingleys, and Elizabeth is greatly impressed by her stoicism and good-natured view of others. With the departure of Mr. Bingley, Mrs. Bennet has begun almost to despair of ever having any of her daughters married. The only thing that lifts the gloom from Longbourn at this time is the regular presence of George Wickham, whose attachment to Elizabeth is fast becoming a settled thing. His supposed mistreatment by Darcy is now a widely known story in the locality, and all take pleasure in seeing their first impressions of Darcy confirmed by it. Only Jane Bennet, who typically likes to think well of everyone, reserves judgment on him. Thus we see that while Elizabeth will later be proved right about Caroline Bingley and wrong about Darcy, Jane will later be proved wrong about Caroline Bingley and right about Darcy.

Mr. and Mrs. Gardiner, Mrs. Bennet's brother and his wife, come to stay at Longbourn for Christmas. Mr. Gardiner is a successful tradesman, and he and his family live in a commercial part of London near his warehouses. The Gardiners are both intelligent and well bred, and Mrs. Gardiner is a particular favorite with Jane and Elizabeth. She discusses recent events with Elizabeth, and she also later advises her to be prudent in her developing relationship with Wickham. The Gardiners invite Jane to come back to London with them when they leave, and she gladly accepts, hoping that she may be able to see something of the Bingleys while she is there, despite the fact that they will be in a more fashionable part of the city. Charlotte Lucas marries Mr. Collins and then departs for Kent but not before securing a promise from Elizabeth that she will come to visit her at Hunsford Parsonage along with Charlotte's father and sister in March. In London, Jane sees nothing of Mr. Bingley, and, though she sees

Caroline Bingley twice, she is clearly snubbed by her and finally realizes that Elizabeth has been right in suspecting her of duplicity. Jane's hopes of renewing her intimacy with Bingley are further dashed when she gathers that he may now give up Netherfield altogether.

Elizabeth, too, now experiences disillusion when she finds that Wickham has suddenly turned his attentions elsewhere—to a Miss King, who has recently inherited a fortune of £10,000. However, she still does not doubt what he has told her about Mr. Darcy, and she is surprisingly lenient in her attitude toward his evidently mercenary behavior in the light of her strong censure of Charlotte Lucas for a similar thing. But Elizabeth is not strongly affected by Wickham's inconstancy, and it rather confirms to her that she never really had any strong feelings for him. (As we hear later on, Wickham does not succeed in his pursuit of Miss King, and she is eventually sent away to live with an uncle in Liverpool.)

On the way to visit Charlotte Lucas in Kent, Elizabeth spends a night with Jane and the Gardiners. Before she leaves again, she is invited to accompany the Gardiners on their summer tour, during which they hope to go as far as the Lake District. At Hunsford, Elizabeth is greeted warmly by Charlotte and "with ostentatious formality" by Mr. Collins, who seems eager to show off all the things she might have had if she had married him. Elizabeth is unimpressed by his pompous show, of course, but when shown around the house by Charlotte, she is genuinely impressed—and surprised—to see just how contented Charlotte seems to be in the comfort of her own home. Hunsford Parsonage lies just on the edge of Rosings Park and about half a mile away from Rosings House, the home of Mr. Collins' self-important and overbearing patroness, Lady Catherine de Bourgh. The Lucas party are invited to dinner at Rosings on the third day of their visit, and Mr. Collins is almost beside himself with the excitement of so soon being able to display "the grandeur of his patroness to his wondering visitors." At Rosings, Sir William Lucas and Maria Lucas are, indeed, overwhelmed by the grandeur of the house and overawed by the haughtiness of Lady Catherine, but Elizabeth refuses to be impressed merely by rank and money, and she remains sufficiently composed to be able to cast a cool, critical eye on her surroundings and on Lady Catherine and her sickly daughter, Miss de Bourgh. Lady Catherine exhibits all the characteristics Elizabeth has been led to expect from her: she is arrogant, vain, domineering, and absolutely status-bound. She dictates the conversation, talks down to everybody, and is shocked to find that Elizabeth has the temerity to speak openly and boldly to her. Miss de Bourgh is little more than a shadow of her mother, physically emaciated, passive in manner, and almost wholly silent.

During Elizabeth's visit to Hunsford, Mr. Darcy arrives to stay with his aunt, along with his cousin, Colonel Fitzwilliam. On the occasions that Darcy is in the same company with Elizabeth, they renew their verbal fencing with one another, but he is now clearly more attentive to Elizabeth and evidently more appreciative of her charms. She also notes that he seems to have no interest at all in Miss de Bourgh. Interestingly, when at Rosings, there is something of a reversal in their positions, for while Elizabeth was previously embarrassed by her mother's vulgarity, he is now embarrassed by his ill-mannered and (in different ways) equally vulgar aunt. Darcy and Fitzwilliam often call at the parsonage, and although Darcy remains a little aloof, it seems clear to us that he is in love with Elizabeth. For her part, she still resents his earlier treatment of her and continues to view him with suspicion in relation to his part in Bingley's sudden departure from Netherfield.

Elizabeth develops a lively friendship with Colonel Fitzwilliam, and they talk candidly with one another. On one occasion, the subject turns to marriage, and Fitzwilliam inadvertently confirms Elizabeth's suspicions that Mr. Darcy was responsible for the rupture in Jane's relationship with Bingley when he tells her that Darcy has recently saved a friend, possibly Bingley, from an imprudent marriage. Later the same day, Elizabeth is alone at the parsonage brooding over Jane's unhappiness and Darcy's partial responsibility for it when Mr. Darcy himself arrives. He is in an agitated state but eventually blurts out his feelings of love for her and asks her to marry him. She is too shocked to respond at first, and so, taking this as a good sign, he continues to explain, at length, how he has struggled with his pride to overcome "his sense of her inferiority" and how he has finally decided to sacrifice his principles to his passion by asking for her hand. Elizabeth becomes increasingly angry as she hears herself being effectively demeaned by Darcy's class snobbery, and as she realizes his arrogant presumption in assuming that she will automatically accept him. She composes herself, however, and when he has finished she coolly but clearly refuses him. He is taken aback by this and presses her to explain a little, and she then takes the opportunity to berate him for his harsh judgment of her sister, his high-handed interference in Bingley's affairs, his ill treatment of Wickham, and his patronizing opinion of herself.

Next day, Elizabeth receives a letter from Darcy in which he defends himself against two of the accusations she has leveled at him. First, his letter explains that his reason for separating Jane and Bingley was mainly that, judging from Jane's composed and serene air at the Netherfield ball, he believed that her affections had not been as deeply or truly engaged as Bingley's had for her. He acknowledges, however, that he may have been mistaken in this belief. As an additional consideration, he admits, he was also concerned about the Bennet family's lack of consequence and, most important, about their lack of "propriety," as manifested consistently by Mrs. Bennet, Kitty, Lydia, and Mary and occasionally even by Mr. Bennet—but he specifically excludes Jane and Elizabeth from this charge. Second, his letter explains the true history of his relationship with George Wickham. We learn that Wickham is the son of the former trusted and valued steward of the Darcys' Pemberley estate in Derbyshire. The elder Darcy had come to bestow favors on him, partly in gratitude for his father's efficient administration of the estate and partly because of his own surface charms. In this way, he had received a gentleman's education and the promise of a church living on the estate if he were to fulfill his stated ambition of becoming a clergyman. Also, on the death of Mr. Darcy (some five years ago), he was left a legacy of £1,000 and an informal promise of Fitzwilliam Darcy's good offices. But Wickham was not at all the character he had presented himself as to the elder Mr. Darcy, as the younger Darcy knew only too well; he was, in fact, an unscrupulous flatterer and wastrel with "vicious propensities." No sooner had his patron died, than he reverted to type: he threw up the intention of going into the church and, through Darcy, exchanged the promise of the Pemberley living for a sum of money. This he then spent in "a life of idleness and dissipation." When all the money was gone, he asked Darcy to present him with the Pemberley living after all, but Darcy steadfastly refused to give him any further help, and Wickham has resented him for this ever since. In the previous summer, moreover, Wickham had tried to gain access to the Darcy fortune by other means, by attempting to elope with Darcy's fifteen-year-old sister, Georgiana. This would have provided him with sweet revenge, too, of course, but luckily Darcy had foiled the attempt at the last minute.

At first, Elizabeth is reluctant to accept Darcy's explanations, but the more she thinks about the details of what he has said, the more she becomes convinced of his sincerity and truthfulness. As she does so, she also starts to question her own attitude toward him. She thinks now that she was perhaps too hard on him in responding to his marriage proposal and that she has been too prejudiced against him generally. Elizabeth's feelings for Darcy remain confused, but she is now inclined to think better and more warmly of him, and this is an important step in the overall development of her feelings for him.

It is now May, and Elizabeth and Jane both return to Longbourn. Elizabeth tells Jane about Darcy's proposal and about the parts of his letter dealing with Wickham. As Wickham's regiment is shortly leaving Meryton for Brighton, they decide not to try to expose his true character to anyone else—not that anyone in Meryton would now easily believe Darcy to be good and Wickham bad. (If Jane and Elizabeth had told the truth about Wickham at this point, of course, events may have turned out differently later on.)

Lydia Bennet is delighted to find herself invited to Brighton by Mrs. Forster, the recently married wife of Colonel Forster, the commander of Wickham's militia regiment. Elizabeth argues with her father that he should not allow the sixteen-year-old Lydia to go alone under the dubious protection of Mrs. Forster, who is not dissimilar to Lydia in age and temperament. Aware of the damage to the family reputation that Lydia's flirtatious behavior has already caused, Elizabeth believes that, in Brighton, with no effective check to her conduct, Lydia will become "the most determined flirt that ever made herself and her family ridiculous." While essentially agreeing with Elizabeth, Mr. Bennet complacently rationalizes the situation and justifies himself in not taking a firmer line with Lydia. He allows her to go to Brighton, and among the various half-convincing reasons he gives for his decision, one suspects that the decisive one for him is that "We shall have no peace at Longbourn if Lydia does not go."

The time for Elizabeth's summer tour with the Gardiners now approaches, and Elizabeth hears that the trip has had to be curtailed because of Mr. Gardiner's business commitments. They will not now be able to go as far as the Lake District and will tour Derbyshire instead. It is around mid-July when they finally set off on the tour. In Derbyshire, they find themselves in the vicinity of Pemberley, Darcy's estate. The Gardiners suggest visiting the house and grounds, and Elizabeth agrees to this when she discovers that Darcy is not in residence. Volume 3 of the novel opens with Elizabeth and the Gardiners making their way to Pemberley and receiving their first sight of the impressive estate. Elizabeth is delighted by what she sees and "at that moment she felt, that to be mistress of Pemberley might be something!" The guided tour of the house is conducted by the housekeeper, Mrs. Reynolds. She has known Darcy from birth, and as they go over the house, she casually reveals facets of Darcy's character that Elizabeth has been unaware of. In particular, Elizabeth is surprised to hear Mrs. Reynolds' high praise for his generous, charitable, and warmhearted nature and for his responsible stewardship of the estate. Elizabeth warms to Darcy even more now, and when she contemplates a portrait of him in the picture gallery, she feels "a more gentle sensation towards the original, than she had ever felt in the height of their acquaintance." Mr. Darcy unexpectedly returns to Pemberley during their visit, and Elizabeth is understandably embarrassed at being found there. However, Darcy behaves extremely courteously to her and to the Gardiners, and Elizabeth marvels at the change in his manner from when she knew him before. It is a consolation to Elizabeth, though, that she can now introduce him to at least two of her relatives who are cultured and intelligent, and she is extremely pleased to see how well they all relate to one another. Darcy invites Mr. Gardiner to visit Pemberley again to fish in the lake and later brings his sister and Bingley to visit Elizabeth and the Gardiners at their lodgings at a local inn. Elizabeth is relieved to find Georgiana Darcy amiable and unassuming and not at all proud, as rumor would have it; and she is relieved also to find that there is no particular attachment between Miss Darcy and Bingley. Bingley asks after Elizabeth's family, and she is pleased to detect distinct traces of his former regard for Jane in some of his inquiries.

The Gardiner party are invited to dinner at Pemberley, but before this event can take place, Elizabeth receives two disturbing letters from Jane. The first breaks the news that Wickham and Lydia have eloped together from Brighton, apparently with the intention of going to Scotland to be married. The second corrects the latter impression, following information given by Mr. Denny and Colonel Forster, and informs Elizabeth that the errant couple have not gone to Scotland after all but to London and that Wickham seems to have no intention whatsoever of marrying Lydia. Darcy arrives at the inn just as Elizabeth finishes reading the letters. She confides in him, reproaching herself for not exposing what she knew of Wickham's character to the rest of her family. Darcy says little but seems to be deep in thought. Elizabeth imagines that he must once more be thinking of how disreputable her family is and of how impossible it would be for him to become associated with it. Ironically, "when all love must be vain," she realizes for the first time that "she could have loved him." Darcy says a few comforting words and then departs, leaving Elizabeth ruefully to wonder if she will ever see him again.

Elizabeth and the Gardiners now make a rapid return to Hertfordshire. Mrs. Gardiner stays at Longbourn to console Mrs. Bennet and her daughters, while Mr. Gardiner follows Mr. Bennet to London to assist him in his search for Lydia and Wickham. Information about Wickham's profligate character is now received from all quarters. Colonel Forster reports on the vast debts he has left behind him in Brighton, while Mrs. Phillips cannot visit Longbourn without some fresh story from Meryton about Wickham's "extravagance or irregularity." Mr. Collins sends a somewhat gloating letter, ostensibly of condolence, advising Mr. Bennet to renounce Lydia and smugly pointing out that the other girls are now unlikely to attract offers of marriage. Mr. Bennet returns from London without having found Lydia. He regrets now having allowed her to go to Brighton, but he still shows little real determination to engage actively in the management and guidance of his daughters.

Mr. Gardiner writes to say that Lydia and Wickham have finally been found, and a marriage between the two arranged. It is obvious that Wickham has received a substantial bribe, presumably from the pocket of Mr. Gardiner, to the concern of Elizabeth and her father. Her mother has no such concerns and stupidly rejoices to have a daughter married at last! Elizabeth, meanwhile, reflects on her ruined chances of marriage.

After the wedding has taken place, Lydia and Wickham return to Longbourn to visit the family. Their behavior is entirely tactless, and Lydia, who shows no signs of remorse whatsoever, boasts of her newfound consequence as the first of the sisters to marry. She insists on describing the wedding, and in the process she lets slip that Mr. Darcy was present at the ceremony. Considerably surprised by this information, Elizabeth writes to her aunt seeking more information. In her response Mrs. Gardiner explains that Mr. Darcy had tracked down Wickham and had persuaded him to marry Lydia by offering to pay his debts and to provide a cash sum with which to start married life. Darcy and Mr. Gardiner had then arranged the wedding together. Mrs. Gardiner tells her niece that she believes Darcy behaved so generously and gallantly for Elizabeth's sake.

Soon after, both Mr. Bingley and Mr. Darcy return to Netherfield and visit Longbourn at the first opportunity. Elizabeth, only too aware of her family's obligation to Darcy, is ashamed to hear her mother boast about Lydia's marriage in front of him and then literally to add insult to injury by purposely slighting him. Darcy remains largely silent and grave, and Elizabeth is unsure of his present attitude to her. On the other hand, a renewal of Mr. Bingley's courtship of Jane soon ensues, and this leads quickly to their engagement. Mrs. Bennet's joy is boundless at the prospect of having two married daughters.

Lady Catherine de Bourgh, having heard rumors of an imminent engagement between Elizabeth and Darcy, arrives at Longbourn to insist that Elizabeth should make a promise *not* to become engaged to Darcy. Elizabeth is indignant at Lady Catherine's presumption and insolence, and she responds with great verve, categorically refusing to make any such commitment. When Lady Catherine in exasperation tells Darcy about all this, she has the opposite effect she intends, as he is simply given fresh hope that Elizabeth may look favorably on a second proposal from him. When the couple meet again, his declaration of love is as passionate as it was before, but without the pride. This time, Elizabeth, no longer prejudiced against him, responds in kind and passionately describes the changes that have taken place in her feelings for him. Darcy's renewed proposal is thus accepted, and they agree to marry. News of their engagement comes as a surprise to all the Bennets, but Mrs. Bennet in particular finds no difficulty in rapidly altering her opinion of Mr. Darcy.

Main Characters: Mr. and Mrs. Bennet, Elizabeth Bennet, Jane Bennet, Kitty Bennet, Lydia Bennet, Mary Bennet, Mr. Bingley, Louisa Bingley (Hurst), Caroline Bingley, Mr. Collins, Mr. Fitzwilliam Darcy, Georgiana Darcy, Lady Catherine de Bourgh, Anne de Bourgh, Colonel Fitzwilliam, Mr. and Mrs. Gardiner, Charlotte Lucas, Mr. Wickham.

Minor Characters: Mrs. Annesley, Captain Carter, Mr. Chamberlayne, Old Mr. Darcy, Lady Anne Darcy, Dawson, Mr. Denny, Colonel and Mrs. Forster, William Goulding, Miss Grantley, Haggerston, the Harringtons, Mrs. Hill, Mr. Hurst, Mrs. Jenkinson, two servants called John, Mr. Jones, Miss Mary King, Mrs. Long, Sir William and Lady Lucas, Maria Lucas, Lady Metcalfe, Colonel Millar, Mr. Morris, Mrs. Nicholls, Mr. and Mrs. Phillips, Miss Pope, Mr. Pratt, Richard, Mrs. Reynolds, Mr. Robinson, Sarah, Sally, Mr. Stone, Miss Watson, the Miss Webbs, Old Mr. Wickham, Mrs. Younge.

Volume and chapter divisions (numbers in brackets are for editions with continuous chapter numbers): Volume 1: Chapters 1–23, volume 2: Chapters 1–19 [24–42], volume 3: Chapters 1–19 [43–61].

See: Allen 1985, Beasley 1973–1974, Bevan 1987b, *Birtwistle and Conklin 1995, Bloom 1987c*, Boles 1981, *Booth 1963*, Brower 1951, Burlin 1983, Carr 1991, Caywood 1984, *Clark 1994*, Crundell 1941, *Dalglish 1962*, Derry 1991, *Folsom 1993*, Fraiman 1989, Gibson 1990, Giles 1988, Goodwin 1990, *Gray 1966*, Halperin 1989a, Harris 1991, Heldman 1990, Hennelly 1983, Heydt 1985, Hirsch 1992, Horwitz 1993, Ives 1987, Kelly 1984, Kliger 1946–1947, Knuth 1989a, Koppel 1989, Lacour 1992, Lellis and Bolton 1981, Litz 1979, *Lobb 1962*, Maugham 1948, McAleer 1989a, McMaster 1996, Michaelson 1990, Moler 1983b, c, *Moler 1989*, Neumann 1986, *O'Brien 1975*, Olsen 1986, Parker 1990, *Petersen 1979*, Rossdale 1980, *Rubinstein 1969*, Satz 1983, Schneider 1993, J. Smith 1993, *Southam 1976b*, Stovel 1987a, 1989, Tempest 1993, Turan 1989, Wiesenfarth 1984, 1989, Wingard 1989, Zelicovici 1985.

Prince, Miss (*Emma* Ch.4; I:4:29). A teacher at Mrs. Goddard's school.

Purvis, Mr. (*The Watsons, Minor Works* 316). Elizabeth Watson's former suitor and a close friend of Robert Watson. Elizabeth had expected to marry Mr. Purvis, but her younger sister, Penelope, had separated them in trying to win him for herself, and he had then married someone else entirely.

R

Ravenshaw, Lord (*Mansfield Park* Ch.13; I:13:121). Mr. Yates arrives at Mansfield Park from a visit to Ecclesford, the seat of the Right Hon. Lord Ravenshaw in Cornwall. The house party there, which had been on the verge of mounting a private production of *Lovers' Vows*, was abruptly ended on the news of the death of Lord Ravenshaw's grandmother. Lord Ravenshaw was going to act the part of Baron Wildenheim, though Mr. Yates thought it remarkable "that he should have so mistaken his powers," being "a little man, with a weak voice, always hoarse after the first ten minutes!"

Rebecca (*Mansfield Park* Ch.38; III:7:377). Mrs. Price's troublesome servant who, judging from all the complaints made about her, seems to Fanny to be "without a single recommendation."

Repton, Mr. Humphrey (*Mansfield Park* Ch.6; I:6:53). A real person (1752–1818) and renowned landscape gardener of the period. Mr. Rushworth considers hiring him to "improve" the grounds at Sotherton Court after having seen the impressive alterations carried out by him at Mr. Smith's Compton estate—"a mere nothing before Repton took it in hand." Repton's terms are five guineas a day, according to Rushworth.

Reynolds, Mrs. (*Pride and Prejudice* Ch.43; III:1:246–51). The friendly and dignified old housekeeper at Pemberley who shows Elizabeth Bennet and the Gardiners around the house and who surprises Elizabeth by her warm praise of Mr. Darcy.

Richard (*Pride and Prejudice* Ch.14; I:14:68). A servant who is apparently to be dismissed by Mr. Phillips and taken on by Colonel Forster.

Richard, Cousin (*Sense and Sensibility* Ch.38; III:2: 272). A cousin of the Miss Steeles.

Richards, Rev. Dr. (*The Watsons, Minor Works* 344). One of the clergymen at the religious visitation that Mr. Watson attends.

Richardson, Miss (*Emma* Ch.4; I:4:29). A teacher at Mrs. Goddard's school.

Richardsons, the (*Sense and Sensibility* Ch.38; III:2:274). Acquaintances of the Steeles who take Anne Steele to Kensington Gardens. She tells Elinor, whom she meets there, that they are "very genteel" and rich enough to keep their own coach.

Robert (*Mansfield Park* Ch.23; II:5:212). Robert is the Grants' nurseryman at Mansfield parsonage. Mrs. Grant complains about him for leaving her plants outside overnight when there may be a sudden frost at any time.

Robert—, Sir (*Sense and Sensibility* Ch.36; II:14). Uncle of Edward and Robert Ferrars.

Robinson (*Northanger Abbey* Ch.26; II:11:214). When Catherine Morland admires a little cottage on the grounds of Henry Tilney's Woodston Parsonage, General Tilney tells his son to speak to Robinson about it, to ensure it stays there. Robinson, therefore, would seem to be a groundsman of some sort, possibly the head gardener.

Robinson, Mr. (*Persuasion* Ch.7; I:7:54–55). The apothecary at Uppercross who treats Charles Musgrove for his dislocated collarbone.

Robinson, Mr. (*Pride and Prejudice* Ch.5; I:5:19). A gentleman at the Meryton assembly who is overheard to ask Mr. Bingley who he thinks is the prettiest woman in the room; he receives the reply, "the eldest Miss Bennet beyond a doubt."

Rooke, Nurse (*Persuasion* Chs.17, 21; II:5:155–56; II:9:205–8). Mrs. Smith's erstwhile nurse and present friend and confidante. As the sister of Mrs. Smith's landlady at Westgate Buildings, Nurse Rooke was on hand to take care of Mrs. Smith when she first arrived in Bath and fell ill. Nurse Rooke had taught Mrs. Smith how to knit, and now Mrs. Smith makes a little money by selling knitted items, through Nurse Rooke, to any of the latter's patients who can afford to buy them. According to Mrs. Smith, Nurse Rooke is a "shrewd, intelligent, sensible" woman who, because of her work, has a good understanding of human nature. But she is also clearly a gossip who has no professional qualms about preserving the confidentiality of her patients, as she regularly reports on their private lives and discussions to Mrs. Smith. This, then, is the source of Mrs. Smith's information about Mr. Elliot's machinations regarding his uncle and cousins, as Nurse Rooke is attending the wife of Mr. Elliot's close friend, Colonel Wallis, during the time of the main action at Bath.

Rose, Mr. (*Sense and Sensibility* Ch.21; I:21:123). A clerk in Exeter known to the Miss Steeles.

Ross, Flora. *See* Stornaway, Lady.

Ross, Janet. *See* Fraser, Mrs.

Rushworth, Mr. (deceased) (*Mansfield Park* Ch.9; I:9:86). The father of James and referred to only briefly by Mrs. Rushworth when showing the Mansfield Park party around the old family chapel at Sotherton Court. Family prayers had been held there regularly since James II's time, but the late Mr. Rushworth, she tells them, ended this tradition. This "improvement," as Austen ironically has Mary Crawford call it, is of a piece with James Rushworth's plans for "improving" the grounds of Sotherton, in that both father and son seem thoughtlessly to destroy venerable aspects of their family's estate without adding anything of value to it.

Rushworth, Mr. James (*Mansfield Park* Ch.4; I:4:38). Mr. Rushworth has recently inherited Sotherton Court, ten miles from Mansfield Park and "one of the largest estates and finest places in the country." It soon becomes clear that the "heavy" in the initial description of him as "a heavy young man," refers as much to the laborious workings of his wit as to his physique, and though the narrator, with typical ironic understatement, tells us that he has "not more than common sense," Edmund is much blunter in wryly declaring, "If this man had not twelve thousand a year, he would be a very stupid fellow." He falls for the beautiful but inconstant Maria Bertram, and they become engaged. When the urbane, witty, and charming Henry Crawford appears on the scene, however, Mr. Rushworth pales into insignificance for Maria, and it becomes quite evident that she has agreed to marry him only for his money and status. During the preparations and rehearsals for *Lovers' Vows*, Mr. Rushworth's lumbering and lackluster personality is sharply exposed by his inability to learn his lines, by his childish delight in the fine costumes, and by his poor acting.

Rushworth, Mrs. (*Mansfield Park* Ch.4; I:4:39). Mr. Rushworth's mother is a well-meaning, dignified, slightly pompous old lady. She takes great pride in Sotherton Court, and she has made great efforts to learn all about its history so that she can show guests around the house with an informed commentary.

Rushworth, Mrs. Maria (*Mansfield Park*). *See* Bertram, Maria.

Russell, Lady (*Persuasion* Ch.1; I:1:5). The widow of Sir Henry Russell and a
near neighbor and old acquaintance of the Elliot family. She had been an intimate friend of the late Lady Elliot, and, after the latter's death, she became the
close friend and mentor of her goddaughter, Anne Elliot, whom she recognizes
as the only one of the Elliot daughters to have inherited their mother's qualities
of good sense and judgment. Lady Russell herself is generally admired and
respected for being a well-judging, rational, refined, and principled woman,
"most correct in her conduct, strict in her notions of decorum, and with manners
that were held a standard of good-breeding." However, if we are alert to Jane
Austen's fine discriminations, especially between morals and manners, the latter
quotation's stress on outward decorum should give us pause for thought. Indeed,
we soon realize, not that Lady Russell has a flawed morality as such, but that
her judgment can become clouded by externals, specifically by her prejudices
on the side of "ancestry . . . rank and consequence." We are also told that her
judgment is "sound" rather than "quick." Thus, through the figure of Lady
Russell, we are already carefully prepared for the novel's central concern with
questions of judgment and discrimination when we hear of how, eight years
ago, she had "persuaded" Anne Elliot to break off her engagement to Captain
Wentworth because of his lack of wealth and social consequence. This prudent
but snobbish act of persuasion sets the novel's main plot in motion, of course,
but its ethical implications reverberate through to the end of the novel as, along
with Anne Elliot, we try to assess the relative rights and wrongs of Lady Russell's advice, as well as the relative responsibilities of adviser and advised in
the final decision that Anne actually took. The element of social snobbery in
Lady Russell's character and its influence over her judgment are manifested
again later in the novel when she badly misjudges Mr. Elliot because of his
surface charms and status—though by then Anne has learned that "she and her
excellent friend could sometimes think differently" (Ch.16; II:4:146–47). At the
same time, however, it is still the case that Anne does consider Lady Russell as
an "excellent friend" and perhaps the only one of her acquaintance who genuinely cares for her welfare and happiness. Anne acknowledges that, like a
mother, Lady Russell's advice to her is always disinterested and well intended,
and she never seriously blames or criticizes her friend for her misjudgments—
therefore, the reader, too, is never seriously alienated from Lady Russell. Moreover, at the end of the novel, Lady Russell demonstrates her integrity—and the
fact that "she loved Anne better than . . . her own abilities"— when she admits
her mistakes and fully accepts Captain Wentworth as a type of son-in-law.

Russell, Sir Henry (deceased) (*Persuasion* Chs.2, 17; I:2:11; II:5:158). The late
husband of Lady Russell. His title derives from his being a knight rather than
a baronet like Sir Walter, hence Lady Russell's deference to the latter.

S

Sally (*Mansfield Park* Ch.38; III:7:383). A girl of "inferior appearance," she is the lower of the two servants in the Price household in Portsmouth.

Sally (*Pride and Prejudice* Ch.47; III:5:292). A maidservant at Mrs. Forster's house in Brighton. When Lydia writes to Mrs. Forster after leaving with Wickham, she asks her to tell Sally to mend one of her muslin gowns before packing up her clothes.

Sally (*Sense and Sensibility* Ch.47; III:11:354). One of the maidservants at Barton Park. Because the Dashwoods' manservant, Thomas, has a message to deliver from Sally at the New London Inn at Exeter, he sees the newlywed Lucy Steele there and is able to report on her marriage to Mr. Ferrars when he returns to Barton Cottage.

Sam (*Sanditon, Minor Works* 407). An old servant at Sanditon hotel who helps the Parker "invalids" with their luggage.

Sandersons, the (*Sense and Sensibility* Ch.30; II:8:192). London friends of Mrs. Jennings.

Sanditon. Jane Austen began this unfinished novel on 17 January 1817 and abandoned it after twelve chapters and about 24,000 words on 18 March of the same year, owing to the illness that eventually killed her. The novel was posthumously titled by the Austen family, though Jane Austen's intended title seems to have been "The Brothers."

Very different from her major novels, it in some ways harks back to an earlier comic-burlesque strain in the author's development in its blending of literary satire (on sentimental fiction, melodramatic and "sublime" Romanticism, the discursive novel of ideas) with social satire (on business speculation, love of money, hypochondria, quack medicines, the rise of the seaside resort); and in its somewhat schematic characterization and disposition of characters. But *Sanditon* also suggestively looks forward to the Victorian novel in its broader social focus and in its concern with *types* of characters set against *trends* of social change (there are also distinct hints of Dickens in some of the novel's eccentric characters and comic episodes).

The opening scene has two genteel travelers on their way from London to the Sussex coast betweeen Hastings and Eastbourne. They have taken a detour off the high road for some business reason; the road rapidly deteriorates in quality, and, after passing the only major house in the vicinity, the surface becomes so poor that the carriage overturns, throwing the gentleman and lady out. They are not seriously hurt, but the man sprains his ankle in the course of extricating himself and his wife from the fallen carriage. Help is soon at hand as a group of haymakers from a field next to the house come over to see what has happened. They are led by the gentleman of the house, Mr. Heywood, who immediately offers the travelers assistance and hospitality. The injured man thanks Mr. Heywood but seems keen to have a surgeon sent for; he has seen a cottage a little way off and makes clear that he believes a surgeon lives there. Mr. Heywood, who has lived in this village, Willingden, for all his fifty-seven years, assures the traveler that there is no surgeon either at the cottage or anywhere else nearby. He is somewhat taken aback by the traveler's insistence that there is, indeed, a surgeon at Willingden. To prove the point, the traveler shows him an advertisement on a newspaper clipping clearly indicating a Willingden surgeon. When Mr. Heywood looks over the advertisement, however, the confusion is explained as he quickly sees that it refers not to this Willingden, but to Great Willingden, seven miles away. The traveler acknowledges his blunder, and he and his wife accept Mr. Heywood's offer of hospitality. He only now introduces himself as Mr. Parker, a landowner from the village of Sanditon on the nearby coast. It later emerges that he had diverted to Willingden in order to follow up the surgeon's advertisement in the hope of being able to persuade him to move to Sanditon. Mr. Parker is something of a property speculator, working to promote Sanditon as a fashionable seaside resort, and he believes his cause will be aided if he can establish a resident surgeon in the village.

This opening to Jane Austen's last work is striking for a number of reasons. Unlike any of her major novels, the initial focus is not on a scene-setting personal or family history of a named protagonist or group of protagonists; the main novels typically prepare us for the action to come by a type of narratorial prologue that always announces the family name of the principal characters on the first page, whereas here, unusually, the initial focus is on an action already in progress, and no one is named until after the dramatic event of the accident. (*Pride and Prejudice* is the most similar to *Sanditon* in this respect, as it, too, could be said to start in the middle of a developing action, in the sense that dialogue is action; but the Bennets are named immediately, and the dialogue between Mr. and Mrs. Bennet at the start is still, to some extent, a prologue to later events rather than an event in its own right.) There is also no initial stability of location, no sense of a fixed, rooted home and way of life, as we have in all Austen's previous novels (*Persuasion* is clearly a precursor of *Sanditon* in its focus on the Elliots' forced removal from Kellynch and, through this, on postwar economic challenges to landed society); the unknown travelers are, precisely, away from home, on the move—and, in fact, *lost*, confused by the existence of two places with the same name within a few miles of each other. Typically modern concerns with questions of identity and belonging are signaled here, but also the sense that this novel is going to be about society at large, seen from a detached perspective, rather than (as with Austen's previous novels) about the manners and mores of one fixed and tightly knit community seen from within. This suggestion of a more sociological approach is reinforced when we learn of Thomas Parker's business at Willingden. For, though in one sense lost, in another sense he is merely exploring, adventuring; as a type of semicomic pioneer of entrepreneurial speculation, his spirited, if risky, departure from the high road is suggestive of his more general departure from tradition and of his search for new ways of doing things—it is symbolic, perhaps, of his search for a shortcut to the future, the economic future he himself projects for Sanditon and the economic future that was actually in the offing for nineteenth-century Britain. But speculation *is* risky, of course (as Jane Austen knew only too well from the experiences of her brother, Henry, whose banking business had collapsed just nine months before she started *Sanditon*), and Thomas Parker's inauspicious accident is also suggestive of the financial crash he may yet have suffered if the novel had been completed. Such a symbolic reading of this scene may seem overingenious, but, regardless of how we actually interpret it, it does appear to be designed to be read symbolically, foregrounded as it is by being placed at the start of the novel and with its anonymous figures, unfixed location, and sharply realized action. There are, of course, examples of symbolism to be found in Austen's other novels (most notably, perhaps, in *Persuasion*), but never in quite this form or in such a pronounced way, and the scene provokes its own speculations about the new directions Austen may have taken with her writing if she had lived longer.

Mr. Parker's sprained ankle turns out to be quite serious, and the Parkers stay with the Heywoods for two weeks, and the two families come to know and like each other. We hear more—a lot more—about Mr. Parker's hopes for Sanditon, for, on the subject of that place, he is "a complete Enthusiast." Sanditon had not long ago been only a quiet village, but Mr. Parker and another local landowner had suddenly recognized its potential as a profitable speculation and had acted to develop it into a fashionable resort. It had by now become reasonably well established, but Thomas Parker has come to live for its increased growth and prosperity, and he never tires of extolling its virtues and of encouraging people to visit. He is fond of Mrs. Parker and their four children, but Sanditon is like a second wife and set of children to him, almost as dear and "certainly more engrossing.'' He tries hard to persuade his new friends, the Heywoods, to come to stay with him there, but Mr. and Mrs. Heywood are homely folk of settled habits and rarely leave Willingden; having brought up fourteen children, they have become used to a quiet and prudent lifestyle at home. However, they are only too happy for their children to make visits away from home, and it is agreed, at the end of the Parkers' sojourn with the Heywoods, that one of the latter's daughters, twenty-two-year-old Charlotte, will accompany the Parkers back to Sanditon.

On the journey to Sanditon, Mr. Parker completes such of the social picture of the place as Charlotte has not yet heard about, and in particular he tells her of his principal partner in speculation, the rich Lady Denham of Sanditon House. With her title and fortune, she is the ''great Lady'' of the neighborhood, and, because she is elderly (seventy years of age), her various relatives are now apparently vying for her favor in order to ensure their share of whatever legacy she eventually leaves. Although born to wealth herself (though not to education, Mr. Parker bluntly tells Charlotte), Lady Denham has clearly done her own fair share of fortune hunting through her two marriages: from her first, much older husband, Mr. Hollis, she had inherited extensive properties, including a large part of the parish of Sanditon; from her second, Sir Harry Denham, she had acquired her title. Mr. Parker goes on to give his own assessment of the current form of the various contenders for her wealth, and once again it may be noted how much has changed in Jane Austen's style here, for although money matters loom large in all her novels, and all contain ironic reflections on avarice and materialism, never have these things been talked of in quite such an open and direct manner as Mr. Parker talks of them. The initial favorite in what we might call the ''Lady Denham stakes'' was the present Denham baronet, Sir Edward Denham, the nephew of Sir Harry and an enthusiastic supporter of the ''improvement'' of Sanditon. The rank outsiders are the relatives of Mr. Hollis, who seem to have expressed their suspicions of the then-Mrs. Hollis at the time of their relative's death. Somewhere in between these two sets is an upcoming poor relation from Lady Denham's own family, the Breretons. Following a trip to London, where she had been kindly treated by some cousins, Lady Denham had invited a dependent niece, the young and beautiful Clara Brereton, to spend the winter with her at Sanditon, and, with her mild manners and gentle good sense, Clara had soon become a general favorite with her aunt and with everyone else in the village, so that at the end of the originally agreed six months, she had been allowed to stay on as Lady Denham's companion.

Two miles or so from Sanditon proper, the carriage passes the Parkers' old family home nestling snugly in a valley and surrounded by a mature garden, orchard, and meadows. Charlotte immediately admires it and compares it to her own family home at Willingden. The house is where Mr. Parker and all his siblings were brought up, and, until the recent building of his new home, Trafalgar House, it is where he and Mrs. Parker started their married life and brought up the first three of their four children. Mrs. Parker looks back fondly at the cozy old house and seems rather to regret having had to move to the more exposed position of their new dwelling on the cliff tops at Sanditon proper. But Mr. Parker soon dispels any sense of nostalgia with his enthusiasm for the modern conveniences of their new position. As they pass through the village of Sanditon, Mr. Parker is overjoyed to see that one of the shops, William Heeley's, has fashionable blue shoes and nankeen boots displayed in the window, as this demonstrates that his development plans for Sanditon are having an effect. However, it also becomes clear that his development plans do not actually concern the old village as such, for it is only on the hill and down above the village that he has started to build new houses and encourage fashionable shops and amenities. Here, too, on the highest ground on the down and about a hundred yards from the cliff edge, Trafalgar House stands, "a light elegant Building, standing in a small lawn with a very young plantation round it." The house overlooks a row of new houses known as the Terrace, and these have a broad walk in front of them "aspiring to be the Mall of the Place." The best milliner's shop, the circulating library, the hotel and billiard room, and the access to the beach and bathing machines are all on or near to the Terrace, and "this was therefore the favourite spot for Beauty & Fashion."

Mr. Parker has already mentioned his brothers and sisters in passing. Diana and Susan have been described as invalids (and we shortly hear of another invalid in the family, the youngest brother, Arthur, though it soon becomes clear that all three are really only hypochondriacs); while Sidney Parker has been referred to as a witty, worldly, and dashing young man with an independent fortune inherited separately from Mr. Parker's own. Before dinner, Mr. Parker finds that he has not had an expected letter from Sidney, but he has had one from his sister Diana. He reads this aloud to give Charlotte a sense of Diana's good character, but, in fact, it merely demonstrates the extent to which she is obsessed with matters of ill health, and this now introduces the other major motif in the novel apart from those of speculation and money—hypochondria. Diana herself has been suffering from a severe attack of "Spasmodic Bile," she reports; Arthur is tolerably well but liverish, and Susan has had a headache, for which she has had six leeches a day for ten days; finding that these were ineffective, she had three teeth drawn, which cured the headache but deranged her nerves! Charlotte is horrified at these extreme measures, and, though Mr. Parker is keen to praise the fortitude of his sisters, he has to agree with his wife when she echoes Charlotte's response and says that the Miss Parkers carry their self-doctoring too far at times, probably inducing their imagined illnesses in the process. Mr. and Mrs. Parker also agree in regretting that the twenty-one-year-old Arthur has succumbed to the influence of his sisters and now considers himself too sickly to pursue any profession. Also in Diana's letter is the news that, although she and her fellow invalids are too delicate to travel and will therefore not be coming to Sanditon themselves this summer, she has managed, through a series of intermediaries, to persuade two large families to come, one a rich family from Surrey who had made their fortune in the West Indies and

another made up of a girls' boarding school from Camberwell. This news delights Mr. Parker, of course, and reinforces his view of his sisters as "excellent
Women."

After dinner, Charlotte and the Parkers visit the library so that Charlotte can
enter her name to become a borrower and make some general purchases (libraries often also served as general stores), but also so that Mr. Parker can check
how many subscribers there are so far this season, as this is a quick way of
ascertaining how many visitors Sanditon has attracted and of what sort (he is
keen to attract a genteel clientele). He is disappointed to find that the list of
subscribers is neither numerous nor particularly distinguished, but he consoles
himself by reflecting that it is still only July and that most people will arrive in
the following two months. As they leave the library, they meet Lady Denham
and Clara Brereton, and these two ladies return to Trafalgar House for tea.
Charlotte finds Clara Brereton as "beautiful & bewitching" as any fictional
heroine might be, and she also notes her graceful and modest manners. Lady
Denham has a mixture of qualities: good-humored and cordial, on one hand,
but also self-satisfied and somewhat affectedly keen to demonstrate her lack of
affectation by adopting a "downright & abrupt" manner.

The next day, Charlotte also meets with Sir Edward Denham and his sister,
Miss Denham. The latter is haughty and reserved, but the former briefly sweeps
Charlotte off her feet with his handsome looks and eloquent address. She is
flattered by his eager attention to her and initially impressed by his range of
conversation. However, when, through the window, he sees Lady Denham and
Clara Brereton walking along the Terrace, his manner abruptly changes, and he
leaves with his sister almost immediately. Charlotte revises her judgment now
and reflects more coolly on his manner toward her. Her suspicion that he had
been flattering her merely for effect is confirmed when she and the Parkers later
join the Denham party on the Terrace, and she sees quite clearly that he has
designs on Clara Brereton—though Charlotte also sees that Clara does not seem
to be responding to him in like manner. When Sir Edward sees Charlotte, however, he instantly leaves Clara and walks beside her. He launches into a long
peroration on the sea and then on poetry, staggering Charlotte with the number
of his quotations and bewildering her with his convoluted sentences and pseudo-
Romantic jargon. Charlotte begins to think him "downright silly" and quickly
sees through his attempt to make Clara jealous by walking and talking with her.
When he praises the poetry of Burns and then defends the passions of the actual
poet against Charlotte's reference to his personal immorality, he elicits a memorable putdown for Burns from Austen through Charlotte: "He felt & he wrote
& he forgot." Austen's hilarious parody of sentimentalism and of contemporary
discourses on the sublime continues a little later on when Sir Edward, after
visiting the library, talks to her also of fiction. Here, his speech is even more
riddled with the jargon of the sublime, and his sentences are almost literally
nonsensical. Charlotte concludes that he has read "more sentimental Novels than
agreed with him" and that from other literature he had gathered "only hard

words & involved sentences.'' His aim in life, we are told, is to be a seducer in the mold of Samuel Richardson's Lovelace (*Clarissa*), and his tendency to rhapsodize and flatter when in the company of young women is part and parcel of this conceit. But he has serious designs only on Clara, partly (if not largely) because she is his rival for the inheritance of Lady Denham, though Clara seems to have seen through him long ago and has ''not the least intention of being seduced.''

While Sir Edward and the others are in the library, Charlotte walks alone with Lady Denham and comes to understand her better. She had initially thought her to be relatively kindly and good-natured, but now, as she hears her talk coldly about her relatives and calculatingly about her money, Charlotte finally decides that Lady Denham is not good-natured at all but a mean and sordid old woman whose manipulative ways make everyone associated with her mean, too. Charlotte becomes increasingly indignant about Lady Denham and only just manages to maintain a civil attitude toward her until they are rejoined by the others.

We now meet the trio of Parker ''invalids,'' for, despite having been too ill to travel only a few days ago, Diana Parker has suddenly taken it upon herself to come to Sanditon to arrange accommodations for the West Indian and boarding school families she has drawn to the resort. Although Mr. Parker is again full of admiration for the exertions of his sister for the good of others (and of Sanditon in particular), Charlotte is mainly taken with Diana's officiousness in interfering in other people's affairs. She is also amused to see just how active, energetic, and garrulous this so-called invalid appears.

When she is introduced to Susan and Arthur Parker, she finds them to be in relatively good health, too, although the former is quite thin and nervous (mainly, Charlotte suspects, because of her dependence on quack medicines), and the latter is set fair to becoming obese through love of eating and hate of exercise. She also finds them as talkative as Diana and Thomas Parker and decides that a ''superfluity of sensation'' must be a family trait, one that is channeled by Thomas into his speculative improvements of Sanditon and by the others into ''the invention of odd complaints.''

When the expected West Indian family arrives in Sanditon, it emerges that it is one and the same as the boarding school family from Camberwell, and far from being a large family who will require the largest house in Sanditon, as Diana Parker has arranged for them, there are only four in the party, and they require only modest lodgings. The reason for the misunderstanding is that Diana Parker had been in communication with the family in such an indirect way, through a long chain of friends and friends of friends, that there had been a Chinese-whisper effect that had distorted the information she had received about them. Thus, her overactive efforts to attract business to Sanditon for her brother have backfired. She, Susan, and Arthur have made an unnecessary journey from Hampshire, Thomas is all the more disappointed for having had his expectations raised, and Diana now has the expense of the large house she has taken on the family's behalf. We are briskly introduced to the newcomers. Mrs. Griffiths is a genteel woman who supports herself by taking in girls while they finish their education, and she has brought three of the girls currently in her charge to Sanditon for the summer: a young West Indian heiress, Miss Lambe (hence the confusion about a rich West Indian family) and two frivolous, fashion-conscious Miss Beauforts.

After ten days in Sanditon, Charlotte has still not seen the inside of Sanditon House, Lady Denham's home, and Mrs. Parker decides to take her there early one morning. As they walk along the road to the house, they meet a smart carriage on its way into Sanditon, and Mrs. Parker is pleasantly surprised to find it driven by her brother-in-law, Sidney Parker. He has come over from East-bourne and is planning to stay for a few days at the hotel, where he is to be joined by some friends. Charlotte is struck by his good manners and his easy, fashionable air, and, as he drives on, the two women cheerfully discuss him as they continue on their way. As they enter the grounds of Sanditon House, Char-lotte, who is taller than Mrs. Parker, looks over the palings and sees Clara Brereton sitting at the foot of a bank apparently in intimate conversation with Sir Edward Denham. Charlotte assumes that this is a secret lovers' meeting, and she immediately withdraws without saying anything to Mrs. Parker. She briefly muses on the difficulties lovers experience in finding appropriate places to meet alone. She and Mrs. Parker are admitted to the house and shown into a handsome sitting room, where, while they wait for Lady Denham, Mrs. Parker points out the portraits of Lady Denham's late husbands: a full-length one of Sir Harry Denham in pride of place over the mantelpiece and a miniature of Mr. Hollis almost lost among several other miniatures. The manuscript ends with Char-lotte's sympathizing with poor Mr. Hollis, who is "obliged to stand back in his own House & see the best place by the fire constantly occupied by Sir H. D.''

Main Characters: Clara Brereton, Lady Denham née Brereton, Sir Edward Denham, Bart., Miss Denham, Charlotte Heywood, Arthur Parker, Diana Parker, Sidney Parker, Susan Parker, Mrs. Mary Parker, Mr. Thomas Parker,

Minor Characters: Andrew, Mr. Beard, Miss and Letitia Beaufort, Dr. and Mrs. Brown, Miss Capper, Mrs. Darling, Mrs. Davis, Sir Harry Denham, Bart. (deceased), Mrs. Charles Dupuis, Mrs. and Miss Jane Fisher, Mrs. Griffiths, Rev. Hanking, William Heeley, Mr. Heywood, Mrs. Heywood, Mr. and Mrs. Hillier, Jebb, Miss Lambe, Captain Little, Mathews family, Miss Merryweather, Morgan, Mullins family, Fanny Noyce, Parker children (including Mary), Rich-ard Pratt, Sam, Miss Scroggs, Mrs. Sheldon, Lieutenant Smith, Mr. Stringer and son, Miss Whitby, Mrs. Whitby, Woodcock.

See: Ebbatson 1992, Halperin 1983b, Le Faye 1987a, MacDonagh 1987, *Sacco 1995, Southam 1964.*

Sarah (*Persuasion* Ch.13; II:1:122). The Musgrove family's old nursemaid at Uppercross Hall. She has become redundant as such, now that the youngest Musgrove, Harry, has left for school, though she continues to live with the

Musgroves, making herself useful by mending clothes and nursing minor ailments among the family. She is delighted to be of use again when she is taken to Lyme to nurse Louisa Musgrove after her fall.

Sarah (*Pride and Prejudice* Ch.45; III:13:344). One of the Bennets' maidservants at Longbourn.

Saunders, John (*Emma* Ch.27; II:9:236). When the rivet falls out of Mrs. Bates' spectacles, Miss Bates means to take them to John Saunders for mending but does not have time to do so before Frank Churchill offers to do it instead (thus taking the opportunity to spend a little more time with Jane Fairfax).

Scholey, Old (*Mansfield Park* Ch.38; III:7:380). A friend of Mr. Price in Portsmouth.

"Scraps" (*Volume the Second*). These five short pieces are dedicated to Jane Austen's newborn niece Fanny and were therefore presumably written around the time of the latter's birth on 23 January 1793 (though they may have been written earlier and simply copied from the lost originals at this time). The pieces that make up "Scraps" are as follows. "The Female Philosopher—A Letter": this is a letter from Arabella Smythe to Louisa Clarke giving a description of some mutual acquaintances, the Millar family; the "female philosopher" is the eighteen-year-old Julia Millar, who has "Sentiments of Morality" and "sensible reflections" ready for all occasions.

"The First Act of a Comedy" has four very short scenes, which introduce four characters on their way to London, along with various servants and inn personnel. A misunderstanding seems to be in the offing, as Pistoletta's father, Popgun, is taking her to London to marry Strephon, while that character is traveling with the intention of marrying Chloe, who is also on her way to London expecting to marry Strephon.

"A Letter from a Young Lady, Whose Feelings Being Too Strong for Her Judgement Led Her into the Commission of Errors Which Her Heart Disapproved.—" The young lady in question is Anna Parker, and her letter is a breezy catalog of her many heinous crimes, including the murder of her mother and father, serial perjury, and forgery. She signs off, "I am now going to murder my Sister."

"A Tour through Wales—in a Letter from a Young Lady—." This is a burlesque on the fashion for "picturesque" travelogues in Jane Austen's time. The letter is to Clara from Elizabeth Johnson, describing how she and her sister, Fanny, have been running through Wales behind their mother, who has been galloping all the way on a horse. Fanny has been making many "beautiful" landscape drawings as she runs along, and they have both worn out two pairs of shoes. They stopped to have these mended in Carmarthen, but they eventually wore out completely, and they then had to make do with just one pair of their mother's satin slippers between them, which meant that they "hopped home from Hereford delightfully."

"A Tale," roughly a page long, once more seems to be making fun of fashionable upper-class trends of the day—this time, the craze for the picturesque country "cottage" is parodied. The joke here is that while what the upper classes meant by "cottage" was by no means a small dwelling such as laboring country folk might have lived in, it *is* the latter type of dwelling that the main character, Wilhelminus, buys in this tale: a small cottage with only two rooms and a closet. When his brother, Robertus, brings his wife, Cecilia, her two sisters, Arabella and Marina, and all their servants to stay, there is, of course, no room for them, and Wilhelminus has to put up two makeshift tents for them. (See also Robert Ferrars' prating disquisition on the subject of cottages in *Sense and Sensibility*, Ch.36; II:14:251–52.)

Scroggs, Miss (*Sanditon, Minor Works* 389). A visitor to Sanditon from Limehouse, noted by Mr. Parker in the subscription list at the circulating library. *See* Beard, Mr.

Sense and Sensibility. The first version of this novel was probably written in 1795, which makes it the first of Jane Austen's major novels to be drafted. At that time, it was a novel in letters entitled "Elinor and Marianne," but little else is known about this version, as the manuscript has not survived. It was rewritten in the form of *Sense and Sensibility*, as a narrated novel, between November 1797 and, probably, sometime in 1798. There is no definite evidence of when Jane Austen took up the novel again, but it was further revised, probably sometime between August 1809 and late 1810. In late 1810 or early 1811, it was accepted for publication by the London publisher Thomas Egerton. Jane Austen corrected proofs in April and May 1811, and *Sense and Sensibility*, "By a Lady," was published on 30 October of the same year, the first of Jane Austen's works to appear in print. A second edition, with some corrections by the author, was published in October 1813.

Perhaps more than with any other of Jane Austen's major works, the title here provides a fairly reliable indication of the main concerns of the novel if we look at it in straightforward terms. We are presented with two apparently contrasting sisters, Elinor and Marianne, the one representing qualities of "sense"—reason, restraint, social responsibility—and the other representing qualities of "sensibility"—emotion, spontaneity, individualism. Or, in other words, Elinor represents the Johnsonian qualities we would conventionally associate with eighteenth-century neo-classicism (rationality, discrimination, judgment, moderation and balance in all things and a stoical adherence to basic Christian values of honesty, humility, charity, and duty); while Marianne represents the qualities associated with the contemporaneous cult of sensibility—roughly the qualities we would now conventionally associate with Romanticism (feeling, imagination, idealism, excess, and an allegiance to nature and "natural'' morality as opposed to culture and conventional morality). (Properly speaking, of course, ''the Age of Sensibility''—usually considered as the period 1745–1798—precedes Romanticism, but there are clear continuities in both movements' opposition to narrow rationalism.) But just as Jane Austen, in general, is best understood as dialogizing rationalism and romanticism (both broadly defined), so *Sense and Sensibility* should not be seen as *contrasting* its title terms so much as dialogizing them. To be sure, in its more extreme forms, the cult of sensibility—celebrating strong and openly expressed emotion, extreme sensitivity, and a passionate responsiveness to the sublime and the beautiful in nature and art—is a constant butt of Jane Austen's satire from her earliest juvenilia to her last works. But here, the satire on sensibility as represented by Marianne is of a relatively gentle kind, and it is clear from the beginning that we are intended to see Marianne not as a foolish character with whom we can have no sympathy but as an appealing, though immature, young girl who is simply misled by her overenthusiastic espousal of sensibility and by her complacent neglect of the common sense and reason that she evidently possesses in abundance. As such, the aim of the novel is not so much to disparage the qualities associated with sensibility, as to advocate the need for a balanced rapport between sensibility and sense, passion and reason. The same principle applies to Elinor, of course: she may be the representative of rational good sense, but that is not at all to say that she lacks passion; on the contrary, she exhibits many of the same powerful feelings as her sister, but she is able to control those feelings rather than being controlled by them. But to advocate a balance between sense and sensibility is not to say that any ideal balance is possible, and that is why the word ''dialogue'' is perhaps better here than either ''contrast'' or ''balance''; Jane Austen, we can say, puts sense and sensibility into dialogue with one another throughout the novel, and though we have a deeper and more sharply defined understanding of both modes by the end of the novel (and though, in terms of the plot, sense comes out on top overall), neither mode emerges as entirely superior to (or, indeed, separate from) the other or as entirely sufficient by itself (this is illustrated by the more one-dimensional characters in the novel who *do* represent extremes of sense or sensibility). As Tony Tanner puts it in his stimulating introduction to the Penguin edition of the novel (Harmondsworth 1969: 7–34):

Admittedly the title and the use of the two sisters does seem to indicate a fairly primitive schematization, but the stuff of a novel may well belie the apparent simplicity of its structuring. The fact that Marianne has plenty of sense and Elinor is by no means devoid of sensibility should alone convince us that Jane Austen was already enough of a novelist to know that nothing comes unmixed, that qualities which may exist in pure isolation as abstractions only occur in people in combination, perhaps in confusion, with other qualities, in configurations which can be highly problematical. (9)

The novel opens with the problems of inheritance that arise after the deaths, in quick succession, of old Mr. Dashwood of Norland Park in Sussex and his nephew and immediate heir, Mr. Henry Dashwood. By his first marriage, Henry Dashwood had a son, John, and this son and *his* son, the four-year-old Harry, had been made legal heirs to Henry by a provision in old Mr. Dashwood's will. Mr. Dashwood had made this arrangement despite knowing that the John Dashwoods were already rich (John had inherited his mother's fortune, and his wife, Fanny, née Ferrars, had come to the marriage with £10,000 settled on her), and despite the fact that Henry Dashwood had a second family who were totally dependent on him, namely, his second wife and their three daughters, Elinor and Marianne (the heroines of the novel) and Margaret.

No sooner is Henry Dashwood buried, than the selfish and unfeeling John Dashwoods move into Norland Park, leaving Mrs. Dashwood and her daughters with no permanent home of their own and with a very limited income (Henry Dashwood had urged his son to make some provision for his stepmother and half sisters, but John Dashwood is soon persuaded out of any such sense of obligation by his wife's self-serving sophistry). Mrs. Dashwood and her daughters continue to live at Norland for the present, however, though Fanny Dashwood loses no opportunity to emphasize their provisional status there. Elinor develops a high regard for Fanny Dashwood's visiting brother, Edward Ferrars, but she knows he is financially dependent on his mother, and she therefore strives to contain her hopes of marrying him. Her sensible caution seems all the more justified when Fanny haughtily tells Mrs. Dashwood that such a marriage would never be acceptable to the wealthy Mrs. Ferrars (who, as we later learn, is as much of a self-important snob as Fanny is). Mrs. Dashwood now finally loses patience with the cold and supercilious treatment she and her daughters receive from John and Fanny, and she decides that they should leave Norland as soon as possible.

A distant relation of Mrs. Dashwood, Sir John Middleton of Barton Park in Devonshire, invites them to become tenants of Barton Cottage on his estate. Although Elinor is unhappy to leave Edward, she appreciates the sense of moving to a small and economical house away from Norland, and, typically, she hides her own feelings and encourages her mother to accept Sir John's offer. Mrs. Dashwood accepts Elinor's advice and makes all the necessary arrangements for their removal. John and Fanny only lightly disguise their great pleasure at being finally rid of the Dashwood women, and they offer only minimal assistance with the costs of the removal. Mrs. Dashwood coolly invites them to visit at Barton, but, to make it absolutely clear to Fanny that she disdains her class snobbery regarding Elinor and Edward, she makes a point of very warmly urging Edward to do so, too.

The Dashwoods move to Devonshire and meet their landlord, Sir John Middleton, a hearty, jovial man who greets them warmly and shows great solicitude for their comfort and convenience. Indeed, he is so concerned to be sociable and neighborly that he presses them, ''to a point of perseverance beyond civility,'' to dine at Barton Park every day until they are settled. Lady Middleton comes to see the newcomers on the following day, and the Dashwoods find her quite friendly, too, but colder and more reserved than her husband. When the Dashwoods return the visit at Barton Park, they are introduced to Mrs. Jennings, Lady Middleton's mother, and Sir John's friend, Colonel Brandon of Delaford in Dorsetshire. Colonel Brandon, alone of the company, listens attentively and appreciatively to Marianne's performance on the piano, and this is the start of his evident attraction to her. Marianne respects him for his musical taste, but, after the visit, she makes it clear that, at thirty-five, Colonel Brandon is too old and dull for her to consider him eligible as a potential suitor.

The Dashwoods settle into a quiet country life at Barton, mainly mixing only with the Middletons and otherwise simply enjoying their own pursuits in the cottage and its garden, with regular walks in the surrounding countryside. One showery morning, Marianne typically interprets a brief spell of sunshine as promise of fair weather for the rest of the day, and she persuades Margaret to come out walking on the downs with her. After a short time congratulating themselves on every little patch of blue sky they see and exulting in "the animating gales of an high south-westerly wind," a driving rain sets in once more, and they are forced to turn back. They console themselves by enjoying the sensation of running down the hill to their garden gate as fast as possible. Before reaching the bottom, however, Marianne slips and twists her ankle. A young gentleman out shooting happens to be passing at that moment, and he comes to Marianne's rescue. As she cannot stand on the injured foot, he picks her up and carries her back to the cottage, where he eventually introduces himself as Mr. John Willoughby, currently staying at nearby Allenham. He asks to be able to call again the next day to inquire after Marianne's progress and then leaves. The dramatic circumstances of their meeting and Willoughby's gallant action, charming manners, and good looks all cause Marianne to view him almost immediately as the type of romantic hero she has read about in fiction and fantasized about meeting in real life. These thoughts are not dispelled by Marianne's hearing from Sir John that Willoughby is a very high-spirited young man who seems to live up to her ideal that whatever a man's pursuits, "his eagerness in them should know no moderation." We also learn from Sir John, in his own blunt phrase, that Willoughby is "well worth catching," as he has his own property in Somersetshire and is heir to his elderly aunt (Mrs. Smith) of Allenham Court, a mile and a half away.

The relationship between Marianne and Willoughby develops as Willoughby becomes a frequent visitor at Barton Cottage. He and Marianne start to display an intimacy of behavior that leads Elinor to believe them to be secretly engaged. This view is supported by Margaret's information that Marianne has given Willoughby a lock of her hair. Elinor generally humors Marianne's infatuation with Willoughby, though she tries discreetly to warn her about the dangers of committing herself too hastily to someone she has known for only a very short time. Elinor is not generally mistrustful of Willoughby, but she is critical of his excessively forthright and forward manners and of his lack of respect for social propriety. She is particularly troubled by his insensitive and, to her mind, unjust and unwarranted criticisms of Colonel Brandon, whom Elinor has come to admire and respect. Elinor feels especially sorry for Colonel Brandon when she hears him being disparaged by Willoughby and Marianne, because she now accepts what she earlier doubted when it was suggested by Mrs. Jennings and the others—that Colonel Brandon has fallen in love with Marianne.

As Willoughby and Marianne continue to flaunt their attachment to one another, Elinor starts to become concerned that they have not yet seen fit to announce their engagement publicly. But then suddenly Willoughby announces to the Dashwoods that he must leave for London on business. He makes this announcement in a rather embarrassed and awkward way and then leaves in haste without making any clear commitment to return. Elinor and Mrs. Dashwood do not know what to make of his behavior, and Marianne is greatly distressed by his departure. Her distress deepens as she waits in vain for a letter from him. Edward Ferrars then comes to stay at Barton Cottage for a week, but his behavior, too, is somewhat cold and reserved, and Elinor is both puzzled and disappointed by his uneasy manner. However, unlike Marianne's ''violence of affliction'' at Willoughby's absence, Elinor exercises self-control here and does not make a show of her true feelings. She responds stoically and sensibly to her disappointment and even tries to rationalize Edward's changed behavior.

Anne and Lucy Steele, two recently discovered relations of Mrs. Jennings, arrive at Barton Park as guests of the Middletons. They are fashionable young women who are clearly keen to ingratiate themselves with Lady Middleton by flattering her and indulging her children. Anne Steele is nearly thirty, plain in looks, and rather simple-minded; while her younger sister is shrewd, smart, and good-looking, though lacking in real elegance or grace and, beneath her veneer of knowingness, uneducated. Elinor is intrigued to learn that the Miss Steeles are acquainted with one of the Ferrars brothers, and she assumes this is Edward's brother, Robert. However, to her great astonishment and dismay, she is later informed by Lucy that not only does she know Edward, but she has been secretly engaged to him for four years. Edward had been a pupil of Lucy's uncle in Plymouth, and that is where their relationship began; they have had to keep the engagement a secret, Lucy tells Elinor, because Lucy has no fortune, and Edward's mother would never agree to the match. Elinor is at first disbelieving and cannot accept that Edward would ever attach himself to someone as shallow as Lucy, but Lucy's convincing account of the relationship and her evident familiarity with Edward gradually force Elinor to accept the truth of the matter, and the first volume of the novel ends with her slim hopes of eventually marrying Edward apparently dashed once and for all. However, although Elinor is, of course, deeply upset at Lucy's revelations, she once again retains her external composure and does not allow her inner distress to show. Indeed, the teasing hints here of a Marianne-style emotional crisis do not carry over into the second volume, for, as is typical of her, Elinor coolly reflects on what she has heard and soon begins to reason out the situation for herself. Trusting to her own intimate knowledge of Edward and to her strong conviction that his feelings for her are genuine, Elinor deduces that his engagement to Lucy was probably the result of a youthful infatuation that has long since died. She guesses that his maturing judgment must have been increasingly offended by Lucy's lack of refinement and intelligence, and she even manages to make herself feel sorry for what she imagines must be an awkward predicament for Edward. On a subsequent visit to Barton Park, Elinor draws Lucy into conversation in order to test her hypotheses, and she does gradually confirm her suspicion that though both Edward and Lucy have tired of their secret engagement, Edward is too honorable to break his promise, while Lucy is too grasping to let the chance of a wealthy match slip through her hands.

Elinor and Marianne are now invited to spend the winter season with Mrs. Jennings in London. Elinor is as anxious to refuse for fear of finding herself in company with Edward and Lucy, as Marianne is anxious to accept in anticipation of meeting up with Willoughby once again. (Marianne knows nothing of the engagement between Lucy and Edward, as Elinor has promised Lucy to keep the matter confidential; this means not only that Marianne cannot understand Elinor's reluctance to go to London but also that, from now on, Elinor must suffer the loss of Edward in silence while Marianne can openly share her anxieties over Willoughby with Elinor.) Eventually, with the support of Mrs. Dashwood, Marianne's passionate "eagerness" prevails over Elinor's prudence, and the invitation is fully accepted. They leave with Mrs. Jennings in the first week of January. In London Marianne writes to Willoughby but receives no response from him. She becomes increasingly agitated as her expectations of a visit or some other communication are repeatedly disappointed. When the Middletons arrive in London, they organize a small, impromptu ball. At the end of the evening, Marianne's fear that Willoughby may be purposely avoiding her is strengthened when she hears that he had been invited to the event but had failed to show up. A few days later, Elinor and Marianne attend a large party with Lady Middleton, and here they finally meet with Willoughby. He is with a fashionable young woman and is evidently embarrassed at having to acknowledge Marianne, whom he greets in a cool and offhand way before leaving the room. Marianne is badly shocked by Willoughby's cruel rebuff and unable to conceal her emotions; wildly agitated while talking to him, she then turns white and almost faints as he moves away from her, before recovering sufficiently to have to be restrained by Elinor from chasing after him to demand an explanation as he leaves the room. Elinor tells Lady Middleton that Marianne is unwell, and they all return home immediately, with Marianne in "silent agony."

The next day, Marianne, in a distraught state, writes to Willoughby as soon as she wakes up, and his reply is received immediately after breakfast. In the same cool tones of his manner on the previous evening, he pleads ignorance of any slight he might have given her at the party, and he brazenly denies ever having given her cause to think that he was attached to her; as she has requested in her letter, he returns her previous letters to him along with the lock of hair she had given him at Barton; and he informs her of his engagement and imminent marriage to someone else. Mrs. Jennings returns from her morning visits armed with the latest gossip gleaned from her acquaintances; she confirms the news that Willoughby is shortly to be married and explains to Elinor that he has apparently squandered all his fortune and has therefore attached himself to an heiress, Miss Grey.

Colonel Brandon throws fresh light on the true character of Willoughby when he tells Elinor about Willoughby's casual seduction and callous desertion of Colonel Brandon's sixteen-year-old charge, Eliza Williams, the illegitimate daughter of Colonel Brandon's late sister-in-law and former sweetheart, Elizabeth Brandon. Willoughby's real character is now fully exposed as being "expensive, dissipated, and worse than both." Elinor and Colonel Brandon hope that when Marianne hears this story, she will at least find some consolation in reflecting on her narrow escape from a fate that may have been similar to that of the young Eliza; but Marianne is, in fact, thrown into an even greater depression by realizing that she has lost not only Willoughby's heart but also the romantic ideals she had projected onto his character. Marianne does, however, become better disposed toward Colonel Brandon from this point on, as she now views him with "compassionate respect."

Elinor and Marianne are persuaded to stay on in London by their mother, who judges that Marianne will be freshly reminded of her romance if she now returns to Barton and that she is more likely to be distracted from her sorrows, if only accidentally, in London. Moreover, Mrs. Dashwood has also learned that the John Dashwoods will be in town shortly, and she thinks it only proper, therefore, that her daughters should remain to spend some time with them. Early in February, some two weeks after Willoughby's final letter to Marianne, his marriage to Miss Grey takes place, and he and his bride leave London. Now that there is no chance of bumping into Willoughby again, Elinor hopes to be able to persuade Marianne to venture outdoors occasionally. Anne and Lucy Steele arrive in London, as do the John Dashwood family. Elinor and Marianne go to a jeweler's shop one morning and, without knowing who it is, observe the foppish Robert Ferrars fussily choosing a toothpick case. They also bump into John Dashwood, who makes lame excuses for not having already called on them; he arranges to do so the next day, making a special point of asking to be introduced to the well-to-do Middletons. He arrives alone at Mrs. Jennings' house the next day with "a pretence of an apology" from his wife, Fanny (who, we later learn, feels that Mrs. Jennings is too "low" for her to visit). While here, he meets Colonel Brandon and then walks with Elinor to the Middletons' house. During the walk, his mercenary attitudes are clearly exposed as he encourages Elinor to seek a match with Colonel Brandon for his money, talks of Marianne's reduced chances of marrying above "five or six hundred a-year" now that she looks so sickly, and talks about his money-making plans for his estate (including the enclosure of Norland Common). He also informs Elinor of Mrs. Ferrars' plans for marrying off Edward Ferrars to an heiress, the Hon. Miss Morton. John Dashwood takes back to his wife such favorable reports of Mrs.

Jennings and, in particular, of Lady Middleton, that Fanny Dashwood does, after all, condescend to pay her respects to these two ladies. She and Lady Middleton are mutually attracted by their shared "cold hearted selfishness . . . insipid propriety of demeanour, and a general want of understanding," and Fanny invites the Middletons to dinner. As Anne and Lucy Steele are now staying with the Middletons, they are invited also, along with Mrs. Jennings, Elinor, Marianne, and Colonel Brandon. Fanny's mother, Mrs. Ferrars, is to be at the dinner party, and this increases Elinor's interest in the event, though she is relieved to learn from Lucy that Edward will not be there, though he is in London at present. At the dinner party, Elinor finds Mrs. Ferrars to be a haughty and ill-natured old woman determined to assert her superiority over others and in particular to show her dislike of Elinor. Fanny and Mrs. Ferrars both clearly suspect Elinor of still harboring designs on Edward, and they do their best to humble her by making a show of preferring Lucy Steele over her. Elinor is more amused than insulted by their rudeness, especially as she appreciates the irony of their paying attention to someone whose actual engagement to Edward they would be horrified to learn about. When Mrs. Ferrars slights Elinor's drawing—which is admired by everyone else—by comparing it unfavorably with the work of Miss Morton, Marianne loses all patience with the old lady and speaks sharply to her in defense of Elinor. Mrs. Ferrars bristles with anger at what she sees as Marianne's impudence, and even Elinor is somewhat embarrassed by the vehemence of Marianne's outburst—but Colonel Brandon is clearly full of admiration for what he sees as evidence of Marianne's "affectionate heart."

John and Fanny Dashwood invite Anne and Lucy Steele to stay at their house in Harley Street, partly as a means of avoiding the need to invite Elinor and Marianne to stay with them. Elinor sees in this sign of favor toward Lucy an indication that perhaps Fanny has been won over by Lucy's flattery and that she is prepared to support her in making a public announcement of the engagement with Edward. Volume 2 of the novel thus ends with Elinor's resignedly expecting such an announcement at any moment. However, volume 3 opens with a different sort of announcement, brought to Elinor by Mrs. Jennings. At Harley Street, it emerges, Anne Steele has inadvertently let slip the secret of Lucy's engagement to Edward, and Fanny Dashwood has reacted to the news with horror, falling into a fit of "violent hysterics" and throwing both the Steele girls out of the house without further ado. Elinor is now forced to explain her own lovelorn situation for the first time to Marianne, who suddenly realizes just how strong and forbearing Elinor has been in comforting her while silently suffering from the same sort of unhappiness. Mrs. Ferrars, we learn, has given Edward an invidious ultimatum: if he insists on marrying Lucy, he will be disowned and disinherited by her; if he breaks off the engagement and agrees to marry Miss Morton instead, she will increase the fortune settled on him. Edward, however, has made it clear that he will abide by his word and honor the commitment he has made to Lucy. He has therefore been dismissed from his mother's house, and she has arranged with her lawyers to transfer the estate destined for Edward to his younger brother, Robert. Three days later, Elinor meets Anne Steele, who tells her that Edward had earlier that day offered Lucy a release from the engagement if she felt he would now be too poor for her but that she had remained resolute in her commitment to him; he intends to be ordained shortly, and they have now apparently agreed to be married as soon as he is able to gain a living. The next morning, however, Elinor receives a letter from Lucy herself, in which she says that *she* had offered Edward the chance of a release from the engagement if he desired it but that he would not hear of such a thing.

Colonel Brandon has heard of Edward's financial problems and, knowing him to be a worthy young man and wanting to be of assistance to him also because of his friendship with Elinor, offers Edward the vacant living on his estate at Delaford. Elinor is very grateful to Colonel Brandon for his kindness to Edward, though she reflects ruefully on the fact that now the next time she sees Edward, he will almost certainly be married to Lucy.

It is now early April, and Elinor and Marianne leave London for Barton once more. They have, however, accepted an invitation from the Palmers to visit them at Cleveland in Somersetshire on their way to Devon, and they travel there together with Mrs. Jennings. At Cleveland, Marianne, acutely aware of being only thirty miles away from Willoughby's seat at Combe Magna, finds that the picturesque gardens accord well with her state of romantic melancholia. Over the first few days here, despite some heavy rainfall, she takes solitary walks in the grounds at every available opportunity, and, as a result, she is taken ill with a severe cold. The cold develops into what appears to be pneumonia, and Marianne becomes dangerously ill. Colonel Brandon leaves to fetch Mrs. Dashwood from Barton, while Elinor stays with Marianne, who is ineffectually treated by the Palmers' apothecary, Mr. Harris.

Gradually, Elinor's careful nursing helps Marianne through the worst of her illness, and she seems out of danger on the fifth day after the start of her illness. Late in the evening on that day, just before the expected time of Mrs. Dashwood's arrival with Colonel Brandon, Elinor hears a carriage and rushes down to greet her mother; to her dismay, however, she finds that the carriage has brought not her mother and Colonel Brandon but John Willoughby. He has heard that Marianne is dying and has traveled from London to try to explain his previous behavior and to seek some sort of forgiveness from Marianne. He admits to what we already know about him in relation to Eliza Williams and to his mercenary marriage to Miss Grey, and he tells Elinor that his last letter to Marianne was, in fact, dictated to him by his wife, for whom, he makes clear, he has little love or respect. Elinor cannot entirely absolve Willoughby of his crimes, and she remains critical of his basic lack of integrity and his weak principles—as ever, too, she finds his manner and speech somewhat intemperate; but she is inclined to give him credit for the genuine love he evidently still feels for Marianne and to accept that he is sincere in regretting his past actions and in wishing to be forgiven for them. She pities him, moreover, for the unhappy and loveless marriage he has entered into—over the years, this will punish him for his misdemeanors more effectively than anything she or Marianne can say now. She grants him her own forgiveness and speaks kindly to him; she agrees to repeat his story to Marianne once her health has improved sufficiently.

Shortly after Willoughby's departure, Mrs. Dashwood finally arrives with Colonel Brandon, and they are both relieved and delighted to find that Marianne is out of danger. Now, with her mother close at hand, Marianne's recovery continues apace, and she is soon almost back to normal. As soon as Mrs. Dashwood has a moment alone with Elinor after her arrival at Cleveland, she tells Elinor that on the journey there with Colonel Brandon he had confided in her about his love for Marianne, and she had assured him that, if Marianne survived, she would do all in her power to promote the match. Elinor listens with amusement as her mother now tries to make up for her mistaken encouragement of Willoughby at Barton by extolling the virtues of Colonel Brandon and emphasizing his great superiority over Willoughby as a suitor for Marianne.

Marianne and Elinor now return to Barton with Mrs. Dashwood. Here, Marianne soberly takes stock of her experiences and behavior over the past six months in the light of her recent illness and narrow escape from death. She realizes that her emotional excesses over Willoughby have been selfish and insensitive rather than romantic, especially when compared to the stoicism and selflessness exhibited by Elinor in the face of similar circumstances; she reproaches herself for the distress she has caused to her family and friends, and she determines to show greater humility in the future and to be more restrained and rational in her behavior. To this end, she tells Elinor, she will undertake a course of serious study over the coming months, devoting herself to music and literature for six hours each day. Elinor admires Marianne's new resolve, though she smiles to herself to see her sister's eager temperament transforming excessive sensibility into its opposite as she introduces "excess into a scheme of such rational employment and virtuous self-controul [*sic*]." Marianne is also now able to think of Willoughby more rationally and without regrets, though she admits that her mind would be easier if she could know that his feelings for her had been genuine for at least some of their time together. This gives Elinor the cue she has been waiting for to recount what Willoughby had told her at Cleveland when he had come from London to seek Marianne's forgiveness on what he thought might be her deathbed. Marianne hears Elinor's narration with rising emotion, and in the end she cannot withhold her tears entirely; but she remains essentially calm and in control of her feelings. After thanking Elinor for setting her mind at rest, she retires to her room to seek a "reasonable" solitude in which to think over what she has heard. Later that day, she talks candidly to Elinor and Mrs. Dashwood about her conclusions; she realizes now that she could never have been happy with Willoughby, whose true character she would have inevitably discovered sooner or later, and she is now content with matters as they stand: "I wish for no change," she repeats with equanimity.

Thomas, Mrs. Dashwood's manservant, returns from an errand to Exeter with the news that he has seen Edward Ferrars and Lucy Steele and that they are now married; he had seen the couple in their carriage and had talked to Lucy, though he had not talked directly to Edward. On hearing this news, Marianne—evidently still in the grip of sensibility where the interests of her sister are concerned—falls into a fit of hysterics and removes to a neighboring room. Elinor's response is not so demonstrative, but her distressed expression reveals to her mother for the first time just how much she has been suffering over recent months. Mrs. Dashwood realizes now that she has actually been neglectful of her more stoical daughter because she had been too ready to believe the self-denying reassurances Elinor had given her in her letters and because she had been too absorbed in the ''more acknowledged'' afflictions of Marianne. Elinor herself finds the news all the more galling for the realization it brings that, ''in spite of herself,'' she has continued to hope against hope that Edward might still break off the engagement with Lucy in her favor; now, all hope is gone, and she condemns her own heart for its ''lurking flattery.'' However, there has been a mistake. Edward now arrives at Barton, and, though Elinor thinks he has come to break the news of his marriage to her, it soon emerges that Thomas had seen Lucy Steele with *Robert* Ferrars, not Edward. Lucy, it appears, had quickly transferred her allegiance to Robert when she saw that he had gained Edward's inheritance; Robert's foolishness and vanity had made him easy prey to Lucy's flattery, and she had led him to the altar even before writing to Edward to break off their engagement. Lucy and Robert had purposely tricked Thomas in Exeter in order ''to go off with a flourish of malice'' against Edward.

In fact, then, Edward has now come to Barton to ask Elinor to marry him, and she, of course, is only too delighted to accept. Mrs. Ferrars is eventually partially reconciled with Edward—though she unaccountably continues to favor Robert and to maintain the legal settlement of the estate on him despite his marriage to Lucy—and she grudgingly gives her consent to Edward's match with Elinor. They are married at Barton in the autumn and settle at Delaford, where Colonel Brandon improves the parsonage to accommodate both of them comfortably. Mrs. Dashwood ensures that she and Marianne visit Delaford regularly so as to promote an attachment between Marianne and Colonel Brandon, and Edward and Elinor happily collaborate with this scheme. ''With such a confederacy against her'' and with her growing appreciation of his good character and of his real love for her, Marianne is, indeed, finally persuaded to accept Colonel Brandon's offer of marriage, and they are married within a year of Elinor and Edward's marrying. The two couples live happily together at Delaford and maintain close links with Mrs. Dashwood and Margaret at Barton. The felicity of this group contrasts sharply with the squabbling discontent that continues to characterize the lives of Lucy, Robert and Mrs. Ferrars, John Willoughby and his wife, and John and Fanny Dashwood.

Main Characters: Colonel Brandon, Mrs. Dashwood, Elinor Dashwood, Fanny Dashwood, John Dashwood, Margaret Dashwood, Marianne Dashwood, Edward Ferrars, Robert Ferrars, Miss Sophia Grey, Mrs. Jennings, Lady Middleton, Sir John Middleton, Miss Anne Steele, Miss Lucy Steele, John Willoughby.

Minor Characters: Betty, Miss Fanny Brandon, Mr. Brandon, Old Mr. Brandon, Mrs. Eliza Brandon, Mrs. Burgess, the Careys, Cartwright, Mrs. Clarke, Lord Courtland, Old Mr. Dashwood, Miss Dashwood, First Mrs. Dashwood, Harry Dashwood, Henry Dashwood, Doctor Davies, Mrs. Dennison, Mr. Donavan, Sir Elliott, Lady Elliott, the Ellisons, Mrs. Ferrars, Old Gibson, the Gilberts, Miss Godby, Gray's, Mr. Harris, Biddy Henshawe, Mr. Jennings, the four young Middletons, Lord Morton, the Hon. Miss Morton, Mr. Thomas Palmer, Mrs. Charlotte Palmer, the Parrys, Mr. Pratt, Cousin Richard (Steele family), the Richardsons, Sir Robert—, Mr. Rose, Sally, the Sandersons, Martha Sharpe, Mr. Simpson, Mrs. Smith, Miss Sparks, Mrs. Taylor, Thomas, Miss Walker, the Westons, the Whittakers, Miss Eliza Williams, Eliza Williams (Brandon).

Volume and chapter divisions (numbers in brackets are for editions with continuous chapter numbers): Volume 1: Chapters 1–22, volume 2: Chapters 1–14 [23–36], volume 3: Chapters 1–14 [37–50].

See: Armstrong 1994, Benedict 1990, Boyd 1983, Brissenden 1984, *Clark 1994*, Conger 1987, Derry 1993, 1994, Easton 1993, Fisher 1987, Haggerty 1988, Harding 1993, C. Johnson 1983b, Kaplan 1983, Kaplan and Kaplan 1990, Kaufmann 1992, Kroeber 1990, Lock 1979, Melander 1949–1950, Nollen 1984, Reinstein 1983, Ruoff 1979, *Ruoff 1992*, Saisselin 1994, Shaffer 1994, Shoben 1982–1983, M. Smith 1987, P. Smith 1993, *Southam 1976b*, Thompson 1990, Thomsen 1990, Tomkins 1940, Tsomondo 1990, Watt 1981.

Serle (*Emma* Chs.3, 21; I:3:24; II:3:172). The Woodhouses' cook at Hartfield, cited by Mr. Woodhouse as an expert at boiling an egg and a pork leg.

Sharpe, Martha (*Sense and Sensibility* Ch.38; III:2:274). Anne Steele's close friend of a year or two ago. They used to have secrets that they kept from Lucy Steele so that she had taken to eavesdropping to hear what they said together. Anne Steele uses this fact to justify her own eavesdropping on Lucy and Edward.

Shaw, Mrs. (*The Watsons, Minor Works* 317). Penelope Watson's friend in Chichester and niece of Dr. Harding.

Sheldon, Mrs. (*Sanditon, Minor Works* 386). In her letter to her brother, Thomas, where she discusses his sprained ankle and recommends "friction," Diana Parker mentions once visiting a friend, Mrs. Sheldon, whose coachman had just sprained *his* ankle; she rubbed it for six hours without a break, and he was well in three days, she reports.

Shepherd, Mr. John (*Persuasion* Ch.1; I:1:9). A lawyer from a market town near Kellynch Hall, father of Mrs. Clay, and Sir Walter Elliot's estate agent.

Mr. Shepherd is a civil and cautious man who diplomatically humors Sir Walter's vanity whenever discussing business matters. He shrewdly prepares Sir Walter for the possibility of their attracting a naval tenant for Kellynch when they put the hall up for rent.

Shirley, Dr. (*Persuasion* Ch.9; I:9:78). The elderly rector of Uppercross. He has been "zealously" discharging his duties for over forty years but has now grown too infirm to continue in his customary manner and is considering appointing a curate, a position he appears to have promised to Charles Hayter.

Shirley, Mrs. (*Persuasion* Ch.12; I:12:102). Wife of Dr. Shirley. Henrietta Musgrove talks of the Shirleys as "excellent people . . . who have been doing good all their lives." Thinking of her marriage to Charles Hayter, however, Henrietta wishes that Dr. Shirley would retire and move to Lyme, where Mrs. Shirley has cousins and many other acquaintances; then Charles could become resident curate of Uppercross.

Simpson, Mr. (*Sense and Sensibility* Ch.21; I:21:123). The employer of Mr. Rose known to the Steele girls in Exeter.

Sir Charles Grandison or The Happy Man, a Comedy in Five Acts. This burlesque condensation of Samuel Richardson's massive novel *The History of Sir Charles Grandison* (1753–1754) had traditionally been ascribed to Jane Austen's niece, Anna Austen, but when the manuscript came to auction in 1977, it became open to scholarly inspection for the first time and was reascribed by B. C. Southam to Jane Austen on the basis of its style, length, and apparent chronology of composition. It seems to have been begun around 1791–1792 and completed by about 1799–1800, with intermittent work done on it from around 1796. The evidence for the play's reascription is not absolutely conclusive, nor is the suggested dating of the work's composition, but Anna Austen was born in 1793, and even if it had been entirely written in 1800, when she was just seven, it seems unlikely that she would have had sufficient grasp of Richardson's novel by that time to make the sort of informed summary of it that the play represents. Brian Southam's edition of the play (Oxford, 1980) does, however, draw attention to the many revisions and additions to the manuscript, some of which are in a childish hand; and it seems likely, as he suggests, that the work was a collaboration, probably between Jane and Anna Austen, though possibly with the involvement of other family members, too. The play itself is not particularly edifying in any critical sense beyond confirming the fact that Jane Austen greatly admired Richardson's novel and had a detailed knowledge of it. Neither is the play particularly funny as it stands (it would seem that it was originally a rough working text for a family performance of the play, and some of the humor may have been in the nature of private jokes recognizable only within the Austen family). The main joke really lies in the absurdity of reducing one of the longest novels in the language to what is effectively a playlet, though the local effects of such reduction (sudden changes of topic and scene and indirections of dialogue) are also sometimes quite amusing. Otherwise, there is little of Jane Austen's usual sharpness of wit, and much of the dialogue is quite wooden. Moreover, the roughness and discontinuity of the writing inevitably prevent any strong sense of dramatic pace or structure from emerging, although the plot of Richardson's novel is quite neatly pared down to its essentials, and this at least gives the play a clear direction. Samuel Richardson's novel is in letter form and the main story line is as follows (Jane Austen's play takes some liberties with this and recasts it in a comic mode, but the main line of development is the same). Harriet Byron, the beautiful and virtuous heroine, arrives in London and soon attracts the attentions of the rakish Sir Hargrave Pollexfen. Harriet resists his advances, and so he kidnaps her from a masked ball and tries to force her into a secret marriage. She continues to defy him, and he sends her in a carriage to his country estate. On the journey, however, she is rescued by the wealthy Sir Charles Grandison, who is presented as a perfect gentleman and paragon of virtue. Harriet and Grandison fall in love but cannot marry because Grandison is already attached to an Italian noblewoman, Clementina della Porretta. He has not already married Clementina because of their different religions, and now the tensions this has caused lead Clementina to suffer a nervous breakdown. Grandison goes to Italy, and she is restored to health on seeing him again, but she finally decides that it would be wrong for either of them to have to sacrifice beliefs for the sake of personal desire. Grandison is thus released from his obligation to her and is able to return to England to marry Harriet with a clear conscience. They both reap the rewards of their virtuous behavior and live happily ever after.

Characters (in the play): Deborah Awberry, Mrs. Awberry, Sally Awberry, Bridget, Harriet Byron, Clergyman, Clerk (to Clergyman), Footman, Frederic, Lord G., Sir Charles Grandison, Charlotte Grandison (younger sister of Charles Grandison), Jenny, Emily Jervois (ward of Charles Grandison), John, Lord L., Lady Caroline L. (elder sister of Charles Grandison), a Milliner, Sir Hargrave Pollexfen, Mr. Reeves, Mrs. Reeves (cousin of Harriet Byron), Sally, Mr. Selby, Mrs. Selby (aunt of Harriet Byron), Lucy Selby, Nancy Selby, Mr. Smith, Thomas, William.

See: Speirs 1985.

"Sir William Mountague" (*Volume the First* of Jane Austen's juvenilia). Described in the dedication to Charles Austen as "an unfinished performance," this piece was probably written sometime in 1788. It is a little over a page and a half in length and is mainly a catalog of the rich Sir William's absurdly rapid succession of love affairs. He falls in love at the drop of a hat, and even when he finally marries Emma Stanhope (whose brother he has killed for the love of Miss Arundel), it is only two weeks before "he became again most violently in love" on seeing the sister of one of his earlier fiancées.

Characters: Miss Arundel, Mr. Brudenell, the three Miss Cliftons, Emma Stanhope, Sir William Mountague, Lady Percival, Mr. Stanhope, Miss Wentworth.

Skinner, Dr., and family (*Northanger Abbey* Chs.2, 8; I:2:22; I:8:54). Neighbors of the Allens at Fullerton who had been to Bath for three months the winter previous to Catherine Morland's visit. Dr. Skinner had gone for his health and, according to Mrs. Allen, had come away "quite stout."

Smallridge, Mrs. (*Emma* Ch.42; III:6:380). The lady with whom Mrs. Elton arranges a position for Jane Fairfax. She is a wealthy neighbor of the Sucklings and urgently requires a governess for her three young daughters.

Smith (*Mansfield Park* Ch.6; I:6:53). Mr. Smith of Compton is a friend of Mr. Rushworth's from a neighboring county. He has just had his estate "improved" by Humphrey Repton.

Smith, Charles (*Lady Susan, Minor Works* 248, 264). Charles Smith is Reginald De Courcy's friend and the source of his original information about the outrageous behavior of Lady Susan at Langford. When Reginald later falls under the sway of Lady Susan, he questions the veracity of his friend's "scandalous tales," though he eventually comes to rue these doubts.

Smith, Charles (deceased) (*Persuasion* Chs.17, 21; II:5:152; II:9:199–200). The wealthy, happy-go-lucky husband of Mrs. Smith. He had married her not long after she had left school, where she had been friendly with Anne Elliot, and they had had a happy, if somewhat reckless, life together, until he died after about ten years (some two years before the main action of the novel). From Mrs. Smith's account of her husband, Anne Elliot deduces an amiable man "of warm feelings, easy temper, careless habits, and not strong understanding." He had been a close friend of Mr. William Walter Elliot since before his marriage to Mrs. Smith, and he had clearly treated Mr. Elliot with great generosity when the latter was still without any fortune of his own. When Mr. Elliot became rich himself, he had encouraged his old friend to live even further beyond his means than he customarily did, and this eventually led to financial ruin for the Smiths, though Charles died without realizing the full extent of it. He had been foolish enough, moreover, to entrust the execution of his will to Mr. Elliot, and this greatly aggravated the situation for his wife, as Mr. Elliot heartlessly refused to act for her.

Smith, Harriet (*Emma* Ch.3; I:3:22–25). The artless young girl who becomes Emma's protégée and the focus of her matchmaking fantasies. She is seventeen years old at the start of the novel and a parlor-boarder at Mrs. Goddard's school. Nothing much is known of her past except that she is "the natural daughter of somebody.'' Although, at the end of the novel, this somebody is revealed to be only a respectable tradesman, Emma imagines a more genteel heritage for her and determines to introduce her—and marry her—into ''good'' society. Harriet is generally admired for her beauty, simple good nature, and lack of conceit; but she is docile, lacking in understanding, and ''certainly not clever,'' and therefore she is easily persuaded by Emma to fall in with her misconceived schemes; and, of course, the comedy of errors that ensues provides the main lines of the plot for a large part of the book. Although a somewhat weak and naive character for most of the novel, she, like Emma, gains in self-awareness through her various mistakes and humiliations, and she is finally able to admit that ''she had been presumptuous and silly, and self-deceived.'' Her basic good nature and generosity of spirit are confirmed here by the fact that she takes all the blame for her own misfortunes, despite the determining influence of Emma in her ''self-deception.''

Smith, Lieutenant (*Sanditon, Minor Works* 389). A naval officer visiting Sanditon, as noted by Mr. Parker in the subscription list at the circulating library. *See* Beard, Mr.

Smith, Miss (*Northanger Abbey* Chs.8, 10; I:8:58; I:10:73). A young lady at the Bath assembly—an acquaintance of Mrs. Hughes—who dances with Henry Tilney just as Catherine Morland becomes free to dance with him herself. She had earlier been forced to refuse his offer to dance because of a prior engagement with John Thorpe, and she is then disappointed to see him leading Miss Smith onto the dance floor just as she is hoping he will repeat the offer.

Smith, Mrs. (*Sense and Sensibility* Ch.9; I:9:40 & 44). John Willoughby's infirm elderly cousin, on whom he is financially dependent. She is the owner of Allenham Court, Devon, which Willoughby hopes to inherit after her death, and he is staying there when he first meets Elinor and Marianne.

Smith, Mrs., née Hamilton (*Persuasion* Chs.17, 21; II:5:152–55; II:9:192–211). As the seventeen-year-old Miss Hamilton, Mrs. Smith had been a good friend to Anne Elliot during Anne's first year at school. Anne had been sent there on the death of her mother, when she was fourteen, and the older girl had taken her under her wing, recognizing how much Anne was suffering from the loss of her mother and from being away from home for the first time. Miss Hamilton had left school a year later, at the age of eighteen, and had married Mr. Charles Smith not long after. Anne has not seen her old friend for twelve years when, while at Bath, she hears from her former governess that Mrs. Smith is in lodgings at Westgate Buildings and that she is now a widow of about two years' standing, poor, and crippled by severe rheumatic fever. When Anne goes to see Mrs. Smith, she is pleased to find that she is still the sensible, warmhearted, and cheerful person she remembers from the past, despite the various misfortunes she has suffered. Indeed, Anne is astonished at the resilience of her friend, given her circumstances, and she decides that Mrs. Smith's positive-minded and cheerful stoicism—what is later referred to as ''the glow of her spirits''—is ''the choicest gift of Heaven.'' Mrs. Smith had loved her husband and had been happily married, though she now regrets their somewhat dissipated life together, as they had been part of ''a thoughtless, gay set'' living only for immediate enjoyment. Although her husband had been very wealthy to begin with, he had been led into increasingly extravagant expenditure by a close friend who had suddenly become rich through marriage, Mr. William Walter Elliot, and Mr. Smith had eventually died in financial ruin, leaving his wife almost destitute. Her situation had been aggravated by the fact that Mr. Elliot had been made the executor of her husband's will but had refused to act for her, even though she believed a West Indian property of her husband's might have been recovered and might have alleviated her plight. But Mrs. Smith's past acquaintance with Mr. Elliot at least enables her now to reveal his true character to Anne, as well as to give the latter a clearer idea of his motives in apparently paying court to her. After Anne marries Captain Wentworth at the end of the novel, Mrs. Smith is their earliest visitor, and she remains one of their closest friends. Captain Wentworth helps her to recover her husband's West Indian property, and both her finances and her health gradually improve once more.

Sneyds, the (*Mansfield Park* Ch.5; I:5:51). Sneyd, a friend of Tom Bertram, once introduced the latter to his mother and sisters when they were together in Ramsgate, and Tom describes what happened as part of his discussion with Mary Crawford and Edmund on the perplexing subject of girls being ''out'' or ''not out.'' Apparently, he paid his attentions to the youngest of the Miss Sneyds, Augusta, who, unknown to him, was *not* out and thereby ''excessively offended'' the elder daughter, who *was* out.

Sophia (*Northanger Abbey* Ch.14; I:14:115). One of Anne Thorpe's two new friends, acquired very rapidly on the morning of the excursion to Clifton from which she had been excluded. *See* Emily.

Sparks, Miss (*Sense and Sensibility* Ch.38; III:2:272). An acquaintance of Anne Steele in London.

Speed, Mrs. (*Persuasion* Ch.21; II:9:197). Mrs. Smith's landlady at Westgate Buildings in Bath. Her sister, Mrs. Rooke, nurses and befriends Mrs. Smith.

Spicers, the (*Persuasion* Ch.9; I:9:76). Friends of the Hayter family who may be able to use their influence with the Bishop to gain a good living for Charles Hayter.

Stanley, Camilla ("Catharine," *Minor Works* 197–98). The frivolous, preening, and vapid daughter of the Stanleys who has acquired many accomplishments but lacks understanding, taste, and judgment. When she comes to stay with Catharine, she at first promises to be a lively and entertaining companion, but her fund of wit and conversation is soon exhausted, and she has little to fall back on except social tittle-tattle and fashion gossip.

Stanley, Edward ("Catharine," *Minor Works* 213). The handsome, gadabout son of the Stanleys who appears at Chetwynde out of the blue and almost literally whisks Catharine Percival off her feet (though he pauses in the process for half an hour to powder and pomatum himself). He has returned from France on hearing of the sickness of his favorite hunting mare, and he has decided to call at Chetwynde on his way back. He seems to have picked up some rather radical notions on his travels, and he takes great delight in cocking a snook at conventions of decorum. He fails to introduce himself to Catharine and yet talks to her in a very familiar manner; he is happy to take Catharine to the Dudleys' ball in his carriage without a chaperon and then to gate-crash into the ball without even introducing himself to the hosts; once there, he blithely overlooks all the other ladies and, to add insult to injury, leads Catharine to the head of the dance floor to lead off the dancing. Mrs. Percival is none too happy to have him stay at her house, but he stays anyway and then plays an elaborate game with both Catharine and her aunt, seducing the emotions of the one while playing on the fears of the other. Then, when he has caused various forms of mayhem in the carefully ordered world of Chetwynde, he dashes off once more toward France; as Mrs. Percival might say, "every thing is going to sixes & sevens and all order will soon be at an end throughout the Kingdom."

Stanley, Mr. and Mrs. ("Catharine," *Minor Works* 197). Wealthy and fashionable relatives of the Percivals who come to stay at Chetwynde with their daughter, Camilla. Mr. Stanley is a member of Parliament, and he and Mrs. Percival discuss politics together.

Steele, Miss Anne (*Sense and Sensibility* Ch.21; I:21:118–26). The silly and simple elder sister of Lucy Steele. Almost thirty, "with a very plain and not a sensible face," Anne is as obsequious and calculating as her sister, but in cruder and less skillful ways. She is another of Jane Austen's effusive and empty talkers, and through her garrulity Fanny Dashwood learns of Lucy's secret engagement to Edward.

Steele, Miss Lucy (*Sense and Sensibility* Chs.21, 22; I:21:118–26; I:22:127). About twenty-two or -three when we first meet her, Lucy is a "considerable beauty" and smart and fashionable with it. She is also "naturally clever" and sharp-witted and apparently always good-humored and agreeable. However, as with so many Austen characters, she is not all she seems at first, and Elinor

Dashwood soon recognizes her for what she is: an artful, scheming, and syco-phantic fortune hunter who joins "insincerity with ignorance." Although other characters are taken in by Lucy's simpering and flattering ways, Elinor imme-diately registers her lack of true elegance and refinement and, most important, her lack of "rectitude, and integrity of mind." In her dealings with Elinor, whom she recognizes as a potential rival for Edward Ferrars' hand and fortune, she shows herself to be cunning and deceitful, and her mercenary motives are seen most clearly when, toward the end of the novel, she secretly marries Ed-ward's brother, Robert, after Edward has been effectively disinherited by Mrs. Ferrars.

Stephen (*Mansfield Park* Ch.19; II:1:189). One of the Mansfield Park grooms capable of driving the Bertrams' coach.

St. Ives, Lord (*Persuasion* Ch.3; I:3:19). The son of a lowly country curate who, because of his services to the navy, has achieved a higher social rank than Sir Walter Elliot; this offends Sir Walter's snobbish sense of propriety.

Stokes, Jack (*The Watsons, Minor Works* 341). A local acquaintance of the Watson family; his uncle has offered to deliver Elizabeth's letter to Sam at Guildford.

Stokes, Mrs. (*Emma* Ch.29; II:11:252). The landlady of the Crown Inn. Mr. Woodhouse doubts if she can be trusted to keep her rooms well aired, even though he apparently knows nothing about her!

Stone, Mr. (*Pride and Prejudice* Ch.51; III:9:319). Mr. Stone is a business associate of Mr. Gardiner's in London. He detains Mr. Gardiner for ten minutes on Lydia Bennet's wedding day, and Lydia describes him as a "horrid man," complaining that when he gets together with Mr. Gardiner, "there is no end of it."

Stornaway, Lady Flora, née Ross (*Mansfield Park* Ch.36; III:5:359–61). An old London friend of Mary Crawford, formerly her "most particular friend" of the two Ross sisters (see also Mrs. Fraser). Mary appears not to care much for either of the sisters while she is at Mansfield Park, ostensibly because of their loveless marriages. According to Mary, Flora had been "dying for Henry" when she first came "out"; then, later, she jilted a young soldier in the Blues (Royal Horse Guards) for "that horrid Lord Stornaway." Later on in London, however, Mary describes Lady Stornaway more positively, "in high spirits, and very happy."

Stornaway, Lord (*Mansfield Park* Ch.36; III:5:361–62). At Mansfield Park, Mary Crawford tells Fanny that she had had her doubts about this man even before her friend Flora married him; since the marriage, these doubts have been confirmed, and she now considers him "horrid," with "about as much sense . . . as Mr. Rushworth, but much worse looking, and with a blackguard character." However, when in London once more, Mary writes to Fanny that "I fancy Lord S. is very good-humoured and pleasant in his own family."

Stringer, Mr. (*Sanditon, Minor Works* 381, 382). Proprietor, with his son, of a fruit and vegetable business at Sanditon. He was encouraged to set up there by Mr. Parker, who is now having qualms about not giving the Stringers enough of his own custom.

Styles, Mr. (*The Watsons, Minor Works* 337). A member of Captain Hunter's regiment.

Suckling, Mr. (*Emma* Chs.22, 32; II:4:183; II:14:272). Mrs. Elton's wealthy brother-in-law, owner of Maple Grove near Bristol and of *two* carriages, one being the famous barouche-landau that Mrs. Elton boasts about.

Suckling, Mrs., née Hawkins (*Emma* Chs.22, 32; II:4:183; II:14:272). Mrs. Elton's elder sister, Selina.

Summers, Miss (*Lady Susan, Minor Works* 246). Miss Summers runs the expensive boarding school in Wigmore Street, London, where Lady Susan sends her daughter, Frederica. After Frederica runs away, Miss Summers cannot be prevailed upon to accept her back at the school.

"Susan." Jane Austen's original manuscript title for the novel that was titled and published as *Northanger Abbey* after her death. "Susan" was first written in 1798–1799 and sold to the publisher Crosby and Company in 1803. However, Crosby never issued the book, and not until 1816 was Jane Austen able to buy back the manuscript and copyright and consider finding another publisher for it. At this point she changed the title to "Catherine," possibly because a novel with the title *Susan* had already been published in 1809. By March 1817, however, she seems to have given up hope of having the work published, and it was left to her brother, Henry, to see it through the press under its better-known title in December 1817. "Susan" may have been revised in 1802–1803, when Jane Austen sold the manuscript after apparently making a second copy of it; and it may have been revised at any time after this, if a second copy existed. In 1809, Jane Austen made inquiries about it to Crosby, and this may suggest she had taken it up again at this time. However, in the Preface she wrote to the work in 1816, ''Advertisement, by the Authoress,'' she states that it had been finished in 1803 and suggests that there had been only slight revisions since that date.

Susan, Lady (''Catharine,'' *Minor Works* 211). She gives Augusta Barlow a new Regency walking dress.

T

Taylor, Miss (*Emma*). *See* Weston, Mrs. Anna.

Taylor, Mrs. (*Sense and Sensibility* Ch.30; II:8:192). A gossiping acquaintance of Mrs. Jennings who tells her about Willoughby's impending marriage to Sophia Grey.

Themes and Concerns. In addition to their protofeminist concern with women's issues and their self-conscious interest in the forms and functions of fiction, Jane Austen's novels have four outstanding themes in common: marriage, morals, manners, and money. Each of these themes has a complex range of reference within Austen's world, and they are all closely interrelated.

Marriage. The theme of marriage should perhaps be called a structural theme in that, including the process of courtship that leads to it, marriage provides Austen with her typical plot structure, and through this structure all other themes emerge and gain significance. The marriage plot is, of course, a conventional device with an ancient pedigree in romance and comedy; as such, it has certain built-in dramatic and thematic possibilities that Austen is able to activate in her own use of it. The conventional pattern of the marriage plot is one in which, with a pair or set of young lovers, we follow the vicissitudes of their progress toward marriage in the face of various types of obstacle, difficulty, misunderstanding, or opposition (often from elderly parents or similar authority figures). Such a pattern provides a ready-made structure or rhythm of suspense, tension, and release that was easily assimilable to the newly emerging domestic novel in the eighteenth century, and it was skillfully adapted for her own (sometimes subversive) purposes by Austen in her fictional comedies of manners. Thematically, the conventional marriage plot can be seen, in terms of romance, to encode archetypal rituals of personal and social renewal, enacting both the individual's rites of passage from youth to maturity and the social regulation of sexual desire with its promise of stability and continuity for the community. In this vein, Jane Austen particularly tends to emphasize the symbolic significance of marriage as a process of balancing the demands of self and society; and several other typically Austenian oppositions tend to be involved in this process—heart and head, desire and duty, imagination and reason, romance and reality.

The archetypal quest-and-learning structure of the marriage plot is also highly functional to Austen's purposes, for her peculiarly modern emphasis is gained through her close analysis of character and, in particular, of the self-interrogating consciousnesses of her heroines as they struggle for self-knowledge on their uneasy journeys toward the goal of marriage (which, in this sense, is merely a convenient, conventional device for narrative closure, subordinate to Austen's own goal of female character analysis). Indeed, as we start to probe the marriage plot not for what it already carries with it as a structure of meanings but for how Austen adapts it to her own purposes, we begin to see that, for her heroines, the so-called goal of marriage is a highly ambivalent one. Marriage is a key theme for Austen not only, or even primarily, because it enables her to encode a comic, Christianized romance-vision of life as ultimately benevolent and harmonious, but also because it provides her with the occasion for a searching critique of her society, particularly of its subordination of women. The paradox of marriage for middle-class women in Austen's time and in her novels was that it represented everything that disempowered them and made them dependent on men but at the same time offered them their only escape from profound material insecurity and an even more constrained and burdensome dependence on the family (if there was a family to offer support). Also, in the period of being ''out'' and available for courtship and, to some extent, during courtship, women might also enjoy a brief period of (largely illusory) power and freedom in choosing suitors and negotiating a relationship with their future husband. But women's lack of autonomy in this period was precisely the result of their status in the marriage market as a type of financial or consumer commodity central to the process of social mobility among genteel families. Their value was seen, in a sense, in inverse proportion to their uselessness (and, effectively, powerlessness), in that their genteel credentials—and the fact that they had reliable credit to bring to a marriage—were validated by the fact that they did not earn their own living. Therefore, to have value and a certain type of power in the marriage stakes, middle-class women could not earn their own living; but this obviously placed them in an economically vulnerable position where they were always actually at the mercy of the male world's decisions about their ''investment'' value: fathers would decide how much to settle on them, and the open market of prospective husbands would then decide if it was enough. To appear marriageable, women also had to conform to other conventions of gentility that further disequipped them for independence. Their education, such as it was, was strictly limited to female ''accomplishments'' (a common butt of Austen's satire), and serious reading or other intellectually demanding study was frowned upon as unbecoming to a woman; and women were generally required to be passive and reticent and not to exhibit any "manly" robustness of mind or body (hence, Austen's many caricatures of the sickly, simpering woman figure). Through focusing so intensively on courtship and marriage rituals, Austen's novels inevitably bring all these paradoxical aspects of female experience to light and, at least implicitly, provide a thoroughly materialist analysis of gender inequalities of the time—even while simultaneously exploiting the full romance potential of the marriage plot.

Meenakshi Mukherjee concisely summarizes the rich potential of the marriage plot for Austen, adding certain thematic features not yet mentioned. For Austen, as for all the major eighteenth-century novelists apart from Defoe and Sterne, she writes, marriage offered

a nodal point on which several areas of human experience converged. The particularly British concern with class divisions and the limited opportunities for social mobility, the rich narrative potential of property inheritance, issues of social conformity, parental authority and individual rebellion, economic survival and moral choice, sexual attraction and emotional drama—all these could be subsumed under one central trope, marriage, which became the ritual ending of most novels . . . till the end of the nineteenth century. (*Mukherjee 1991*: 29)

Morals. In his influential *The Great Tradition* (1948), F. R. Leavis identified Jane Austen's "intense moral interest" as the defining feature of her greatness as a novelist:

The principle of organization, and the principle of development, in her work is an intense moral interest of her own in life that is in the first place a preoccupation with certain problems that life compels on her as personal ones. She is intelligent and serious enough to be able to impersonalize her moral tensions as she strives, in her art, to become more fully conscious of them, and to learn what, in the interests of life, she ought to do with them. Without her intense moral preoccupation she wouldn't have been a great novelist.

   This account of her would . . . [be] my case for calling Jane Austen, and not anyone later, "the first modern novelist." . . . Jane Austen, in fact, is the inaugurator of the great tradition of the English novel." (*The Great Tradition* [Harmondsworth: Penguin, 1972], p. 16)

As the daughter of a clergyman and as a devout Christian, it would perhaps be surprising if morality did not play a significant part in Austen's art, and each of her novels undoubtedly deals with specific moral questions that are intended to exercise our understanding, judgment, and discrimination. It is fairly clear that Austen's own values, as represented by the novels, are directly in line with the basic principles of Enlightenment rationalism and of the established church of her time. However, as is often noted, her novels are actually remarkably free of explicit moralizing, and, when critics talk of her "moral interest," they are referring not so much to the specific moral issues she raises (though these are obviously part of what they are talking about), as to her interest both in the *need* to make moral judgments as a matter of course and in the *processes* by which they are arrived at. This dual interest helps to reveal the full significance of the technical advances Austen made in the art of fiction in her use of a "free indirect style" of character presentation. This method of "filtering" a character's consciousness through the "central authorial intelligence," in a sort of "submerged speech" or semidramatic thought summary (Skilton 1977: 87–8), enabled Austen to show and implicitly analyze the moment-by-moment thought processes of her heroines as they grapple with the problems that confront them. That the individual *is* confronted constantly by moral problems in the modern world and *needs* to resolve them intelligently is part of her point and part of what makes her "the first modern novelist."

The fact that "the individual" in her novels is actually a woman should also be noted as a key part of her "moral interest." As Margaret Kirkham explains, in an age when women were generally considered incapable of "rational, principled, moral judgement, independent of personal interest," Austen's development of a free, indirect style enabled her (in one fairly imperceptible stroke) to demonstrate that women are capable—because they are presented simply doing it—of "stringent rational reflection" whereby "they learn to judge aright of their own conduct and that of other people, including those in higher places" (*Kirkham 1983*: 173). Of course, even apart from this technique, the very nature of Austen's powerful heroines—as rational, autonomous, intelligent, independent-minded, and physically robust characters—stands as a challenge to the period's gender stereotyping and asserts a strong moral claim of its own: "Jane Austen's heroines are not self-conscious feminists, yet they are all exemplary of the first claim of Enlightenment feminism: that women share the same moral nature as men, ought to share the same moral status, and exercise the same responsibility for their own conduct" (*Kirkham 1983*: 84). Particularly from a feminist perspective, then, the novel as the new literary form of the age, especially as it was developed by Jane Austen, was "both a new art and a new form of moral discourse" (*Kirkham 1983*: xvii). To men and women alike, Austen's novels continue to reveal "the ethical basis of everyday life" and the need to maintain "a constant alertness of will and intellect to control the self and understand others" (Skilton 1977: 81).

Manners. For Austen, as an essentially rationalistic Augustan, the manners or conventions of a civilized society ought to be a type of codification of the right reason and morality underlying that society. But, there are two opposing dangers that her novels constantly warn of that can break the link between morality and manners and eventually lead to a corruption in basic values. On one hand, manners can become reified—rigid, empty forms that have lost their original point and significance but that continue to carry status as a badge of gentility. Austen's novels are, of course, full of characters who wear this badge with bravado but whose outward manner is gradually shown to be an empty front for more or less vicious motives of self-advancement. The dangers of accepting manners at face value, of judging people by conventional forms rather than by reference to underlying moral principles, is often precisely at the heart of the learning process that Austen's heroines must undergo. On the other hand, manners can be carelessly flouted with no regard for their underlying regulative function in society. This, for Austen, is the lesser of the dangers—and the flouting of manners in a spirit of openness, warmth of feeling, or "candour" is never censured by her—but it remains a danger, nonetheless, in that it represents (in her world of microcosmic symbolism) a potentially anarchic threat to the rational order of society. The flouting of manners in the novels is usually associated with selfish or insensitive characters who pay no heed to the cares and concerns of others; it represents a lack of rational restraint and of good judgment—sometimes connected with romantic excess, as with Marianne in *Sense and Sensibility*—and it invariably has painful consequences for the characters involved.

Money. Austen's acute understanding of the economic basis of society and the "amorous effects of 'brass,'" as W. H. Auden put it in his famous poetic comment on Austen ("Letter to Lord Byron," quoted in *Southam 1987*: 299), is part and parcel of both her realism and her moralism. On one hand, Austen—herself a single woman with no independent income—had no illusions about the economic vulnerability of women in her time, and she was perfectly tough-minded and unsentimental in showing in her novels that there could be no happiness or fulfillment for her heroines without at least modest material security and comfort, something that could be attained, for the majority of middle-class women, only by marrying well. Austen also lived at a time of growing consumerism among the aspiring middle classes—with women in the paradoxical position of being both major domestic consumers and, in the marriage market, types of commodity—and it is merely part of her formal realism to reflect this by openly stating characters' incomes (usually on first introduction) and, among other things, systematically tabulating their rank, status, and income by careful reference to various sorts of consumer goods and related economic indicators (furniture, dress, horses, carriages, servants, and so on). Thus money, simply as a material feature of everyday life, is ubiquitous in Austen's novels.

On the other hand, while Austen acknowledges hard economic realities and tries to represent these objectively in her fiction, she does not accept them uncritically. As a moralist, she is, of course, constantly at pains to attack mere money values, ostentatious consumerism, and any form of behavior motivated purely by materialistic considerations; indeed, almost all her unsympathetic characters are condemned by their avaricious natures. As a feminist moralist, moreover, it is also central to her art that she should systematically expose and challenge unequal power relations between the sexes based on the economic subordination of women. As Edward Copeland sums up: "From the start of her career, Austen is a shrewd observer of the economic terrain of her class, though always from the chilly and exposed position of an economically marginal female member of it. . . . In fact, the shadow of the single woman without money, Charlotte Lucas syndrome, continues to haunt her works to the end" (Copeland 1997: 145–46).

To conclude this brief consideration of Jane Austen's themes, it may be useful as a stimulus to the reader's own reflections on Austen to present, without comment, two other short overviews of her achievement, one representative of a lifetime's devotion to the subject and the other representative of more contemporary modes of reading Austen.

It is with Jane Austen that the novel takes on its distinctively modern character in the realistic treatment of unremarkable people in the unremarkable situations of everyday life. In her six novels . . . Austen created the comedy of manners of middle-class life in the England of her time, revealing the possibilities of "domestic" literature. Her repeated fable of a young woman's voyage to self-discovery on the passage through love to marriage focuses upon easily recognizable aspects of life. It is this concentration upon character and personality and upon the tensions between her heroines and their society that relates her novels more closely to the modern world than to the traditions of the 18th century. It is this modernity, together with the wit, realism, and timelessness of her prose style; her shrewd, amused sympathy; and the satisfaction to be found in stories so skillfully told, in novels so beautifully constructed, that helps to explain her continuing appeal for readers of all kinds. (Brian C. Southam, "Jane Austen," *Encyclopaedia Britannica*, 1996)

To read her novels as entirely realistic and unequivocal records of the life she knew is wilfully to overlook the different kinds of tension in her work . . . between subversive parodic strategies and mimetic representations of life; between stasis and spatial enclosure on the one hand and mobility and expansion on the other; between the private domain of emotion and imagination, and the public arena of propriety and property; between a woman's need to define her individual self and society's demand that she should conform to the familial and gender mould; between liberal sympathies and anti-Jacobin orthodoxy. Jane Austen's persistently non-polemical stand and her ideological reticence open out the novels to a range of equivocal meanings, while her sure syntax, concise dialogue and perfectly synchronised formal structures point towards a univocal certainty, baffling the critic who must coax a coherent system out of these elusive texts. (*Mukherjee 1991*: 141)

See also "Themes" in the Index for themes as they are cross-referenced to text and character entries throughout the rest of the book.

See the entry for "Criticism" for a comprehensive guide to some of the most useful works to consult in this large area. Some suggested references for the specific themes mentioned here, in addition to those already cited in the article, are as follows. On marriage and related matters: Adams 1982, Allen 1985, Astell 1987, *Beer 1974, Berglund 1993*, Bloom 1994, Bowden 1992, Brown 1982, Cohen 1987, relevant entries in *De Rose and McGuire 1982, Dhatwalia 1988*, Fowler 1980, Gordon 1988, Gornall 1966–1967, *Halperin 1988, Handler and Segal 1990, Hardy 1984*, Honan 1984a, Hunt 1986, *Hudson 1992*, Kaufmann 1986, Kern 1986, Lundeen 1990, Macey 1983, Magee 1975, 1987, *McMaster 1978*, Millard 1980, *Mooneyham 1988*, Newman 1983, Okin 1983–1984, *Polhemus 1990*, Rzepka 1994, Shaffer 1992, 1994, Stout 1982, *Sulloway 1989*, Thompson 1986a, Ty 1986, *Vasudeva Reddy 1987b, Weldon 1984*, White 1995.

On morals, values, and related matters: any general study of Austen will discuss these—see the entry on "Criticism" for a guide and also *Butler 1975, Collins 1994, De Rose 1980, Devlin 1975, Duckworth 1971*, Dunn 1995, Dussinger 1990, *Ehrenpreis 1980, Fergus 1983, Gillie 1974*, Harding 1940, Heldman 1988, Heyns 1986, Kastely 1991,

Keener 1983, Koppel 1988, Koppel 1989, *Lerner 1967*, Miller 1992, *Monaghan 1980*, Nardin 1988, *Odmark 1981, Poovey 1984*, Reinstein 1983, Shoben 1982–1983, *Tave 1973*, Tobin 1990, Willis 1987.

On manners and related matters: Brissenden 1984, Brown 1996, Brownstein 1982, Buck 1971, *Byrde 1979, Cecil 1978*, Elsbree 1960–1961, Fowler 1974, Goold 1987, *Grey 1986* (relevant entries), *Jenkins 1938*, Kaufmann 1992, Kearney 1988, 1990, La Rue 1994, *Lane 1986, 1996*, David Marshall 1989, McAleer 1989, McKenzie 1985, *Nardin 1973*, Nardin 1988, Richards 1990, Saisselin 1994, *Schapera 1977*, Schneider 1993, *Singh 1981, Wallace 1983, Wilks 1978*.

On money: Copeland 1989, 1993, 1996, 1997, Dodds 1949, Dorsey 1990, *Fergus 1991*, Frost 1991, Heldman 1990, Holway 1992, Hopkins 1994, Macey 1983, Okin 1983–1984, *Pool 1993*, Porter 1992, *Scheuermann 1993*, Terry 1988, Thompson 1984, 1990, Tobin 1990, Webb 1981, Woolf 1942.

On free indirect style, see the section on language under the entry for ''Criticism'' and Finch and Bowen 1990, Flavin 1987, 1991, Neumann 1986, Pascal 1977, Shaw 1990, Tandrup 1983.

Thomas (*Sense and Sensibility* Ch.38; III:2:353). The Dashwoods' manservant, brought with them from Norland to Barton Cottage. His ''voluntary communication'' of the marriage between Lucy Steele and Mr. Ferrars (information gleaned from a business errand to Exeter) provides for a moment of raised dramatic tension near the end of the novel when Elinor's (and the reader's) hopes of her marrying Edward Ferrars seem to be dashed once and for all. (To everybody's great relief, of course, we are soon to learn that the Mr. Ferrars in question is not Edward but his younger brother Robert.)

Thorpe, Anne (*Northanger Abbey* Chs.4, 14; I:4:32; I:14:115). Anne is Mrs. Thorpe's second daughter and the one left behind by the Clifton excursion party. She has clearly been peeved by this, but in typical Thorpe style, she exaggerates her unconcern and displaces her frustration by attaching herself to ''two of the sweetest girls in the world, who had been her dear friends all the morning.''

Thorpe, Edward (*Northanger Abbey* Ch.4; I:4:32). Mrs. Thorpe's second son, mentioned only in passing as being at Merchant-Taylors' School.

Thorpe, Isabella (*Northanger Abbey* Chs.4, 13, 27; I:4:32–34; I:13:97–98; II: 12:216–19). At twenty-one, the eldest of the three Thorpe sisters and the most handsome. The speed with which she affects to be Catherine Morland's intimate friend is only a little greater than the speed with which she breaks off her engagement to James Morland when she realizes his lack of fortune and sees the prospect of making a more profitable match; both circumstances clearly illustrate the shallowness of this character, and the latter circumstance also demonstrates how determinedly self-seeking and mercenary she is, for all her veneer of affable ''sweetness.'' Catherine is at first taken in by this older and more worldly girl, finding her vacuous chatter about fashion and flirtation initially fascinating and her exaggerated interest in gothic novels infectious. But Isabella's inability to read anything more serious than popular romances (illustrated by a dismissive comment about Samuel Richardson's *Sir Charles Grandison*); her officious and manipulative attempts to pair off Catherine with her oafish brother, John, and to separate Catherine from the Tilneys; and, later, her patent duplicity over her flirtation with Frederick Tilney and her treatment of James Morland—all gradually accumulate to expose her "strain of shallow artifice" to Catherine, who finally dismisses her as a heartless and hypocritical "coquette."

Thorpe, John (*Northanger Abbey* Chs.4, 7; I:4:32–33; I:7:45–50). John Thorpe is the eldest of Mrs. Thorpe's children and studying at Oxford in the same college as his friend, James Morland. Totally inept in his social manner, "easy where he ought to be civil, and impudent where he might be allowed to be easy," John Thorpe is a caricature of the foppish man-about-town. He is boorish and boastful about his possessions, particularly about his horse and carriage, and constantly trying to impress others by exaggerated claims about his wealth and social consequence—indeed, through his meddlesome bragging General Tilney gains his false ideas about Catherine Morland's background (first, that she is an heiress and then, that she is very poor). He also tries to impress others, Catherine Morland in particular, with a woefully misplaced confidence in his own charms; in fact, he is plain in looks, clumsy in movements and manners, and wholly witless in conversation. Catherine is confounded by his illogical speeches and at first mildly amused at his gauche attempts to woo her. But she becomes more seriously alarmed and indignant about his behavior when he presses his claim more importunately and, like his sister, seeks to control her movements and decisions by dishonestly interfering in her arrangements with the Tilneys. Thus, although John Thorpe is, in many ways, a harmless figure of fun, the implications and consequences of some of his actions draw attention to an element of serious moral critique in Jane Austen's depiction of this type of character.

Thorpe, Maria (*Northanger Abbey* Chs.4, 14; I:4:32; I:14:115). The youngest of Mrs. Thorpe's three daughters. She and Anne pretend to be as handsome as their elder sister, Isabella, and they imitate her in dress and manner—which suggests that they are as silly and affected as she is.

Thorpe, Mrs. (*Northanger Abbey* Ch.4; I:4:31–34). Mrs. Thorpe of Putney is an old school friend of Mrs. Allen. They have not seen each other for fifteen years and happen to bump into each other at the pump-room in Bath. A widow with six grown-up children, Mrs. Thorpe is a talkative, "good-humoured, well-meaning woman, and a very indulgent mother." She is a widow and has her three daughters at Bath with her.

Thorpe, William (*Northanger Abbey* Ch.4; I:4:32). Mrs. Thorpe's third son, mentioned only in passing as being at sea.

"The Three Sisters, a Novel" (*Volume the First* of Jane Austen's juvenilia). Jane Austen dedicated this piece to her brother, Edward, and this suggests that it may have been loosely inspired by the three elder sisters of the Bridges family into which he married in December 1791; he married the youngest of the three, Elizabeth, but her two elder sisters, Fanny and Sophia, were also engaged and married in the same year. This and the relative maturity of the writing would then support the date usually given for the composition of "The Three Sisters"—1792 (though, for the suggestion of 1790, see *Jan Fergus 1991*: 53). The work consists of four letters, two each from the sisters Mary and Georgiana Stanhope to their friends Fanny and Anne, respectively. Mary is the eldest of the three Stanhope girls, and she has been proposed to by their rich but unpleasant neighbor, Mr. Watts. She cannot bear him, but she can bear even less the possibility that if she refuses him—and his money—he may marry one of her younger sisters or even one of the girls of a neighboring family, the Duttons. She is thus strongly attracted by the security and consequence such a marriage might bring her, but she is almost as strongly repelled by the idea of having to live with the odious Mr. Watts: "If I accept him I know I shall be miserable all the rest of my Life." The stark choice between security and happiness is treated comically here, as there is little doubt from the start which option the foolish and avaricious Mary will take, but, clearly, the basic dilemma was a serious one for women at the time and one that Jane Austen would explore in much greater depth in her major novels. Mrs. Stanhope makes it clear to Mary that she does not intend to lose this chance of having at least one of her daughters settled securely, though she does not much mind which one it is, and the more Mary feels that she is in danger of being passed over in the marriage stakes, the more she is inclined to accept Mr. Watts. Georgiana's two letters then pick up the story and present it from a different perspective. She is the youngest of the sisters and obviously sharper and more sensible than Mary, whose foolishness she makes fun of. Georgiana and her other sister, Sophy, agree with Mary (and everyone else, it seems) about Mr. Watts' deficiencies— "Hideous in his person and without one good Quality to make amends for it"— but they are absolutely unequivocal in their determination never to marry him "were Beggary the only alternative." In order to ensure their own safety from Mr. Watts, Georgiana and Sophy pretend to Mary that they *would* accept him if she were to pass up the opportunity. The thought of being upstaged by her younger sisters finally pushes Mary into deciding to accept Mr. Watts. When he calls to receive her decision later that day, the wholly materialistic basis of the match is made clear as they haggle late into the night over the details of the marriage settlement. Mary makes bold demands for a new carriage, new horses, clothes, furniture, and servants as well as for "an infinite number of the most valuable Jewels" and an agreement that she should be able to spend seasons in

Bath and London and on holiday tours. But Mr. Watts drives a hard bargain, too: he refuses almost all of her terms and eventually carries the day with a much more modest agreement after bluntly threatening to withdraw his proposal in favor of Sophy if Mary were to persist in her demands. The next day, Mary goes to visit the Duttons in order to boast of her coming marriage, but it is clear that Kitty and Jemima, like Georgiana and Sophy, do not envy her in the slightest, particularly as they have with them a handsome and well-mannered young man, Mr. Brudenell, who stands as a stark contrast to the odious Mr. Watts.

As B. C. Southam argues (*1964*: 34–35), in the sequence of juvenile pieces, "The Three Sisters" represents a significant advance in Jane Austen's technique and vision:

With its firm design and neatly-turned plot it reads like a short episode from a full-scale novel. Jane Austen now avoids lengthy passages of narrative or reported speech, and employs direct conversation. The effect is dramatic, and hits the tone of social comedy. Her subject—marriage for an establishment—was a crucial problem at this time, posing the question of expediency and idealism. . . . The direction of Jane Austen's art is clearly marked. . . . Her aim is to show how character is formed and defined in the events of ordinary life, and how speech and behaviour are determined by a complex of personal and social considerations.

Frances Beer, in her excellent introduction to a selection of the juvenilia (*The Juvenilia of Jane Austen and Charlotte Brontë*. Harmondsworth: Penguin, 1986, pp. 7–19), also identifies this work as a key development away from simple burlesque and toward serious moral criticism:

The movement away from a strict neoclassical reaction to a series of isolated foibles—and toward a romantic response to the individual as potential victim of a materialistic, claustrophobic society—is crucial to Austen's artistic development, and will be carried over and refined in her novels. Her romanticism, if such we can call it, will not take her so far as to abandon her toughness on the question of personal responsibility, or to justify the extremes of rebellion or despair. But in the straits faced by the Dashwood or the Bennet girls—the narrowness of their lives, the apparent obligation to marry, no matter whom, to survive—and even more in the melancholy and quiet desperation of Fanny Price, or Jane Fairfax, or Anne Elliott [*sic*.], we see a crystallization of a negative view of society that first begins to be articulated in *The Three Sisters*. (16)

Main Characters: Mr. Brudenell, Kitty and Jemima Dutton, Mrs. Stanhope and her daughters, Mary, Sophy and Georgiana Stanhope, Mr. Watts.

Tilney, Eleanor (*Northanger Abbey* Ch.8; I:8:53–56). The elegant and dignified sister of Henry Tilney who becomes a close friend and confidante of Catherine Morland. Eleanor stands in stark contrast to Catherine's false friend Isabella Thorpe: where the latter is frivolous, affected, selfish, and hypocritical, Eleanor is sensible and sincere, genuinely kind and openhearted. In contrast to the "decided pretension" and "resolute stilishness" of Isabella, Eleanor has "real elegance'' and ''good breeding.'' One of the ironies in the novel is that, though Jane Austen pokes fun at the conventions of gothic romance through her heroine's fantasies while at Northanger Abbey, she still makes positive use of certain gothic and romance conventions herself, and Northanger *does* become the source of both ''horrid'' sensation and romantic intrigue, though not of the sorts that Catherine originally envisaged. The sensation comes with Catherine's unseemly eviction by General Tilney; but the romance comes, in displaced form, when, right at the end of the novel, we learn of Eleanor's clandestine meetings at the abbey with her impoverished lover and of the fairy tale ending to their affair when this ''most charming young man in the world'' unexpectedly inherits a fortune and title and is finally able to marry her.

Tilney, Frederick (*Northanger Abbey* Chs.14, 16; I:14:113; II:1:131). Eldest son of General Tilney and a captain in the army. A handsome, fashionable young man with an assuming air and a roving eye. His blatant flirtation with Isabella Thorpe leads to the breaking off of her engagement to James Morland, though Frederick Tilney clearly has no intention of marrying her himself and soon transfers his attentions to another woman (Charlotte Davis). Catherine Morland judges his looks and manners to be ''decidedly inferior'' to those of Henry Tilney, and, from his behavior and the comments of others, it is clear that Frederick is a vain and thoughtless gadabout.

Tilney, General (*Northanger Abbey* Chs.10, 13, 20, 29; I:10:73, 80; I:13:102–3; II:5:156; II:14:237–38). Owner of Northanger Abbey in Gloucesterhire, a widower of nine years' standing, and father of Frederick, Henry, and Eleanor Tilney. When Catherine first sees him at Bath, she is mainly struck by his handsome looks and imposing demeanor; she is a little overawed when she is introduced to him, but he quickly puts her at ease by his polite and gallant manner toward her. Indeed, he seems exaggeratedly concerned to impress her and to encourage her friendship with his son and daughter. As Mrs. Allen later says, at this time, he seemed to be ''such an agreeable, worthy man.'' However, almost as soon as he leaves Bath, his evidently cultivated public manner begins to slip, and, on the journey to Northanger, Catherine begins to notice how he is ''always a check upon his children's spirits.'' At Northanger, his irritability shows in his impatience over mealtimes, and, when Catherine starts to speculate about the death of Mrs. Tilney, she draws on these previous hints of a darker personality as, in her imagination, she transforms him into a truly heinous figure after the model of the villains she has read about in gothic romances. The irony of such imaginings is that the General eventually does turn out to be a type of villain, though not quite of the gothic sort. For when he discovers that Catherine is not the heiress he had been led to believe she was by John Thorpe, he angrily dismisses her from his house and sends her on the long journey home with no escort. His superficial charm and apparent benevolence toward Catherine are thus exposed as part of a calculated attempt to bring money into the family by promoting a match with his son, Henry. General Tilney's true character is now revealed to be that of an ill-tempered tyrant, driven by purely mercenary motives—though his gullibility in being taken in by the foolish John Thorpe should also be noted.

Tilney, Henry (*Northanger Abbey* Ch.3; I:3:25). The younger son of General Tilney and the incumbent of Woodston, twenty miles from Northanger Abbey. Twenty-four or twenty-five when we first meet him, Henry Tilney is the hero of the novel who eventually marries Catherine Morland. Tall and good-looking, with "a pleasing countenance" and "a very intelligent and lively eye," he is well read and well educated, witty, urbane, and eloquent. He enjoys teasing Catherine with clever wordplay and mischievously makes fun of her fanciful romantic notions. But there is never any doubt but that he values her for her openness, sincerity, and good nature, as well as for her essential good sense and steadiness of principle.

Tilney, Mrs., née Drummond (deceased) (*Northanger Abbey* Ch.9; I:9:68–69). Originally from a very rich family (her father, Mr. Drummond, gave her £20, 000 on her marriage, as well as £500 for her wedding clothes), Mrs. Tilney died nine years before the time of the main action, after a short and sudden illness described as "a bilious fever." A large part of the mock-gothic comedy at Northanger Abbey centers on Catherine Morland's overwrought imaginings about what might have been the true fate of Mrs. Tilney.

Tom ("Catharine," *Minor Works* 213). Mrs. Percival's servant.

Tom (*Emma* Ch.44; III:8:383). A young servant at Randalls, the home of the Westons, who is sent to collect the chaise from the Crown for Frank Churchill's peremptory return to Richmond following the Box Hill party.

Tomlinson, Mr. (*The Watsons, Minor Works* 322, 336–37). The banker of D. with a newly erected house on the edge of the town. His wife and two sons are mentioned later on in relation to the ball.

Trent, Governor (*Persuasion* Ch.3; I:3:23). Formerly a resident at Monkford, in the neighborhood of Kellynch, mentioned briefly by Sir Walter Elliot and defined by him as a "gentleman" because of his being a man of property.

Tupmans, the (*Emma* Ch.36; II:18:310). Acquaintances of Mrs. Elton who live at West Hall in the neighborhood of the Sucklings' Maple Grove near Bristol. Without any self-irony whatsoever, she uses them as examples of "upstarts" who, despite only a recently made fortune and "many low connections," consider themselves on a par with "the old established families." Quite apart from anything else, Mrs. Elton says, they come from Birmingham, "not a place to promise much, you know ... I always say there is something direful in the sound.''

Turner, Mrs. (*The Watsons, Minor Works* 315, 321). Emma Watson's aunt in Shropshire, by whom Emma was brought up from an early age. Her first husband died about two years ago, and she has recently married Captain O'Brien and removed to Ireland.

Turner's (*Mansfield Park* Ch.38; III:7:380). An actual naval shop in Portsmouth at the time, situated at 85 High Street. Mr. Price orders William's mess there for his forthcoming service on the *Thrush*.

V

Vernon, Charles (*Lady Susan, Minor Works* 243, 246–47). Charles Vernon is the younger brother of Lady Susan's late husband. He is a mild-mannered and kindly man and therefore easily imposed upon by the predatory Lady Susan, who quickly notes the signs of "plenty & elegance" when she arrives at his house.

Vernon children (*Lady Susan, Minor Works* 243, 250). There appears to be an abundance of Vernon children, but only Catherine and Frederic are named. Lady Susan tries to ingratiate herself with the Vernons by being especially nice to the children.

Vernon, Frederic (deceased) (*Lady Susan, Minor Works* 244, 249). Lady Susan's late husband, former owner of Vernon Castle in Staffordshire, and elder brother of Charles Vernon.

Vernon, Frederica Susanna (*Lady Susan, Minor Works* 244, 269–70, 279). Lady Susan's neglected sixteen-year-old daughter. Lady Susan constantly disparages Frederica and makes her sound stupid, stubborn, and ill tempered. But when she actually appears, a very different picture emerges of a timid and withdrawn but well-disposed girl who has been cruelly treated by her mother. As the Vernons treat her kindly, so she starts to come out of herself a little and to display a lively mind and affectionate disposition. Mrs. Vernon soon realizes that Lady Susan's original account of Frederica was a self-rationalizing travesty, and such an unnatural attitude to one's own child sets Mrs. Vernon even more definitely against Lady Susan. The immediate occasion for Lady Susan's harsh treatment of Frederica is the latter's unwillingness to marry the wealthy Sir James Martin, but Frederica finds him repulsive and would, she says, rather work for her upkeep than marry him. As this suggests, although Frederica is clearly cowed by her domineering mother, she does show signs of a plucky spirit—other examples are when she runs away from her boarding school and when she dares to write to Reginald De Courcy to ask for his help in opposing Lady Susan's marriage plans for her. While staying with the Vernons, Frederica falls in love with Reginald De Courcy, and we are given to understand that she later marries him, once the threat of Sir James Martin has been lifted by Lady Susan's marrying him herself and after she has been taken in as a permanent member of the Vernon family at Churchill.

Vernon, Lady Susan (*Lady Susan, Minor Works* 243). The eponymous heroine—or antiheroine—of the novel: wife of the late Frederic Vernon, mother of Frederica, and lover of, variously, Mr. Manwaring, Reginald De Courcy, and Sir James Martin. The main problem for most critics and readers of *Lady Susan* has been how to understand its tone of voice in relation to Lady Susan. Cold, callous, and calculating in most of her actions and attitudes (and she has been seen as a type of psychopath by some), she is nevertheless a highly intelligent, independent-minded, and sexually liberated woman who can be admired for her flouting of the male-dominated morals and mores of a cold, callous, and calculating social order. She is undoubtedly deceitful and duplicitous in her behavior, and she treats others, including her own daughter, with a ruthless disregard for their feelings and well-being, but some of her letters display a disarming honesty about her own motives and the hypocrisies of others, and she has a charm, wit, and vivacity that make her a peculiarly alluring femme fatale who gains grudging admiration from even her worst enemies.

Vernon, Mrs. Catherine, née De Courcy (*Lady Susan, Minor Works* 243, 246). The wife of Lady Susan's brother-in-law and sister of Reginald De Courcy. Lady Susan comes to Mrs. Vernon's house at Churchill with some trepidation, as she had originally (six years ago) tried to prevent her brother-in-law from marrying his wife for fear of losing control of some of the Vernon family's fortune. The fact that Lady Susan failed in this endeavor reflects the strength of Mrs. Vernon's character, and Lady Susan knows she cannot fool or manipulate her as easily as she can fool and manipulate others, including Mr. Vernon. Indeed, Mrs. Vernon is never really taken in by Lady Susan's beguiling manners at Churchill, even though there are brief moments when she doubts her own judgment. Mrs. Vernon makes strenuous efforts to prevent her brother from being seduced by Lady Susan, and she quickly and compassionately intervenes to help Frederica when she sees how cruelly her mother is treating her, later effectively adopting Frederica as her own. In determinedly opposing Lady Susan, Mrs. Vernon is the heroine of the novel to her antagonist's antiheroine, and she acts in some ways as the resisting and questioning voice of the reader—the resisting moral voice of the text—in the face of Lady Susan's sometimes bewitching appeal.

Verses. Although Jane Austen seems never to have made a serious or sustained effort to write in poetic form, she clearly enjoyed producing occasional light verses, and examples of these survive from more or less every period of her life. Her verses all seem to have been written solely for family and friends, and, with one or two exceptions (the most notable being "To the Memory of Mrs. Lefroy"), they are mostly of a humorous and whimsical nature. Of course, the fact that Austen did not write poetry *as such* does not mean that she could not write *poetically*, and many passages in her novels, particularly in *Emma* and *Persuasion*, clearly exhibit their own form of poetic lyricism.

The verses, most of them titled posthumously, are as follows: "I Am in a Dilemma," "Lines on Maria Beckford," "Lines *Supposed* to Have Been Sent to an Uncivil Dressmaker," "Lines to Martha Lloyd," "A Middle-Aged Flirt," "Mock Panegyric on a Young Friend," "Mr. Gell and Miss Gill," "My Dearest Frank, I Wish You Joy" (letter in verse), "On Sir Home Popham's Sentence, April 1807," "On the Weald of Kent Canal Bill," "On a Headache," "See They Come, Post Haste from Thanet," "To the Memory of Mrs. Lefroy," "To Miss Bigg with Some Pockethandkerchiefs," "Venta," "Verses to Rhyme with 'Rose,' " "Verses Given with a Needlework Bag to Mrs. James Austen." (With her own alterations, Jane Austen also copied out one of Byron's poems, "Napoleon's Farewell"—first printed in the *Examiner* of 30 July 1815, as "Lines of Lord Byron, in the Character of Buonaparté.")

All the known poems of Jane Austen, along with a selection written by various members of her family, can be found in the authoritative *Jane Austen: Collected Poems and Verse of the Austen Family*, edited by David Selwyn (Manchester: Carcanet Press, 1996). This contains detailed textual and explanatory notes by the editor on all the poems. Most of Austen's poems are also printed together in *Minor Works*, pp. 440–52, along with three of Austen's charades (see also my entry under *Charades*): this section of the volume also prints two falsely attributed verses, "On the Universities" and "On Capt. Foote's Marriage with Miss Patton." Slight verses incidental to the juvenilia can be found on pp. 5, 9, 10, 34, 50, and 174 of *Minor Works*, along with the more substantial sixteen-line "Ode to Pity" on pp. 74–75. "Lines *Supposed* to Have . . ." can be found on p. 132 of *Le Faye 1989*; "See They Come . . ." and "My Dearest Frank . . ." can be found in the *Letters*, 3d ed., 1995, pp. 113–14 and 175–78; "Lines of Lord Byron . . ." are referred to in the *Family Record*, p. 199 and in the Appendix to the authoritative article by David Gilson, "Jane Austen's Verses," *The Book Collector* 33 (Spring 1984): 25–37. (Note that here and throughout this book I have used the titles as given in Austen's verses in *Minor Works* as these are likely to be most familiar to Austen scholars; but David Selwyn's edition of the poems, mentioned here, establishes several new titles, for good reasons.)

Viscount, the (*Northanger Abbey* Ch.28; II:13:251). The long-standing lover of Eleanor Tilney who, lacking status and wealth, is unable to marry her until, at the end of the novel, he unexpectedly inherits a title and fortune. Their marriage and the "accession of dignity" it brings have the consequence of putting General Tilney in good spirits, and he is then finally prepared to give his blessing to the marriage of Henry and Catherine. We also learn at the end that the laundry bills that Catherine had found in her bedroom cabinet at Northanger Abbey—the ones she had initially imagined to be a precious manuscript—belonged to the Viscount and had been left behind by his negligent servant following one of his visits to the house.

"The Visit, a Comedy in 2 Acts" (*Volume the First* of Jane Austen's juvenilia). Dedicated to James Austen, it is likely that this little playlet was inspired by the theatricals largely organized by him at the Steventon rectory during Jane Austen's youth between 1782 and 1789. There is a quotation here from one of the plays performed at Steventon over Christmas 1788–1789, and this suggests a date of possible composition around that time. The play contains only four very short scenes and seems comically designed to lead to the triple marriage alliance at the end as quickly as possible. As there are insufficient seats to go round for all of Lord Fitzgerald's house guests, they are forced into a fairly rapid intimacy with one another by having to sit on each other's laps. Then, after a brisk dinner of fried cowheel and onion, red herrings, tripe, liver and crow, the happy ending is upon us as, one after another, the various characters make their bald confessions of love: Lord Fitzgerald proposes to Sophy Hampton, and Stanly proposes to Cloe Willoughby, but Miss Fitzgerald has the last word by brazenly proposing to Mr. Willoughby.

Characters: Lord Fitzgerald, Miss Fitzgerald, Sir Arthur Hampton, Lady Hampton, Sophy Hampton, Stanly, Mr. Willoughby, Cloe Willoughby.

W

Walker, Miss (*Sense and Sensibility* Ch.30; II:8:194). A gossiping friend of Mrs. Jennings' gossiping friend Mrs. Taylor.

Wallis, Colonel (*Persuasion* Ch.15; II:3:139). Mr. Elliot's close friend who lives "in very good style" at Marlborough Buildings in Bath. He first informs Mr. Elliot of Mrs. Clay's apparent designs on Sir Walter Elliot and then collaborates closely with Mr. Elliot in his attempts to preserve his Elliot inheritance. In addition to his friendship with the duplicitous Mr. Elliot, Colonel Wallis also has the dubious merit of being admired by Sir Walter Elliot, partly for his style of living and partly for his fine military figure (apart from his sandy hair!). Although Mrs. Smith assumes Colonel Wallis to be a sensible and discerning character from what Nurse Rooke tells her about him, he is clearly not sensible or discerning enough to realize that his wife repeats everything he tells her to Nurse Rooke.

Wallis family (*Emma* Ch.27; II:9:236). The bakers of Highbury. Mrs. Wallis bakes the Bates' apples for them in her oven.

Wallis, Mrs. (*Persuasion* Ch.15; II:3:139, 141). Mrs. Wallis, Colonel Wallis' wife, is reputed to be charming and very beautiful, but we hear from Nurse Rooke, via Mrs. Smith, that she is a silly and showy woman, concerned only with money and fashion. She also gossips unthinkingly to Nurse Rooke, repeating things her husband has told her, and this is how Mrs. Smith learns of Mr. Elliot's attempts to ingratiate himself with his uncle and cousins.

Walsh, Captain (*Mansfield Park* Ch.38; III:7:380). A Portsmouth friend of Fanny's father, Mr. Price.

Watson, Augusta (*The Watsons, Minor Works* 350). The young daughter of Robert and Jane Watson who is left behind in Croydon when they come to stay at Stanton.

Watson, Elizabeth (*The Watsons, Minor Works* 315). At twenty-eight, Elizabeth is the eldest of the Watson girls and the one whose company Emma finds most congenial. At the start of the novel, Elizabeth kindly agrees to stay at home with Mr. Watson so that the newly returned Emma can go to her first ball in the area. As she drives her sister to the town, she provides her (and the reader) with a brief history of recent family affairs and prepares her for some of the local people she is to meet at the ball. She also makes Emma reflect somberly on the family's relatively low social and economic status in the community by repeated references to the family's chances in the marriage market.

Watson, Emma (*The Watsons, Minor Works* 315). Emma Watson is clearly intended to be the heroine of the novel, but her character is not fully developed because the work was never finished. She has been brought up in genteel circumstances by her aunt Turner in Shropshire since the age of five and now returns to her family in Stanton, Surrey, at the age of nineteen. It seems that she had been expecting to continue living with her aunt and eventually to inherit something from her. However, her aunt had recently remarried, and her new husband, Captain O'Brien, had not wanted Emma to go to live with them in Ireland. Emma is effectively disinherited by her aunt's second marriage, and, on her return to Stanton, she is acutely aware of a fall in her social standing. She is shocked to realize just how desperate her sisters are to marry into wealth and to realize just how important money is in the marriage market. As the novel progresses, she becomes more and more depressed by her general sense of the arbitrary importance of money in society—something that is emphasized by her contact with the rich but shallow society of Tom Musgrave and Lord Osborne. Only her brief encounter and conversation at the ball with the intelligent and cultured Mr. Howard provide her with a sense of potential that might lift her above both idle money and her enervating domestic circumstances.

Watson, Jane (*The Watsons, Minor Works* 319). Emma's materialistic, pompous, and showy sister-in-law from Croydon.

Watson, Margaret (*The Watsons, Minor Works* 317). The third Watson daughter whose "artificial Sensibility" when she is trying to impress visitors contrasts sharply with her "common voice" of fretful bad temper. She mistakenly believes that Tom Musgrave is seriously courting her when he calls at her home, but it is Emma he actually wants to see.

Watson, Miss (*Pride and Prejudice* Ch.7; I:7:30). An inhabitant of Meryton, mentioned only briefly when Lydia reports some gossip from her aunt Phillips about the movements of the Meryton officers.

Watson, Mr. (*The Watsons, Minor Works* 315). Mr. Watson of Stanton in Surrey is the invalid widower father of Emma Watson and her five brothers and sisters. He is an educated and sensible man, and Emma later finds solace in attending him in his sick chamber away from the petty captiousness of the other members of her family.

Watson, Penelope (*The Watsons, Minor Works* 316). Emma's second eldest sister. She would do anything to get married, according to Elizabeth Watson, and she does not appear in the course of the novel, as she is in Chichester trying to "catch" wealthy old Dr. Harding. Elizabeth warns Emma not to trust Penelope, as she still remembers with bitterness the fact that Penelope had once separated her from a lover in trying to win him for herself, and he had then married someone else entirely.

Watson, Robert (*The Watsons, Minor Works* 316). Emma's eldest brother and the husband of Jane Watson. He is a prosperous attorney in Croydon and very smug and self-satisfied about both that and the fact that he had married his former employer's only daughter, who had brought a fortune of £6,000 with her. His mind habitually turns to money matters, and his insensitive comments about Emma's aunt and uncle and her newly precarious financial position bring her nearly to tears.

Watson, Samuel (*The Watsons, Minor Works* 320). Emma's younger brother. He is a surgeon at Guildford and a would-be suitor of Mary Edwards.

The Watsons An unfinished novel of about 17,500 words, titled posthumously by J. E. Austen-Leigh in the 1871 edition of his *Memoir of Jane Austen*. It was begun probably sometime in 1804 (though possibly in 1803) and abandoned in early 1805, possibly around the time of the death of Jane Austen's father (27 January). The surviving manuscript is a heavily revised first draft with leaves watermarked 1803. Precisely why Jane Austen never finished this work is not clear. Three main possibilities are usually put forward, two to do with her personal circumstances at the time and one to do with the inherent nature of the material she was dealing with. First of all, it would be reasonable to assume that she was too distressed and distracted by the death of her father to continue with the novel at that time, especially given that her state of mind would already have been unsettled by the tragic accidental death of her close friend, Madam Lefroy, only a month or so before, on 16 December 1804. Second, it is often suggested that she was unable to settle to any sustained writing throughout the whole of the period after leaving Steventon in 1801 and moving to Chawton in

1809 because her domestic life was generally unsettled, with many changes of dwelling, much traveling, and, after the death of her father, a relatively uncertain economic position; moreover, it would seem that she was at her happiest, both personally and in her writing, when she was living in the country, and most of her homes in this period were in towns. Finally, Austen's inability to complete the novel may have been to do with the formal and thematic difficulties of what she was attempting. Lacking her customary flashes of comedy, *The Watsons* is an experiment in a type of somber social realism that Austen had not seriously grappled with before, and she may simply have been defeated by the difficulties of sustaining a new style and focus: "[P]robably Jane Austen's failure to continue the work later was in recognition of its serious flaws; perhaps, too, she felt out of sympathy with the almost unrelieved bleakness of the social picture, and the asperity of the satire. . . . she was telling the story of a distressed heroine, the staple character of sentimental and Gothic fiction. It is hardly surprising that at a first attempt she should meet some difficulty in appropriating this subject to her own kind of domestic comedy" (*Southam 1964*: 63–65).

The Watson family live in the village of Stanton, Surrey, three miles from the town of D. (presumably Dorking). They are a genteel family but are relatively poor and cannot afford to keep a closed carriage. Their friends, the Edwards family (sometimes written Edwardes in the manuscript), are richer and are able to keep their own coach; they live in the town and always issue an invitation to the Watsons to dress, dine, and sleep at their house when there is to be a ball in the town. The first winter assembly of the season is about to take place, on Tuesday, 13 October, and all the important families of the area are expected to attend, including the most important of all, that of Lord Osborne of Osborne Castle. On this occasion, only two of the Watson children are at home, and only one of them, Emma, will be able to attend the ball and accept the Edwards family's invitation. Her sister, Elizabeth, who is twenty-eight and the eldest daughter, will have to stay behind to look after their sickly widowed father.

Emma is nineteen and has only recently returned to the family after fourteen years in Shropshire, so this will be her first public appearance in the neighborhood. Emma had left when she was five to be brought up by her aunt and uncle Turner, but her uncle had died two years ago, and her aunt had now remarried and removed to Ireland with her second husband, Captain O'Brien, who did not want Emma to come to live with them. (It may be that O'Brien was a fortune hunter: we learn later—though the unworldly Emma thinks little of it herself—that, as Mr. Turner left his fortune in the hands of his wife without making any direct provision for Emma, this second marriage of her aunt's has effectively disinherited Emma of the £8,000 or £9,000 she might have expected on her aunt's death had she remained a widow. Repeated references to her aunt's foolishness would seem to support this view, though Emma only speaks positively of her erstwhile guardians.)

Elizabeth, while driving with Emma into town on the morning of the ball, prepares her for the occasion by telling her what to expect of the Edwards family and of the various people she is likely to meet, including the womanizing Tom Musgrave, who, "an universal favourite," seems to have flirted with every girl in the neighborhood, including herself. As Elizabeth chatters away about the various romantic entanglements that she and her other two sisters, Penelope and Margaret, have been involved in, Emma is somewhat disconcerted to realize that the only matter of concern to her sisters is to find an eligible husband, which to them seems to mean no more than his having a comfortable income. In voicing her concern about this, Emma concisely expresses one of the central themes in all Jane Austen's fiction: "To be so bent on Marriage—to pursue a Man merely for the sake of situation—is a sort of thing that shocks me; I cannot understand it. Poverty is a great Evil, but to a woman of Education & feeling it ought not, it cannot be the greatest.—I would rather be a Teacher at a school (and I can think of nothing worse) than marry a Man I did not like." On hearing this, Elizabeth concludes that Emma has been brought up by her aunt to be too refined for her own good and suggests that such an attitude may lead to unhappiness. Elizabeth, in any case, continues in a similar vein, this time talking of their brother Sam's hopes of marrying Mary Edwards, whom he has loved for two years. Sam is a surgeon in "Guilford" (presumably Guildford) and cannot be there for the ball, so Elizabeth urges Emma to notice with whom Mary dances and, in particular, to see if she dances more than once with a Captain Hunter, about whom Elizabeth has her fears. Mary Edwards is an only child with at least £10,000 settled on her, and Elizabeth fears that Sam stands little chance of marrying her, given his lack of fortune—though Elizabeth hopes Sam may be as lucky as their eldest brother, Robert, a successful attorney in Croydon, who managed to marry someone with £6,000. Again, Emma is aggrieved to find that money counts for so much in marriage, and she is increasingly uncomfortable at the thought of her family's apparently lowly status.

In this frame of mind, Emma arrives at the house of the Edwards family apprehensive of how she might be thought of by this rich family who have met her, briefly, only once before. Although Mrs. and Miss Edwards receive her in a friendly manner, they are rather stiff and reserved with her and seem to have little conversation. She is put more at ease when Mr. Edwards arrives, as he is more relaxed and talkative. He brings the news that the Osbornes will certainly be at the ball, as horses for two carriages have been ordered by them. As Emma and Mary dress for the ball together, they become better acquainted and easier with one another; Emma finds that, despite her earlier reserve, Mary has "the shew of good sense, a modest unpretending mind, & a great wish of obliging." Back in the parlor, the girls' dresses are inspected and admired, and Mary shyly asks Emma if she is often likened to her brother, Sam. Mr. and Mrs. Edwards clearly bristle at this remark and exaggeratedly insist that there is no resemblance whatsoever and that such a comparison cannot be very flattering to Emma. At dinner, Mr. Edwards, who is something of a gossip and keen to glean whatever new information he can, asks Emma about her aunt's recent second marriage and then goes on to make some pointed remarks about the need for elderly ladies to be careful in choosing second husbands.

The Edwards family party arrive early at the ball, and Emma has her first glimpse of Tom Musgrave as they pass through a gallery leading to the assembly room. She learns from Mary that he is no favorite with her or her parents, as he is considered to be of "rather an unsettled turn." When the dancing begins, Mary is engaged for the first two dances by the very Captain Hunter that Elizabeth had earlier talked of; Emma dances with a fellow officer of his and begins to enjoy herself. As a new and pretty face at the assembly, Emma is carefully observed by all and generally admired for her vigorous good looks.

There is a stir as the Osborne party finally arrives. It consists of Lady Osborne, her son Lord Osborne, and her daughter Miss Osborne; the daughter's friend, Miss Carr, Mr. Howard, Lord Osborne's former tutor, and now a local clergyman, his widowed sister, Mrs. Blake, and her ten-year-old son, Charles; and also Tom Musgrave, who seems to have delayed his entrance to coincide with that of the Osbornes. Emma overhears Lady Osborne, a handsome, dignified woman of about fifty, remark to someone that they had come early to the ball for the sake of little Charles Blake, who is extremely fond of dancing. Shortly after this, Emma finds herself seated among the Osbornes, and she enjoys watching the excitement with which Charles Blake anticipates his first dances, promised to him by Miss Osborne. As the orchestra strikes up, however, Miss Osborne quickly excuses herself from this obligation and dances instead with a Colonel Beresford, one of the smartest of the officers present. Little Charles is clearly mortified at this, and he seems close to tears when Emma comes to the rescue and offers to dance with him in Miss Osborne's place. He accepts very readily and is immediately restored to his previous high spirits. Mrs. Blake, too, is most grateful to Emma for her spontaneous kindness. As they dance, the unusual couple become a major focus of attention, and even the previously aloof Lord Osborne makes a point of coming over to talk to Charles to gain a better impression of his partner.

After tea, Mrs. Blake introduces Emma to her brother, Mr. Howard, and he engages her for the next two dances. Before these, however, Emma is flattered and amused to overhear Lord Osborne sending Tom Musgrave to dance with "that beautiful Emma Watson" so that he might later be introduced to her if "she does not want much Talking to." As Emma is already spoken for by Mr. Howard, however, she is relieved to be able to refuse Tom Musgrave when he approaches her on his errand, and she enjoys seeing him discomfited by her cool and collected manner toward him, used as he has been to the overeager attentions of her sisters. When she dances with Mr. Howard, she finds him an intelligent and agreeable partner and regrets the shortness of their two dances together, especially as the Osborne party leave almost immediately thereafter. However, the evening has been a great success for Emma, and she goes to bed that night "in charming Spirits, her head full of Osbornes, Blakes & Howards."

The next morning brings a steady stream of visitors to Mrs. Edwards' house,

all keen to see more of the young lady who had been so admired by Lord
Osborne. Then Tom Musgrave arrives with a note from Emma's sister, Elizabeth, informing her that her father has taken the carriage for the day to attend
a religious visitation and that she will have to find her own way home somehow.
Tom Musgrave then adds "a verbal postscript" to the effect that Elizabeth had
agreed that he should bring Emma back home in his curricle. Emma steadfastly
refuses this offer, however, and Mrs. Edwards supports her by offering her the
services of the family coach, which Emma gladly accepts. Back with Elizabeth,
Emma relates the events of the preceding evening, and Elizabeth is greatly
impressed to hear of her sister's friendship with the Osbornes and in equal
measure surprised to hear her censure of Tom Musgrave as being vain, conceited, and ridiculous in his attempts to curry favor with people. When Mr.
Watson arrives home later that evening, he talks admiringly of the preacher he
had heard that day, and this preacher turns out to have been none other than
Mr. Howard. Mr. Watson also reports that Mr. Howard had helped him up some
stairs to dinner and had inquired after one of his daughters, though he could not
say which of them he meant.

Three days after the day of the ball, Lord Osborne and Tom Musgrave unexpectedly call at the Watsons' house as Emma and Elizabeth are preparing for
an early informal dinner in the parlor. Emma is flattered by a visit that she takes
as a compliment to herself but embarrassed by her unpreparedness and the general inelegance of her surroundings. Tom sits near to Elizabeth and talks animatedly to her, as usual, while Lord Osborne, with Emma, struggles to sustain
a desultory conversation, though it is clear that he would like to impress her.
The awkward visit is brought to an end when the housekeeper, Nanny, comes
in to remind them that Mr. Watson, who is ill in bed, is still waiting for his
dinner. Afterward, Emma reflects, "among other unsatisfactory feelings," that
the visit might at least have been more agreeable if Mr. Howard had come as
well.

Some two weeks later, Margaret Watson is brought home from Croydon by
her brother Robert and his wife, Jane, and they remain at Stanton for a few days
to become better acquainted with Emma. Emma finds both her sister and sister-
in-law irritatingly affected and insincere, and she is brought almost to tears by
her brother when, thinking only of money like almost everyone else, he talks
harshly of her beloved aunt and late uncle.

Later that evening, Tom Musgrave calls at the house on his way home from
London, and, though Emma would not normally be glad to see him, she finds
that he adds a welcome degree of variety, humor, and good manners to a family
party that may otherwise have grown tedious and fretful. Before he leaves,
Margaret, who believes his visit was intended for her, prompts Elizabeth to
invite him to dinner for the following evening. He agrees to come if he can,
but he will not commit himself, and he departs, "delighted with the uncertainty
in which he had left it." Margaret excitedly spends the whole of the next day
supervising preparations for this dinner, but when Musgrave fails to show, she

becomes extremely vexatious and peevish, and this sours the atmosphere in the house for the remainder of Robert and Jane's stay. Emma retreats to her father's sick chamber. He, at least, is "a Man of Sense and Education," and she can have an intelligent conversation with him when he is well enough to talk. At other times, she can at least find some peace and quiet and some respite "from the dreadful mortifications of unequal Society, & family Discord—from the immediate endurance of Hard-hearted prosperity, low-minded Conceit, & wrong-headed folly, engrafted on an untoward Disposition."

When Robert and Jane leave, they invite Emma to come back with them to Croydon, but, unsurprisingly, she declines and they depart without her.

(The manuscript ends here. Cassandra Austen is said to have told some of her nieces how Jane Austen intended to continue the story: after the death of Mr. Watson, Emma would become dependent on her brother and sister-in-law for a home; she would decline an offer of marriage from Lord Osborne and eventually marry Mr. Howard.)

Main Characters: Rev. Mr. Howard, Tom Musgrave, Lord Osborne, Mr. Watson, Emma Watson, Jane Watson, Elizabeth Watson, Robert Watson.

Minor Characters: Colonel Beresford, Betty, Mrs. Blake, Charles Blake, Fanny Carr, Mr. Curtis, Mr. Edwards, Mrs. Edwards, Mary Edwards, Dr. Harding, Mr. Hemmings, Captain Hunter, James, Mr. Marshall, Nanny, Mr. Norton, Captain O'Brien, Mrs. Osborne, Miss Osborne, Mr. Purvis, Rev. Dr. Richards, Mrs. Shaw, Jack Stokes, Mr. Styles, Mr. Tomlinson, Mrs. Tomlinson, James Tomlinson, Mrs. Turner, Augusta Watson, Margaret Watson, Penelope Watson, Samuel Watson.

See: Heldman 1986, McMaster 1986, 1994, Norris 1986, Pickrel 1988, *Southam 1964*, Wiesenfarth 1984.

Webbs, the Miss (*Pride and Prejudice* Ch.29; II:6:164). Acquaintances of Lady Catherine de Bourgh's, referred to by her as comparing favorably with the Bennet girls for *all* having learned music.

Wentworth, Captain Frederick (*Persuasion* Ch.4; I:4:26–28). The central male character in the novel, Frederick Wentworth is thirty-one when we first meet him and a warm, open, well-mannered man, highly successful and respected in his professional life and quietly self-assured, but with no trace of conceit or affectation. He has just (in the summer of 1814) returned from active service in the navy at the end of the Napoleonic Wars, during which he has made a substantial fortune (of about £25,000). Eight years previously, as "a remarkably fine young man, with a great deal of intelligence, spirit and brilliancy," he had been engaged to Anne Elliot. However, at that time, he was not yet a captain, and his prospects were uncertain; Lady Russell had therefore persuaded Anne that it would be imprudent to marry him, and she had broken off the engagement. He had been indignant at this decision and had left the country shortly afterward, never to see Anne again until the present time. In the intervening years, Anne has thought a great deal about her decision and has developed a mature and balanced view of it; she deeply regrets accepting Lady Russell's advice, but she believes she acted dutifully in doing so and in the best interests of Wentworth himself. However, his view of the event has remained arrested at the stage it was eight years ago: he has not forgiven Anne for her action, is still bitter about it, and is proudly determined not to think of her again as a potential partner. As such, we have an unusual situation for a Jane Austen novel, where from the outset the heroine has already learned her lessons and already has a mature and clear-sighted outlook on life, while the hero undergoes a process of learning about himself and his judgment of others, most particularly about his true feelings for Anne. As the novel progresses, therefore, it traces (largely through Anne Elliot's eyes, of course) Wentworth's gradual shift in feeling and judgment, from a stubborn and studied refusal to acknowledge his continuing desire for Anne, through his self-deceiving flirtation with Louisa Musgrove, to a passionate, open avowal of love for Anne and an admission of his own fool-ishness in not seeking to renew their relationship earlier (when he had first been made a captain two years after their separation).

Wentworth, Edward (*Persuasion* Ch.3; I:3:23). Captain Wentworth's brother. He had held the curacy of Monkford, near Kellynch, for two or three years (possibly from 1805 to 1808) before moving to a new living in Shropshire several years before the time at the start of the novel (i.e., the summer of 1814). During his time at Monkford, in the summer of 1806, Anne Elliot had first met Captain Wentworth, who was then staying with his brother. Edward Wentworth was the only person of Captain Wentworth's acquaintance to know anything of the latter's brief engagement to Anne, and she feels sure that, as Edward was a sensible and discreet man, he would never have told anybody else about it.

Weston, Anna (*Emma* Ch.53; III:17:461–62). The Westons' newborn child.

Weston, Mr. (*Emma* Chs.1, 2; I:1:6; I:2:15–17). Mr. Weston is "a straight-forward, open-hearted man," with a cheerful disposition and outgoing person-ality. Born and bred in Highbury, he was from a respectable family that had been steadily "rising into gentility and property." As a young man with a small independence, he satisfied his active nature by joining the county militia, where, as Captain Weston, he was "a general favourite." His marriage to the rich Miss Churchill of Enscombe, Yorkshire, produced a son, Frank, but "did not produce much happiness" and left him, when Mrs. Weston died after three years, "rather a poorer man than at first." His immediate difficulties were eased somewhat when he agreed, apparently with "some scruples and some reluctance," to the adoption of Frank by the Churchills. He then left the militia and went into trade, as his brothers had already done and, over about twenty years, gradually remade his fortune until he could afford to buy the small estate of Randalls and to set up a new home there with his second wife, Miss Taylor, whom he has just married at the start of the novel. Mr. Weston has maintained regular contact with his son, seeing him every year in London and growing proud of him, but the rather distant relationship he has had with Frank also perhaps reflects a certain shallowness of feeling in his character; as John Knightley observes, "Mr. Weston is rather an easy, cheerful tempered man, than a man of strong feelings; he takes things as he finds them, and makes enjoyment of them somehow or other."

Weston, Mrs. Anna, née Taylor (*Emma* Ch.1; I:1:5). The novel opens with the marriage of Miss Taylor to Mr. Weston and the melancholic reflections of Emma and Mr. Woodhouse at having "lost" their much-loved governess and friend of sixteen years. She had brought up Emma and her sister almost like a mother, and then, after Isabella's marriage when Emma was about fourteen, she had become less of a governess and more of a friend and companion to Emma and one "such as few possessed, intelligent, well-informed, useful, gentle . . . one to whom she [Emma] could speak every thought as it arose, and who had such an affection for her as could never find fault." Indeed, if Miss Taylor had a fault of her own, it was this overindulgence of Emma in her early womanhood, allowing her to have "rather too much her own way" and failing to direct her education and opinions a little more forcefully and purposefully. Mr. Knightley, who otherwise respects Mrs. Weston as "a rational unaffected woman," criticizes her for just this, for too often submitting to Emma's will when she should have been asserting her own; she makes a better wife than a governess, he says, for, rather than educating Emma, she received "a very good education from *her*, on the very matrimonial point of . . . doing as you were bid." But Mrs. Weston continues to champion Emma, and she gives as good as she gets in her discussion with Knightley on Emma's character and behavior. As later events show, Knightley is right to worry about the dangers of Emma's having things rather too much her own way, but Mrs. Weston is also later vindicated in her confident, motherly (or sisterly) trust in Emma: "[S]he has qualities which may be trusted; she will never lead any one really wrong; she will make no lasting blunder."

Weston, Mrs., née Churchill (deceased) (*Emma* Ch.2; I:2:15). Originally from the rich Churchill family of Enscombe, Yorkshire, she was the first wife of Mr. (then Captain) Weston and, by him, mother of Frank Churchill. Her brother and sister-in-law, Mr. and Mrs. Churchill, strongly disapproved of the match with Mr. Weston and, after the marriage, "threw her off with due decorum." Although strong-willed enough to defy her family over the match, she was later not strong-willed enough "to refrain from unreasonable regrets . . . nor from missing the luxuries of her former home," and the marriage was not a very happy one. The couple lived beyond their means, and, when Mrs. Weston died after three years, Mr. Weston was left in straitened circumstances. (This partly explains why he was willing to have Frank adopted by the Churchills.)

Westons, the (*Sense and Sensibility* Ch.20; I:20:110). Some friends of the Palmers who are to visit them at Cleveland.

Whitaker family (*Sense and Sensibility* Ch.18; I:18:100). Local acquaintances of the Middletons in Barton.

Whitaker, Mrs. (*Mansfield Park* Ch.10; I:10:104–5). The housekeeper at Sotherton who shows Mrs. Norris around the dairy and gives her a recipe for a cream cheese, as well as, later on, an actual cream cheese and four pheasant eggs. It is a moot point as to whether these were "forced" on Mrs. Norris, as she avers, or "spunged," as Maria Bertram suggests.

Whitby, Miss (*Sanditon, Minor Works* 390). The daughter of Mrs. Whitby who looks after the general sales department of the circulating library (which retailed many things besides books). She is a fashion-conscious young girl with glossy curls and smart trinkets and clearly preoccupied with her own appearance as she has to be hurried down from her toilette to serve Charlotte Heywood.

Whitby, Mrs. (*Sanditon, Minor Works* 381, 389). The proprietor of the circulating library at Sanditon. When Charlotte Heywood and the Parkers call there on their first evening back in Sanditon, Mrs. Whitby is "sitting in her inner room, reading one of her own Novels, for want of Employment."

Wickham, Mr. (deceased) (*Pride and Prejudice* Ch.16; I:16:81). The father of George Wickham and the elder Mr. Darcy's steward at Pemberley. He had started his professional life as an attorney but had then devoted all his time to the management of the Pemberley estates. He discharged his duties so conscientiously and honorably there that he was held in the highest esteem by old Mr. Darcy, who came to rely on him as a close and confidential friend. Mr. Wickham died about five years prior to the main action of the story.

Wickham, Mr. George (*Pride and Prejudice* Ch.15; I:15:74). Mr. Wickham is initially presented in almost wholly positive terms, as a handsome, dashing, and well-bred gentleman who appears all the more glamorous to the Bennet girls by having recently accepted a commission as lieutenant in Colonel Forster's militia regiment. His true character, however, turns out to be very different from the first impressions he creates. He is, in fact, a thoroughly deceitful and scheming character, mercenary, dishonest, and wholly selfish and unscrupulous in his dealings with women. In the past, as we eventually discover, he had duped his father's employer, the elder Mr. Darcy, into bequeathing him money; he had squandered that money through a life of gambling and general dissipation; and then, when the young Fitzwilliam Darcy had refused to give him any more help, he had tried to cheat his way into the family's fortune by attempting to seduce Darcy's fifteen-year-old sister, Georgiana. When he later elopes with Lydia Bennet, his main motive in leaving Brighton is, in fact, to evade having to pay the large gambling debts he has incurred there; he has no intention of marrying her, and he gives no thought whatsoever to her reputation or to the damage he may be causing to her family. Of course, he is eventually forced to marry her by Mr. Darcy, but only after he has struck a deal about his debts and a wedding settlement. Wickham's lies to Elizabeth Bennet about how he has been mistreated by Darcy clearly reflect on his bad character, but they also serve a broader plot function in reinforcing Elizabeth's existing prejudices against Darcy and thus in delaying the development of their relationship. But as Elizabeth learns the truth about Wickham, so her estimate of Darcy improves, and her romance with him is able to advance. We see, then, a clear contrast not only between the inherent characters of Wickham and Darcy but also between Elizabeth's first and later impressions of the two men (note that "First Impressions" was the title of the early version of the novel).

Wilcox (*Mansfield Park* Chs.8, 20; I:8:77; II:2:189–90). The old coachman at Mansfield Park. Mrs. Norris (when in Sir Thomas' hearing, at least) appears to be extremely solicitous for "good old Wilcox" and his "noble" horses; she nurses his rheumatism in winter and even gets out of the carriage (she *says*) to save the horses at Sandcroft Hill on the way to Sotherton with Mrs. Bertram. Wilcox had apparently insisted on driving them on that trip, "out of his great love and kindness," despite suffering from a bad bout of his rheumatism and despite having been specially sought out by Mrs. Norris to advise him not to venture out (which rather suggests that, in fact, Mrs. Norris had harried him to come!). When plans are being laid for the party to Sotherton, Maria Bertram, keen to be driven by Henry Crawford in his barouche, coldly states that "Wilcox is a stupid old fellow, and does not know how to drive."

William (*Northanger Abbey* Ch.28; I:13:102–3). General Tilney's servant who is briefly suspected of negligence for allowing Catherine Morland to make her own way into the drawing room at the Tilneys' Bath residence. But Catherine's own "rapidity" was to blame, as she rushed in to the house straight past William, so eager was she to correct the message given to Eleanor Tilney by John Thorpe about Catherine's planned walk with Eleanor.

Williams, Eliza (*Sense and Sensibility*). See Brandon, Eliza.

Williams, Miss Eliza (*Sense and Sensibility* Ch.13; I:13:209). The illegitimate daughter of Mrs. Eliza Brandon. Colonel Brandon had taken her into his care on the death of her mother. He sent her to school and visited her whenever he could; after he inherited Delaford, she frequently visited him there, and this gave rise to suspicions that she was *his* "natural" daughter. When she was fourteen, she was placed under the care of a respectable lady in Dorsetshire. At sixteen, after a visit to Bath with some friends and about nine months before

Brandon's first acquaintance with the Dashwoods, she disappeared. It later emerges that she had eloped to London with John Willoughby, where she was seduced and then abandoned by him. Her letter to Colonel Brandon, communicating this, is the cause of his sudden departure from the Middletons' home on the morning of the proposed party to Whitwell. When he arrives in London, he finds Eliza on the point of giving birth to Willoughby's child. He fights an inconclusive duel with Willoughby over his behavior with Eliza and then takes her and the child into the country.

Willoughby, John (*Sense and Sensibility* Chs.9, 10, 31, 44; I:9:42–45; I:10:46–49; II:9: 209–10; III:8:317–32). Willoughby is the first in a line of trickster figures in Jane Austen's major fiction (to be followed by George Wickham, Henry Crawford, Frank Churchill, and William Walter Elliot): a type of character initially presented in glamorous terms as charming, attractive, witty, and intelligent but who turns out to be a deceiver, at best a thoughtless fibster and play-actor (Frank Churchill), at worst totally fraudulent and mendacious (George Wickham). Willoughby interestingly encompasses both extremes. On one hand, he seems genuinely to possess "every advantage of person and talents . . . a disposition naturally open and honest, and a feeling, affectionate temper." These are the considered later views of the rational Elinor, and they suggest that the heroic figure that the romantic Marianne falls in love with is not altogether a sham. On the other hand, Elinor's early suspicions about Willoughby's "lack of caution" are more than vindicated by what we later hear of his dissipated past and, in particular, of his callous seduction and abandonment of Eliza Williams, as well as by his cruel cutting off of Marianne in mercenary favor of the rich Miss Grey. There is thus an undeniably vicious streak in what might otherwise seem an attractive, though impetuous, character. Elinor explains this somewhat paradoxical conjunction as the result of "too early an independence and its consequent habits of idleness, dissipation, and luxury" (though one cannot help wondering if, to some extent, it also reflects some uncertainty in Jane Austen's technique and vision in this, her first published novel).

Willoughby, Mrs. (*Sense and Sensibility*). *See* Grey, Miss Sophia.

Wilson (*Lady Susan, Minor Works* 284). Lady Susan's maid.

Wingfield, Mr. (*Emma* Ch.11; I:11:92). Isabella Knightley's apothecary in London and the source of much consternation on the part of Mr. Woodhouse, who questions his medical advice, citing instead the opinions of his own Mr. Perry.

Woodcock (*Sanditon, Minor Works* 407). The proprietor of the resort hotel at Sanditon.

Woodhouse, Emma (*Emma* Ch.1; I:I:5). The eponymous young heroine of the novel, Emma Woodhouse, is initially presented as uniting "some of the best blessings of existence." She has good looks, intelligence, a happy disposition, great wealth, and a high status in the community. But, though we are positioned by the author to like Emma for her quick mind and warm feelings, we soon realize that she has been spoiled by all these so-called blessings and that, having had "rather too much her own way" for most of her twenty-one years, she has become quite conceited, with a tendency to arrogance and snobbery in her attitudes to others. In particular, she has an exaggerated sense of her own superiority in the community, a brash overconfidence in her own opinions and judgments, and a complacent lack of critical self-awareness. In fact, the opening portrayal of her character represents partly how *she* perceives, or rather misperceives, herself; and the novel's progress can be seen largely in terms of the successive shocks of recognition that Emma experiences on the hard road to self-discovery and objective self-understanding as each of her matchmaking fantasies fails and exposes her misjudgment and self-deception. But we retain sympathy for Emma, because she is honest and intelligent enough to acknowledge her own foolishness once it is revealed to her and because she has the integrity and strength of character to learn from her experiences and to strive to improve herself. By the end of the novel, largely by her own careful self-scrutiny (though sometimes aided by the criticisms of Mr. Knightley), she has come to recognize her "insufferable vanity" and "unpardonable arrogance" in trying to control the destiny of others; she realizes that she has been "universally mistaken" and that she must become less of an "imaginist" and "more rational, more acquainted with herself." The ironic repetition of the phrase "the best blessings of existence" at this late stage of the novel (at the end of Ch.48; III:12) emphasizes just how far Emma's character has traveled in self-understanding since the beginning. But, formulated by Emma in reference to Harriet Smith's prospects of marrying Knightley, the phrase here also reminds us that Emma's story is as much a love story as a story of formation or self-discovery. It is one of the masterly structural ironies of the novel that Emma's hasty and misplaced plans for the romance of others are ironically counterpointed throughout by the slow growth and gradual awakening of her unsuspected and unimagined love for Mr. Knightley. As she registers this love, "with the speed of an arrow," so she registers the truth about all those misplaced plans and what such a truth tells her about herself. One aspect of Emma's development that remains ambiguous even at the end of the novel (though perhaps it rather reflects an ambivalence of Jane Austen's) is the extent to which she learns to modify her class-conscious snobbery. On one hand (to take just one example), where she had originally dismissed the farmer Robert Martin as entirely beneath her notice and as an unsuitable match for a gentleman's daughter (which she imagines Harriet to be), she is finally happy to acknowledge his true "sense and worth" and to attend the wedding between him and Harriet. On the other hand, where Emma had originally been intimate with Harriet, an orphan of unknown parentage, she now views her as a farmer's wife and accepts unquestioningly an inevitable social distance between them: her intimacy with Harriet ''must sink,'' for what ''ought to be . . . must be.'' Emma's continuing snobbery is also reflected by the wonderfully ironic representation of her response to finding that Harriet's father is a tradesman. She thinks with horror at what might have been the consequences if Harriet had, indeed, married any one of the three men Emma had tried to match her up with; she would have been responsible for introducing into their families ''the stain of illegitimacy, unbleached by nobility or wealth.''

Woodhouse, Mr. Henry (*Emma* Ch.1; I:1:5). Mr. Woodhouse is the wealthy owner of Hartfield in Highbury, Surrey, a widower of long standing and the ''affectionate, indulgent'' father of Emma and Isabella. Emma loves her father dearly, but when Miss Taylor leaves to get married, and they are left to themselves, Emma is, we hear, ''in danger of suffering from intellectual solitude,'' for her father is a rather simple-minded man and cannot ''meet her in conversation, rational or playful.'' Indeed, ''though everywhere beloved for the friendliness of his heart and his amiable temper, his talents could not have recommended him at any time.'' A valetudinarian all his life, ''without activity of mind or body,'' he appears to be much older than he actually is, an impression accentuated by his nervous disposition, his horror of even the slightest change to daily routines, and his obsessive concern with questions of health. Mr. Woodhouse is one of Jane Austen's great comic creations, but, kindly and querulous by turn, he also serves the serious purpose (like Miss Bates) of testing the tolerance and understanding of the other characters.

Wright (*Emma* Ch.38; III:2:283). The Eltons' housekeeper at the vicarage.

Wynne, Cecilia (''Catharine,'' *Minor Works* 193–95). Along with her younger sister, Mary, Cecilia was the intimate childhood friend of Catharine Percival. After the death of her father, she became dependent on a relation, Sir George Fitzgibbon, who paid for her passage to India, where she was married to Mr. Lascelles, a man she felt no love for. (As frequently noted by critics, the fate of Cecilia Wynne mirrors that of Jane Austen's aunt Philadelphia Hancock.)

Wynne, Charles (''Catharine,'' *Minor Works* 206). The eldest of the Wynne boys. His father had intended him to enter the church, and this had been his own favored option, but after Mr. Wynne's death, the Bishop of M—had perversely arranged for him to join the army as a lieutenant.

Wynne, Mary (''Catharine,'' *Minor Works* 193–95). The younger of the two Wynne girls. After the death of Mr. Wynne, Mary is taken in by Lady Halifax as a companion to her daughters, and she goes to live with them in Scotland.

Her subsequent letters to Catharine convey a sense of unhappiness and a suggestion that she is coldly treated by the Halifaxes.

Wynne, Rev. (deceased) (''Catharine,'' *Minor Works* 193–94). The former incumbent of the Chetwynde parish and a close friend of the Percivals.

Y

Yates, the Honourable John (*Mansfield Park* Chs.12, 13; I:12:117 & 119; I: 13:121–22). After ten days spent in the same company at Weymouth, Tom Bertram makes a new "intimate friend" in the Honourable John Yates, and he invites him to come to Mansfield Park whenever he can manage it. Mr. Yates duly arrives, earlier than expected, directly from another house party in Cornwall. There, he had been on the verge of taking part in a private theatrical production of *Lovers' Vows* when a sudden bereavement brought the party to an untimely end; he comes to Mansfield Park, therefore "on the wings of disappointment, and with his head full of acting," and he soon becomes the moving force behind the Mansfield Park theatricals. A boastful and boorish dandy with little sense and less self-awareness, he is quickly established, especially during the rehearsals, as a comical figure to rival that of the oafish Mr. Rushworth. He believes himself to be a good actor but lacks all talent and taste and is generally considered "to rant dreadfully" (Mary Crawford later exclaims, "[I]f his rents were but equal to his rants!"); when Julia Bertram flirts with him, he totally fails to realize that she is only using him to try to provoke jealousy in her real target, Henry Crawford. In fact, Mr. Yates has little to recommend him "beyond habits of fashion and expense, and being the younger son of a lord with a tolerable independence." He is, it appears, one of many similar such friends with whom Tom Bertram fritters away his time and money when he is away from home, and it is clear that Sir Thomas would not have welcomed him at Mansfield Park had he been there when Mr. Yates arrived, for he considers him "trifling and confident, idle and expensive" and "the worst object" connected with the theatricals. Sir Thomas is certainly glad to see the back of him when he finally leaves and relieved to rid the house of what he sees as a pernicious influence, particularly as it bears on his elder son and younger daughter; "as the friend of Tom and the admirer of Julia he became offensive." However, Mr. Yates reappears later in the novel when, in London, he once more pays court to Julia Bertram. At first he is unsuccessful, as before, but then, in the immediate aftermath of the scandal involving Maria and Henry when Julia fears greater severity and restraint at home, he finally persuades her to elope with him to Scotland, and they marry soon after. Their match turns out to be "a less desperate business" than it initially appears to Sir Thomas, however; Mr. Yates' fortune turns out to be greater than was thought, and though he is still "not very solid," there is a hope of his becoming "less trifling" and "at least tolerably domestic and quiet."

Younge, Mrs. (*Pride and Prejudice* Ch.11; I:11:202). When Georgiana Darcy was first sent to live in London, at the age of fifteen, Mrs. Younge was appointed as her companion and chaperon. But Mr. Darcy later finds that he had been deceived as to her good character, and she appears to have colluded with Mr. Wickham (with whom she had been intimate in the past) in his attempted elopement with Miss Darcy. When the plan was discovered, however, Mrs. Younge was dismissed. She reappears in the story later on, as the landlady of a lodging house in Edward Street in London, when Darcy goes to her to find out the whereabouts of Wickham and Lydia. At first she will not tell him anything, but after two or three days and, it is implied, some bribery, she finally admits that Wickham had been there, and she reveals his present location.

Part III
BIBLIOGRAPHIES

4

Works by Jane Austen

For the modern, scholarly edition of Jane Austen's major novels, see here under *The Novels of Jane Austen*. Details of other contemporary editions of the novels are not given, as in almost all cases these rely on the texts of the scholarly edition, with only minor editorial adjustments. Separate entries for each novel are also given in order to provide details of the first English and American editions and of the first translation in each case. After initial publication in Britain between 1813 and 1817–1818, the novels next appeared in Bentley's *Standard Novels* series in 1833, after the London publisher Richard Bentley had bought the copyright of all six novels: the copyright for *Pride and Prejudice* from the publisher Thomas Egerton for £40 and the other five copyrights from Cassandra Austen for £210. Later in 1833, Bentley also issued all six novels in their first collected edition, and this was reprinted in 1837, 1856, 1866, and 1869.

As all the works here are by Jane Austen, the list runs alphabetically according to titles, although in one or two cases I have broken or manipulated the alphabetical order so as to keep certain kindred works together (e.g., in the case of the volumes of letters). At the end of the list, I append three texts that are not by Jane Austen, as these contain the first publication of a number of Jane Austen's works or letters (or extracts from them).

"Amelia Webster" and "The Three Sisters": Epistolary "Novels" by Jane Austen. English Department of the University of Alberta: Juvenilia Press, 1993.

Catharine and Other Writings. Edited by Margaret Anne Doody and Douglas Murray. Oxford: Oxford University Press, 1993.

Charades, Written a Hundred Years Ago by Jane Austen and Her Family. London: 1895. Includes three charades (out of twenty-two) by Jane Austen (reprinted in the Oxford Edition, *Minor Works*, 1954, p. 450).

Emma. 3 vols. London: John Murray, December 1815 (title page dated 1816). First U.S.

edition, Philadelphia: Mathew Carey, 1816. First translation, into French as *La Nouvelle Emma*, 1816.

Frederic and Elfrida: A Novel. With illustrations by Edward Bawden. Moreton-in-Marsh: Kit-Cat, 1987. 20 pp. Limited edition of 350. The first of the juvenilia from *Volume the First*.

"The History of England" by Jane Austen: A Facsimile of Her Manuscript Written Aged Sixteen and Illustrated by Her Sister Cassandra with an Introduction by Deirdre Le Faye and a Transcript of the Text. London: British Library, 1993.

The History of England from the Reign of Henry the 4th to the Death of Charles the 1st. Chapel Hill, NC: Algonquin Books, 1993. Introduction by A. S. Byatt.

Jane Austen: Collected Poems and Verse of the Austen Family. Edited by David Selwyn. Manchester: Carcanet/Fyfield Books in association with the Jane Austen Society, 1996.

Jane Austen's "Lady Susan": A Facsimile of the Manuscript in the Pierpont Morgan Library and the 1925 Printed Edition. Preface by A. Walton Litz. New York and London: Garland, 1989.

Jane Austen's "Sir Charles Grandison." Transcribed and edited by Brian Southam. Oxford: Clarendon Press, 1980. This provides a reading text and a transcription of the manuscript of Jane Austen's burlesque play "Sir Charles Grandison or The Happy Man, a Comedy in Five Acts." Although in Jane Austen's hand, the play had traditionally been ascribed to Jane Austen's second niece, Anna. However, when the manuscript came to auction in the autumn of 1977 and became open to scholarly inspection for the first time, its length, nature, and apparent chronology of composition provided strong (though not conclusive) evidence of Jane Austen's authorship.

Lady Susan. Edited by R. W. Chapman. Oxford: Clarendon Press, 1925.

Letters of Jane Austen. 2 vols. Edited by Edward, Lord Brabourne. London: Richard Bentley and Son, 1884. The first collection, printing eighty-nine letters and some verses for the first time.

[Letters] Jane Austen's Letters to Her Sister Cassandra and Others. 2 vols. Edited by R. W. Chapman. Oxford: Oxford University Press, 1932. This printed all the letters then known. A second edition in 1952 added five letters. A third edition, edited and collected by Deirdre Le Faye as *Jane Austen's Letters* (Oxford: Oxford University Press, 1995), represents a thorough revision of Chapman's edition, adding further letters and bringing the record right up-to-date; this edition contains 161 letters by Jane Austen.

[Letters] Jane Austen: Selected Letters. Edited by R. W. Chapman. Oxford: Oxford University Press, 1955. A representative selection from the preceding two-volume edition. Reprinted in 1985, with an introduction by Marilyn Butler.

[Letters] Jane Austen: "My Dear Cassandra." London: Collins and Brown, 1990. An illustrated selection of the letters edited by Penelope Hughes-Hallett.

"Lines *Supposed to* Have Been Sent to an Uncivil Dressmaker" (April 1805) and Jane Austen's verses on Frank Austen's marriage to Mary Gibson (July 1806). Edited by Deirdre Le Faye. *Times Literary Supplement* (20 February 1987): 185.

"Lines to Martha Lloyd." Edited by Donald Greene. *Nineteenth-Century Fiction* 30 (1975–1976): 257–60. First complete publication of the manuscript, including all eleven stanzas, where the version in the *Minor Works* prints only three.

Love and Freindship. [*sic*] London: Chatto and Windus, 1922. This is the first publication of the whole of *Volume the Second* and contains an introduction by G. K. Chesterton. For the scholarly text, see under *Volume the Second*.

Mansfield Park. 3 vols. London: T. Egerton, May 1814. 2d edition, London: John Murray, February 1816. First U.S. edition, in 2 vols., Philadelphia: Carey and Lea, December 1832. First translation, into French as *Le Parc de Mansfield*, 1816.

Minor Works. Edited by R. W. Chapman. Oxford: Oxford University Press, 1954. Reprinted in 1958, with revisions in 1963 and 1965, and with further revisions by B. C. Southam in 1969 and at several subsequent dates. Vol. 6 in the Oxford edition of Jane Austen (see under *The Novels* . . .), this collects all Jane Austen's writings (then available) apart from the six novels and the letters.

Northanger Abbey and *Persuasion*. 4 vols. London: John Murray, December 1817 (1818 on title page). First U.S. editions: separate publication, each novel in 2 vols., Philadelphia: Carey and Lea, November 1832 (*Persuasion*) and 1833 (*Northanger Abbey*). First translations, into French, *Persuasion* as *La Famille Elliot* 1821, *Northanger Abbey* as *L'Abbaye de Northanger*, 1824. *Persuasion* was also translated into German in 1822.

The Novels of Jane Austen. 5 vols. Edited by R. W. Chapman. Oxford: Oxford University Press, 1923. (1. *Sense and Sensibility*. 2. *Pride and Prejudice*. 3. *Mansfield Park*. 4. *Emma*. 5. *Northanger Abbey* and *Persuasion*.) Reprinted with revisions and corrections (but from the 1923 plates), in 1926 and in 1932–1934 as the second and third editions, respectively; and reprinted many times since, with further revisions, corrections, and additions. The first scholarly edition, now generally considered authoritative. In 1954 it was extended to six vols., as *The Works of Jane Austen*, with the publication of the *Minor Works* (see earlier).

Plan of a Novel, according to Hints from Various Quarters. Edited by R. W. Chapman, Oxford: Clarendon Press, 1926. First publication in full and accompanied by the first printing of Jane Austen's collection of comments, ''Opinions of *Mansfield Park*,'' and ''Opinions of *Emma*'' and also her notes on the dates of composition of three novels and on profits from her novels to March 1817.

Pride and Prejudice. 3 vols. London: T. Egerton, January 1813. 2d edition, October 1813. 3d edition, in 2 vols., 1817. First U.S. edition, entitled *Elizabeth Bennet*, Philadelphia: Carey and Lea, August 1832. First translation, into French as *Orgueil et Prejugé*, 1822.

[*Sanditon*] *Fragment of a Novel by Jane Austen, January–March 1817*. Edited by R. W. Chapman. Oxford: Clarendon Press, 1925. First publication in full of the unfinished novel we now know as *Sanditon*.

Sanditon: An Unfinished Novel by Jane Austen: Reproduced in Facsimile from the Manuscript in the Possession of King's College Cambridge. Introduction by B. C. Southam. Oxford: Clarendon Press; London: Scolar Press, 1975.

Sense and Sensibility. 3 vols. London: T. Egerton, October 1811. 2d edition, October 1813. First U.S. edition, in 2 vols., Philadelphia: Carey and Lea, 1833. First translation, into French as *Raison et Sensibilité*, 1815.

Three Evening Prayers. Edited by W. M. Roth. San Francisco: Roth, 1940.

''To the Memory of Mrs. Lefroy.'' In Sir John Henry Lefroy's *Notes and Documents Relating to the Family of Loffroy . . . by a Cadet*. Woolwich: Privately printed, 1868, pp. 117–18. Jane Austen's verses printed here for the first time.

Two Chapters of Persuasion. Edited by R. W. Chapman. Oxford: Clarendon Press, 1926. Reprints the original manuscript ending of the novel (Chapters 10 and 11 of vol.

2). It corrects errors in the transcript of Chapter 10 that was included in J. E. Austen-Leigh's 1871 *Memoir* (see end of this list) and points out that not all of this chapter had been "canceled" (as suggested by the *Memoir*); it also reveals that the manuscript Chapter 11 differs in details from its printed version (where it becomes Chapter 12) and that there had therefore been some further revision of this chapter, too.

Two Poems by Jane Austen. 1926. First publication of "Mr. Gill and Miss Gell" and "On a Headache."

Volume the First. Edited by R. W. Chapman. Oxford: Clarendon Press, 1933.

Volume the Second. Edited by B. C. Southam. Oxford: Clarendon Press, 1963. Recollated from the original. See also under *Love and Freindship* [*sic*].

Volume the Third. Edited by R. W. Chapman. Oxford: Clarendon Press, 1951.

The Watsons: A Fragment. Edited by R. W. Chapman. Oxford: Clarendon Press, 1927.

WORKS BY OTHER AUTHORS CONTAINING MATERIAL BY JANE AUSTEN

Austen-Leigh, James Edward. *A Memoir of Jane Austen.* London: Richard Bentley and Son, 1870 (actually issued in December 1869); 2d revised and enlarged edition, 1871 (reprinted, edited by R. W. Chapman, Oxford: Clarendon Press, 1926, 1951). The first edition printed thirty-six of Jane Austen's letters and some of her verses for the first time. The second edition included the first publication of *Lady Susan, The Watsons*, the so-called canceled chapter from *Persuasion*, "The Mystery" (*Volume the First*), further letters, and extracts from *Plan of a Novel* and from "The Last Work" (*Sanditon*).

Austen-Leigh, William, and Richard Arthur Austen-Leigh. *Jane Austen: Her Life and Letters, a Family Record.* London: Smith, Elder, 1913. Written by J. E. Austen-Leigh's son and the latter's nephew, this book was based on the 1869–1871 *Memoir* but drew on newly available material and many unpublished family papers, including ten new letters from Jane Austen. The book is a largely factual biography and has come to be seen as the standard *Life* of the author and as a primary source of reference for Austen scholarship. Drawing on R. A. Austen-Leigh's own much-annotated copy of the book and on further papers collected by him (and, indeed, on the complete Austen family archive) and incorporating new material published since 1913, along with findings from her own original researches, Deirdre Le Faye has recently revised and enlarged this work as *Jane Austen: A Family Record.* London: British Library, 1989.

Hubback, J. H., and E. C. Hubback. *Jane Austen's Sailor Brothers.* London: 1906. Written by Frank Austen's grandson and the latter's daughter, this work provided much new family information and printed, for the first time, five of Jane Austen's letters to her brother, along with the poem "Venta."

5

Books and Pamphlets on Jane Austen, with a Chronological Summary

With the exclusion of short study guides, the following list is, to the best of my knowledge, a complete list of critical and biographical books and pamphlets on Jane Austen up to 1996. To give a sense of the development of Austen scholarship through time, I provide an abbreviated chronological listing of all these works at the end of the alphabetical list.

Aaron Blake Publishers. *The Jane Austen Map of England.* Aaron Blake, 1987.
Adams, Oscar Fay. *The Story of Jane Austen's Life.* Chicago: A. C. McClurg, 1891. (2d ed., Boston: Lee and Shepard, 1897, reprinted, Norwood, PA: Norwood Editions, 1976.)
Aldington, Richard. *Jane Austen.* Pasadena: Ampersand Press, 1948.
Alexander, Samuel. *The Art of Jane Austen.* Manchester: Manchester University Press, 1928. A pamphlet, 22 pp., based on a talk and printed first as an article with the same title in *Bulletin of the John Rylands Library* 12 (1928): 314–35.
Amis, Kingsley. *What Became of Jane Austen? and Other Questions.* London: Cape, 1970, pp. 13–17. Reprint of "What Became of Jane Austen?" *Spectator* 199 (1957): 439–40.
Apperson, George Latimer. *A Jane Austen Dictionary.* London: Cecil Palmer, 1932. (Reprinted, New York: Haskell House, 1968.)
Armstrong, Isobel. *Jane Austen, "Mansfield Park."* Harmondsworth: Penguin, 1988. (Penguin Critical Studies)
———. *Jane Austen: "Sense and Sensibility."* Harmondsworth: Penguin, 1994. (Penguin Critical Studies)
Ashton, Helen. *Parson Austen's Daughter.* London: Collins, 1949. A novel.
Austen, Caroline Mary Craven. *My Aunt Jane Austen: A Memoir.* Alton, Hampshire: Jane Austen Society, 1952. (Written in 1867; reprinted, 1991.)
———. *Reminiscences of Caroline Austen.* Edited by Deirdre Le Faye. Chawton, Hampshire: Jane Austen Society, 1986.
Austen, Jane. *Selected Letters 1796–1817.* Edited by R. W. Chapman. Oxford and New York: Oxford University Press, 1985.

Austen-Leigh, Emma. *Jane Austen and Steventon.* London: Spottiswoode, Ballantyne, 1937. This and the following item are reprinted in *Jane Austen: Family History.* Edited by Louise Ross. London: Routledge/Thoemmes Press, 1995.

———. *Jane Austen and Bath.* London: Spottiswoode, Ballantyne, 1939. (Reprinted, Norwood, PA: Norwood Editions, 1976.)

Austen-Leigh, James Edward. *A Memoir of Jane Austen.* London: Richard Bentley and Son, 1870 (actually issued in December 1869); 2d revised and enlarged edition, 1871 (reprinted, edited by R. W. Chapman, Oxford: Clarendon Press, 1926, 1951).

Austen-Leigh, Mary Augusta. *Personal Aspects of Jane Austen.* London: J. Murray, 1920. (Reprinted, Folcroft, PA: Folcroft Library Editions, 1974.)

Austen-Leigh, Richard Arthur. *Pedigree of Austen of Horsmonden, Broadford, Grovehurst, Kippington, Capel Manor etc.* London: Privately printed by Spottiswoode, Ballantyne, 1940. Traces the family from 1522 to 1940.

———. *Jane Austen and Lyme Regis.* London: Spottiswoode, Ballantyne, 1941. (Reprinted, Norwood, PA: Norwood Editions, 1976; and in *Jane Austen: Family History.* Edited by Louise Ross. London: Routledge/Thoemmes Press, 1995.)

———. *Austen Papers, 1704–1856.* London: Spottiswoode, Ballantyne, 1942.

———. *Jane Austen and Southampton.* London: Spottiswoode, Ballantyne, 1949. (Reprinted in *Jane Austen: Family History.* Edited by Louise Ross. London: Routledge/Thoemmes Press, 1995.)

Austen-Leigh, William, and Richard Arthur Austen-Leigh. *Jane Austen, Her Life and Letters: A Family Record.* London: Smith, Elder, 1913. Revised and enlarged by Deirdre Le Faye as *Jane Austen: A Family Record.* London: British Library, 1989.

Babb, Howard S. *Jane Austen's Novels: The Fabric of Dialogue.* Columbus: Ohio State University Press, 1962.

Bailey, John Cann. *Introductions to Jane Austen.* London: Oxford University Press, 1931. (Reprinted, Folcroft, PA: Folcroft Library Editions, 1969.)

Barfoot, C. C. *The Thread of Connection: Aspects of Fate in the Novels of Jane Austen and Others.* Amsterdam: Rodopi, 1982.

Barr, John, and W. Hilton Kelliher. *Jane Austen, 1775–1817: Catalogue of an Exhibition Held in the King's Library, British Library Reference Division, 9 December 1975 to 29 February 1976.* London: British Museum Publications, 1975.

Batey, Mavis. *Jane Austen and the English Landscape.* London: Barn Elms, 1996.

Becker, May L. *Presenting Miss Jane Austen.* New York: Dodd, Mead, 1952.

Beer, Patricia. *Reader, I Married Him: A Study of the Women Characters of Jane Austen, Charlotte Brontë, Elizabeth Gaskell, and George Eliot.* New York: Barnes and Noble, 1974, pp. 45–83.

Berendsen, Marjet. *Reading Character in Jane Austen's "Emma."* Assen, Holland: Van Gorcum, 1991.

Berglund, Birgitta. *Woman's Whole Existence: The House as an Image in the Novels of Ann Radcliffe, Mary Wollstonecraft, and Jane Austen.* Lund: Lund University Press, 1993.

Birtwistle, Sue, and Susie Conklin. *The Making of "Pride and Prejudice."* Harmondsworth: Penguin and BBC Books, 1995. On the making of the BBC television serial.

———. *The Making of Jane Austen's "Emma."* Harmondsworth: Penguin, 1996.

Black, Maggie, and Deirdre Le Faye. *The Jane Austen Cookbook*. London: British Museum Press, 1995.

Bloom, Harold, ed. *Jane Austen*. New York: Chelsea House, 1986. (Modern Critical Views)

———. *Jane Austen's "Emma."* New York: Chelsea House, 1987a. (Modern Critical Interpretations)

———. *Jane Austen's "Mansfield Park."* New York: Chelsea House, 1987b. (Modern Critical Interpretations)

———. *Jane Austen's "Pride and Prejudice."* New York: Chelsea House, 1987c. (Modern Critical Interpretations)

Boardman, Michael M. *Narrative Innovation and Incoherence: Ideology in Defoe, Goldsmith, Austen, Eliot, and Hemingway*. Durham, NC: Duke University Press, 1992.

Bonnell, Henry Houston. *Charlotte Brontë, George Eliot, Jane Austen: Studies in Their Works*. New York: Longmans, Green, 1902.

Booth, Bradford Allen, ed. *"Pride and Prejudice": Text, Backgrounds, Criticism*. New York and Burlingame: Harcourt, Brace, and World, 1963.

Brabourne, Edward. *Letters of Jane Austen*. 2 vols. London: Richard Bentley and Son, 1884.

Bradbrook, Frank W. *Jane Austen: "Emma."* London: Edward Arnold, 1961.

———. *Jane Austen and Her Predecessors*. Cambridge: Cambridge University Press, 1966.

Brade-Birks, Stanley Graham. *Jane Austen and Godmersham*. Godmersham: Parochial Church Council, 1938. 12-p. pamphlet.

Brown, Ivor. *Jane Austen and Her World*. London: Lutterworth Press, 1966.

Brown, Julia Prewitt. *Jane Austen's Novels: Social Change and Literary Form*. Cambridge: Harvard University Press, 1979.

Brown, Lloyd W. *Bits of Ivory: Narrative Techniques in Jane Austen's Fiction*. Baton Rouge: Louisiana State University Press, 1973.

Brüggemeier, Luise-Marie. *The Journey of the Self: Studien zum Reisemotiv im Roman Jane Austens*. Frankfurt and Bern: Lang, 1981.

Burrows, J. F. *Jane Austen's "Emma."* Sydney: Sydney University Press, 1968.

———. *Computation into Criticism: A Study of Jane Austen's Novels and an Experiment in Method*. Oxford: Clarendon Press, 1987.

Bush, Douglas. *Jane Austen*. London and New York: Macmillan, 1975. (Masters of World Literature)

Bussby, Canon Frederick. *Jane Austen in Winchester*. 3d edition. Winchester: Friends of Winchester Cathedral, 1979. (1st edition, 1969; 2d edition, 1975.)

Butler, Marilyn. *Jane Austen and the War of Ideas*. Oxford: Clarendon Press, 1975.

Byrde, Penelope. *A Frivolous Distinction: Fashion and Needlework in the Works of Jane Austen*. Bath: Bath City Council, 1979.

Cahoon, Herbert. *Jane Austen: Letters and Manuscripts in the Pierpont Morgan Library*. New York: Pierpont Morgan Library, 1975.

Canby, Henry Siedel. *Emma and Mr. Knightley: A Critical Essay*. New York: Saturday Press, 1931. 7-p. pamphlet; not wholly devoted to Jane Austen.

Carpenter, T. Edward. *The Story of Jane Austen's Chawton Home*. Chawton, Hampshire: Jane Austen Memorial Trust, 1954.

Castellanos, Gabriela. *Laughter, War, and Feminism: Elements of Carnival in Three of Jane Austen's Novels*. New York: Peter Lang, 1994.

Cecil, David. *Jane Austen*. Cambridge: Cambridge University Press, 1935.

————. *A Portrait of Jane Austen*. London: Constable, 1978.

Chapman, R. W. *Jane Austen: Facts and Problems*. Oxford: Clarendon Press, 1948; revised edition, 1950.

————. *Jane Austen: A Critical Bibliography*. Oxford: Clarendon Press, 1953; revised edition, 1955.

————, ed. *Jane Austen's Letters to Her Sister Cassandra and Others*. Oxford: Oxford University Press, 1932; 2d edition, 1952; 3d edition, collected and edited by Deirdre Le Faye as *Jane Austen's Letters*, 1995.

Chessell, Henry. *Jane Austen in Lyme*. Lyme Regis, Dorset: Lyme Regis Printing, 1975, 10 pp. Short biographical sketch followed by a dramatized scene about the author in Lyme.

Clark, Robert, ed. *"Sense and Sensibility" and "Pride and Prejudice": Jane Austen*. New York: St. Martin's Press, 1994. (New Casebooks)

Clarke, Isabel Constance. *Six Portraits*. London: Hutchinson, 1935. Madame de Staël, Jane Austen, pp. 93–134, George Eliot, Mrs. Oliphant, John Oliver Hobbes/Mrs. Craigie, Katherine Mansfield.

Coates, James R. *"Persuasion" (Jane Austen)*. Oxford: Basil Blackwell, 1969. (Notes on English Literature)

Collins, Irene. *Jane Austen and the Clergy*. London and Rio Grande, OH: Hambledon Press, 1994.

Cookson, Linda, and Bryan Loughrey, eds. *Critical Essays on "Emma," Jane Austen*. London and New York: Longman, 1988.

Copeland, Edward, and Juliet McMaster, eds. *The Cambridge Companion to Jane Austen*. Cambridge: Cambridge University Press, 1997.

Cornish, Francis Warre. *Jane Austen*. London: Macmillan, 1913. (English Men of Letters series. Reprinted, Freeport, NY: Books for Libraries Press, 1971.)

Cottom, Daniel. *The Civilized Imagination: A Study of Ann Radcliffe, Jane Austen, and Sir Walter Scott*. Cambridge: Cambridge University Press, 1985.

Cox, Richard Anthony. *"Mansfield Park" (Jane Austen)*. Oxford: Basil Blackwell, 1970. (Notes on English Literature)

Craik, W. A. *Jane Austen: The Six Novels*. London: Methuen, 1965.

————. *Jane Austen in Her Time*. London: Nelson, 1969.

Dalglish, Jack. *"Pride and Prejudice" (Jane Austen)*. Oxford: Basil Blackwell, 1962. (Notes on English Literature)

De Rose, Peter L. *Jane Austen and Samuel Johnson*. Washington, DC: University Press of America, 1980.

De Rose, Peter L., and S. W. McGuire. *A Concordance to the Works of Jane Austen*. 3 vols. New York: Garland, 1982.

Devlin, D. D. *Jane Austen and Education*. New York: Barnes and Noble, 1975.

Dhatwalia, H. R. *Familial Relationships in Jane Austen's Novels*. New Delhi: National Book Organisation, 1988.

Duckworth, Alistair M. *The Improvement of the Estate: A Study of Jane Austen's Novels*. Baltimore: Johns Hopkins University Press, 1971.

Duffy, J. A. M., Jr. "Jane Austen and the Nineteenth-Century Critics of Fiction 1812–1913." Diss., University of Chicago, 1954.

Dussinger, John A. *In the Pride of the Moment: Encounters in Jane Austen's World*. Columbus: Ohio State University Press, 1990.

Dwyer, June. *Jane Austen*. New York: Continuum, 1989.

Edwards, Anne-Marie. *In the Steps of Jane Austen: Town and Country Walks*. London: BBC, 1979; 2d edition, enlarged and illustrated, Southampton: Arcady Books, 1985.

Ehrenpreis, Irvin. *Acts of Implication: Suggestion and Covert Meaning in the Works of Dryden, Swift, Pope, and Austen*. Berkeley and Los Angeles: University of California Press, 1980. "Austen: The Heroism of the Quotidian," pp. 112–45, enlarged from his "Jane Austen and Heroism," *New York Review of Books* (8 February 1979): 37–43.

Evans, Mary. *Jane Austen and the State*. London and New York: Tavistock, 1987.

Farrar, Sydney. *Jane Austen: "Northanger Abbey."* London: Hulton Educational, 1962. (Guides to English Literature)

Fast, Howard. *The Novelist: A Romantic Portrait of Jane Austen*. London: S. French, 1992.

Fergus, Jan S. *Jane Austen and the Didactic Novel: "Northanger Abbey," "Sense and Sensibility," and "Pride and Prejudice."* London: Macmillan, 1983.

————. *Jane Austen: A Literary Life*. London: Macmillan, 1991.

Firkins, Oscar W. *Jane Austen*. New York: H. Holt, 1920. (Reprinted, New York: Russell and Russell, 1965.)

Fitzgerald, P. H. *Jane Austen: A Criticism and Appreciation*. London: Jarrold and Sons, 1912.

Fleishman, Avrom. *A Reading of Mansfield Park: An Essay in Critical Synthesis*. Minneapolis: University of Minnesota Press, 1967.

Folsom, Marcia McClintock, ed. *Approaches to Teaching Austen's "Pride and Prejudice."* New York: Modern Language Association of America, 1993. 17 essays, with other material.

Freeman, Jean Todd. *Jane Austen in Bath*. Alton, Hampshire: Jane Austen Society, 1969.

Freeman, Kathleen. *T'other Miss Austen*. London: MacDonald, 1956.

Gard, Roger. *Jane Austen: "Emma" and "Persuasion."* Harmondsworth: Penguin, 1985. (Penguin Critical Studies)

————. *Jane Austen's Novels: The Art of Clarity*. New Haven, CT, and London: Yale University Press, 1992.

Gillie, Christopher. *A Preface to Jane Austen*. London: Longman, 1974. (Revised edition, 1985.)

Gilson, David. *A Bibliography of Jane Austen*. Oxford: Clarendon Press, 1982.

Gooneratne, Yasmine. *Jane Austen*. Cambridge: Cambridge University Press, 1970.

Gorman, Anita G. *The Body in Illness and Health: Themes and Images in Jane Austen*. New York: Peter Lang, 1993.

Gould, Jean. *Jane*. Boston: Houghton Mifflin, 1947. Jane Austen's life for children.

Gray, Donald J., ed. *Pride and Prejudice: An Authoritative Text, Backgrounds, Reviews, and Essays in Criticism*. New York: Norton, 1966.

Greene-Armytage, E. L. *A Map of Bath in the Time of Jane Austen, with Comments and Descriptions from Her Letters and Novels*. Bath: Pitman Press, 1968.

Grey, J. David, ed. *The Jane Austen Companion*. New York: Macmillan, 1986. (Consultant editors Brian Southam and A. Walton Litz. Published in Britain as *The Jane Austen Handbook*, London: Athlone Press, 1986.)

————. *Jane Austen's Beginnings: The Juvenilia and Lady Susan*. Ann Arbor: UMI Research Press, 1989.

Halperin, John. *The Life of Jane Austen.* Baltimore: Johns Hopkins University Press, 1984.

————. *Jane Austen's Lovers: And Other Studies in Fiction and History from Austen to le Carré.* New York: St. Martin's Press, 1988.

————, ed. *Jane Austen: Bicentenary Essays.* New York and Cambridge: Cambridge University Press, 1975.

Halperin, John, and Janet Kunert. *Plots and Characters in the Fiction of Jane Austen, the Brontës, and George Eliot.* Hamden, CT: Archon Books, 1976.

Hampshire County Library. *Jane Austen in Southampton: Reproductions of Old Prints.* Southampton: Hampshire County Library, 1978. 16-p. pamphlet.

Handler, Richard, and Daniel Segal. *Jane Austen and the Fiction of Culture: An Essay on the Narration of Social Realities.* Tucson: University of Arizona Press, 1990.

Handley, Graham. *Jane Austen.* New York: St. Martin's Press, 1992. (Criticism in Focus)

Hardwick, Michael. *A Guide to Jane Austen.* New York: Scribner's, 1973. Published in Britain as *The Osprey Guide to Jane Austen.* Reading, Berks.: Osprey, 1973.

Hardy, Barbara. *A Reading of Jane Austen.* London: Peter Owen, 1975.

Hardy, John P. *Jane Austen's Heroines: Intimacy in Human Relationships.* London: Routledge and Kegan Paul, 1984.

Harris, Jocelyn. *Jane Austen's Art of Memory.* Cambridge: Cambridge University Press, 1989.

Havely, Cicely Palser. *A Study Guide to "Mansfield Park."* Bletchley, Bucks.: Open University Press, 1973.

Hawkridge, Audrey. *Jane Austen and Hampshire.* Winchester: Hampshire County Council, 1995.

Heath, William W. *Discussions of Jane Austen.* Boston: Heath, 1961.

Helm, W. H. *Jane Austen and Her Country-House Comedy.* London: Eveleigh Nash, 1909. (Reprinted, New York: Haskell House, 1973.)

Hickman, Peggy. *A Jane Austen Household Book, with Martha Lloyd's Recipes.* Newton Abbot, Devon: David and Charles, 1977.

Hill, Constance. *Jane Austen: Her Homes and Her Friends.* London and New York: John Lane, 1902 (issued November 1901).

Hinkley, Laura Lois. *Ladies of Literature: Fanny Burney, Jane Austen, Charlotte and Emily Brontë, Elizabeth Barrett Browning, George Eliot.* New York: Hastings House, 1946, pp. 59–118.

Hodge, Jane Aiken. *The Double Life of Jane Austen.* London: Hodder and Stoughton, 1972. (Published in the United States with the title *Only a Novel: The Double Life of Jane Austen.* New York: Coward, McCann, and Geogheghan.)

Hodgkins Booksellers. *A Catalogue of Books by and about the Brontë Family, Jane Austen, and Other Literary Ladies of the Nineteenth Century.* Catalog 24. Stroud, Gloucestershire: Hodgkins, 1981.

Honan, Park. *Jane Austen: Her Life.* London: Weidenfeld and Nicholson, 1987.

Horwitz, Barbara Jane. *Jane Austen and the Question of Women's Education.* New York: Peter Lang, 1991.

Howard, Tom. *Austen Country.* London: Grange Books, 1995.

Hubback, J. H., and Edith C. Hubback. *Jane Austen's Sailor Brothers: Being the Adventures of Sir Francis Austen, G.C.B., Admiral of the Fleet, and Rear-Admiral Charles Austen.* London: J. Lane, 1906. (Reprinted, Norwood, PA: Norwood Editions, 1976.)

Hubback, John Austen. *The Parents in Jane Austen's Novels*. Kenley, Surrey: Privately printed, 1960.

Hudson, Glenda A. *Sibling Love and Incest in Jane Austen's Fiction*. London: Macmillan, 1992.

Hughes-Hallett, Penelope, ed. *Jane Austen: "My Dear Cassandra."* London: Collins and Brown, 1990. Illustrated selection of letters.

Innes, Kathleen Elizabeth Royds. *Hampshire Pilgrimages: Men and Women Who Have Sojourned in Hampshire: Jane Austen, Charlotte Mary Yonge, Florence Nightingale, Gilbert White, William Cobbett, Dr. Joseph Stevens [and] Lovers of Test and Itchen*. London: William Sessions, 1948, pp. 1–10.

Irons, Keith. *Steventon and the Austens*. Steventon, Hampshire: Jane Austen Bicentenary Committee, 1975.

Isaacs, Enid. *In Jane Austen's Country*. Canberra: Mulini Press, 1975.

Jack, Adolphus Alfred. *Essays on the Novel as Illustrated by Scott and Miss Austen*. London: Macmillan, 1897, pp. 232–97.

James, Selma. *The Ladies and the Mammies: Jane Austen and Jean Rhys*. Bristol: Falling Wall Press, 1983.

Jane Austen's England: A Literary Tour Guide. Footsteps Map, 1997.

Jane Austen Society. *Jane Austen and Jane Austen's House*. Alton: Jane Austen Society, 1949, 12 pp. Mainly on Jane Austen and Chawton.

————. *Collected Reports of the Jane Austen Society, 1949–1965*. Folkestone: William Dawson and Son, 1967.

————. *Jane Austen Bicentenary, 1775–1975: Loan Exhibition, Jane Austen's House, Chawton, 2nd July–31st August*. Alton, Hampshire: Jane Austen Society, 1975.

————. *Collected Reports of the Jane Austen Society, 1966–1975*. Folkestone: William Dawson and Son, 1977.

————. *Collected Reports of the Jane Austen Society, 1976–1985*. Overton, Hampshire: Jane Austen Society, 1989. See also continuing annual reports, 1986 onward.

Jane Austen Society of North America. *Persuasions: Journal of the Jane Austen Society of North America*. 1979–.

Jarvis, William. *Jane Austen and Religion*. Stonesfield, Witney, Oxfordshire: Stonesfield Press, 1996.

Jefferson, Douglas. *Jane Austen's "Emma": A Landmark in English Fiction*. London: Chatto and Windus for Sussex University Press, 1977.

Jenkins, Elizabeth. *Jane Austen: A Biography*. London: Victor Gollancz, 1938.

Johnson, Claudia L. *Jane Austen: Women, Politics, and the Novel*. Chicago and London: University of Chicago Press, 1988.

————. *Equivocal Beings: Politics, Gender, and Sentimentality in the 1790s: Wollstonecraft, Radcliffe, Burney, Austen*. Chicago and London: University of Chicago Press, 1995.

Johnson, R. Brimley. *The Women Novelists*. London: Collins, 1918, pp. 66–130 and passim.

————. *Jane Austen*. London: Sheed and Ward, 1927. (Reprinted, Folcroft, PA: Folcroft Library Editions, 1972.)

————. *Jane Austen: Her Life, Her Work, Her Family, and Her Critics*. London and Toronto: J. M. Dent and Sons, 1930. See also under Villard in this bibliography.

Jones, Ann H. *Ideas and Innovations: Best Sellers of Jane Austen's Age*. New York: AMS Press, 1986.

Jones, Vivien. *How to Study a Jane Austen Novel.* 2d edition. London: Macmillan, 1997 (first published, 1987).

Kaplan, Charles, ed. *The Overwrought Urn: A Potpourri of Parodies of Critics Who Triumphantly Present the Real Meaning of Authors from Jane Austen to J. D. Salinger.* New York: Pegasus, 1969. "Mrs. Bennet and the Dark Gods: The Key to Jane Austen," by D. Bush, pp. 102–7, reprinted from *Sewanee Review* 64 (1957): 591–96.

Kaplan, Deborah. *Jane Austen among Women.* Baltimore: Johns Hopkins University Press, 1992.

Kaye-Smith, Sheila, and G. B. Stern. *Talking of Jane Austen.* London: Cassell, 1943.

———. *More Talk of Jane Austen.* London: Harper, 1949.

Keener, Frederick M. *The Chain of Becoming: The Philosophical Tale, the Novel, and a Neglected Realism of the Enlightenment: Swift, Montesquieu, Voltaire, Johnson, and Austen.* New York: Columbia University Press, 1983. "The Philosophical Tale, Jane Austen, and the Novel," pp. 241–307.

Kennedy, Margaret. *Jane Austen.* London: A. Barker, 1950.

Kenyon, Katherine Mary Rose. *Jane Austen Out of Doors.* Capivard Press, 1959, 9 pp.

Kestner, Joseph A. *Jane Austen: Spatial Structure of Thematic Variations.* Salzburg: Institut für Englische Sprache und Literatur, Universität Salzburg, 1974.

Keynes, Geoffrey. *Jane Austen: A Bibliography.* London: Nonesuch Press, 1929.

Kirkham, Margaret. *Jane Austen, Feminism and Fiction.* Brighton: Harvester Press, 1983.

Konigsberg, Ira. *Narrative Technique in the English Novel: Defoe to Austen.* Hamden, CT: Archon Books, 1985.

Koppel, Gene. *The Religious Dimension of Jane Austen's Novels.* Ann Arbor, MI: UMI Research Press, 1988.

Kroeber, Karl. *Styles in Fictional Structure: The Art of Jane Austen, Charlotte Brontë, George Eliot.* Princeton: Princeton University Press, 1971.

Kuwahara, Kuldip Kaur. *Jane Austen at Play: Self-Consciousness, Beginnings, Endings.* New York: Peter Lang, 1993.

Lane, Maggie. *The Jane Austen Quiz and Puzzle Book.* Bristol: Abson, 1982.

———. *Jane Austen's Family: Through Five Generations.* London: Robert Hale, 1984.

———. *Jane Austen's England.* London: Robert Hale, 1986.

———. *A Charming Place: Bath in the Life and Times of Jane Austen.* Bath: Millstream, 1988.

———. *Jane Austen and Food.* London and Rio Grande: Hambledon Press, 1994.

———. *Jane Austen's World: The Life and Times of England's Most Popular Author.* London: Carlton Books, 1996.

Lascelles, Mary. *Jane Austen and Her Art.* London: Oxford University Press, 1939.

Laski, Marghanita. *Jane Austen and Her World.* London: Thames and Hudson, 1969. (Revised, 1975.)

Lauber, John. *Jane Austen.* New York: Twayne, 1993. (English Authors Series)

Lauritzen, Monica. *Jane Austen's "Emma" on Television: A Study of a BBC Classic Serial.* Göteborg: Acta Universitatis Gothoburgensis, 1981. (Gothenburg Studies in English, 48)

Le Faye, Deirdre. *Jane Austen: A Family Record.* London: British Library, 1989. (Revised, enlarged, and effectively rewritten version of W. Austen-Leigh and R. A. Austen-Leigh 1913, op. cit.)

Le Faye, Deirdre, ed. *Jane Austen's Letters*. 3d edition. Oxford and New York: Oxford University Press, 1995. See under R. W. Chapman for first two editions.

Lee, James W., ed. *Studies in the Novel* 7 (Spring 1975). (Jane Austen Special Number. 11 essays.)

Leeming, Glenda. *Who's Who in Jane Austen and the Brontës*. New York: Taplinger, 1974.

Lerner, Laurence. *The Truthtellers: Jane Austen, George Eliot, D. H. Lawrence*. London: Chatto and Windus, 1967.

Liddell, Robert. *The Novels of Jane Austen*. London: Longmans, 1963.

Link, Frederick Martin. "The Reputation of Jane Austen in the Twentieth Century, with an Annotated Enumerative Bibliography of Austen Criticism from 1811 to June, 1957." Diss., Boston University, 1958.

Litz, A. Walton. *Jane Austen: A Study of Her Artistic Development*. New York: Oxford University Press, 1965.

Llewelyn, Margaret. *Jane Austen: A Character Study*. London: Kimber, 1977.

Lobb, Kenneth Martyn. *Jane Austen: "Pride and Prejudice."* Amersham, Buckinghamshire: Hulton Educational, 1962.

Lock, F. P., and D. J. Gilson, eds. *Five Letters from Jane Austen to Her Sister Cassandra, 1813*. Brisbane: Locks' Press, 1981.

Lodge, David, ed. *Jane Austen: Emma: A Casebook*. London: Macmillan, 1968.

Looser, Devoney, ed. *Jane Austen and Discourses of Feminism*. New York: St. Martin's Press, 1995.

Lucas, Victor. *Jane Austen*. Andover, Hampshire: Pitkin, 1996. 19-p. guidebook.

MacDonagh, Oliver. *Jane Austen: Real and Imagined Worlds*. New Haven, CT, and London: Yale University Press, 1991.

MacKinnon, Frank Douglas, ed. *Grand Larceny: Being the Trial of Jane Leigh Perrot, Aunt of Jane Austen*. London: Oxford University Press, 1937. See also Sidney Ives, *The Trial of Mrs. Leigh Perrot . . . to Which Are Added, Some Circumstances Attendant on That Interesting Trial*. Boston: Club of Odd Volumes, 1980.

Malden, S. F. *Jane Austen*. London: W. H. Allen, 1889. (Reprinted, Norwood, PA: Norwood Editions, 1976.)

Mallinson, Anne. *Chawton Commemorates Jane Austen: An Account of the Commemoration of the 15th Anniversary of the Death of Jane Austen—Chawton, July 14th–18th, 1967*. Selborne: The author, 1967, 20 pp.

Mansell, Darrel. *The Novels of Jane Austen: An Interpretation*. London: Macmillan, 1973.

Marsh, Honoria D., and Peggy Hickman. *Shades from Jane Austen*. London: Perry Jackman, 1975.

May, J. C. C. *"Persuasion," Jane Austen: A Critical Introduction*. Dublin: Scepter, 1970.

McMaster, Juliet. *Jane Austen on Love*. Victoria, British Columbia: University of Victoria, 1978.

———. *Jane Austen the Novelist: Essays Past and Present*. London: Macmillan, 1996.

———, ed. *Jane Austen's Achievement: Papers Delivered at the Jane Austen Bicentennial Conference at the University of Alberta, 1975*. London: Macmillan, 1976. 6 essays.

McMaster, Juliet, and Bruce Stovel, eds. *Jane Austen's Business: Her World and Her Profession*. London: Macmillan; New York: St. Martin's Press, 1996. 15 essays and a short story by Margaret Drabble.

Menon, K. R. *A Guide to Jane Austen's "Northanger Abbey."* Singapore: India Publishing House, 1956, 100 pp.

Milligan, Ian. *Studying Jane Austen.* London: Longman, 1988.

Mitton, G. E. *Jane Austen and Her Times.* London: Methuen, 1905. (Reprinted, Port Washington, NY: Kennikat Press, 1970.)

Modert, Jo, ed. *Jane Austen's Manuscript Letters in Facsimile: Reproductions of Every Known Extant Letter, Fragment, and Autograph Copy, with an Annotated List of All Known Letters.* Carbondale and Edwardsville: Southern Illinois University Press, 1990.

Moler, Kenneth L. *Jane Austen's Art of Allusion.* Lincoln: University of Nebraska Press, 1968.

————. *"Pride and Prejudice": A Study in Artistic Economy.* New York: Twayne, 1989.

Monaghan, David. *Jane Austen: Structure and Social Vision.* London: Macmillan, 1980.

————, ed. *Jane Austen in a Social Context.* London: Macmillan, 1981.

————. *"Emma": Jane Austen.* New York: St. Martin's Press, 1992. (New Casebooks)

Mooneyham, Laura G. *Romance, Language, and Education in Jane Austen's Novels.* London: Macmillan, 1988.

Morgan, Susan. *In the Meantime: Character and Perception in Jane Austen's Fiction.* Chicago: University of Chicago Press, 1980.

Morris, Ivor. *Mr. Collins Considered: Approaches to Jane Austen.* London: Routledge and Kegan Paul, 1987.

Mudrick, Marvin. *Jane Austen: Irony as Defense and Discovery.* Princeton: Princeton University Press, 1952.

Mukherjee, Meenakshi. *Jane Austen.* London: Macmillan, 1991. (Women Writers)

Myer, Valerie Grosvenor. *Jane Austen.* Glasgow: Blackie, 1980. (Authors in Their Age)

————. *Obstinate Heart: Jane Austen: A Biography.* London: Michael O'Mara Books, 1997.

Nardin, Jane. *Those Elegant Decorums: The Concept of Propriety in Jane Austen's Novels.* Albany: State University of New York Press, 1973.

Nicolson, Nigel. *The World of Jane Austen.* London: Weidenfeld and Nicolson, 1991. Photographs by Steven Colover.

————. *Godmersham Park Kent before, during and after Jane Austen's Time.* Alton, Hampshire: Jane Austen Society, 1996.

Nineteenth-Century Fiction 30 (December 1975). (Jane Austen Special Issue.) 10 essays and editorial foreword.

Nokes, David. *Jane Austen.* London: Fourth Estate, 1997.

Norris, William Basil. *Jane Austen and Steventon.* Steventon, Hampshire: Jane Austen Bi-Centenary Commmittee, 1975, 20 pp.

O'Brien, F. V. *Pride and Prejudice: An Inaugural Lecture Delivered . . . on 23 April 1975.* Belfast: Queen's University of Belfast, 1975.

Odmark, John. *An Understanding of Jane Austen's Novels: Character, Value and Ironic Perspective.* Totowa, NJ: Barnes and Noble, 1981.

Odom, Keith C. *Jane Austen: Rebel of Time and Place.* Arlington, TX: Liberal Arts Press, 1991.

O'Neill, Judith, ed. *Critics on Jane Austen.* Coral Gables, FL: University of Miami Press, 1970.

Page, Norman. *The Language of Jane Austen.* Oxford: Basil Blackwell, 1972.

Paris, Bernard J. *Character and Conflict in Jane Austen's Novels: A Psychological Approach*. Detroit: Wayne State University Press, 1978.

Parrish, Stephen Maxfield, ed. *Emma: An Authoritative Text, Backgrounds, Reviews, and Criticism*. New York: Norton, 1972.

Payne, Susan. *The Strange within the Real: The Function of Fantasy in Austen, Brontë and Eliot*. Rome: Bulzoni, 1992.

Pellew, W. George. *Jane Austen's Novels*. Boston: Cupples, Upham, 1883, 50 pp.

Petersen, Per Serritslev, ed. "On the First Sentence of *Pride and Prejudice*: A Critical Discussion of the Theory and Practice of Literary Interpretation." *Dolphin* 1 (February 1979). 6 essays on the sentence and novel with discussion of methods of approach.

Phelps, William Lyon. [*Introduction to "The Novels of Jane Austen"*]. Separate printing of fifty copies of the introduction, pp. ix–lix, to an edition of Austen's novels edited by R. Brimley Johnson—New York: Frank S. Holby, 1906. (Reprinted in Phelps' *Essays on Books*. New York: Macmillan, 1914, pp. 129–77.)

Phillipps, K. C. *Jane Austen's English*. London: Deutsch, 1970.

Piggott, Patrick. *The Innocent Diversion: A Study of Music in the Life and Writings of Jane Austen*. London: Cleverdon, 1979.

Pilgrim, Constance. *Dear Jane: A Biographical Study of Jane Austen*. London: Kimber, 1971. (2d edition. Edinburgh: Pentland Press, 1991.)

———. *This Is Illyria, Lady*. Edinburgh: Pentland Press, 1989.

Pinion, F. B. *A Jane Austen Companion: A Critical Survey and Reference Book*. London: Macmillan, 1973.

Polhemus, Robert M. *Comic Faith: The Great Tradition from Austen to Joyce*. Chicago: University of Chicago Press, 1980.

———. *Erotic Faith: Being in Love from Jane Austen to D. H. Lawrence*. Chicago: University of Chicago Press, 1990.

Pollock, Frederick. *Jane Austen Centenary Memorial: A Record of the Ceremony of Its Unveiling at Chawton, Hampshire*. London: John Lane, 1917, 16 pp.

Pollock, Walter Herries. *Jane Austen: Her Contemporaries and Herself, an Essay in Criticism*. London: Longmans, Green, 1899. The contemporaries are Fanny Burney, Maria Edgeworth, and Susan Ferrier. (Reprinted, New York: Haskell House, 1970.)

Pool, Daniel. *What Jane Austen Ate and Charles Dickens Knew: From Fox Hunting to Whist: The Facts of Daily Life in Nineteenth-Century England*. New York: Simon and Schuster, 1993.

Poovey, Mary. *The Proper Lady and the Woman Writer: Ideology as Style in the Works of Mary Wollstonecraft, Mary Shelley, and Jane Austen*. Chicago: University of Chicago Press, 1984. "Ideological Contradictions and the Consolations of Form: The Case of Jane Austen," pp. 172–207; " 'The True English Style,' " pp. 208–40.

Radovici, Nadia. *A Youthful Love: Jane Austen and Tom Lefroy*. Braunton: Merlin, 1995.

Ragg, Laura Marie. *Jane Austen in Bath*. London: Alexander Moring, 1938.

Ram, Atma. *Heroines in Jane Austen: A Study in Character*. New Delhi: Kalyani, 1982.

———. *Woman as a Novelist: A Study of Jane Austen*. Delhi: Doaba House, 1989.

Rathburn, Robert Charles, and Martin Steinmann, Jr., eds. *From Jane Austen to Joseph Conrad: Essays Collected in Memory of James T. Hillhouse*. Minneapolis: University of Minnesota Press, 1958. "The Makers of the British Novel," by R. C.

Rathburn, 1–23. "The Background of *Mansfield Park*," by C. Murrah, pp. 24–34. "Critical Realism in *Northanger Abbey*," by A. D. McKillop, pp. 35–45.

Rawlence, Guy. *Jane Austen*. London: Duckworth, 1934. (Reprinted, Folcroft, PA: Folcroft Library Editions, 1970.)

Rees, Joan. *Jane Austen: Woman and Writer*. New York: St. Martin's Press, 1976.

Rhydderch, David. *Jane Austen, Her Life and Art*. London: J. Cape, 1932.

Roberts, Warren. *Jane Austen and the French Revolution*. London: Macmillan, 1979. (Reprinted, London and Atlantic Highlands, NJ: Athlone Press, 1995.)

Ross, Louise, ed. *Jane Austen: Family History*. London: Routledge/Thoemmes Press, 1995. Reprints of works on Jane Austen by members of her family: see under Emma Austen-Leigh and R. A. Austen-Leigh.

Røstvig, Maren-Sofie, ed. *Fair Forms: Essays in English Literature from Spenser to Jane Austen*. Totowa, NJ: Rowman and Littlefield, 1975. "Mistaken Conduct and Proper Feeling: A Study of Jane Austen's *Pride and Prejudice*," by Grete Ek, pp. 178–202.

Roth, Barry. *An Annotated Bibliography of Jane Austen Studies, 1973–83*. Charlottesville: University Press of Virginia, 1985.

Roth, Barry, and Joel Weinsheimer. *An Annotated Bibliography of Jane Austen Studies, 1952–1972*. Charlottesville: University Press of Virginia, 1973.

Rubinstein, Elliot. *Jane Austen's Novels: The Metaphor of Rank. Literary Monographs*, vol. 2. Edited by Eric Rothstein and Richard N. Ringler. Madison: University of Wisconsin Press, 1969, pp. 101–193, 218–25.

———, ed. *Twentieth Century Interpretations of "Pride and Prejudice": A Collection of Critical Essays*. Englewood Cliffs, NJ: Prentice-Hall, 1969.

Ruderman, Anne Crippen. *The Pleasures of Virtue: Political Thought in the Novels of Jane Austen*. Lanham, MD: Rowman and Littlefield, 1995.

Ruoff, Gene W. *Jane Austen's "Sense and Sensibility."* New York: St. Martin's Press, 1992. (Critical Studies of Key Texts)

———, ed. *The Wordsworth Circle* 7 (Autumn 1976). (Jane Austen special number) 6 essays.

Sacco, Terran Lee. *A Transcription and Analysis of Jane Austen's Last Work, "Sanditon."* Lewiston, NY, and Lampeter, Wales: Edwin Mellen Press, 1995.

Sadleir, Michael. *The Northanger Novels: A Footnote to Jane Austen*. Oxford: Oxford University Press for the English Association, 1927. Identifies and discusses the seven "horrid" novels mentioned by Isabella Thorpe in *Northanger Abbey* (p. 40).

Sales, Roger. *Jane Austen and Representations of Regency England*. London: Routledge, 1994.

Schapera, Isaac. *Kinship Terminology in Jane Austen's Novels*. London: Royal Anthropological Institute of Great Britain and Ireland, 1977, 24 pp.

Scheuermann, Mona. *Her Bread to Earn: Women, Money, and Society from Defoe to Austen*. Lexington: University Press of Kentucky, 1993.

Scott, Peter J. M. *Jane Austen. A Reassessment*. London: Vision, 1982.

Selwyn, David, ed. *Jane Austen: Collected Poems and Verse of the Austen Family*. Manchester: Carcanet, 1996.

Seymour, Beatrice K. *Jane Austen: Study for a Portrait*. London: M. Joseph, 1937.

Sherif, Abla. *Jane Austen's "Persuasion."* Zürich: Juris-Verlag, 1968. (Diss., University of Zürich, 97 pp.)

Sherry, Norman. *Jane Austen*. London: Evans Brothers, 1966.

Simons, Judy, ed. *"Mansfield Park" and "Persuasion."* New York: St. Martin's Press, 1997. (New Casebook Series.)

Singh, Sushila. *Jane Austen: Her Concept of Social Life*. New Delhi: S. Chand, 1981.

Sisson, Rosemary Anne. *The Young Jane Austen*. London: Max Parrish, 1962. Jane Austen's life up to 1801, for children.

Smith, Goldwin, and John Parker Anderson. *Life of Jane Austen*. London: Walter Scott, 1890. (Reprinted, New York: Kennikat Press, 1972.)

Smith, LeRoy W. *Jane Austen and the Drama of Woman*. New York: St. Martin's Press, 1983.

Smith, Ross S. *Fanny Bertram: The Structure of "Mansfield Park."* Townsville, Queensland, Australia: James Cook University of North Queensland, 1978.

Smithers, David Waldron. *Jane Austen in Kent*. Westerham, Kent: Hurtwood, 1981.

Southam, B. C. *Jane Austen's Literary Manuscripts: A Study of the Novelist's Development through the Surviving Papers*. London: Oxford University Press, 1964.

———. *Jane Austen*. Harlow, Essex: Longman for the British Council, 1975. (Writers and Their Work, no. 241)

———, ed. *Critical Essays on Jane Austen*. London: Routledge and Kegan Paul, 1968a.

———. *Jane Austen: The Critical Heritage*. London: Routledge and Kegan Paul, 1968b.

———. *Jane Austen: "Northanger Abbey" and "Persuasion": A Casebook*. London: Macmillan, 1976a.

———. *Jane Austen: "Sense and Sensibility," "Pride and Prejudice," and "Mansfield Park": A Casebook*. London: Macmillan, 1976b.

———. *Jane Austen: The Critical Heritage*. Vol. 2: 1870–1940. London: Routledge and Kegan Paul, 1987.

Spacks, Patricia Ann Meyer, ed. *Persuasion: Authoritative Text, Backgrounds and Contexts, Criticism*. New York: W. W. Norton, 1995.

Sparks, Graham. *Jane Austen: Her Hampshire Days*. Winchester: Sarsen Press, 1985. 16-p. pamphlet.

Spencer, Jane. *The Rise of the Woman Novelist: From Aphra Behn to Jane Austen*. Oxford: Basil Blackwell, 1986.

Spender, Dale. *Mothers of the Novel: 100 Good Women Writers before Jane Austen*. London: Pandora, 1986.

Steeves, Harrison R. *Before Jane Austen: The Shaping of the English Novel in the Eighteenth Century*. New York: Holt, Rinehart, and Winston, 1965.

Stevenson, John A. *The British Novel, Defoe to Austen: A Critical History*. New York: Twayne, 1990.

Stewart, Maaja A. *Domestic Realities and Imperial Fictions: Jane Austen's Novels in Eighteenth-Century Contexts*. Athens, GA, and London: University of Georgia Press, 1993.

Stokes, Myra. *The Language of Jane Austen: A Study of Some Aspects of Her Vocabulary*. London: Macmillan, 1991.

Stout, Janis P. *Strategies of Reticence: Silence and Meaning in the Works of Jane Austen, Willa Cather, Katherine Anne Porter, and Joan Didion*. Charlottesville: University Press of Virginia, 1990.

Studies in the Novel 7 (Spring 1975). (Jane Austen special number).

Sulloway, Alison G. *Jane Austen and the Province of Womanhood.* Philadelphia: University of Pennsylvania Press, 1989.

Tanner, Tony. *Jane Austen.* Cambridge: Harvard University Press, 1986.

Tave, Stuart M. *Some Words of Jane Austen.* Chicago: University of Chicago Press, 1973.

Ten Harmsel, Henrietta. *Jane Austen: A Study in Fictional Conventions.* The Hague: Mouton, 1964.

Thackeray, Anne I. *A Book of Sibyls: Mrs. Barbauld, Miss Edgeworth, Mrs. Opie, Miss Austen.* London: Smith, Elder, 1883, pp. 197–229. (Revised version of "Jane Austen." *Cornhill Magazine* 34 [1871]: 158–74; reprinted in her *Toilers and Spinsters and Other Essays.* London: Smith, Elder, 1874, pp. 35–71.)

Thompson, Emma. *Sense and Sensibility: The Sense and Sensibility Screenplay and Diaries.* New York: Newmarket Press, 1995.

Thompson, James. *Between Self and World: The Novels of Jane Austen.* University Park: Pennsylvania State University Press, 1988.

Thomson, Clara L. *Jane Austen: A Survey.* London: Horace Marshall and Son, 1929.

Todd, Janet M., ed. *Jane Austen: New Perspectives.* New York: Holmes and Meier, 1983. 19 essays.

Tomalin, Claire. *Jane Austen: A Life.* London and New York: Viking, 1997.

Trowbridge, Hoyt. *From Dryden to Jane Austen: Essays on English Critics and Writers, 1660–1818.* Albuquerque: University of New Mexico Press, 1977. "Mind, Body, and Estate: Jane Austen's System of Values," pp. 275–92.

Tucker, George Holbert. *A Goodly Heritage: A History of Jane Austen's Family.* Manchester: Carcanet New Press, 1983.

———. *Jane Austen: The Woman: Some Biographical Insights.* New York: St. Martin's Press, 1994.

Tytler, Sarah (pseudonym of Henrietta Keddie). *Jane Austen and Her Works.* London: Cassell, Petter, Galpin, 1880. (Reprinted, Folcroft, PA: Folcroft Library Editions, 1976.) For younger readers.

Varma, Devendra P., ed. *The Northanger Set of Jane Austen Horrid Novels.* 7 vols. London: Folio Society, 1968.

Vasudeva Reddy, T. *Jane Austen: The Dialectics of Self Actualisation in Her Novels.* New York: Envoy Press, 1987a.

———. *Jane Austen: The Matrix of Matrimony.* Bohra, 1987b.

Villard, Léonie. *Jane Austen: A French Appreciation by Léonie Villard, Translated by Veronica Lucas, with a New Study of Jane Austen by R. Brimley Johnson.* London: George Routledge and Sons, 1924. (Reprinted, New York: B. Blom, 1971. Translated from *Jane Austen: sa vie et son oeuvre.* Saint-Étienne: Société Anonyme de l'Imprimerie Mulcey, 1915.)

Vipont, Elfrida. *A Little Bit of Ivory: A Life of Jane Austen.* London: Hamish Hamilton, 1977.

Voss-Clesly, Patricia. *Tendencies of Character Depiction in the Domestic Novels of Burney, Edgeworth, and Austen: A Consideration of Subjective and Objective World.* 3 vols. Salzburg: Institut für Anglistik und Amerikanistik, Universität Salzburg, 1979.

Wallace, Robert K. *Jane Austen and Mozart: Classical Equilibrium in Fiction and Music.* Athens: University of Georgia Press, 1983.

Wallace, Tara Ghoshal. *Jane Austen and Narrative Authority.* London: Macmillan, 1995.

Warner, Sylvia Townsend. *Jane Austen, 1775–1817*. Harlow, Essex: Longmans, Green, 1951, 35 pp.

Watkins, Susan. *Jane Austen: In Style*. London: Thames and Hudson, 1990.

Watson, Winifred. *Jane Austen in London*. Alton, Hampshire: Jane Austen Society, 1960.

Watt, Ian P., ed. *Jane Austen: A Collection of Critical Essays*. Englewood Cliffs, NJ: Prentice-Hall, 1963.

Weinsheimer, Joel, ed. *Jane Austen Today*. Athens: University of Georgia Press, 1975.

Weldon, Fay. *Letters to Alice on First Reading Jane Austen*. London: Michael Joseph, 1984.

Whitten, Benjamin. *Jane Austen's Comedy of Feeling: A Critical Analysis of "Persuasion."* Ankara: Hacettepe University Press, 1974.

Wiesenfarth, Joseph. *The Errand of Form: An Assay of Jane Austen's Art*. New York: Fordham University Press, 1967.

Wilks, Brian. *Jane Austen*. London and New York: Hamlyn, 1978. Illustrated biography.

Williams, A. Susan. *Jane Austen*. Hove, E. Sussex: Wayland, 1989.

Williams, Michael. *Jane Austen: Six Novels and Their Methods*. London: Macmillan, 1986.

Wilson, Mona. *Jane Austen and Some Contemporaries*. London: Cresset Press, 1938. Contemporaries: Eliza Fletcher (1770–1858), Anne Woodrooffe (1766–1830), Mary Martha Butt (1775–1795), Mary Anne Schimmelpenninck (1778–1856), Charlotte Elizabeth Tonna (1790–1846), Mary Somerville (1780–1872), Harriet Grote (1792–1878). (Reprinted, New York: Kennikat Press, 1966.)

Wilt, Judith. *Ghosts of the Gothic: Austen, Eliot, and Lawrence*. Princeton: Princeton University Press, 1980. "Jane Austen: The Anxieties of Common Life," pp. 121–72.

Wiltshire, John. *Jane Austen and the Body: "The Picture of Health."* Cambridge: Cambridge University Press, 1992.

Wodehouse, Edmond Robert. *Miss Austen*. Bath: Herald Office, 1886, 32 pp. (Paper read to the Bath Literary and Philosophical Association on 29 January 1886, reprinted from the *Bath Herald*.)

Wood, Nigel, ed. *"Mansfield Park."* Buckingham and Philadelphia: Open University Press, 1993. (Theory in Practice)

Wordsworth Circle 7 (Autumn 1976). (Jane Austen special issue).

Wright, Andrew H. *Jane Austen's Novels: A Study in Structure*. London: Chatto and Windus, 1953. (2d edition, 1961.)

Chronological Summary

The following is an abbreviated, chronological list of the preceding bibliography designed to provide a quick overview of the development of Austen criticism. Authors are listed in alphabetical order under each date, and full publication details of all the works cited can be found in the preceding bibliography.

1870	Austen-Leigh, James Edward. *A Memoir of Jane Austen.*
1880	Tytler, Sarah (pseudonym of Henrietta Keddie). *Jane Austen and Her Works.*
1883	Pellew, W. George. *Jane Austen's Novels.*
	Thackeray, Anne I. *A Book of Sibyls: Mrs. Barbauld, Miss Edgeworth, Mrs. Opie, Miss Austen.*
1884	Brabourne, Edward. *Letters of Jane Austen.*
1886	Wodehouse, Edmond Robert. *Miss Austen.*
1889	Malden, S. F. *Jane Austen.*
1890	Smith, Goldwin, and John Parker Anderson. *Life of Jane Austen.*
1891	Adams, Oscar Fay. *The Story of Jane Austen's Life.*
1897	Jack, Adolphus Alfred. *Essays on the Novel as Illustrated by Scott and Miss Austen.*
1899	Pollock, Walter Herries. *Jane Austen: Her Contemporaries and Herself, an Essay in Criticism.*
1902	Bonnell, Henry Houston. *Charlotte Brontë, George Eliot, Jane Austen: Studies in Their Works.*
	Hill, Constance. *Jane Austen: Her Homes and Her Friends.*
1905	Mitton, G. È. *Jane Austen and Her Times.*
1906	Hubback, J. H., and Edith C. Hubback. *Jane Austen's Sailor Brothers.*
	Phelps, William Lyon. [*Introduction to "The Novels of Jane Austen"*].
1909	Helm, W. H. *Jane Austen and Her Country-House Comedy.*
1912	Fitzgerald, P. H. *Jane Austen: A Criticism and Appreciation.*
1913	Austen-Leigh, William, and Richard Arthur Austen-Leigh. *Jane Austen, Her Life and Letters: A Family Record.*
	Cornish, Francis Warre. *Jane Austen.*
1917	Pollock, Frederick. *Jane Austen Centenary Memorial.*
1918	Johnson, R. Brimley. *The Women Novelists.*
1920	Austen-Leigh, Mary Augusta. *Personal Aspects of Jane Austen.*
	Firkins, Oscar W. *Jane Austen.*

1924	Villard, Léonie. *Jane Austen: A French Appreciation . . . with a New Study of Jane Austen by R. Brimley Johnson.*
1927	Johnson, R. *Jane Austen.*
	Sadleir, Michael. *The Northanger Novels: A Footnote to Jane Austen.*
1928	Alexander, Samuel. *The Art of Jane Austen.*
1929	Keynes, Geoffrey. *Jane Austen: A Bibliography.*
	Thomson, Clara L. *Jane Austen: A Survey.*
1930	Johnson, R. *Jane Austen: Her Life, Her Work, Her Family, and Her Critics.*
1931	Bailey, John Cann. *Introductions to Jane Austen.*
	Canby, Henry Siedel. *Emma and Mr. Knightley: A Critical Essay.*
1932	Apperson, George Latimer. *A Jane Austen Dictionary.*
	Chapman, R. W., ed. *Jane Austen's Letters to Her Sister Cassandra and Others.*
	Rhydderch, David. *Jane Austen, Her Life and Art.*
1934	Rawlence, Guy. *Jane Austen.*
1935	Cecil, David. *Jane Austen.*
	Clarke, Isabel Constance. *Six Portraits.*
1937	Austen-Leigh, Emma. *Jane Austen and Steventon.*
	MacKinnon, Frank Douglas, ed. *Grand Larceny: Being the Trial of Jane Leigh Perrot, Aunt of Jane Austen.*
	Seymour, Beatrice K. *Jane Austen: Study for a Portrait.*
1938	Brade-Birks, Stanley Graham. *Jane Austen and Godmersham.*
	Jenkins, Elizabeth. *Jane Austen: A Biography.*
	Ragg, Laura Marie. *Jane Austen in Bath.*
	Wilson, Mona. *Jane Austen and Some Contemporaries.*
1939	Austen-Leigh, Emma. *Jane Austen and Bath.*
	Lascelles, Mary. *Jane Austen and Her Art.*
1940	Austen-Leigh, Richard Arthur. *Pedigree of Austen.*
1941	Austen-Leigh, Richard Arthur. *Jane Austen and Lyme Regis.*
1942	Austen-Leigh, Richard Arthur. *Austen Papers, 1704–1856.*
1943	Kaye-Smith, Sheila, and G. B. Stern. *Talking of Jane Austen.*
1946	Hinkley, Laura Lois. *Ladies of Literature: Fanny Burney, Jane Austen, Charlotte and Emily Brontë, Elizabeth Barrett Browning, George Eliot.*
1947	Gould, Jean. *Jane.*
1948	Aldington, Richard. *Jane Austen.*
	Chapman, R. W. *Jane Austen: Facts and Problems.*
	Innes, Kathleen Elizabeth Royds. *Hampshire Pilgrimages: Men and Women Who Have Sojourned in Hampshire: Jane Austen,. . . .*

1949   Ashton, Helen. *Parson Austen's Daughter.*

                Austen-Leigh, Richard Arthur. *Jane Austen and Southampton.*

                Jane Austen Society. *Jane Austen and Jane Austen's House.*

                Kaye-Smith, Sheila, and G. B. Stern. *More Talk of Jane Austen.*

1950   Kennedy, Margaret. *Jane Austen.*

1951   Warner, Sylvia Townsend. *Jane Austen, 1775–1817.*

1952   Austen, Caroline Mary Craven. *My Aunt Jane Austen: A Memoir.*

                Becker, May L. *Presenting Miss Jane Austen.*

                Mudrick, Marvin. *Jane Austen: Irony as Defense and Discovery.*

1953   Chapman, R. W. *Jane Austen: A Critical Bibliography.*

                Wright, Andrew H. *Jane Austen's Novels: A Study in Structure.*

1954   Carpenter, T. Edward. *The Story of Jane Austen's Chawton Home.*

                Duffy, J. A. M., Jr. "Jane Austen and the Nineteenth-Century Critics
                of Fiction 1812–1913."

1956   Freeman, Kathleen. *T'other Miss Austen.*

                Menon, K. R. *A Guide to Jane Austen's "Northanger Abbey."*

1958   Link, Frederick Martin. "The Reputation of Jane Austen in the Twen-
                tieth Century, with an Annotated Enumerative Bibliography of Aus-
                ten Criticism from 1811 to June, 1957."

                Rathburn, Robert Charles, and Martin Steinmann, Jr., eds. *From Jane
                Austen to Joseph Conrad: Essays Collected in Memory of James T.
                Hillhouse.*

1959   Kenyon, Katherine Mary Rose. *Jane Austen Out of Doors.*

1960   Hubback, John Austen. *The Parents in Jane Austen's Novels.*

                Watson, Winifred. *Jane Austen in London.*

1961   Bradbrook, Frank, W. *Jane Austen: "Emma."*

                Heath, William W. *Discussions of Jane Austen.*

1962   Babb, Howard S. *Jane Austen's Novels: The Fabric of Dialogue.*

                Dalglish, Jack. *"Pride and Prejudice" (Jane Austen).*

                Farrar, Sydney. *Jane Austen: "Northanger Abbey."*

                Lobb, Kenneth Martyn. *Jane Austen: "Pride and Prejudice."*

                Sisson, Rosemary Anne. *The Young Jane Austen.*

1963   Booth, Bradford Allen, ed. *"Pride and Prejudice": Text, Back-
                grounds, Criticism.*

                Liddell, Robert. *The Novels of Jane Austen.*

                Watt, Ian P., ed. *Jane Austen: A Collection of Critical Essays.*

1964   Southam, B. C. *Jane Austen's Literary Manuscripts.*

                Ten Harmsel, Henrietta. *Jane Austen: A Study in Fictional Conven-
                tions.*

1965	Craik, W. A. *Jane Austen: The Six Novels.*
	Litz, A. Walton. *Jane Austen: A Study of Her Artistic Development.*
	Steeves, Harrison R. *Before Jane Austen: The Shaping of the English Novel in the Eighteenth Century.*
1966	Bradbrook, Frank W. *Jane Austen and Her Predecessors.*
	Brown, Ivor. *Jane Austen and Her World.*
	Gray, Donald J., ed. *Pride and Prejudice: An Authoritative Text, Backgrounds, Reviews, and Essays in Criticism.*
	Sherry, Norman. *Jane Austen.*
1967	Fleishman, Avrom. *A Reading of Mansfield Park: An Essay in Critical Synthesis.*
	Jane Austen Society. *Collected Reports of the Jane Austen Society, 1949–1965.*
	Lerner, Laurence. *The Truthtellers: Jane Austen, George Eliot, D. H. Lawrence.*
	Mallinson, Anne. *Chawton Commemorates Jane Austen.*
	Wiesenfarth, Joseph. *The Errand of Form: An Assay of Jane Austen's Art.*
1968	Burrows, J. *Jane Austen's "Emma."*
	Greene-Armytage, E. L. *A Map of Bath in the Time of Jane Austen, with Comments and Descriptions from Her Letters and Novels.*
	Lodge, David, ed. *Jane Austen: Emma: A Casebook.*
	Moler, Kenneth L. *Jane Austen's Art of Allusion.*
	Sherif, Abla. *Jane Austen's "Persuasion."*
	Southam, B. C., ed. *Jane Austen: The Critical Heritage.*
	Southam, B. C., ed. *Critical Essays on Jane Austen.*
	Varma, Devendra P., ed. *The Northanger Set of Jane Austen Horrid Novels.*
1969	Coates, James R. *"Persuasion" (Jane Austen).*
	Craik, W. A. *Jane Austen in Her Time.*
	Freeman, Jean Todd. *Jane Austen in Bath.*
	Kaplan, Charles, ed. *The Overwrought Urn: A Potpourri of Parodies of Critics . . . of Authors from Jane Austen to J. D. Salinger.*
	Laski, Marghanita. *Jane Austen and Her World.*
	Rubinstein, Elliot. *Jane Austen's Novels: The Metaphor of Rank.*
	Rubinstein, Elliot, ed. *Twentieth Century Interpretations of "Pride and Prejudice": A Collection of Critical Essays.*
1970	Amis, Kingsley. *What Became of Jane Austen? and Other Questions.*
	Cox, Richard Anthony. *"Mansfield Park" (Jane Austen).*

Gooneratne, Yasmine. *Jane Austen.*

May, J. C. C. *"Persuasion," Jane Austen: A Critical Introduction.*

O'Neill, Judith, ed. *Critics on Jane Austen.*

Phillipps, K. C. *Jane Austen's English.*

1971   Duckworth, Alistair M. *The Improvement of the Estate: A Study of Jane Austen's Novels.*

Kroeber, Karl. *Styles in Fictional Structure: The Art of Jane Austen, Charlotte Brontë, George Eliot.*

Pilgrim, Constance. *Dear Jane: A Biographical Study of Jane Austen.*

1972   Hodge, Jane Aiken. *The Double Life of Jane Austen.*

Page, Norman. *The Language of Jane Austen.*

Parrish, Stephen Maxfield, ed. *Emma: An Authoritative Text, Backgrounds, Reviews, and Criticism.*

1973   Brown, Lloyd W. *Bits of Ivory: Narrative Techniques in Jane Austen's Fiction.*

Hardwick, Michael. *A Guide to Jane Austen.*

Havely, Cicely Palser. *A Study Guide to "Mansfield Park."*

Mansell, Darrel. *The Novels of Jane Austen: An Interpretation.*

Nardin, Jane. *Those Elegant Decorums: The Concept of Propriety in Jane Austen's Novels.*

Pinion, F. B. *A Jane Austen Companion: A Critical Survey and Reference Book.*

Roth, Barry, and Joel Weinsheimer. *An Annotated Bibliography of Jane Austen Studies, 1952–1972.*

Tave, Stuart M. *Some Words of Jane Austen.*

1974   Beer, Patricia. *Reader, I Married Him: A Study of the Women Characters of Jane Austen, Charlotte Brontë, Elizabeth Gaskell, and George Eliot.*

Gillie, Christopher. *A Preface to Jane Austen.*

Kestner, Joseph A. *Jane Austen: Spatial Structure of Thematic Variations.*

Leeming, Glenda. *Who's Who in Jane Austen and the Brontës.*

Whitten, Benjamin. *Jane Austen's Comedy of Feeling: A Critical Analysis of "Persuasion."*

1975   Bush, Douglas. *Jane Austen.*

Butler, Marilyn. *Jane Austen and the War of Ideas.*

Cahoon, Herbert. *Jane Austen: Letters and Manuscripts in the Pierpont Morgan Library.*

Chessell, Henry. *Jane Austen in Lyme.*

Devlin, D. D. *Jane Austen and Education.*

Halperin, John, ed. *Jane Austen: Bicentenary Essays.*

Hardy, Barbara. *A Reading of Jane Austen.*

Irons, Keith. *Steventon and the Austens.*

Isaacs, Enid. *In Jane Austen's Country.*

Jane Austen Society. *Jane Austen Bicentenary, 1775–1975: Loan Exhibition.*

Marsh, Honoria D., and Peggy Hickman. *Shades from Jane Austen.*

Nineteenth-Century Fiction 30 (December 1975). *(Jane Austen special issue)*

Norris, William Basil. *Jane Austen and Steventon.*

O'Brien, F. V. *Pride and Prejudice: An Inaugural Lecture.*

Røstvig, Maren-Sofie ed. *Fair Forms: Essays in English Literature from Spenser to Jane Austen.*

Southam, B. *Jane Austen.*

Studies in the Novel 7 (Spring 1975). (Jane Austen special number)

Weinsheimer, Joel, ed. *Jane Austen Today.*

1976   Barr, John, and W. Hilton Kelliher. *Jane Austen, 1775–1817: Catalogue of an Exhibition.*

Halperin, John, and Janet Kunert. *Plots and Characters in the Fiction of Jane Austen, the Brontës, and George Eliot.*

McMaster, Juliet, ed. *Jane Austen's Achievement: Papers Delivered at the Jane Austen Bicentennial Conference . . . 1975.*

Rees, Joan. *Jane Austen: Woman and Writer.*

Ruoff, Gene W., ed. *The Wordsworth Circle* 7 (Autumn 1976). (Jane Austen special number)

Southam, B., ed. *Jane Austen: "Northanger Abbey" and "Persuasion": A Casebook.*

Southam, B., ed. *Jane Austen: "Sense and Sensibility," "Pride and Prejudice," and "Mansfield Park": A Casebook.*

1977   Hickman, Peggy. *A Jane Austen Household Book, with Martha Lloyd's Recipes.*

Jane Austen Society. *Collected Reports of the Jane Austen Society, 1966–1975.*

Jefferson, Douglas. *Jane Austen's "Emma": A Landmark in English Fiction.*

Llewelyn, Margaret. *Jane Austen: A Character Study.*

Schapera, Isaac. *Kinship Terminology in Jane Austen's Novels.*

Trowbridge, Hoyt. *From Dryden to Jane Austen: Essays on English Critics and Writers, 1660–1818.*

Vipont, Elfrida. *A Little Bit of Ivory: A Life of Jane Austen.*

1978   Cecil, David. *A Portrait of Jane Austen.*

Hampshire County Library. *Jane Austen in Southampton: Reproductions of Old Prints.*

McMaster, Juliet. *Jane Austen on Love.*

Paris, Bernard J. *Character and Conflict in Jane Austen's Novels: A Psychological Approach.*

Smith, Ross S. *Fanny Bertram: The Structure of "Mansfield Park."*

Wilks, Brian. *Jane Austen.*

1979   Brown, Julia Prewitt. *Jane Austen's Novels: Social Change and Literary Form.*

Bussby, Canon Frederick. *Jane Austen in Winchester.*

Byrde, Penelope. *A Frivolous Distinction: Fashion and Needlework in the Works of Jane Austen.*

Edwards, Anne-Marie. *In the Steps of Jane Austen: Town and Country Walks.*

Jane Austen Society of North America. *Persuasions: Journal of the Jane Austen Society of North America* (begins publication).

Petersen, Per Serritslev, ed. "On the First Sentence of *Pride and Prejudice*. . . ." *Dolphin* 1 (February 1979). (6 essays.)

Piggott, Patrick. *The Innocent Diversion: A Study of Music in the Life and Writings of Jane Austen.*

Roberts, Warren. *Jane Austen and the French Revolution.*

Voss-Clesly, Patricia. *Tendencies of Character Depiction in the Domestic Novels of Burney, Edgeworth, and Austen.*

1980   De Rose, Peter L. *Jane Austen and Samuel Johnson.*

Ehrenpreis, Irvin. *Acts of Implication: Suggestion and Covert Meaning in the Works of Dryden, Swift, Pope, and Austen.*

Monaghan, David. *Jane Austen: Structure and Social Vision.*

Morgan, Susan. *In the Meantime: Character and Perception in Jane Austen's Fiction.*

Myer, Valerie Grosvenor. *Jane Austen.*

Polhemus, Robert M. *Comic Faith: The Great Tradition from Austen to Joyce.*

Wilt, Judith. *Ghosts of the Gothic: Austen, Eliot, and Lawrence.*

1981   Brüggemeier, Luise-Marie. *The Journey of the Self: Studien zum Reisemotiv im Roman Jane Austens.*

Hodgkins Booksellers. *A Catalogue of Books by and about the Brontë Family, Jane Austen and Other Literary Ladies.*

Lauritzen, Monica. *Jane Austen's "Emma" on Television: A Study of a BBC Classic Serial.*

Monaghan, David, ed. *Jane Austen in a Social Context.*

Odmark, John. *An Understanding of Jane Austen's Novels: Character, Value and Ironic Perspective.*

Singh, Sushila. *Jane Austen: Her Concept of Social Life.*

Smithers, David Waldron. *Jane Austen in Kent.*

1982 Barfoot, C. C. *The Thread of Connection: Aspects of Fate in the Novels of Jane Austen and Others.*

De Rose, Peter L., and S. W. McGuire. *A Concordance to the Works of Jane Austen.*

Gilson, David. *A Bibliography of Jane Austen.*

Lane, Maggie. *The Jane Austen Quiz and Puzzle Book.*

Ram, Atma. *Heroines in Jane Austen: A Study in Character.*

Scott, Peter J. M. *Jane Austen. A Reassessment.*

1983 Fergus, Jan S. *Jane Austen and the Didactic Novel: "Northanger Abbey," "Sense and Sensibility," and "Pride and Prejudice."*

James, Selma. *The Ladies and the Mammies: Jane Austen and Jean Rhys.*

Keener, Frederick M. *The Chain of Becoming: The Philosophical Tale, the Novel, and a Neglected Realism of the Enlightenment: Swift, Montesquieu, Voltaire, Johnson, and Austen.*

Kirkham, Margaret. *Jane Austen, Feminism and Fiction.*

Smith, LeRoy W. *Jane Austen and the Drama of Woman.*

Todd, Janet M., ed. *Jane Austen: New Perspectives.*

Tucker, George Holbert. *A Goodly Heritage: A History of Jane Austen's Family.*

Wallace, Robert K. *Jane Austen and Mozart: Classical Equilibrium in Fiction and Music.*

1984 Halperin, John. *The Life of Jane Austen.*

Hardy, John P. *Jane Austen's Heroines: Intimacy in Human Relationships.*

Lane, Maggie. *Jane Austen's Family: Through Five Generations.*

Poovey, Mary. *The Proper Lady and the Woman Writer: Ideology as Style in the Works of Mary Wollstonecraft, Mary Shelley, and Jane Austen.*

Weldon, Fay. *Letters to Alice on First Reading Jane Austen.*

1985 Austen, Jane. *Selected Letters 1796–1817.*

Cottom, Daniel. *The Civilized Imagination: A Study of Ann Radcliffe, Jane Austen, and Sir Walter Scott.*

Gard, Roger. *Jane Austen: "Emma" and "Persuasion."*

Konigsberg, Ira. *Narrative Technique in the English Novel: Defoe to Austen.*

Roth, Barry. *An Annotated Bibliography of Jane Austen Studies, 1973–83.*

Sparks, Graham. *Jane Austen: Her Hampshire Days.*

1986   Austen, Caroline Mary Craven. *Reminiscences of Caroline Austen.*

Bloom, Harold, ed. *Jane Austen.*

Grey, J. David, ed. *The Jane Austen Companion.*

Jones, Ann H. *Ideas and Innovations: Best Sellers of Jane Austen's Age.*

Lane, Maggie. *Jane Austen's England.*

Spencer, Jane. *The Rise of the Woman Novelist: From Aphra Behn to Jane Austen.*

Spender, Dale. *Mothers of the Novel: 100 Good Women Writers before Jane Austen.*

Tanner, Tony. *Jane Austen.*

Williams, Michael. *Jane Austen: Six Novels and Their Methods.*

1987   Aaron Blake Publishers. *The Jane Austen Map of England.*

Bloom, Harold, ed. *Jane Austen's "Emma."*

Bloom, Harold, ed. *Jane Austen's "Mansfield Park."*

Bloom, Harold, ed. *Jane Austen's "Pride and Prejudice."*

Burrows, J. F. *Computation into Criticism: A Study of Jane Austen's Novels and an Experiment in Method.*

Evans, Mary. *Jane Austen and the State.*

Honan, Park. *Jane Austen: Her Life.*

Jones, Vivien. *How to Study a Jane Austen Novel* (2d ed. 1997).

Morris, Ivor. *Mr. Collins Considered: Approaches to Jane Austen.*

Southam, B., ed. *Jane Austen: The Critical Heritage.* Vol. 2: 1870–1940.

Vasudeva Reddy, T. *Jane Austen: The Dialectics of Self Actualisation in Her Novels.*

Vasudeva Reddy, T. *Jane Austen: The Matrix of Matrimony.*

1988   Armstrong, Isobel. *Jane Austen, "Mansfield Park."*

Cookson, Linda, and Bryan Loughrey, eds. *Critical Essays on "Emma," Jane Austen.*

Dhatwalia, H. R. *Familial Relationships in Jane Austen's Novels.*

Halperin, John. *Jane Austen's Lovers: And Other Studies in Fiction and History from Austen to le Carré.*

Johnson, Claudia L. *Jane Austen: Women, Politics, and the Novel.*

Koppel, Gene. *The Religious Dimension of Jane Austen's Novels.*

Lane, Maggie. *A Charming Place: Bath in the Life and Times of Jane Austen.*

Milligan, Ian. *Studying Jane Austen.*

Mooneyham, Laura G. *Romance, Language, and Education in Jane Austen's Novels.*

Thompson, James. *Between Self and World: The Novels of Jane Austen.*

1989 Dwyer, June. *Jane Austen.*

Grey, J., ed. *Jane Austen's Beginnings: The Juvenilia and Lady Susan.*

Harris, Jocelyn. *Jane Austen's Art of Memory.*

Jane Austen Society. *Collected Reports of the Jane Austen Society, 1976–1985.*

Moler, Kenneth L. *"Pride and Prejudice": A Study in Artistic Economy.*

Pilgrim, Constance. *This Is Illyria, Lady.*

Ram, Atma. *Woman as a Novelist: A Study of Jane Austen.*

Sulloway, Alison G. *Jane Austen and the Province of Womanhood.*

Williams, A. Susan. *Jane Austen.*

1990 Dussinger, John A. *In the Pride of the Moment: Encounters in Jane Austen's World.*

Handler, Richard, and Daniel Segal. *Jane Austen and the Fiction of Culture: An Essay on the Narration of Social Realities.*

Hughes-Hallett, Penelope, ed. *Jane Austen: "My Dear Cassandra."*

Modert, Jo., ed. *Jane Austen's Manuscript Letters in Facsimile.*

Polhemus, Robert M. *Erotic Faith: Being in Love from Jane Austen to D. H. Lawrence.*

Stevenson, John A. *The British Novel, Defoe to Austen: A Critical History.*

Stout, Janis P. *Strategies of Reticence: Silence and Meaning in the Works of Jane Austen, Willa Cather, Katherine Anne Porter, and Joan Didion.*

Watkins, Susan. *Jane Austen: In Style.*

1991 Berendsen, Marjet. *Reading Character in Jane Austen's "Emma."*

Fergus, Jan S. *Jane Austen: A Literary Life.*

Horwitz, Barbara Jane. *Jane Austen and the Question of Women's Education.*

MacDonagh, Oliver. *Jane Austen: Real and Imagined Worlds.*

Mukherjee, Meenakshi. *Jane Austen.*

Nicolson, Nigel. *The World of Jane Austen.*

Odom, Keith C. *Jane Austen: Rebel of Time and Place.*

Stokes, Myra. *The Language of Jane Austen: A Study of Some Aspects of Her Vocabulary.*

1992   Boardman, Michael M. *Narrative Innovation and Incoherence: Ideology in Defoe, Goldsmith, Austen, Eliot, and Hemingway.*

Fast, Howard. *The Novelist: A Romantic Portrait of Jane Austen.*

Gard, Roger. *Jane Austen's Novels: The Art of Clarity.*

Handley, Graham. *Jane Austen.*

Hudson, Glenda A. *Sibling Love and Incest in Jane Austen's Fiction.*

Kaplan, Deborah. *Jane Austen among Women.*

Monaghan, David, ed. *"Emma": Jane Austen.*

Payne, Susan. *The Strange within the Real: The Function of Fantasy in Austen, Brontë and Eliot.*

Ruoff, Gene W. *Jane Austen's "Sense and Sensibility."*

Wiltshire, John. *Jane Austen and the Body: "The Picture of Health."*

1993   Berglund, Birgitta. *Woman's Whole Existence: The House as an Image in the Novels of Ann Radcliffe, Mary Wollstonecraft, and Jane Austen.*

Folsom, Marcia McClintock, ed. *Approaches to Teaching Austen's "Pride and Prejudice."*

Gorman, Anita G. *The Body in Illness and Health: Themes and Images in Jane Austen.*

Kuwahara, Kuldip Kaur. *Jane Austen at Play: Self-Consciousness, Beginnings, Endings.*

Lauber, John. *Jane Austen.*

Pool, Daniel. *What Jane Austen Ate and Charles Dickens Knew . . . The Facts of Daily Life in Nineteenth-Century England.*

Scheuermann, Mona. *Her Bread to Earn: Women, Money, and Society from Defoe to Austen.*

Stewart, Maaja A. *Domestic Realities and Imperial Fictions: Jane Austen's Novels in Eighteenth-Century Contexts.*

Wood, Nigel, ed. *"Mansfield Park."*

1994   Armstrong, Isobel. *Jane Austen: "Sense and Sensibility."*

Castellanos, Gabriela. *Laughter, War, and Feminism: Elements of Carnival in Three of Jane Austen's Novels.*

Clark, Robert, ed. *"Sense and Sensibility" and "Pride and Prejudice": Jane Austen.*

Collins, Irene. *Jane Austen and the Clergy.*

Lane, Maggie. *Jane Austen and Food.*

Sales, Roger. *Jane Austen and Representations of Regency England.*

Tucker, George Holbert. *Jane Austen: The Woman: Some Biographical Insights.*

1995   Birtwistle, Sue, and Susie Conklin. *The Making of "Emma."*

Black, Maggie, and Deirdre Le Faye. *The Jane Austen Cookbook.*

Hawkridge, Audrey. *Jane Austen and Hampshire.*

Howard, Tom. *Austen Country.*

Johnson, Claudia L. *Equivocal Beings: Politics, Gender, and Sentimentality in the 1790s: Wollstonecraft, Radcliffe, Burney, Austen.*

Le Faye, Deirdre, ed. *Jane Austen's Letters.*

Looser, Devoney, ed. *Jane Austen and Discourses of Feminism.*

Radovici, Nadia. *A Youthful Love: Jane Austen and Tom Lefroy.*

Ross, Louise, ed. *Jane Austen: Family History.*

Ruderman, Anne Crippen. *The Pleasures of Virtue: Political Thought in the Novels of Jane Austen.*

Sacco, Terran Lee. *A Transcription and Analysis of Jane Austen's Last Work, "Sanditon."*

Spacks, Patricia Ann Meyer, ed. *Persuasion: Authoritative Text, Backgrounds and Contexts, Criticism.*

Thompson, Emma. *Sense and Sensibility: The Sense and Sensibility Screenplay and Diaries.*

Wallace, Tara Ghoshal. *Jane Austen and Narrative Authority.*

1996   Batey, Mavis. *Jane Austen and the English Landscape.*

Birtwistle, Sue, and Susie Conklin. *The Making of "Pride and Prejudice."*

Jarvis, William. *Jane Austen and Religion.*

Lane, Maggie. *Jane Austen's World: The Life and Times of England's Most Popular Author.*

Lucas, Victor. *Jane Austen.*

McMaster, Juliet. *Jane Austen the Novelist: Essays Past and Present.*

McMaster, Juliet, and Bruce Stovel, eds. *Jane Austen's Business: Her World and Her Profession.*

Nicolson, Nigel. *Godmersham Park Kent before, during and after Jane Austen's time.*

Selwyn, David, ed. *Jane Austen: Collected Poems and Verse of the Austen Family.*

1997   Copeland, Edward, and Juliet McMaster, eds. *The Cambridge Companion to Jane Austen.*

Myer, Valerie Grosvenor. *Obstinate Heart: Jane Austen: A Biography*.

Nokes, David. *Jane Austen*.

Simons, Judy, ed. *"Mansfield Park" and "Persuasion."*

Tomalin, Claire. *Jane Austen: A Life*.

6

Essays on Jane Austen

There is no room here to provide a comprehensive listing of the many hundreds of essays and articles that have been published on Jane Austen since the nineteenth century, and what follows is a representative selection only (though a fairly generous one). It should be noted that I have given more space to works published after 1983 than to those published earlier, as pre-1983 works are already comprehensively documented in existing bibliographies (see Southam 1969 and *Roth and Weinsheimer 1973, Gilson 1982, and Roth 1985*).

The journal *Persuasions: Journal of the Jane Austen Society of North America* is abbreviated to *Persuasions* throughout.

NINETEENTH CENTURY

(Extracts and/or commentary on most of the following essays can be found in the two volumes edited by B. C. Southam, *Jane Austen: The Critical Heritage*, 1968, 1987.)

Anonymous. [Review of *Sense and Sensibility.*] *Critical Review* 4th series 1 (February 1812): 149–57.
———. [Notice of *Sense and Sensibility.*] *British Critic* 39 (May 1812): 527.
———. [Notice of *Pride and Prejudice.*] *British Critic* 41 (February 1813): 189–90.
———. [Review of *Pride and Prejudice.*] *Critical Review* 4th series 3 (March 1813): 318–24.
———. [Review of *Pride and Prejudice*]. *The New Review* 1 (April 1813): 393–96.
———. [Review of *Emma.*] *The Champion*, no. 168 (Sunday, 31 March 1816): 102–3.
———. [Review of *Emma.*] *Augustan Review* 2, no. 13 (May 1816): 484–86.
———. [Notice of *Emma.*] *Morgenblatt für gebildete Stände*, Tübingen, Supplement to Jg.10, no. 137 (Friday, 7 June 1816), "Uebersicht der neueste Literatur," no. 9, p. 33.

———. [Notice of *Emma.*] *Jenaische Allgemeine Literature-Zeitung*, Jg. 13, 1816, Intelligenzblatt no.37 (June 1816): col. 293.

———. [Notice of *Emma.*] *Vestnik Evropi*, Moscow, 87 no. 12 (June 1816): 319–20.

———. [Notice of *Emma.*] *British Critic* n.s. 6 (July 1816): 96–98.

———. [Notice of *Emma.*] *Monthly Review* 80 (July 1816): 320.

———. [Notice of *Emma.*] *British Lady's Magazine and Monthly Miscellany* 4 (September 1816): 180–81.

———. [Notice of *Emma.*] *Gentleman's Magazine* 86 (September 1816): 248–49.

———. [Notice of *Emma.*] *Literary Panorama* 6 (1 June 1817): col. 418.

———. [Review of *Northanger Abbey* and *Persuasion.*] *British Critic* 9 (March 1818): 293–301.

———. [Review of *Northanger Abbey* and *Persuasion.*] *Blackwood's Edinburgh Magazine and Literary Miscellany* n.s. 2 (May 1818): 453–55.

———. [Notice of *Northanger Abbey* and *Persuasion.*] *The Gentleman's Magazine* 88 (July 1818): 52–53.

———. "Miss Austen's Novels." *The Printing Machine* no. 4 (19 April 1834): 77–78.

———. "Miss Austen [Female Novelists. No. 1]." *New Monthly Magazine* 95 (May 1852): 17–23.

———. "Miss Austen's Novels." *Littell's Living Age* 45 (1855): 205–7.

———. "Miss Austen." *Englishwoman's Domestic Magazine* 3d series 2 (1866): 237–40, 278–82.

———. "Jane Austen." *St. Paul's Magazine* 5 (March 1870): 631–43.

Armitt, Annie. "Jane Austen and Charlotte Brontë: A Contrast." *Modern Review* 3 (1882): 384–96.

Austen, Henry. "Biographical Notice of the Author." Preface to *Northanger Abbey and Persuasion* by Jane Austen. London: John Murray, 1817 (1818 on title page).

Childe-Pemberton, Harriet L. "Women of Intellect: Jane Austen." *Girl's Own Paper* 3 (1882): 378–79.

Clymer, W.B.S. "A Note on Jane Austen." *Scribner's Magazine* (February 1891).

Conant, Samuel Stillman. "Jane Austen." *New Monthly Magazine* 41 (1870): 225–33.

Elwood, Anne Katharine. *Memoirs of the Literary Ladies of England, from the Commencement of the Last Century.* 2 vols. London: Henry Colburn, 1843, vol. 2, pp. 174–86. (Reprinted, New York: AMS Press, 1973.)

Forsyth, William. *The Novels and Novelists of the Eighteenth Century.* London: John Murray, 1871, pp. 328–37, and passim.

Hutton, R. H. "The Memoir of Miss Austen." *Spectator* (25 December 1869): 1533–35.

———. "Miss Austen's Posthumous Pieces." *Spectator* (22 July 1871): 891–92. (Review of the 1871 edition of Austen-Leigh's *Memoir.*)

———. "The Charm of Miss Austen." *Spectator* 64 (1890): 403–4. (Review of G. Smith, *Jane Austen*, 1890.)

Kavanagh, Julia. "Miss Austen's Six Novels." In her *English Women of Letters.* Leipzig: B. Tauchnitz, 1862, pp. 251–74.

Kebbel, Thomas Edward. "Miss Austen and George Eliot." *National Review* 2 (1883): 259–73.

King, Alice. "Jane Austen." *Argosy* 34 (1882): 187–92.

Lefroy, Fanny Caroline. "Hunting for Snarks at Lyme Regis." *Temple Bar* 57 (1879): 391–97.

Lewes, George Henry. "The Lady Novelists." *Westminster Review* 58, no. 2 (1852): 129–41.

————. "The Novels of Jane Austen." *Blackwood's Edinburgh Magazine* 86 (1859): 99–113.

Luyster, Isaphen M. "Jane Austen's Novels." *Christian Examiner* 74, 5th series 12 (1863): 400–421.

Murch, Jerom. *Mrs. Barbauld and Her Contemporaries.* London: Longmans, Green, 1877, pp. 19–23.

Oliphant, Margaret. "Miss Austen and Miss Mitford." *Blackwood's Edinburgh Magazine* 107 (March 1870): 294–305.

————. *The Literary History of England.* 3 vols. London: Macmillan, 1882, vol. 3, pp. 221–37.

Pollock, William Frederick. "British Novelists—Richardson, Miss Austen, Scott." *Fraser's Magazine* 61 (1860): 20–38.

Scott, Walter. "*Emma; a Novel. By the Author of Sense and Sensibility, Pride and Prejudice, &c.*" *Quarterly Review* 14 (October 1815): 188–201. Though dated October 1815, the issue was not actually published until March 1816. Scott's review appeared anonymously—and its title was not quite accurate, as *Emma*'s title page did not mention *Sense and Sensibility.*

Simpson, Richard. "Review of *A Memoir of Jane Austen* by J.-E. Austen-Leigh." *North British Review* 52 (April 1870): 129–52. Published anonymously, this review actually ranged much more widely over the works of Jane Austen and represents a landmark in the development of serious criticism of the author.

Thackeray, Anne I. "Jane Austen." *Cornhill Magazine* 34 (1871): 158–74. (Reprinted in her *Toilers and Spinsters* and, in revised form, *A Book of Sibyls*; see entry in preceding bibliography.)

Ward, Mary Augusta (Mrs. Humphry Ward). "Style and Miss Austen." *Macmillan's Magazine* 51 (1885): 84–91. Critical review of Lord Brabourne's edition of *Letters of Jane Austen*, 1884.

Waterston, Anna. "Jane Austen." *Atlantic Monthly* 11 (1863): 235–40.

Whately, Archbishop Richard. "*Northanger Abbey* and *Persuasion*." *Quarterly Review* 21 (January 1821): 352–76. Unsigned review that, with Scott's, remains one of the few pieces of serious criticism of Austen in the early nineteenth century and helps to set the tone of much later criticism.

TWENTIETH CENTURY

Adams, Timothy Dow. "To Know the Dancer from the Dance: Dance as a Metaphor of Marriage in Four Novels of Jane Austen." *Studies in the Novel* 14 (Spring 1982): 55–65.

Aers, David. "Community and Morality: Towards Reading Jane Austen." In *Romanticism and Ideology: Studies in English Writing, 1765–1830.* Edited by David Aers, Jonathan Cook, and David Punter. London: Routledge, 1981, pp. 118–36, 184–86.

Ahmad, Syed Nasim. "Point of View in *Mansfield Park*." *The Aligarh Journal of English Studies* 14 (October 1989): 172–88.

Alexander, Peter F. " 'Robin Adair' as a Musical Clue in Jane Austen's Emma." *Review of English Studies* 39 (February 1988): 84–86.

Allen, Brooke. "Jane Austen for the Nineties." *The New Criterion* 14 (September 1995): 15–22.

Allen, Dennis W. "No Love for Lydia: The Fate of Desire in *Pride and Prejudice.*" *Texas Studies in Literature and Language* 27 (Winter 1985): 425–43.

Anderson, Beatrice. "The Unmasking of Lady Susan." In *Jane Austen's Beginnings: The Juvenilia and Lady Susan.* Edited by J. David Grey. Ann Arbor: UMI Research Press, 1989, pp. 193–203.

Anderson, Misty G. " 'The Different Sorts of Friendship': Desire in *Mansfield Park.*" In *Jane Austen and Discourses of Feminism.* Edited by Devoney Looser. New York: St. Martin's Press, 1995, pp. 167–83.

Anderson, Walter E. "From Northanger to Woodston: Catherine's Education to Common Life." *Philological Quarterly* 63 (Fall 1984): 493–509.

Andrews, S. M. *Jane Austen: Some Aspects of Her Work, Together with Her Tonbridge Connections.* Tonbridge: Tonbridge Free Press, 1949, 18 pp.

Armstrong, Nancy. "Inside Greimas's Square: Literary Characters and Cultural Constraints." In *The Sign in Music and Literature.* Edited by Wendy Steiner. Austin: University of Texas Press, 1981, pp. 52–66.

———. "The Nineteenth-Century Jane Austen: A Turning Point in the History of Fear." *Genre* 23 (1990): 227–46.

Astell, Ann W. "Anne Elliot's Education: The Learning of Romance in *Persuasion.*" *Renascence: Essays on Value in Literature* 40 (Fall 1987): 2–14.

Auerbach, Nina. "Jane Austen's Dangerous Charm: Feeling as One Ought about Fanny Price." *Women and Literature* 3 (1983): 208–23.

Austen-Leigh, Joan. "The Austen Leighs and Jane Austen or 'I have always maintained the importance of Aunts.' " *Women and Literature* 3 (1983): 11–28.

———. "New Light Thrown on Jane Austen's Refusal of Harris Bigg-Wither." *Persuasions* 8 (December 1986): 34–36.

———. "The Juvenilia: A Family 'View.' " In *Jane Austen's Beginnings: The Juvenilia and Lady Susan.* Edited by J. David Grey. Ann Arbor: UMI Research Press, 1989a, pp. 173–79.

———. "My Aunt, Jane Austen." *Persuasions 11* (December 1989b): 28–36.

———. "Forms of Address and Titles in Jane Austen." *Persuasions* 12 (December 1990): 35–37.

Baguley, David. "A Possible Source for Jane Austen's Names." *Notes and Queries,* n.s. 29 (June 1982): 206.

Bald, Marjory A. "Jane Austen." In her *Women Writers of the Nineteenth Century.* Cambridge: University of Cambridge Press, 1923, pp. 1–27.

Bander, Elaine. "A Possible Source for Jane Austen's Names." *Notes and Queries* 29 (227) (June 1982): 206.

———. "Jane Austen and the Uses of Silence." In *Literature and Ethics. Essays Presented to A. E. Malloch.* Edited by Gary Wihl and David Williams. Montreal: McGill-Queen's University Press, 1988, pp. 46–61.

———. "Blair's Rhetoric: And the Art of *Persuasion.*" *Persuasions* 15 (December 1993): 124–30.

Banerjee, A. "Dr. Johnson's Daughter: Jane Austen and *Northanger Abbey.*" *English Studies* (April 1990).

Barfoot, C. C. "The Gist of the Gothic in English Fiction; or, Gothic and the Invasion of Boundaries." In *Exhibited by Candlelight: Sources and Developments in the Gothic Tradition.* Edited by Valeria Tinkler-Villani, Peter Davidson, and Jane Stevenson. Amsterdam: Rodopi, 1995, pp. 159–72.

Barker, Gerard A. *Grandison's Heirs: The Paragon's Progress in the Late Eighteenth-Century English Novel*. Newark: University of Delaware Press, 1985, pp. 146–50.

Barry, Elizabeth. "Jane Austen and Lord Byron: Connections." *Persuasions* 8 (December 1986): 39–41.

Bayley, John. "Kundera and Jane Austen." *The Review of Contemporary Fiction* 9 (Summer 1989): 58–64.

Beasley, Jerry C. "Fanny Burney and Jane Austen's *Pride and Prejudice*." *English Miscellany* 24 (1973–1974): 153–66.

Benedict, Barbara M. "Jane Austen's *Sense and Sensibility*: The Politics of Point of View." *Philological Quarterly* 69 (Fall 1990): 453–70.

———. "A Source for the Names in *Persuasion*." *Persuasions* 14 (December 1992): 68–69.

Benson, Arthur C. "Jane Austen at Lyme Regis." *Cornhill Magazine* (1909).

Benson, Mary Margaret. "Mothers, Substitute Mothers, and Daughters in the Novels of Jane Austen." *Persuasions* 11 (December 1989): 117–24.

Bernard, Kenneth. "The Raw Squirmy Thing: Some Reflections on Drama, Packaging, and Jane Austen." *Widener Review* 8 (1991): 96–111.

Bertelsen, Lance. "Jane Austen's Miniatures: Painting, Drawing, and the Novels." *Modern Language Quarterly* 45 (December 1984): 350–72.

Bevan, C. Knatchbull. "Personal Identity in *Mansfield Park*: Forms, Fictions, Role-Play, and Reality." *SEL: Studies in English Literature, 1500–1900* 27 (Autumn 1987a): 595–608.

———. "The Rhetoric of Syntax in *Pride and Prejudice*." *Language and Style: An International Journal* 20 (Fall 1987b): 396–410.

Bilger, Audrey. "Goblin Laughter: Violent Comedy and the Condition of Women in Frances Burney and Jane Austen." *Women's Studies* 24 (March 1995): 323–40.

Birkhead, Edith. "Sentiment and Sensibility in the Eighteenth Century Novel." *Essays and Studies by the English Association* 11 (1925): 92–116.

Birrell, Augustine. "Elementary Jane." In his *More Obiter Dicta*. London: Heinemann, 1924, pp. 36–42.

Bittner, Donald F. "Jane Austen and Her Officers: A Portrayal of the Army in English Literature." *Journal of the Society for Army Historical Research* 72 (Summer 1990): 76–91.

Bizzaro, Patrick. "Global and Contextual Humor in *Northanger Abbey*." *Persuasions* 7 (December 1985): 82–88.

Bloom, Donald A. "Dwindling into Wifehood: The Romantic Power of the Witty Heroine in Shakespeare, Dryden, Congreve, and Austen." In *Look Who's Laughing: Gender and Comedy*. Edited by Gail Finney. Langhorne, PA: Gordon and Breach, 1994, pp. 53–79.

Bodenheimer, Rosemarie. "Looking at the Landscape in Jane Austen." *SEL: Studies in English Literature, 1500–1900* 21 (Autumn 1981): 605–23.

Boles, Carolyn G. "Jane Austen and the Reader: Rhetorical Techniques in *Northanger Abbey, Pride and Prejudice*, and *Emma*." *Emporia State University Research Studies* 30 (Summer 1981).

Booth, James W. "What We Have Here Is a Failure to Communicate: A Rogerian Analysis of *Northanger Abbey* and *Persuasion*." *Journal of Evolutionary Psychology* 9 (August 1988): 248–55.

Booth, Wayne C. "Emma, *Emma*, and the Question of Feminism." *Persuasions* 5 (December 1983): 29–40.

Boren, Lynda S. "The Performing Self: Psychodrama in Austen, James and Woolf." *The Centennial Review* 30 (Winter 1986): 1–24.

Bowden, Jean K. "Living in Chawton Cottage." *Persuasions* 12 (December 1990): 79–86.

Bowden, Martha F. "What Does Lady Bertram Do?" *English Language Notes* 30 (December 1992): 30–33.

Boyd, Zelda. "The Language of Supposing: Modal Auxiliaries in *Sense and Sensibility*." *Women and Literature* 3 (1983): 142–54.

———. "Jane Austen's 'Must': The Will and the World." *Nineteenth Century Literature* 39 (September 1984): 127–43.

Bradbrook, Frank W. "Jane Austen and Choderlos de Laclos." *Notes and Queries* 199 (1954): 75.

Bradley, A. C. "Jane Austen. A Lecture." *Essays and Studies by Members of the English Association*. Vol. 2. Collected by H. C. Beeching. Oxford: Clarendon Press, 1911, pp. 7–36.

Breihan, John, and Clive Caplan. "Jane Austen and the Militia." *Persuasions* 14 (December 1992): 16–26.

Brissenden, R. F. "*Mansfield Park*: Freedom and the Family." In *Jane Austen: Bicentenary Essays*. Edited by John Halperin. New York: Cambridge University Press, 1975, pp. 156–71.

———. "The Task of Telling Lies: Candor and Deception in *Sense and Sensibility*." In *Greene Centennial Studies: Essays Presented to Donald Greene in the Centennial Year of the University of Southern California*. Edited by Paul J. Korshin and Robert R. Allen. Charlottesville: University Press of Virginia, 1984, pp. 442–57.

Bronson, Larry L. "*Loiterer, The*." In *British Literary Magazines: The Romantic Age, 1789–1836*. Edited by Alvin Sullivan. Westport, CT: Greenwood Press, 1983, pp. 284–87.

Brower, Reuben A. "Light and Bright and Sparkling: Irony and Fiction in *Pride and Prejudice*." In his *The Fields of Light: An Experiment in Critical Readiing*. New York: Oxford University Press, 1951, pp. 164–81. (Rewritten version of "The Controlling Hand: Jane Austen and *Pride and Prejudice*." *Scrutiny* 13 [1945–1946]: 99–111. Reprinted in Southam, *Sense and Sensibility . . . A Casebook* [1976]: 169–85.)

———. "From the *Iliad* to Jane Austen, via *The Rape of the Lock*." In *Jane Austen: Bicentenary Essays*. Edited by John Halperin. New York: Cambridge University Press, 1975, pp. 43–60. (Also in Brower's *Mirror on Mirror: Translation, Imitation, Parody*. Cambridge: Harvard University Press, 1974, pp. 77–95.)

Brown, Carole O. "Dwindling into a Wife: A Jane Austen Heroine Grows Up." *International Journal of Women's Studies* 5 (November–December 1982): 460–69.

Brown, Julia Prewitt. "Jane Austen's England." *Persuasions* 10 (December 1988): 53–58.

———. "The Feminist Depreciation of Austen: A Polemical Reading." *Novel: A Forum on Fiction* 23 (Spring 1990): 303–13.

————. "Private and Public in *Persuasion*." In *Jane Austen's Business: Her World and Her Profession*. Edited by Juliet McMaster and Bruce Stovel. New York: St. Martin's Press, 1996, pp. 168–77.

Brown, Lloyd W. "Jane Austen and the Feminist Tradition." *Nineteenth-Century Fiction* 28 (1973): 321–38.

Brownstein, Rachel M. "Getting Married: Jane Austen." In her *Becoming a Heroine: Reading about Women in Novels*. New York: Viking Press, 1982, pp. 79–134.

————. "Jane Austen: Irony and Authority." *Women's Studies: An Interdisciplinary Journal* 15, nos. 1–3 (1988): 57–70. (Special Issue: "Last Laughs: Perspectives on Women and Comedy")

Buck, Anne. "The Costume of Jane Austen and Her Characters." *The So-Called Age of Elegance: Costume 1785–1820. Proceedings of the Fourth Annual Conference of the Costume Society, 1970*. London: Costume Society, 1971, pp. 36–45.

Burlin, Katrin R. " 'Pictures of Perfection' at Pemberley: Art in *Pride and Prejudice*." *Women and Literature* 3 (1983): 155–70.

Burrows, J. F. "*Persuasion* and Its 'Sets of People.' " Sydney Studies in English 2 (1976–1977): 3–23.

————. "Modal Verbs and Moral Principles: An Aspect of Jane Austen's Style." *Literary and Linguistic Computing: Journal of the Association for Literary and Linguistic Computing* 1 (1986): 9–23.

Burton, Antoinette. " 'Invention Is What Delights Me': Jane Austen's Remaking of 'English' History." In *Jane Austen and Discourses of Feminism*. Edited by Devoney Looser. New York: St. Martin's Press, 1995, pp. 35–50.

Butler, Marilyn. "The Woman at the Window: Ann Radcliffe in the Novels of Mary Wollstonecraft and Jane Austen." In *Gender and Literary Voice*. Edited by Janet Todd. New York: Holmes and Meier, 1980, pp. 128–48.

————. "Disregarded Designs: Jane Austen's Sense of the Volume." In *Jane Austen in a Social Context*. Edited by David Monaghan. London: Macmillan, 1981a, pp. 49–65.

————. "Novels for the Gentry: Austen and Scott." In her *Romantics, Rebels, and Reactionaries: English Literature and Its Background, 1760–1830*. New York: Oxford University Press, 1981b, pp. 94–112.

Butte, George. "Shame or Espousal? *Emma* and the New Intersubjectivity of Anxiety in Austen." In *Jane Austen's Business: Her World and Her Profession*. Edited by Juliet McMaster and Bruce Stovel. New York: St. Martin's Press, 1996, pp. 54–65.

Caine, Barbara. "G. H. Lewes and 'The Lady Novelists.' " *Sydney Studies in English* 7 (1981–1982): 85–101.

Carr, Jean Ferguson. "The Polemics of Incomprehension: Mother and Daughter in *Pride and Prejudice*." In *Tradition and the Talents of Women*. Edited by Florence Howe. Urbana: University of Illinois Press, 1991, pp. 68–86.

Caywood, Cynthia L. "*Pride and Prejudice* and the Belief in Choice: Jane Austen's Fantastical Vision." In *Portraits of Marriage in Literature*. Edited by Anne C. Hargrove and Maurine Magliocco. Macomb, IL: Essays in Literature, 1984, pp. 31–37.

Chaber, Lois A. "Transgressive Youth: Lady Mary, Jane Austen, and the Juvenilia Press." *Eighteenth Century Fiction* 8 (October 1995): 81–88.

Cheng, Yung-Hsiao T. "Clergymen in Jane Austen's Novels." *Fu Jen Studies: Literature and Linguistics* 11 (1978): 25–40.

Child, Harold. H. "Jane Austen." In *The Cambridge History of English*. Vol. 12, *The Nineteenth Century (I)*. Cambridge: Cambridge University Press, 1915, pp. 231–44. (Bibliography, pp. 446–47, by A. T. Bartholomew.)

Citron, Jo Ann. "Running the Basepaths: Baseball and Jane Austen." *Journal of Narrative Technique* 18 (Fall 1988): 269–77.

Clark, Lorrie. "Transfiguring the Romantic Sublime in *Persuasion*." In *Jane Austen's Business: Her World and Her Profession*. Edited by Juliet McMaster and Bruce Stovel. New York: St. Martin's Press, 1996, pp. 30–41.

Cleere, Eileen. "Reinvesting Nieces: *Mansfield Park* and the Economics of Endogamy." *Novel: A Forum on Fiction* 28 (Winter 1995): 113–30.

Cohen, Paula Marantz. "Stabilizing the Family System at *Mansfield Park*." *ELH: English Literary History* 54 (Fall 1987): 669–93.

———. "The Anorexic Syndrome and the Nineteenth-Century Domestic Novel." In *Disorderly Eaters: Texts in Self-Empowerment*. Edited by Lilian R. Furst and Peter W. Graham. University Park: Pennsylvania State University Press, 1992, pp. 125–39.

———. "Jane Austen's Rejection of Rousseau: A Novelistic and Feminist Initiation." *Papers on Language and Literature: A Journal for Scholars and Critics of Language and Literature* 30 (Summer 1994): 215–34.

Collins, Barbara Bail. "Jane Austen's Victorian Novel." *Nineteenth-Century Fiction* 4 (1949–1950): 175–85. (*Mansfield Park*.)

Collins, K. K. "Prejudice, *Persuasion*, and the Puzzle of Mrs. Smith." *Persuasions* 6 (December 1984): 40–43.

Conger, Syndy McMillen. "Austen's Sense and Radcliffe's Sensibility." *Gothic* 2 (1987): 16–24.

———. "Reading *Lovers' Vows*: Jane Austen's Reflections on English Sense and German Sensibility." *Studies in Philology* 85 (Winter 1988): 92–113.

Conrad, Peter. "Introduction" to *Emma*. Edited by Mary Lascelles. New York: Dutton, 1980, pp. v–xxx.

Cope, Sir Zachary. "Who Was Sophia Sentiment? Was She Jane Austen?" *Book Collector* 15 (1966): 143–51. (See responses by Gore and Jenkins, both 1977.)

Copeland, Edward. "The Burden of Grandison: Jane Austen and Her Contemporaries." *Women and Literature* 3 (1983): 98–106.

———. "Fictions of Employment: Jane Austen and the Woman's Novel." *Studies in Philology* 85 (Winter 1988): 114–24.

———. "Money Talks: Jane Austen and the Lady's Magazine." In *Jane Austen's Beginnings: The Juvenilia and Lady Susan*. Edited by J. David Grey. Ann Arbor: UMI Research Press, 1989, pp. 153–71.

———. "The Economic Realities of Jane Austen's Day." In *Approaches to Teaching Austen's "Pride and Prejudice."* Edited by Marcia McClintock Folsom. New York: Modern Language Association of America, 1993, pp. 33–45.

———. "The Austens and the Elliots: A Consumer's Guide to *Persuasion*." In *Jane Austen's Business: Her World and Her Profession*. Edited by Juliet McMaster and Bruce Stovel. New York: St. Martin's Press, 1996, pp. 136–53. (Revised version of essay first published in *Persuasions* 15 [December 1993]: 111–23.)

———. "Money." In Edward Copeland and Juliet McMaster, eds. *The Cambridge Companion to Jane Austen*. Cambridge: Cambridge University Press, 1997, pp. 131–48. (See also Copeland's *Women Writing about Money: Women's Fiction in England, 1790–1820*. Cambridge: Cambridge University Press, 1995.)

Cottom, Daniel. "The Novels of Jane Austen: Attachments and Supplements." *Novel: A Forum on Fiction* 14 (Winter 1981): 152–67.

Crawford, Thomas. "Boswell's Temple and the Jane Austen World." *Scottish Literary Journal* 10 (December 1983): 53–67.

Crosby, Christina. "Facing the Charms of *Emma*." *New Orleans Review* 16 (Spring 1989): 88–97.

Crundell, H. W. "Pride and Prejudice." *Notes and Queries* 180 (1941): 258. (Uses of the phrase before Austen's novel in Burney's *Cecilia*, Jeremy Taylor's *Holy Living* [1650], Edward Gibbon and Mrs. Thrale.)

Daiches, David. "Jane Austen, Karl Marx, and the Aristocratic Dance." *American Scholar* 17 (1947–1948): 289–96.

Darwin, Francis. *Rustic Sounds, and Other Studies in Literature and Natural History*. London: J. Murray, 1917, pp. 61–77.

Dash, Irene G. "*Emma* Crosses the Channel." *Names: Journal of the American Name Society* 31 (September 1983): 191–96.

Davies, J. M. Q. "*Emma* as Charade and the Education of the Reader." *Philological Quarterly* 65 (Spring 1986): 231–42.

Davis, Patricia D. "Jane Austen's Use of Frank Churchill's Letters in *Emma*." *Persuasions* 10 (December 1988): 34–38.

Davison, Trevor. "Jane Austen and the 'Process' of *Persuasion*." *Durham University Journal* 77 (December 1984): 43–47.

De Bruyn, Frans. "Edmund Burke's Gothic Romance: The Portrayal of Warren Hastings in Burke's Writings and Speeches on India." *Criticism: A Quarterly for Literature and the Arts* 29 (Fall 1987): 415–38.

———. "Jane Austen and the Common Reader." *Review* 16 (1994): 31–39.

DeForest, Mary. "Mrs. Elton and the Slave Trade." *Persuasions* 9 (December 1987): 11–13.

———. "Jane Austen and the Anti-Heroic Tradition." *Persuasions* 10 (December 1988): 11–21.

Demoor, Marysa. "Male Monsters or Monstrous Males in Victorian Women's Fiction." In *Exhibited by Candlelight: Sources and Developments in the Gothic Tradition*. Edited by Valeria Tinkler-Villani, Peter Davidson, and Jane Stevenson. Amsterdam: Rodopi, 1995, pp. 173–82.

De Rose, Peter L. "Imagination in *Northanger Abbey*." *University of Mississippi Studies in English* 4 (1983): 62–76.

Derry, Stephen. "The Ellesmeres and the Elliots: Charlotte Smith's Influence on *Persuasion*." *Persuasions* 12 (December 1990a): 69–70.

———. "Jane Austen's Reference to Hannah More in 'Catharine.' " *Notes and Queries*, n.s. 37 (March 1990b): 20.

———. "Sources of Jane Austen's *Love and Freindship*: A Note." *Notes and Queries*, n.s. 37 (March 1990c): 18–19.

———. "Jane Austen's Use of *The Vicar of Wakefield* in *Pride and Prejudice*." *English Language Notes* 28 (March 1991): 25–27.

———. "Harriet Smith's Reading." *Persuasions* 14 (December 1992): 70–72.

———. "Jane Austen's Use of *Measure for Measure* in *Sense and Sensibility.*" *Persuasions* 15 (December 1993): 37–41.

———. "Robert Bage's *Barham Downs* and *Sense and Sensibility.*" *Notes and Queries* n.s. 41 (September 1994): 325–26.

Dillon, Brian. "Circumventing the Biographical Subject: Jane Austen and the Critics." *Rocky Mountain Review of Language and Literature* 46:4 (1992): 213–21.

Dodds, M. H. "Jane Austen and Charlotte M. Yonge." *Notes and Queries* 193 (1948): 476–78.

———. "Hours of Business, 1780 to 1820." *Notes and Queries* 194 (1949): 436–37. Information on shops and shopping with reference to Austen.

Doody, Margaret Anne. "Jane Austen's Reading." In *The Jane Austen Companion.* Edited by J. David Grey. New York: Macmillan, 1986, pp. 347–63.

Dorsey, Shelly. "Austen, Forster, and Economics." *Persuasions* 12 (December 1990): 54–59.

Drabble, Margaret. "The Dower House at Kellynch: A Somerset Romance." In *Jane Austen's Business: Her World and Her Profession.* Edited by Juliet McMaster and Bruce Stovel. New York: St. Martin's Press, 1996, pp. 206–22.

Drew, Philip. "Jane Austen and Bishop Butler." *Nineteenth-Century Fiction* 35 (1980): 127–49.

Duckworth, Alistair M. "Prospects and Retrospects." In *Jane Austen Today.* Edited by Joel Weinsheimer. Athens: University of Georgia Press, 1975, pp. 1–32.

———. "Fiction and Some Uses of the Country House Setting from Richardson to Scott." In *Landscape in the Gardens and the Literature of Eighteenth-Century England: Papers Read at a Clark Library Seminar, 18 March 1978.* Edited by David C. Streatfield and Alistair M. Duckworth. Los Angeles: William Andrews Clark Memorial Library, University of California, 1981, pp. 91–128.

———. "Jane Austen and the Conflict of Interpretations." *Women and Literature* 3 (1983): 39–52.

———. "Jane Austen's Accommodations." *Persuasions* 7 (December 1985): 67–77.

———. "Jane Austen and the Construction of a Progressive Author." *College English* 53: 1 (1991): 77–90.

Duncan-Jones, E. E. "Jane Austen and Crabbe." *Review of English Studies* n.s. 5 (1954): 174.

Dunn, Allen. "The Ethics of *Mansfield Park*: MacIntyre, Said, and Social Context." *Soundings: An Interdisciplinary Journal* 78 (Fall–Winter 1995): 483–500.

Dussinger, John A. "Jane Austen's Political Silence." *Dolphin* 19 (Autumn 1990): 32–42.

Easton, Celia A. "*Sense and Sensibility* and the Joke of Substitution." *Journal of Narrative Technique* 23 (Spring 1993): 114–26.

Ebbatson, Roger. "*Sanditon.*" *Critical Survey* 4:1 (1992): 45–51.

Edgecombe, Rodney Stenning. "Legitimate Hyperbole in *Northanger Abbey.*" *University of Dayton Review* 22 (Spring 1993): 147–48.

Edwards, Thomas R. "Embarrassed by Jane Austen." *Raritan: A Quarterly Review* 7 (Summer 1987): 62–80.

Ehrenpreis, Anne Henry. "*Northanger Abbey*: Jane Austen and Charlotte Smith." *Nineteenth Century Fiction* 25 (1970–1971): 343–48.

Elsbree, Langdon. "Jane Austen and the Dance of Fidelity and Complaisance." *Nineteenth-Century Fiction* 15 (1960–1961): 113–36.

Epstein, Julia L. "Jane Austen's Juvenilia and the Female Epistolary Tradition." *Papers on Language and Literature* 21 (Fall 1985): 399–416.

Erickson, Joyce Quiring. "Public and Private in Jane Austen's Novels." *Midwest Quarterly: A Journal of Contemporary Thought* 25 (Winter 1984): 201–19.

Erickson, Lee. "The Economy of Novel Reading: Jane Austen and the Circulating Library." *SEL: Studies in English Literature, 1500–1900* 30 (Autumn 1990): 573–90.

Farrer, Reginald. "Jane Austen, *ob.* July 18, 1817." *Quarterly Review* 228 (July 1917): 1–30.

Faulkner, Karen. "Anthony Trollope's Apprenticeship." *Nineteenth Century Literature* 38 (September 1983): 161–88.

Fergus, Jan. " 'My Sore-Throats, You Know, Are Always Worse than Anybody's': Mary Musgrove and Jane Austen's Art of Whining." In *Jane Austen's Business: Her World and Her Profession*. Edited by Juliet McMaster and Bruce Stovel. New York: St. Martin's Press, 1996, pp. 69–80. (First published in *Persuasions* 15 [December 1993]: 139–47.)

Ferguson, Moira. "*Mansfield Park*: Slavery, Colonialism, and Gender." *The Oxford Literary Review* 13:1–2 (1991): 118–39.

Fielding, Anita. "Macaulay and Miss Austen." *Persuasions* 15 (December 1993): 24–29.

Finch, Casey, and Peter Bowen. " 'The Tittle-Tattle of Highbury': Gossip and the Free Indirect Style in *Emma.*" *Representations* 31 (Summer 1990): 1–18.

Fischer, Doucet Devin. "Byron and Austen: Romance and Reality." *The Byron Journal* 21 (1993): 71–79.

Fisher, Judith Warner. "All the 'Write' Moves; Or, Theatrical Gesture in *Sense and Sensibility.*" *Persuasions* 9 (December 1987): 17–23.

Fitzgerald, Jennifer. "Jane Austen's *Persuasion* and the French Revolution." *Persuasions* 10 (December 1988): 39–43.

Flahiff, F. T. "Place and Replacement in *Mansfield Park.*" *University of Toronto Quarterly: A Canadian Journal of the Humanities* 54 (Spring 1985): 221–33.

Flavin, Louise. "*Mansfield Park*: Free Indirect Discourse and the Psychological Novel." *Studies in the Novel* 19 (Summer 1987): 137–59.

———. "Free Indirect Discourse and the Clever Heroine of *Emma.*" *Persuasions* 13 (December 1991): 50–57.

Fleishman, Avrom. "Two Faces of *Emma.*" *Women and Literature* 3 (1983): 248–56.

Fletcher, Loraine. "Emma: The Shadow Novelist." *Critical Survey* 4:1 (1992): 36–44.

Footerman, Sharon. "The First Fanny Price." *Notes and Queries* n.s. 25 (1978): 217–19.

Fowler, Kathleen L. "Apricots, Raspberries, and Susan Price! Susan Price!: *Mansfield Park* and Maria Edgeworth." *Persuasions* 13 (December 1991): 28–32.

Fowler, Marian E. "The Courtesy-Book Heroine of *Mansfield Park.*" *University of Toronto Quarterly* 44 (1974): 31–46.

———. " 'Substance and Shadow': Conventions of the Marriage Market in *Northanger Abbey.*" *English Studies in Canada* 6 (1980): 277–91.

Fraiman, Susan. "The Humiliation of Elizabeth Bennet." In *Refiguring the Father: New*

Feminist Readings of Patriarchy. Edited by Patricia Yaeger and Beth Kowaleski-Wallace. Urbana: University of Illinois Press, 1989, pp. 168–87.

―――. "Jane Austen and Edward Said: Gender, Culture, and Imperialism." *Critical Inquiry* (Summer 1995).

Frank, Maude Morrison. *Great Authors in Their Youth*. New York: Holt, 1915, pp. 265–91.

Frazer, June M. "Stylistic Categories of Narrative in Jane Austen." *Style* 17 (Winter 1983): 16–26.

Frost, Cy. "Autocracy and the Matrix of Power: Issues of Propriety and Economics in the Work of Mary Wollstonecraft, Jane Austen, and Harriet Martineau." *Tulsa Studies in Women's Literature* 10 (Fall 1991): 253–71.

Fullbrook, Kate. "Jane Austen and the Comic Negative." In *Women Reading Women's Writing*. Edited by Sue Roe. Brighton, Sussex: Harvester, 1987, pp. 37–57.

Galperin, William. "Byron, Austen and the 'Revolution' of Irony." *Criticism: A Quarterly for Literature and the Arts* 32 (Winter 1990): 51–80.

―――. "The Theatre at *Mansfield Park*: From Classic to Romantic Once More." *Eighteenth Century Life* 16 (November 1992): 247–71.

Gamble, David E. "Pragmatic Sympathy in Austen and Eliot." *College Language Association Journal* 32 (March 1989): 348–60.

Gard, Roger. "*Mansfield Park*, Fanny Price, Flaubert and the Modern Novel." *English: The Journal of the English Association* 38 (Spring 1989a): 1–33.

―――. "*Lady Susan* and the Single Effect." *Essays in Criticism: A Quarterly Journal of Literary Criticism* 39 (October 1989b): 305–25.

Gardiner, Ellen. "Privacy, Privilege, and 'Poaching' in *Mansfield Park*." In *Jane Austen and Discourses of Feminism*. Edited by Devoney Looser. New York: St. Martin's Press, 1995, pp. 151–66.

Garnett, Christopher Browne, Jr. *Taste: An Essay in Critical Imagination*. Jericho, NY: Exposition Press, 1968, pp. 35–42 and passim.

Garside, P. D. "Jane Austen and Subscription Fiction." *British Journal for Eighteenth Century Studies* 10 (Autumn 1987): 175–88.

Garside, Peter, and Elizabeth McDonald. "Evangelicalism and *Mansfield Park*." *Trivium* 10 (1975): 34–50.

Gay, Penelope. "Theatricals and Theatricality in *Mansfield Park*." *Sydney Studies in English* 13 (1987–1988): 61–73.

―――. "A Changing View: Jane Austen's Landscape." *Sydney Studies in English* 15 (1989–1990): 47–62.

Gibbon, Frank. "The Antiguan Connection: Some New Light on *Mansfield Park*." *The Cambridge Quarterly* 11 (1982): 298–305.

Gibbs, Christine. "Absent Fathers: An Examination of Father–Daughter Relationships in Jane Austen's Novels." *Persuasions* 8 (December 1986): 45–50.

Gibson, Walker. "Contrarieties of Emotion: Or, Five Days with *Pride and Prejudice*." In *Conversations: Contemporary Critical Theory and the Teaching of Literature*. Edited by Charles Moran and Elizabeth F. Penfield. Urbana, IL: National Council of Teachers of English, 1990, pp. 114–19.

Gilbert, Sandra M., and Susan Gubar. "Shut Up in Prose: Gender and Genre in Austen's Juvenilia." *The Madwoman in the Attic: The Woman Writer and the Nineteenth Century Literary Imagination*. New Haven, CT, and London: Yale University Press, 1979, pp. 107–45.

Giles, Paul. "The Gothic Dialogue in *Pride and Prejudice.*" *Text and Context: A Journal of Interdisciplinary Studies* 2 (Spring 1988): 68–75.

Gillis, Christina Marsden. "Garden, Sermon, and Novel in *Mansfield Park*: Exercises in Legibility." *Novel: A Forum on Fiction* 18 (Winter 1985): 117–25.

Gillooly, Eileen. "Rehabilitating Mary Crawford: *Mansfield Park* and the Relief of 'Throwing Ridicule.' " In *Feminist Nightmares: Women at Odds: Feminism and the Problem of Sisterhood.* Edited by Susan Ostrov Weisser and Jennifer Fleischner. New York: New York University Press, 1994, pp. 328–42.

Gilson, David J., and J. David Grey. "Jane Austen's *Juvenilia* and *Lady Susan*: An Annotated Bibliography." In *Jane Austen's Beginnings: The Juvenilia and Lady Susan.* Edited by J. David Grey. Ann Arbor: UMI Research Press, 1989, pp. 243–62.

Giobbi, Giuliana. "Sisters Beware of Sisters: Sisterhood as a Literary Motif in Jane Austen, A. S. Byatt and I. Bossi Fedrigotti." *Journal of European Studies* 22 (September 1992): 241–58.

Giordano, Julia. "The Word as a Battleground in Jane Austen's *Persuasion.*" In *Anxious Power: Reading, Writing, and Ambivalence in Narrative by Women.* Edited by Carol J. Singley and Susan Elizabeth Sweeney. New York: State University of New York Press, 1993, pp. 107–23.

Giuffre, Giulia. "Sex, Self and Society in *Mansfield Park.*" *Sydney Studies in English* 9 (1983–1984): 76–93.

Goodwin, Sarah Webster. "Knowing Better: Feminism and Utopian Discourse in *Pride and Prejudice, Villette,* and 'Babette's Feast.' " In *Feminism, Utopia, and Narrative.* Edited by Libby Falk Jones and Sarah Webster Goodwin. Knoxville: University of Tennessee Press, 1990, pp. 1–20.

Goold, Patrick. "Obedience and Integrity in *Mansfield Park.*" *Renascence: Essays on Value in Literature* 39 (Summer 1987): 452–69.

Gordon, Jan B. "A-filiative Families and Subversive Reproduction: Gossip in Jane Austen." *Genre* 21 (Spring 1988): 5–46.

Gore, John. " 'Sophia Sentiment': Jane Austen?" In *Collected Reports of the Jane Austen Society 1966–75.* Folkestone: Dawson and Sons, 1977, pp. 9–12. (Response to Cope 1966.)

Gornall, J. F. G. "Marriage, Property, and Romance in Jane Austen's Novels." *Hibbert Journal* 65 (1966–1967): 151–56; 66 (1966–1967): 24–29. (Shorter version reprinted in *History Today* 17 [1967]: 805–11.)

Graham, Peter W. "*Emma*'s Three Sisters." *Arizona Quarterly: A Journal of American Literature, Culture, and Theory* 43 (Spring 1987): 39–52.

Grant, John E. "Shows of Mourning in the Text of Jane Austen's *Persuasion.*" *Modern Philology: A Journal Devoted to Research in Medieval and Modern Literature* 80 (February 1983): 283–86.

Greene, Donald. "Jane Austen and the Peerage." *PMLA: Publications of the Modern Language Association* 68 (1953): 1017–31.

———. "A Partial Pedigree of Jane Austen." *Persuasions* 6 (December 1984): 31–33.

Greenfield, Susan C. "Fanny's Misreading and the Misreading of Fanny: Women, Literature, and Interiority in *Mansfield Park.*" *Texas Studies in Literature and Language* (Fall 1994).

Grey, J. David. "Sibling Relationships in *Mansfield Park.*" *Persuasions* 2 (December 1980): 28–29.

Griffin, Cynthia. "The Development of Realism in Jane Austen's Early Novels." *ELH* 30 (1963): 36–52.

Gross, Gloria. "Mentoring Jane Austen: Reflections on 'My Dear Dr. Johnson.' " *Persuasions* 11 (December 1989): 53–60.

———. "Jane Austen and Psychological Realism: 'What Does a Woman Want?' " In *Reading and Writing Women's Lives: A Study of the Novel of Manners.* Edited by Bege K. Bowers and Barbara Brothers. Ann Arbor: UMI Research Press, 1990, pp. 19–33.

———. "Flights into Illness: Some Characters in Jane Austen." *Literature and Medicine during the Eighteenth Century.* Edited by Marie Mulvey Roberts and Roy Porter. London: Routledge, 1993, pp. 188–99.

Grove, Robin. "Jane Austen's Free Enquiry: *Mansfield Park.*" *The Critical Review* 25 (1983): 132–50.

Groves, David. "The Two Picnics in *Emma.*" *Persuasions* 5 (December 1983): 6–7.

———. "Knowing One's Species Better: Social Satire in *Persuasion.*" *Persuasions* 6 (December 1984): 13–15.

Grundy, Isobel. "*Persuasion:* or, The Triumph of Cheerfulness." In *Jane Austen's Business: Her World and Her Profession.* Edited by Juliet McMaster and Bruce Stovel. New York: St. Martin's Press, 1996, pp. 3–16.

Gunn, Daniel P. "In the Vicinity of Winthrop: Ideological Rhetoric in *Persuasion.*" *Nineteenth Century Literature* 41 (March 1987): 403–18.

Haddow, G. C. "England's Jane." *Dalhousie Review* 24 (1944–1945): 379–92.

Haggerty, George E. "The Sacrifice of Privacy in *Sense and Sensibility.*" *Tulsa Studies in Women's Literature* 7 (Fall 1988): 221–37.

Halperin, John. "The Worlds of *Emma*: Jane Austen and Cowper." In *Jane Austen: Bicentenary Essays.* Edited by John Halperin. New York: Cambridge University Press, 1975, pp. 197–206.

———. "The Novelist as Heroine in *Mansfield Park*: A Study in Autobiography." *Modern Language Quarterly* 44 (June 1983a): 136–56.

———. "Jane Austen's Anti-Romantic Fragment: Somes Notes on *Sanditon.*" *Tulsa Studies in Women's Literature* 2 (Fall 1983b): 183–91.

———. "Jane Austen's Lovers." *SEL: Studies in English Literature, 1500–1900* 25 (Autumn 1985): 719–36.

———. "Inside *Pride and Prejudice.*" *Persuasions* 11 (December 1989a): 37–45.

———. "Unengaged Laughter: Jane Austen's Juvenilia." In *Jane Austen's Beginnings: The Juvenilia and Lady Susan.* Edited by J. David Grey. Ann Arbor: UMI Research Press, 1989b, pp. 29–44.

Haney, John Louis. "*Northanger Abbey.*" *Modern Language Notes* 16 (1901): 223–24. First identification of the seven "horrid" novels mentioned by Isabella Thorpe in Chapter 6 of the novel.

Harding, D. W. "Regulated Hatred: An Aspect of the Work of Jane Austen." *Scrutiny* 7 (March 1940): 346–62.

———. "The Supposed Letter Form of *Sense and Sensibility.*" *Notes and Queries* 40: 238 (December 1993): 464–66.

Harris, Jocelyn. "Anne Elliot, the Wife of Bath, and Other Friends." *Women and Literature* 3 (1983): 273–93.

———. "The Influence of Richardson on *Pride and Prejudice.*" In *Approaches to*

Teaching Austen's "Pride and Prejudice." Edited by Marcia McClintock Folsom. New York: Modern Language Association of America, 1993, pp. 94–99.

———. "Jane Austen and the Burden of the (Male) Past: The Case Reexamined." In *Jane Austen and Discourses of Feminism.* Edited by Devoney Looser. New York: St. Martin's Press, 1995, pp. 87–100.

Harris, Laurie Lanzen, ed. "Jane Austen, 1775–1817." *Nineteenth-Century Literature Criticism: Excerpts from Criticism of the Works of Novelists, Poets, Playwrights, Short Story Writers, and Other Creative Writers Who Lived between 1800 and 1900, from the First Published Critical Appraisals to Current Evaluations.* Detroit: Gale Research, 1981, pp. 29–68.

Harris, R. Allen. "Social Definition in *Pride and Prejudice*: An Exercise in Extensional Semantics." *English Studies in Canada* 17 (June 1991): 163–76.

Hart, John. "Jane Austen's Sailors: Gentlemen in the Military Capacity." *Persuasions* 4 (December 1982): 18–20.

Havely, Cicely Palser. "*Emma*: Portrait of the Artist as a Young Woman." *English: The Journal of the English Association* 42 (Fall 1993): 221–37.

Hayes, E. N. "*Emma*: A Dissenting Opinion." *Nineteenth-Century Fiction* 4 (1949–1950): 1–20.

Heldman, James. "Where Is Jane Austen in The Watsons?" *Persuasions* 8 (December 1986): 84–91.

———. "Kipling, 'Jane's Marriage,' and 'the Janeites.' " *Persuasions* 10 (December 1988): 44–47.

———. "How Wealthy Is Mr. Darcy—Really? Pounds and Dollars in the World of *Pride and Prejudice.*" *Persuasions* 16 (December 1990): 38–49.

———. "The Crofts and the Art of Suggestion in *Persuasion*: A Speculation." *Persuasions* 15 (December 1993): 46–52.

Hennelly, Mark M., Jr. "*Pride and Prejudice*: The Eyes Have It." *Women and Literature* 3 (1983): 187–207.

Herbert, David. "Place and Society in Jane Austen's England." *Geography* 76 (July 1991): 193–208.

Heydt, Jill. " 'First Impressions' and Later Recollections: The Place of the Picturesque in *Pride and Prejudice.*" *Studies in the Humanities* 12 (December 1985): 115–24.

Heydt-Stevenson, Jill. " 'Unbecoming Conjunctions': Mourning the Loss of Landscape and Love in *Persuasion.*" *Eighteenth Century Fiction* 8 (October 1995): 51–71.

Heyns, Michiel. "Shock and Horror: The Moral Vocabulary of *Mansfield Park.*" *English Studies in Africa: A Journal of the Humanities* 29:1 (1986): 1–18.

Hildebrand, Enid G. "Jane Austen and the Law." *Persuasions* 4 (December 1982): 34–41.

Hilliard, Raymond F. "*Emma*: Dancing without Space to Turn In." In *Probability, Time, and Space in Eighteenth-Century Literature.* Edited by Paula R. Backscheider. New York: AMS Press, 1979, pp. 275–98.

Hirsch, Gordon. "Shame, *Pride and Prejudice*: Jane Austen's Psychological Sophistication." *Mosaic: A Journal for the Interdisciplinary Study of Literature* 25 (Winter 1992): 63–78.

Hoeveler, Diane. "Vindicating *Northanger Abbey*: Mary Wollstonecraft, Jane Austen, and Gothic Feminism." In *Jane Austen and Discourses of Feminism*. Edited by Devoney Looser. New York: St. Martin's Press, 1995, pp. 117–36.

Hogan, Charles Beecher. "*Lovers' Vows* and Highbury." In *Collected Reports of the Jane Austen Society, 1966–1975*. Folkestone: Dawson, 1977, pp. 227–35.

Holly, Grant I. "*Emma*grammatology." In *Studies in Eighteenth Century Culture*. Vol. 19. Edited by Leslie Ellen Brown and Patricia Craddock. East Lansing, MI: Colleagues Press, 1989, pp. 39–51.

Holstein, Suzy Clarkson. "Out of the Estate and into the Rescue Boat." *Persuasions* 15 (December 1993): 53–56.

Holway, Tatiana M. "The Game of Speculation: Economics and Representation." *Dickens Quarterly* 9 (September 1992): 103–14.

Honan, Park. "Jane Austen and Marriage." *Contemporary Review* 245 (November 1984a): 253–59.

———. "Sterne and the Formation of Jane Austen's Talent." In *Laurence Sterne: Riddles and Mysteries*. Edited by Valerie Grosvenor Myer. London: Vision, 1984b, pp. 161–71.

———. "Jane Austen and the American Revolution." *University of Leeds Review* 28 (1985–1986): 181–95.

———. "Richardson's Influence on Jane Austen (Some Notes on the Biographical and Critical Problems of an 'Influence')." In *Samuel Richardson: Passion and Prudence*. Edited by Valerie Grosvenor Myer. London: Vision, 1986, pp. 165–77.

———. "Jane's Fighting Ships." *History Today* 37 (August 1987): 40–46.

———. "The Austen Brothers and Sisters." *Persuasions* 10 (December 1988): 59–64.

Hopkins, Annette Brown. "Jane Austen's *Love and Freindship*: A Study in Literary Relations." *South Atlantic Quarterly* 34 (1925): 34–49.

Hopkins, Lisa. "Jane Austen and Money." *The Wordsworth Circle* 25 (Spring 1994): 76–78.

Hopkins, Robert. "General Tilney and Affairs of State: The Political Gothic of *Northanger Abbey*." *Philological Quarterly* 57 (1978): 213–24.

Hopkinson, David. "The Naval Career of Jane Austen's Brother." *History Today* 26 (1976): 576–83.

Horwitz, Barbara. "Lady Susan: The Wicked Mother in Jane Austen's Work." In *Jane Austen's Beginnings: The Juvenilia and Lady Susan*. Edited by J. David Grey. Ann Arbor: UMI Research Press, 1989, pp. 181–91.

———. "*Pride and Prejudice* and *Framley Parsonage*: A Structural Resemblance." *Persuasions* 15 (December 1993): 32–36.

Hudson, Glenda A. "Incestuous Relationships: *Mansfield Park* Revisited." *Eighteenth Century Fiction* 4 (October 1991): 53–68.

———. "Consolidated Communities: Masculine and Feminine Values in Jane Austen's Fiction." In *Jane Austen and Discourses of Feminism*. Edited by Devoney Looser. New York: St. Martin's Press, 1995, pp. 100–114.

Hunt, John Dixon. "Sense and Sensibility in the Landscape Designs of Humphrey Repton." *Studies in Burke and His Time* 19 (1978): 3–28.

Hunt, John Dixon, and Peter Willis, eds. "Jane Austen (1775–1817)." In their *The Genius of the Place: The English Landscape Garden, 1620–1820*. New York: Harper and Row, 1975, pp. 372–75.

Hunt, Linda C. "A Woman's Portion: Jane Austen and the Female Character." In *Fetter'd or Free? British Women Novelists, 1670–1815*. Edited by Mary Anne Schofield and Cecilia Macheski. Columbus: Ohio University Press, 1986, pp. 8–28. (See also her book *A Woman's Portion: Ideology, Culture, and the British Female Novel Tradition.* New York: Garland, 1988.)

Hutcheson, John. "Subdued Feminism: Jane Austen, Charlotte Brontë, and George Eliot." *International Journal of Women's Studies* 6 (May–June 1983): 230–57.

Hyams, Edward. *Capability Brown and Humphrey Repton.* London: J. M. Dent and Sons, 1971, passim.

Ives, Sidney. "The Withering Eye, the Transmuting Hand, the Alchemies of *Pride and Prejudice*." *Persuasions* 9 (December 1987): 41–45.

Jackel, David. "*Leonora* and *Lady Susan*: A Note on Maria Edgeworth and Jane Austen." *English Studies in Canada* 3 (1977): 278–88.

Jackson, Michael. "Jane Austen's View of the Clergy." *Theology* 78 (1975): 531–38.

Jarvis, W. A. M. "The Ships in *Mansfield Park*." *Persuasions* 10 (December 1988): 31–33.

Jenkins, Elizabeth. "A Footnote to 'Sophia Sentiment.' " In *Collected Reports of the Jane Austen Society 1966–75.* Folkestone: Dawson and Sons, 1977, pp. 12–13. (Response to Cope 1966.)

———. "Some Notes on Background." In *Collected Reports of the Jane Austen Society, 1976–1985.* Chawton: Jane Austen Society, 1989, pp. 152–68.

Jerinic, Maria. "In Defense of the Gothic: Rereading *Northanger Abbey*." In *Jane Austen and Discourses of Feminism.* Edited by Devoney Looser. New York: St. Martin's Press, 1995, pp. 137–50.

Johnson, Claudia L. "The 'Operations of Time, and the Changes of the Human Mind': Jane Austen and Dr. Johnson Again." *Modern Language Quarterly* 44 (March 1983a): 23–38.

———. "The 'Twilight of Probability': Uncertainty and Hope in *Sense and Sensibility*." *Philological Quarterly* 62 (Spring 1983b): 171–86.

———. " 'The Kingdom at Sixes and Sevens': Politics and the *Juvenilia*." In *Jane Austen's Beginnings: The Juvenilia and Lady Susan.* Edited by J. David Grey. Ann Arbor: UMI Research Press, 1989a, pp. 45–58.

———. "A 'Sweet Face as White as Death': Jane Austen and the Politics of Female Sensibility." *Novel: A Forum on Fiction* 22 (Winter 1989b): 159–74.

Johnson, Eric. "Oxford Electronic Text Library Edition of the Complete Works of Jane Austen." *Computers and the Humanities* (August–October 1994).

Johnson, Judy Van Sickle. "The Bodily Frame: Learning Romance in *Persuasion*." *Nineteenth Century Literature* 38 (June 1983): 43–61.

Jones, W. S. Handley. "Jane and Charlotte." *London Quarterly and Holborn Review* 170, 6th series 14 (1945): 347–50. Austen and Brontë.

Jordan, Elaine. "Pulpit, Stage, and Novel: *Mansfield Park* and Mrs. Inchbald's *Lovers' Vows*." *Novel: A Forum on Fiction* 20 (Winter 1987): 138–48.

Juhasz, Suzanne. "Bonnets and Balls: Reading Jane Austen's Letters." *The Centennial Review* 31 (Winter 1987): 84–104.

Kaplan, Deborah. "Achieving Authority: Jane Austen's First Published Novel." *Nineteenth Century Literature* 37 (March 1983): 531–51.

———. "The Disappearance of the Woman Writer: Jane Austen and Her Biographers." *Prose Studies* 7 (September 1984): 129–47.

———. "Female Friendship and Epistolary Form: *Lady Susan* and the Development of

Jane Austen's Fiction.'' *Criticism: A Quarterly for Literature and the Arts* 29 (Spring 1987): 163–78.

———. ''The Family Influence on Jane Austen's Juvenilia.'' *Persuasions* 10 (December 1988a): 65–69.

———. ''Representing Two Cultures: Jane Austen's Letters.'' In *The Private Self: Theory and Practice of Women's Autobiographical Writings*. Edited by Shari Benstock. Chapel Hill: University of North Carolina Press, 1988b, pp. 211–29.

———. ''Domesticity at Sea: The Example of Charles and Fanny Austen.'' *Persuasions* 14 (December 1992): 113–21.

Kaplan, Laurie. ''Jane Austen and the Uncommon Reader.'' In *Jane Austen's Beginnings: The Juvenilia and Lady Susan*. Edited by J. David Grey. Ann Arbor: UMI Research Press, 1989, pp. 73–82.

———. ''*Persuasion*: The Accidents of Human Life.'' *Persuasions* 15 (December 1993): 157–63.

Kaplan, Laurie, and Richard S. Kaplan. ''What Is Wrong with Marianne? Medicine and Disease in Jane Austen's England.'' *Persuasions* 12 (December 1990): 117–30.

Kastely, James L. ''*Persuasion*: Jane Austen's Philosophical Rhetoric.'' *Philosophy and Literature* 15 (April 1991): 74–88.

Katz, Richard A. ''The Comic Perception of Jane Austen.'' In *Voltaire, the Enlightenment and the Comic Mode: Essays in Honor of Jean Sareil*. Edited by Maxine G. Cutler. New York: Peter Lang, 1990, pp. 65–87.

Kaufmann, David. ''Closure in *Mansfield Park* and the Sanctity of the Family.'' *Philological Quarterly* 65 (Spring 1986): 211–29.

———. ''Law and Propriety, *Sense and Sensibility*: Austen on the Cusp of Modernity.'' *ELH: English Literary History* 59 (Summer 1992): 385–408.

Kavanagh, Julia. *English Women of Letters: Biographical Sketches*. Leipzig: Bernhard Tauchnitz, 1962, pp. 247–74.

Kear, Celine M. ''Travelling in the Steps of Jane Austen.'' *Persuasions* 9 (December 1987): 31–33.

Kearney, J. A. ''Tumult of Feeling, and Restraint, in *Mansfield Park*.'' *Theoria: A Journal of Studies in the Arts, Humanities and Social Sciences* 71 (May 1988): 35–45.

———. ''Jane Austen and the Reason–Feeling Debate.'' *Theoria: A Journal of Studies in the Arts, Humanities and Social Sciences* 75 (May 1990): 107–22.

Keith, Rhonda. ''Jane Austen and Shakespeare.'' *Persuasions* 6 (December 1984): 30.

Kelly, Gary. ''Reading Aloud in *Mansfield Park*.'' *Nineteenth Century Literature* 37 (June 1982): 29–49.

———. ''The Art of Reading in *Pride and Prejudice*.'' *English Studies in Canada* 10 (June 1984): 156–71.

———. ''Jane Austen and the English Novel of the 1790s.'' In *Fetter'd or Free? British Women Novelists, 1670–1815*. Edited by Mary Anne Schofield and Cecilia Macheski. Athens: Ohio University Press, 1986, pp. 285–306.

———. ''Jane Austen, Romantic Feminism, and Civil Society.'' In *Jane Austen and Discourses of Feminism*. Edited by Devoney Looser. New York: St. Martin's Press, 1995, pp. 19–34.

———. ''Jane Austen's Real Business: The Novel, Literature and Cultural Capital.'' In *Jane Austen's Business: Her World and Her Profession*. Edited by Juliet McMaster and Bruce Stovel. New York: St. Martin's Press, 1996, pp. 154–67.

Kenney, Catherine. "The Mystery of *Emma*: Or, the Consummate Case of the Least Likely Heroine." *Persuasions* 13 (December 1991): 138–45.

Kent, Christopher. "Learning History with, and from, Jane Austen." In *Jane Austen's Beginnings: The Juvenilia and Lady Susan*. Edited by J. David Grey. Ann Arbor: UMI Research Press, 1989, pp. 59–72.

Kern, Jean B. "The Old Maid; Or, 'To Grow Old, and Be Poor, and Laughed At.' " In *Fetter'd or Free? British Women Novelists, 1670–1815*. Edited by Mary Anne Schofield and Cecilia Macheski. Columbus: Ohio University Press, 1986, pp. 201–14.

Kilroy, G. J. F. "*Mansfield Park* in Two Volumes." *English: The Journal of the English Association* 34 (Summer 1985): 115–29.

Kinkead-Weekes, Mark. "The Old Maid: Jane Austen Replies to Charlotte Brontë and D. H. Lawrence." *Nineteenth Century Fiction* 31 (1976): 188–205.

Kirkham, Margaret. "The Theatricals in *Mansfield Park* and 'Frederick' in *Lovers' Vows*." *Notes and Queries*, n.s. 22 (1975): 388–90.

Kirkland, Janice J. "Jane Austen and Bonomi." *Notes and Queries* 34: 232 (March 1987): 1, 24–25.

Kliger, Samuel. "Jane Austen's *Pride and Prejudice* in the Eighteenth-Century Mode." *University of Toronto Quarterly* 16 (1946–1947): 357–70.

Knoepflmacher, U. C. "The Importance of Being Frank: Character and Letter-Writing in *Emma*." *Studies in English Literature 1500–1900* 7 (1967): 639–58.

Knox-Shaw, Peter. "*Persuasion*, Byron, and the Turkish tale." *Review of English Studies* 44 (February 1993): 47–69.

Knuth, Deborah J. " 'We Fainted Alternately on a Sofa': Female Friendship in Jane Austen's Juvenilia." *Persuasions* 9 (December 1987): 64–71.

———. "Sisterhood and Friendship in *Pride and Prejudice*: Need Happiness Be 'Entirely a Matter of Chance'?" *Persuasions* 11 (December 1989a): 99–109.

———. " 'You, Who I Know Will Enter into All My Feelings': Friendship in Jane Austen's *Juvenilia* and *Lady Susan*." In *Jane Austen's Beginnings: The Juvenilia and Lady Susan*. Edited by J. David Grey. Ann Arbor: UMI Research Press, 1989b, pp. 95–106.

———. " 'There Is So Little Real Friendship in the World!': 'Distant Civility,' Conversational 'Treat(s),' and Good Advice in *Persuasion*." *Persuasions* 15 (December 1993): 148–56.

Koppel, Gene. "The Role of Contingency in *Mansfield Park*: The Necessity of an Ambiguous Conclusion." *Southern Review: Literary and Interdisciplinary Essays* 15 (November 1982): 306–13.

———. "The Mystery of the Self in *Persuasion*." *Persuasions* 6 (December 1984): 48–54.

———. "*Pride and Prejudice*: Conservative or Liberal Novel—Or Both? (A Gadamerian Approach)." *Persuasions* 11 (December 1989): 132–39.

Kroeber, Karl. "Jane Austen as an Historical Novelist: *Sense and Sensibility*." *Persuasions* 12 (December 1990): 10–18.

Lacour, Claudia Brodsky. "Austen's *Pride and Prejudice* and Hegel's 'Truth in Art': Concept, Reference, and History." *ELH: English Literary History* 59 (Fall 1992): 597–623.

Lamont, Claire. "Jane Austen's Gothic Architecture." In *Exhibited by Candlelight: Sources and Developments in the Gothic Tradition*. Edited by Valeria Tinkler-

Villani, Peter Davidson, and Jane Stevenson. Amsterdam: Rodopi, 1995, pp. 107–15.

La Rue, Helene. "Music, Literature and Etiquette: Musical Instruments and Social Identity from Castiglione to Austen." In *Ethnicity, Identity and Music: The Musical Construction of Place.* Edited by Martin Stokes. Oxford: Berg, 1994, pp. 189–205.

Latkin, Patricia. "Looking for Jane in All the Wrong Places: Collecting Books in Gilson's Category J." *Persuasions* 15 (December 1993): 63–72.

Lau, Beth. "Madeline at Northanger Abbey: Keats's Antiromances and Gothic Satire." *Journal of English and German Philology* 84:1 (1985): 30–50.

Laurence, Patricia. "Women's Silence as a Ritual of Truth: A Study of Literary Expressions in Austen, Brontë, and Woolf." *Listening to Silences: New Essays in Feminist Criticism.* Edited by Elaine Hedges and Shelley Fisher Fishkin. London and New York: Oxford University Press, 1994, pp. 156–67.

Le Faye, Deirdre. "Jane Austen and Her Hancock Relatives." *Review of English Studies* n.s. 30 (February 1979): 12–27.

———. "Jane Austen and Mrs. Hunter's Novel." *Notes and Queries* 32 (230) (September 1985a): 335–36.

———. "Three Austen Family Letters." *Notes and Queries* 32 (230) (September 1985b): 329–35.

———. "*Sanditon*: Jane Austen's Manuscript and Her Niece's Continuation." *Review of English Studies* n.s. 38 (February 1987a): 56–61.

———. "Jane Austen's Verses." *Times Literary Supplement* (20 February 1987b): 185.

———. "Jane Austen and William Hayley." *Notes and Queries* 34 (232) (March 1987c): 1, 25–26.

———. "Jane Austen's Verses and Lord Stanhope's Disappointment." *The Book Collector* 37 (Spring 1988a): 86–91.

———. "Anna Lefroy's Original Memories of Jane Austen." *Review of English Studies* n.s. 39 (August 1988b): 417–21.

———. "Jane Austen: New Biographical Comments." *Notes and Queries* 39 (237) (June 1992a): 2, 162–63.

———. "Jane Austen's Letters." *Persuasions* 14 (December 1992b): 76–88.

Leavis, F. R. *The Great Tradition.* Harmondsworth: Penguin, 1972, pp. 9–39. (First published, London: Chatto and Windus 1948.)

Leavis, L. R., and J. M. Blom. "A Return to Jane Austen's Novels." *English Studies: A Journal of English Language and Literature* 62 (August 1981): 313–23.

Leavis, Q. D. "A Critical Theory of Jane Austen's Writings." *Scrutiny* 10 (1941–1942a): 61–87.

———. "A Critical Theory of Jane Austen's Writings (II): *Lady Susan* into *Mansfield Park*." *Scrutiny* 10 (1941–1942b): 114–42, 272–94.

———. "A Critical Theory of Jane Austen's Writings (III): *The Letters*." *Scrutiny* 12 (1944–1945): 104–19.

Lee, Judith. " 'Without Hate, without Bitterness, without Fear, without Protest, without Preaching': Virginia Woolf Reads Jane Austen." *Persuasions* 12 (December 1990): 111–16.

Leighton, Angela. "Sense and Silences: Reading Jane Austen Again." *Women and Literature* 3 (1983): 128–41.

Lellis, George, and H. Philip Bolton. "Pride but No Prejudice." In *The English Novel and the Movies*. Edited by Michael Klein and Gillian Parker. New York: Ungar, 1981, pp. 44–51.

Lenta, Margaret. "Jane Austen's Feminism: An Original Response to Convention." *Critical Quarterly* 23 (Autumn 1981a): 27–36.

———. "Jane Fairfax and Jane Eyre: Educating Women." *Ariel: A Review of International English Literature* 12 (October 1981b): 27–41.

———. "Androgyny and Authority in *Mansfield Park*." *Studies in the Novel* 15 (Fall 1983): 169–82.

Lescinski, Joan. "Heroines under Fire: Rebels in Austen and James." *CEA Critic: An Official Journal of the College English Association* 49 (Winter–Summer 1986–1987): 60–69.

Levine, George. "Translating the Monstrous: *Northanger Abbey*." *Nineteenth-Century Fiction* 30 (December 1975): 335–50.

Levine, Jay Arnold. "*Lady Susan*: Jane Austen's Character of the Merry Widow." *Studies in English Literature 1500–1900* 1 (1961): 23–34.

Lew, Joseph. " 'That Abominable Traffic': *Mansfield Park* and the Dynamics of Slavery." In *History, Gender and Eighteenth-Century Literature*. Edited by Beth Fowkes Tobin. Athens: University of Georgia Press, 1994, pp. 271–300.

Lewis, Lisa A. F. "Kipling's Jane: Some Echoes of Austen." *English Literature in Transition 1880–1920* 29:1 (1986): 76–82.

Liddell, Robert. *A Treatise on the Novel*. London: Cape, 1947, passim. An appendix, pp. 146–63, on Ivy Compton-Burnett suggests her affinities with Jane Austen.

Litvak, Joseph. "Reading Characters: Self, Society, and Text in *Emma*." *PMLA: Publications of the Modern Language Association of America* 100 (October 1985): 763–73.

———. "The Infection of Acting: Theatricals and Theatricality in *Mansfield Park*." *ELH: English Literary History* 53 (Summer 1986): 331–55.

Litz, A. Walton. "*The Loiterer*: A Reflection on Jane Austen's Early Environment." *Review of English Studies* n.s. 12 (1961): 251–61.

———. "The Picturesque in *Pride and Prejudice*." *Persuasions* 1 (December 1979): 13–15, 20–24.

———. "Jane Austen: The *Juvenilia*." In *Jane Austen's Beginnings: The Juvenilia and Lady Susan*. Edited by J. David Grey. Ann Arbor: UMI Research Press, 1989, pp. 1–6.

Lock, F. P. "*Camilla, Belinda*, and Jane Austen's 'Only a Novel.' " *Notes and Queries* n.s. 23 (1976): 105–6.

———. "The Geology of *Sense and Sensibility*." *Yearbook of English Studies* 9 (1979): 246–55.

Lodge, David. *Language of Fiction*. London and New York: Routledge, 1966, pp. 94–113.

Looser, Devoney. "(Re)Making History and Philosophy: Austen's *Northanger Abbey*." *European Romantic Review* 4 (Summer 1993): 34–56.

———. "Introduction: Jane Austen and Discourses of Feminism." In *Jane Austen and Discourses of Feminism*. Edited by Devoney Looser. New York: St. Martin's Press, 1995, pp. 1–16.

Lougy, Robert E. "A Colder Room: Place and Memory in *Mansfield Park* and *Great Expectations*." *West Virginia University Philological Papers* 34 (1988): 23–30.

Lovell, Terry. "Jane Austen and the Gentry: A Study in Literature and Ideology." In

The Sociology of Literature: Applied Studies. Edited by Diane Laurenson. Keele: University of Keele, 1978, pp. 15–37.

Loveridge, Mark. "Francis Hutcheson and Mr. Weston's Conundrum in *Emma.*" *Notes and Queries* n.s. 30 (June 1983): 214–16.

———. "*Northanger Abbey*: Or, Nature and Probability." *Nineteenth Century Literature* 56 (June 1991): 1–29.

Lucas, John, ed. "Jane Austen and Romanticism." *Critical Survey* 4:1 (1992); Special issue. (In fact, only two essays—*Sanditon* and *Emma*—are devoted solely to Jane Austen.)

Lundeen, Kathleen. "A Modest Proposal? Paradise Found in Jane Austen's Betrothal Scenes." *Review of English Studies* 41 (February 1990): 65–75.

Lynd, Robert. "Jane Austen: Natural Historian." In his *Old and New Masters.* London: T. Fisher Unwin, 1919, pp. 17–24.

MacCarthy, Bridget. *The Later Woman Novelists, 1744–1818.* Cork: Cork University Press, 1947, pp. 235–81.

MacDonagh, Oliver. "The Church in *Mansfield Park*: A Serious Call?" *Sydney Studies in English* 12 (1986–1987): 36–55.

———. "*Sanditon*: A Regency Novel." In *The Writer as Witness: Literature as Historical Evidence.* Edited by Tom Dunne. Cork: Cork University Press, 1987, pp. 114–32.

MacDonald, Susan Peck. "Jane Austen and the Tradition of the Absent Mother." In *The Lost Tradition: Mothers and Daughters in Literature.* Edited by Cathy N. Davidson and E. M. Broner. New York: Ungar, 1980, pp. 58–69.

Macey, Samuel L. "Austen: Gaining a Sufficient Competence with an Insufficient Dowry." In his *Money and the Novel: Mercenary Motivation in Defoe and His Immediate Successors.* Victoria, British Columbia: Sono Nis Press, 1983, pp. 146–64. (Revised version of his "Clocks and Chronology in the Novels from Defoe to Austen." *Eighteenth Century Life* 7 [January 1982]: 96–104.)

Magee, William H. "The Happy Marriage: The Influence of Charlotte Smith on Jane Austen." *Studies in the Novel* 7 (Spring 1975): 104–19.

———. "Instrument of Growth: The Courtship and Marriage Plot in Jane Austen's Novels." *Journal of Narrative Technique* 17 (Spring 1987): 198–208.

Mallett, Phillip. "On Liking Emma." *Durham University Journal* 53 (July 1992): 249–54.

Mandel, Miriam B. "Fiction and Fiction-Making: *Emma.*" *Persuasions* 13 (December 1991): 100–103.

Marie, Beatrice. "*Emma* and the Democracy of Desire." *Studies in the Novel* 17 (Spring 1985): 1–13.

Marshall, Christine. " 'Dull Elves' and Feminists: A Summary of Feminist Criticism of Jane Austen." *Persuasions* 14 (December 1992): 39–45.

Marshall, David. "True Acting and the Language of Real Feeling: *Mansfield Park.*" *The Yale Journal of Criticism: Interpretation in the Humanities* 3 (Fall 1989): 87–106.

Marshall, Mary Gaither. "Jane Austen's Manuscripts of the *Juvenilia* and *Lady Susan*: A History and Description." In *Jane Austen's Beginnings: The Juvenilia and Lady Susan.* Edited by J. David Grey. Ann Arbor: UMI Research Press, 1989, pp. 107–21.

Marshall, P. Scott. "Techniques of Persuasion in *Persuasion*: A Lawyer's Viewpoint." *Persuasions* 6 (December 1984): 44–47.

Martin, Carol A. " 'These Would Have Been All My Friends': Lyme Regis and Jane Austen's Elliot." *Weber Studies: An Interdisciplinary Humanities Journal* 11 (Spring–Summer 1994): 127–32.

Martin, Ellen E. "The Madness of Jane Austen: Metonymic Style and Literature's Resistance to Interpretation." In *Jane Austen's Beginnings: The Juvenilia and Lady Susan*. Edited by J. David Grey. Ann Arbor: UMI Research Press, 1989, pp. 83–94.

Maugham, W. Somerset. "*Pride and Prejudice*." *Atlantic* 181 (May 1948): 99–104. (Reprinted in *Great Novelists and Their Novels: Essays on the Ten Greatest Novels in the World, and the Men and Women Who Wrote Them*. Philadelphia: John C. Winston, 1948, pp. 77–93.)

Maxwell, J. C. "Jane Austen and *Belinda*." *Notes and Queries* n.s. 21 (1974): 175–76.

McAleer, John. "The Comedy of Social Distinctions in *Pride and Prejudice*." *Persuasions* 11 (December 1989a): 70–76.

———. "What a Biographer Can Learn about Jane Austen from Her Juvenilia." In *Jane Austen's Beginnings: The Juvenilia and Lady Susan*. Edited by J. David Grey. Ann Arbor: UMI Research Press, 1989b, pp. 7–27.

———. "What a Biographer Can Learn about Jane Austen from *Emma*." *Persuasions* 13 (December 1991): 69–81.

McCawley, Dwight. "Assertion and Aggression in the Novels of Jane Austen." *Persuasions* 11 (December 1989a): 77–84.

———. "Hostility and Aggression: Jane Austen's Inner Plot." *Mid Hudson Language Studies* 12 (1989b): 16–26.

McCullough, Bruce. "The Novel of Character: Jane Austen." In his *Representative English Novelists: Defoe to Conrad*. New York: Harper and Brothers, 1946, pp. 97–112.

McDonnell, Jane. " 'A Little Spirit of Independence': Sexual Politics and the Bildungsroman in *Mansfield Park*." *Novel: A Forum on Fiction* 17 (Spring 1984): 197–214.

McGowan, John P. "Knowledge/Power and Jane Austen's Radicalism." *Mosaic: A Journal for the Interdisciplinary Study of Literature* 18 (Summer 1985): 1–15.

McKellar, Hugh D. " 'The Profession of a Clergyman.' " *Persuasions* 7 (December 1985): 28–34.

———. "Muted Merriment: Christmas Celebrations in Jane Austen." *Persuasions* 8 (December 1986): 12–16.

———. "*Lady Susan*: Sport or Cinderella?" In *Jane Austen's Beginnings: The Juvenilia and Lady Susan*. Edited by J. David Grey. Ann Arbor: UMI Research Press, 1989, pp. 205–14.

———. "Canadian Connections of Jane Austen and Her Circle." *Persuasions* 13 (December 1991): 82–87.

McKenzie, Alan T. "The Derivation and Distribution of 'Consequence' in *Mansfield Park*." *Nineteenth Century Literature* 40 (December 1985): 281–96.

McLean, Barbara. "Professional Persuasion: Dr. Anne Elliot." *Persuasions* 15 (December 1993): 170–77.

McMaster, Juliet. "The Continuity of Jane Austen's Novels." *Studies in English Literature* 10 (1970): 723–39.

————. " 'God Gave Us Our Relations': The Watson Family." *Persuasions* 8 (December 1986): 60–72.

————. " 'The Beautifull Cassandra' Illustrated." *Persuasions* 10 (December 1988): 99–103.

————. "Teaching *Love and Freindship.*" In *Jane Austen's Beginnings: The Juvenilia and Lady Susan.* Edited by J. David Grey. Ann Arbor: UMI Research Press, 1989, pp. 135–51.

————. "The Secret Languages of *Emma.*" *Persuasions* 13 (December 1991): 119–31.

————. "The Children in *Emma.*" *Persuasions* 14 (December 1992): 62–67.

————. "The Adventures of 'The Beautifull Cassandra' and the Beautiful Jane." *Persuasions* 15 (December 1993): 178–83.

————. "Emma Watson: Jane Austen's Uncompleted Heroine." In *Critical Reconstructions: The Relationship of Fiction and Life.* Edited by Robert M. Polhemus and Roger B. Henkle. Stanford, CA: Stanford University Press, 1994, pp. 212–30.

————. "Talking about Talk in *Pride and Prejudice.*" In *Jane Austen's Business: Her World and Her Profession.* Edited by Juliet McMaster and Bruce Stovel. New York: St. Martin's Press, 1996, pp. 81–94.

Melander, Martin. "An Unknown Source of Jane Austen's *Sense and Sensibility.*" *Studia Neophilologica* 22 (1949–1950): 146–70.

Mellor, Anne K. "Why Women Didn't Like Romanticism: The Views of Jane Austen and Mary Shelley." In *The Romantics and Us: Essays on Literature and Culture.* Edited by Gene W. Ruoff. New Brunswick, NJ: Rutgers University Press, 1990, pp. 274–87.

Merrett, Robert James. "The Concept of Mind in *Emma.*" *English Studies in Canada* 6 (1980): 39–55.

Meyers, Kate Beaird. "Jane Austen's Use of Literary Allusion in the Sotherton Episode of *Mansfield Park.*" *Papers on Language and Literature: A Journal for Scholars and Critics of Language and Literature* 22 (Winter 1986): 96–99.

Meyersohn, Marylea. "What Fanny Knew: A Quiet Auditor of the Whole." *Women and Literature* 3 (1983): 224–30.

————. "Jane Austen's Garrulous Speakers: Social Criticism in *Sense and Sensibility, Emma,* and *Persuasion.*" In *Reading and Writing Women's Lives: A Study of the Novel of Manners (Challenging the Literary Canon).* Edited by Bege K. Bowers and Barbara Brothers. Ann Arbor: UMI Research Press, 1990, pp. 35–48.

Michaelson, Patricia Howell. "Reading *Pride and Prejudice.*" *Eighteenth Century Fiction* 3 (October 1990): 65–76.

Millard, Mary. "The Outs and Not Outs." *Persuasions* 2 (December 1980): 24–25.

Miller, D. A. "The Late Jane Austen." *Raritan* 10 (Summer 1990): 55–79.

————. "Austen's Attitude." *Yale Journal of Criticism* 8 (Spring 1995): 1–5.

Miller, Nancy W. "Sloth: The Moral Problem in Jane Austen's *Mansfield Park.*" *International Journal of Moral and Social Studies* 7 (Autumn 1992): 255–66.

Miller, Pamela Cook. "Jane Austen and the Power of the Spoken Word." *Persuasions* 7 (December 1985): 35–38.

————. " 'Will You Dance, Miss Austen?' A One-Woman Show." *Literature in Performance: A Journal of Literary and Performing Art* 8 (November 1988): 65–75.

Millgate, Jane. "Prudential Lovers and Lost Heirs: *Persuasion* and the Presence of Scott." In *Jane Austen's Business: Her World and Her Profession.* Edited by Juliet McMaster and Bruce Stovel. New York: St. Martin's Press, 1996, pp. 109–

23. (Revised version of essay first published in *Persuasions* 15 [December 1993]: 184–95.)

Moffat, Wendy. "Identifying with Emma: Some Problems for the Feminist Reader." *College English* 53:1 (1991): 45–76.

Molan, Ann. "Persuasion in *Persuasion*." *The Critical Review* 24 (1982): 16–29.

Moler, Kenneth L. " 'Only Connect': Emotional Strength and Health in *Mansfield Park*." *English Studies: A Journal of English Language and Literature* 64 (April 1983a): 144–52.

———. "The Balm of Sisterly Consolation: *Pride and Prejudice* and *Sir Charles Grandison*." *Notes and Queries* 30 (228) (June 1983b): 216–17.

———. "The Olive Branch Metaphor in *Pride and Prejudice*." *Notes and Queries* 30 (228) (June 1983c): 214.

———. "Some Verbal Tactics of General Tilney." *Persuasions* 6 (December 1984): 10–12.

———. "Miss Price All Alone: Metaphors of Distance in *Mansfield Park*." *Studies in the Novel* 17 (Summer 1985): 189–93.

———. " 'Group Voices' in Jane Austen's Narration." *Persuasions* 13 (December 1991): 7–12.

Monaghan, David. "*Mansfield Park* and Evangelicalism: A Reassessment." *Nineteenth-Century Fiction* 33 (1978): 215–30.

———. "The Complexity of Jane Austen's Novels." *Women and Literature* 3 (1983): 88–97.

Monk, Leland. "Murder She Wrote: The Mystery of Jane Austen's *Emma*." *Journal of Narrative Technique* 20 (Fall 1990): 342–53.

Moon, E. B. " 'A Model of Female Excellence': Anne Elliot, *Persuasion*, and the Vindication of a Richardsonian Ideal of the Female Character." *AUMLA: Journal of the Australasian Universities Language and Literature Association* 67 (May 1987): 25–42.

Moore, Susan. "The Heroine of *Mansfield Park*." *English Studies: A Journal of English Language and Literature* 63 (April 1982): 139–44.

Morgan, Susan. "Why There's No Sex in Jane Austen's Fiction." *Studies in the Novel* 19 (Fall 1987): 346–56.

———. "Letter Writing, Cassandra, and the Conventions of Romantic Love." *Persuasions* 14 (December 1992): 104–12.

Morgan, Susan, and Susan Kneedler. "Austen's Sexual Politics." *Persuasions* 12 (December 1990): 19–23.

Morrison, Paul. "Enclosed in Openness: *Northanger Abbey* and the Domestic Carceral." *Texas Studies in Literature and Language* 33 (1991): 1–23.

Morrison, Sarah R. "Of Woman Borne: Male Experience and Feminine Truth in Jane Austen's Novels." *Studies in the Novel* 26 (Winter 1994): 337–49.

Morrow, Patrick D. "Sublime or Sensible: *The Mysteries of Udolpho* and *Northanger Abbey*." In his *Tradition, Undercut, and Discovery: Eight Essays on British Literature*. Amsterdam: Rodopi, 1980, pp. 93–117.

Murray, Douglas. "Gazing and Avoiding the Gaze." In *Jane Austen's Business: Her World and Her Profession*. Edited by Juliet McMaster and Bruce Stovel. New York: St. Martin's Press, 1996, pp. 42–53.

Myer, Valerie Grosvenor. " 'Caro Sposo' at the Ball: Jane West and Jane Austen's *Emma*." *Notes and Queries* n.s. 29 (June 1982): 208.

————. "Jane Austen and 'The Soul of a Prostitute.' " *Notes and Queries* n.s. 35 (September 1988): 305.

Nardin, Jane. "Children and Their Families in Jane Austen's Novels." *Women and Literature* 3 (1983): 73–87.

————. "Propriety vs. Morality in Jane Austen's Novels." *Persuasions* 10 (December 1988): 70–75.

Nath, Prem. "Dr. Johnson and Jane Austen." *Notes and Queries* n.s. 27 (1980): 55–56.

Neill, Edward. "Between Deference and Destruction: 'Situations' of Recent Critical Theory and Jane Austen's *Emma.*" *Critical Quarterly* 29 (Autumn 1987): 39–54.

————. "The Politics of 'Jane Austen.' " *English: The Journal of the English Association* 40 (Autumn 1991): 205–13.

Neumann, Anne Waldron. "Characterization and Comment in *Pride and Prejudice*: Free Indirect Discourse and 'Double-Voiced' Verbs of Speaking, Thinking, and Feeling." *Style* 20 (Fall 1986): 364–94.

Newman, Karen. "Can This Marriage Be Saved: Jane Austen Makes Sense of an Ending." *ELH: English Literary History* 50 (Winter 1983): 693–710.

Nollen, Elizabeth M. "Ann Radcliffe's *A Sicilian Romance*: A New Source of Jane Austen's *Sense and Sensibility.*" *English Language Notes* 22 (December 1984): 30–37.

————. "Female Detective Figures in British Fiction: Coping with Madness and Imprisonment." *Clues: A Journal of Detection* 15 (Fall–Winter 1994): 39–49.

Nordhjem, Bent. *What Fiction Means: An Inquiry into the Nature of Fiction with a Study of Three Comic Novels.* Copenhagen: University of Copenhagen; Philadelphia: Coronet Books, 1987.

Norris, John. " 'Sam Is Only a Surgeon, You Know.' " *Persuasions* 8 (December 1986): 92–95.

Odom, Keith C. "Jane Austen's Rise to Fame." *Conference of College Teachers of English Studies* 54 (September 1989): 47–52.

O'Keefe, Bernard. "*Emma*: Reading and Misreading." *English Review* 5 (September 1994): 6–9.

Okin, Susan Moller. "Patriarchy and Married Women's Property in England: Questions on Some Current Views." *Eighteenth Century Studies* 17 (Winter 1983–1984): 121–38.

Olsen, Stein Haugom. "Appreciating *Pride and Prejudice*." In *The Nineteenth-Century British Novel.* Edited by Jeremy Hawthorn. London: Edward Arnold, 1986, pp. 1–16.

O'Neill, John H. "The Experience of Error: Ironic Entrapment in Augustan Narrative Satire." *Papers on Language and Literature: A Journal for Scholars and Critics of Language and Literature* 18 (Summer 1982): 278–90.

Orange, Michael. "Aspects of Narration in *Persuasion.*" *Sydney Studies in English* 15 (1989–1990): 63–71.

Orr, Bridget. " 'Blushing for Her Mother': Jane Austen's Embarrassed Representation of Maternity." In *Remembering Representation.* Edited by Howard McNaughton. Canterbury, Kent: Department of English, University of Canterbury, 1993, pp. 52–64.

O'Toole, Tess. "Reconfiguring the Family in *Persuasion.*" *Persuasions* 15 (December 1993): 200–206.

Page, Alex. " 'Straightforward Emotions and Zigzag Embarrassments' in Austen's

Emma.'' In *Johnson and His Age.* Edited by James Engell. Cambridge: Harvard University Press, 1984, pp. 559–74.

Parker, Jo Alyson. ''*Pride and Prejudice*: Jane Austen's Double Inheritance Plot.'' *REAL: The Yearbook of Research in English and American Literature* 7 (1990): 159–90.

Parke, Catherine. ''Vision and Revision: A Model for Reading the Eighteenth-Century Novel of Education.'' *Eighteenth Century Studies* 16 (Winter 1982–1983): 162–74.

———. '' 'The Experiment Just Begun': Virginia Woolf's Reading of Jane Austen's *Persuasion.*'' *Publications of the Missouri Philological Association* 8 (1983): 31–35.

Parker, Keiko. ''Illustrating Jane Austen.'' *Persuasions* 11 (December 1989): 22–27.

———. ''Sense and 'Non-Sense' in Eight Jane Austen Biographies.'' *Persuasions* 12 (December 1990): 24–34.

Parker, Mark. ''The End of *Emma*: Drawing the Boundaries of Class in Austen.'' *Journal of English and Germanic Philology* 91 (July 1992): 344–59.

Parsons, Farnell. ''Fact and Fantasy: Jane Austen's Childhood Reading.'' *Persuasions* 10 (December 1988): 90–98.

Pascal, Roy. ''Early Accomplishment.'' In his *The Dual Voice: Free Indirect Speech and Its Functioning in the Nineteenth-Century European Novel.* Totowa, NJ: Rowman and Littlefield, 1977, pp. 37–66.

Patteson, Richard F. ''Truth, Certitude, and Stability in Jane Austen's Fiction.'' *Philological Quarterly* 60 (Fall 1981): 455–69.

Paulson, Ronald. ''Gothic Fiction and the French Revolution.'' *ELH: English Literary History* 48 (Fall 1981): 532–54.

Pedley, Colin. '' 'The Inward Dispositions of the Heart': Jane Austen and Jane West.'' *Notes and Queries* n.s. 36 (June 1989): 169–71.

———. '' 'Terrific and Unprincipled Compositions': The Reception of *Lovers' Vows* and *Mansfield Park.*'' *Philological Quarterly* 74 (Summer 1995): 297–316.

Perkins, Pam. ''A Subdued Gaiety: The Comedy of *Mansfield Park.*'' *Nineteenth Century Literature* 48 (June 1993): 1–25.

Perry, Ruth. ''Interrupted Friendships in Jane Austen's *Emma.*'' *Tulsa Studies in Women's Literature* 5 (Fall 1986): 185–202.

———. ''Clarissa's Daughters, or the History of Innocence Betrayed: How Women Writers Rewrote Richardson.'' *Women's Writing* 1 (1994): 5–24.

Person, Leland S., Jr. ''Playing House: Jane Austen's Fabulous Space.'' *Philological Quarterly* 59 (Winter 1980): 62–75.

Pickrel, Paul. ''*Emma* as Sequel.'' *Nineteenth Century Literature* 40 (September 1985a): 135–53.

———. ''Lionel Trilling and *Emma*: A Reconsideration.'' *Nineteenth Century Literature* 40 (December 1985b): 297–311.

———. ''Lionel Trilling and *Mansfield Park.*'' *SEL: Studies in English Literature 1500–1900* 27 (Autumn 1987): 609–21.

———. '' 'The Watsons' and the Other Jane Austen.'' *ELH: English Literary History* 55 (Summer 1988): 443–67.

Pilgrim, Constance. ''The Unknown Lover.'' *Persuasions* 9 (December 1987): 37–40.

Pinch, Adela. ''Lost in a Book: Jane Austen's *Persuasion.*'' *Studies in Romanticism* Spring 32 (1993): 97–117.

Pinion, F. B. "A Sterne Echo in 'Love and Freindship.' " *Notes and Queries* n.s. 24 (1977): 320–21.

Pittock, Joan. "The Novelist in Search of a Fiction: *Northanger Abbey.*" *Etudes Anglaises: Grande Bretagne, Etats-Unis* 40 (April–June 1987): 142–53.

Polletta, Gregory T. "The Author's Place in Contemporary Narratology." In *Contemporary Approaches to Narrative.* Edited by Antony Mortimer. Tübingen: Narr, 1984, pp. 109–23. Barthean approach to *Emma.*

Poovey, Mary. "*Persuasion* and the Promises of Love." In *The Representation of Women in Fiction.* Edited by Carolyn Heilbrun and Margaret R. Higonnet. Baltimore: Johns Hopkins University Press, 1983a, pp. 152–79.

———. "The True English Style." *Persuasions* 5 (December 1983b): 48–51.

Porter, Roy. "Pre-Modernism and the Art of Shopping." *Critical Quarterly* 34 (Winter 1992): 3–14.

Postlethwaite, Diana. "Sometimes I Feel like a Motherless Child: Austen's Anne Elliot and Freud's Anna O." In *The Anna Book: Searching for Anna in Literary History.* Edited by Mickey Pearlman. Westport, CT: Greenwood Press, 1992, pp. 37–48.

Potter, Tiffany F. " 'A Low but Very Feeling Tone': The Lesbian Continuum and Power Relations in Jane Austen's *Emma.*" *English Studies in Canada* 20 (June 1994): 187–203.

Preus, Nicholas E. "Sexuality in *Emma*: A Case History." *Studies in the Novel* 23 (Summer 1991): 196–216.

Ragg, Laura M. "What Jane Austen Read." *English* 2 (1938): 167–74.

———. "Jane Austen and the War of Her Time." *Contemporary Review* 158 (1940): 544–49.

Ram, Atma. "Frail and Weak: A Portrait of Fanny Price." *Panjab University Research Bulletin (Arts)* 8 (April–October 1977a): 27–34.

———. "Jane Austen and Mary Wollstonecraft." *Indian Journal of English Studies* 12 (1977b): 149–51.

———. "The Feminine Point of View before Jane Austen." *Panjab University Research Bulletin (Arts)* 16 (October 1985): 67–74.

Ray, Joan Klingel. "Jane Austen's Case Study of Child Abuse: Fanny Price." *Persuasions* 13 (December 1991): 16–26.

———. "In Defense of Lady Russell; or, The Godmother Knew Best." *Persuasions* 15 (December 1993): 207–15.

Redmond, Luanne Bethke. "Land, Law and Love." *Persuasions* 11 (December 1989): 46–52.

Reid-Walsh, Jacqueline. "Governess or Governor?: The Mentor/Pupil Relation in *Emma.*" *Persuasions* 13 (December 1991): 108–17.

———. " 'She Learned Romance as She Grew Older': From Conduct Book Propriety to Romance in *Persuasion.*" *Persuasions* 15 (December 1993): 216–25.

Reinstein, P. Gila. "Moral Priorities in *Sense and Sensibility.*" *Renascence: Essays on Value in Literature* 35 (Summer 1983): 269–83.

Restuccia, Frances L. "A Black Morning: Kristevan Melancholia in Jane Austen's *Emma.*" *American Imago* 51 (Winter 1994): 447–69.

Richards, Bernard. "Jane Austen and Manners." *English Review* 1 (November 1990): 16–19.

Robbins, Susan Pepper. "Jane Austen's Epistolary Fiction." In *Jane Austen's Begin-*

nings: The Juvenilia and Lady Susan. Edited by J. David Grey. Ann Arbor: UMI Research Press, 1989, pp. 215–24.

Roberts, Bette B. "The Horrid Novels: *The Mysteries of Udolpho* and *Northanger Abbey*." *Gothic Fictions: Prohibition/Transgression*. Edited by Kenneth W. Graham. New York: AMS, 1989, pp. 89–111.

Roberts, Janene. "Literature on PBS: Three 'Masterpiece Theatre' Productions of Nineteenth-Century British Novels." *Text and Performance Quarterly* 9 (October 1989): 311–21.

Robinson, Lillian S. "Why Marry Mr. Collins?" In her *Sex, Class, and Culture*. New York and London: Methuen, 1986 (first published, 1978), pp. 178–99. (See also Robinson's next essay, "On Reading Trash," pp. 200–222, in which she discusses Jane Austen in relation to the Regency romances of the historical novelist Georgette Heyer.)

Rogers, Pat. " 'Caro Sposo': Mrs. Elton, Burneys, Thrales, and Noels." *Review of English Studies: A Quarterly Journal of English Literature and the English Language* 45 (February 1994): 70–75.

Rogers, Winfield H. "The Reaction against Melodramatic Sensibility in the English Novel, 1796–1830." *Proceedings of the Modern Language Association* 49 (1934): 98–122.

Rosenbaum, Barbara, and Pamela White. "Jane Austen." In their *Index of Literary Manuscripts*. Vol. 4: 1800–1900. Part 1. London: Mansell, 1982, pp. 21–31.

Rosmarin, Adena. " 'Misreading' *Emma*: The Powers and Perfidies of Interpretive History." *ELH: English Literary History* 51 (Summer 1984): 315–42.

Rossdale, P. S. A. "What Caused the Quarrel between Mr. Collins and Mr. Bennet? Observations on the Entail of Longbourn." *Notes and Queries* 27 (1980): 503–4.

Roth, Barry. "Review Essay: The Once and Future Austen." *Studies in the Novel* 17 (Summer 1985): 218–25.

———. "Heart of Darkness: Recent Readings of Jane Austen." *Studies in the Novel* 26 (Winter 1994): 420–27.

Royle, Nicholas. "Telepathy: From Jane Austen and Henry James." *The Oxford Literary Review* 10 (1988): 43–60.

Rumrich, John Peter. "The Importance of Being Frank." *Essays in Literature* 8 (Spring 1981): 97–104.

Ruoff, Gene W. "The Sense of a Beginning: *Mansfield Park* and Romantic Narrative." *The Wordsworth Circle* 10 (1979): 174–86.

———. "The Triumph of *Persuasion*: Jane Austen and the Creation of Woman." *Persuasions* 6 (December 1984): 54–61.

Rzepka, Charles J. "Making It in a Brave New World: Marriage, Profession, and Anti-Romantic Ekstasis in Austen's *Persuasion*." *Studies in the Novel* 26 (Summer 1994): 99–120.

Sabor, Peter. " 'Finished up to Nature': Walter Scott's Review of *Emma*." *Persuasions* 13 (December 1991): 88–99.

———. " 'Staring in Astonishment': Portraits and Prints in *Persuasion*." In *Jane Austen's Business: Her World and Her Profession*. Edited by Juliet McMaster and Bruce Stovel. New York: St. Martin's Press, 1996, pp. 17–29.

Said, Edward W. "Jane Austen and Empire." In *Raymond Williams: Critical Perspectives*. Edited by Terry Eagleton. Boston: Northeastern University Press, 1989, pp. 150–64. (Reprinted in *Contemporary Marxist Literary Criticism*. Edited by Francis Mulhern. London: Longman, 1992, pp. 97–113.)

Saisselin, Remy G. "The Man of Taste as Social Model, or, *Sense and Sensibility*." In *The Crisis of Courtesy: Studies in the Conduct-Book in Britain, 1600–1900*. Edited by Jacques Carre. Leiden: Brill, 1994, pp. 119–27.

Sandock, Mollie. "Imagining Jane Austen." *Review* 15 (1993): 103–13.

Satz, Martha. "An Epistemological Understanding of *Pride and Prejudice*: Humility and Objectivity." *Women and Literature* 3 (1983): 171–86.

Schmidt, Kari Anne Rand. "Male and Female Language in Jane Austen's Novels." In *Papers from the First Nordic Conference for English Studies, Oslo, 17–19 September, 1980*. Edited by Stig Johansson and Bjorn Tysdahl. Oslo: Institute of English Studies, University of Oslo, 1981, pp. 198–210.

Schneider, Matthew. "Card-Playing and the Marriage Gamble in *Pride and Prejudice*." *Dalhousie Review* 73 (Spring 1993): 5–17.

Scholes, Robert. "Dr. Johnson and Jane Austen." *Philological Quarterly* 54 (1975): 380–90.

Schorer, Mark. "Fiction and the 'Matrix of Analogy.' " *Kenyon Review* 11 (1949): 539–60. (Reprinted in his *The World We Imagine: Selected Essays*. New York: Farrar, Straus, and Giroux, 1968, pp. 24–45.) On *Persuasion, Wuthering Heights*, and *Middlemarch*.

Schott, Max. "The Scene at the White Hart Inn." *Spectrum* (University of California, Santa Barbara) 27 (1985): 87–92.

Searle, Catherine. "Outdoor Scenes in Jane Austen's Novels." *Thought: A Review of Culture and Ideas* 59 (December 1984): 419–31.

Sedgwick, Eve Kosofsky. "Jane Austen and the Masturbating Girl." *Critical Inquiry* 17 (1991): 818–37.

Shaffer, Julie A. "Not Subordinate: Empowering Women in the Marriage-Plot—The Novels of Frances Burney, Maria Edgeworth, and Jane Austen." *Criticism: A Quarterly for Literature and the Arts* 34 (Winter 1992): 51–73.

———. "The Ideological Intervention of Ambiguities in the Marriage Plot: Who Fails Marianne in Austen's *Sense and Sensibility*?" In *A Dialogue of Voices: Feminist Literary Theory and Bakhtin*. Edited by Karen Hohne and Helen Wussow. Minneapolis: University of Minnesota Press, 1994, pp. 128–51.

Shaw, Narelle. "Free Indirect Speech and Jane Austen's 1816 Revision of *Northanger Abbey*." *SEL: Studies in English Literature, 1500–1900* 30 (Autumn 1990): 591–601.

Shields, Carol. "Jane Austen Images of the Body: No Fingers, No Toes." *Persuasions* 13 (December 1991): 132–37.

Shoben, Edward Joseph, Jr. "Impulse and Virtue in Jane Austen: *Sense and Sensibility* in Two Centuries." *The Hudson Review* 35 (Winter 1982–1983): 521–39.

Showalter, Elaine. "Retrenchments." In *Jane Austen's Business: Her World and Her Profession*. Edited by Juliet McMaster and Bruce Stovel. New York: St. Martin's Press, 1996, pp. 181–91.

Simpson, Janice C. "Fanny Price as Cinderella: Folk and Fairy-Tale in *Mansfield Park*." *Persuasions* 9 (December 1987): 25–30.

Singh, Sushila. "The French Revolution and Jane Austen." In *The French Revolution: Ideology and Influence on Literature*. Edited by T. R. Sharma. Meerut, India: Shalabh Prakashan, 1991, pp. 160–70.

Siskin, Clifford. "A Formal Development: Austen, the Novel, and Romanticism." *The Centennial Review* 28–29 (Fall–Winter 1984–1985): 1–28.

———. "Jane Austen and the Engendering of Disciplinarity." In *Jane Austen and Discourses of Feminism.* Edited by Devoney Looser. New York: St. Martin's Press, 1995, pp. 51–67.

Skilton, David. "Jane Austen." In his *The English Novel: From Defoe to the Victorians.* Newton Abbott: David and Charles, 1977, pp. 81–90.

Skinner, John. "Exploring Space: The Constellations of *Mansfield Park.*" *Eighteenth Century Fiction* 4 (January 1992): 125–48.

Smith, Amy Elizabeth. " 'Julias and Louisas': Austen's *Northanger Abbey* and the Sentimental Novel." *English Language Notes* 30 (September 1992): 33–42.

Smith, Johanna H. " 'My Only Sister Now': Incest in *Mansfield Park.*" *Studies in the Novel* 19 (Spring 1987): 1–15.

———. " 'I Am a Gentleman's Daughter': A Marxist-Feminist Reading of *Pride and Prejudice.*" In *Approaches to Teaching Austen's "Pride and Prejudice."* Edited by Marcia McClintock Folsom. New York: Modern Language Association of America, 1993, pp. 67–73.

Smith, Mack. "The Document of Falsimilitude: Frank's Epistles and Misinterpretation in *Emma.*" *Massachusetts Studies in English* 9:4 (1984): 52–70.

Smith, Muriel. " 'Everything to My Wife': The Inheritance Theme in *The Moonstone* and *Sense and Sensibility.*" *Wilkie Collins Society Journal* 7 (1987): 13–18.

Smith, Peter. "*Mansfield Park* and the World Stage." *The Cambridge Quarterly* 23:3 (1994): 203–29.

Smith, Phoebe A. "*Sense and Sensibility* and 'The Lady's Law': The Failure of Benevolent Paternalism." *CEA Critic: An Official Journal of the College English Association* 55 (Spring–Summer 1993): 3–25.

Snyder, William C. "Mother Nature's Other Natures: Landscape in Women's Writing, 1770–1830." *Women's Studies: An Interdisciplinary Journal* 21:2 (1992): 143–62.

Southam, Brian C. "The Manuscript of Jane Austen's *Volume the First.*" *The Library* 5th series 17 (1962): 231–37.

———. "Jane Austen, 1775–1817." In *New Cambridge Bibliography of English Literature.* Vol. 3: 1800–1900. Edited by George Watson. Cambridge: Cambridge University Press, 1969, columns 692–700. Before the publication of Gilson (1982), the most complete listing of criticism up to 1967.

———. "General Tilney's Hot-Houses: Some Recent Jane Austen Studies and Texts." *Ariel: A Review of International English Literature* 2:4 (1971): 52–62.

———. "Jane Austen." In *The English Novel: Select Bibliographical Guides.* Edited by A. E. Dyson. London: Oxford University Press, 1974, pp. 145–63.

———. "The Silence of the Bertrams: Slavery and the Chronology of *Mansfield Park.*" *Times Literary Supplement* (17 February 1995): 13–14.

Spacks, Patricia Meyer. "The Talent of Ready Utterance: Eighteenth-Century Female Gossip." In *Women and Society in the Eighteenth Century.* Edited by Ian Duffy. Bethlehem, PA: Lawrence Henry Gipson Institute, 1983, pp. 1–14.

———. "Sisters." In *Fetter'd or Free? British Women Novelists, 1670–1815.* Edited by Mary Anne Schofield and Cecilia Macheski. Athens: Ohio University Press, 1986, pp. 136–151.

———. "Female Resources: Epistles, Plot, and Power." *Persuasions* 9 (December

1987): 88–98. (Reprinted in *Writing the Female Voice: Essays on Epistolary Literature.* Edited by Elizabeth Goldsmith. Evanston, IL: Northwestern University Press, 1989, pp. 63–76.)

———. "Austen's Laughter." *Women's Studies* 15:1–3 (1988): 71–85. (Special Issue: "Last Laughs: Perspectives on Women and Comedy.")

———. "Plots and Possibilities: Jane Austen's Juvenilia." In *Jane Austen's Beginnings: The Juvenilia and Lady Susan.* Edited by J. David Grey. Ann Arbor: UMI Research Press, 1989a, pp. 123–34.

———. "Women and Boredom: The Two Emmas." *The Yale Journal of Criticism: Interpretation in the Humanities* 2 (Spring 1989b): 191–205. Emma Bovary and Emma Woodhouse.

———. "The Problem of the Interesting." *Persuasions* 12 (December 1990): 71–78.

Speirs, Logan. *"Sir Charles Grandison or the Happy Man, a Comedy." English Studies: A Journal of English Language and Literature* 66 (February 1985): 25–35.

Spence, Jon. "The Abiding Possibilities of Nature in *Persuasion." SEL: Studies in English Literature, 1500–1900* 21 (Autumn 1981): 625–36.

Spring, David. "Interpreters of Jane Austen's Social World: Literary Critics and Historians." *Women and Literature* 3 (1983): 53–72.

Steele, Pamela. "In Sickness and in Health: Jane Austen's Metaphor." *Studies in the Novel* 14 (Summer 1982): 152–60.

Stepankowsky, Paula, and Conrad K. Harper. "Views from Both Directions: Courtship and Marriage in Letters and Diaries from the Age of Jane Austen." *Persuasions* 10 (December 1988): 117–26.

Stewart, Ralph. "Fairfax, Churchill, and Jane Austen's *Emma." University of Hartford Studies in Literature: A Journal of Interdisciplinary Criticism* 14:3 (1982): 96–100.

Stokes, Myra. " 'Smart' Talk by Miss Austen." In *Medieval Literature and Antiquities: Studies in Honour of Basil Cottle.* Edited by Myra Stokes and T. L. Burton. Cambridge: Brewer, 1987, pp. 187–97.

Stout, Janis P. "Jane Austen's Proposal Scenes and the Limitations of Language." *Studies in the Novel* 14 (Winter 1982): 316–26.

Stovel, Bruce. " 'A Contrariety of Emotion': Jane Austen's Ambivalent Lovers in *Pride and Prejudice." International Fiction Review* 14 (Winter 1987a): 27–33.

———. "Subjective to Objective: A Career Pattern in Jane Austen, George Eliot, and Contemporary Women Novelists." *Ariel: A Review of International English Literature* 18 (January 1987b): 55–61.

———. "Secrets, Silence, and Surprise in *Pride and Prejudice." Persuasions* 11 (December 1989): 85–91.

———. "Emma's Search for a True Friend." *Persuasions* 13 (December 1991): 58–67.

———. " 'The Sentient Target of Death': Jane Austen's Prayers." In *Jane Austen's Business: Her World and Her Profession.* Edited by Juliet McMaster and Bruce Stovel. New York: St. Martin's Press, 1996, pp. 192–205.

St. Peter, Christine. "Jane Austen's Creation of the Sister." *Philological Quarterly* 66 (Fall 1987): 473–92.

Sulloway, Alison G. "Emma Woodhouse and *A Vindication of the Rights of Woman." The Wordsworth Circle* 7 (Autumn 1976): 320–32.

———. "Jane Austen's Mediative Voice." In *Nineteenth-Century Women Writers of the English-Speaking World.* Edited by Rhoda B. Nathan. Westport, CT: Greenwood Press, 1986, pp. 194–99.

Sutherland, Eileen. "Dining at the Great House: Food and Drink in the Time of Jane Austen." *Persuasions* 12 (December 1990): 88–98.

———. "The Rise and Fall of the House of Elliot." *Persuasions* 15 (December 1993): 57–62.

Sutherland, Kathryn. "Jane Eyre's Literary History: The Case for *Mansfield Park.*" *ELH: English Literary History* 59 (Summer 1992): 409–40.

Swingle, L. J. "The Poets, the Novelists, and the English Romantic Situation." *The Wordsworth Circle* 10:2 (1979): 118–28.

Swords, Barbara W. " 'Woman's Place' in Jane Austen's England 1770–1820." *Persuasions* 10 (December 1988): 76–82.

Tandrup, Birthe. "Free Indirect Style and the Critique of the Gothic in *Northanger Abbey.*" *The Romantic Heritage: A Collection of Critical Essays.* Edited by Karsten Engelberg. Copenhagen: University of Copenhagen, 1983, pp. 81–92.

Tayler, Irene. "Afterword: Jane Austen Looks Ahead." In *Fetter'd or Free? British Women Novelists, 1670–1815.* Edited by Mary Anne Schofield and Cecilia Macheski. Athens: Ohio University Press, 1986, pp. 426–33.

Taylor, Roselle. "Point of View and Estrangement in *Persuasion.*" *Publications of the Arkansas Philological Association* 15 (April 1989): 97–108.

Tempest, Richard. "The Girl on the Hill: Parallel Structures in *Pride and Prejudice* and *Eugene Onegin.*" *Elementa: Journal of Slavic Studies and Comparative Cultural Semiotics* 1:2 (1993): 197–213.

Tempska, Urszula. "The Spatial Aspects of Five Chosen Novels by Jane Austen and Charlotte and Emily Brontë: A Comparative Study of *Pride and Prejudice, Mansfield Park, Jane Eyre, Villette, Wuthering Heights.*" *Studia Anglica Posnaniensia: An International Review of English Studies* 20 (1987): 197–212.

Terry, Judith. " 'Knit Your Own Stuff'; Or, Finishing Off Jane Austen." *Persuasions* 8 (December 1986): 73–83.

———. "Seen but Not Heard: Servants in Jane Austen's England." *Persuasions* 10 (December 1988): 104–16.

———. "The Slow Process of *Persuasion.*" In *Jane Austen's Business: Her World and Her Profession.* Edited by Juliet McMaster and Bruce Stovel. New York: St. Martin's Press, 1996, pp. 124–35. (First published in *Persuasions* 15 [December 1993]: 226–34.)

Thaden, Barbara Z. "Figure and Ground: The Receding Heroine in Jane Austen's *Emma.*" *South Atlantic Review* 55 (January 1990): 47–62.

Thomas, B. C. "Portsmouth in Jane Austen's Time." *Persuasions* 12 (December 1990): 61–66.

Thomas, Keith G. "Jane Austen and the Romantic Lyric: *Persuasion* and Coleridge's Conversational Poems." *ELH: English Literary History* 54 (Winter 1987): 893–924.

Thompson, James. "Jane Austen's Clothing: Things, Property, and Materialism in Her Novels." *Studies in Eighteenth Century Culture* 13 (1984): 217–31.

———. "The Art of Courtship; Or, Business in a Bad Market." *Postscript* 3 (1986a): 35–43.

———. "Jane Austen and History." *Review* 8 (1986b): 21–32.

————. "Jane Austen and the Limits of Language." *Journal of English and Germanic Philology* 85 (October 1986c): 510–31.

————. "*Sense and Sensibility*: Finance and Romance." In *Sensibility in Transformation: Creative Resistance to Sentiment from the Augustans to the Romantics*. Essays in Honor of Jean H. Hagstrum. Edited by Syndy McMillen Conger. London and Toronto: Associated University Presses, 1990, pp. 147–71.

————. "Jane Austen." In *The Columbia History of the British Novel*. Edited by John Richetti et al. New York: Columbia University Press, 1994, pp. 275–99.

Thomsen, Inger Sigrun. "Dangerous Words and Silent Lovers in *Sense and Sensibility*." *Persuasions* 12 (December 1990): 134–38.

————. "*Persuasion* and Persuadibility: When Vanity Is a Virtue." *Persuasions* 15 (December 1993): 235–44.

————. "Words 'Half-Dethroned': Jane Austen's Art of the Unspoken." In *Jane Austen's Business: Her World and Her Profession*. Edited by Juliet McMaster and Bruce Stovel. New York: St. Martin's Press, 1996, pp. 95–106.

Thrower, Norman J. W. "A New Map of the New World, 1808." *Persuasions* 14 (December 1992): 132–35.

Tobin, Mary-Elizabeth Fowkes. "Aiding Impoverished Gentlewomen: Power and Class in *Emma*." *Criticism: A Quarterly for Literature and the Arts* 30 (Fall 1988): 413–30.

————. "The Moral and Political Economy of Property in Austen's *Emma*." *Eighteenth Century Fiction* 2 (April 1990): 229–54.

Todd, Janet. "Who's Afraid of Jane Austen?" *Women and Literature* 3 (1983): 107–27.

————. "Jane Austen, Politics and Sensibility." In *Feminist Criticism: Theory and Practice*. Edited by Susan Sellers, Linda Hutcheon, and Paul Perron. Toronto: University of Toronto Press, 1991, pp. 71–87.

Tompkins, J. M. S. "*Elinor and Marianne*: A Note on Jane Austen." *Review of English Studies* 16 (1940): 33–43. The influence of Jane West's *A Gossip's Story* on *Sense and Sensibility*.

Trickett, Rachel. "*Mansfield Park*." *The Wordsworth Circle* 17 (Spring 1986): 87–95.

Trilling, Lionel. "*Mansfield Park*." *Encounter* 3 (September 1954): 9–19. (Also in *Partisan Review* 21 [1954]: 492–511; and reprinted in his *The Opposing Self*. New York: Viking 1955, pp. 206–30.)

————. "*Emma*." *Encounter* 8 (June 1957): 49–59. (Reprinted in his *Beyond Culture*. New York: Viking, 1965, pp. 31–55.)

Tsomondo, Thorell. "Representation, Context and Cognition, and Jane Austen." *Theoria: A Journal of Studies in the Arts, Humanities and Social Sciences* 64 (May 1985): 65–75.

————. "*Emma*: A Study in Textual Strategies." *English Studies in Africa: A Journal of the Humanities* 30:2 (1987): 69–82.

————. "Imperfect Articulation: A Saving Instability in *Sense and Sensibility*." *Persuasions* 12 (December 1990): 99–110.

Tumbleson, Ray. " 'It is like a Woman's Writing': The Alternative Epistolary Novel in *Emma*." *Persuasions* 14 (December 1992): 141–43.

Turan, Kenneth. "*Pride and Prejudice*: An Informal History of the Garson–Olivier Motion Picture." *Persuasions* 11 (December 1989): 140–43.

Ty, Eleanor. "Ridding Unwanted Suitors: Jane Austen's *Mansfield Park* and Charlotte Smith's *Emmeline*." *Tulsa Studies in Women's Literature* 5 (Fall 1986): 327–28.

Uphaus, Robert W. "Jane Austen and Female Reading." *Studies in the Novel* 19 (Fall 1987): 334–45.

Vanita, Ruth. "*Mansfield Park* in Miranda House." In *The Lie of the Land: English Literary Studies in India*. Edited by Rajeswari Sunder Rajan. Delhi: Oxford University Press, 1992, pp. 90–98.

Vick, Robin. "Some Unexplained References in Jane Austen's Letters." *Notes and Queries* 41 (239) (September 1994): 318–21.

Viveash, C. F. "Jane Austen and Madame de Staël." *Persuasions* 13 (December 1991): 39–40.

Waldron, Mary. "The Frailties of Fanny: *Mansfield Park* and the Evangelical Movement." *Eighteenth Century Fiction* 6 (April 1994): 259–82.

Walton, James. "*Mansfield Park*: The Circle Squared." In *Studies in Nineteenth Century Literature*. Salzburg: Institut für Anglistik und Amerikanistik, Universität Salzburg, pp. 44–108.

Warhol, Robyn R. "The Look, the Body, and the Heroine: A Feminist-Narratological Reading of *Persuasion*." *Novel: A Forum on Fiction* 26 (Fall 1992): 5–19.

Warren, Leland E. "The Conscious Speakers: Sensibility and the Art of Conversation Considered." *Sensibility in Transformation: Creative Resistance to Sentiment from the Augustans to the Romantics. Essays in Honor of Jean H. Hagstrum.* Edited by Syndy McMillen Conger. Rutherford, NJ.: Fairleigh Dickinson University Press, 1990, pp. 25–42.

Watt, Ian. "Jane Austen and the Traditions of Comic Aggression: *Sense and Sensibility*." *Persuasions* 3 (December 1981): 14–15, 25–28.

Webb, Igor. *From Custom to Capital: The English Novel and the Industrial Revolution*. Ithaca, NY: Cornell University Press, 1981, pp. 49–72, 101–23, 158–77, and passim. On *Pride and Prejudice* and *Mansfield Park*.

Webb, Mary. [Review of 2d edition of Oxford edition of Jane Austen.] *Bookman* 71 (1927): 256–58.

Weedon, Margaret. "Jane Austen and William Enfield's *The Speaker*." *British Journal for Eighteenth Century Studies* 11 (Autumn 1988): 159–62.

Weinsheimer, Joel. "*Emma* and Its Critics: The Value of Tact." *Women and Literature* 3 (1983): 257–72.

Weissman, Cheryl. "Doubleness and Refrain in Jane Austen's *Persuasion*." *The Kenyon Review* 10 (Fall 1988): 87–91.

White, Laura Mooneyham. "Jane Austen and the Marriage Plot: Questions of Persistence." In *Jane Austen and Discourses of Feminism*. Edited by Devoney Looser. New York: St. Martin's Press, 1995, pp. 71–86.

Wiesenfarth, Joseph. "The Case of *Pride and Prejudice*." *Studies in the Novel* 16 (Fall 1984): 261–73.

———. "*The Watsons* as Pretext." *Persuasions* 8 (December 1986): 101–11.

———. "Violet Hunt Rewrites Jane Austen: *Pride and Prejudice* (1813) and *Their Lives* (1916)." *Persuasions* 11 (December 1989): 61–65.

Wilkes, G. A. "Unconscious Motives in Jane Austen's *Emma*." *Sydney Studies in English* 13 (1987–1988): 74–89.

Wilkes, Joanne. "Jane Austen: The Novelist as Historian." *Sydney Studies in English* 17 (1991–1992): 121–24.

Wilkie, Brian. "Structural Layering in Jane Austen's Problem Novels." *Nineteenth Century Literature* 46 (March 1992a): 517–44.

———. "Jane Austen: Amor and Amoralism." *Journal of English and Germanic Philology* 91 (October 1992b): 529–55.

Williams, Michael. "*Northanger Abbey*: Some Problems of Engagement." *Unisa English Studies* 25:2 (1987): 8–17.

Willis, Lesley. "Religion in Jane Austen's *Mansfield Park*." *English Studies in Canada* 13 (March 1987): 65–78.

Wilt, Judith. "Jane Austen's Men: Inside/Outside 'the Mystery.' " *Women and Literature* 2 (1982): 59–76.

———. "The Powers of the Instrument: Or Jane, Frank, and the Pianoforte." *Persuasions* 5 (December 1983): 41–47.

Wiltshire, John. "The World of *Emma*." *The Critical Review* 27 (1985): 84–97.

Wingard, Sara. "Reversal and Revelation: The Five Seasons of *Pride and Prejudice*." *Persuasions* 11 (December 1989): 92–98.

———. "Folks That Go A Pleasuring." *Persuasions* 14 (December 1992): 122–31.

Woolf, Leonard. "The Economic Determination of Jane Austen." *New Statesman and Nation* 24 (1942): 39–41.

Woolf, Virginia. "Jane Austen." In her *The Common Reader*. London: Hogarth Press, 1925, pp. 168–83.

Worthington, Pepper. "Jane Austen's Image of Female Character and Personality in *Mansfield Park*." *Mount Olive Review* 6 (Spring 1992): 61–76.

Wright, Andrew. "Jane Austen Adapted." *Nineteenth-Century Fiction* 30 (December 1975): 421–53.

Yarrow, Dorothy F. "*Mansfield Park* and *Wives and Daughters*." *Gaskell Society Newsletter* 12 (August 1991): 4–5.

Yeazell, Ruth Bernard. "The Boundaries of *Mansfield Park*." *Representations* 7 (Summer 1984): 133–52.

York, Lorraine M. " 'The Pen of the Contriver' and the Eye of the Perceiver: *Mansfield Park*, the Implied Author and the Implied Reader." *English Studies in Canada* 13 (June 1987): 161–73.

Zaal, J. "Is *Emma* Still Teachable?" *CRUX: A Journal on the Teaching of English* 22 (August 1988): 61–68.

Zelicovici, Dvora. "The Inefficacy of *Lovers' Vows*." *ELH: English Literary History* 50 (Fall 1983): 531–40.

———. "Reversal in *Pride and Prejudice*." *Studies in the Humanities* 12 (December 1985): 106–14.

Index

About the Author

PAUL POPLAWSKI is Senior Lecturer in English at Trinity College Carmarthen in Wales. He has taught widely in 19th- and 20th-century literature and specializes in Jane Austen, Modernism, and Post-Colonial literatures. His four previous books include: *Promptings of Desire: Creativity and the Religious Impulse in the Works of D. H. Lawrence* (Greenwood, 1993) and *D. H. Lawrence: A Reference Companion* (Greenwood, 1996).